The SIS Football Rookie Handbook 2019

Comprehensive Scouting and Analytics Guide

Sports Info Solutions

Edited by Matt Manocherian

ACTA SPORTS

The SIS Football Rookie Handbook 2019
Comprehensive Scouting and Analytics Guide
Sports Info Solutions
Edited by Matt Manocherian

Cover Design by Tom A. Wright and Corey March

First Edition: February 2019

Published by:
ACTA Sports, a division of ACTA Publications
4848 North Clark Street
Chicago, IL 60640
(800) 397-2282
www.actasports.com www.actapublications.com

ISBN: 978-0-87946-671-8

Printed in the United States of America by McNaughton & Gunn

Table of Contents

Introduction

Throughout my time with the Saints, we would always take a picture of our draft board in February and tell the same joke:

"Remember what it looks like now because we are about to spend the next two months ruining it!"

In February, the draft board is pure. It is based on the work of the scouts who dedicate themselves to studying these players year-round. It is based on film study, projecting players based on how they perform on the football field. And just as importantly, the February draft board knows nothing of the "Underwear Olympics" that we call the Combine and Pro Days, has heard no input from biased coaches competing over draft resources, and hasn't yet ruled out players with whom the medical staff is uncomfortable.

The February draft board is the answer to the question: *Based on their play on the field, who do our full-time college scouts think will make the best pro players?*

With this book, we present to you our February draft board. Sports Info Solutions has the largest collection of football scouts under one roof—bigger than any NFL team—with over 50 Video Scouts grinding the proverbial tape from every college football game in the Football Bowl Subdivision (FBS). They have watched all the film, studied the players, and written the reports, all based off best practices that I learned from my time in the scouting departments of Mickey Loomis' New Orleans Saints and Michael Lombardi's Cleveland Browns. So, if you are looking for the most professional scouting reports that look like what the teams are using, you have come to the right place.

While this all makes this book unique, there is more. After all, we are Sports Info Solutions, and we have built our reputation as the groundbreaking researchers and analysts who help both teams and the public understand sports on a deeper level. From our flagship baseball stat, Defensive Runs Saved, which is the gold standard defensive metric in baseball, to our brand-new NFL division of credit metric, Total Points, we are always pushing the cutting edge of research and analytics. *The SIS Football Rookie Handbook* will be no different.

For the first time, we will be sharing some of our proprietary college football metrics with the public. All of the statistics that you see in this book are based on charting data collected by our Video Scouts in our office in Coplay, Pennsylvania—hometown of former top draft pick Saquon Barkley. Every game is charted by no fewer than four scouts before it goes through auditing by our full-time Operations staff. From there, our Research and Development team slices, dices, and analyzes the data, putting together automated and customized reports for our clients, including professional teams, leading media providers like ESPN, Football Outsiders, Sharp Football, and more. And now, we have curated a selection of our unique statistics that are most relevant for every position group in this book, and you will be able to see brand new analytics along with our professional scouting reports, side-by-side.

Our premise is that scouting and analytics are both integral parts of team-building and decision-making in football. Without scouts, we would be trying to reduce a complex, interdependent sport involving imperfect humans into an equation. Without analytics, we are turning our back on modern best practices, ignoring the opportunity to improve our decision making. Perhaps most importantly, from my perspective, is that our data covers every game that was played by an FBS team, which means that the data can "see" all the games. I don't care how much tape you think you grind: there is no scout in the world who can say that.

With that in mind, please enjoy the first edition of *The SIS Football Rookie Handbook*. Whether you are a tape junkie, a number cruncher, or you are just looking for the most comprehensive information on what your NFL team's rookies did while they were playing college football, this book has what you are looking for and more. Before we dive into the players, our Research & Development staff has assembled some of their most interesting analysis into the early pages, and then my Scouting Lieutenants, Nathan Cooper and John Todd (who, along with the tireless execution of Brian Reiff, have been as instrumental to this book as anyone), will explain how our NFL-style scouting process takes us from a list of thousands of names to the best of the next.

As we say every day when we hit the practice field, the tape, or the database: Let's go to work!

Matt Manocherian
Coplay, PA
January 31, 2019

A Statistical Comparison of Outland Winners Quinnen Williams and Ed Oliver

Bryce Rossler

For the first time in six years, the NFL Draft will feature two Outland Trophy winners, both of whom figure to be selected early. But, this occurrence is especially strange because both players in question, Houston's **Ed Oliver** and Alabama's **Quinnen Williams**, are defenders (the award is given to the best interior linemen, on offense or defense).

The last time that two defensive winners of the trophy were in the same draft was 1978, which featured Notre Dame's Ross Brown and Texas's Brad Shearer. And perhaps that's fitting since the defensive line is considered the strength of this class, a group that Oliver and Williams still manage to stand out from.

For most of last offseason, Oliver was billed by some as the surefire top selection in the class, but that was before Williams ascended to the throne with a dominant 2018 campaign. Whereas the former has been a known commodity for some time now, the latter seemingly came out of nowhere. Both of Williams' running mates at Alabama, Isaiah Buggs and Raekwon Davis, were certainly attracting more attention in preseason. But, once he hit the field, Williams quickly became the focus of opposing teams.

The Crimson Tide sophomore ranked first in run stuff rate (i.e. solo tackles for non-positive yardage) among 339 defensive tackles with at least 100 run snaps. His rate of 6.8 percent was a full percentage point higher than the next-best interior player, South Alabama's Tyree Turner (5.8). And in case you were wondering - his Outland predecessor ranked third with a rate of 5.3 percent.

That difference is even further accentuated when you consider that teams aimed runs towards Williams on 19 percent of their rushing attempts, as opposed to 29 percent of the time for Oliver. And when teams did run at Williams, he caused the ballcarrier to bounce the play 43 percent of the time - nearly ten-plus percentage points more often than Oliver did (34 percent).

Williams was an even bigger difference-maker as a pass-rusher, boasting a hurry rate of 13.8 percent. That dwarfs the second-highest figure, which belongs to San Jose State's Boogie Roberts, by 2.8 percentage points. Oliver once again ranks fourth with a still-excellent hurry rate of 10.5 percent. But, to give you an idea of just how impactful Williams was, his hurry rate outpaced that of several edge rushers who will merit first round consideration in April, namely: Clemson's Clelin Ferrell (12.1 percent), Florida State's Brian Burns (11.5), Mississippi State's Montez Sweat (10.5), and Michigan's Rashan Gary (9.5).

While the NFL will present a new set of challenges for Williams, his hurry rate this year was comparable to Aaron Donald's at the NFL level. This doesn't mean that he'll be able to maintain that productivity on Sundays, but it does serve to illustrate his level of collegiate dominance. (If anything, it should serve to illustrate how futile the search for the next Aaron Donald is.)

The bottom line is that both players project to be three-down difference-makers early in their careers. The advanced metrics seem to favor Williams, but an argument could be made that the already-established and obviously-talented Oliver suffered from a junior-year drop off as Jadeveon Clowney and Myles Garrett once did, and that he was capable of imposing his will more often. At any rate, statistics can only begin to contextualize a player's performance, and film is what tells the full story.

What to do on 2nd-and-10? Let's look at the numbers

Bryce Rossler

Expected Points Added (EPA) is a valuable measure that can contextualize performance proportionally to include points and turnovers in measures of efficiency and advise us of what the most prudent course of action is most of the time. But, we can't stop there.

Take, for example, the case of the much-maligned second-and-10 run. Whereas conventional wisdom holds that a team should run to set up a more manageable third down, EPA frowns upon the decision to run and suggests that teams should pass instead.

Dating back to 2016, the average EPA/attempt in such situations is -0.29, compared to -0.11 for a pass (note that here and moving forward, we're excluding all plays in which either team had a lead larger than eight points in the fourth quarter). For these reasons, the play call is widely regarded by the analytics community as the coward's way out and, in some ways, it is. But, blanket EPA is only part of the story.

Risk management is undeniably a component of decision-making in football. So, perhaps a more reasonable theory about second-and-10 playcalling is that most teams should pass most of the time. Something that should be taken into consideration is eventual first down rate (EFDR), which indicates that running it on second-and-10 isn't the end of the world. In fact, if a team runs on second-and-10, it is still more likely than not to convert that set of downs.

Since 2016, there have been 2,129 designed runs on second-and-10. And in 1,095 (51 percent) of those instances, the team in question ultimately moved the chains. Now, EFDR still favors passing; over that same time period, teams took to the air 3,025 times and eventually picked up a first down 57 percent of the time. However, passing has risk factors that running does not, namely sacks and interceptions.

For example, the turnover rate on such rushing plays is 0.5 percent whereas the interception rate for passing is over three times that figure -- 1.8 percent. Sacks also occur on 5.6 percent of those plays, and strip sacks recovered by the defense bump the turnover rate to 2.2 percent. There's also the problem of incompletions and checkdowns that go for zero or negative yards. Second-and-10 dropbacks produce non-positive yardage 39 percent of the time, and the mode yardage for passing plays is 0, whereas the counterpart figures for rushing are 18 percent and 3, respectively.

EPA failures on passing plays are also far less manageable than EPA failures for rushes. Compare the average EPA value on the set of passing plays with negative EPA values (-0.92) to that of rushing plays (-0.69), and it becomes apparent why some coaches favor conservative decision-making in these scenarios.

Now that we've properly quantified some of the motivations for why coaches may elect to run on 2nd & 10, let's examine some third-down hypotheticals tailored to the data presented above.

Since the most common rushing gain on second-and-10 is three yards, we'll examine 3rd-and-7 situations, of which there have been 1,144 instances since 2016. Passing is generally more optimal in this scenario, and 481 of 1,117 third-and-7 dropbacks lead to eventual first downs, a rate of 43 percent.

Good luck if you gain no yardage on a run or throw an incompletion on second-and-10 though. Of the 1,175 third-and-10's, teams only converted through the air at a rate of 33 percent on 1,143 passes -- a stark difference of 10 percentage points. It's even worse if you get sacked on a second-and-10 dropback. The mode yardage lost on sacks is 7 yards, and 176 third-and-17 situations imposed a daunting 18 percent conversion rate on 148 dropbacks.

Now, to retrace our steps, conventional wisdom tells us that running on second-and-10 can give a team a more manageable third down. This is true if we're only considering yards-to-go, but we must consider how down and distance can affect pressure rates. The pressure rates in third-and-7 and third-and-10 are 30 percent and 31 percent, both high figures. This can likely be attributed to the predictability of the pass inherent in those set-ups.

Quarterbacks on second-and-10, however, are pressured just 22 percent of the time. Therefore, it can be prudent to go ahead and pass if a coach is worried about his quarterback's ability to perform under pressure. Generally speaking, a coach should certainly factor his team's personnel when making any decision. The difference in pressure rate is already built into some of the analysis above, but it's worth mentioning here to give a sense for why performance declines on third-and-long.

The conclusions we can draw from this can be summarized thusly:

1. EPA and EFDR favor passing, and
2. Most teams should still pass most of the time on second-and-10, but
3. Rushing on second-and-10 is still more likely than not to eventually result in a first down, and
4. Second-and-10 passing is a bimodal proposition which has risks that merit consideration, and
5. Some teams should run at a rate above league average on second-and-10.

I intend to do further research that will analyze these components on a team level and how the above assertions comport to organizational trends, indicating that most coaches are more efficient decision-makers than we may believe.

Play-calling Boom or Bust Potential

Alex Vigderman and Bryce Rossler

If you've ever played a game of Madden, you're likely familiar with the infamous Engage Eight defense, a hyper-aggressive blitz which features three defenders playing deep zone while the other eight rush the quarterback. The playcall has generated many virtual turnovers and sacks, but the savvy gamer usually finds a way to exploit it for big plays. And yet, the closest thing to a real-life equivalent, Cover 0, was surprisingly successful at the NFL level in 2018. In fact, it was far and away the best coverage on an Expected Points Added (EPA) basis, with offenses generating an average EPA of -0.16 against it. Compare that to the more-prevalent Cover 1, which yields about 0.02 EPA per dropback, and it's easy to wonder why more teams don't run Cover 0, right?

Of course not.

The proposition of six rushers with five defenders in coverage is intuitively dangerous, and if you suggested to an NFL head coach that they employ it with regularity, they'd look at you as if you were your 12-year-old cousin who calls Engage Eight every time in Madden.

In football analysis, we must do a better job of considering what analysts in other domains do: variability and risk management. Take, for example, the run-pass equilibrium that the analytics community has recently adopted as their pet cause. Generally the argument goes, "Even as passing has become more prevalent in today's NFL, pass plays are still much more efficient than run plays, so teams should be cutting back on running the ball even more."

The basic statistical backing for that argument is that the Net Yards Per Attempt on called passes (a figure that includes sacks and scrambles) is more than two yards higher than the average on called runs. In terms of EPA, which accounts for the turnover rates of each play type, the difference is comparatively smaller. But, the narrative is the same: pass more.

Per-Play Performance by Called Play Type 2018

	Yards	EPA
Pass	6.4	0.05
Run	4.2	-0.08

Based on these figures, it would seem that passing is generally more valuable than rushing. And that's true. Generally. But, as with anything that seems too good to be true, there's a catch: passing is much more of a boom-bust proposition than running is. A good measurement of these extreme results is the rate of plays with EPA values above 1.00 (boom) or below -1.00 (bust), as they are nice, round numbers that about two-thirds of plays fall within:

Per-Play Performance and Variability by Called Play Type, 2018		
	Boom Rate	**Bust Rate**
Pass	23%	16%
Run	9%	9%

As this table illustrates, run plays may not provide the same upside as passing plays, but they are more stable.

Additional Uses for Risk-Reward Analysis

Below are a few more examples of situations in which considering the variability in outcomes is important when analyzing a tactic, player, or situation.

Run Types

Run type is one such factor to consider. Below is a table showing the performance of runs with and without pulls. Runs with at least one puller perform a little better on average, which can likely be attributed to a higher boom rate and a lower bust rate.

Per-Rush Performance and Variability by Run Blocking 2018			
	EPA/Att	**Bust Rate**	**Boom Rate**
Pull(s)	-0.02	8%	10%
No pulls	-0.09	9%	8%

This trend exists independently of run direction. Inside, off tackle, and outside runs all skew the same way, but the difference with outside runs is particularly stark. Pulling linemen outside the tackles has a similar advantage over zone blocking, largely because it has more boom potential and a lower bust rate:

Per-Rush Performance and Variability by Run Blocking, Outside Runs, 2018			
	EPA/Att	**Bust Rate**	**Boom Rate**
Pull(s)	0.01	9%	12%
No pulls	-0.07	12%	11%

Coverage Schemes

Circling back to coverage schemes, below is a chart that helps visualize how certain coverages are used with variability and risk in mind. It isn't surprising, for example, that Prevent defense allows the fewest boom plays, with Cover 0 and Cover 1 on the other end of that spectrum. In fact, the three most boom-or-bust coverages are all man schemes (the aforementioned two plus Man Cover 2).

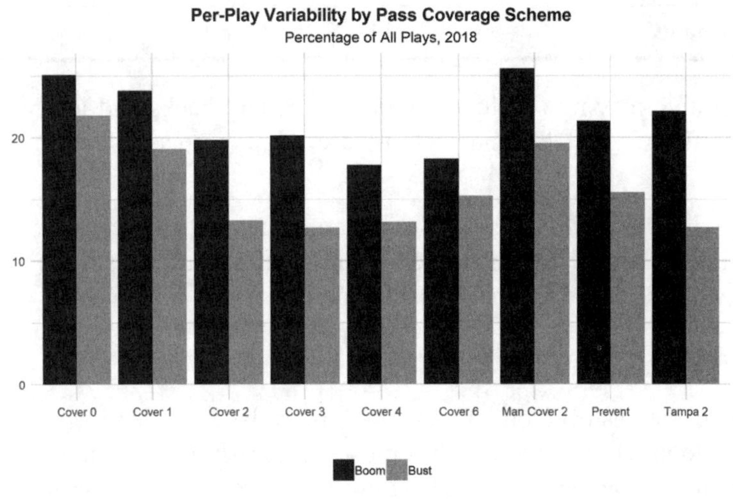

Interestingly, Man Cover 2 is the most extreme of them all, producing a big play one way or the other nearly half the time (27% boom rate, 20% bust rate). Despite having two deep safeties, Man Cover 2 is susceptible to double moves, broken play opportunities, and deep routes.

Another finding is that Tampa 2 is the worst coverage type on average, as it represents a +0.12 EPA/play proposition for the offense. Although it's traditionally thought of as a conservative coverage, it often fails to live up to its billing, yielding boom plays at an above average rate of 24%. It also fails to force the offense into bust plays at a desirable rate (only 14%).

Player Evaluation - Running Backs

As we've already outlined, big plays are less frequent in the running game, so the occasional 70-yard score greatly skews antiquated statistics like yards-per-carry. Therefore, it makes sense to use more stable measures like positive play rate (an EPA-based success rate) to evaluate running backs. Even then, this table illustrates why that metric alone doesn't tell the full story:

Rushing Leaders, Positive Play Rate, 2018 (min. 100 carries)				
	Positive Play Rate	**EPA/Att**	**Bust Rate**	**Boom Rate**
Todd Gurley	51%	0.09	7%	12%
Gus Edwards	50%	0.10	2%	9%
Austin Ekeler	49%	0.04	7%	9%
Aaron Jones	49%	0.04	6%	9%
Mark Ingram	49%	-0.01	7%	7%

The leaders in positive play rate include a mix of excellent backs and low-volume rushers who have been very efficient. Just beyond this list are Alvin Kamara, Kareem Hunt, and Melvin Gordon.

This demonstrates how a player's distribution of outcomes must be considered when evaluating him. Mark Ingram's relatively low EPA/attempt and boom/bust ratio pale in comparison to most backs who rank within the top 25 in positive play percentage.

Conclusion

As we've outlined, the distribution of outcomes must be considered given the complex and dynamic nature of football. Because coaches must weigh risk in addition to reward when making decisions, understanding the volatility and stability of certain tactics is crucial, and EPA fails to provide such insight as a standalone. It is similarly important to contextualize player performance not only by how often they produce positive plays, but their distribution of outcomes, as well. And when we can combine the EPA framework with SIS's charting data, we can gain a deeper understanding of these components and, therefore, the game and its agents.

Evaluating Goal-to-Go Strategy with Expected Points

Spencer Harrison

Those who are really good at knowing what to call in a given situation contend for Super Bowl titles (so long as they have the talent that can execute their wishes). Those who aren't good in that area may frequently be riding the coaching carousel. With that in mind, it is possible to ascertain what the most successful play calls for a given situation are using Expected Points Added (EPA) as the tool for evaluation.

As an example, here are looks at the most effective routes and run schemes in goal-to-go situations.

Route Types

How often have you seen a quarterback throwing a fade into the end zone with his team close to the goal line and the ball sails over or off the receiver's outstretched arms as he jumps to try to make the play?

Dating to 2016, the Fade (combining both traditional and back-shoulder varieties) is the second-most-targeted route type in goal-to-go situations. However, EPA suggests that this is one of the most inefficient throws a quarterback can make in these situations.

Over the past three seasons, there have been fourteen route types (as classified by Sports Info Solutions Video Scouts) to garner at least 50 targets in goal-to-go situations. Of those route types, six average a positive EPA per target. The routes that do well tend to be shorter and more lateral with higher completion percentages. Drags work best in this situation, followed by throws into the flat.

Best Performing Targets, 2016-18				Worst Performing Targets, 2016-18			
Type	Tgt	EPA	Positive Play%	Type	Tgt	EPA	Positive Play%
Drag	145	0.35	52%	Fade	275	-0.26	29%
Flat	290	0.14	48%	Seam	59	-0.21	36%
Out	241	0.10	47%	Whip	63	-0.14	44%
Slant	267	0.09	50%	Corner	145	-0.04	41%
Dig	122	0.03	40%	Curl	166	-0.02	43%

Curl, Corner, Whip, Seam, and Fade routes all result in a negative EPA per target, with Fades typically costing a team the most. Fade routes in goal-to-go situations are completed just 29 percent of the time, so they very frequently result in a loss of down or worse.

Run Schemes

There is a similar disconnect in goal-to-go situations between the most frequently used run schemes and the highest average EPA run schemes.

Among schemes with at least 30 plays, Inside and Outside Zone runs have been called most frequently since 2016, with Inside Zone runs accounting for more than 40 percent of all runs in goal-to-go situations.

The most successful runs tend to be those by quarterbacks, including scrambles, though those plays (which aren't called by an offensive coordinator) put the most important player on the field at greater risk. (As a result, those plays have been removed from the table below.)

When the ball is put into the running back's hands, the most effective run schemes in goal-to-go situations tend to involve pulls, with Power, Trap, Pitch, and Sweep all performing well.

Best Performing Rush Types, 2016-18				Worst Performing Rush Types, 2016-18			
Type	**Rushes**	**EPA**	**Positive%**	**Type**	**Rushes**	**EPA**	**Positive%**
Power	239	0.10	50%	FB Dive	40	-0.16	50%
Trap	40	0.09	50%	Stretch	66	-0.08	42%
Zone Read Handoff	98	0.08	47%	Counter	56	-0.06	41%
Pitch	77	0.06	49%	Lead	208	0.01	45%
Sweep	32	0.05	41%	Inside Zone	1043	0.01	50%

One fear with pull scheme runs might be the possibility of a defender shooting the gap and blowing up the play for a loss. However, the rate at which those runs cost a team at least one expected point is in line with most other runs, while outside zone runs like Stretch and Lead plays tend to get blown up slightly more frequently than others.

Inside Zone is essentially neutral from an EPA perspective, but actually produces a positive outcome more often than some of the schemes that fall above it in average EPA per play.

Lamar Jackson, Scrambles, and Two-Man

Keegan Abdoo

This article appeared on Football Outsiders *before the start of the 2018 NFL sesaon. Since then, Lamar Jackson took over as the starting QB of the Ravens.*

Lamar Jackson was frequently compared to Michael Vick in last year's pre-draft process, and for good reason. Both are quarterbacks from ACC schools who have strong arms and inconsistent accuracy, but the most distinct point of comparison that binds the two is that Jackson possesses the rare combination of breathtaking speed, elusiveness, and athleticism that has not been seen in an elite quarterback prospect since Vick.

While Vick's career ended up being quite the rollercoaster, it seems clear that some of his on-field struggles in his early seasons came from his coaching staff trying to force him into a more traditional offense. On the other hand, Vick's career year with the Eagles in 2010 came with the creative coaching of offensive coordinator Marty Mornhinweg and head coach Andy Reid, who adapted their scheme to take advantage of Vick's unique skill set. It will be paramount for Jackson's new coaching staff -- including Greg Roman (who coached Colin Kaepernick in San Francisco) and the aforementioned Morningwheg -- to craft an offensive scheme to cater to Jackson's electric athleticism. Part of this task will include understanding the schematic advantage that having a quarterback with rare agility can give an offense.

In the weeks leading up to the draft, Matt Bowen of ESPN brought up an anecdote from his career as a defensive back in the NFL during an appearance on the Bill Barnwell Podcast. When Bowen played for the Packers, they faced Vick twice one season, and their defensive gameplanning during the practice week leading up to those games was complicated by Vick's elite ability to make big plays with his legs in addition to his arm. "There are certain things against a quarterback with an electric skill set like Lamar or Michael Vick that impacts your defensive game plan so much you can't do certain things," Bowen said. For example, a defense "cannot play two-man. The cornerbacks are already taught to be in a trail position, looking at the receiver, they're not watching the quarterback. The safeties are already 15 yards deep at the snap to start and pedaling. So you have no one, if the quarterback gets out of the pocket, it's an automatic first down."

For the other two main man coverage schemes, Cover-1 and Cover-0, a defense can usually employ a spy who has enough speed to deter a mobile quarterback from breaking the pocket and scrambling. While this takes away a player in coverage or a pass-rusher, it's a better alternative to the quarterback tucking the ball and taking off for a first down. However, as Bowen explains, when it comes to a quarterback with Jackson's or Vick's exceptional athletic profile, Cover-1/-0 with a spy "looks great on the chalkboard, it looks awesome on Friday practice vs. the scout team. Guess what? You better have someone that can match a Michael Vick or Lamar Jackson athletically. And you don't."

Essentially, having a quarterback with that speed can force a defense to be more one-dimensional and use less man coverage and more zone coverage. Defenders in zone coverage will have their eyes in the backfield reading the quarterback instead of sticking with a receiver and thus will be able to react more quickly if the quarterback tucks the ball and takes off scrambling. While this theory makes plenty of intuitive sense, it is important to verify it through statistical analysis. Luckily, at Sports Info Solutions (SIS), we have the ability to do this, as we identify quality control information for every play in the NFL and college football's FBS. Utilizing our rich database of charting data that includes coverages and scramble types, we can test the conventional wisdom out in a few steps.

1. Examining league-wide scramble tendencies and efficiencies vs. different coverages to see how Man Cover-2 (or "two-man") compares to other coverages.

2. Looking at how Jackson's opponents changed their usage of Man Cover-2 against Jackson and see if there is a noticeable difference.

3. Analyzing Jackson's performance vs. Man Cover-2 to see if the coverage was warranted.

Nationwide Scrambling: Man Cover-2 vs. Other Coverages

During the 2017 season, FBS teams employed Man Cover-2 on 3,507 total dropbacks. That represented 6.1 percent of all dropbacks, making two-man the seventh-most frequently used coverage. Opposing quarterbacks scrambled 313 times vs. two-man, which gave the coverage a scramble rate of 8.9 percent. This was the highest rate of the seven high-volume coverages (over 1,000 total dropbacks). The only coverage overall that had a higher rate of scrambles per dropback was Tampa-2 at 10.8 percent, but that was on one-fifth the sample size (only 650 dropbacks).

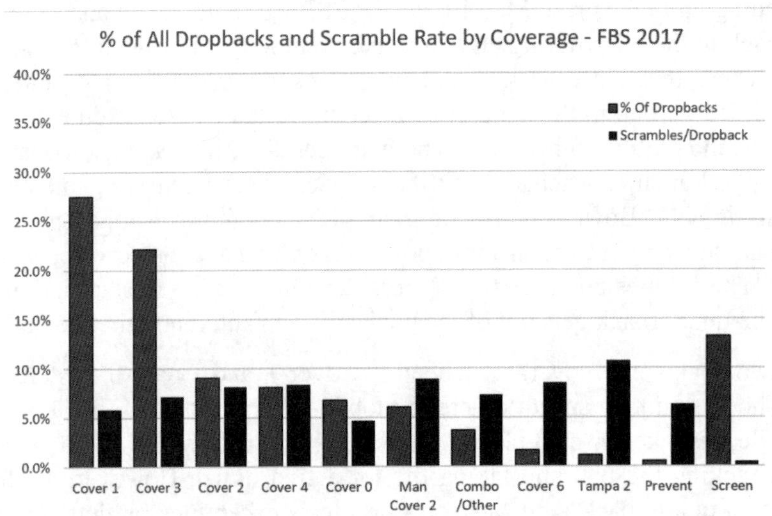

So the first part of the theory bears itself out in the data. Quarterbacks do scramble against Man Cover-2 at a higher rate than any other high-volume coverage. The next question we should ask is, does this happen for a good reason? Our next chart shows the success rate and yards per play of all coverage schemes that saw over 50 scrambles in 2017.

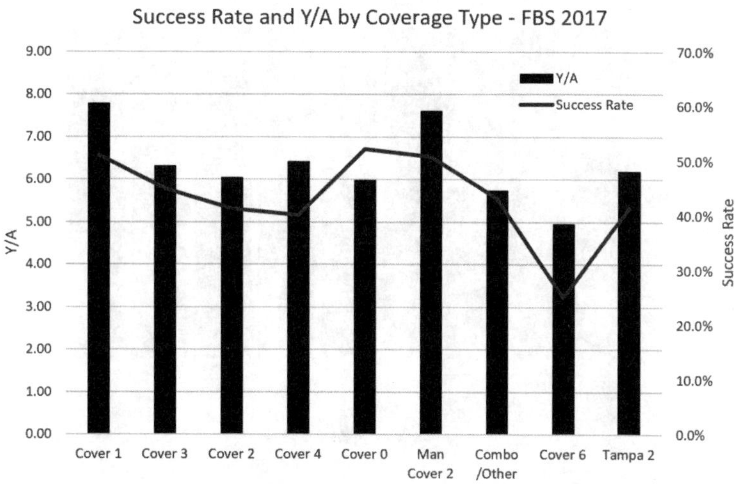

Two-man allowed one of the highest efficiencies on scrambles of any coverage last season, the third-highest Success Rate (50.8 percent) and the second-highest yards per attempt (7.6). Another thing to note in this chart is that the top three coverages by Success Rate allowed were the three types of man coverage (Cover-0, Cover-1, and Man Cover-2). In 2016, two-man allowed the highest success rate (50.7 percent) by a full two percentage points and highest Y/A (7.95) by 0.9 yards (Cover-1 was second in both).

At SIS, we classify the primary reason for every scramble. There are three categories of scrambles: coverage, pressure, and open rushing lane. In the FBS last season, pressure scrambles were the most frequent (44.6 percent of all scrambles), followed by coverage scrambles (33.3 percent), and then open rush lane scrambles (22.1 percent). From an efficiency standpoint, when a quarterback scrambled because he saw an open lane, he was most efficient, averaging 8.7 Y/A and 59.6 percent success rate. Pressure scrambles were the second most explosive (6.4 Y/A compared to 5.8 Y/A for coverage scrambles), but their efficiency was almost identical to coverage scrambles (41.4 percent vs. 41.7 percent success rate).

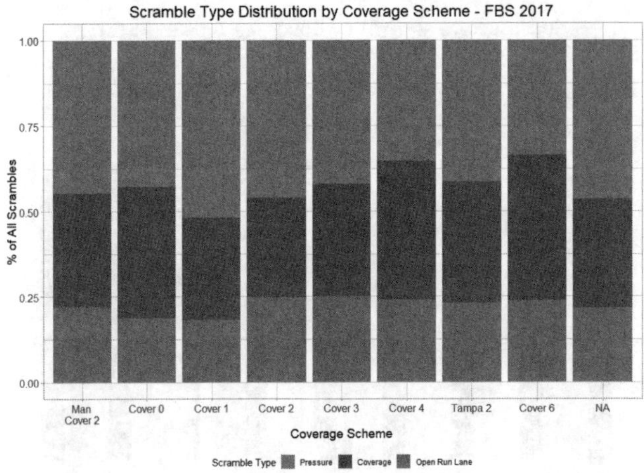

Looking at the scramble type distribution between the nine main coverages (all had at least 70 scrambles), Man Cover-2 has the fourth-highest rate of pressure scrambles (45 percent), fifth-highest rate of coverage scrambles (33 percent), and sixth-highest open run lane scramble rate (22 percent). All nine coverages had at least 25 coverage scrambles, but Man Cover-2 really stood out as being especially susceptible to this scramble type on a large sample (104 rushes). It gave up a 52.9 percent success rate and 7.3 Y/A, which gave it a substantial lead over second place Cover-1 (47 percent success rate and 6.3 Y/A). This makes a lot of sense given Bowen's explanation earlier, as the cornerbacks are in trail technique and not looking at the quarterback. If they are locking down their matchups, the quarterback can pull the ball and break the pocket and will have a whole lot of open field in front of him. Cover-1 presents a similar issue, but often has at least one underneath zone or spy defender.

NFL Scrambling: Man Cover-2 vs. Other Coverages

Man Cover-2 was also the coverage most susceptible to scrambles in 2017 at the NFL level, where the coverage was even more popular. It was employed on 1,642 dropbacks last season, which represented 8.1 percent of dropbacks. This made it the fourth-most popular coverage (not including screens) in the NFL last year. Nine teams employed two-man on more than 10 percent of the dropbacks they faced. These teams include the Steelers (10.2 percent), Buccaneers (11.2 percent), Titans (11.4 percent), and Broncos (11.5 percent), all of whom the Ravens are scheduled to face in the 2018 regular season. Another AFC North rival, the Bengals, ranked 11th at 9.2 percent. Opposing quarterbacks scrambled 111 times vs. Man Cover-2, which was the highest rate (6.8 percent) of any coverage by a considerable amount.

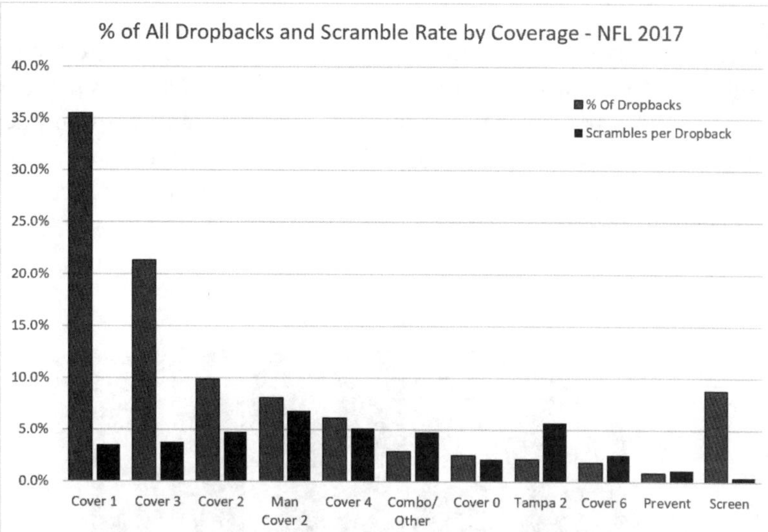

Again, we should check the efficiency of scrambles vs. each type of coverage to see if quarterbacks are making rational decisions by scrambling so often vs. Man Cover-2. In the NFL, two-man was the worst defense in containing scrambles. Of the seven coverages that faced at least 25 scrambles last season, Man Cover-2 allowed the highest Y/A (8.5) and Success Rate (67.6 percent). (Note that Success Rate is calculated differently for college than the NFL, with a 50%/70%/100% threshold for yards to go for college instead of 45%/60%/100% for the NFL).

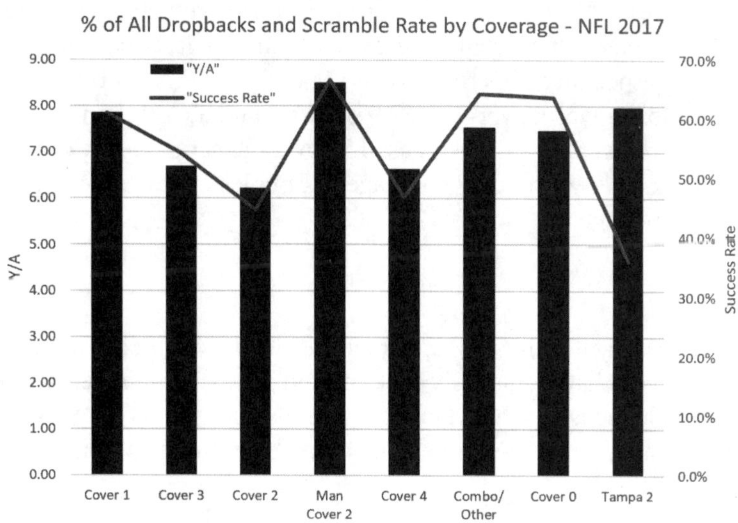

Clearly, the league-wide data backs up our hypothesis: two-man is the coverage that leaves defenses most susceptible to success by scrambles. It repeats itself across both the NFL and FBS, and the good news for Jackson is that the Man Cover-2 is used in the NFL at 133 percent the rate that it is used in the FBS.

Scramble types follow a pretty similar distribution at the NFL level. Pressure scrambles once again are the most common (45.4 percent), followed by coverage scrambles (29.8 percent) and then open rushing lane scrambles (24.8 percent). When quarterbacks scramble with an open running lane, they have a ridiculous 69.3 percent success rate and 8.5 Y/A. Scrambles that are forced by pressure are more efficient (53.8 percent success rate and 7.3 Y/A) than those forced by coverage (48.3 percent success rate and 6.4 Y/A).

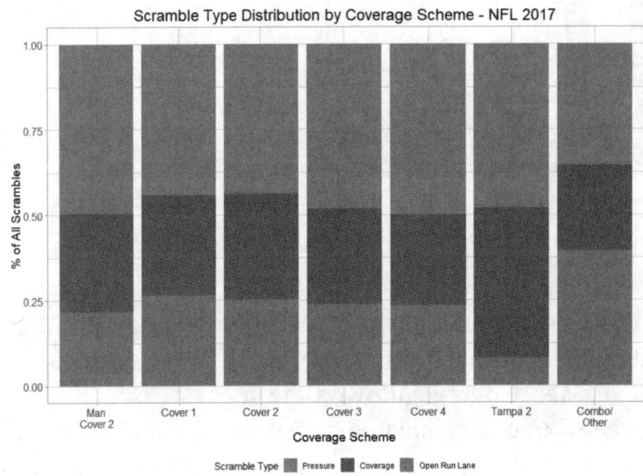

Man Cover-2 had the second-highest relative pressure scramble rate (49 percent), fourth-highest rate of coverage scrambles (29 percent), and sixth-highest open run lane scramble rate (22 percent) of any of the seven coverages that faced at least 25 scrambles last season. Just like in the FBS, coverage scrambles are especially effective against Man Cover-2, with by far the highest success rate (75 percent; next closest was Cover-4 at 52.9 percent) and Y/A (9.0; next closest was Cover-3 with 6.0) of the five coverages that saw at least 15 coverage scrambles. Combining this with the larger-sample FBS data, it is clear that coverage scrambles are a huge weakness that can be exploited in two-man coverage.

Lamar Jackson

Looking at the 2017 season, it is readily apparent that teams avoided playing Man Cover-2 vs. Jackson last season. Given that teams only face around 10 to 14 opponents in a season and the diversity in talent and scheme is vast between the 100-plus teams in the FBS, it is important to take into account each opponent's relative tendencies when examining the distribution of coverages each quarterback faced.

For my sample in this analysis, I took the 123 FBS quarterbacks who had over 200 dropbacks in 2017. Before I explain this process for this opponent adjustment, I created a flow chart to illustrate it:

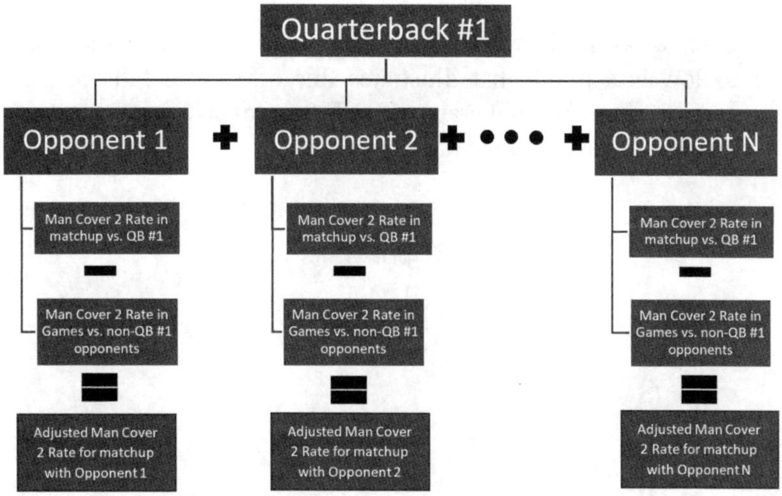

The steps for this are as follows:

1. For each qualifying quarterback, find the Man Cover-2 rate in each of their matchups.

2. For each matchup, calculate the Man Cover-2 rate used by the opponent in all of their games that season against teams other than the quarterback's team.

3. Take the difference between these two rates in each matchup.

4. Calculate an average (weighted by dropbacks by the quarterback in each game) of that difference, and you have the Opponent-Adjusted Man Cover-2 Rate Faced for each quarterback.

The Opponent-Adjusted Man Cover-2 Rate Faced represents the general change in two-man coverage strategy of defensive coordinators when facing a specific quarterback over the course of a season.

After doing calculations, we once again find evidence that teams avoided playing two-man against Lamar Jackson. Interestingly, enough, Jackson's opponents used Man Cover-2 in their games against other teams at the fourth-highest rate in the sample (9.1 percent). However, in their games vs. Louisville, they only employed the coverage on 5.2 percent of dropbacks (52nd-lowest rate). Jackson's Opponent-Adjusted Man Cover-2 Rate Faced was -4.4 percent, which was the eighth biggest discrepancy in the sample. Clearly, defensive coordinators were limited in matchups against Jackson and were forced to scheme away from using Man Cover-2.

We can be even more confident that this deterrence effect is signal and not noise by looking at 2016 to see if the trend repeats itself. There were 118 quarterbacks who had at least 200 dropbacks in the FBS during the 2016 season. Jackson's 2016 opponents played Man Cover-2 in their other games at a rate of 8.1 percent (38th-highest rate), which was still above average. Jackson only saw Man Cover-2 at a 4.9 percent rate (31st-lowest). His aggregated opponent-adjusted Man Cover-2 rate was -3.1 percent in 2016, which was the 17th-biggest discrepancy in the sample. Jackson ranking in the top 20 in back-to-back years just confirms that teams avoided using the coverage against him.

Combining both years, Jackson clearly sticks out as a quarterback who forced teams to avoid playing two-man. Below is a graph that illustrates this effect. He falls in the quadrant where opponents usually employed an above-average rate of Man Cover-2, but when they played Jackson they used the coverage at a below-average rate.

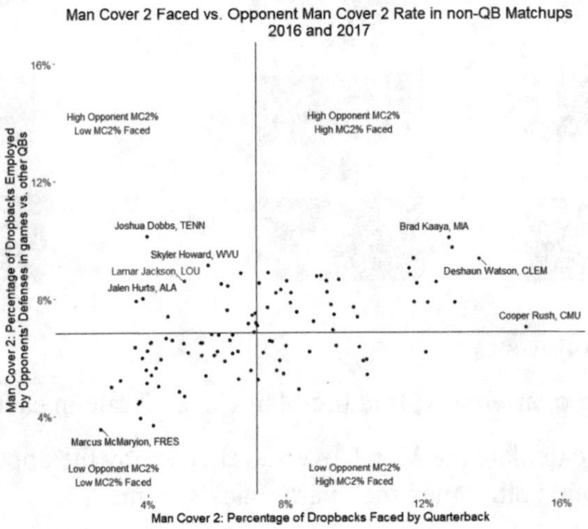

We can also use the Opponent-Adjusted Man Cover-2 Rate Faced to see if this deterrence effect extends beyond Jackson to any quarterback with a tendency to scramble against the coverage. Below is a graph of the 104 quarterbacks who had at least 400 dropbacks over the past two seasons, with their Opponent-Adjusted Man Cover-2 Rate Faced plotted against their scramble rate against the coverage.

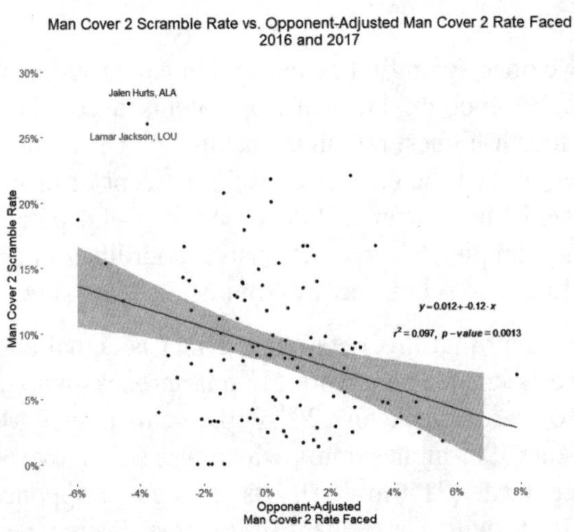

Jackson is clearly an outlier, with a ridiculous scramble rate of 26 percent. Beyond him, there exists a statistically significant relationship between a quarterback's tendency to scramble against two-man and their deterrence effect with the coverage, as seen in the graph. The threat of a given quarterback scrambling against two-man accounts for about ten percent of an opponent's likelihood to employ that coverage scheme against him above or below their normal tendency. If you look at the top 10 and bottom 10 in the Opponent-Adjusted Man Cover-2 Rate Faced, it becomes pretty clear that a quarterback's scramble rate plays a role in how often Defensive Coordinator's employ two-man against them.

Player	College	DropBacks	Scrambles	Scr/DB	M2 Scr/DB	OAM2R	Rank
Joshua Dobbs	Tennessee	401	30	7.5%	18.8%	-6.0%	1
Jason Driskel	Florida Atlantic	695	28	4.0%	15.4%	-5.1%	2
Jake Bentley	South Carolina	655	45	6.9%	12.5%	-4.5%	3
Jalen Hurts	Alabama	753	97	12.9%	27.6%	-4.4%	4
Lamar Jackson	Louisville	987	100	10.1%	26.0%	-3.8%	5
Alex Hornibrook	Wisconsin	545	11	2.0%	4.0%	-3.4%	6
Skyler Howard	West Virginia	417	21	5.0%	8.3%	-3.1%	7
DeShone Kizer	Notre Dame	413	26	6.3%	6.7%	-2.8%	8
Mckenzie Milton	UCF	879	62	7.1%	14.3%	-2.7%	9
Darell Garretson	Oregon State	408	16	3.9%	16.7%	-2.6%	10
Eric Dungey	Syracuse	776	74	9.5%	16.7%	3.4%	95
Deshaun Watson	Clemson	624	25	4.0%	4.7%	3.6%	96
Chase Litton	Marshall	849	17	2.0%	4.7%	3.8%	97
Kyle Shurmur	Vanderbilt	810	25	3.1%	3.2%	4.1%	98
Zach Smith	Baylor	434	14	3.2%	3.6%	4.2%	99
Ryan Finley	NC State	883	23	2.6%	4.7%	4.7%	100
Mike White	Western Kentucky	1123	14	1.2%	3.5%	4.8%	101
Conner Manning	Georgia State	822	31	3.8%	2.4%	4.8%	102
Ross Bowers	California	481	14	2.9%	1.7%	5.5%	103
Cooper Rush	Central Michigan	494	21	4.3%	6.8%	7.9%	104

Other than Alex Hornibrook and Skyler Howard, all of the quarterbacks in the top 10 had either an above-average overall scramble rate or two-man scramble rate. In the bottom 10, all of the quarterbacks scrambled at a below-average rate both overall and against Man Cover-2, other than Eric Dungey. It appears that not only are defensive coordinators discouraged from using the coverage against scrambling quarterbacks, but they also increase their usage against quarterbacks who do not scramble often.

Jackson's Dominance vs. Man Cover-2

After providing ample evidence that teams did in fact shy away from playing two-man vs. Jackson, naturally the next question to ask is was it warranted? The answer to that is: absolutely. Jackson dominated Man Cover-2 with his legs. He faced two-man on 50 dropbacks and he scrambled on 13 of those (26 percent). Small sample aside, his numbers are incredible. He had a ridiculous 84.6 percent Success Rate and 15.2 yards per attempt on scrambles. If you look at all of his dropbacks vs. two-man, his success rate was 51.9 percent, which ranked ninth out of the 85 quarterbacks who faced the coverage on at least 30 dropbacks over the past two seasons. This is visualized in the graph below, which plots the Opponent-Adjusted Man Cover-2 Rate Faced against each quarterback's success rate on all dropbacks vs. the coverage. Jackson falls in one of the "rational" quadrants, where he was very efficient when facing two-man and defensive coordinators reacted accordingly.

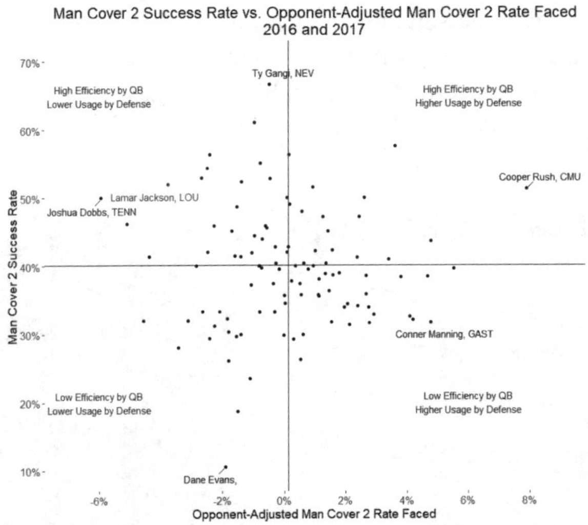

Jackson was able to recognize the vulnerability in this coverage and take full advantage, as evidenced by his outlier scramble rate vs. two-man (which was three times the FBS average). This highlights Jackson's ability to process information quickly and make optimal decisions. Contrary to some popular narratives, Jackson was adept at moving through his reads playing in Bobby Petrino's pro-style offense. Given his experience in Petrino's system, it shouldn't be much of a surprise that Baltimore Ravens offensive coordinator Marty Mornhinweg recently said that Jackson has done "an outstanding job" at training camp so far and is "way ahead of the curve."

According to Benjamin Solak's incredibly detailed charting project, Contextualized Quarterbacking, Jackson stands out in two aspects that illustrate his football intelligence: ball placement and moving beyond first read. Jackson had great placement at every level past the line of scrimmage; out of the 13 quarterback prospects who Solak charted, he ranked:

- fourth in placement (75.3 percent) from 0 to 9 yards;
- third in placement (69.2 percent) from 10 to 19 yards;
- and first in placement (60.4 percent) at 20-plus yards.

As Solak explains, this shows that Jackson "is acutely aware of where the ball belongs relative to the coverage" when he throws. Furthermore, Jackson threw the highest share of his attempts moving past his first read (21.7 percent), and on these throws led the sample by a substantial amount in placement (72.2 percent; Kyle Lauletta was second at 67.1 percent). This exemplifies Jackson's "ability to retain his head post-snap … the playbook understanding, poise, and self-control to shred a defense with whatever they give him."

Jackson's experience in a pro-style offense with complex reads can be further seen in the distribution of his snap-to-throw time on his shotgun dropbacks, where he had highest median of all the drafted quarterbacks we timed.

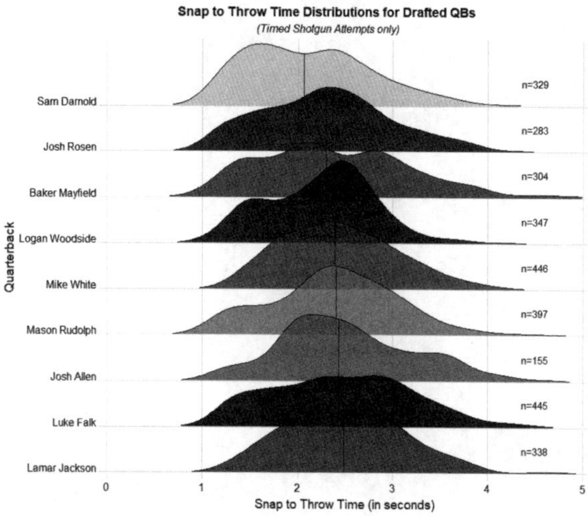

Summary

After looking at how often each qualifying quarterback faced Man Cover-2 relative to their opponent's tendencies, it is evident that defensive coordinators avoided using the coverage when playing Jackson. We also noticed that the other quarterbacks clustered around Jackson who faced a low opponent-adjusted two-man rate almost all had above-average scramble rates; conversely, the quarterbacks who faced a high adjusted two-man rate almost all scrambled less than average. Looking at Jackson's performance against the coverage, it is clear that he scrambled often and was hyper-efficient on those scrambles. Even including passes, Jackson was one of the most successful quarterbacks in the FBS over the past two seasons vs. Man Cover-2, so defensive coordinators were acting rationally by decreasing their use of the coverage against Louisville.

The Secret Behind the Rams' Rushing Success

Nate Weller

The late-season resurgence of C.J. Anderson in Los Angeles, who played a large role in propelling the Rams through the playoffs, added fuel to the debate about the relevance of running backs in the modern NFL.

This came in a season in which James Conner gained close to 1,500 scrimmage yards in only 13 games, and a 33-year-old Adrian Peterson got back over the 1,000 yard mark for the first time since 2015. Meanwhile, teams like the Jaguars, whose run game carried them to a conference championship only a year ago, failed to have a single 100-yard rusher.

Based on pretty much any metric, passing provides more value than running, but what that really means for play calling is still hotly debated. And if it's so inefficient, why were the Rams, Chiefs, and Patriots able to win this weekend by dominating on the ground?

Stop Trying to Establish the Run

Conventional wisdom has always stated that establishing the run is crucial to an offense's success. Even if you aren't running the ball particularly well, you should stick with it because you will wear down the defense and have more success as the game wears on.

To look at this, we compared a team's first half carries versus their positive play percentage (Positive%) on second half carries. (Positive% is an Expected Points-based metric that represents the percentage of plays a player earned a positive Expected Points Added value.) Establishing the run in the first half shows almost no correlation to second half success. In fact, it actually shows a small negative correlation, indicating at some level that rushing performance actually *decreases* the more carries are forced onto a running back early in the game.

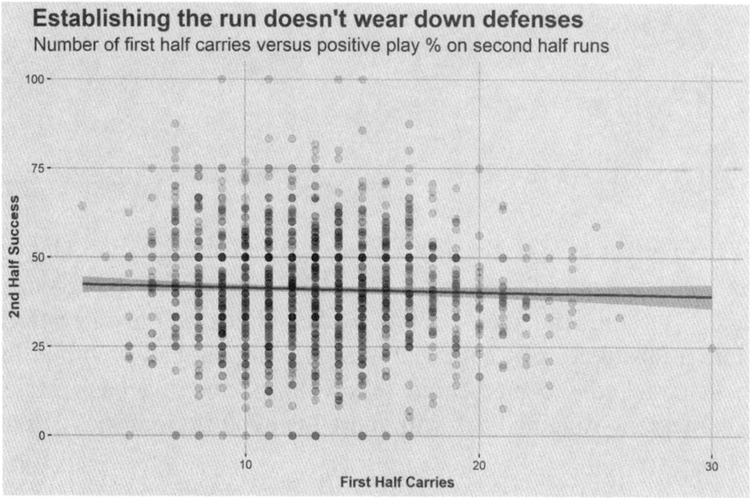

This potentially indicates a few things: that running the ball a lot early does not cause the defense to fatigue more than a normal offensive split, at least not enough to affect performance in a meaningful way, and that predictable play calling can lead to decreased offensive performance.

Despite this, coaches continue to stick by this strategy. In their playoff exit, the Seahawks ran the ball 24 times for 3.0 yards per carry, waiting until the final quarter to open up the pass game. This is despite Russell Wilson averaging 8.6 yards per attempt and posting a QB Rating of 115.3.

This also illustrates another important point: passing success generally acts independent of rushing success. Since 2016, the correlation between a teams Positive% on the ground and their Positive% through the air is close to zero, and this correlation even holds true when looking at play action. On average, success rate on play action passes tended to stay around 50 percent, with some noise on either side, regardless of a team's success on the ground.

Creating Mismatches at the Line of Scrimmage

Teams that are successful on the ground in the modern NFL are not doing so by staying patient, or "establishing the run" early. They are doing so by putting their running backs and linemen in advantageous situations.

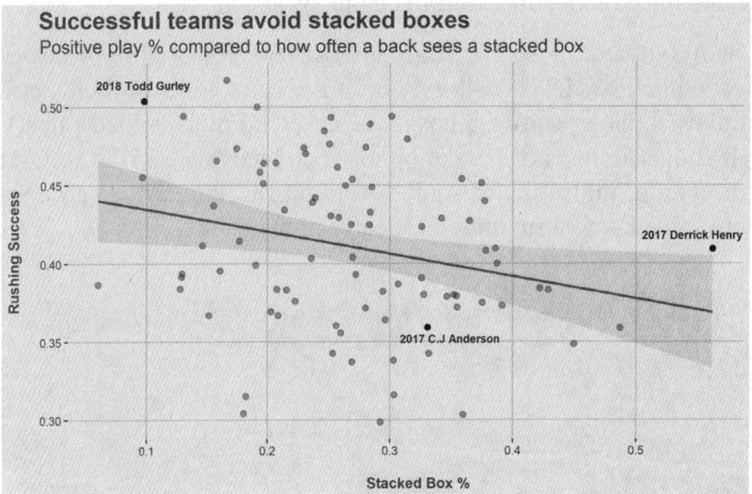

C.J. Anderson is the perfect case study. During his 2017 campaign with Denver, Anderson ran into a stacked box on 33 percent of attempts, and had a Positive% of 36 percent. In weeks 16 and 17 with the Rams this season, Anderson ran into a stacked box on only 19 percent of his carries, and flipped that into a Positive% of 62 percent. Among running backs with at least 25 carries in that time period, that ranked second behind fellow Rams running back Malcolm Brown (69 percent). Put into context, no running back with more than 100 attempts in 2018 had a success rate above 50 percent.

Even without considering that he was unemployed for most of the season, Anderson has been impressive, and McVay's creative play calling deserves a lot of credit. While the Rams predominantly stick to one personnel grouping, they use a wide variety of formations and move players around a lot to generate mismatches, including some of the most creative use of motion in the league.

Nobody Uses Motion More Effectively Than the Rams

In 2018, teams averaged 1.6 yards before contact (YBC) and 4.1 yards per attempt (Y/A) on runs that didn't use motion. When using motion in any capacity those numbers jumped to 1.9 and 4.5, and jumped further to 2.2 and 4.9 on plays using jet motion (YBC and Y/A exclude jet sweeps and QB scrambles).

No team made use of this more than the Rams, who led the league in jet motion usage by a long shot. In total, the Rams used jet motion on 17 percent of offensive snaps in 2018. The next closest teams were the Chargers and Titans who used jet motion on 14 and 8 percent of offensive snaps respectively.

The Rams averaged an astonishing 2.7 YBC on plays utilizing jet motion, significantly better than their overall average on runs plays of 2.0, and almost a full yard better than the average run play in the NFL (1.8).

There's more to this than simply using jet motion more, and having a talented running back certainly adds value, but the point is that scheme plays an important role too. Nobody will argue that Anderson is a better running back than Ezekiel Elliott, but Elliott wasn't good enough against the Rams in the divisional round to overcome facing a stacked box on 40 percent of his carries.

Running the ball still has an important role in modern offenses, but for teams to be successful they need to start moving away from the more traditional ground-and-pound methods. The Rams are creating a blueprint; now it's time for other teams to start using it.

Our Scouting Process

John Todd

This is the first version of *The SIS Football Rookie Handbook,* but the wheels were put into motion years ago. Sports Info Solutions has produced *The Bill James Handbook* for nearly two decades, compiling the baseball statistics and insights that have driven the sport into its modern age. More recently, a scout of ours, Nathan Cooper (you'll hear from him shortly…), started putting together an NFL Draft guide as a side-project on his own time. With some assistance from co-workers and his parents, he put together his own book for each of the past two offseasons, and the bones of this venture were established. Under the guidance of our Director of Football and former NFL scout, Matt Manocherian, we were able to build our own version of an NFL scouting department in Coplay, Pennsylvania.

Besides the training that all scouts receive when they come to SIS, we help with weekly "Scout School" sessions in the fall, where we discuss everything from how to watch film and what to look for in different positions, to report-writing structure and creating a common language for player evaluations. The grading scales and report formats seen in these pages are adapted from what Matt learned with two NFL front offices. Practice reports at each position were written, edited, and revised through the season. Countless hours of film were watched, and thousands of players were considered. Gradually over the next few months, over 400 different players were evaluated and cross-checked. Nathan and I, serving as over-the-top scouts, have synthesized and finalized the reports and stacked the players to ultimately present scouting reports on 254 of the best players in the 2019 NFL Draft.

Sports Info Solutions, at its core, is an analytics provider. We chart every FBS and NFL game each season, logging specific data points, tracking player assignments, and creating deep-dive statistical analyses to better understand the game of football. With that in mind, it was important to stay true to our data roots in creating this book. Combining scouting and analytics is an increasingly hot topic in league circles, and we hope offering both—side-by-side—for each player in this handbook will help illustrate the importance of considering these perspectives in tandem.

On The Road with SIS

Nathan Cooper

This season, Sports Info Solutions partnered with the College Gridiron Showcase, a postseason all-star event for NFL Draft hopefuls, to use some of the data found in this handbook to suggest invitees. CGS is the first stop on the pre-draft circuit, where scouts get to evaluate and interact with hundreds of players who may not have previously had the same exposure as more highly-thought-of prospects. We were given a selection of players to choose from, ran the numbers on each of them, and watched film to back up our findings to come up with around 100 players to recommend. The data on these players suggested they were playing at a higher level than public expectations, and we believed each of them was deserving of an opportunity to prove himself. After invites to other events were accepted, injuries, and other factors, nine of our players made their way to Fort Worth, Texas for a week of meetings with scouts, seminars, practices, and a controlled scrimmage. It was a successful week for all of them, and discussions with NFL personnel confirmed that many helped themselves with solid weeks. You will find a report on our CGS Player of the Week, McKinley Whitfield, later in this handbook.

Additionally, for the second straight season, Sports Info Solutions Video Scouts descended on Mobile, Alabama for Senior Bowl week. After months of writing reports on the top players in the 2019 Draft, we had over twenty of our scouts in attendance to see them in person. Many of these scouts have aspirations of careers in scouting, and working at SIS and on this *Handbook* was their first exposure into that field. The Senior Bowl is a great place to evaluate players, but it is also a congregation of the NFL's front office professionals, making it a fantastic networking opportunity. Despite the rain, the experience was a great one! Jim Nagy and his staff have done a great job of opening the week up to current and future scouts alike.

Sports Info Solutions Grading Scale

Before we get into the reports, it's important that we explain how our grading scale works. As a scouting staff, we use a common terminology to grade every trait that we evaluate. We use a 1-9 scale with a 1 representing a "Reject" grade and a 9 meaning a "Rare" grade for whatever trait we are evaluating. We spend a lot of time in Scout School making sure that our scales are calibrated with one another, and this common scale and set of language is a key aspect to ensuring that our evaluations are consistent (that…and cross-checks).

As you look at the scale, note that there is a bold line separating Good (6) from Sufficient (5). Good signifies a trait that wins at the NFL level most of the time. It is the minimum target that needs to be met in order to build a Super Bowl-level roster.

Grade	Definition
9	Rare
8	Excellent
7	Very Good
6	Good
5	Sufficient
4	Mediocre
3	Poor
2	Terrible
1	Reject

Additionally, as you get to the beginning of each position in the book, you will notice that there are positional grading scales. As opposed to grading traits, these scales apply to stacking the final grades for each prospect. For example, on the next page, you can see our Quarterback Grading Scale.

The final grades are listed in the left column (unlike trait grades, these have decimals), but you won't find traditional round-based grades here. Like certain teams, we organize our scale based on how the players project to contribute, not based on the traditional, "he looks like a third rounder," which we think can lead to confusion. For quarterbacks (and at every position), the top grade level is 9.0-7.0, which signifies a perennial Pro Bowl-level player (not an alternate!). The rest of our draftable grades flow down from there.

One final note: all of these grades and descriptions refer to where the player is projected to be by the first game of their second season in the NFL. Sound complicated? Like most things football, you'll see that it's actually quite simple.

QUARTERBACK

Quarterback Grading Scale

GRADE	DESCRIPTION
9.0 – 7.0	Pro Bowl level player. Difference-maker.
6.9 – 6.7	Strong starter. One of the reasons you win.
6.6 – 6.5	Sufficient starter. You can win with him.
6.4 – 6.2	Circumstantial starter or high-quality backup.
6.1 – 6.0	Developmental. Top traits but needs time.
5.9 – 5.8	Backup with limited upside.
5.7	3rd-string or practice squad candidate.

Quarterback Rankings

Rank	Name	Grade	Page
1	Dwayne Haskins	6.8	32
2	Kyler Murray	6.8	34
3	Daniel Jones	6.5	36
4	Ryan Finley	6.4	38
5	Will Grier	6.4	40
6	Drew Lock	6.3	42
7	Jarrett Stidham	6.3	44
8	Brett Rypien	6.3	46
9	Gardner Minshew II	6.3	48
10	Tyree Jackson	6.2	50
11	Clayton Thorson	6.2	52
12	Easton Stick	5.9	54
13	Taylor Cornelius	5.8	56
14	Trace McSorley	5.8	58

Dwayne Haskins

Ohio State Buckeyes

Final Grade: 6.8 QB Rank: 1 of 14

Height	Weight	Year	Jersey #	Hometown
6021	220	3SO	7	Potomac, MD

One-Liner

Haskins is a strong pocket passer who has all of the physical tools to be a starter at the next level, but could elevate even further with more consistent footwork.

Overall

Haskins played quarterback in Ohio State's spread offense, exclusively out of shotgun. He is a two-year player, but 2018 was his first year as a starter. Haskins is a good athlete with the size necessary to withstand NFL-caliber hits and punishment. Haskins is a competitor who has shown the ability to command an offense.

Pass Game

In the pass game, Haskins improved drastically over the course of his first season as the starting quarterback. Haskins shows good spot-on accuracy short, with very good ball placement down the field. He's a high volume short-level passer. He has very good arm strength when he steps into his throws, but occasionally will not step into them when driving down the field. He rarely puts the ball in dangerous situations and reads his progressions well. He also has the ability to move outside the pocket and makes good decisions when deciding whether to run, pass or throw the ball away. He frequently makes awkward throws, but sometimes he forces himself into that situation with his footwork. He takes a lot of short, choppy steps and doesn't look natural throwing on the move. He's an upper-body thrower and doesn't always step into his passes. He lifts his back foot as he throws and tends to fall off at times. He displays ideal pocket mobility and poise in the pocket. He protects the ball and works the pocket around defenders, but doesn't reset his base to throw. He often fails to throw from a consistent base when under duress, sometimes forcing inaccurate throws. Haskins has the ability to stand in the pocket and deliver the ball with accuracy while pressure is in his face. Haskins is a clutch performer who can step up on the biggest stages for his team. He also improved on third down in game situations throughout his sophomore season. Having only one season of starting experience at a major college, while highly successful, may lead to a steeper learning curve when dealing with adversity at the next level.

Run Game

Haskins isn't a threat in the run game, but is sufficient enough to gain yardage on designed run calls and scrambles. While he possesses the ability to run and break down defenses with his legs, Haskins is not a run-first quarterback.

Last Word

Dwayne Haskins is a young quarterback who has a very high ceiling because he is still developing, as seen by his growth this season. He projects to be a high-end "win-with" starting quarterback by year two who can consistently contribute to the success of his team.

– Brian Rogers

Strengths	Weaknesses
• Decision making	• Consistent base/footwork
• Pocket mobility	• Experience
• Off-platform throws	

Critical Factors

Accuracy	Decision Making / Mental	Clutch Performance
6	7	6

Positional Factors

Short Accuracy	Deep Accuracy	Pocket Awareness	Footwork
6	7	7	5
Under Pressure	**Mobility**	**Arm Strength**	**Release**
6	5	7	6
Awkward Throw	**Eye Discipline**	**Leadership**	**Body Composition**
7	7	6	7

Basic

	Passing									
Year	Att	Comp	Comp%	Yards	Air Yards	Y/A	TD	Int	Sacks	Rating
2017	57	40	70.2%	565	298	9.9	4	1	3	117.9
2018	534	374	70.0%	4839	2348	9.1	50	8	20	123.2
	591	414	70.1%	5404	2646	9.1	54	9	23	122.7

Advanced

	Passing Analytics				Rushing (Excluding Sacks)			
Year	IQR	On-Target%	Catchable%	Avg Throw Depth	Att	Yards	Y/A	Scrambles
2017	124.5	-	78.6%	7.3	21	107	5.1	5
2018	125.8	78.1%	82.1%	7.9	58	211	3.6	29
	125.7	78.1%	81.7%	7.8	79	318	4.0	34

Deep Dive

	EPA			IQR Detail				
Year	Total	EPA Per Dropback	Rush EPA	Deep Throws	Under Pressure	No Pressure	vs. Man Cov	vs. Zone Cov
2017	2.9	0.22	-10.7	158.3	112.0	126.6	157.1	120.1
2018	137.0	0.26	-17.0	119.6	83.9	135.3	116.7	120.0
	139.8	0.25	-27.7	123.0	85.8	134.4	121.0	120.0

Kyler Murray

Oklahoma Sooners
Final Grade: 6.8 QB Rank: 2 of 14

Height	Weight	Year	Jersey #	Hometown
5096	195	4JR	1	Allen, TX

One-Liner
Murray is a rare playmaker at the quarterback position with the requisite mental capacity to maximize his arm talent and mobility, but may need to rework his release as a pro to mitigate size concerns.

Overall
Murray played quarterback in Oklahoma's Air Raid-influenced system, heavy in RPOs and play action, which commonly featured concepts such as mesh, hitch-seam, and Y-cross. He was a one-year starter for the Sooners and appeared in 29 career games going back to his time at Texas A&M. Murray is significantly undersized in terms of height and frame but makes up for it with electric athleticism and playmaking ability in the open field. He has good footwork and sets up quickly in the pocket. He benefitted from a very strong offensive line and a scheme that allowed him to get the ball out quickly or run.

Pass Game
Murray considerably improved his ability to effectively and quickly diagnose coverages and work through his progressions over the course of the season and was good in that regard by year's end. He has sufficient awareness of the rush and has rare mobility to extend plays and avoid sacks when the protection breaks down. Murray prefers to break the pocket and scramble rather than navigate the rush from within structure. He will take sacks trying to keep plays alive for too long, but overall makes good decisions with the ball in his hands. He flashes the ability to move defenders with his eyes. He tends to throw falling away when a rusher is bearing down on him. He has a baseball-style release which features a false pump and an occasional looping motion from the hip which, when combined with his body composition, will result in some batted balls and pass deflections at the pro level. He has very good arm strength and is able to access tight windows, make the landmark throws and push the ball downfield accurately. Murray displays the necessary touch, as well as the ability to plant his back leg and drive the ball with velocity. During his load, his front foot twists toward his target after it has planted, instead of before it lands. He shows good accuracy short and frequent spot-on accuracy deep to hit receivers in stride. He's able to access a variety of arm slots and is comfortable throwing off-platform and on the move. He performs very well in clutch situations and shows mental toughness to recover from mistakes.

Run Game
In the run game, Murray is an exceptional threat as both an improvisational and designed ballcarrier, due to excellent short area quickness and change-of-direction skills. His acceleration to top speed is explosive when he decides to take off, and he needs to be heavily accounted for on the ground by defenses.

Last Word
Murray projects as a solid starting "win-with" quarterback in the NFL, with flashes of elite "win because of" playmaking ability. His size will always be an issue and he will need more reps, but he has the inherent quarterbacking skills and intangibles necessary to succeed.

– Bryce Rossler

Strengths	Weaknesses
• Mobility/acceleration	• Size
• Arm strength	• Experience
• Clutch playmaking ability	• Inconsistent release

Critical Factors

Accuracy	Decision Making / Mental	Clutch Performance
6	6	7

Positional Factors

Short Accuracy	Deep Accuracy	Pocket Awareness	Footwork
6	7	6	6
Under Pressure	**Mobility**	**Arm Strength**	**Release**
5	9	7	5
Awkward Throw	**Eye Discipline**	**Leadership**	**Body Composition**
6	6	6	3

Basic

	Passing									
Year	Att	Comp	Comp%	Yards	Air Yards	Y/A	TD	Int	Sacks	Rating
2017	21	18	85.7%	359	129	17.1	3	0	0	158.3
2018	377	260	69.0%	4361	2264	11.6	42	7	18	137.2
	398	278	69.8%	4720	2393	11.9	45	7	18	140.1

Advanced

	Passing Analytics				Rushing (Excluding Sacks)			
Year	IQR	On-Target%	Catchable%	Avg Throw Depth	Att	Yards	Y/A	Scrambles
2017	158.3	-	90.0%	8.0	14	142	10.1	3
2018	143.2	79.2%	84.0%	10.6	122	1110	9.1	40
	145.7	79.2%	84.3%	10.5	136	1252	9.2	43

Deep Dive

	EPA			IQR Detail				
Year	Total	EPA Per Dropback	Rush EPA	Deep Throws	Under Pressure	No Pressure	vs. Man Cov	vs. Zone Cov
2017	25.1	0.93	3.0	143.8	158.3	155.8	158.3	151.9
2018	236.9	0.47	61.4	106.8	113.8	148.6	138.5	133.4
	262.0	0.50	64.4	108.5	119.1	149.6	145.0	134.4

Daniel Jones

Duke Blue Devils
Final Grade: 6.5 QB Rank: 3 of 14

Height	Weight	Year	Jersey #	Hometown
6052	220	4JR	17	Charlotte, NC

One-Liner
Jones has the arm talent, mobility, and poise under pressure to succeed at the next level, but he'll need to improve his decision-making ability and overall accuracy.

Overall
Jones was the QB in Duke's spread offense that centered around the quick passing game. He was a three-year starter, playing in 36 career games for the Blue Devils and started all of them. He is a good athlete with a big, semi-lanky frame. He shows exceptional toughness by fighting through contact, executing throws with rushers bearing down on him, and quickly bouncing back from being hit hard.

Pass Game
In the pass game, he flashes consistent spot-on accuracy overall. His short accuracy is good, as he consistently optimizes YAC for his receivers via his placement. On deep balls, he's inconsistent and off-target, throwing a lot of pre-determined passes that were questionable decisions. He has the mobility to extend plays consistently. Although he makes some quick, one-read throws, he does use good eye discipline to manipulate the safety. He ties his upper half and lower half together, and he consistently resets and throws with a good base. He has unorthodox footwork in his drops and and often initiates them with a hop. He will have to develop the ability to take snaps under center in the pros. He stands in to deliver throws with pressure in his face. He flashes the ability to throw on the run with some accuracy, although he's inconsistent throwing off-platform. Jones was affected by breaking his clavicle, as there was less zip on his ball and his release became elongated. He also began to pat the ball more often to get in rhythm. He showed a lack of arm strength and control in precipitious conditions. Jones attempts some questionable throws, especially when he pre-determines his targets.

Run Game
In the run game, he has good speed, quickness, and vision, with the size and physicality to withstand hits. Duke used him on many designed QB runs and he showed that he was able to gain yardage down the field and run away from defenders.

Last Word
Jones projects to be a sufficient "win-with" starting QB at the next level. He has the physical tools to develop into a solid QB if he can take to NFL coaching and make the fixes that are required.

– Ben Hrkach

Strengths	**Weaknesses**
• Arm talent	• Decision making
• Eye discipline	• Inconsistent accuracy
• Mobility	• Pocket awareness

Critical Factors

Accuracy	Decision Making / Mental	Clutch Performance
5	5	6

Positional Factors

Short Accuracy	Deep Accuracy	Pocket Awareness	Footwork
6	5	5	6
Under Pressure	**Mobility**	**Arm Strength**	**Release**
6	6	6	6
Awkward Throw	**Eye Discipline**	**Leadership**	**Body Composition**
5	7	6	6

Basic

	Passing									
Year	Att	Comp	Comp%	Yards	Air Yards	Y/A	TD	Int	Sacks	Rating
2016	429	269	62.7%	2781	1285	6.5	15	9	29	84.3
2017	453	257	56.7%	2691	1277	5.9	14	11	28	74.3
2018	392	237	60.5%	2674	1289	6.8	22	9	28	90.0
	1274	763	59.9%	8146	3851	6.4	51	29	85	82.5

Advanced

	Passing Analytics				Rushing (Excluding Sacks)			
Year	IQR	On-Target%	Catchable%	Avg Throw Depth	Att	Yards	Y/A	Scrambles
2016	89.5	-	77.3%	7.5	112	637	5.7	27
2017	74.4	-	74.1%	7.9	132	715	5.4	24
2018	99.5	74.5%	79.6%	8.1	76	494	6.5	23
	87.3	74.5%	76.9%	7.8	320	1846	5.8	74

Deep Dive

	EPA			IQR Detail				
Year	Total	EPA Per Dropback	Rush EPA	Deep Throws	Under Pressure	No Pressure	vs. Man Cov	vs. Zone Cov
2016	-34.2	-0.07	-0.1	65.8	87.0	91.1	74.1	104.2
2017	-61.3	-0.16	32.5	62.8	65.7	77.9	66.3	66.9
2018	-18.3	-0.07	17.6	87.5	52.0	120.4	104.3	88.9
	-113.7	-0.10	49.9	75.9	67.4	95.5	81.3	84.4

Ryan Finley

NC State Wolfpack
Final Grade: 6.4 QB Rank: 4 of 14

Height	Weight	Year	Jersey #	Hometown
6040	208	6SR	15	Phoenix, AZ

One-Liner

Finley has the arm, anticipatory instincts, and clutch production that are necessary to succeed at the next level, but his inconsistent footwork and follow-through may lead to accuracy issues early in his career.

Overall

Finley was the quarterback in North Carolina State's West Coast offense. He played in 47 games with 42 starts between his time at Boise State and NC State. He transferred to NC State as a graduate after three years at Boise State (2013-15). He's a solid, but lanky, athlete with good body composition for the quarterback position. He's tough and a competitor, having played six seasons at the college level due to a season-ending injury before leaving Boise State.

Pass Game

He has good overall spot-on accuracy, but struggles some in the short-to-intermediate area of the field. Some of his accuracy issues can be attributed to his release and footwork. He doesn't always have a consistent drop back and his feet will get erratic. He starts with his right foot offset and behind his left foot, and then takes his first drop step with the right, not gaining any ground. Although they mostly run out of shotgun, there was one instance when he got a foot stepped on by his offensive lineman trying to get out from under center. He has a tendency to throw off of his back foot even when he has the room to step into his throw. He has a quick, compact release, but doesn't always follow through. He tends to try to guide or place the ball instead of throwing it, which leads to some off-target passes. He makes good decisions overall, but will try to force some passes by throwing back across his body over the middle. When he throws with anticipation, he shows good instincts and accuracy. He does a good job going through reads, but at times will get locked onto a receiver. He has the arm strength to make every throw on the field, but needs to follow through on his release. In the clutch, he performed well by converting 3rd downs and scoring touchdowns late in games. He shows the ability to make awkward throws off platform and still deliver a ball with accuracy. Under pressure he will lose some poise at times, but overall does a good job escaping and keeping his eyes downfield.

Run Game

Although he isn't a threat to the defense as a runner, and is more of the prototypical pocket passer, he still has enough mobility to work the pocket, keep plays alive, and even scramble for yardage on brief occasion.

Last Word

Finley projects as a top-end backup at the next level with some "win-with" traits who can start given the right circumstance. He's a quiet leader that lets his play do the talking, but can take command of a huddle.

– Nathan Cooper

Strengths	**Weaknesses**
• Throws with anticipation	• Short accuracy
• Off-platform accuracy	• Follow-through
• Clutch performance	• Footwork on drops

Critical Factors

Accuracy	Decision Making / Mental	Clutch Performance
6	6	6

Positional Factors

Short Accuracy	Deep Accuracy	Pocket Awareness	Footwork
5	6	6	5
Under Pressure	**Mobility**	**Arm Strength**	**Release**
5	5	6	5
Awkward Throw	**Eye Discipline**	**Leadership**	**Body Composition**
6	6	6	6

Basic

	Passing									
Year	Att	Comp	Comp%	Yards	Air Yards	Y/A	TD	Int	Sacks	Rating
2016	403	243	60.3%	3053	1284	7.6	18	8	15	90.5
2017	478	310	64.9%	3513	1805	7.3	17	6	14	93.4
2018	484	326	67.4%	3928	2572	8.1	25	11	11	99.8
	1365	879	64.4%	10494	5661	7.7	60	25	40	94.8

Advanced

	Passing Analytics				Rushing (Excluding Sacks)			
Year	IQR	On-Target%	Catchable%	Avg Throw Depth	Att	Yards	Y/A	Scrambles
2016	96.1	-	77.4%	7.8	58	192	3.3	13
2017	100.4	-	80.0%	8.5	55	289	5.3	10
2018	103.5	79.0%	81.4%	9.4	32	99	3.1	9
	100.2	79.0%	79.7%	8.6	145	580	4.0	32

Deep Dive

	EPA			IQR Detail				
Year	Total	EPA Per Dropback	Rush EPA	Deep Throws	Under Pressure	No Pressure	vs. Man Cov	vs. Zone Cov
2016	8.0	0.05	-11.1	74.1	67.0	101.3	103.4	91.0
2017	69.3	0.11	21.7	108.9	104.6	99.5	107.8	94.4
2018	94.5	0.18	6.7	93.4	77.4	111.7	123.9	89.9
	171.8	0.11	17.3	95.8	82.7	104.3	111.9	91.6

Will Grier

West Virginia Mountaineers
Final Grade: 6.4 QB Rank: 5 of 14

Height	Weight	Year	Jersey #	Hometown
6024	218	5SR	7	Charlotte, NC

One-Liner
Grier shows accuracy and arm strength to throw to all levels of the field, but questions about his ability to process post-snap, handle pressure, and perform in the clutch may prevent him from ascending to a high-level starter.

Overall
Grier played quarterback almost exclusively out of the shotgun in West Virginia's Air Raid-inspired, RPO-based system. He spent his first two collegiate years at Florida, where he played in six games and started five, before transferring to the Mountaineers and posting big numbers over the last two seasons. He shows fairly good size for the position along with sufficient athleticism.

Pass Game
Grier is a rhythm passer who is at his best when he can get a clean pre-snap read and distribute the ball quickly. He shows good accuracy and arm strength to make throws to all levels of the field. He flashes a great deep ball along with the ability to throw to open receivers, but he needs to develop more consistency in these areas to be a high-level NFL starter. Grier plays with a gunslinger mentality and is quick to take advantage of a favorable one-on-one matchup. That said, when the play breaks down or he needs to improvise, Grier shows some struggles. He doesn't respond well to pressure, makes poor decisions in the pocket, and takes too many sacks. He needs to improve on his ability to make plays when his first read isn't available, and I worry that he over-relies on predetermining his throws in his simple college offense.

Run Game
Grier is not a strong threat as a runner, but he shows sufficient mobility to pick up easy first downs with his legs. He won't be involved in designed-run concepts, but he moves decently within the pocket and shows some ability to keep the play alive.

Last Word
Grier shows the ability to spread the ball around the field and accumulate yardage, but his poise under pressure, and when his team needed him to step up, leave questions about his ability to be a top-tier quarterback on the next level. Overall, he projects in the range of a lower-level starter or high-quality backup, depending on where he ends up. He shows some traits that remind me of both Derek Carr and Ryan Nassib when they were in college, with good size, arm talent, and production but question marks about how they handle pressure.

– Matt Manocherian

Strengths	Weaknesses
• Arm talent	• Struggles under pressure
• Productivity	• Inconsistent in clutch
• First-read throws	• Second- and third- read throws

Critical Factors

Accuracy	Decision Making / Mental	Clutch Performance
6	5	5

Positional Factors

Short Accuracy	Deep Accuracy	Pocket Awareness	Footwork
6	6	5	6
Under Pressure	**Mobility**	**Arm Strength**	**Release**
4	5	6	6
Awkward Throw	**Eye Discipline**	**Leadership**	**Body Composition**
5	5	6	6

Basic

	Passing									
Year	Att	Comp	Comp%	Yards	Air Yards	Y/A	TD	Int	Sacks	Rating
2017	388	250	64.4%	3490	2057	9.0	34	12	14	109.6
2018	397	266	67.0%	3864	2033	9.7	37	8	24	121.1
	785	516	65.7%	7354	4090	9.4	71	20	38	115.4

Advanced

	Passing Analytics				Rushing (Excluding Sacks)			
Year	IQR	On-Target%	Catchable%	Avg Throw Depth	Att	Yards	Y/A	Scrambles
2017	114.9	-	82.5%	11.5	49	214	4.4	30
2018	127.9	78.7%	83.1%	9.8	24	85	3.5	13
	121.5	78.7%	82.8%	10.6	73	299	4.1	43

Deep Dive

	EPA			IQR Detail				
Year	Total	EPA Per Dropback	Rush EPA	Deep Throws	Under Pressure	No Pressure	vs. Man Cov	vs. Zone Cov
2017	53.0	0.15	-10.6	95.1	88.3	119.5	106.3	113.5
2018	140.1	0.32	-1.3	116.1	84.8	136.3	124.1	123.6
	193.1	0.24	-11.9	98.1	87.2	128.6	115.2	120.4

Drew Lock

Missouri Tigers

Final Grade: 6.3 QB Rank: 6 of 14

Height	Weight	Year	Jersey #	Hometown
6036	223	4SR	3	Lee's Summit, MO

One-Liner

Lock is a tough, poised passer who can win deep, but struggles to progress through reads, throw with anticipation, and make good decisions.

Overall

Lock was the starting QB who operated almost exclusively out of the shotgun in Missouri's no-huddle offense. His primary passing concepts were Tosser, Ohio, Stick, All-Curl, screens, and RPOs (slant, fade, screen, out). He was mainly tasked with making one-read and half-field reads out of 0/1- and 3-step drops. He was a 4-year starter who started 46 of the 50 games he played in for the Tigers. He has good athleticism and is a tough, demonstrative leader who plays with confidence. He has a good body comp for the QB position and is built well to withstand hits.

Pass Game

In the passing game, he demonstrates good eye discipline and has a feel for navigating the pocket and feeling the rush while keeping his eyes downfield. However, he lacks sufficient anticipation and is often guilty of staring down his targets. He has good play strength and can escape arm tackles in the pocket. He possesses a good release with a quick, compact throwing motion and the ability to access different arm slots. Lock demonstrates sufficient ability to maintain baseline accuracy under duress. He demonstrates good toughness to stand in and drive throws in the face of oncoming rushers. Despite the offense he played in, he has flashed the ability to progress through multiple reads. He possesses good arm strength to hit the landmark throws with velocity, drive the ball from awkward positions, and while on the move. He throws an accurate deep ball to both the outside and middle of the field. If he extends the play outside of the pocket and nothing is open, he will throw the ball away. He can break contain and extend the play or scramble for significant yardage and has ability to be used on designed runs. His footwork is sloppy outside of RPO drops. His athleticism suggests that he's capable of improving his footwork. He is too content to settle for tight-window throws to his initial read and must improve his ability to work through progressions. His decision making is generally sufficient, but he takes too many risks and negative plays. He often fails to find his checkdown when pressured. He does not demonstrate sufficient processing speed against zone and is late to recognize throwing windows. His accuracy to the short and intermediate areas is inconsistent and he often makes throws that require his receivers to break stride/adjust or allow defenders to make plays on the ball. His clutch production against top competition leaves something to be desired.

Run Game

In the run game, he has enough mobility to extend plays and even gain positive yardage when scrambling.

Last Word

Lock projects as a backup/circumstantial starter at the next level.

– Bryce Rossler

Strengths	Weaknesses
• Deep accuracy	• Progression movement
• Arm strength	• Short accuracy
• Pocket awareness	• Anticipation

Critical Factors

Accuracy	Decision Making / Mental	Clutch Performance
5	5	5

Positional Factors

Short Accuracy	Deep Accuracy	Pocket Awareness	Footwork
4	6	6	4
Under Pressure	**Mobility**	**Arm Strength**	**Release**
5	6	6	6
Awkward Throw	**Eye Discipline**	**Leadership**	**Body Composition**
6	6	5	6

Basic

	Passing									
Year	Att	Comp	Comp%	Yards	Air Yards	Y/A	TD	Int	Sacks	Rating
2016	434	237	54.6%	3399	1763	7.8	23	10	13	88.3
2017	419	242	57.8%	3964	2181	9.5	44	13	11	111.7
2018	437	275	62.9%	3493	1889	8.0	28	8	13	101.6
	1290	754	58.4%	10856	5833	8.4	95	31	37	100.4

Advanced

	Passing Analytics				Rushing (Excluding Sacks)			
Year	IQR	On-Target%	Catchable%	Avg Throw Depth	Att	Yards	Y/A	Scrambles
2016	97.1	-	75.8%	11.5	39	215	5.5	10
2017	125.7	-	79.4%	11.1	33	182	5.5	8
2018	110.7	73.4%	79.5%	8.5	42	268	6.4	13
	111.0	73.4%	78.2%	10.4	114	665	5.8	31

Deep Dive

	EPA			IQR Detail				
Year	Total	EPA Per Dropback	Rush EPA	Deep Throws	Under Pressure	No Pressure	vs. Man Cov	vs. Zone Cov
2016	-37.8	-0.09	-3.0	77.2	31.3	107.0	92.6	84.4
2017	59.5	0.13	0.8	106.0	101.8	130.1	123.6	116.3
2018	60.0	0.12	11.7	135.4	85.2	117.0	105.7	125.0
	81.6	0.05	9.6	108.0	83.7	117.5	110.0	111.1

Jarrett Stidham

Auburn Tigers

Final Grade: 6.3 QB Rank: 7 of 14

Height	Weight	Year	Jersey #	Hometown
6023	214	3JR	8	Stephenville, TX

One-Liner

Stidham has the overall accuracy, decision making, and mobility to be effective at the next level, but his inability to produce under pressure or hit the deep ball with consistency may ultimately keep him from being a starter.

Overall

Stidham started at quarterback in Auburn's pro-style offense, which incorporates some spread concepts in it as well. He started 27 games for the Tigers the past two seasons, after transferring from Baylor where he appeared in 10 games during the 2015 season. He possesses good size and speed for the position. He's a solid athlete, which stems from running track and playing basketball in high school. He possesses good toughness and durability, as he has been a reliable starter.

Pass Game

In the passing game, Stidham delivers a good ball with a fluid throwing motion. He displays the ability to be spot-on in the short levels of the field and gives his receivers chances to make plays after the catch. He will lose some mechanics and accuracy when trying to get rid of the ball hot or on quick screens. He struggles when throwing the ball deep and tends to overshoot his receivers way too often, as evidenced in the Mississippi State game. He shows good arm strength as he is able to make all of the throws on the field and make throws in tight windows. His decision making is good when given time to make his reads and progressions, but if under pressure, he seems to panic and make careless decisions. His clutch performance is just sufficient because he has been a mixed bag in big situations. His footwork is clean and his mobility allows him to extend plays outside the pocket. That said, he shows inconsistency in keeping his eyes downfield when the pocket collapses.

Run Game

In the run game, Stidham isn't flashy, but he is able to make some plays. He's able to scramble when needed and not only gains positive yardage but gains much more. Auburn used him in the power run game on occasion as well.

Last Word

Stidham projects as a backup QB at the next level with the ability to start under some circumstances. He isn't going to be a guy who you win because of, but you can win with him in the right situation.

– Cole Ratliff

Strengths	**Weaknesses**
• Short accuracy	• Deep accuracy
• Mechanics	• Inconsistent eye discipline
• Arm strength	• Under pressure

Critical Factors

Accuracy	Decision Making / Mental	Clutch Performance
6	5	5

Positional Factors

Short Accuracy	Deep Accuracy	Pocket Awareness	Footwork
6	4	5	6
Under Pressure	**Mobility**	**Arm Strength**	**Release**
4	6	6	6
Awkward Throw	**Eye Discipline**	**Leadership**	**Body Composition**
6	5	6	6

Basic

	Passing									
Year	Att	Comp	Comp%	Yards	Air Yards	Y/A	TD	Int	Sacks	Rating
2017	369	246	66.7%	3157	1247	8.6	18	6	35	102.8
2018	369	224	60.7%	2794	1075	7.6	18	5	24	94.8
	738	470	63.7%	5951	2322	8.1	36	11	59	98.8

Advanced

	Passing Analytics				Rushing (Excluding Sacks)			
Year	IQR	On-Target%	Catchable%	Avg Throw Depth	Att	Yards	Y/A	Scrambles
2017	106.0	-	80.1%	8.6	68	366	5.4	39
2018	104.8	77.4%	81.0%	7.1	48	175	3.6	23
	105.4	77.4%	80.5%	7.9	116	541	4.7	62

Deep Dive

	EPA			IQR Detail				
Year	Total	EPA Per Dropback	Rush EPA	Deep Throws	Under Pressure	No Pressure	vs. Man Cov	vs. Zone Cov
2017	-18.8	-0.01	-14.5	110.3	48.8	118.8	93.4	106.1
2018	-9.6	-0.02	-6.9	116.7	65.5	116.4	93.7	124.1
	-28.4	-0.02	-21.4	113.1	56.9	118.5	93.5	115.4

Brett Rypien

Boise State Broncos

Final Grade: 6.3 QB Rank: 8 of 14

Height	Weight	Year	Jersey #	Hometown
6016	204	4SR	4	Spokane, WA

One-Liner

Rypien is a quality backup who wins with decision making and accuracy, but he has limited upside, which will prevent him from developing into a long-term starter.

Overall

Rypien is a quarterback who played in Boise State's pro-style offense. He was a four-year starter, starting 49 of the 50 games he appeared in. Rypien is an average athlete with a slender, lean build, who possesses average height and below-average weight for the position. He is competitive and shows good mental toughness.

Pass Game

In the pass game, he shows good spot-on accuracy and the ability to consistently hit receivers in stride on short and long routes. He possesses good anticipation and touch to deliver the ball without making his receivers adjust and places the ball where only his receivers can catch it. Rypien possesses good decision-making and mental-processing skills. He has the ability to diagnose the defense pre-snap, understand the coverage, and make correct reads in order to take advantage of favorable matchups, all while getting the ball out quickly. Rypien has good clutch production, with an ability to make completions at critical points in the game and sustain drives. He possesses the ability to complete throws under pressure, maintain good eye level as the pocket collapses, climb the pocket to avoid sacks, and stand tall in the pocket as he is hurried. He also has good vision and awareness with an ability to scan the field and work through his progressions. Rypien has sufficient mobility and is often able to climb the pocket to avoid pressure, but he does not possess the ability to escape the pocket. His accuracy struggles when he leaves the pocket to roll out, scrambles, or tries to throw off-platform. He is careless with the football at times, leading to fumbles and interceptions when he tries to keep the play alive. Overall, Rypien has good instincts and possesses good football intelligence, often making the right decisions and not forcing throws or making incorrect reads. He shows sufficient arm strength, putting velocity on his balls in the short and intermediate routes, but relying on touch, timing, and anticipation on deep routes, where his spot-on accuracy is questionable. He has a quick release despite his long throwing motion.

Run Game

In the run game, Rypien does not pose as a threat to the defense, lacks quickness and mobility outside the pocket, and lacks effectiveness on designed quarterback runs.

Last Word

Rypien projects as a good quality backup who is seen as a game manager. Despite his good decision making and ability under pressure, Rypien has a relatively low ceiling due to merely sufficient size, mobility, and arm strength.

– SIS Scouting Staff

Strengths	**Weaknesses**
• Experience	• Spot-on deep accuracy
• Toughness	• Mobility
• Decison making under pressure	• Slender frame

Critical Factors

Accuracy	Decision Making / Mental	Clutch Performance
6	6	6

Positional Factors

Short Accuracy	Deep Accuracy	Pocket Awareness	Footwork
6	5	6	6
Under Pressure	**Mobility**	**Arm Strength**	**Release**
6	5	5	6
Awkward Throw	**Eye Discipline**	**Leadership**	**Body Composition**
6	6	6	5

Basic

	Passing									
Year	Att	Comp	Comp%	Yards	Air Yards	Y/A	TD	Int	Sacks	Rating
2016	394	244	61.9%	3646	2018	9.3	24	8	19	104.1
2017	348	218	62.6%	2878	1567	8.3	16	6	20	96.9
2018	448	301	67.2%	3705	2357	8.3	30	7	33	108.3
	1190	763	64.1%	10229	5942	8.6	70	21	72	103.6

Advanced

	Passing Analytics				Rushing (Excluding Sacks)			
Year	IQR	On-Target%	Catchable%	Avg Throw Depth	Att	Yards	Y/A	Scrambles
2016	109.4	-	77.1%	12.1	29	100	3.4	17
2017	102.6	-	79.1%	9.2	17	113	6.6	10
2018	116.1	74.8%	76.6%	10.3	52	194	3.7	26
	109.9	74.8%	77.5%	10.6	98	407	4.2	53

Deep Dive

	EPA			IQR Detail				
Year	Total	EPA Per Dropback	Rush EPA	Deep Throws	Under Pressure	No Pressure	vs. Man Cov	vs. Zone Cov
2016	72.3	0.16	0.3	109.0	64.6	119.5	100.9	118.4
2017	33.8	0.13	-10.8	114.9	94.1	106.1	101.4	103.2
2018	76.5	0.15	3.9	120.6	93.0	122.7	122.1	111.1
	182.6	0.15	-6.5	118.8	87.2	117.4	109.0	111.0

Gardner Minshew II

Washington State Cougars
Final Grade: 6.3 QB Rank: 9 of 14

Height	Weight	Year	Jersey #	Hometown
6007	224	5SR	16	Brandon, MS

One-Liner
Minshew has the overall accuracy, instincts, and leadership qualities to be an eventual low-end starter at the next level, but his footwork and inconsistency in the short-to-intermediate passing game may force him into being a backup.

Overall
Minshew played quarterback in an Air Raid offense at Washington State. He began his career at Northwest Mississippi CC in 2015, where he led the team to an NJCAA National Championship. He transferred to East Carolina and played in 17 games with 7 starts over two seasons. He then transferred as a graduate to Washington State in 2018 and started all 13 games. He's played on teams that run plays exclusively out of shotgun, so he hasn't taken many snaps from under center. He's a good athlete and competitor. He has below-average body composition/height for the position, and that translated to quite a few batted balls at the line of scrimmage in college.

Pass Game
He has good overall accuracy, but has some issues in the short to intermediate areas of the field. Most of his accuracy issues come from lack of proper footwork, but some off-target passes were due to miscommunications. He also throws off his back foot a lot, even when there isn't pressure in his face. He fails to reset his base on most occasions, and relies heavily on his upper body for arm strength. On downfield throws, he shows good arm strength and ball placement. When he sets his base and steps into his throws, he has enough arm strength to make all of the throws on the field. Although he uses good eye discipline and goes through his reads, his decision making is suspect at times and he will force some passes. However, he has good instincts and there are many cases where he throws with very good anticipation before the receiver has even gotten into his break. His release is quick and compact, allowing him to get the ball out of his hand quickly. That quick release helps when he is under duress. He knows when to throw the ball away, but can make accurate throws under pressure and on the run. He's able to make on-target throws off platform and allow the receiver to catch the ball in stride to gain yards after the catch. He has good poise in the pocket, but there are times that he will sense some false pressure and escape when he doesn't need to. He makes plays in clutch situations. He was strong on 3rd down, and made throws when they counted late in games.

Run Game
Minshew is not a threat as a runner, but he's mobile enough in the pocket to improvise and scramble for yardage when the situation calls for it.

Last Word
Minshew is a leader on and off of the field. He projects as a quality backup and circumstantial starter in his first two seasons at the next level, and shows traits to eventually become a low-end "win-with" player.

– Nathan Cooper

Strengths
- Throws with anticipation
- Makes throws off platform
- Quick, compact release

Weaknesses
- Consistent short accuracy
- Footwork/doesn't always reset base
- Senses false pressure at times

Critical Factors

Accuracy	Decision Making / Mental	Clutch Performance
6	5	6

Positional Factors

Short Accuracy	Deep Accuracy	Pocket Awareness	Footwork
5	6	6	4
Under Pressure	**Mobility**	**Arm Strength**	**Release**
5	5	6	6
Awkward Throw	**Eye Discipline**	**Leadership**	**Body Composition**
6	6	6	5

Basic

	Passing									
Year	Att	Comp	Comp%	Yards	Air Yards	Y/A	TD	Int	Sacks	Rating
2016	202	119	58.9%	1347	716	6.7	8	4	9	83.9
2017	302	174	57.6%	2140	999	7.1	16	7	9	87.6
2018	662	468	70.7%	4779	1918	7.2	38	9	13	104.5
	1166	761	65.3%	8266	3633	7.1	62	20	31	96.6

Advanced

	Passing Analytics				Rushing (Excluding Sacks)			
Year	IQR	On-Target%	Catchable%	Avg Throw Depth	Att	Yards	Y/A	Scrambles
2016	89.0	-	78.1%	7.8	11	24	2.2	8
2017	86.6	-	76.0%	9.0	10	18	1.8	3
2018	109.7	78.4%	83.0%	5.7	45	194	4.3	32
	100.1	78.4%	80.4%	6.9	66	236	3.6	43

Deep Dive

	EPA			IQR Detail				
Year	Total	EPA Per Dropback	Rush EPA	Deep Throws	Under Pressure	No Pressure	vs. Man Cov	vs. Zone Cov
2016	-15.0	-0.06	-5.3	118.1	45.1	99.6	75.7	92.2
2017	7.8	0.03	-4.3	86.1	49.5	100.8	79.3	75.3
2018	96.0	0.13	10.8	123.6	69.5	117.0	131.3	92.6
	88.8	0.07	1.2	108.9	55.6	111.1	111.8	88.7

Tyree Jackson

Buffalo Bulls
Final Grade: 6.2 QB Rank: 10 of 14

Height	Weight	Year	Jersey #	Hometown
6070	249	4JR	3	Norton Shores, MI

One-Liner
Jackson is an upside player with the size, arm strength, and mobility to develop into a circumstantial starter, but his issues with accuracy and mechanics may hinder his ability to ascend an NFL depth chart.

Overall
Jackson played in Buffalo's spread offensive scheme. He started in 31 of 32 career games. He has very good size for the position. He's got the frame and sturdiness to withstand hits and contact in the NFL. He's a good athlete and showcases his athletic traits as a runner. He is a long strider with good straight-line speed. He's a competitor and leader that finds a way to win games.

Pass Game
In the passing game, he displays very good arm strength. Jackson can generate plenty of zip and velocity behind his throws. He has the height to see over the offensive line and deliver passes down the field. With his arm strength, he tries to fire it in too much and struggles with touch passes. His build allows him to shake sacks and extend plays outside the pocket. His overall accuracy is average and he misses too many easy throws. He can deliver a sufficient deep ball as he flashes the ability to drop deep dimes and hit guys in stride. His accuracy is average when he is asked to complete shorter throws. He has difficulty hitting with consistency on rhythm throws. He struggles to consistently replicate mechanics and footwork. His release is average and noticeably elongated. He takes a long time to load up. He'll continuously over-stride and pick his back leg up on his follow through. This gives him extra strength, but leads to his being inaccurate. He locks onto his first read and stares him down too often. He needs to be quicker with working through progressions. He plays with sufficient pocket awareness and usually displays enough poise in the pocket to notice when defenders are present.

Run Game
In the running game, he displays enough mobility, especially for his size. He isn't a true dual threat, but he can be a threat to defenses as a runner. He has the ability to be utilized in designed quarterback run concepts. His size helps him pick up necessary yardage on quarterback sneaks.

Last Word
Jackson flashes sufficient decision making ability, however, he can make poor decisions when put under pressure. He has the arm strength to make awkward throws at an above-average rate. Jackson projects as a quality backup and circumstantial starter at the next level, especially once he gets the coaching needed.

– Alex O'Brien

Strengths	Weaknesses
• Arm strength	• Overall accuracy
• Clutch	• Under-pressure throws
• Body composition	• Elongated release

Critical Factors

Accuracy	Decision Making / Mental	Clutch Performance
4	5	6

Positional Factors

Short Accuracy	Deep Accuracy	Pocket Awareness	Footwork
4	5	5	5
Under Pressure	**Mobility**	**Arm Strength**	**Release**
5	5	7	4
Awkward Throw	**Eye Discipline**	**Leadership**	**Body Composition**
6	5	6	7

Basic

	Passing									
Year	Att	Comp	Comp%	Yards	Air Yards	Y/A	TD	Int	Sacks	Rating
2016	311	165	53.1%	1772	970	5.7	9	9	10	67.6
2017	237	143	60.3%	2096	1249	8.8	12	3	9	100.8
2018	407	225	55.3%	3131	1958	7.7	28	12	17	90.9
	955	533	55.8%	6999	4177	7.3	49	24	36	85.8

Advanced

	Passing Analytics				Rushing (Excluding Sacks)			
Year	IQR	On-Target%	Catchable%	Avg Throw Depth	Att	Yards	Y/A	Scrambles
2016	63.9	-	67.3%	10.8	89	460	5.2	24
2017	103.0	-	75.8%	11.4	38	263	6.9	4
2018	96.5	65.4%	71.7%	12.4	38	264	6.9	25
	87.4	65.4%	71.3%	11.6	165	987	6.0	53

Deep Dive

	EPA			IQR Detail				
Year	Total	EPA Per Dropback	Rush EPA	Deep Throws	Under Pressure	No Pressure	vs. Man Cov	vs. Zone Cov
2016	-66.7	-0.18	-9.8	28.1	55.1	63.8	68.0	39.2
2017	57.8	0.19	10.4	115.5	66.7	111.8	97.3	105.1
2018	45.0	0.09	20.7	89.6	84.5	99.5	82.2	99.8
	36.1	0.02	21.4	82.8	70.0	91.5	81.2	83.7

Clayton Thorson

Northwestern Wildcats
Final Grade: 6.2 QB Rank: 11 of 14

Height	Weight	Year	Jersey #	Hometown
6036	226	5SR	18	Wheaton, IL

One-Liner
Thorson shows decision-making and leadership qualities to be a circumstantial starter or quality backup, but needs to improve his spot-on accuracy and poise under pressure to become a solid starter on the next level.

Overall
Thorson played quarterback in Northwestern's spread offense, and has been introduced to some pro-style aspects throughout his career. He was a four-year starter at Northwestern, starting all 53 games he played in. Thorson is a pocket quarterback with average mobility outside the pocket. He is a tough competitor that is willing to stand in the pocket and take a hit, as well as move outside the pocket to make plays.

Pass Game
In the pass game, his short accuracy is good when he has a clean pocket, but under duress it drops to sufficient. Thorson's deep accuracy is average, as he has trouble connecting on deep passes with or without a clean pocket. He makes good decisions and rarely puts the ball in dangerous situations on first and second down. He will throw the ball away or tuck and run instead of forcing a bad throw. Thorson's accuracy under duress is sufficient, but again it is much better on short passes. He has above-average clutch performance ability, knowing where the sticks are on third downs, and tries to make any play he can to get first downs. His coach puts the ball in his hands to make decisions late in the fourth quarter and on third downs. Thorson has not displayed good mobility this season, mainly due to coming off an ACL injury, but his instincts and footwork are good, allowing him to move efficiently in and out of the pocket.

Run Game
In the run game, Thorson was not a threat as a runner his senior season, but was a threat through his first three seasons. A knee injury in his bowl game as a junior is most likely the cause of the decline in his running ability.

Last Word
Thorson has the abilities as a passer to contribute to a team as a quality backup and circumstantial starter at the next level, and if his mobility returns to his pre-ACL form, he is a threat with his legs as well.

– Brian Rogers

Strengths	**Weaknesses**
• Decision making	• Deep accuracy
• Footwork	• Mobility (post-ACL)
• Release	• Under pressure

Critical Factors

Accuracy	Decision Making / Mental	Clutch Performance
5	6	5

Positional Factors

Short Accuracy	Deep Accuracy	Pocket Awareness	Footwork
5	4	5	6
Under Pressure	**Mobility**	**Arm Strength**	**Release**
4	5	5	6
Awkward Throw	**Eye Discipline**	**Leadership**	**Body Composition**
5	5	6	6

Basic

	Passing									
Year	Att	Comp	Comp%	Yards	Air Yards	Y/A	TD	Int	Sacks	Rating
2016	478	280	58.6%	3182	1840	6.7	22	9	38	86.1
2017	434	262	60.4%	2844	1624	6.6	15	12	30	79.7
2018	489	298	60.9%	3186	1762	6.5	17	15	34	78.8
	1401	840	60.0%	9212	5226	6.6	54	36	102	81.6

Advanced

	Passing Analytics				Rushing (Excluding Sacks)			
Year	IQR	On-Target%	Catchable%	Avg Throw Depth	Att	Yards	Y/A	Scrambles
2016	93.2	-	74.6%	9.0	59	309	5.2	17
2017	85.9	-	78.6%	8.0	57	232	4.1	19
2018	79.6	71.3%	78.7%	7.8	43	142	3.3	16
	86.1	71.3%	77.3%	8.2	159	683	4.3	52

Deep Dive

	EPA			IQR Detail				
Year	Total	EPA Per Dropback	Rush EPA	Deep Throws	Under Pressure	No Pressure	vs. Man Cov	vs. Zone Cov
2016	-3.3	0.00	-4.6	81.5	71.6	96.1	83.1	91.6
2017	-26.8	-0.08	25.6	53.2	48.1	99.1	86.8	85.5
2018	-68.5	-0.15	5.1	95.4	57.4	88.0	76.2	86.4
	-98.6	-0.07	26.1	79.8	59.9	94.1	81.9	87.7

Easton Stick

North Dakota State Bison
Final Grade: 5.9 QB Rank: 12 of 14

Height	Weight	Year	Jersey #	Hometown
6013	217	4SR	12	Omaha, NE

One-Liner
Stick shows some traits, such as eye discipline, footwork and mobility, but he needs to improve his overall accuracy and poise to succeed at the next level.

Overall
Stick was the QB in North Dakota State's pro-style offense. He started 50 of his 53 career games. He was 47-3 as a starter and won three FCS Championships. He shows glimpses of good accuracy, but his spot-on accuracy is only sufficient on a consistent basis. He's a good athlete who competes with toughness. He has good body composition and a sturdy build.

Pass Game
In the pass game, he shows good decision making and mental processing. He uses solid eye discipline to go through his reads and showed a great amount of improvement in terms of decision making from 2017 to 2018. He performs in the clutch, having led his team to two scores in the last four minutes against No. 11 ranked Iowa in 2016. That includes a successful drive that started with 1:53 left in the game and ended with a game-winning field goal as time expired. Stick shows above-average short accuracy but can get inaccurate on mid-level throws. He has good arm strength and can make all the throws necessary for a quarterback at the next level. Stick gets a little uneasy when the pocket collapses but shows good footwork and mobility in the pocket. However, he hangs in the pocket with defenders closing in and will take a hit in order to make the throw. He struggles to throw with consistent accuracy on the run and on off-platform throws, and makes sure to reset his base most times. He has a good release and smooth throwing motion. He is a very good leader as a three-time team captain and directs his offense well through his pre-snap communication.

Run Game
In the run game, his mobility is very good as he can easily maneuver in the pocket and is a strong runner down the field. He runs the zone-read well and can beat the defense with his legs.

Last Word
Stick projects as a career No. 2 that has versatility as a passer and rusher. He brings some intangibles to the table that could help an offense at the next level.

– Jeremy Percy

Strengths	Weaknesses
• Arm strength	• Short/intermediate accuracy
• Mobility	• Pocket awareness
• Eye discipline	• Throws on the run

Critical Factors

Accuracy	Decision Making / Mental	Clutch Performance
5	6	6

Positional Factors

Short Accuracy	Deep Accuracy	Pocket Awareness	Footwork
5	6	5	6
Under Pressure	**Mobility**	**Arm Strength**	**Release**
5	7	6	6
Awkward Throw	**Eye Discipline**	**Leadership**	**Body Composition**
5	6	7	6

LOOKING AHEAD

Two of the top quarterbacks in college football aren't even draft-eligible yet. They happen to be the two who started the national championship game: Alabama's Tua Tagovailoa and Clemson's Trevor Lawrence.

Tagovailoa had the second-highest Independent Quarterback Rating in FBS, trailing only Oklahoma's Kyler Murray. He had the highest completion percentage on passes thrown at least 20 yards downfield (57 percent) of anyone with more than 30 attempts. He made plenty of passes of that type too, connecting on 31, sixth-most in FBS. This feat is especially impressive considering he managed to do so against SEC teams replete with secondary talent. And on top of that, the Alabama standout was nursing a bum knee for much of the season.

His counterpart, Lawrence, showed strong anticipation and good decision-making skills in his freshman season, throwing only four interceptions in 399 attempts. His 137.0 IQR against man coverage ranked third, trailing only Murray and Tagovailoa. The Clemson wunderkind also demonstrated next-level accuracy and poise unbecoming of a true freshman during their championship run. He threw 75 percent of his passes on target in the title game win over Alabama, the second-highest percentage for a quarterback against the Crimson Tide last season (Nick Fitzgerald, 90 percent).

Taylor Cornelius

Oklahoma State Cowboys
Final Grade: 5.8 QB Rank: 13 of 14

Height	Weight	Year	Jersey #	Hometown
6057	220	5SR	14	Bushland, TX

One-Liner
Cornelius has upside in terms of size, movement skills, and arm talent, but questions about his mental processing ability are exacerbated by his lack of college experience.

Overall
Cornelius was the quarterback in Oklahoma State's up-tempo spread system, which features 10 and 11 personnel, RPOs, and vertical passing concepts. He was a one-year starter for the Cowboys, starting 13 of 21 total games in his career after backing up Mason Rudolph for multiple years. He is an above-average athlete with a lean, slender build who possesses very good height and weight for the position. Cornelius is a competitive player who possesses sufficient mental toughness and leadership qualities. He showed a consistent ability to move his team down the field and into the end zone, and he properly communicates the play call and audibles to the offense while operating in a no-huddle.

Pass Game
In the pass game, Cornelius shows sufficient spot-on accuracy, displaying the ability hit receivers in stride on short, intermediate, and deep routes fairly consistently. His mental processing ability has limitations, as he is decisive but lacks anticipation on his throws, doesn't play in a progression offense, and can struggle to read defenses. He does not currently display good field vision or judgement, which will limit his potential at the next level. He is a decent player in the clutch who does well to keep his team on the field on third and fourth downs, and who delivers catchable balls in critical moments. Cornelius completes throws under pressure fairly well, maintaining good eye level downfield as the pocket collapses. He has also shown flashes of accuracy on the move outside the pocket. His size allows him to take hits and shrug off weaker sack attempts. He fails to identify open receivers at times, but some of this has to do with half-field reads and the overall scheme he is in. Cornelius' footwork in the pocket needs refinement, as he has a tendency to get off balance and throw from unnecessarily shaky platforms. He does have a solid, high release he can get off quickly. He can make most throws with arm strength and has the ability to fit intermediate balls into tight windows as well as throw deep with touch.

Run Game
In the run game, Cornelius is effective as a designed runner on read-option keepers, flashing quickness to get up field as well as power and size to break tackles. He possesses good maneuverability in the pocket and while scrambling, showing an ability to keep plays alive and pick up first downs with his legs.

Last Word
Cornelius projects as an eventual career backup because his mental processing is questionable. He hasn't had the playing time as a starter to get a strong feel for the position at a higher level of competition. However, he flashes positive traits across the board and has the desired size to hold up.

– Nick Giella

Strengths	Weaknesses
• Release	• Mental processing
• Mobility	• Field vision
• Body composition	• Footwork

Critical Factors

Accuracy	Decision Making / Mental	Clutch Performance
5	5	5

Positional Factors

Short Accuracy	Deep Accuracy	Pocket Awareness	Footwork
5	5	5	4
Under Pressure	**Mobility**	**Arm Strength**	**Release**
5	6	5	6
Awkward Throw	**Eye Discipline**	**Leadership**	**Body Composition**
5	5	5	7

Basic

	Passing									
Year	Att	Comp	Comp%	Yards	Air Yards	Y/A	TD	Int	Sacks	Rating
2016	9	7	77.8%	64	44	7.1	0	0	0	96.3
2017	10	6	60.0%	148	92	14.8	0	0	1	104.2
2018	485	288	59.4%	3978	2425	8.2	32	13	31	96.6
	504	301	59.7%	4190	2561	8.3	32	13	32	96.9

Advanced

	Passing Analytics				Rushing (Excluding Sacks)			
Year	IQR	On-Target%	Catchable%	Avg Throw Depth	Att	Yards	Y/A	Scrambles
2016	104.8	-	100.0%	7.3	6	28	4.7	2
2017	104.2	-	60.0%	16.8	6	83	13.8	2
2018	98.5	71.1%	75.1%	11.5	91	619	6.8	19
	99.2	71.1%	75.1%	11.5	103	730	7.1	23

Deep Dive

	EPA			IQR Detail				
Year	Total	EPA Per Dropback	Rush EPA	Deep Throws	Under Pressure	No Pressure	vs. Man Cov	vs. Zone Cov
2016	12.4	0.63	5.7	0.0	0.0	104.8	108.3	108.3
2017	10.7	0.45	3.7	95.8	116.7	94.4	109.7	104.2
2018	84.6	0.11	37.1	81.7	69.2	108.6	110.1	84.7
	107.7	0.13	46.4	82.2	71.6	108.7	112.3	86.2

Trace McSorley

Penn State Nittany Lions
Final Grade: 5.8 QB Rank: 14 of 14

Height	Weight	Year	Jersey #	Hometown
6002	200	5SR	9	Ashburn, VA

One-Liner
McSorley shows toughness, mobility, and unquestioned leadership. However, he lacks ideal size, and he will need to improve his overall accuracy and pocket presence to succeed at the next level.

Overall
McSorley was a three-year starter at QB in Penn State's spread offense. He played in 47 games during his career with the Nittany Lions. He has a somewhat slender frame for a QB, but overall is well-built. He is a very good athlete and competes with toughness on every play.

Pass Game
In the pass game, his spot-on accuracy is adequate in the short to intermediate range, and he thrived on throwing slants and outs. He is good at getting the ball out of his hands quickly on bubble screens and quick routes. Deep accuracy is something he struggles with and will need work on. While McSorley has the ability to make a great deep ball throw, he also throws some head-scratching ones, which might be attributed to his lack of arm strength. He makes decent decisions most of the time but will throw some questionable balls into traffic. He made some big anticipation throws during the Ohio State game, and his clutch production has shown in big-time games. Coach James Franklin usually puts the ball in McSorley's hands when the game is on the line and there's something to be said for that. His accuracy under duress is inconsistent. He doesn't have great poise in the pocket and sometimes gets happy feet. He works the pocket well, as he steps up in the pocket to find throwing windows. McSorley keeps his eyes downfield when pressured, but sometimes looks to run right away, relying on his speed and athleticism. He shows good instincts to feel out pressure and has very good ball security, rarely turning the ball over. He is a natural leader at Penn State and galvanizes his teammates. He shows good body language and mental toughness.

Run Game
In the run game, McSorley is a real threat due to his speed and athleticism, which stem from his background in basketball and lacrosse. He has a smooth-running style which allows him to run the read-option and make big plays with his legs. His lack of size could get him in trouble with his fearless running style.

Last Word
McSorley projects as an eventual backup at the next level. His leadership and ability to take command of a huddle will give him a shot.

– Drew Schweitzer

Strengths	**Weaknesses**
• Mobility	• Deep accuracy
• Leadership	• Footwork
• Toughness	• Eye discipline

Critical Factors

Accuracy	Decision Making / Mental	Clutch Performance
5	5	6

Positional Factors

Short Accuracy	Deep Accuracy	Pocket Awareness	Footwork
5	3	5	5
Under Pressure	**Mobility**	**Arm Strength**	**Release**
5	7	5	6
Awkward Throw	**Eye Discipline**	**Leadership**	**Body Composition**
5	5	8	4

Basic

	Passing									
Year	Att	Comp	Comp%	Yards	Air Yards	Y/A	TD	Int	Sacks	Rating
2016	387	224	57.9%	3614	2092	9.3	29	8	23	105.6
2017	427	284	66.5%	3570	1718	8.4	28	10	27	104.4
2018	361	192	53.2%	2530	1501	7.0	18	7	27	84.1
	1175	700	59.6%	9714	5311	8.3	75	25	77	98.6

Advanced

	Passing Analytics				Rushing (Excluding Sacks)			
Year	IQR	On-Target%	Catchable%	Avg Throw Depth	Att	Yards	Y/A	Scrambles
2016	118.7	-	81.1%	11.7	122	543	4.5	41
2017	111.8	-	83.5%	8.0	117	629	5.4	25
2018	96.1	69.4%	72.4%	9.9	143	959	6.7	44
	109.2	69.4%	79.3%	9.8	382	2131	5.6	110

Deep Dive

	EPA			IQR Detail				
Year	Total	EPA Per Dropback	Rush EPA	Deep Throws	Under Pressure	No Pressure	vs. Man Cov	vs. Zone Cov
2016	40.0	0.12	-8.1	113.9	107.1	118.3	112.7	104.5
2017	101.3	0.20	11.9	115.7	83.9	120.1	118.9	96.1
2018	-33.9	-0.13	23.9	78.8	86.8	99.4	100.5	90.5
	107.4	0.07	27.8	111.9	93.6	113.9	110.9	96.3

Glossary

Air Yards
The number of yards the ball travels downfield from the line of scrimmage to where the wide receiver catches the ball

Catchable%
The number of catchable throws a quarterback makes divided by the total number of pass attempts

Deep Throws (IQR Detail split)
Throws that travel at least 15 yards downfield before being touched or hitting the ground

IQR
Sports Info Solutions' proprietary quarterback metric builds on the traditional Passer Rating formula by considering the value of a quarterback independent of results outside of the his control such as dropped passes, dropped interceptions, throwaways, etc.

On-Target%
The number of on-target throws a quarterback makes divided by the total number of pass attempts

Rating
Traditional Passer Rating

Y/A (Passing split)
Yards per pass attempt

Y/A (Rushing split)
Yards per rush attempt, not counting sacks

Quarterback Leaderboards

Pass Yards Per Attempt Leaders			
Rank	Player	School	Y/A
1	Kyler Murray	Oklahoma	11.6
2	Will Grier	West Virginia	9.7
3	Dwayne Haskins	Ohio State	9.1
4	Brett Rypien	Boise State	8.3
5	Taylor Cornelius	Oklahoma State	8.2
6	Ryan Finley	NC State	8.1
7	Drew Lock	Missouri	8.0
8	Tyree Jackson	Buffalo	7.7
9	Jarrett Stidham	Auburn	7.6
10	Gardner Minshew II	Washington State	7.2

Total Expected Points Added Leaders			
Rank	Player	Team	Total EPA
1	Kyler Murray	Oklahoma	236.9
2	Will Grier	West Virginia	140.1
3	Dwayne Haskins	Ohio State	137.0
4	Gardner Minshew II	Washington State	96.0
5	Ryan Finley	NC State	94.5
6	Taylor Cornelius	Oklahoma State	84.6
7	Brett Rypien	Boise State	76.5
8	Drew Lock	Missouri	60.0
9	Tyree Jackson	Buffalo	45.0
10	Jarrett Stidham	Auburn	-9.6

On-Target Percentage Leaders			
Rank	Player	School	On Target %
1	Kyler Murray	Oklahoma	79.2%
2	Ryan Finley	NC State	79.0%
3	Gardner Minshew II	Washington State	78.4%
4	Will Grier	West Virginia	78.4%
5	Dwayne Haskins	Ohio State	78.1%
6	Jarrett Stidham	Auburn	77.4%
7	Brett Rypien	Boise State	74.8%
8	Daniel Jones	Duke	74.5%
9	Drew Lock	Missouri	73.4%
10	Clayton Thorson	Northwestern	71.3%

Expected Points Added Per Dropback Leaders			
Rank	Player	Team	EPA Per Dropback
1	Kyler Murray	Oklahoma	0.47
2	Will Grier	West Virginia	0.32
3	Dwayne Haskins	Ohio State	0.26
4	Ryan Finley	NC State	0.18
5	Brett Rypien	Boise State	0.15
6	Gardner Minshew II	Washington State	0.13
7	Drew Lock	Missouri	0.12
8	Taylor Cornelius	Oklahoma State	0.11
9	Tyree Jackson	Buffalo	0.09
10	Jarrett Stidham	Auburn	-0.02

Independent Quarterback Rating Leaders			
Rank	Player	School	IQR
1	Kyler Murray	Oklahoma	143.2
2	Will Grier	West Virginia	127.9
3	Dwayne Haskins	Ohio State	125.8
4	Brett Rypien	Boise State	116.1
5	Drew Lock	Missouri	110.7
6	Gardner Minshew II	Washington State	109.7
7	Jarrett Stidham	Auburn	104.8
8	Ryan Finley	NC State	103.5
9	Daniel Jones	Duke	99.5
10	Taylor Cornelius	Oklahoma State	98.5

Rushing Expected Points Added Leaders			
Rank	Player	Team	Rush EPA
1	Kyler Murray	Oklahoma	61.4
2	Taylor Cornelius	Oklahoma State	37.1
3	Trace McSorley	Penn State	23.9
4	Tyree Jackson	Buffalo	20.7
5	Daniel Jones	Duke	17.6
6	Drew Lock	Missouri	11.7
7	Gardner Minshew II	Washington State	10.8
8	Ryan Finley	NC State	6.7
9	Clayton Thorson	Northwestern	5.1
10	Brett Rypien	Boise State	3.9

RUNNING BACK

Running Back Grading Scale

GRADE	DESCRIPTION
9.0 – 7.0	High-end 3 down starter. Pro Bowl level.
6.9 – 6.7	Strong starter who plays on all 3 downs.
6.6 – 6.5	Lower-end starter. Starting player on early downs.
6.3	Role playing starter. 3rd down difference maker.
6.2	Backup who can play on all 3 downs.
6.1 – 6.0	Developmental. Top traits but needs time.
5.6 – 5.5	Backup. Either base or 3rd down role.

Running Back Rankings

Rank	Name	Grade	Page
1	Josh Jacobs	7.1	64
2	Devin Singletary	6.8	66
3	Damien Harris	6.8	68
4	Rodney Anderson	6.8	70
5	Trayveon Williams	6.7	72
6	Miles Sanders	6.7	74
7	Devine Ozigbo	6.6	76
8	Justice Hill	6.5	78
9	David Montgomery	6.3	80
10	D.J. Knox	6.3	82
11	Jalin Moore	6.3	84
12	Darrell Henderson	6.3	86
13	Myles Gaskin	6.3	88
14	James Williams	6.3	90
15	Benny Snell Jr.	6.2	92
16	Bryce Love	6.2	94
17	Elijah Holyfield	6.2	96
18	Ryquell Armstead	6.2	98
19	Darrin Hall	6.2	100
20	Nick Brossette	6.2	102
21	Alexander Mattison	6.2	104
22	Karan Higdon	6.2	106
23	Mike Weber	6.2	108
24	Qadree Ollison	6.2	110

Josh Jacobs

Alabama Crimson Tide

Final Grade: 7.1 RB Rank: 1 of 24

Height	Weight	Year	Jersey #	Hometown
5091	216	3JR	8	Tulsa, OK

One-Liner

Jacobs plays with elite tenacity, and with his lower-body strength and quick footwork, has the makings of a future star.

Overall

Jacobs was a running back in Alabama's balanced offense that used a mix of zone and power blocking schemes, as well as their primary kickoff returner. He played in 42 career games as a rotational back since the start of his true freshman season, with a few spot starts. He is a bit short, but a well-built, strong athlete with a thick lower half and very good feet. His competitive toughness is excellent, and he plays with added motivation due to having to fight for recognition since high school and for playing time each week in Tuscaloosa.

Run Game

Jacobs plays with good vision, although he can unnecessarily bounce some runs, his instincts and feel for his blockers and where holes will come open are excellent. He has had some pre-snap alignment issues he'll need to clean up. He is quick to the line while still being patient for his blocks to set up, and does a good job of pressing holes to force decisions. Jacobs' footwork behind the line is very good and he has explosive acceleration to burst into openings and defenders at contact. His downhill tendency makes him a great fit in power, but he has the traits to succeed in zone schemes as well. Jacobs runs with great ball security and body lean to get skinny through holes. He is very elusive in open space for his build, but he can choose finesse over power too often. His low center of gravity and strength give him excellent contact balance to drive through arm tackles. Jacobs' elite tenacity combined with his lower body strength make him a powerful runner despite his overall size. He is an aggressive lead blocker and top special teams contributor, as he participated on all units for the Crimson Tide.

Pass Game

In the pass game, he has good hands and route traits when made an early option, but he needs to work harder as an available checkdown target. He shows high-end awareness and aggression as a pass protector, and with better form can become a strong contributor in this area.

Last Word

Jacobs projects as an NFL contributor in any scheme on all four downs with high upside due to his low collegiate usage. He has only seven career double-digit carry games and one 100-yard rushing performance. He is only scratching the surface of his potential.

– John Todd

Strengths	**Weaknesses**
• Tenacity in all phases • Footwork and acceleration • Leg drive and finishing runs	• Checkdown availability • Form blocking

Critical Factors

Instincts / Vision	Contact Balance	Passing Game Impact
7	8	6

Positional Factors

Play Speed	Elusiveness	Power
7	7	7
Playmaker	**Catching Skill**	**Pass Protection**
7	6	7
Ball Security	**Ruggedness / Toughness**	**Special Teams Value**
6	8	8

Basic

	Rushing				Receiving				
Year	Att	Yds	Y/A	TD	Targets	Rec	Yds	Y/Trgt	TD
2016	85	567	6.7	4	19	14	156	8.2	0
2017	46	284	6.2	1	14	14	168	12.0	2
2018	120	639	5.3	10	26	20	247	9.5	3
	251	1490	5.9	15	59	48	571	9.7	5

Advanced

	Yards Per Carry				Per 100 Touches		EPA		
Year	Inside	Off-Tackle	Outside	After Contact	Fumbles	Broken Tackles	Rush	Rec	Total
2016	5.6	8.9	4.9	4.6	2.0	41	10.5	6.0	16.5
2017	6.9	4.3	8.0	3.4	0.0	33	6.2	7.9	14.0
2018	6.9	5.1	3.5	3.6	0.7	38	29.2	12.7	41.9
	6.3	6.0	5.1	3.9	1.0	38	45.9	26.6	72.5

Deep Dive

	Receiving / Blocking			Positive Play %			Usage	
Year	Routes Run	Yards Per Route Run	Blown Block %	Overall	Zone Blocking	Gap Blocking	Split Out %	Heavy Box %
2018	104	2.4	0.4%	59.2%	55.7%	65.9%	10.5%	15.8%

Devin Singletary

Florida Atlantic Owls
Final Grade: 6.8 RB Rank: 2 of 24

Height	Weight	Year	Jersey #	Hometown
5086	200	3JR	5	Deerfield Beach, FL

One-Liner
Singletary has the contact balance, instincts, and playmaking ability to be a solid starting back at the next level, but his lack of consistent impact in the passing game may limit his effectiveness on third downs early on.

Overall
Singletary was the primary ballcarrier in FAU's hurry-up offense. Singletary played in all 38 games for Florida Atlantic during his three years on campus. In 2017, Singletary led the NCAA in rushing TDs and total TDs, and he averaged 6 yards per carry for his career. Singletary is a quick-twitch athlete who plays with a tough running style.

Run Game
Singletary is a powerful and elusive runner with a low center of gravity. His contact balance is his defining trait. He is a tough runner who never shies away from contact, lowering his shoulder to finish runs and keep on his feet for extra yardage. His combination of elusiveness, balance, and power make him very difficult to bring down as he bounces off tackles on almost every play. He is a patient runner, using his vision and instincts to find a hole and accelerate through it with burst.

Pass Game
In the pass game, Singletary runs good routes, but he doesn't show natural hands. He's shown some ability in pass protection, but will need to work on his recognition and strength at the POA to be someone that can be counted on in passing situations at the next level.

Last Word
Singletary projects as a starting RB at the next level who can play on all three downs. By his second year, he can contribute early in the running game and develop his passing game skills to become a solid three-down starter. On 3rd downs, he has the skill set to be a threat in the passing game, but needs to develop as a rookie. As a physical player with good play speed, he could contribute on some special teams units if asked.

– Gennady Gusak

Strengths

- Contact balance
- Instincts
- Elusiveness

Weaknesses

- Natural hands
- Pass protection

Critical Factors

Instincts / Vision	Contact Balance	Passing Game Impact
7	8	5

Positional Factors

Play Speed	Elusiveness	Power
6	7	7
Playmaker	**Catching Skill**	**Pass Protection**
7	5	5
Ball Security	**Ruggedness / Toughness**	**Special Teams Value**
6	6	6

Basic

	Rushing				Receiving				
Year	Att	Yds	Y/A	TD	Targets	Rec	Yds	Y/Trgt	TD
2016	150	1015	6.8	12	31	26	163	5.3	0
2017	302	1923	6.4	32	24	19	198	8.3	1
2018	261	1348	5.2	22	14	6	36	2.6	0
	713	4286	6.0	66	69	51	397	5.8	1

Advanced

	Yards Per Carry				Per 100 Touches		EPA		
Year	Inside	Off-Tackle	Outside	After Contact	Fumbles	Broken Tackles	Rush	Rec	Total
2016	6.5	8.6	4.8	3.9	0.0	30	30.8	-16.1	14.6
2017	5.7	8.0	4.4	3.9	1.2	37	57.6	5.7	63.3
2018	4.2	5.6	7.0	3.6	0.4	41	4.4	-7.8	-3.4
	5.4	7.2	5.5	3.8	0.7	37	92.7	-18.2	74.5

Deep Dive

	Receiving / Blocking			Positive Play %			Usage	
Year	Routes Run	Yards Per Route Run	Blown Block %	Overall	Zone Blocking	Gap Blocking	Split Out %	Heavy Box %
2018	61	0.6	0.0%	40.4%	41.6%	20.0%	0.7%	6.5%

Damien Harris

Alabama Crimson Tide
Final Grade: 6.8 RB Rank: 3 of 24

Height	Weight	Year	Jersey #	Hometown
5096	215	4SR	34	Richmond, KY

One-Liner
Harris is an instinctive runner with a low center of gravity and natural receiving ability who has the skill set to be a complete back at the next level.

Overall
Harris was Alabama's starting running back in its power/man blocking scheme. He played in 56 games and made 34 starts for the Tide. He is a great athlete who shows incredible lower-body strength, good speed, and great balance. He can make people miss with ease and run through them. He is a fierce competitor that always keeps his feet moving and churning, fighting for every yard. He's a very tough player who loves making contact and driving through people, and almost never falls backwards.

Run Game
In the run game, he wins in a variety of ways. When he sees the hole open he has very good burst to hit the hole. Harris is a very elusive player, especially for his size. He plays with good instincts and vision, although sometimes he looks for the home-run play and tries to cut back instead of hitting the designed hole.

Pass Game
In the passing game, he shows natural receiving ability and had the most productive year of his career in 2018. He has good hands and a lot of linebackers struggle to cover him. He shows the ability to be a threat in the passing game, as he shows natural hands. He's very good as a pass protector and knows his assignments. He'll sometimes uses his shoulder instead of hands to block, but when he squares up with good technique, he stuns defenders.

Last Word
Harris projects as a 4-down player who can contribute in the run and pass game and will be a difference maker on special teams. Damien is a good special teams player and has received multiple Alabama special teams Player of the Week awards during his time there.

– Austin Cochran

Strengths	Weaknesses
• Natural receiver	• Upright runner at times
• Aggression as a blocker	• Blocking technique
• Good footwork	• Looks for the cut back too much

Critical Factors

Instincts / Vision	Contact Balance	Passing Game Impact
6	6	7

Positional Factors

Play Speed	Elusiveness	Power
6	6	6
Playmaker	**Catching Skill**	**Pass Protection**
6	6	7
Ball Security	**Ruggedness / Toughness**	**Special Teams Value**
6	6	7

Basic

	Rushing				Receiving				
Year	Att	Yds	Y/A	TD	Targets	Rec	Yds	Y/Trgt	TD
2016	146	1042	7.1	2	16	14	99	6.2	2
2017	135	1000	7.4	11	14	12	91	6.5	0
2018	150	876	5.8	9	28	22	204	7.3	0
	431	2918	6.8	22	58	48	394	6.8	2

Advanced

	Yards Per Carry				Per 100 Touches		EPA		
Year	Inside	Off-Tackle	Outside	After Contact	Fumbles	Broken Tackles	Rush	Rec	Total
2016	6.2	8.4	7.6	3.5	1.3	24	27.8	1.1	28.9
2017	7.3	7.5	7.5	4.7	0.0	29	35.8	1.4	37.2
2018	6.2	5.6	5.6	3.0	0.0	20	7.8	6.5	14.4
	6.5	7.0	6.8	3.7	0.4	24	71.4	9.0	80.5

Deep Dive

	Receiving / Blocking			Positive Play %			Usage	
Year	Routes Run	Yards Per Route Run	Blown Block %	Overall	Zone Blocking	Gap Blocking	Split Out %	Heavy Box %
2018	104	2.0	0.6%	47.3%	52.0%	38.5%	3.2%	13.3%

Rodney Anderson

Oklahoma Sooners

Final Grade: 6.8 RB Rank: 4 of 24

Height	Weight	Year	Jersey #	Hometown
6005	220	4JR	24	Katy, TX

One-Liner

Anderson is a strong runner that is very tough to bring down, who also shows natural receiving ability, but concerns about his injury history, elusiveness, and pass protection ability may keep him from seeing the field as much as his traits warrant.

Overall

Anderson lined up at running back in Oklahoma's spread offense. He had only one full year of starting experience after two season-ending lower-body injuries in 2016 and 2018. He shows sufficient athleticism with a strong build for the position. He is an aggressive ball carrier who plays with good overall effort but has serious durability concerns.

Run Game

In the run game, he shows good instincts and vision up to the line, and has very good footwork behind the line of scrimmage. He is a patient runner allowing blockers to create space, then has good one-cut ability to get into the second level. He has decent enough speed to break away and can hit an extra gear when he sees open field. Anderson's best attribute is his toughness with the ball in his hands. He runs behind his pads, and can absorb contact and bounce off defenders. He is not the most fluid lateral athlete, but he does have some wiggle in his running style, which he parlays into avoiding direct physical contact and forcing broken tackles. Anderson did benefit from running through huge running lanes at OU, but he contributed plenty of his own created yards with his excellent contact balance and power. Anderson takes good care of the ball, covering with two hands when running through traffic and at contact. He shows very good power fighting for extra yards and is difficult to keep from falling forward. Anderson does have good playmaking ability, but he also benefited from the talent around him and the defensive schemes he faced.

Pass Game

In the pass game, Anderson has very natural catching skills, and was a featured member of the Sooners' passing game. As a blocker in pass protection he is sufficient, but will need to improve his anchor as his lower body power doesn't translate well in passive situations and can be overpowered.

Last Word

He does not project well as an impact special teams contributor. Anderson has the skill set of a three-down starting running back in the league, but his injury history and durability concerns are red flags. With a clean bill of health and improved lateral agility, as well as developing in secondary areas such as pass protection and special teams, he can have a bright future.

– Jordan Edwards

Strengths	Weaknesses
• Contact balance • Natural receiving ability	• Elusiveness • Play strength in pass protection • Durability

Critical Factors

Instincts / Vision	Contact Balance	Passing Game Impact
6	8	7

Positional Factors

Play Speed	Elusiveness	Power
6	5	7
Playmaker	**Catching Skill**	**Pass Protection**
6	7	5
Ball Security	**Ruggedness / Toughness**	**Special Teams Value**
6	6	4

Basic

	Rushing				Receiving				
Year	Att	Yds	Y/A	TD	Targets	Rec	Yds	Y/Trgt	TD
2017	188	1161	6.2	13	21	17	281	13.4	5
2018	11	119	10.8	3	1	0	0	0.0	0
	199	1280	6.4	16	22	17	281	12.8	5

Advanced

	Yards Per Carry				Per 100 Touches		EPA		
Year	Inside	Off-Tackle	Outside	After Contact	Fumbles	Broken Tackles	Rush	Rec	Total
2017	6.0	7.1	3.4	3.9	0.0	26	23.3	17.9	41.1
2018	10.0	4.6	22.0	5.3	0.0	27	5.0	-0.6	4.4
	6.1	7.0	5.4	3.9	0.0	26	28.2	17.3	45.5

Deep Dive

	Receiving / Blocking			Positive Play %			Usage	
Year	Routes Run	Yards Per Route Run	Blown Block %	Overall	Zone Blocking	Gap Blocking	Split Out %	Heavy Box %
2018	12	0.0	0.0%	54.5%	50.0%	57.1%	2.8%	27.3%

Trayveon Williams

Texas A&M Aggies
Final Grade: 6.7 RB Rank: 5 of 24

Height	Weight	Year	Jersey #	Hometown
5091	200	3JR	5	Houston, TX

One-Liner
Williams has the contact balance and passing game impact to be a solid 3-down back, but his lack of speed and footwork may give him some issues early on.

Overall
Williams was the primary running back in Texas A&M's pro-style offense. He played in 38 games for the Aggies and started in 31 of them. He was the primary running back all three years. He's a good athlete that competes with toughness in his running style. He has sufficient play speed but shows the elusiveness to make guys miss.

Run Game
In the run game, he runs hard with very good power and balance. He has a compact frame with a low center of gravity. He makes quick cuts with good vision to find the open hole and has the acceleration and burst to get through quickly. Williams does a great job of getting downhill and doesn't have any wasted moves. He secures the ball when hitting the hole and as a result has good ball security, rarely putting the ball on the ground. He is a very physical runner who consistently breaks arm tackles and uses his balance to continue to fight for extra yardage. With that, he does a great job of falling forward to get the extra yards on the vast majority of his carries.

Pass Game
In the passing game, Williams is very good at pass protection. He knows blocking schemes and knows where and when to pick up blitzing defenders. He is strong at the POA and can sustain blocks instead of just giving one initial blow. As a receiver, he shows good hands with the ability to have a major impact in the passing game. He is patient on screens and allows his blocks to setup before hitting the hole. He has clear upside as a receiver as his routes, while limited, are well defined.

Last Word
Williams projects to be a starting 3-down back at the next level. He's a very capable 3rd down back due to his pass protection and hands. He may not make a huge impact on special teams, but he has some kick return experience.

– SIS Scouting Staff

Strengths	Weaknesses
• Strong runner/ contact balance	• Slow feet
• Elusive	• Play speed
• Pass protection	• Heavy college workload

Critical Factors

Instincts / Vision	Contact Balance	Passing Game Impact
6	7	7

Positional Factors

Play Speed	Elusiveness	Power
5	6	7
Playmaker	**Catching Skill**	**Pass Protection**
6	6	7
Ball Security	**Ruggedness / Toughness**	**Special Teams Value**
6	6	5

Basic

	Rushing				Receiving				
Year	Att	Yds	Y/A	TD	Targets	Rec	Yds	Y/Trgt	TD
2016	156	1056	6.8	8	27	19	91	3.4	0
2017	173	798	4.6	8	35	20	192	5.5	0
2018	271	1760	6.5	18	38	27	278	7.3	1
	600	3614	6.0	34	100	66	561	5.6	1

Advanced

	Yards Per Carry				Per 100 Touches		EPA		
Year	Inside	Off-Tackle	Outside	After Contact	Fumbles	Broken Tackles	Rush	Rec	Total
2016	6.0	9.9	4.3	3.5	1.1	18	3.4	-6.7	-3.2
2017	5.0	3.2	5.6	2.6	0.5	10	-18.7	-9.9	-28.6
2018	5.6	7.4	6.2	3.8	1.0	23	35.1	-1.9	33.2
	5.5	6.9	5.6	3.4	0.9	18	19.9	-18.5	1.4

Deep Dive

	Receiving / Blocking			Positive Play %			Usage	
Year	Routes Run	Yards Per Route Run	Blown Block %	Overall	Zone Blocking	Gap Blocking	Split Out %	Heavy Box %
2018	241	1.2	1.1%	45.4%	47.8%	40.0%	2.6%	18.8%

Miles Sanders

Penn State Nittany Lions
Final Grade: 6.7 RB Rank: 6 of 24

Height	Weight	Year	Jersey #	Hometown
5111	215	3JR	24	Pittsburgh, PA

One-Liner
Sanders is a well-rounded football player with impressive contact balance and playmaking ability, who should compete for snaps early and can become a solid NFL starter.

Overall
Sanders was a running back in Penn State's shotgun-based, read option-heavy offense. He played in 38 career games, only becoming the feature back his final season at State College. He has very good size with a thick lower body, as well as plenty of athleticism, quickness, and strength.

Run Game
He is patient off the snap, letting his blocks setup in front of him during the mesh point read, then shows explosion into the hole. Sanders runs with great pad level and body lean, which contribute to his high-end contact balance. He bounces off tacklers very well and consistently gets yards after contact. He shows good power when necessary in short yardage, but is more of an elusive and glancing runner in space. He uses spin moves and can stick his foot in the ground to change directions very quickly. Sanders does get in trouble by trying to bounce too many runs to the outside, creating negative plays. He does a good job of making defenders miss, but while his speed is good, it isn't elite to consistently pull away from secondary players. He moves freely behind the line and can create yards for himself.

Pass Game
In the passing game, Sanders runs mostly screens, swings and checkdown routes. He wasn't a high-volume pass catcher in the Nittany Lions' offense, but he was capable of more. He doesn't create consistent separation from defenders on downfield routes. He is good in pass protection, as he possesses a good anchor picking up blitzing linebackers and reads defenders with good awareness. His balance is evident in pass protection, as well, where he rarely gets caught off balance and can attack rushers without lunging.

Last Word
Sanders projects as an NFL starter with skills to compete for reps on all three downs early in his career. He is a well-balanced athlete whose predecessor has transitioned well from this offense to the NFL.

– Evan Butler

Strengths	Weaknesses
• Contact balance	• Limited receiving experience
• Playmaking ability	• Bouncing runs
• Pass protection	• Breakaway speed

Critical Factors

Instincts / Vision	Contact Balance	Passing Game Impact
6	7	6

Positional Factors

Play Speed	Elusiveness	Power
6	6	6
Playmaker	**Catching Skill**	**Pass Protection**
7	6	6
Ball Security	**Ruggedness / Toughness**	**Special Teams Value**
6	6	6

Basic

	Rushing				Receiving				
Year	Att	Yds	Y/A	TD	Targets	Rec	Yds	Y/Trgt	TD
2016	25	184	7.4	1	3	2	24	8.0	1
2017	31	191	6.2	2	12	6	30	2.5	0
2018	220	1274	5.8	9	34	24	139	4.1	0
	276	1649	6.0	12	49	32	193	3.9	1

Advanced

	Yards Per Carry				Per 100 Touches		EPA		
Year	Inside	Off-Tackle	Outside	After Contact	Fumbles	Broken Tackles	Rush	Rec	Total
2016	4.2	14.1	2.7	5.2	7.4	33	-5.5	2.2	-3.3
2017	6.5	6.3	4.8	4.2	2.7	46	3.8	-3.5	0.3
2018	6.6	5.2	4.5	3.5	1.6	23	7.6	-14.0	-6.4
	6.4	6.0	4.2	3.7	2.3	26	5.9	-15.3	-9.4

Deep Dive

	Receiving / Blocking			Positive Play %			Usage	
Year	Routes Run	Yards Per Route Run	Blown Block %	Overall	Zone Blocking	Gap Blocking	Split Out %	Heavy Box %
2018	210	0.7	0.9%	45.5%	48.2%	37.0%	3.4%	2.7%

Devine Ozigbo

Nebraska Cornhuskers

Final Grade: 6.6 RB Rank: 7 of 24

Height	Weight	Year	Jersey #	Hometown
5105	219	4SR	22	Sachse, TX

One-Liner

Ozigbo's combination of size, vision, and elusiveness project to make him a two-down starter in the NFL, but his lack of impact in the pass game hinders his ability to contribute on third down.

Overall

Ozigbo was a running back in Nebraska's shotgun RPO-based offense where they ran a mix of zone and power blocking schemes. He played in 44 career games, and never came into a season as the starter, but due to injuries or his own superior play, ended his junior and senior years as the Huskers' leading rusher. He has a thick lower half, strong arms, and decent athleticism for his build. Ozigbo is a good competitor who had to fight for his playing time for four years, and he uses his strength to finish runs well.

Run Game

His best trait is his vision between the tackles. He does a very good job of pressing the hole and forcing linebackers and blocked linemen to show their hand. Especially for his size, he has very impressive lateral jump cut ability, short-area quickness, and feel to bounce into cutbacks and open space. He has an innate ability to create yards when none seem to be available by making unblocked defenders miss in the backfield, getting skinny through tight spaces, and falling forward at contact. He attacks defenders like a much smaller back, more often relying on his elusiveness than lowering his shoulder and churning through contact. He does not possess top-end long speed, but he has enough burst to score from distance. He doesn't bounce off blocks like he looks like he should, but he has thick thighs and good leg drive to finish with an extra yard or two. He seemed to lose some juice as his senior year went on during his heaviest collegiate workload.

Pass Game

In the pass game, Ozigbo is inexperienced but flashes ability. He is a good and savvy route runner out of the backfield, but he isn't a natural receiver of the football and will drop some catchable balls, limiting his downfield passing game impact. However, he can usually be relied upon to haul in short screens and check downs. Ozigbo has surprisingly sound technique and is a strong pass protector, despite limited reps in this area.

Last Word

Ozigbo's skill set suggests he'd be a strong special teams contributor on multiple units. He projects as a strong starting caliber two-down contributor by his second year.

– John Todd

Strengths	Weaknesses
• Ballcarrier vision	• Breakaway speed
• Lateral agility	• Catching skills
• Manufacturing yards	• Passing game experience

Critical Factors

Instincts / Vision	Contact Balance	Passing Game Impact
7	6	6

Positional Factors

Play Speed	Elusiveness	Power
5	7	6
Playmaker	**Catching Skill**	**Pass Protection**
7	5	7
Ball Security	**Ruggedness / Toughness**	**Special Teams Value**
7	6	7

Basic

	Rushing				Receiving				
Year	Att	Yds	Y/A	TD	Targets	Rec	Yds	Y/Trgt	TD
2016	97	412	4.2	5	11	5	100	9.1	0
2017	129	493	3.8	3	19	16	123	6.5	0
2018	155	1082	7.0	12	37	23	203	5.5	0
	381	1987	5.2	20	67	44	426	6.4	0

Advanced

	Yards Per Carry				Per 100 Touches		EPA		
Year	Inside	Off-Tackle	Outside	After Contact	Fumbles	Broken Tackles	Rush	Rec	Total
2016	4.6	3.6	4.6	2.6	1.0	11	-11.0	-1.9	-12.9
2017	4.0	3.5	4.0	2.8	1.4	19	-19.9	-9.2	-29.1
2018	6.5	6.5	9.2	4.1	0.0	28	31.4	-10.6	20.8
	5.1	4.7	7.1	3.3	0.7	21	0.5	-21.7	-21.2

Deep Dive

	Receiving / Blocking			Positive Play %			Usage	
Year	Routes Run	Yards Per Route Run	Blown Block %	Overall	Zone Blocking	Gap Blocking	Split Out %	Heavy Box %
2018	142	1.4	1.1%	51.6%	54.3%	43.6%	12.7%	5.2%

Justice Hill

Oklahoma State Cowboys
Final Grade: 6.5 RB Rank: 8 of 24

Height	Weight	Year	Jersey #	Hometown
5096	190	3JR	5	Tulsa, OK

One-Liner
Hill's third-down ability isn't natural and needs improvement, but he possesses high-end vision, lateral agility, burst, and overall playmaking skills to succeed as a starting-caliber ballcarrier.

Overall
Hill was a running back in Oklahoma State's spread offense. He was a three-year starter and played in 36 career games. He has good size with decent lower-body thickness. Hill is a very good athlete with lateral agility, speed and playmaking ability in space. He is a tough runner who finishes plays and gives good effort.

Run Game
Hill has very impressive vision in the backfield. He does a great job of hitting holes, being patient for blocks to develop, and eyeing cutback lanes to make a play on his own. He will have some negative plays trying to extend a run instead of taking the easy yards. He has impressive lateral agility, which makes it difficult to bring him down]. Hill is a slalom, one-cut runner, with excellent jump cuts and evasive jukes to make defenders whiff, as well as great burst and acceleration into open space. Despite his slender frame, he does a good job of finishing runs with physicality when necessary and falling forward. He has solid lower-body strength and balance to keep his feet moving and run through tackles.

Pass Game
In the pass game, Hill wasn't used often. He has been reliable on checkdowns but doesn't look to be a natural receiver. His pass protection effort is there, but his anchor and technique need improvement to stay on the field as a third down option.

Last Word
Hill offers kick return versatility and his ability in open space should allow him to make an immediate impact there. By his second year, he projects as a two-down starter in zone blocking scheme, where he can use his vision, burst and quickness to make big plays for an offense. He would do well to improve his third-down skills, as he is an ideal space player.

– Drew Schweitzer

Strengths	**Weaknesses**
• Vision and instincts	• Natural receiving traits
• Lateral agility	• Pass protection
• Acceleration	

Critical Factors

Instincts / Vision	Contact Balance	Passing Game Impact
7	6	5

Positional Factors

Play Speed	Elusiveness	Power
7	7	6
Playmaker	**Catching Skill**	**Pass Protection**
7	5	5
Ball Security	**Ruggedness / Toughness**	**Special Teams Value**
6	7	6

Basic

	Rushing				Receiving				
Year	Att	Yds	Y/A	TD	Targets	Rec	Yds	Y/Trgt	TD
2016	206	1144	5.6	6	6	5	46	7.7	0
2017	268	1467	5.5	15	44	31	190	4.3	1
2018	158	930	5.9	9	17	13	68	4.0	0
	632	3541	5.6	30	67	49	304	4.5	1

Advanced

	Yards Per Carry				Per 100 Touches		EPA		
Year	Inside	Off-Tackle	Outside	After Contact	Fumbles	Broken Tackles	Rush	Rec	Total
2016	4.9	6.2	5.2	3.1	1.4	19	-1.1	1.4	0.3
2017	5.1	5.6	6.1	3.1	0.7	22	15.8	-7.6	8.3
2018	7.2	5.0	4.6	2.8	0.0	27	-1.8	-1.5	-3.4
	5.6	5.7	5.5	3.0	0.7	23	12.8	-7.7	5.2

Deep Dive

	Receiving / Blocking			Positive Play %			Usage	
Year	Routes Run	Yards Per Route Run	Blown Block %	Overall	Zone Blocking	Gap Blocking	Split Out %	Heavy Box %
2018	101	0.7	0.9%	40.5%	40.6%	40.0%	3.3%	8.9%

David Montgomery

Iowa State Cyclones

Final Grade: 6.3 RB Rank: 9 of 24

Height	Weight	Year	Jersey #	Hometown
5096	216	3JR	32	Cincinnati, OH

One-Liner

Montgomery is a strong, patient runner with good pass-catching ability, whose lack of impactful play speed may limit him to a role-playing position in the NFL.

Overall

Montgomery was a running back in Iowa State's offense. He played in 37 career games as the starting running back since late in his freshman season. He has solid size and is a decent athlete for the position, who lacks elite speed but shows solid quickness and footwork on cuts.

Run Game

In the run game, he plays with very good vision and patience to wait for blocks to develop and holes to open up. Montgomery isn't extremely athletic or elusive, but he has a good amount of short area wiggle in tight areas to make defenders miss in the hole and burst into open space. He does a good job of taking contact and falling forward. Montgomery won't outrun many second-level defenders, but he can break tackles in different ways and works hard for extra yards.

Pass Game

In the pass game, he is a high-volume, solid receiver. He runs very sharp routes out of the backfield to make himself available as a checkdown, as well as win with separation as an early option. As a pass protector, he plays with a strong base but can improve on his technique and awareness.

Last Word

He was moved around and schemed open as a Cyclone, and has proven to be a reliable third-down contributor. Montgomery's skillset projects as a low-end starter at the next level, who may not be able to make a difference every down, but has the versatility and vision to play a role.

– SIS Scouting Staff

Strengths	Weaknesses
• Patience behind the line • Sharp route running • Contact balance	• Pass protection consistency • Breakaway speed

Critical Factors

Instincts / Vision	Contact Balance	Passing Game Impact
7	7	6

Positional Factors

Play Speed	Elusiveness	Power
5	6	6
Playmaker	**Catching Skill**	**Pass Protection**
6	6	5
Ball Security	**Ruggedness / Toughness**	**Special Teams Value**
6	6	5

Basic

	Rushing				Receiving				
Year	Att	Yds	Y/A	TD	Targets	Rec	Yds	Y/Trgt	TD
2016	109	563	5.2	2	17	13	129	7.6	0
2017	258	1146	4.4	11	47	36	296	6.3	0
2018	257	1216	4.7	13	25	22	157	6.3	0
	624	2925	4.7	26	89	71	582	6.5	0

Advanced

	Yards Per Carry				Per 100 Touches		EPA		
Year	Inside	Off-Tackle	Outside	After Contact	Fumbles	Broken Tackles	Rush	Rec	Total
2016	4.9	4.9	7.9	3.5	0.8	29	-2.2	-0.4	-2.6
2017	3.9	5.0	5.3	3.3	0.3	44	-22.6	-5.8	-28.4
2018	4.6	4.7	5.8	3.1	0.4	33	-4.7	-2.7	-7.4
	4.3	4.9	5.9	3.3	0.4	37	-29.5	-9.0	-38.5

Deep Dive

	Receiving / Blocking			Positive Play %			Usage	
Year	Routes Run	Yards Per Route Run	Blown Block %	Overall	Zone Blocking	Gap Blocking	Split Out %	Heavy Box %
2018	112	1.4	0.0%	42.0%	43.1%	38.2%	2.2%	10.9%

D.J. Knox

Purdue Boilermakers
Final Grade: 6.3 RB Rank: 10 of 24

Height	Weight	Year	Jersey #	Hometown
5065	210	5SR	1	Fairburn, GA

One-Liner
Knox is a very quick-footed and tough running back with great lower-body strength and contact balance who has the ability to impact an offense on any down, despite his height.

Overall
Knox was a 4-year player for Purdue, making starts in three seasons, while often splitting time. Knox is a solid athlete who shows playmaking ability, elusiveness, and very good contact balance.

Run Game
In the running game, Knox is a one-cut back with good instincts and the patience to find open lanes. Knox's biggest strength is his balance and ability to bounce off tacklers. He consistently gained extra yardage based on his thick lower half and low center of gravity. Knox's ball security is sufficient as he does not fumble often, but he carries the ball a bit too loosely to continue that trend in the NFL. Purdue rotates its backs frequently, so stamina could be an issue at the next level in addition to his size.

Pass Game
In the passing game, Knox has good hands and demonstrates playmaking ability in space. He is good with the ball in his hands, and his combination of elusiveness and power will help him to contribute on screens and quick passes. He occasionally lined up in the slot for Purdue, but he is not used prominently in this role. Knox is sufficient in pass protection, but not for lack of effort and aggression. He is a very willing blocker, but his size will likely limit him in this area at the next level.

Last Word
Knox is a talented back, but his size limitations and inconsistency with playing speed will likely relegate him to a change-of-pace back early, but his toughness and will could see him as a low-end starter down the road.

– Ronan Potts

Strengths	Weaknesses
• Toughness • Contact balance and body lean • One-cut ability	• Pass pro anchor • Burst

Critical Factors

Instincts / Vision	Contact Balance	Passing Game Impact
6	7	6

Positional Factors

Play Speed	Elusiveness	Power
5	6	6
Playmaker	**Catching Skill**	**Pass Protection**
6	6	5
Ball Security	**Ruggedness / Toughness**	**Special Teams Value**
5	7	7

Basic

	Rushing				Receiving				
Year	Att	Yds	Y/A	TD	Targets	Rec	Yds	Y/Trgt	TD
2017	90	561	6.2	2	22	16	147	6.7	2
2018	158	883	5.6	8	31	27	180	5.8	1
	248	1444	5.8	10	53	43	327	6.2	3

Advanced

	Yards Per Carry				Per 100 Touches		EPA		
Year	Inside	Off-Tackle	Outside	After Contact	Fumbles	Broken Tackles	Rush	Rec	Total
2017	6.9	5.1	7.4	3.4	0.9	24	4.4	4.3	8.8
2018	6.3	5.1	5.7	3.4	0.5	21	2.4	1.5	3.9
	6.6	5.1	6.2	3.4	0.7	22	6.8	5.9	12.7

Deep Dive

	Receiving / Blocking			Positive Play %			Usage	
Year	Routes Run	Yards Per Route Run	Blown Block %	Overall	Zone Blocking	Gap Blocking	Split Out %	Heavy Box %
2018	179	1.0	1.3%	40.1%	40.7%	39.4%	5.8%	9.6%

Jalin Moore

Appalachian State Mountaineers
Final Grade: 6.3 RB Rank: 11 of 24

Height	Weight	Year	Jersey #	Hometown
5095	207	5SR	25	Shelby, NC

One-Liner
Moore has a slender frame, but uses his toughness, balance, and effort to make plays against all competition, and should become a nice rotational role player in the league.

Overall
Moore was a running back in Appalachian State's multiple offense. He played in 42 games in his decorated career and has been an impactful player since late in his freshman season. He has decent size and is a very good athlete with great lateral agility, contact balance, and acceleration. This allow him to make people miss against all levels of competition. He plays with a high level of toughness and has rehabbed hard from his season-ending ankle injury to prepare for the pre-draft process. He was often the best player on the field for the Mountaineers and raised his game against top competition.

Run Game
His vision is inconsistent, he runs with his head down up the middle while also occasionally bouncing or reversing field outside, resulting in negative plays. This running style leads to great playmaking ability, however, as he'll give you big-chunk yardage. Moore has good elusiveness in the open field, but his contact balance between the tackles is his best trait. He uses his low base along with an aggressive temperament and good pad level to run through arm tackles and bounce off tacklers, despite his average size. Moore is not a powerful runner, but his toughness and body lean allow him to get skinny and fall forward often.

Pass Game
In the passing game, he is a very quick route runner out of the backfield and can be a mismatch for linebackers. His hands are average and inconsistent downfield, but he gets himself open and can make plays once the the ball is in his hands. Moore is an impressive pass protector for his size, showing excellent willingness and solid awareness of blitzing fronts. He attacks with a good base, but he lunges at times to compensate for his size.

Last Word
He best projects as a difference-making role player at the next level, based on his toughness, playmaking ability, and combination of contact balance and agility. He will need to prove he is healthy leading up to the draft.

– SIS Scouting Staff

Strengths	Weaknesses
• Contact balance	• Catching skill
• Toughness	• Inconsistent vision
• Playmaking ability	

Critical Factors

Instincts / Vision	Contact Balance	Passing Game Impact
5	7	6

Positional Factors

Play Speed	Elusiveness	Power
6	6	5
Playmaker	**Catching Skill**	**Pass Protection**
7	4	6
Ball Security	**Ruggedness / Toughness**	**Special Teams Value**
6	7	5

Basic

	Rushing				Receiving				
Year	Att	Yds	Y/A	TD	Targets	Rec	Yds	Y/Trgt	TD
2016	237	1402	5.9	10	9	5	32	3.6	0
2017	184	1040	5.7	12	19	12	163	8.6	1
2018	64	400	6.3	6	9	6	40	4.4	0
	485	2842	5.9	28	37	23	235	6.4	1

Advanced

	Yards Per Carry				Per 100 Touches		EPA		
Year	Inside	Off-Tackle	Outside	After Contact	Fumbles	Broken Tackles	Rush	Rec	Total
2016	6.0	5.8	6.9	2.9	0.4	19	6.7	-5.4	1.3
2017	4.8	7.2	3.9	2.7	0.5	23	12.7	-0.3	12.4
2018	6.7	6.5	4.0	3.6	0.0	40	5.5	-0.8	4.6
	5.6	6.3	4.9	2.9	0.4	21	24.8	-6.5	18.3

Deep Dive

	Receiving / Blocking			Positive Play %			Usage	
Year	Routes Run	Yards Per Route Run	Blown Block %	Overall	Zone Blocking	Gap Blocking	Split Out %	Heavy Box %
2018	31	1.3	0.0%	42.2%	42.2%	-	0.6%	12.5%

Darrell Henderson

Memphis Tigers
Final Grade: 6.3 RB Rank: 12 of 24

Height	Weight	Year	Jersey #	Hometown
5085	200	3JR	8	Batesville, MS

One-Liner
Henderson wins with speed, and shows excellent acceleration along with great vision to become a home run hitting role player at the next level.

Overall
Henderson was the feature running back in Memphis' offense. He played in 35 career games, making starts since his freshman season. He has had a nationally recognized, record-breaking career with the Tigers. He has a slight frame but good lower-body thickness. He is a very explosive athlete with the long speed to run away from defenders at the next level.

Run Game
In the run game, Henderson is best on stretch plays where he can probe the defense and explode through the hole. He has very good vision and knows when to put his foot in the ground and get upfield, as well as cutback and weave through a defense at the second level. He accelerates quickly to his top speed and is difficult to catch from behind. Henderson produces some missed tackles with elusiveness, but he usually beats defenders by outrunning angles more than through or around them. His contact balance is better than his ability to run with power, but neither is a facet of his game. Henderson is a true home run hitter in the open field.

Pass Game
In the pass game, he flashes the ability to run good routes. He was not asked to do much more than screens and swing routes at Memphis. He was split out occasionally and can burst past linebackers in man coverage. His pass protection anchor and positioning are questionable, but he doesn't shy from contact.

Last Word
Henderson did return kicks at Memphis and could be a very good returner at the next level because of his speed and open-field vision. Overall, he projects to be a high level change-of-pace back. He has good enough hands to become an employable third-down receiver and can pick up chunk plays frequently if put in the position to do so.

– Ben Hrkach

Strengths	Weaknesses
• Burst and acceleration	• Pass protection
• Vision	• Running with power
• Big play ability	

Critical Factors

Instincts / Vision	Contact Balance	Passing Game Impact
7	5	5

Positional Factors

Play Speed	Elusiveness	Power
7	6	4
Playmaker	**Catching Skill**	**Pass Protection**
7	5	4
Ball Security	**Ruggedness / Toughness**	**Special Teams Value**
6	6	6

Basic

	Rushing				Receiving				
Year	Att	Yds	Y/A	TD	Targets	Rec	Yds	Y/Trgt	TD
2016	87	482	5.5	5	26	20	237	9.1	3
2017	129	1148	8.9	9	33	24	226	6.8	2
2018	214	1909	8.9	22	24	19	295	12.3	3
	430	3539	8.2	36	83	63	758	9.1	8

Advanced

	Yards Per Carry				Per 100 Touches		EPA		
Year	Inside	Off-Tackle	Outside	After Contact	Fumbles	Broken Tackles	Rush	Rec	Total
2016	4.8	7.2	4.4	2.5	0.0	13	5.2	9.0	14.3
2017	8.8	9.8	7.0	5.7	1.3	23	23.6	5.0	28.6
2018	8.1	10.0	7.5	6.0	0.4	24	61.2	10.4	71.6
	7.4	9.5	6.7	5.2	0.6	22	90.0	24.4	114.4

Deep Dive

	Receiving / Blocking			Positive Play %			Usage	
Year	Routes Run	Yards Per Route Run	Blown Block %	Overall	Zone Blocking	Gap Blocking	Split Out %	Heavy Box %
2018	106	2.8	0.0%	48.6%	49.5%	47.7%	4.3%	5.6%

Myles Gaskin

Washington Huskies
Final Grade: 6.3 RB Rank: 13 of 24

Height	Weight	Year	Jersey #	Hometown
5091	193	4SR	9	Lynnwood, WA

One-Liner
Gaskin is an elusive, shifty runner who has been a high-volume workhorse throughout his record-breaking collegiate career, but is better suited for a change-of-pace role in the NFL.

Overall
Gaskin was a running back in Washington's balanced offense. He was a four-year starter who played 52 games in his decorated collegiate career. He has a slender frame but has avoided major injury. He is tough despite his size and has logged a record number of carries and yards in his time as a Husky.

Run Game
Gaskin has good vision behind the line, as he follows pulling linemen well and is patient in zone to let plays develop. He doesn't have explosive acceleration or elite long speed, and his history as a track athlete doesn't always translate to the field, but he hits holes hard. He has great footwork to and through the line of scrimmage and he ties his eyes to his feet well. His footwork helps his contact balance and especially his shiftiness. Gaskin is very elusive in the open field and regularly makes players miss at the second level. He has good contact balance for his size, but it's fair to question if this will hold up against NFL defenders at his current playing weight. He doesn't always run with power, but he has flashed some surprising pop.

Pass Game
In the pass game, Gaskin is a player who needs accounting for. His receiving numbers are dwarfed by his rushing statistics, but he has had success out of the backfield as well. This is where he projects to be utilized, but his anchor will need improvement to hold up against stronger rushers in the league.

Last Word
While he has a clear history of high-volume usage, he best projects as a change-of-pace back in the NFL due to his size, where his speed, elusiveness and receiving skills can provide a spark.

– SIS Scouting Staff

Strengths	Weaknesses
• One-cut vision	• Power
• Elusiveness	• Pass protection anchor
• Natural receiver	• Explosiveness

Critical Factors

Instincts / Vision	Contact Balance	Passing Game Impact
6	6	6

Positional Factors

Play Speed	Elusiveness	Power
6	7	5
Playmaker	**Catching Skill**	**Pass Protection**
6	6	5
Ball Security	**Ruggedness / Toughness**	**Special Teams Value**
6	6	6

Basic

	Rushing				Receiving				
Year	Att	Yds	Y/A	TD	Targets	Rec	Yds	Y/Trgt	TD
2016	237	1373	5.8	10	26	19	137	5.3	1
2017	222	1380	6.2	21	24	19	232	9.7	3
2018	259	1268	4.9	12	30	21	77	2.6	1
	718	4021	5.6	43	80	59	446	5.6	5

Advanced

	Yards Per Carry				Per 100 Touches		EPA		
Year	Inside	Off-Tackle	Outside	After Contact	Fumbles	Broken Tackles	Rush	Rec	Total
2016	5.3	6.6	5.3	2.9	0.0	30	18.3	-2.8	15.6
2017	5.3	7.3	6.2	2.8	0.8	26	32.4	7.1	39.5
2018	4.3	4.3	6.6	2.9	0.4	22	2.6	-11.2	-8.6
	5.0	6.0	6.1	2.9	0.4	26	53.3	-6.8	46.5

Deep Dive

	Receiving / Blocking			Positive Play %			Usage	
Year	Routes Run	Yards Per Route Run	Blown Block %	Overall	Zone Blocking	Gap Blocking	Split Out %	Heavy Box %
2018	116	0.7	0.2%	41.3%	37.6%	47.9%	3.1%	22.4%

James Williams

Washington State Cougars
Final Grade: 6.3 RB Rank: 14 of 24

Height	Weight	Year	Jersey #	Hometown
5111	205	4JR	32	Burbank, CA

One-Liner
Williams is a quick, elusive back with good contact balance, very good receiving skills and lack of power in the run game which tabs him as a difference maker on 3rd downs at the next level.

Overall
Williams was a RB in Washington State's Air Raid offense where he thrived not just as a runner, but as a receiver, where he lead the team in receptions. He played in 39 games for the Cougars and started in 18 of them. Williams has very good athleticism that he illustrates through his elusiveness, playmaking ability and high impact in the passing game. He competes in his play, especially when tabbed as a receiver out of the backfield.

Run Game
In the run game, Williams shows good play speed and elusiveness in the hole and even though he isn't the largest back, he does play with sufficient power and toughness. He also has his eyes connected to his feet well as he uses good vision when looking for open running lanes. He is best when he makes one cut and hits the hole.

Pass Game
In the pass game, Williams is a game-changer. Throughout his career, he has proved to impact the passing game with his catching skills. He's dynamic out of the backfield and can be a mismatch when LBs or bigger DBs are manned up on him. He doesn't have much experience staying in to block and struggles to anchor against power.

Last Word
Williams doesn't have the 3-down ability to be a starter, but projects as a 3rd down difference maker at the next level. He will make most of his impact as a pass catcher on third down, in two-minute drills or any other situation where a receiving threat in the backfield is needed. Due to his athleticism and catching ability, he should also be able to provide good special teams value whether it is covering kicks/punts or returning them.

– Mark Johnson

Strengths	Weaknesses
• Passing-game impact • Contact balance • Playmaking ability	• Pass protection • Power in the run game

Critical Factors

Instincts / Vision	Contact Balance	Passing Game Impact
6	6	7

Positional Factors

Play Speed	Elusiveness	Power
6	6	5
Playmaker	**Catching Skill**	**Pass Protection**
6	7	4
Ball Security	**Ruggedness / Toughness**	**Special Teams Value**
6	5	6

Basic

	Rushing				Receiving				
Year	Att	Yds	Y/A	TD	Targets	Rec	Yds	Y/Trgt	TD
2016	102	584	5.7	6	60	48	342	5.7	1
2017	92	395	4.3	1	81	71	482	6.0	3
2018	122	560	4.6	12	93	83	613	6.6	4
	316	1539	4.9	19	234	202	1437	6.1	8

Advanced

	Yards Per Carry				Per 100 Touches		EPA		
Year	Inside	Off-Tackle	Outside	After Contact	Fumbles	Broken Tackles	Rush	Rec	Total
2016	5.6	5.7	6.2	3.7	0.7	37	12.5	-1.7	10.8
2017	6.1	4.3	2.7	2.9	0.6	42	-9.7	0.8	-8.9
2018	5.1	3.5	4.5	2.7	1.0	36	11.1	12.3	23.4
	5.4	4.7	3.5	3.1	0.8	38	14.0	11.3	25.3

Deep Dive

	Receiving / Blocking			Positive Play %			Usage	
Year	Routes Run	Yards Per Route Run	Blown Block %	Overall	Zone Blocking	Gap Blocking	Split Out %	Heavy Box %
2018	345	1.8	1.6%	50.0%	50.0%	50.0%	4.9%	0.0%

Benny Snell Jr.

Kentucky Wildcats
Final Grade: 6.2 RB Rank: 15 of 24

Height	Weight	Year	Jersey #	Hometown
5096	223	3JR	26	Westerville, OH

One-Liner
Snell is a tough, physical runner with a strong history as an SEC workhorse, but his third-down limitations and lack of breakaway speed may keep him to a backup role.

Overall
Snell, Jr. was a running back in Kentucky's run-heavy offense, which incorporated both power and zone blocking concepts. He was has also featured in Wildcat packages this past season. Snell was a three-year starter who played in 39 career games. Snell is a good athlete with a stocky, thick build. He has average height and above average weight for the position. He is extremely competitive, constantly wants the ball late in games, and displays very good mental and physical toughness.

Run Game
In the run game, Snell is a powerful running back who has good vision to identify open holes and make decisive cuts to get upfield. He shows good patience to allow his blockers to open holes and let the play develop. He has decent foot speed and short-area quickness but isn't a home run hitter. He has plenty of wiggle to supplement his strength and uses it to evade defenders and force missed tackles. His best trait is his contact balance. He consistently falls forward, keeps positive momentum after contact, and rarely goes down with first contact. He possesses good power with an ability to maintain a low center of gravity, keep his pad level low, and run through arm tackles. Snell is a tough runner who looks for, and embraces contact, while also keeping the ball close to his chest as he engages defenders. He has a strong stiff-arm move and is able to occasionally flash a spin move to avoid tacklers in the open field. He lacks the breakaway speed to turn the corner and pull away and won't beat second-level angles at the next level.

Pass Game
In the pass game, Snell is frequently used as a receiver out of the backfield, often only asked to catch simple checkdown passes. He hasn't shown the natural hands or experience to win on third downs. He is sufficient in pass protection with the stoutness to hold up against blitzers but possesses only average technique and awareness.

Last Word
By his second season, Snell should at least be a solid backup with the ability to add a spark if allowed to get into a rhythm. Snell churns out tough yards and is capable of being a workhorse, but he lacks the playmaking ability and pass-game production to be a three-down player at the next level. He possesses the strength and toughness to bring special teams value to multiple units.

– Nick Giella

Strengths	**Weaknesses**
• Interior instincts	• Limited receiving ability
• Contact balance and toughness	• Breakaway speed
• Evasiveness for size	• Third-down versatility

Critical Factors

Instincts / Vision	Contact Balance	Passing Game Impact
6	7	5

Positional Factors

Play Speed	Elusiveness	Power
5	6	6
Playmaker	**Catching Skill**	**Pass Protection**
5	4	5
Ball Security	**Ruggedness / Toughness**	**Special Teams Value**
6	7	6

Basic

	Rushing				Receiving				
Year	Att	Yds	Y/A	TD	Targets	Rec	Yds	Y/Trgt	TD
2016	186	1091	5.9	13	3	2	39	13.0	0
2017	262	1333	5.1	19	16	10	72	4.5	0
2018	289	1454	5.0	16	22	17	105	4.8	0
	737	3878	5.3	48	41	29	216	5.3	0

Advanced

	Yards Per Carry				Per 100 Touches		EPA		
Year	Inside	Off-Tackle	Outside	After Contact	Fumbles	Broken Tackles	Rush	Rec	Total
2016	5.9	5.4	8.8	3.5	1.1	22	32.8	2.7	35.4
2017	5.0	5.0	6.4	3.1	0.7	22	-8.3	-10.3	-18.6
2018	5.4	4.5	4.5	3.2	0.7	19	7.4	-2.4	5.1
	5.4	4.9	6.0	3.2	0.8	21	31.9	-10.0	21.9

Deep Dive

	Receiving / Blocking			Positive Play %			Usage	
Year	Routes Run	Yards Per Route Run	Blown Block %	Overall	Zone Blocking	Gap Blocking	Split Out %	Heavy Box %
2018	66	1.6	0.7%	42.6%	44.2%	37.5%	1.2%	11.1%

Bryce Love

Stanford Cardinal
Final Grade: 6.2 RB Rank: 16 of 24

Height	Weight	Year	Jersey #	Hometown
5091	202	4SR	20	Wake Forest, NC

One-Liner
Love is a tough, instinctual runner that has the short-area quickness and elusiveness to create and make plays at the next level, but his power and play strength will hold him back.

Overall
Love was a running back in Stanford's heavy gap-blocking run game. He played in 49 career games, playing through some with injury in 2017 and tearing his ACL the final regular season game of 2018. He has decent size for the position and is a good athlete. He exemplifies toughness and is a competitor as he has continued to played through multiple injuries, although his ankle injuries have affected him and been the reason why he was not as explosive in 2018 as he was in 2017.

Run Game
In the run game, he shows that he's an excellent downhill runner with acceleration and burst through the hole and the speed to break off long runs. He has very good elusiveness and his vision in space allows him to make defenders miss with regularity. He has sufficient contact balance as he is able to run through most arm and hand tackles, but can run with a high pad level at times, which prevents him from taking advantage of his power. He has good ball security and rarely put the ball on the ground in college. He is a very good playmaker and can create some yards after contact because of his build, strength and burst. He has the proven stamina to be a more effective runner as the game goes on and has shown he can be an every down back throughout the rigors of a season.

Pass Game
In the pass game, he is sufficient at pass protection, as he doesn't always use good technique or strength at the POA. He shows good hands catching the ball out of the backfield, but the offense at Stanford did not call for him to do these things as often as he should be asked to at the next level.

Last Word
Love projects as a change of pace back who can play on 1st and 2nd down with some limited 3rd down ability early in his career. He has impact in the passing game, but needs to improve pass pro and overall impact to warrant starting ability. Given his speed and elusiveness, he could contribute some on special teams, although he was used sparingly as a returner in college.

– Cole Ratliff

Strengths	Weaknesses
• Shows burst through the line	• Play strength
• Short-area quickness/elusive	• Bounces too many runs
• Pass protection awareness	• Needs to play with more power

Critical Factors

Instincts / Vision	Contact Balance	Passing Game Impact
7	5	6

Positional Factors

Play Speed	Elusiveness	Power
7	7	4
Playmaker	**Catching Skill**	**Pass Protection**
7	6	5
Ball Security	**Ruggedness / Toughness**	**Special Teams Value**
6	7	6

Basic

	Rushing				Receiving				
Year	Att	Yds	Y/A	TD	Targets	Rec	Yds	Y/Trgt	TD
2016	111	783	7.1	2	13	8	83	6.4	1
2017	262	2104	8.0	19	9	6	33	3.7	0
2018	165	736	4.5	6	26	20	99	3.8	0
	538	3623	6.7	27	48	34	215	4.5	1

Advanced

	Yards Per Carry				Per 100 Touches		EPA		
Year	Inside	Off-Tackle	Outside	After Contact	Fumbles	Broken Tackles	Rush	Rec	Total
2016	5.6	7.7	8.5	4.4	0.8	26	15.0	0.2	15.1
2017	6.3	9.1	10.0	5.0	1.1	33	34.8	-3.5	31.3
2018	3.8	4.1	6.6	3.3	0.5	28	-34.0	-10.4	-44.4
	5.4	7.3	8.3	4.4	0.9	30	15.8	-13.8	2.0

Deep Dive

	Receiving / Blocking			Positive Play %			Usage	
Year	Routes Run	Yards Per Route Run	Blown Block %	Overall	Zone Blocking	Gap Blocking	Split Out %	Heavy Box %
2018	102	1.0	1.1%	32.7%	32.9%	32.5%	1.6%	26.1%

Elijah Holyfield

Georgia Bulldogs
Final Grade: 6.2 RB Rank: 17 of 24

Height	Weight	Year	Jersey #	Hometown
5095	215	3JR	13	College Park, GA

One-Liner
Holyfield is a physical, downhill runner with good vision, patience, and contact balance, but his limited ability in the passing game likely relegates him to only early-down duties.

Overall
Holyfield played running back in Georgia's pro-style offense. He started in 10 of his 32 career games played, primarily being used as a backup for the Bulldogs during his time there. He has sufficient height for the position, but enough sturdiness to withstand NFL hits. There is not much wear and tear on his body due to small career workload. He has good play speed and burst for the position and possesses good foot quickness with fluid hips. He's deceptively agile in short areas. He's a tough player that is not afraid to lower his shoulder and embrace contact.

Run Game
In the run game, he displays a downhill running style. He has good contact balance and runs with a low center of gravity. He does a good job of racking up yards after contact by keeping his legs churning. He has the strength, balance, and base to run through tacklers. Holyfield is a smart runner that makes good decisions with a north-south mentality that allows him to fall forward and gain positive yards. He displays good ball security, and usually keeps the ball tight to his frame and covers it in traffic. He shows good patience and vision, and lets blocks develop in front of him. He sets up his blocks and bursts through openings into the second level. He rarely takes unnecessary risks and will work to gain what yards he can if he has no other options. He has enough speed to bounce it outside when necessary and turn the corner. He flashes sufficient elusiveness but is smooth in and out of his cuts. He made some guys miss in the hole but did not shake many guys in the open field. He has a good jump cut that he uses to get himself into space. He has above average playmaking ability and is capable of busting 10+ yard runs with some regularity, but doesn't have that extra gear to pull away in the open field.

Pass Game
In the pass game, he has limited experience as a receiver. In the reps he had, he showed sufficient hands with the ability to turn upfield and get yards post-catch. He has the physical ability to be sufficient in pass protection, but he needs further development in his technique. He is a face-up blocker that showed decent blitz awareness. There were some occasions where he saw the blitz too late and missed his assignment.

Last Word
Holyfield projects as a change-of-pace back with 2-down ability at the next level and limited impact on 3rd downs early on. He has the speed and toughness to offer good special teams value on most units.

– Alex O'Brien

Strengths	Weaknesses
• Vision	• Catching skills
• Contact balance	• Pass protection
• Power runner	• Elusiveness

Critical Factors

Instincts / Vision	Contact Balance	Passing Game Impact
7	6	5

Positional Factors

Play Speed	Elusiveness	Power
6	5	6
Playmaker	**Catching Skill**	**Pass Protection**
5	4	5
Ball Security	**Ruggedness / Toughness**	**Special Teams Value**
6	6	6

Basic

	Rushing				Receiving				
Year	Att	Yds	Y/A	TD	Targets	Rec	Yds	Y/Trgt	TD
2016	6	29	4.8	0	1	1	19	19.0	0
2017	50	293	5.9	2	1	1	4	4.0	0
2018	159	1018	6.4	7	7	5	40	5.7	0
	215	1340	6.2	9	9	7	63	7.0	0

Advanced

	Yards Per Carry				Per 100 Touches		EPA		
Year	Inside	Off-Tackle	Outside	After Contact	Fumbles	Broken Tackles	Rush	Rec	Total
2016	0.0	2.0	6.8	3.7	0.0	43	1.4	1.9	3.3
2017	5.8	6.5	1.0	3.9	2.0	33	9.7	-0.5	9.3
2018	6.9	4.3	7.4	4.3	0.6	23	20.6	-0.3	20.3
	6.6	4.8	6.8	4.2	0.9	26	31.8	1.0	32.9

Deep Dive

	Receiving / Blocking			Positive Play %			Usage	
Year	Routes Run	Yards Per Route Run	Blown Block %	Overall	Zone Blocking	Gap Blocking	Split Out %	Heavy Box %
2018	36	1.1	0.4%	50.3%	51.0%	25.0%	0.7%	10.7%

Ryquell Armstead

Temple Owls

Final Grade: 6.2 RB Rank: 18 of 24

Height	Weight	Year	Jersey #	Hometown
5112	223	4SR	7	Millville, NJ

One-Liner

Armstead is a powerful, downhill runner who possesses the vision and contact balance needed at the next level, but his overall lacking in the passing game could hold him back from being a starter.

Overall

Armstead is a running back in Temple's zone running offense. He played in 49 games during his four years with the Owls. He is a good athlete that competes with toughness and runs with toughness.

Run Game

In the run game, he brings power in between the tackles. He has good speed and can make the edge on occasion, but he's primarily as a one-cut, downhill runner who runs between the tackles. His vision and instincts allow him to find the smallest of holes to get through the line. He shows burst through the hole and gets into another gear going through the second and third levels. Sometimes his feet don't always keep up with the rest of his body, but he generally shows good footwork in the backfield. He brings some elusiveness, but his hips seem a little stiff when trying to get lateral. He likes to use a spin move on defenders when in space and will usually back his way upfield for extra yardage. He's able to keep his legs driving through tackles and almost always falls forward. In terms of ball security, he's fumbled some throughout his college career and looks to hold the ball a little loose.

Pass Game

In the passing game, he lacks overall impact, but shows solid traits. He struggles at the POA in pass protection. He gets good initial contact, but his strength at the POA is almost always unable to sustain the block. As a receiver, he wasn't utilized much in the passing game. He ran quite a few routes out of the backfield, but was only targeted a small percentage of the time. He shows sufficient hands when he has caught passes and is able to gain some yardage after the catch.

Last Word

Armstead projects as a change-of-pace back in a one-cut, zone scheme at the next level, mainly on 1st and 2nd down. His traits suggest that he can be successful on some special team's units.

– Nathan Cooper

Strengths	Weaknesses
• Instincts/Vision • Runs with power • Contact balance	• Not a threat in passing game • Pass protection • Holds ball a little loose

Critical Factors

Instincts / Vision	Contact Balance	Passing Game Impact
7	6	5

Positional Factors

Play Speed	Elusiveness	Power
6	5	6
Playmaker	**Catching Skill**	**Pass Protection**
5	5	4
Ball Security	**Ruggedness / Toughness**	**Special Teams Value**
5	6	6

Basic

	Rushing				Receiving				
Year	Att	Yds	Y/A	TD	Targets	Rec	Yds	Y/Trgt	TD
2016	155	914	5.9	14	7	5	41	5.9	0
2017	157	620	3.9	5	20	14	75	3.8	0
2018	211	1098	5.2	13	14	8	52	3.7	0
	523	2632	5.0	32	41	27	168	4.1	0

Advanced

	Yards Per Carry				Per 100 Touches		EPA		
Year	Inside	Off-Tackle	Outside	After Contact	Fumbles	Broken Tackles	Rush	Rec	Total
2016	6.5	5.5	6.1	3.4	0.0	19	20.0	-1.1	18.9
2017	3.6	4.7	3.3	2.2	1.8	17	-25.9	-2.8	-28.7
2018	5.8	5.2	3.9	3.1	0.5	16	6.5	-4.9	1.6
	5.3	5.2	4.3	2.9	0.7	17	0.6	-8.7	-8.2

Deep Dive

	Receiving / Blocking			Positive Play %			Usage	
Year	Routes Run	Yards Per Route Run	Blown Block %	Overall	Zone Blocking	Gap Blocking	Split Out %	Heavy Box %
2018	109	0.5	0.0%	44.5%	46.4%	34.4%	5.5%	3.8%

Darrin Hall

Pittsburgh Panthers
Final Grade: 6.2 RB Rank: 19 of 24

Height	Weight	Year	Jersey #	Hometown
5115	217	4SR	22	Youngstown, OH

One-Liner
Hall is a strong back with good vision and acceleration in the running game, but lacks much passing-game impact to be a 3-down back early on at the next level.

Overall
Hall played running back in Pitt's pro style offense with a zone blocking scheme. He was a 4-year player who played in 48 games and started in 8 of them. He was part of a RB rotation during his four years at Pitt. He's a solid athlete who plays with toughness.

Run Game
In the run game, he shows his ability as a one-cut runner. He is a big, strong back who has a great burst of acceleration and hits the hole downhill with speed and power. He has good footwork and can work his way into tight holes and make something out of nothing. He's a decisive runner and doesn't spend time dancing in the backfield. When he sees the hole, he plants his foot and he hits it with force. When he sees the hole is not there, he puts his head down and gets what he can. He is a tough runner who muscles his way through contact and drives would be tacklers backwards. He has excellent vision and trust in his offensive line. He seems to know where the hole is going to open before it actually happens. He has great acceleration and short-distance speed to get around defenders on the edge. His long-distance speed leaves a little to be desired, but he will rarely get tracked down from behind.

Pass Game
In the passing game, he was rarely used. When he is called upon, he shows sufficient hands but doesn't seem natural as a pass catcher. He does an adequate job in pass protection but is not asked to be a key contributor in the passing game. He has the ability to be a sufficient receiver out of the backfield.

Last Word
Hall projects to be a solid change-of-pace back, especially on 1st and 2nd down. On 3rd down, he won't see much action early on, but could if he develops his hands and improves his pass protection. As a tough runner with some solid speed, he could contribute on some special teams units.

– Austin Cochran

Strengths	Weaknesses
• Burst/acceleration through hole • Good footwork • Decisive runner	• Unnatural hands • Overall passing-game impact

Critical Factors

Instincts / Vision	Contact Balance	Passing Game Impact
6	7	5

Positional Factors

Play Speed	Elusiveness	Power
6	6	6
Playmaker	**Catching Skill**	**Pass Protection**
6	4	5
Ball Security	**Ruggedness / Toughness**	**Special Teams Value**
6	6	6

Basic

	Rushing				Receiving				
Year	Att	Yds	Y/A	TD	Targets	Rec	Yds	Y/Trgt	TD
2016	36	160	4.4	0	5	2	14	2.8	0
2017	128	629	4.9	9	20	16	157	7.9	1
2018	153	1144	7.5	10	20	15	66	3.3	0
	317	1933	6.1	19	45	33	237	5.3	1

Advanced

	Yards Per Carry				Per 100 Touches		EPA		
Year	Inside	Off-Tackle	Outside	After Contact	Fumbles	Broken Tackles	Rush	Rec	Total
2016	4.1	5.6	2.8	2.3	0.0	11	0.4	0.0	0.4
2017	3.6	5.9	3.0	2.3	0.7	19	-7.6	7.1	-0.5
2018	7.2	5.6	12.8	4.0	0.6	21	26.4	-7.2	19.2
	5.3	5.7	8.6	3.1	0.6	19	19.2	-0.2	19.1

Deep Dive

	Receiving / Blocking			Positive Play %			Usage	
Year	Routes Run	Yards Per Route Run	Blown Block %	Overall	Zone Blocking	Gap Blocking	Split Out %	Heavy Box %
2018	67	1.0	2.1%	51.0%	45.7%	59.0%	0.8%	15.7%

Nick Brossette

LSU Tigers

Final Grade: 6.2 RB Rank: 20 of 24

Height	Weight	Year	Jersey #	Hometown
5111	217	4SR	4	Baton Rouge, LA

One-Liner

Brossette brings a tough, balanced skillset to a backfield, but without a difference-making trait or ability as a receiving mismatch, he may be relegated to a backup role and special teams contributor in the NFL.

Overall

Brossette was a running back in LSU's run-heavy, pro-style offense. He played in 47 total games with 12 career starts, first becoming the Tigers' primary back his senior year. He has very good size with a thick, athletic frame.

Run Game

Brossette runs behind his pads with good speed and power, and decent elusiveness. He can avoid defenders with his jump cuts behind the line of scrimmage and in tight spaces, but is best as a downhill runner with leverage to fall forward for tough yards. He has good vision and patience through holes, allowing his blocks to set up. LSU runs a good amount of power, and while he can move laterally and hit holes in zone, his running style is best suited in man schemes. He runs with very good ball security and keeps the ball high and tight on his chest running through contact. He runs with good balance and body lean at the point of attack. He's a tough, hard runner who is not easily brought down against one defender.

Pass Game

In the pass game, Brossette is very good in pass protection. He's a good cut blocker and can pick up blitzes, as well as anchor against stronger rushers. He has solid hands to catch screens out the backfield, but isn't a good route runner and isn't much of a mismatch against most linebackers. Brossette has some playmaking ability for a running back, but his talent and skillset profile better as a consistent runner who churns out tough yards.

Last Word

He is a solid overall back who doesn't have many game-breaking traits but works hard and brings a toughness to a backfield and multiple special teams units. Brossette's skillset profiles more as a back who will carry the load, but his lack of top traits suggests he is best suited as a backup at the next level.

– Brian Hammond

Strengths	**Weaknesses**
• Power and toughness	• Route running
• Pass protection	• Shiftiness
• Reliability and consistency	• Playmaking

Critical Factors

Instincts / Vision	Contact Balance	Passing Game Impact
6	6	5

Positional Factors

Play Speed	Elusiveness	Power
6	5	6
Playmaker	**Catching Skill**	**Pass Protection**
5	5	7
Ball Security	**Ruggedness / Toughness**	**Special Teams Value**
7	6	6

Basic

	Rushing				Receiving				
Year	Att	Yds	Y/A	TD	Targets	Rec	Yds	Y/Trgt	TD
2016	15	145	9.7	0	0	0	0	-	0
2017	19	96	5.1	0	1	0	0	0.0	0
2018	240	1039	4.3	14	19	14	78	4.1	0
	274	1280	4.7	14	20	14	78	3.9	0

Advanced

	Yards Per Carry				Per 100 Touches		EPA		
Year	Inside	Off-Tackle	Outside	After Contact	Fumbles	Broken Tackles	Rush	Rec	Total
2016	4.4	15.7	-	7.2	0.0	27	5.0	0.0	5.0
2017	3.4	6.3	2.0	2.8	5.3	26	-4.1	-0.7	-4.8
2018	5.1	3.6	3.9	2.6	0.4	15	-8.0	-6.2	-14.2
	5.0	4.7	3.8	2.9	0.7	16	-7.1	6.9	-14.0

Deep Dive

	Receiving / Blocking			Positive Play %			Usage	
Year	Routes Run	Yards Per Route Run	Blown Block %	Overall	Zone Blocking	Gap Blocking	Split Out %	Heavy Box %
2018	64	1.2	0.6%	40.6%	42.5%	35.4%	0.3%	21.8%

Alexander Mattison

Boise State Broncos

Final Grade: 6.2 RB Rank: 21 of 24

Height	Weight	Year	Jersey #	Hometown
5111	219	3JR	22	San Bernadino, CA

One-Liner
Mattison is a tough back with a solid overall skillset, who doesn't excel in any one area but has a volume of carries in his history and can be utilized in multiple schemes.

Overall
Mattison's primary position is running back, having spent two of his three collegiate seasons as the featured back at Boise State. He has great size and strength and is a very good athlete, showing quick feet and smooth movements, as well as displaying very good balance and flexibility. He shows good competitive toughness, as he wants the ball in key situations and has shouldered a high volume of carries for the Broncos.

Run Game
In the run game, Mattison has the ability to read developing blocks and alter his course accordingly. Mattison runs with a wide base, which allows him to balance well and run with power. He has experience as a one-cut and a downhill runner, and has a blend of the necessary skills to succeed in multiple schemes. He has good elusiveness and power, both stemming from his athleticism and contact balance.

Pass Game
In the pass game, Mattison was underutilized as a receiver, but is capable of making plays for the offense. He is adequate in pass protection, showing the ability to identify his responsibility, engage the defender, and sustain the block, but he could face difficulties at the next level handling high end speed rushers or overpowering physical interior defenders. Mattison has good hands and shows the ability to catch balls at a high level, making routine catches as well as catching poorly thrown balls. He can pluck away from his body and has the ability to make plays after the catch. His route tree is limited, mostly consisting of options and out-breaking routes.

Last Word
At the NFL level, Mattison projects to be a three-down backup whose talents best translate to early downs but can be a sufficient third-down substitute, as well. He isn't dynamic in space, but he grinds out tough yards and brings a workhorse mentality when allowed to get in a rhythm.

– Aaron Gray

Strengths

- Size and strength
- Tough yard creation

Weaknesses

- Speed and burst
- Short area quickness
- Top traits

Critical Factors

Instincts / Vision	Contact Balance	Passing Game Impact
6	6	5

Positional Factors

Play Speed	Elusiveness	Power
5	5	6
Playmaker	**Catching Skill**	**Pass Protection**
6	6	5
Ball Security	**Ruggedness / Toughness**	**Special Teams Value**
6	7	5

Basic

	Rushing				Receiving				
Year	Att	Yds	Y/A	TD	Targets	Rec	Yds	Y/Trgt	TD
2016	67	329	4.9	4	6	5	54	9.0	0
2017	212	1086	5.1	12	35	28	284	7.7	1
2018	302	1413	4.7	17	34	27	173	5.1	0
	581	2828	4.9	33	75	60	511	6.6	1

Advanced

	Yards Per Carry				Per 100 Touches		EPA		
Year	Inside	Off-Tackle	Outside	After Contact	Fumbles	Broken Tackles	Rush	Rec	Total
2016	3.8	5.8	7.1	2.8	0.0	22	4.4	1.1	5.5
2017	5.9	3.3	7.3	3.1	0.8	22	-3.7	2.6	-1.1
2018	5.1	4.4	3.7	2.6	0.0	19	-1.2	-8.3	-9.5
	5.3	4.2	5.6	2.8	0.3	21	-0.5	-4.6	-5.1

Deep Dive

	Receiving / Blocking			Positive Play %			Usage	
Year	Routes Run	Yards Per Route Run	Blown Block %	Overall	Zone Blocking	Gap Blocking	Split Out %	Heavy Box %
2018	179	1.0	0.2%	47.4%	45.7%	51.1%	4.8%	22.8%

Karan Higdon

Michigan Wolverines
Final Grade: 6.2 RB Rank: 22 of 24

Height	Weight	Year	Jersey #	Hometown
5090	203	4SR	22	Sarasota, FL

One-Liner
Higdon is a quick, decisive, one-cut runner who works hard in pass protection, but he lacks upside and goes down on first contact too often to be be an ideal starter at the next level.

Overall
Higdon was a running back in Michigan's pro-style offense. He played in 39 career games with 19 starts. He has a slightly below-average height, but a decent frame for the position. He plays with sufficient toughness on the field but has often taken more time than expected to return from injuries.

Run Game
Higdon is a one-cut runner who can find and hit holes and creases confidently and efficiently. He is instinctive in the open field, and has quick feet, but lacks top-end speed and elusiveness. He has displayed ability to run well in both zone and gap schemes. Due to his size he isn't a consistent tackle breaker and too often goes to ground at first contact. Higdon has flashes of power and yards after contact ability, but he will need improved overall strength to win in this area at the next level.

Pass Game
Higdon has sufficient quickness in the open field, and while not often utilized as a route runner, can make a solid impact on third downs going forward. This area is heightened by his willingness and effort as a pass protector, where, while limited by his size, he shows very good awareness and technique. He stuns rushers with a strong pop and is good at helping with chip assignments.

Last Word
Higdon has special teams experience as a punt protector and should be a good contributor on multiple fourth down units. Higdon projects as a three-down backup by his second year based on his production and experience at a top program, as well as his ability to produce on all downs. He will need more consistency, strength, and toughness moving forward to reach a higher ceiling, but he possesses a natural skill set that should translate well.

– Jake Schwanitz

Strengths	Weaknesses
• Decisiveness	• Yards after contact
• Pass protection	• Toughness and durability
	• Receiving experience

Critical Factors

Instincts / Vision	Contact Balance	Passing Game Impact
6	5	6

Positional Factors

Play Speed	Elusiveness	Power
6	5	5
Playmaker	**Catching Skill**	**Pass Protection**
5	5	7
Ball Security	**Ruggedness / Toughness**	**Special Teams Value**
6	5	6

Basic

	Rushing				Receiving				
Year	Att	Yds	Y/A	TD	Targets	Rec	Yds	Y/Trgt	TD
2016	72	425	5.9	6	1	0	0	0.0	0
2017	164	994	6.1	11	14	8	131	9.4	0
2018	223	1173	5.3	10	10	7	43	4.3	0
	459	2592	5.6	27	25	15	174	7.0	0

Advanced

	Yards Per Carry				Per 100 Touches		EPA		
Year	Inside	Off-Tackle	Outside	After Contact	Fumbles	Broken Tackles	Rush	Rec	Total
2016	5.3	9.4	3.2	2.7	0.0	18	7.2	-6.0	1.2
2017	6.2	6.5	4.9	3.2	1.2	23	13.6	1.9	15.5
2018	4.3	6.6	5.5	2.9	0.4	18	-4.1	-3.5	-7.6
	5.1	6.9	4.9	3.0	0.6	20	16.7	-7.6	9.1

Deep Dive

	Receiving / Blocking			Positive Play %			Usage	
Year	Routes Run	Yards Per Route Run	Blown Block %	Overall	Zone Blocking	Gap Blocking	Split Out %	Heavy Box %
2018	99	0.4	0.3%	38.1%	37.9%	38.4%	4.7%	13.5%

Mike Weber

Ohio State Buckeyes

Final Grade: 6.2 RB Rank: 23 of 24

Height	Weight	Year	Jersey #	Hometown
5085	215	4JR	25	Detroit, MI

One-Liner

Weber is instinctive and has a solid blend of quickness and strength, but his lack of a definitive trait could make it difficult to separate himself at the next level.

Overall

Weber was a rotational running back in Ohio State's offense. He lined up in the backfield, in the slot and out wide. He played in 38 career games, moving from a starting role his freshman season to a backup/change-of-pace back the following years. Weber is a good athlete with a solid combination of speed and contact balance. He has good start-and-stop ability, lateral quickness, and straight-line speed. Weber competes in all 3 phases of the RB position and has taken his reduced role after having early success.

Run Game

In the run game, Weber is a patient runner. He waits for the hole to develop in front of him and attacks it. He shows good instincts to push the hole to force defenders to show their gaps and takes advantage with the created running room. He is elusive in tight quarters and does a nice job of manufacturing yardage. He bounces off contact well for his size and keeps his feet moving to the whistle, although his pure strength and power aren't top traits. He gives good effort as a lead blocker and away from the ball.

Pass Game

In the passing game, Weber has sufficient hands. He receives checkdowns and screens without issue and has decent route-running ability downfield. He ran a wide variety of routes out of the backfield and from different alignments. Weber is a good pass blocker, using his awareness and instincts to read and mirror blitzes and punch with good, strong technique.

Last Word

Weber is a well-rounded back, but doesn't possess a special trait, which may limit his ability to see the field much in the league. He is versatile and experienced as a starter and backup, and offers a complete, albeit unspectacular skillset to a backfield.

– Dan Davis

Strengths	Weaknesses
• Instincts	• Special traits
• Pass protection	• Receiving skills
• Short-area wiggle	• Power

Critical Factors

Instincts / Vision	Contact Balance	Passing Game Impact
6	6	5

Positional Factors

Play Speed	Elusiveness	Power
6	6	5
Playmaker	**Catching Skill**	**Pass Protection**
6	5	6
Ball Security	**Ruggedness / Toughness**	**Special Teams Value**
6	6	5

Basic

	Rushing				Receiving				
Year	Att	Yds	Y/A	TD	Targets	Rec	Yds	Y/Trgt	TD
2016	182	1096	6.0	9	32	23	91	2.8	0
2017	101	626	6.2	10	12	10	94	7.8	0
2018	172	954	5.5	5	29	21	112	3.9	1
	455	2676	5.9	24	73	54	297	4.1	1

Advanced

	Yards Per Carry				Per 100 Touches		EPA		
Year	Inside	Off-Tackle	Outside	After Contact	Fumbles	Broken Tackles	Rush	Rec	Total
2016	5.9	6.0	6.6	3.0	2.0	20	13.7	-14.4	-0.7
2017	7.1	4.7	4.6	2.8	1.8	15	20.0	2.6	22.6
2018	5.9	5.8	4.2	3.0	2.1	23	9.2	-2.0	7.2
	6.2	5.6	5.1	3.0	2.0	20	42.9	-13.8	29.1

Deep Dive

	Receiving / Blocking			Positive Play %			Usage	
Year	Routes Run	Yards Per Route Run	Blown Block %	Overall	Zone Blocking	Gap Blocking	Split Out %	Heavy Box %
2018	148	0.8	0.0%	48.3%	48.1%	48.8%	11.4%	5.2%

Qadree Ollison

Pittsburgh Panthers
Final Grade: 6.2 RB Rank: 24 of 24

Height	Weight	Year	Jersey #	Hometown
6012	225	5SR	30	Niagara Falls, NY

One-Liner
Ollison has the vision, patience and contact balance to be a solid back at the next level, but his lack of passing game impact will most likely limit him to a 1st and 2nd down player early on.

Overall
Ollison is a big, powerful RB who mostly plays on 1st and 2nd downs. He played in 52 games for Pitt, starting in 35 of them. Ollison is a solid athlete, and a tough, physical back who hits the hole hard.

Run Game
Ollison has good instincts as a ball carrier. He identifies holes well and has the ability to run between the tackles or get outside the numbers. He really excels in short-yardage situations and embraces contact. He shows a tremendous ability to break tackles and gain yards after contact. He has very good balance after contact and has the play strength to run through multiple defenders. He has sufficient play speed and elusiveness. Ollison is faster than a traditional power back but does not possess game-changing speed. He shows some shiftiness in the way he avoids defenders. He can run through tackles or make defenders miss at the second level. He has good ball security and rarely puts the ball on the ground.

Pass Game
When Ollison is in during passing situations he is sufficient as a pass protector, and he shows solid strength at the POA. He shows the same kind of ruggedness running the ball as he does blocking. He is not afraid to get in front of a blitzing linebacker. He is not a playmaker in the pass game and is limited as a pass catcher. Ollison shows very limited ability running routes and doesn't show the ball skills or hands to be a consistent pass catcher.

Last Word
Ollison's powerful running style projects as a change-of-pace back at the next level, playing mostly on 1st and 2nd down with some 3rd down contributions. His toughness as a runner, decent play speed, and durability suggest that he may be able to play some special teams, and he will probably need to contribute here early in his career.

– Ian Riley

Strengths

- Patience
- Contact balance
- Tough runner

Weaknesses

- Passing game impact
- Elusiveness

Critical Factors

Instincts / Vision	Contact Balance	Passing Game Impact
6	6	5

Positional Factors

Play Speed	Elusiveness	Power
5	5	6
Playmaker	**Catching Skill**	**Pass Protection**
6	5	5
Ball Security	**Ruggedness / Toughness**	**Special Teams Value**
6	6	5

Basic

	Rushing				Receiving				
Year	Att	Yds	Y/A	TD	Targets	Rec	Yds	Y/Trgt	TD
2016	23	89	3.9	2	5	2	38	7.6	0
2017	90	398	4.4	5	27	23	194	7.2	2
2018	194	1213	6.3	11	16	11	66	4.1	0
	307	1700	5.5	18	48	36	298	6.2	2

Advanced

	Yards Per Carry				Per 100 Touches		EPA		
Year	Inside	Off-Tackle	Outside	After Contact	Fumbles	Broken Tackles	Rush	Rec	Total
2016	3.9	1.8	5.3	1.5	0.0	4	-1.5	-0.4	-1.9
2017	4.3	4.8	3.4	2.7	0.0	21	4.9	6.1	11.1
2018	7.8	5.9	6.4	3.7	0.0	18	24.5	-4.1	20.4
	5.7	5.5	5.5	3.2	0.0	18	28.0	1.6	29.6

Deep Dive

	Receiving / Blocking			Positive Play %			Usage	
Year	Routes Run	Yards Per Route Run	Blown Block %	Overall	Zone Blocking	Gap Blocking	Split Out %	Heavy Box %
2018	80	0.8	0.0%	40.7%	38.2%	43.5%	4.6%	19.1%

Glossary

After Contact
The amount of additional yards the ball carrier achieves after first contact is made by a defender

Blown Block %
Blown Block Rate, the percentage of blocking snaps that the player had a blown block

Broken Tackles
Times where a defender was in position to make a tackle but failed to bring down the ballcarrier. Counts both broken tackles (physical) and missed tackles (elusive)

Gap Blocking (Positive Play % split)
Plays on which there was a pulling lineman

Heavy Box %
Percentage of a running back's carries that came against a heavy box (eight or more defenders at or near the line of scrimmage)

Inside (Yards Per Carry split)
Runs with a designed gap between the left guard and right guard

Off-Tackle (Yards Per Carry split)
Runs with a designed gap off either side of an offensive tackle

Outside (Yards Per Carry split)
Runs with a designed gap outside of the tight end, or, if there is no tight end in the formation, outside of where one would be lined up

Positive Play %
Percentage of carries by the running back with a positive Expected Points Added

Split Out %
Percentage of plays on which the running back did not line up in the backfield

Y/A
Yards per rush attempt

Y/Trgt
Receiving yards per pass attempt in which the receiver is targeted, including incompletions

Zone Blocking (Positive Play % split)
Plays on which there was not a pulling lineman

Running Back Leaderboards

Yards Per Attempt Leaders

Rank	Player	Team	Y/A
1	Darrell Henderson	Memphis	8.9
2	Darrin Hall	Pittsburgh	7.5
3	Devine Ozigbo	Nebraska	7.0
4	Trayveon Williams	Texas A&M	6.5
5	Elijah Holyfield	Georgia	6.4
6	Qadree Ollison	Pittsburgh	6.3
7	Justice Hill	Oklahoma State	5.9
8	Damien Harris	Alabama	5.8
9	Miles Sanders	Penn State	5.8
10	D.J. Knox	Purdue	5.6

Yards Per Route Run Leaders

Rank	Player	Team	Y/RR
1	Darrell Henderson	Memphis	2.8
2	Josh Jacobs	Alabama	2.4
3	Damien Harris	Alabama	2.0
4	James Williams	Washington State	1.8
5	Benny Snell Jr.	Kentucky	1.6
6	Devine Ozigbo	Nebraska	1.4
7	David Montgomery	Iowa State	1.4
8	Trayveon Williams	Texas A&M	1.2
9	Nick Brossette	LSU	1.2
10	Elijah Holyfield	Georgia	1.1

Yards Per Carry After Contact Leaders

Rank	Player	Team	YAC/A
1	Darrell Henderson	Memphis	6.0
2	Elijah Holyfield	Georgia	4.3
3	Devine Ozigbo	Nebraska	4.1
4	Darrin Hall	Pittsburgh	4.0
5	Trayveon Williams	Texas A&M	3.8
6	Qadree Ollison	Pittsburgh	3.7
7	Josh Jacobs	Alabama	3.6
8	Devin Singletary	Florida Atlantic	3.6
9	Miles Sanders	Penn State	3.5
10	D.J. Knox	Purdue	3.4

Positive Play Percentage Leaders

Rank	Player	Team	Positive%
1	Josh Jacobs	Alabama	59.2%
2	Rodney Anderson	Oklahoma	54.5%
3	Devine Ozigbo	Nebraska	51.6%
4	Darrin Hall	Pittsburgh	51.0%
5	Elijah Holyfield	Georgia	50.3%
6	James Williams	Washington State	50.0%
7	Darrell Henderson	Memphis	48.6%
8	Mike Weber	Ohio State	48.3%
9	Alexander Mattison	Boise State	47.4%
10	Damien Harris	Alabama	47.3%

Broken Tackles Per 100 Touches Leaders

Rank	Player	Team	BT/100
1	Devin Singletary	Florida Atlantic	41
2	Josh Jacobs	Alabama	38
3	James Williams	Washington State	36
4	David Montgomery	Iowa State	33
5	Bryce Love	Stanford	28
6	Devine Ozigbo	Nebraska	28
7	Justice Hill	Oklahoma State	27
8	Darrell Henderson	Memphis	24
9	Mike Weber	Ohio State	23
10	Trayveon Williams	Texas A&M	23

Total Expected Points Added Leaders

Rank	Player	Team	EPA
1	Darrell Henderson	Memphis	71.6
2	Josh Jacobs	Alabama	41.9
3	Trayveon Williams	Texas A&M	33.2
4	James Williams	Washington State	23.4
5	Devine Ozigbo	Nebraska	20.8
6	Qadree Ollison	Pittsburgh	20.4
7	Elijah Holyfield	Georgia	20.3
8	Darrin Hall	Pittsburgh	19.2
9	Damien Harris	Alabama	14.4
10	Mike Weber	Ohio State	7.2

WIDE RECEIVER

Wide Receiver Grading Scale

GRADE	DESCRIPTION
9.0 – 7.0	High-end 3 down starter. Pro Bowl level.
6.9 – 6.7	Strong starter who plays on all 3 downs.
6.4	3rd receiver. Role player.
6.1 – 6.0	Developmental. Top traits but needs time.
5.9	4th receiver (with special teams ability).
5.8	5th receiver (with special teams ability).
5.6	4th receiver (no special teams ability).
5.5	5th receiver (no special teams ability).

Wide Receiver Rankings

Rank	Name	Grade	Page
1	N'Keal Harry	6.8	116
2	D.K. Metcalf	6.8	118
3	A.J. Brown	6.8	120
4	Deebo Samuel	6.7	122
5	Marquise Brown	6.7	124
6	Hakeem Butler	6.7	126
7	Parris Campbell	6.7	128
8	David Sills V	6.7	130
9	Kelvin Harmon	6.7	132
10	Emanuel Hall	6.7	134
11	KeeSean Johnson	6.4	136
12	Alex Wesley	6.4	138
13	Hunter Renfrow	6.4	140
14	Miles Boykin	6.4	142
15	Antoine Wesley	6.4	144
16	Lil'Jordan Humphrey	6.4	146
17	Andy Isabella	6.4	148
18	Terry Godwin	6.4	150
19	Riley Ridley	6.4	152
20	Anthony Johnson	6.4	154
21	JJ Arcega-Whiteside	6.4	156
22	Diontae Johnson	6.4	158
23	Emmanuel Butler	6.4	160
24	Stanley Morgan Jr.	6.4	162
25	Jalen Hurd	6.1	164
26	Tony Pollard	5.9	166
27	Jakobi Meyers	5.9	168
28	Greg Dortch	5.9	170
29	Nyqwan Murray	5.9	172
30	Gary Jennings	5.9	174
31	Papi White	5.9	176
32	Felton Davis III	5.9	178
33	Preston Williams	5.9	180
34	John Ursua	5.9	182
35	DaMarkus Lodge	5.9	184

N'Keal Harry

Arizona State Sun Devils
Final Grade: 6.8 WR Rank: 1 of 35

Height	Weight	Year	Jersey #	Hometown
6032	213	3JR	1	Chandler, AZ

One-Liner
Harry is a big receiver who possesses good hands, playmaking ability, and shows physicality as a blocker, but struggles to create consistent separation.

Overall
Harry is primarily a big outside WR who also has some experience playing slot receiver, tight end, and running back. He started all 37 games he played in for the Sun Devils. He is a good athlete who can move around the field smoothly and looks natural going in and out of cuts, especially for someone of his size. Harry does not have the suddenness or speed of smaller WRs, but his body control, flexibility, and change of direction are plus characteristics for a receiver of his size.

Pass Game
In the pass game, Harry is a big, reliable target and big-play threat. It is rare for him to blow a defender off the LOS with explosion, but he can fight through or evade jams at the LOS, leaving DBs who attempt to jam in bad position. Once off the LOS, Harry's biggest weapon is size. He cannot always get separation using speed or route running, but gets open with his size, long arms, and catch radius. His route running is good, as he runs smoothly with long strides and can create a little separation in man coverage. In zone coverage, he shows very good instincts and route savvy for finding the soft spot, and will regularly cut routes short to keep distance from defenders. When the ball is in the air, Harry shows very good body control and tracking. He can adjust to bad passes and take efficient angles when the ball is off target. He will almost always make routine and difficult catches, with flashes of highlight catches. One problem Harry faces is his ability to fight through contact and make contested catches, mainly from his inconsistency in fully extending his arms as the ball arrives. Harry's ability to run after the catch borders on excellent, as he looks faster and more comfortable with the ball in his hands than without. He uses his size to force broken tackles and rarely goes down on first contact; he has the ability to score every time he touches the ball.

Run Game
Harry is a very tough competitor, and it shows in his run blocking. He is a willing and violent blocker, though he will take a play off from time to time in ASU's run-heavy offense. He exhibits physicality and good strength at the POA, but his strength is not on par with his size. He consistently beats DBs but does not always dominate.

Last Word
Harry projects to be a No. 1 by his second year in the NFL. He is best suited for the outside given his size but would also present a mismatch problem on the inside against slot CBs. Furthermore, his ability with the ball in his hands should make him a solid KR and PR on special teams.

– Tony Shields

Strengths	**Weaknesses**
• Solid hands	• Inconsistent separation
• Tracking and balance with ball in the air	• Play speed
• Strong blocker	

Critical Factors

Hands	Separation	Run After Catch
7	5	7

Positional Factors

Tracking / Adjust to Ball	Route Running	Route Savvy
7	6	7
Play Speed	**Playmaker**	**Balance / Body Control**
5	6	7
Clutch Performance	**Blocking**	**Ruggedness / Toughness**
6	7	6

Basic

	Receiving								
Year	Targets	Rec	Comp%	Yards	Air Yards	YAC	TD	Yds/Trgt	Drops
2016	96	58	60.4%	659	329	330	5	6.9	5
2017	124	82	66.1%	1162	705	457	8	9.4	5
2018	117	73	62.4%	1088	567	521	9	9.3	6
	337	213	63.2%	2909	1601	1308	22	8.6	16

Advanced

	Advanced Receiving					EPA	
Year	Catchable Catch %	YAC per Reception	Target Share	Avg Target Depth	Receiver Rating	Total	Per Target
2016	84.1%	5.7	23.1%	9.6	89.7	5.3	0.06
2017	85.4%	5.6	30.3%	11.2	103.6	35.2	0.28
2018	82.0%	7.1	30.4%	10.1	114.9	34.8	0.30
	83.9%	6.1	27.9%	10.4	103.6	75.3	0.22

Deep Dive

		Route Running				Positive Play %		Lined Up
Year	On-Target Catch %	Routes Run	Yards Per Route Run	Deep Percent	Unique Routes	vs. Man	vs. Zone	Slot%
2018	85.1%	396	2.7	47.2%	7	52.9%	40.5%	27.0%

D.K. Metcalf

Ole Miss Rebels
Final Grade: 6.8 WR Rank: 2 of 35

Height	Weight	Year	Jersey #	Hometown
6026	230	3SO	14	Oxford, MS

One-Liner
Metcalf is a big, physical receiver who can get separation with his size, strength, and savvy at the top of his route, but his lack of top-end speed and durability concerns could be an issue.

Overall
Metcalf is a big-bodied X receiver who mainly played outside in Ole Miss's variant of the Air Raid. He only played in 21 games for the Rebels, starting in 19 of them, as he dealt with injuries the past two seasons.

Pass Game
He was used predominantly as a deep-threat in college and ran a limited route tree that consisted almost entirely of flies, fades, and deep curls. He has good athleticism for a big WR but lacks the suddenness or COD quickness to move into the slot. He has good balance and body control, but has not regularly exhibited the required foot speed, or the ability to sink his weight needed to crisply run breaking routes such as digs, outs, or double-moves. He is a very good competitor who shows borderline excellent toughness but has also been noticeably disinterested in instances when his team is losing by a large margin (Alabama and LSU). In the pass game, Metcalf is a big target who uses his size and strength well. He displays a quick release but relies more on beating press coverage at the line with his strength and violent hands. He has good speed and can beat slower DBs deep in man coverage if he wins at the LOS, but does not have speed to run past DBs who are giving up several yards of cushion, or playing in a bail technique. Metcalf uses his size and post-up strength to gain separation, but also uses his off-hand to wall off the DB while the ball is arriving. He shows good ability to track the ball and adjust accordingly in stride but can mistime jumps on occasion. Metcalf generally has good hands and shows the ability to make difficult and contested catches. However, he drops more easy catches than he should, and his lack of awareness near the sideline has resulted in incompletions. Metcalf is good after the catch because of his size and strength but will rarely make defenders miss tackles because of elusiveness.

Run Game
In the run game, Metcalf can be a devastating blocker, but needs to polish his technique. He has the upper-body strength, attitude, and aggression to dominate DBs, but at times will not place his hands properly, or not finish his block. Despite his technique, Metcalf appears to love hitting and does not shy away from contact.

Last Word
On 3rd downs, he fits best outside where he can use his size to post up or box out defenders. He can be an immediate asset on the interior or exterior of any core special teams unit. Metcalf projects as at least a No. 2 receiver by his second season at the next level, playing mainly on the outside.

– Tony Shields

Strengths	Weaknesses
• Physicality/size/strength	• Durability
• Competitiveness	• Route crispness
• Savvy at the top of routes	• Drops

Critical Factors

Hands	Separation	Run After Catch
6	7	6

Positional Factors

Tracking / Adjust to Ball	Route Running	Route Savvy
6	6	7
Play Speed	**Playmaker**	**Balance / Body Control**
6	7	6
Clutch Performance	**Blocking**	**Ruggedness / Toughness**
6	6	7

Basic

	Receiving								
Year	Targets	Rec	Comp%	Yards	Air Yards	YAC	TD	Yds/Trgt	Drops
2016	3	2	66.7%	13	13	0	2	4.3	0
2017	77	39	50.6%	646	429	217	7	8.4	4
2018	41	26	63.4%	569	306	263	5	13.9	3
	121	67	55.4%	1228	748	480	14	10.1	7

Advanced

	Advanced Receiving					EPA	
Year	Catchable Catch %	YAC per Reception	Target Share	Avg Target Depth	Receiver Rating	Total	Per Target
2016	100.0%	0.0	0.6%	14.3	115.3	1.9	0.64
2017	76.5%	5.6	18.2%	13.6	93.3	-0.7	-0.01
2018	78.8%	10.1	9.6%	12.8	136.4	23.4	0.57
	77.9%	7.2	9.1%	13.4	115.3	24.6	0.20

Deep Dive

		Route Running				Positive Play %		Lined Up
Year	On-Target Catch %	Routes Run	Yards Per Route Run	Deep Percent	Unique Routes	vs. Man	vs. Zone	Slot%
2018	78.8%	216	2.6	56.9%	5	50.0%	100.0%	2.1%

A.J. Brown

Ole Miss Rebels
Final Grade: 6.8 WR Rank: 3 of 35

Height	Weight	Year	Jersey #	Hometown
6010	230	3JR	1	Starkville, MS

One-Liner
Brown is a very good receiver who is able to use his size-adjusted athleticism to make plays at different parts of the field and has the ability to produce more after the catch.

Overall
Brown primarily played in the slot for Ole Miss in their variant of the Air Raid offense. He lined up out wide on rare occasions and was also be the benefactor of motions to the backfield for jet sweeps, end arounds and screens. He was a 3-year player and 2-year starter at wide receiver. He started 25 of 36 games in his career at Ole Miss. He is a very good, twitchy athlete, but can lack hustle on plays he is not directly involved in. He has great size for the position, and also possesses very good speed. He plays with toughness and competes in his play.

Pass Game
In the pass game, he runs a limited route tree. He mainly ran outs and corners from the slot position, with occasional fades and seams. When running routes down the field, he is able to create separation with his speed and quickness. At the top of his route, he can sink his hips and change directions quickly. He's a fluid route runner and plays with savvy. He knows how to stem his routes to create separation and find the open holes in zone coverage. He has good hands as a receiver, although he has a few drops and issues with double-catches at times. When in traffic, he has the strength in his hands to make contested catches. He has good body control and is able to adjust to the ball in air. After the catch, Brown is a very good playmaker and creates yards after the catch on his own. His size and athleticism make him incredibly difficult to bring down. He makes some clutch catches, but his inconsistency could affect his success late in games. He makes big plays frequently but tends to struggle against the better SEC teams.

Run Game
In the run game, Brown doesn't lack the willingness, but will let up on some opportunities. He's strong at the POA but needs to use better technique.

Last Word
Brown projects as a No. 2 receiver by his second season who can play any of the receiver positions but is best suited for his abilities in the slot. On 3rd downs, he can use his quickness and playmaking ability out of the slot to create yards and move the chains. He would be a solid contributor on special teams and has experience returning kicks.

– Dillon Josephsen

Strengths	Weaknesses
• Athleticism • Creates after the catch • Savvy route runner	• Shows lack of hustle at times • Blocking inconsistency • Concentration drops

Critical Factors

Hands	Separation	Run After Catch
6	6	7

Positional Factors

Tracking / Adjust to Ball	Route Running	Route Savvy
6	6	7
Play Speed	**Playmaker**	**Balance / Body Control**
7	7	6
Clutch Performance	**Blocking**	**Ruggedness / Toughness**
6	5	7

Basic

	Receiving								
Year	Targets	Rec	Comp%	Yards	Air Yards	YAC	TD	Yds/Trgt	Drops
2016	46	29	63.0%	407	247	160	2	8.8	3
2017	100	75	75.0%	1252	601	651	11	12.5	8
2018	120	85	70.8%	1320	729	591	6	11.0	4
	266	189	71.1%	2979	1577	1402	19	11.2	15

Advanced

	Advanced Receiving					EPA	
Year	Catchable Catch %	YAC per Reception	Target Share	Avg Target Depth	Receiver Rating	Total	Per Target
2016	85.3%	5.5	9.6%	11.9	87.9	4.9	0.11
2017	88.2%	8.7	23.6%	9.5	140.8	52.4	0.52
2018	86.7%	7.0	28.1%	10.7	113.2	37.8	0.32
	87.1%	7.4	20.0%	10.4	119.2	95.1	0.36

Deep Dive

		Route Running				Positive Play %		Lined Up
Year	On-Target Catch %	Routes Run	Yards Per Route Run	Deep Percent	Unique Routes	vs. Man	vs. Zone	Slot%
2018	89.5%	427	3.1	38.6%	7	49.2%	57.5%	56.4%

Deebo Samuel

South Carolina Gamecocks
Final Grade: 6.7 WR Rank: 4 of 35

Height	Weight	Year	Jersey #	Hometown
5114	216	5SR	1	Inman, SC

One-Liner

Samuel is an explosive receiver with the route running and after-the-catch playmaking skills to become a starting receiver in the league; however, he'll need to learn an NFL route tree and become more of a hands catcher.

Overall

Samuel lined up as the outside receiver for South Carolina, but has the skills to play in the slot. He started 27 of 30 games played for the Gamecocks, having struggled to stay healthy before 2018. He is a good athlete with agile feet.

Pass Game

Samuel is a very good route runner who uses his quick feet to set the defender up and cut at an opportune moment. When he does, he's able to create very good separation and make plays. He shows good understanding and route savvy. Samuel runs crisp, concise, and efficient routes and makes it easy for the quarterback to know where he will be. He does a very good job of contorting his body in the best position to make the catch. For being a shorter receiver, he does a great job of high pointing the ball and aggressively going up to get it in traffic while defenders are contesting. Samuel makes some highlight-reel catches, but has some lapses in concentration and will drop some easy passes. Samuel is a huge red zone target for South Carolina and consistently scored in clutch situations. When Samuel gets the ball in his hands with blockers ahead, he does a good job of finding creases to run with and gain extra yardage. He does a solid job of breaking and creating missed tackles and is able to create YAC. Samuel has very good play speed and when he gets in open field, he can break it at any moment.

Run Game

In the run game, Samuel struggles to hold blocks, as blocking is the clearest weakness in his game. At times, Samuel isn't willing and doesn't even attempt to block his defender which leads to his man tackling the ball carrier. If there is a designed play going to a different offensive player (screen, run play, etc.), he shows minimal effort and does not engage the defender.

Last Word

Samuel projects as a solid starting No. 2 receiver that can play outside or in the slot. On 3rd downs, he's best utilized in the slot to maximize his quickness and separation ability in short-areas. On special teams, he should contribute as a returner due to his speed and vision after the catch.

– Elijah Cornejo

Strengths	**Weaknesses**
• Play speed	• Route tree
• Acceleration/deceleration in routes	• Natural hands catching
• Athleticism/lower-body explosion	• Away-from-ball effort

Critical Factors

Hands	Separation	Run After Catch
5	7	7

Positional Factors

Tracking / Adjust to Ball	Route Running	Route Savvy
6	7	6
Play Speed	**Playmaker**	**Balance / Body Control**
7	6	7
Clutch Performance	**Blocking**	**Ruggedness / Toughness**
7	4	5

Basic

	Receiving								
Year	Targets	Rec	Comp%	Yards	Air Yards	YAC	TD	Yds/Trgt	Drops
2016	83	59	71.1%	783	368	415	1	9.4	2
2017	23	15	65.2%	250	108	142	3	10.9	2
2018	100	62	62.0%	882	282	600	11	8.8	5
	206	136	66.0%	1915	758	1157	15	9.3	9

Advanced

	Advanced Receiving					EPA	
Year	Catchable Catch %	YAC per Reception	Target Share	Avg Target Depth	Receiver Rating	Total	Per Target
2016	88.1%	7.0	21.0%	8.6	99.6	20	0.24
2017	83.3%	9.5	6.0%	10.5	123.2	12.6	0.55
2018	78.5%	9.7	23.0%	7.8	114.7	21.4	0.21
	82.9%	8.5	17.0%	8.4	110.0	54.1	0.26

Deep Dive

		Route Running				Positive Play %		Lined Up
Year	On-Target Catch %	Routes Run	Yards Per Route Run	Deep Percent	Unique Routes	vs. Man	vs. Zone	Slot%
2018	85.7%	358	2.5	45.5%	5	35.7%	61.3%	19.6%

Marquise Brown

Oklahoma Sooners

Final Grade: 6.7 WR Rank: 5 of 35

Height	Weight	Year	Jersey #	Hometown
5096	168	3JR	5	Hollywood, FL

One-Liner
Brown is an explosive, albeit undersized athlete and dangerous playmaker with skills that make him more than a gadget player, but needs to get tougher with better awareness in his route running at the next level.

Overall
Brown was primarily used as an outside WR in Lincoln Riley's Air Raid system, but has experience playing in the slot. He played in 27 games, starting 21 of them for the Sooners. His most common routes run were go's, curls, drags, screens, and digs. He's an excellent athlete who competes but needs to get tougher as a route runner.

Pass Game
In the passing game, he shows excellent burst when releasing off the line and breaks down cushion very quickly. He displays excellent play speed. He didn't face press often, but when he did, he flashed ability to win with excellent lateral agility and good hand usage. He does a good job mixing up the pace of his routes and demonstrates good understanding of how to stem and attack defenders' leverage. He's very smooth and sudden in and out of his breaks, and separates using excellent speed, burst, and change of direction skills. His route strength is mediocre and it's uncertain if he'll be able to consistently hold the redline at the NFL level when he fails to stack the defender. Brown does a good job of finding holes in zones, but can become stationary on scramble drills when the quarterback is rolling away from him. His catch radius is limited due to his size, but he exhibits the ability to adjust outside of his frame with good balance / body control. He has very good ability to track the deep ball and make necessary adjustments downfield. He catches the ball at a good rate, but is not a natural hands-catcher due to his small hands. He struggles to secure through contact in the short-to-intermediate areas of the field. His usefulness in the red zone diminishes due to issues with size, play strength, catch radius, and contested catch ability. Brown offers excellent speed/agility/acceleration and good elusiveness as a very good YAC player, but must win with finesse elements due to marginal contact strength.

Run Game
In the run game, he is a willing blocker, but does not have the play strength to sustain blocks at a consistent rate.

Last Word
Brown projects as a No. 2 receiver by his second season who has inside-outside flexibility, but is best-suited outside due to his ability to threaten defenses deep. He could possibly offer some special teams help as a returner with his playmaking ability and speed.

– Bryce Rossler

Strengths	Weaknesses
• Play speed	• Catch radius
• Release	• Size/play strength
• Tracking/adjusting	• Contested catches

Critical Factors

Hands	Separation	Run After Catch
5	7	7

Positional Factors

Tracking / Adjust to Ball	Route Running	Route Savvy
7	6	5
Play Speed	**Playmaker**	**Balance / Body Control**
8	7	6
Clutch Performance	**Blocking**	**Ruggedness / Toughness**
5	4	4

Basic

	Receiving								
Year	Targets	Rec	Comp%	Yards	Air Yards	YAC	TD	Yds/Trgt	Drops
2017	83	57	68.7%	1095	480	615	7	13.2	7
2018	107	75	70.1%	1318	669	649	10	12.3	8
	190	132	69.5%	2413	1149	1264	17	12.7	15

Advanced

	Advanced Receiving					EPA	
Year	Catchable Catch %	YAC per Reception	Target Share	Avg Target Depth	Receiver Rating	Total	Per Target
2017	83.8%	10.8	19.5%	13.8	134.5	35.2	0.42
2018	83.3%	8.7	27.3%	12.4	131.3	60.8	0.57
	83.5%	9.6	23.2%	13.0	133.1	96	0.51

Deep Dive

		Route Running				Positive Play %		Lined Up
Year	On-Target Catch %	Routes Run	Yards Per Route Run	Deep Percent	Unique Routes	vs. Man	vs. Zone	Slot%
2018	85.9%	364	3.6	46.2%	8	58.6%	58.9%	20.8%

Hakeem Butler

Iowa State Cyclones
Final Grade: 6.7 WR Rank: 6 of 35

Height	Weight	Year	Jersey #	Hometown
6046	225	4JR	18	Baltimore, MD

One-Liner
Butler has the physical tools, tracking and playmaking ability to be a solid starter at the next level, but he needs to sure up his hands and be more savvy in his route running to contribute consistently.

Overall
Butler was the X receiver for Iowa State's spread offense, but also played out of the slot during his career. He played in a total of 37 games for the Cyclones. He's a solid athlete that is long and has good size. He competes in his play and exhibits toughness. This was most evident in Iowa State's bowl game against WSU where he took some shots but kept on playing.

Pass Game
In the passing game, Butler makes some incredible catches, but drops a lot of easy ones. He tends to catch passes with his body rather than using his hands. Off the line, he tends to false step, most likely stemming from his wide stance. Against press, he knows how to get off the line, but will sometimes open his chest up and allow more physical DBs to jam him. He's a long strider and has some deceptive speed and wiggle in his route running. He's precise but doesn't always stem to give himself the best leverage. At times, he'll run straight into defenders instead of avoiding contact. He has shown the ability to separate with precise cuts and quickness, with his off-hand at the last second, or by boxing out defenders with the ball in the air. He possesses very good tracking ability and is able to adjust with good balance to an off-target throw. His awareness around the sideline is uncanny, making plenty of catches right on the sideline as he was falling out of bounds. Once the ball is in his hands, he is tough to bring down. He's able to make guys miss or even carry defenders to create extra yards after the catch. He makes plays in the clutch; he made a number of catches late in games and consistently moved the chains on 3rd and 4th down. When lined up as a single receiver, he was the recipient of quite a few double-teams.

Run Game
In the run game, his willingness to block can be hot and cold, but when he wants to, he goes all out. He'll miss some easy blocks on occasion, mainly due to lack of technique or want-to. When he decides to block, he comes off the line and tries to physically punish the defender. In many cases he was able to take his defender to the ground.

Last Word
Butler projects as a No. 2 receiver by his second year and has the capability of playing outside or in the slot. On 3rd down, he fits best out wide, but can slide into the slot to create a mismatch on a smaller DB or LB. He's tough and physical but shouldn't be looked at to contribute on special teams.

– Nathan Cooper

Strengths

- Tracking ability
- Creates after the catch
- Plays physical

Weaknesses

- Too many drops
- Needs more route savvy

Critical Factors

Hands	Separation	Run After Catch
5	6	7

Positional Factors

Tracking / Adjust to Ball	Route Running	Route Savvy
7	6	5
Play Speed	**Playmaker**	**Balance / Body Control**
5	7	6
Clutch Performance	**Blocking**	**Ruggedness / Toughness**
7	6	6

Basic

	Receiving								
Year	Targets	Rec	Comp%	Yards	Air Yards	YAC	TD	Yds/Trgt	Drops
2016	15	9	60.0%	134	90	44	2	8.9	0
2017	72	41	56.9%	697	453	244	7	9.7	9
2018	112	60	53.6%	1318	922	396	9	11.8	12
	199	110	55.3%	2149	1465	684	18	10.8	21

Advanced

	Advanced Receiving					EPA	
Year	Catchable Catch %	YAC per Reception	Target Share	Avg Target Depth	Receiver Rating	Total	Per Target
2016	81.8%	4.9	3.8%	10.0	128.9	8.9	0.59
2017	70.7%	6.0	15.3%	11.8	110.7	21.8	0.30
2018	75.0%	6.6	31.6%	15.9	107.7	29.5	0.26
	73.8%	6.2	16.3%	13.9	110.7	60.1	0.30

Deep Dive

		Route Running				Positive Play %		Lined Up
Year	On-Target Catch %	Routes Run	Yards Per Route Run	Deep Percent	Unique Routes	vs. Man	vs. Zone	Slot%
2018	74.2%	352	3.7	47.2%	6	50.0%	46.3%	24.6%

Parris Campbell

Ohio State Buckeyes
Final Grade: 6.7 WR Rank: 7 of 35

Height	Weight	Year	Jersey #	Hometown
6002	208	5SR	21	Akron, OH

One-Liner
Campbell has top-end speed and good catching ability, but he needs to learn an NFL route tree and improve his toughness to reach his potential on the next level.

Overall
Campbell lined up in the slot and out wide on both sides of the field in Ohio State's pro-style offense. He also returned kicks for the team in 2016 and 2017, and started in 38 of the 48 games he appeared. He is an excellent athlete who has shown the ability to burst out of his breaks and accelerate once he catches the ball. He has very good speed to create separation and pull away from pursuing defenders. He is a tough runner with the ball in his hands, but his toughness is inconsistent when engaging with defenders near the line of scrimmage.

Pass Game
In the passing game, Campbell has the ability to turn short completions into big gains and touchdowns. He has very good run-after-the-catch ability. He is good at creating separation at the top of his routes due to his short-area quickness, and his top-end speed allows him to outrun defenders. He shows route savvy and can beat man or zone coverage. He has decent zone awareness, but doesn't always stem his routes away from defenders. He consistently hauls in catchable passes. He is a patient runner with the ball in his hands who knows how to read blocks and get the most out of every touch.

Run Game
In the run game, he's an average blocker. He showed a few good blocks, but also missed key blocks near the line of scrimmage. Against Penn State, he showed he can be an effective downfield blocker against defensive backs.

Last Word
Campbell projects as a No. 2 NFL starter by year two. He will need time to learn an NFL route tree and improve his blocking ability, but he offers instant special teams value as a kick returner. He can contribute in the passing game early through screens and short, quick passes, and he shows the ability to fit in either on the outside or in the slot on 3rd downs.

– Dan Davis

Strengths	**Weaknesses**
• Speed	• Limited route tree
• Run after catch	• Blocking
• Hands	• Toughness in route running

Critical Factors

Hands	Separation	Run After Catch
6	6	7

Positional Factors

Tracking / Adjust to Ball	Route Running	Route Savvy
6	6	6
Play Speed	**Playmaker**	**Balance / Body Control**
7	7	6
Clutch Performance	**Blocking**	**Ruggedness / Toughness**
6	4	5

Basic

	Receiving								
Year	Targets	Rec	Comp%	Yards	Air Yards	YAC	TD	Yds/Trgt	Drops
2016	26	13	50.0%	121	102	19	0	4.7	2
2017	53	40	75.5%	584	61	523	3	11.0	6
2018	111	91	82.0%	1071	257	814	12	9.6	5
	190	144	75.8%	1776	420	1356	15	9.3	13

Advanced

	Advanced Receiving					EPA	
Year	Catchable Catch %	YAC per Reception	Target Share	Avg Target Depth	Receiver Rating	Total	Per Target
2016	86.7%	1.5	6.5%	12.1	63.1	-3.9	-0.15
2017	81.6%	13.1	12.5%	6.2	129.8	5.4	0.10
2018	92.9%	9.0	19.9%	4.5	139.2	53	0.48
	88.9%	9.4	13.7%	6.0	128.3	54.6	0.29

Deep Dive

		Route Running				Positive Play %		Lined Up
Year	On-Target Catch %	Routes Run	Yards Per Route Run	Deep Percent	Unique Routes	vs. Man	vs. Zone	Slot%
2018	94.8%	303	3.5	32.3%	7	38.1%	62.5%	86.5%

David Sills V

West Virginia Mountaineers
Final Grade: 6.7 WR Rank: 8 of 35

Height	Weight	Year	Jersey #	Hometown
6030	210	4SR	13	Wilmington, DE

One-Liner
Sills is a long, athletic receiver with great body control and red zone ability, who has shown to be a quick learner at the WR position and has more room for growth.

Overall
Sills was primarily an outside receiver in West Virginia's spread offense, with also some schemed snaps from the slot. He played 33 games for the Mountaineers, starting 26, after a storied prep career as a quarterback. He has a long, wiry frame with good athleticism. He shows good aggression in all phases and has worked hard in his position change to become a top wideout.

Pass Game
In the pass game, Sills is the true definition of a red zone threat at the next level. He has an innate ability to make contested catches in close spaces in the end zone, and he shows good awareness to keep his feet inbounds. He has very good balance and body control, and uses his body well to box defenders out on jump balls and in traffic over the middle of the field. Sills does not create separation from defenders with speed, but he has enough length and size to create some separation at the catch point. He is still improving his route running getting in and out of his breaks, but he shows intelligence as a route runner with the savvy to work back to the quarterback in broken play scenarios. West Virginia does a good job of scheming Sills open in their offense as he lines up in the slot regularly to try and create mismatches. He shows flashes of being able to run after the catch, but more with his natural athleticism and effort than refined cuts or elite speed. He lacks top-end speed at the receiver position, but does have decent acceleration and can gain ground with his long strides.

Run Game
In the run game, Sills is a willing blocker on the edge. He's aggressive and isn't afraid to get physical with defenders at contact.

Last Word
Sills projects as a starter by his second year in the NFL based on the progress he's made so far in his receiving career along with his natural athleticism and size. He can line up in multiple positions on the field and brings a specific, desired skillset to a receiving group

– Jordan Edwards

Strengths	**Weaknesses**
• Red zone production	• Separation with speed
• Ball tracking and contested catches	• Route sharpness
• Body control	• Receiving/ route tree experience

Critical Factors

Hands	Separation	Run After Catch
6	5	6

Positional Factors

Tracking / Adjust to Ball	Route Running	Route Savvy
7	6	6
Play Speed	**Playmaker**	**Balance / Body Control**
6	6	7
Clutch Performance	**Blocking**	**Ruggedness / Toughness**
6	6	6

Basic

	Receiving								
Year	Targets	Rec	Comp%	Yards	Air Yards	YAC	TD	Yds/Trgt	Drops
2017	104	60	57.7%	980	639	341	18	9.4	7
2018	117	65	55.6%	986	659	327	15	8.4	10
	221	125	56.6%	1966	1298	668	33	8.9	17

Advanced

	Advanced Receiving					EPA	
Year	Catchable Catch %	YAC per Reception	Target Share	Avg Target Depth	Receiver Rating	Total	Per Target
2017	74.1%	5.7	21.9%	14.0	121.0	32.1	0.31
2018	73.9%	5.0	26.6%	12.8	112.4	31.5	0.27
	74.0%	5.3	24.2%	13.4	116.4	63.6	0.29

Deep Dive

		Route Running				Positive Play %		Lined Up
Year	On-Target Catch %	Routes Run	Yards Per Route Run	Deep Percent	Unique Routes	vs. Man	vs. Zone	Slot%
2018	78.0%	419	2.4	47.3%	7	42.6%	57.4%	34.1%

Kelvin Harmon

NC State Wolfpack
Final Grade: 6.7 WR Rank: 9 of 35

Height	Weight	Year	Jersey #	Hometown
6021	214	3JR	3	Palmyra, NJ

One-Liner
Harmon is a big, physical receiver who lacks deep speed but brings strong hands, contested-catch ability, and a history of productivity.

Overall
Harmon lined up mostly as an outside receiver at NC State, where he had two straight 1,000-yard seasons in his three seasons in Raleigh. He projects to line up on the inside or outside at the next level. He has very good size for the position and is a strong, physical receiver. That said, he has just sufficient play speed and therefore lacks the ability to take the top off the defense.

Pass Game
Harmon is a sharp route runner who understands how to use stems to manipulate the defense, but due to his lack of top-end speed he struggles to separate from man coverage. He is better against zone where he can use his route savvy and body-positioning skills to make himself available to his quarterback. Against man, he maintains his effectiveness by winning contested catches and boxing out defenders. In either case, his skill set requires an accurate quarterback to be successful. Harmon has very good hands, and though he will body catch at times, he usually only does this in situations where he is shielding from defenders. He shows very good body control on sideline catches, balls outside his frame, and especially on back-shoulder fades. His skill set should lend itself to him being a strong performer after the catch, but his broken tackle and YAC production was underwhelming in the films viewed.

Run Game
Harmon's size and physicality help him to be a positive contributor in the run game, and his mental development in this area on the NFL level will be a key aspect to if he can earn time on the field as a Z receiver, who is often required to do a lot of blocking. He shows good toughness, and this area projects to be a strength of his at the next level.

Last Word
Overall, Harmon lacks the speed to be a true No. 1 wide receiver, but his size, body control, and contested-catch ability can be great assets if he lands with a team that can utilize his skills. In terms of play style, he reminds me of a less-explosive Michael Crabtree when he was coming out of Texas Tech.

– Matt Manocherian

Strengths	**Weaknesses**
• Contested catches	• Long speed
• Size/physicality	• Separation
• Productivity	• YAC production

Critical Factors

Hands	Separation	Run After Catch
7	5	6

Positional Factors

Tracking / Adjust to Ball	Route Running	Route Savvy
7	6	7
Play Speed	**Playmaker**	**Balance / Body Control**
5	7	7
Clutch Performance	**Blocking**	**Ruggedness / Toughness**
7	7	6

Basic

	Receiving								
Year	Targets	Rec	Comp%	Yards	Air Yards	YAC	TD	Yds/Trgt	Drops
2016	46	27	58.7%	462	319	143	5	10.0	1
2017	114	69	60.5%	1017	725	292	4	8.9	7
2018	119	81	68.1%	1186	935	251	7	10.0	4
	279	177	63.4%	2665	1979	686	16	9.6	12

Advanced

	Advanced Receiving					EPA	
Year	Catchable Catch %	YAC per Reception	Target Share	Avg Target Depth	Receiver Rating	Total	Per Target
2016	81.8%	5.3	10.6%	14.0	120.0	17.4	0.38
2017	83.1%	4.2	23.8%	13.7	97.7	31.6	0.28
2018	85.3%	3.1	24.6%	14.4	116.4	61.8	0.52
	83.9%	3.9	20.0%	14.1	109.4	110.8	0.40

Deep Dive

		Route Running				Positive Play %		Lined Up
Year	On-Target Catch %	Routes Run	Yards Per Route Run	Deep Percent	Unique Routes	vs. Man	vs. Zone	Slot%
2018	88.8%	393	3.0	49.4%	7	67.4%	56.3%	13.3%

Emanuel Hall

Missouri Tigers
Final Grade: 6.7 WR Rank: 10 of 35

Height	Weight	Year	Jersey #	Hometown
6022	195	4SR	84	Franklin, TN

One-Liner
Hall shows the speed to take the top off of a defense as a No. 2 receiver with good route running and savvy, but his inconsistent hands and lack of down-to-down effort could lead to struggles.

Overall
Hall played WR for Missouri who primarily played on the outside, but also lined up in the slot occasionally. He played in 45 games for the Tigers during his four years on campus. He struggled with injuries in 2018, so his production was inconsistent. When healthy, he's a very good athlete who has very good speed. He lacks consistent effort from down to down, showing a lack of interest running routes when he is not the primary receiver.

Pass Game
In the passing game, his deep-threat ability stands out on film and on the stat sheet. He is able to blow by defenders with his speed and route savvy. His ability to use his speed to close space between him and the defender and then blow by allows him to be an excellent playmaker and a lethal deep threat. His second gear allowed him to average over 20 yards per catch during his career. He mostly uses his speed and quickness to cut in and out of routes to create space, but has shown the ability to use his hands to separate from defenders. His hands are average, as he uses his body to make a lot of his catches; he has dropped quite a few passes due to a lack of concentration.

Run Game
In the run game, he shows minimal effort and willingness to block unless he knows the ball is coming his way.

Last Word
Hall projects as a potential No. 2 receiver at the next level, using his size, speed and quickness to play on the inside and outside and take the top off secondaries. His pure athleticism and skills allow him to be a threat on 3rd down to create yards after the catch and take the top off the defense. He provides little-to-no special teams ability, unless he shows that he'll be able to return kicks, which is something he didn't do in college.

– Ian Berg

Strengths	**Weaknesses**
• Deep threat/playmaking ability	• Consistent effort
• Speed and short-area quickness	• Average hands
• Route running	• Physicality

Critical Factors

Hands	Separation	Run After Catch
4	7	6

Positional Factors

Tracking / Adjust to Ball	Route Running	Route Savvy
7	6	6
Play Speed	**Playmaker**	**Balance / Body Control**
7	8	6
Clutch Performance	**Blocking**	**Ruggedness / Toughness**
6	3	3

Basic

	Receiving								
Year	Targets	Rec	Comp%	Yards	Air Yards	YAC	TD	Yds/Trgt	Drops
2016	33	19	57.6%	307	190	117	2	9.3	3
2017	60	33	55.0%	817	633	184	8	13.6	11
2018	58	37	63.8%	828	577	251	6	14.3	4
	151	89	58.9%	1952	1400	552	16	12.9	18

Advanced

	Advanced Receiving					EPA	
Year	Catchable Catch %	YAC per Reception	Target Share	Avg Target Depth	Receiver Rating	Total	Per Target
2016	79.2%	6.2	7.5%	17.9	109.0	10.4	0.32
2017	68.8%	5.6	14.4%	20.0	139.6	38.9	0.65
2018	80.4%	6.8	13.2%	19.6	141.8	46.6	0.80
	75.4%	6.2	11.6%	19.4	138.6	96	0.64

Deep Dive

		Route Running				Positive Play %		Lined Up
Year	On-Target Catch %	Routes Run	Yards Per Route Run	Deep Percent	Unique Routes	vs. Man	vs. Zone	Slot%
2018	85.0%	212	3.9	44.3%	5	59.0%	62.5%	6.9%

KeeSean Johnson

Fresno State Bulldogs
Final Grade: 6.4 WR Rank: 11 of 35

Height	Weight	Year	Jersey #	Hometown
6011	204	5SR	3	East Palo Alto, CA

One-Liner
Johnson's strong, natural hands, spatial awareness and playmaking ability should allow him to be a No. 2 starting receiver, but his inability to consistently separate may hold him back at the next level.

Overall
Johnson primarily lined up as an outside receiver for Fresno State. He has played in 52 career games for the Bulldogs, starting in 50 of them. Johnson's athleticism doesn't jump off the screen when watching him, but he is a fluid enough athlete that he can play at the next level.

Pass Game
Johnson's quick feet and flexibility make him a good route runner. He competes on every route and is always looking to pick up extra yards after the catch. He has very good hands and rarely drops passes. Johnson shows really good ability to make tough catches in weird angles on the field. He has very good body control and awareness on the field. There were multiple plays throughout the 2018 season where he made tough, contested catches with not only one foot in bounds, but two. He is also a good clean route runner who doesn't waste motion coming in and out of breaks. Johnson won't create much separation at the next level with his speed, but with his combination of length, good route running, and ability to make tough catches, it shouldn't set him back.

Run Game
In the run game, Johnson is not a great blocker on the edge, but he shows a willingness to get physical. He uses decent technique, but doesn't have the play strength to sustain.

Last Word
By his second year in the league, Johnson projects as a No. 3 receiver. On 3rd downs, Johnson would be best suited lined up outside, but he has the versatility to play in the slot as well. In 2016-2017, Johnson returned punts and kicks for Fresno State, and he could potentially add special teams value to an NFL roster.

– Jordan Edwards

Strengths

- Strong hands
- Catch in traffic
- Football intelligence/Awareness

Weaknesses

- Consistent separation
- Blocking on the edge
- Elite athleticism

Critical Factors

Hands	Separation	Run After Catch
7	5	6

Positional Factors

Tracking / Adjust to Ball	Route Running	Route Savvy
6	6	6
Play Speed	**Playmaker**	**Balance / Body Control**
6	6	6
Clutch Performance	**Blocking**	**Ruggedness / Toughness**
6	5	5

Basic

	Receiving								
Year	Targets	Rec	Comp%	Yards	Air Yards	YAC	TD	Yds/Trgt	Drops
2016	100	59	59.0%	691	407	284	4	6.9	8
2017	134	77	57.5%	1018	549	469	8	7.6	3
2018	133	95	71.4%	1342	856	486	8	10.1	6
	367	231	62.9%	3051	1812	1239	20	8.3	17

Advanced

	Advanced Receiving					EPA	
Year	Catchable Catch %	YAC per Reception	Target Share	Avg Target Depth	Receiver Rating	Total	Per Target
2016	84.3%	4.8	29.0%	10.7	80.9	4.1	0.04
2017	88.5%	6.1	31.2%	11.0	92.2	4.3	0.03
2018	88.0%	5.1	30.9%	11.1	117.4	54.3	0.41
	87.2%	5.4	30.5%	11.0	98.3	62.7	0.17

Deep Dive

		Route Running				Positive Play %		Lined Up
Year	On-Target Catch %	Routes Run	Yards Per Route Run	Deep Percent	Unique Routes	vs. Man	vs. Zone	Slot%
2018	89.4%	409	3.3	48.7%	6	53.7%	54.7%	36.9%

Alex Wesley

Northern Colorado Bears
Final Grade: 6.4 WR Rank: 12 of 35

Height	Weight	Year	Jersey #	Hometown
5117	191	5SR	81	Murphy, TX

One-Liner
Wesley has the hands-catching ability, speed, and body control to be a solid contributor at the next level, but his struggles getting into routes against physical press defenders may hold him back.

Overall
Wesley primarily played as an outside receiver for Northern Colorado while also moving down into the slot on certain occasions. He's played in 42 games with 37 starts during his college career. He's a quick-twitch athlete and his track background is easy to see in his play speed. He plays bigger than his size and shows toughness. He had three different quarterbacks throughout the season, yet his production remained consistent.

Pass Game
In the passing game, Wesley possesses very good hands-catching ability. He plucks the ball out of the air and rarely lets it get into his body. Not only can he make on-target catches, but he has the balance and tracking ability to locate the ball outside of his frame. Although, reaching to pick balls off the turf prove troublesome. He's not afraid to come across the middle, as he converted multiple 3rd and 4th downs making tough catches in traffic, and he made several catches in other clutch situations late in games. His route running is precise, and he's able to get in and out of his breaks quickly and easily with some suddenness. However, he does get re-routed at times by more physical DBs. He has a fluid get-off and release, but he struggles with the press at times. Wesley shows the ability to separate, and he can win on deep routes as well as in- and out-breaking cuts. Once he gets the ball in his hands, he runs hard and is able to gain yards after the catch. He's not an especially elusive runner, but he is able to break some tackles and gain extra yards by way of his straight-line speed.

Run Game
In the run game, he shows the willingness to make blocks, but doesn't have the strength or sustainability to be consistently effective.

Last Word
Wesley projects as a No. 3 receiver by year two, playing mainly on the outside, but has the traits to fit best sliding into the slot on 3rd downs. His speed and toughness suggest that he shouldn't have any problem playing on any special teams and he has returning ability.

– Nathan Cooper

Strengths	Weaknesses
• Hands	• Gets re-routed
• Tracking ability	• Press release vs. physical DBs
• Speed	

Critical Factors

Hands	Separation	Run After Catch
7	5	6

Positional Factors

Tracking / Adjust to Ball	Route Running	Route Savvy
6	6	6
Play Speed	**Playmaker**	**Balance / Body Control**
6	6	6
Clutch Performance	**Blocking**	**Ruggedness / Toughness**
6	5	6

Alex Wesley is trying to become the second wide receiver to be drafted from Northern Colorado. The first did pretty well: Vincent Jackson played 12 seasons for the Chargers and Buccaneers and made three Pro Bowls. Wesley is alongside Jackson as one of the top receivers in school history. In his senior season, he led the team with 57 receptions and tied for the team lead with four touchdowns.

One of Wesley's biggest calling cards is his speed. He was the three-time Big Sky outdoor champion in the 400-meter dash. He ended his track career in 2018 as an All-American. Now, a new career may be just beginning.

Hunter Renfrow

Clemson Tigers

Final Grade: 6.4 WR Rank: 13 of 35

Height	Weight	Year	Jersey #	Hometown
5103	175	6SR	13	Myrtle Beach, SC

One-Liner

Renfrow has great hands and a high football IQ with tenacious competitiveness that should make him a reliable No. 3 slot receiver, but he needs to improve his run after catch ability to be more dynamic at the next level.

Overall

Renfrow was a slot receiver in Clemson's quick passing game. He lacks the size to play on the outside with his thin frame and minimal muscle mass. He's played in 55 career games for the Tigers. He is a very good athlete but lacks size and growth in physical projection. He showcases elite competitiveness and tenacity in his play.

Pass Game

In the passing game, Renfrow's biggest assets are his hands and catching ability. He does an excellent job catching passes with his soft hands and dependable catching ability. He also knows when to body catch or catch outside his frame. He secures the ball upon delivery and maintains very good ball security throughout the entirety of the catch. He shows a quick release off the line of scrimmage with solid acceleration into his route. His cuts are fluid in and out of breaks on routes with little to no wasted movement. He shows good agility to change directions quickly. His toughness is evident but lacks strength to break tackles and create yards after the catch. He is very effective on routes on the first level, being used heavily on simple screens, drag, and quick one-cut routes. He does a good job using swim and rip moves in his release to get around press-man corners. He ran a limited route tree at Clemson, so he will have to show the ability to develop the ability of running a full route tree if he is going to be successful in the NFL.

Run Game

In the run game, he displays adequate play strength as a blocker and is much better as a blocker on the move with momentum. The willingness to block is there, but his ability to anchor and maintain balance when blocking becomes difficult due to lack of size and play strength.

Last Word

Renfrow's lack of play strength might limit him, but his mental toughness is off the charts. His play elevates when in clutch situations and is often the go to guy on 3rd downs. He projects to be a strong No. 3 option in the slot with his excellent hands, quick mental processing, and high football IQ. He may be able to play some special teams and shows that he has the ability to return some kicks.

– Noah Gatsik

Strengths	**Weaknesses**
• Hands	• Positional flexibility
• Toughness/competitiveness	• Strength
• Football IQ	• Run-after-the-catch ability

Critical Factors

Hands	Separation	Run After Catch
7	6	5

Positional Factors

Tracking / Adjust to Ball	Route Running	Route Savvy
6	5	6
Play Speed	**Playmaker**	**Balance / Body Control**
6	6	6
Clutch Performance	**Blocking**	**Ruggedness / Toughness**
7	5	6

Basic

	Receiving								
Year	Targets	Rec	Comp%	Yards	Air Yards	YAC	TD	Yds/Trgt	Drops
2016	66	44	66.7%	495	280	215	6	7.5	4
2017	82	60	73.2%	602	342	260	3	7.3	1
2018	67	49	73.1%	544	364	180	1	8.1	2
	215	153	71.2%	1641	986	655	10	7.6	7

Advanced

	Advanced Receiving					EPA	
Year	Catchable Catch %	YAC per Reception	Target Share	Avg Target Depth	Receiver Rating	Total	Per Target
2016	84.6%	4.9	10.7%	9.3	112.9	21.6	0.33
2017	90.9%	4.3	17.8%	6.9	95.7	27.8	0.34
2018	87.5%	3.7	13.5%	9.0	101.8	21.3	0.32
	87.9%	4.3	13.7%	8.3	102.9	70.7	0.33

Deep Dive

		Route Running				Positive Play %		Lined Up
Year	On-Target Catch %	Routes Run	Yards Per Route Run	Deep Percent	Unique Routes	vs. Man	vs. Zone	Slot%
2018	92.3%	290	1.9	40.0%	6	51.7%	58.3%	89.8%

Miles Boykin

Notre Dame Fighting Irish
Final Grade: 6.4 WR Rank: 14 of 35

Height	Weight	Year	Jersey #	Hometown
6025	228	4SR	81	Tinley Park, IL

One-Liner

Boykin wins with size and strength downfield, but his route-running quickness and play speed will keep him off the field in some packages.

Overall

Boykin is an outside wide receiver who played in Notre Dame's RPO-based offense. He occasionally played in the slot for mismatches. He started 14 of his 37 appearances. He is a big target with a wide catch radius and a thick, athletic cut. His ability to box out defenders at the catch point and his tenacious blocking are good examples of his toughness.

Pass Game

In the pass game, Boykin has a knack for making big catches downfield and away from his body. He is a sufficient route runner who is smooth but not quick. He needs to improve his sharp cuts, but he does a good job of coming back to the quarterback for easy throws and making himself available on broken plays. Boykin's strength and catch radius allow him to separate at the catch point. He has very strong hands, and his size and strength can be used to create mismatches against defensive backs. Once the ball is in the air, he is very good at finding and attacking it. He catches the ball away from his body and rarely drops anything. His speed is a weakness, as he doesn't separate well on deep routes, and is often caught from behind after the catch. He isn't an agile athlete with the ball in his hands but falls forward with power.

Run Game

In the run game, Boykin is an aggressive blocker that seeks out contact and punishes smaller secondary defenders. He has the strength to crack inside from the slot and seal linebackers as well.

Last Word

Boykin projects as an outside third receiver at the next level by his second year, especially with improved route running and quickness. He won't blow past anyone in the league, but he can win with size and strong hands in the red zone, and his blocking and aggression project well to a special teams role.

– Ben Hrkach

Strengths	Weaknesses
• Strong hands	• Speed
• Ball tracking and catch radius	• Route running
• Blocking aggression	• Agility after the catch

Critical Factors

Hands	Separation	Run After Catch
7	6	5

Positional Factors

Tracking / Adjust to Ball	Route Running	Route Savvy
7	5	6
Play Speed	**Playmaker**	**Balance / Body Control**
5	6	6
Clutch Performance	**Blocking**	**Ruggedness / Toughness**
6	7	6

Basic

	Receiving								
Year	Targets	Rec	Comp%	Yards	Air Yards	YAC	TD	Yds/Trgt	Drops
2016	15	6	40.0%	81	56	25	1	5.4	3
2017	24	12	50.0%	253	193	60	2	10.5	0
2018	99	59	59.6%	872	651	221	8	8.8	4
	138	77	55.8%	1206	900	306	11	8.7	7

Advanced

	Advanced Receiving					EPA	
Year	Catchable Catch %	YAC per Reception	Target Share	Avg Target Depth	Receiver Rating	Total	Per Target
2016	60.0%	4.2	3.9%	13.7	80.1	-1.8	-0.12
2017	80.0%	5.0	7.1%	19.8	98.1	9.2	0.38
2018	84.3%	3.8	24.3%	14.1	102.8	23.9	0.24
	81.1%	4.0	12.2%	15.0	99.5	31.3	0.23

Deep Dive

		Route Running				Positive Play %		Lined Up
Year	On-Target Catch %	Routes Run	Yards Per Route Run	Deep Percent	Unique Routes	vs. Man	vs. Zone	Slot%
2018	87.5%	415	2.1	53.7%	8	54.2%	54.1%	20.8%

Antoine Wesley

Texas Tech Red Raiders
Final Grade: 6.4 WR Rank: 15 of 35

Height	Weight	Year	Jersey #	Hometown
6041	200	3JR	4	Las Vegas, NV

One-Liner
Wesley is a big-bodied WR with very good hands and body control to make acrobatic catches, but needs to fill out and be more consistent to be a real threat at the next level.

Overall
Wesley primarily played the right WR in Texas Tech's Air Raid offense. He's played in 29 games for the Red Raiders with his first real starting experience coming in 2018. Wesley is a long, wiry wide receiver. He shows good athleticism and competitiveness in his play.

Pass Game
In the passing game, he has very good hands and has shown the ability to make one-handed grabs with a large catch radius. He rarely makes body catches and only does so when necessary. He shows some separation off the line, but lacks explosiveness and acceleration, and relies on his long arms to battle with press coverage. Even when separation is not there, Wesley seems to always have a chance to go up and high-point the football, using his size to box out corners. Wesley shows the ability to create some yards after the catch and can break tackles almost like a running back. Although his acceleration is average, he has good long speed, mainly due to being a long strider. He does a good job of extending his long arms to catch overthrown footballs and can track and adjust to the football in the air. His route running needs work, as he only ran a few different routes in Texas Tech's offensive scheme. In terms of route savvy, he shows good spatial awareness and find open holes in the zone. Although he has good play speed, it shows up inconsistently. He's a playmaker in the Texas Tech offense and makes plays all over the field. He shows very good body control with the ball in the air, and has made a bunch of acrobatic, sideline, and back of the end zone catches. Wesley shows up in big games and in clutch situations.

Run Game
In the run game, he is a willing blocker, but doesn't stand out in that aspect. He isn't strong enough to sustain blocks on a consistent basis.

Last Word
Wesley projects as a No. 3 outside receiver at the next level. He needs to fill out his frame and get stronger. On 3rd down, he is best suited on the outside where he can win one-on-one balls using size. He could play some gunner on special teams.

– Drew Schweitzer

Strengths	Weaknesses
• Hands	• Lacks acceleration
• Body control	• Route tree
• RAC	• Wiry build

Critical Factors

Hands	Separation	Run After Catch
7	5	6

Positional Factors

Tracking / Adjust to Ball	Route Running	Route Savvy
6	5	6
Play Speed	**Playmaker**	**Balance / Body Control**
6	6	7
Clutch Performance	**Blocking**	**Ruggedness / Toughness**
6	5	6

Basic

	Receiving								
Year	Targets	Rec	Comp%	Yards	Air Yards	YAC	TD	Yds/Trgt	Drops
2016	2	0	0.0%	0	0	0	0	0.0	1
2017	12	10	83.3%	138	103	35	1	11.5	0
2018	124	88	71.0%	1404	778	626	9	11.3	4
	138	98	71.0%	1542	881	661	10	11.2	5

Advanced

	Advanced Receiving					EPA	
Year	Catchable Catch %	YAC per Reception	Target Share	Avg Target Depth	Receiver Rating	Total	Per Target
2016	0.0%	-	0.3%	29.0	39.6	-1.7	-0.84
2017	90.9%	3.5	2.3%	11.0	107.3	9	0.75
2018	89.8%	7.1	24.3%	11.6	129.4	58.7	0.47
	88.3%	6.7	8.3%	11.8	126.1	66	0.48

Deep Dive

		Route Running				Positive Play %		Lined Up
Year	On-Target Catch %	Routes Run	Yards Per Route Run	Deep Percent	Unique Routes	vs. Man	vs. Zone	Slot%
2018	90.6%	496	2.8	55.8%	6	51.7%	65.8%	6.7%

Lil'Jordan Humphrey

Texas Longhorns
Final Grade: 6.4 WR Rank: 16 of 35

Height	Weight	Year	Jersey #	Hometown
6036	225	3JR	84	Southlake, TX

One-Liner
Humphrey is a raw, big-bodied receiver who will fit either inside or out and wins in the short/intermediate areas of the field by capitalizing on his RAC ability and size, but still needs to sure up his hands and learn an NFL route tree.

Overall
Humphrey was primarily used out of the slot in Texas' hurry-up spread offense. He played in 36 games with 17 starts for the Longhorns during his three years in Austin. He's a big-framed receiver who possesses power and sneaky speed and wins with physicality. His lack of effort is evident at times, especially when the play isn't going his way or during running situations.

Pass Game
In the pass game, he works well against press and regularly gets the DB on his heels using quick feet and very good hand usage to wipe defender's hands and keep his frame clean. He wasn't asked to run a wide variety of routes, but is effective in the short/intermediate areas. He doesn't effectively sink his weight and hips into his breaks, and he lacks suddenness in his routes. There are times he will slow down to enter breaks which hurts his cushion, but has flashed the ability to put his foot in the ground and burst out of his cut on quick-breaking routes. He often fails to sell his deep routes to work curls/hitches more efficiently, but he does a nice job of incorporating head fakes with hip movement. He gets good separation at the top of his stems by using his hands and size to move the DB. Humphrey shows an understanding of working the DB's hips to his favor, and can create separation this way at times. He has some drops, usually related to taking his eyes off the ball, but for the most part he catches the ball cleanly with both his hands and body. He shows flashes of high-pointing and displays a large catch radius. He has the spatial awareness to work holes in zones to sit for his QB. He's very smooth after the catch and is able to pick up chunk yardage combining, size, power, speed, and elusiveness. His best attribute at the moment is his ability to make defenders miss after the catch, often looking like a running back with the ball in his hands.

Run Game
In the run game, he is very lackluster for his size. He shows that he has the ability to work, but often gets lazy. He doesn't drive his feet and doesn't block with a lot of power. He ran past defenders that ended up making the tackle on more than one occasion.

Last Word
Humphrey projects as a No. 3 receiver at the next level by his second season. On 3rd downs, he'd be most effective in the slot to take advantage of his speed and skill with the ball in his hands. He contributed on special teams at Texas as a punt returner, effectively capitalizing on his RAC ability, something he could possibly do at the next level.

– Zach Fernandez

Strengths	Weaknesses
• Release vs press	• Route tree
• Run after catch	• Tracking ability
• Catch radius	• Concentration drops

Critical Factors

Hands	Separation	Run After Catch
5	6	7

Positional Factors

Tracking / Adjust to Ball	Route Running	Route Savvy
5	5	6
Play Speed	**Playmaker**	**Balance / Body Control**
6	6	6
Clutch Performance	**Blocking**	**Ruggedness / Toughness**
6	4	6

Basic

	Receiving								
Year	Targets	Rec	Comp%	Yards	Air Yards	YAC	TD	Yds/Trgt	Drops
2016	2	2	100.0%	15	8	7	0	7.5	0
2017	60	37	61.7%	431	164	267	1	7.2	3
2018	120	86	71.7%	1176	573	603	9	9.8	6
	182	125	68.7%	1622	745	877	10	8.9	9

Advanced

	Advanced Receiving					EPA	
Year	Catchable Catch %	YAC per Reception	Target Share	Avg Target Depth	Receiver Rating	Total	Per Target
2016	100.0%	3.5	0.5%	4.0	97.9	1.3	0.65
2017	88.1%	7.2	12.6%	7.0	89.0	0.1	0.00
2018	85.1%	7.0	26.0%	9.0	113.8	55.2	0.46
	86.2%	7.0	13.7%	8.3	105.6	56.5	0.31

Deep Dive

		Route Running				Positive Play %		Lined Up
Year	On-Target Catch %	Routes Run	Yards Per Route Run	Deep Percent	Unique Routes	vs. Man	vs. Zone	Slot%
2018	91.0%	450	2.6	50.0%	10	60.8%	47.4%	86.4%

Andy Isabella

UMASS Minutemen

Final Grade: 6.4 WR Rank: 17 of 35

Height	Weight	Year	Jersey #	Hometown
5087	186	4SR	5	Mayfield, OH

One-Liner

Isabella is a small target with excellent play speed and detailed footwork who should carve out a strong role as a slot receiver in the NFL.

Overall

Isabella was a wide receiver who played inside and outside in UMass' offense. He played in 46 career games, starting 35 of them, and did not miss a game in his final three years in college. He is short with decent thickness in his lower body. His elite track background translates well on the field. He has good, quick footwork and short strides with high end acceleration skills. He's very durable for his size and gives great effort in all aspects of the game.

Pass Game

As a route runner, Isabella is very detailed with the intricacies of his assignments. He clearly takes pride in exaggerating his stem, selling his breaks, and setting up defenders, especially on deep routes. His ability to combine his deep speed with his footwork in the secondary allows him to separate in two different ways. He struggles with the ability to decelerate at the top of his route and throttle down for comebacks and true horizontal breaks, often taking an extra step or two to sink his hips and reaccelerate. At the catch point, Isabella is not a natural receiver, in part due to his small hands. He usually relies on body and basket catches when possible, and hands attempts are often double caught. However, he doesn't have a significant problem with drops based on his target share and is a reliable target in most clutch and traffic situations. Isabella has the ability to win deep and short, with good ball tracking skills as well as quick footwork and awareness to sit in coverages and move the chains. He doesn't have the ability to catch outside of his frame, and he doesn't offer much skill after the catch beyond his speed. He will struggle physically releasing and separating from longer secondary players in the NFL.

Run Game

In the run game, despite his high effort, Isabella lacks the size to be an effective blocker against larger secondary players.

Last Word

Isabella carried an extremely high share of UMass' offensive workload, and produced at a high level against small and Power 5 schools alike. He was noticeably the fastest player on the field in nearly every game he played. As a special teams contributor, he will need to continue to prove himself as a returner after minimal experience there in college. Isabella projects as a slot-receiving deep threat at the next level, who can also succeed in bunch and off-man situations where he can be schemed into free releases.

– John Todd

Strengths	Weaknesses
• Long speed • Route savvy	• Top-of-route deceleration • Natural catching skills • Physicality

Critical Factors

Hands	Separation	Run After Catch
5	7	5

Positional Factors

Tracking / Adjust to Ball	Route Running	Route Savvy
6	6	7
Play Speed	**Playmaker**	**Balance / Body Control**
8	6	4
Clutch Performance	**Blocking**	**Ruggedness / Toughness**
6	4	5

Basic

	Receiving								
Year	Targets	Rec	Comp%	Yards	Air Yards	YAC	TD	Yds/Trgt	Drops
2016	90	54	60.0%	678	454	224	6	7.5	2
2017	108	65	60.2%	1020	535	485	10	9.4	8
2018	148	102	68.9%	1698	952	746	13	11.5	8
	346	221	63.9%	3396	1941	1455	29	9.8	18

Advanced

	Advanced Receiving					EPA	
Year	Catchable Catch %	YAC per Reception	Target Share	Avg Target Depth	Receiver Rating	Total	Per Target
2016	87.1%	4.2	23.4%	11.7	91.8	9.8	0.11
2017	79.3%	7.5	24.7%	12.4	122.5	31	0.29
2018	90.3%	7.3	36.5%	11.4	131.0	61.7	0.42
	86.0%	6.6	28.2%	11.8	118.1	102.5	0.30

Deep Dive

		Route Running				Positive Play %		Lined Up
Year	On-Target Catch %	Routes Run	Yards Per Route Run	Deep Percent	Unique Routes	vs. Man	vs. Zone	Slot%
2018	90.3%	403	4.2	50.9%	7	51.1%	54.0%	47.4%

Terry Godwin

Georgia Bulldogs
Final Grade: 6.4 WR Rank: 18 of 35

Height	Weight	Year	Jersey #	Hometown
5113	174	4SR	5	Hogansville, GA

One-Liner
Godwin is an undersized, speedy, inside WR with good hands and inconsistent tracking ability, but he can create separation on deeper routes and projects as an eventual No. 3 WR deep-threat specialist.

Overall
Godwin is an inside receiver who, although undersized, could play outside because of his deep speed. He started 36 of 54 games for Georgia. He is a top athlete with excellent deep speed and very good change-of-direction ability, but he lacks ideal explosion and acceleration. He looks natural and smooth in his movements, and he has good flexibility and body control.

Pass Game
In the pass game, Godwin's primary role is as a deep threat. He shows some explosion off the line of scrimmage but depends on shiftiness and hand fighting to win on his release. He is very good at creating separation on deep routes that require slight cuts, such as posts or corners, and he can dominate on deep double-moves. He shows very good instincts for setting up defenders on double-move routes and seems to make the second move at the most opportune time. Godwin has quick feet and is good on sharper cut routes like digs or outs, even though his acceleration coming out of the cuts is not elite. He is better when these routes are run deeper, so he has a chance to gain separation vertically with speed. If a defender keeps close, he has shown an ability to consistently use his off hand to create a little extra separation. Godwin's tracking ability is inconsistent. He has flashed the ability to track the ball immediately off the QBs hand, adjust, and catch the ball in stride, but has also shown a lack of awareness as to where a pass would land; the ability is there but the inconsistency is problematic. Godwin has good hands, consistently makes clean, on-target hands catches, but has not shown the ability to consistently make contested catches. He does not consistently extend his arms fully, which gives defenders a better chance to contest and break up passes. Godwin is good after the catch, mostly because of speed. He shows the ability to break tackles and stay on his feet against DBs but may not be strong enough to do the same in the NFL.

Run Game
Godwin is a competitor and shows a willingness to block or help the team by any means necessary, even when he is not being targeted in the pass game. Godwin is not afraid to block DBs, but his lack of size/strength make him a limited run blocker. He will typically hold his own but will very rarely show domination.

Last Word
Godwin should be a No. 3 WR by his second year, based on his long speed and deep-threat ability. He has some value on special teams as a KR with speed but is likely not big enough or aggressive enough to cover.

– Tony Shields

Strengths	**Weaknesses**
• Natural hands	• Route tree
• Play speed	• Physicality
• Route savvy	• Tracking

Critical Factors

Hands	Separation	Run After Catch
6	6	6

Positional Factors

Tracking / Adjust to Ball	Route Running	Route Savvy
5	6	7
Play Speed	**Playmaker**	**Balance / Body Control**
7	6	6
Clutch Performance	**Blocking**	**Ruggedness / Toughness**
6	5	5

Basic

	Receiving								
Year	Targets	Rec	Comp%	Yards	Air Yards	YAC	TD	Yds/Trgt	Drops
2016	68	38	55.9%	397	167	230	0	5.8	3
2017	56	38	67.9%	639	396	243	6	11.4	3
2018	35	22	62.9%	373	233	140	3	10.7	1
	159	98	61.6%	1409	796	613	9	8.9	7

Advanced

	Advanced Receiving					EPA	
Year	Catchable Catch %	YAC per Reception	Target Share	Avg Target Depth	Receiver Rating	Total	Per Target
2016	88.4%	6.1	18.1%	8.6	54.6	-15.3	-0.23
2017	90.5%	6.4	18.6%	11.4	141.9	29.7	0.53
2018	91.7%	6.4	10.0%	13.3	115.5	20.2	0.58
	89.9%	6.3	15.5%	10.6	98.8	34.6	0.22

Deep Dive

		Route Running				Positive Play %		Lined Up
Year	On-Target Catch %	Routes Run	Yards Per Route Run	Deep Percent	Unique Routes	vs. Man	vs. Zone	Slot%
2018	91.7%	157	2.4	48.4%	8	70.6%	50.0%	65.8%

Riley Ridley

Georgia Bulldogs

Final Grade: 6.4 WR Rank: 19 of 35

Height	Weight	Year	Jersey #	Hometown
6010	200	3JR	8	Coconut Creek, FL

One-Liner

Ridley has great hands, and plays with route savvy and body control to win at different levels of the field, but he doesn't possess superior athletic traits to dominate as a top target.

Overall

Ridley's primary position was X-receiver in Georgia's spread offense. He started in 19 of his 39 career games played. He has good size and length. His play speed is sufficient, but he doesn't pull away from many defenders in one-on-one situations. He is a smooth mover with good change-of-direction skills. He plays with good effort, but his physicality and toughness are inconsistent.

Pass Game

In the pass game, he flashes decent route-running ability with the ability to sink his weight quickly. He displays good instincts and route savvy against zone coverage to manipulate defenders and find the soft spots in the coverage. He makes smooth breaks at the top of his routes and he does a good job of working back to the ball. He does not have the speed to challenge secondaries vertically. He uses his long strides and acceleration to eat up the cushion quickly against off-man coverage but doesn't have an extra gear to blow by defenders. He displays very good balance and body control when making difficult over-the-shoulder and sideline catches. He is not easily knocked off his route. He showed the ability to make body adjustments in the air to put himself in position to make catches. He has very good, strong hands and uses his large catch radius to make catches away from his frame. He has been a clutch playmaker in numerous big games for the Bulldogs. He only has sufficient separation skills but he uses route deception to open enough of a window to win at the catch point. He can struggle to get separation versus press-man coverage and needs improved hand use off the line with his releases. After the catch, he is not physically imposing enough to break many tackles and does not have the wiggle to force missed attempts. He has little experience in the slot, and despite his route savvy, he isn't twitchy enough to consistently win inside.

Run Game

In the run game, he is a sufficient run blocker. He has some good moments as a blocker but is not very consistent in seeking out contact and has some lapses in technique.

Last Word

Ridley projects as a solid third receiver by his second year, with developed growth in his ability to separate with route running. His speed and agility after the catch should limit him from being a go-to receiver, but his ball skills are an NFL-level trait.

– Alex O'Brien

Strengths	Weaknesses
• Strong hands	• Run after catch
• Body control	• Separation
• Ball tracking	• Long speed

Critical Factors

Hands	Separation	Run After Catch
7	5	4

Positional Factors

Tracking / Adjust to Ball	Route Running	Route Savvy
6	5	6
Play Speed	**Playmaker**	**Balance / Body Control**
5	6	7
Clutch Performance	**Blocking**	**Ruggedness / Toughness**
6	5	5

Basic

	Receiving								
Year	Targets	Rec	Comp%	Yards	Air Yards	YAC	TD	Yds/Trgt	Drops
2016	26	12	46.2%	238	156	82	2	9.2	5
2017	25	14	56.0%	218	186	32	2	8.7	2
2018	62	44	71.0%	570	422	148	9	9.2	2
	113	70	61.9%	1026	764	262	13	9.1	9

Advanced

	Advanced Receiving					EPA	
Year	Catchable Catch %	YAC per Reception	Target Share	Avg Target Depth	Receiver Rating	Total	Per Target
2016	63.2%	6.8	6.9%	19.5	104.3	7.4	0.28
2017	77.8%	2.3	8.3%	16.6	95.1	8.1	0.32
2018	91.7%	3.4	17.8%	11.6	132.4	38.7	0.62
	82.4%	3.7	11.0%	14.5	122.5	54.1	0.48

Deep Dive

		Route Running				Positive Play %		Lined Up
Year	On-Target Catch %	Routes Run	Yards Per Route Run	Deep Percent	Unique Routes	vs. Man	vs. Zone	Slot%
2018	95.5%	290	2.0	60.3%	3	67.6%	57.1%	20.4%

Anthony Johnson

Buffalo Bulls
Final Grade: 6.4 WR Rank: 20 of 35

Height	Weight	Year	Jersey #	Hometown
6021	211	4SR	83	Rock Hill, SC

One-Liner

Johnson has the hands, tracking ability, and body control to be an effective target at the next level, but lacks the over-the-top speed to consistently win deep.

Overall

Johnson plays both outside and inside receiver in a spread system that includes a myriad of vertical and underneath concepts. He is a two-year starter and has played in 25 games for the Bulls, starting 24 of them. He is a fluid athlete who possesses good suddenness, balance, short area quickness and change of direction. Anthony has sufficient competitive toughness with an ability to perform well in clutch moments late in games, but has a tendency to take plays off when he is not the intended target or when there is a run to the opposite side of the field.

Pass Game

In the pass game, he has an understanding of the route tree, possessing very good route running ability from both the outside and slot positions. He does not telegraph his routes and has no wasted motion, displaying speed and balance throughout his stem. He shows suddenness which allows him to quickly stop and decelerate, while also being able to explode out of his breaks and cuts. He struggles to separate with speed on deep routes, but can win at the top of his route and uses timely off-hand help to create separation just before the ball arrives. He has good spatial awareness and understands defensive alignments, which allows him to sit in the hole and find a soft spot in zone coverage. He has a solid release at the line of scrimmage, showing a savvy ability to hand fight and give head and shoulder fakes, to avoid jams against press coverage. He displays good manual dexterity with an ability to make difficult catches with defenders around him and is able to win the contested 1-on-1 matchups. Johnson possesses very good tracking skills, displaying the ability to look back and properly adjust to the ball in the air while running full speed down the field. He also has very good body control with the ball in the air and showing the ability to maintain balance to get his feet down in tight spaces close to the sideline and in the endzone. He flashes playmaking ability, showing good vision and quickness after the catch with the strength to break tackles from smaller secondary defenders.

Run Game

In the run game, Johnson is an average blocker, showing some ability to latch onto defenders and when he does win, he wins with strength. Too often he does not engage physically or move his feet and has trouble shadowing defenders which could lead to blown blocks on the perimeter.

Last Word

Johnson projects as a role-playing receiver by his second season at the next level being used in red zone 3rd down situations. Although he needs to improve toughness, he could bring value on special teams as a returner and an asset on kickoff and punt coverage.

– Nick Giella

Strengths	Weaknesses
• Tracking	• Inconsistent separation
• Body control	• Lacks speed
• Creating after the catch	• Blocking

Critical Factors

Hands	Separation	Run After Catch
6	6	6

Positional Factors

Tracking / Adjust to Ball	Route Running	Route Savvy
7	7	6
Play Speed	**Playmaker**	**Balance / Body Control**
5	6	7
Clutch Performance	**Blocking**	**Ruggedness / Toughness**
6	4	5

Basic

	Receiving								
Year	Targets	Rec	Comp%	Yards	Air Yards	YAC	TD	Yds/Trgt	Drops
2017	129	77	59.7%	1363	831	532	14	10.6	8
2018	98	57	58.2%	1011	727	284	11	10.3	4
	227	134	59.0%	2374	1558	816	25	10.5	12

Advanced

	Advanced Receiving					EPA	
Year	Catchable Catch %	YAC per Reception	Target Share	Avg Target Depth	Receiver Rating	Total	Per Target
2017	80.2%	6.9	32.7%	13.5	122.3	53.3	0.41
2018	85.1%	5.0	23.9%	16.8	109.7	33.5	0.34
	82.2%	6.1	19.0%	14.9	116.9	86.8	0.38

Deep Dive

		Route Running				Positive Play %		Lined Up
Year	On-Target Catch %	Routes Run	Yards Per Route Run	Deep Percent	Unique Routes	vs. Man	vs. Zone	Slot%
2018	90.2%	295	3.4	59.7%	5	46.5%	52.3%	28.5%

JJ Arcega-Whiteside

Stanford Cardinal

Final Grade: 6.4 WR Rank: 21 of 35

Height	Weight	Year	Jersey #	Hometown
6021	225	4SR	19	Inman, SC

One-Liner

Arcega-Whiteside is a big, strong, explosive athlete who excels in the red zone because of his ability to box people out, and he projects to be an outside No. 3 receiver by year two.

Overall

Arcega-Whiteside primarily played outside receiver on both sides of the field and occasionally in the slot in a pro-style offense for Stanford. He played in 34 games and started in 23 for the Cardinal. Arcega-Whiteside is a great athlete, as he was a multi-sport athlete in high school and has a big, explosive, strong body. He is a very tough player that competes in his play.

Pass Game

In the pass game, Arcega-Whiteside possesses good leaping ability and does an excellent job of boxing out defenders. Although he isn't always able to create a lot on his own after the catch, he constantly fights for extra yards. He has good, strong hands, and he rarely drops on-target passes. He can also make some extremely difficult catches because he has very good body control and has a large catch radius. He does a great job of watching the ball all the way into his hands. Overall, he can create some separation, but struggles to separate against press man coverage. He doesn't have the speed to run by anyone and separates almost exclusively using his size and high-point ability. He has very good footwork which helps him in and out of his routes.

Run Game

In the run game, Arcega-Whiteside shows a willingness to block and good strength at the point of attack. He uses good technique and is able to sustain his blocks.

Last Word

Arcega-Whiteside projects to be a role-playing receiver by year two that can come in and contribute early on, especially in the red zone. He should be on the field lined up out wide on 3rd downs. His skill set suggests that he could contribute some on special teams but shouldn't be relied upon.

– Austin Cochran

Strengths	**Weaknesses**
• Big and strong • Excellent red zone threat • Body control with ball in the air	• Struggles to separate vs. press coverage • Lacks top-end speed

Critical Factors

Hands	Separation	Run After Catch
6	5	6

Positional Factors

Tracking / Adjust to Ball	Route Running	Route Savvy
6	6	6
Play Speed	**Playmaker**	**Balance / Body Control**
5	7	7
Clutch Performance	**Blocking**	**Ruggedness / Toughness**
6	6	6

Basic

	Receiving								
Year	Targets	Rec	Comp%	Yards	Air Yards	YAC	TD	Yds/Trgt	Drops
2016	41	24	58.5%	379	262	117	5	9.2	4
2017	79	48	60.8%	781	624	157	9	9.9	3
2018	95	63	66.3%	1059	801	258	14	11.1	1
	215	135	62.8%	2219	1687	532	28	10.3	8

Advanced

	Advanced Receiving					EPA	
Year	Catchable Catch %	YAC per Reception	Target Share	Avg Target Depth	Receiver Rating	Total	Per Target
2016	80.0%	4.9	13.6%	13.4	108.6	18.6	0.45
2017	84.2%	3.3	22.1%	14.8	121.3	38.9	0.49
2018	84.0%	4.1	22.9%	14.0	134.6	60.7	0.64
	83.3%	3.9	20.0%	14.2	125.4	118.2	0.55

Deep Dive

		Route Running				Positive Play %		Lined Up
Year	On-Target Catch %	Routes Run	Yards Per Route Run	Deep Percent	Unique Routes	vs. Man	vs. Zone	Slot%
2018	85.9%	340	3.1	62.6%	6	57.1%	62.9%	11.5%

Diontae Johnson

Toledo Rockets
Final Grade: 6.4 WR Rank: 22 of 35

Height	Weight	Year	Jersey #	Hometown
5096	181	4JR	3	Ruskin, FL

One-Liner
Johnson has the speed, quickness, and playmaking ability to be a solid slot receiver at the next level, but the fact he gets re-routed too often and his lack of physicality may make it difficult for him to find consistent success.

Overall
Johnson played the X receiver for Toledo's Air Raid style offense. He played in 38 games for the Rockets, starting in 28 of them. He's a quick-twitch athlete that possesses very good speed, quickness and acceleration. He competes in his routes and plays tough but isn't incredibly physical. He tends to be a bit hesitant coming across the middle.

Pass Game
In the passing game, his quickness is what allows him to win. He knows how to work the defenders off the line. When he can get a free release, he makes the DB look silly and can usually get into his route rather easily. When physical defenders get their hands on him, it's tough for him to create as he almost always gets neutralized or re-routed. When into his route, he's able to create separation mostly with his speed and quickness. On deep balls, he shows the ability to use his off-hand to create last-second separation. He can track and adjust to the ball thrown over his shoulder near the sideline. He's got good body control and concentration with the ball in the air. He also shows the spatial awareness to get open and stem his route away from defenders. He's a precise route runner, but takes a little bit of time getting out of the top of his route. He looks to drag his feet toward the top of the route when trying to re-direct which slows him down. For a smaller receiver, he uses his hands well to make receptions. He's able to go up and pluck the ball out of the air and catch it at its highest point. However, he doesn't have a large catch radius. His size makes it difficult for him to make too many off-target catches or catches in traffic. He's a space player, so once he gets the ball in his hands, he's able to make defenders miss and create yards after the catch.

Run Game
In the run game, he doesn't show much in the way of blocking. He makes some blocks down the field from time to time, but he seems to miss some key blocks for his teammates on the edge that would allow for bigger gains. Although he's somewhat willing, he doesn't have the size or the strength to sustain many blocks.

Last Word
Johnson projects as a solid No. 3 slot receiver at the next level. He can play some on the outside, but he will be utilized to his best potential in the slot. On 3rd downs, his quickness off the line and in his routes should allow him to win battles to pick up conversions. He's been one of the best returners in college football over the past two seasons, so his return ability will allow him to contribute on special teams.

– Nathan Cooper

Strengths	Weaknesses
• Speed & quickness	• Neutralized by physical DBs
• Spatial awareness	• Too long getting out of top of route
• Playmaking ability	• Hesitant across the middle

Critical Factors

Hands	Separation	Run After Catch
6	5	6

Positional Factors

Tracking / Adjust to Ball	Route Running	Route Savvy
6	5	6
Play Speed	**Playmaker**	**Balance / Body Control**
7	6	6
Clutch Performance	**Blocking**	**Ruggedness / Toughness**
6	4	4

Basic

	Receiving								
Year	Targets	Rec	Comp%	Yards	Air Yards	YAC	TD	Yds/Trgt	Drops
2017	106	74	69.8%	1278	711	567	13	12.1	3
2018	93	49	52.7%	761	345	416	8	8.2	6
	199	123	61.8%	2039	1056	983	21	10.2	9

Advanced

	Advanced Receiving					EPA	
Year	Catchable Catch %	YAC per Reception	Target Share	Avg Target Depth	Receiver Rating	Total	Per Target
2017	92.5%	7.7	25.5%	12.6	142.2	48.9	0.46
2018	76.6%	8.5	24.3%	11.3	104.3	18.2	0.20
	85.4%	8.0	16.4%	12.0	125.2	67.1	0.34

Deep Dive

		Route Running				Positive Play %		Lined Up
Year	On-Target Catch %	Routes Run	Yards Per Route Run	Deep Percent	Unique Routes	vs. Man	vs. Zone	Slot%
2018	81.7%	315	2.4	47.0%	7	42.4%	44.7%	23.4%

Emmanuel Butler

Northern Arizona Lumberjacks
Final Grade: 6.4 WR Rank: 23 of 35

Height	Weight	Year	Jersey #	Hometown
6025	220	5SR	1	Phoenix, AZ

One-Liner
Butler is a big receiver that shows tracking ability, body control, and contested catch skills to be an effective receiving threat, but his lack of consistent separation and creating after the catch likely prevent him from being a consistent starter.

Overall
Butler was mainly the X receiver for Northern Arizona. He's played in 45 games during his time with the Lumberjacks. He is a big-bodied receiver that has good athleticism. He plays with some toughness but doesn't always show it across the middle. However, he competes in his route running. He also tends to take some plays off and not have the highest motor.

Pass Game
In the passing game, he has strong hands to make easy hands catches. Those strong hands also allow him to make catches in traffic. He has good ball skills, tracking ability, and concentration with the ball in the air to go up and make the catch at its highest point. He has the balance in the air and body control around the boundary to make plays on the ball. He has a wide stance on the line which forces him to false step on occasion and be slow off the ball. When he can get a free release, he tends to have more success. He's physical with DBs off the line and in his routes, although he tends to unnecessarily invite the contact instead of avoiding it. When separating, he has the speed to stretch the field and run away from defenders, but will have to separate more with his physicality and size at the next level. Overall, he's inconsistent in his separation ability, but is sufficient enough with speed, size, and off-hand use. Butler is a precise route runner. He is crisp at the top of his routes and doesn't round his routes or have many false movements. He has good spatial awareness to stem routes and work away from defenders in zones. He shows good speed and burst, but doesn't have much playmaking ability to create on his own.

Run Game
In the run game, he is inconsistent in his blocking. When he wants to, he'll get in good position and block effectively with strength. When he takes plays off, he is out of control and rarely makes an effective block.

Last Word
Butler projects as a No. 3 outside receiver by his second season at the next level. He can run some routes out of the slot but shouldn't be placed there consistently. On 3rd downs, he will be best on the outside where he can use his size. He doesn't show much ability as a special teams player and most likely will need to make an impact as a receiver in order to contribute on the next level.

– Nathan Cooper

Strengths	**Weaknesses**
• Tracking ability • Catch in traffic • Body control	• Creating after the catch • Blocking consistency

Critical Factors

Hands	Separation	Run After Catch
6	5	5

Positional Factors

Tracking / Adjust to Ball	Route Running	Route Savvy
6	6	6
Play Speed	**Playmaker**	**Balance / Body Control**
6	5	6
Clutch Performance	**Blocking**	**Ruggedness / Toughness**
6	5	5

High Tide

Which school had the highest average ranking among players we graded? Not surprisingly, it's Nick Saban's Alabama Crimson Tide, whose six players on our board averaged a 6.9 rating. Defensive tackle Quinnen Williams set the pace with a 7.4, the highest score of anyone on the defensive side of the ball. The offensive side was led by running back, Josh Jacobs, who earned a 7.1. Jacobs had the highest grade among skill-position players.

Stanley Morgan Jr.

Nebraska Cornhuskers

Final Grade: 6.4 WR Rank: 24 of 35

Height	Weight	Year	Jersey #	Hometown
5116	200	4SR	8	New Orleans, LA

One-Liner

Morgan Jr. is a good route runner with the quickness and versatility to serve as a flexible, role-playing WR, but needs to improve his speed and toughness to make more of an impact.

Overall

Morgan Jr.'s primary position for Nebraska was on the left side, although he also lined up on the right and in the slot. He played in 49 career games for the Cornhuskers, starting in 35 of them. Morgan Jr. is a solid athlete with good quickness, balance and body control that help make up for his merely sufficient play speed. He is an intelligent player with very good tracking ability, and he has a knack for getting into a position to help his QB when the play breaks down.

Pass Game

In the pass game, Morgan Jr. has good, reliable hands. He routinely makes catches using his hands, and only uses his body when it is necessary. While at Nebraska he demonstrated an ability to use his athleticism to make up for inconsistent QB play. He runs good routes, and makes crisp, clean cuts and gets open efficiently. He looks smooth running short, deep, and intermediate routes, and his ability to execute the entire route tree should not be an issue at the next level. He relies on his quickness for his release, and he consistently creates separation from his opponents. He doesn't have great downfield speed and can occasionally get swallowed up against more physical corners. Morgan Jr. has sufficient toughness for the next level. He is willing to go over the middle of the field, and isn't afraid to make contact with defenders when he has the ball in his hands, but he isn't going to overwhelm most opponents with his physicality.

Run Game

In the run game, Morgan Jr. is a willing blocker. His block strength is sufficient, and he may struggle to sustain his blocks against more physical DBs.

Last Word

In his first two NFL seasons, Morgan Jr. will likely serve best as a role-playing receiver, with the ability to line up both inside and outside in 3 WR sets. Due to his size and speed, Morgan Jr. may project slightly better as a slot receiver, though teams should not shy away from lining him up outside if they see fit.

– Ronan Potts

Strengths	Weaknesses
• Route running	• Physicality
• Adusting to off-target passes	• Breakaway speed
• Quickness	• Toughness

Critical Factors

Hands	Separation	Run After Catch
6	6	6

Positional Factors

Tracking / Adjust to Ball	Route Running	Route Savvy
7	6	6
Play Speed	**Playmaker**	**Balance / Body Control**
5	6	6
Clutch Performance	**Blocking**	**Ruggedness / Toughness**
6	5	5

Basic

	Receiving								
Year	Targets	Rec	Comp%	Yards	Air Yards	YAC	TD	Yds/Trgt	Drops
2016	67	33	49.3%	453	278	175	2	6.8	5
2017	112	61	54.5%	986	680	306	10	8.8	6
2018	113	70	61.9%	1004	602	402	7	8.9	2
	292	164	56.2%	2443	1560	883	19	8.4	13

Advanced

	Advanced Receiving					EPA	
Year	Catchable Catch %	YAC per Reception	Target Share	Avg Target Depth	Receiver Rating	Total	Per Target
2016	75.0%	5.3	16.8%	12.8	75.0	6.1	0.09
2017	74.4%	5.0	24.9%	13.9	99.0	13.4	0.12
2018	90.9%	5.7	28.6%	11.8	104.0	20.7	0.18
	80.8%	5.4	23.5%	12.8	95.4	40.1	0.14

Deep Dive

		Route Running				Positive Play %		Lined Up
Year	On-Target Catch %	Routes Run	Yards Per Route Run	Deep Percent	Unique Routes	vs. Man	vs. Zone	Slot%
2018	93.3%	397	2.5	59.2%	6	47.7%	51.2%	28.2%

Jalen Hurd

Baylor Bears
Final Grade: 6.1 WR Rank: 25 of 35

Height	Weight	Year	Jersey #	Hometown
6046	227	5SR	5	Hendersonville, TN

One-Liner
Hurd is a versatile, ultra-athletic converted running back who has already impressively taken to his position change and has shown great potential given more experience.

Overall
Hurd primarily lined up as a receiver in Baylor's spread offense, both out wide and in the slot, after transferring from Tennessee and transitioning from the running back position. Occasionally, Baylor lined Hurd up as a running back in an I-formation in goal line and short yardage situations. In 3 years at Tennessee, he played in 33 games, starting all but 4 of those, and in 2018 at Baylor he started in 11 of the 12 games he played. Hurd has big hands and is tall, but he is now lankier and thinner than he was in his Volunteer days. He is very competitive and has flashes of high aggression, almost boiling over.

Pass Game
Hurd is a very athletic, quick-twitch, and versatile receiver. He looks to be going 100% on every play, at times to a fault when it would benefit him to change and adjust speeds in and out of routes. As a receiver, he has displayed technically-sound releases off the line and is quick into his routes. Hurd can separate very well in a number of ways - with his size, athleticism to high point, speed, and quickness. He's adept at running routes and surprisingly savvy for being new to the position, showing good zone awareness and the ability to set up defenders on double moves with detailed footwork. Hurd almost always runs his routes at full speed, causing him to round off his cuts or lose control at the breakpoint. He has soft hands and can pluck the ball at its peak, but he isn't a natural catcher of the ball from the receiver position yet as he often braces for contact at the catch point and sacrifices yards after in favor of securing the ball. When given space to run, he taps into his ball carrying background to run through and away from contact.

Run Game
In the run game, he is a willing and strong blocker, but isn't great at keeping defenders engaged down field. When lined up in the backfield, Hurd displays impressive contact balance, vision, and quickness, as well as natural footwork, despite his lanky frame looking a bit out of place.

Last Word
In the NFL, Hurd projects to make an immediate key contribution on special teams, especially as a gunner. As a receiver, he will be a project who can be lined up inside or out. With more time and coaching at the position, his natural athleticism and size suggest a very high ceiling.

– Gennady Gusak

Strengths	Weaknesses
• Athleticism and explosive traits	• Speed adjustment
• Alignment versatility	• Downfield blocking
• Ball-carrying skills	• Project/ inexperience

Critical Factors

Hands	Separation	Run After Catch
5	7	6

Positional Factors

Tracking / Adjust to Ball	Route Running	Route Savvy
5	6	6
Play Speed	**Playmaker**	**Balance / Body Control**
6	6	6
Clutch Performance	**Blocking**	**Ruggedness / Toughness**
5	5	6

Basic

	Receiving								
Year	Targets	Rec	Comp%	Yards	Air Yards	YAC	TD	Yds/Trgt	Drops
2016	16	10	62.5%	81	34	47	2	5.1	1
2018	108	69	63.9%	946	588	358	4	8.8	7
	124	79	63.7%	1027	622	405	6	8.3	8

Advanced

	Advanced Receiving					EPA	
Year	Catchable Catch %	YAC per Reception	Target Share	Avg Target Depth	Receiver Rating	Total	Per Target
2016	76.9%	4.7	4.3%	1.6	88.8	-16.3	-1.02
2018	86.3%	5.2	22.8%	10.2	92.6	35.8	0.33
	84.9%	5.1	9.5%	9.1	92.4	19.6	0.16

Deep Dive

		Route Running				Positive Play %		Lined Up
Year	On-Target Catch %	Routes Run	Yards Per Route Run	Deep Percent	Unique Routes	vs. Man	vs. Zone	Slot%
2018	88.2%	422	2.2	48.3%	9	60.7%	48.6%	86.7%

Tony Pollard

Memphis Tigers

Final Grade: 5.9 WR Rank: 26 of 35

Height	Weight	Year	Jersey #	Hometown
5115	200	4JR	1	Memphis, TN

One-Liner

Pollard is a dynamic return specialist who has sufficient other skills to be utilized in space on offense from a variety of alignments.

Overall

Pollard was a slot receiver and change-of-pace back for Memphis, as well as their decorated return specialist. Pollard saw action in 40 games, starting 26. He has good size for his elite quickness, and he is an explosive athlete in space with the ball in his hands. Pollard plays with a motor, whether he's running routes, blocking, or returning kicks.

Pass Game

Pollard uses his quickness and awareness to create separation from defenders. He isn't the most refined route runner, but his agility helps him get open inside and over the middle. At the catch point, he has big hands but a smaller catch radius. He has some difficulties catching in traffic, preferring more to get the ball clean and short with space to run. He has excellent run-after-catch ability, utilizing vision and explosiveness, as well as solid strength and impressive body control, to make defenders miss in multiple ways.

Run Game

In the run game, he runs with patience and uses his great vision to set up blocks and find run lanes. Once he sees the lane, he explodes through the hole with burst. He gives good effort as a blocker away from the ball.

Last Word

In the NFL, Pollard will contribute immediately as a return specialist. On offense, he doesn't have a defined position fit, but can be used all over the field. His skills probably are best used as a fourth receiver in the slot where he can work downfield and in space as opposed to taking handoffs into the trenches. However, he has shown good vision between the tackles and his size shouldn't prohibit him from getting carries out of the backfield in the league, which adds to his versatility.

– Gennady Gusak

Strengths	Weaknesses
• Speed and playmaking ability	• Catch radius
• Vision	• Route-running details
• Return skills	• True position fit

Critical Factors

Hands	Separation	Run After Catch
5	6	8

Positional Factors

Tracking / Adjust to Ball	Route Running	Route Savvy
5	5	5
Play Speed	**Playmaker**	**Balance / Body Control**
7	7	7
Clutch Performance	**Blocking**	**Ruggedness / Toughness**
6	6	6

Basic

	Receiving								
Year	Targets	Rec	Comp%	Yards	Air Yards	YAC	TD	Yds/Trgt	Drops
2016	44	29	65.9%	298	80	218	2	6.8	3
2017	60	36	60.0%	536	205	331	4	8.9	6
2018	63	39	61.9%	458	207	251	3	7.3	4
	167	104	62.3%	1292	492	800	9	7.7	13

Advanced

	Advanced Receiving					EPA	
Year	Catchable Catch %	YAC per Reception	Target Share	Avg Target Depth	Receiver Rating	Total	Per Target
2016	78.4%	7.5	9.6%	5.0	100.4	3	0.07
2017	80.0%	9.2	12.7%	7.9	97.6	13.3	0.22
2018	81.3%	6.4	15.6%	7.7	93.2	-1	-0.02
	80.0%	7.7	12.5%	7.1	96.7	15.4	0.09

Deep Dive

		Route Running				Positive Play %		Lined Up
Year	On-Target Catch %	Routes Run	Yards Per Route Run	Deep Percent	Unique Routes	vs. Man	vs. Zone	Slot%
2018	90.7%	233	2.0	44.6%	8	34.8%	52.9%	58.9%

Jakobi Meyers

NC State Wolfpack

Final Grade: 5.9 WR Rank: 27 of 35

Height	Weight	Year	Jersey #	Hometown
6016	196	4JR	11	Lithonia, GA

One-Liner

Meyers has the hands, RAC ability and flashes of playmaking ability to earn solid playing time at the next level, but his inability to consistently separate and his need to learn the intricacies of route running may hold him back.

Overall

Meyers primarily lined up in the slot for the Wolfpack. He played in 37 games during his time at NC State. He has good size and speed for the position. He's a good athlete, showcased by the fact that he was a 3-sport athlete in high school. However, Meyers is still raw as a receiver, having been recruited as a quarterback. Although he is still learning the position, he has been increasingly productive year after year for the last three seasons.

Pass Game

In the pass game, he shows the ability to create after the catch. He's able to make guys miss and gain extra yards. He has good hands and is a playmaker both short and deep. Meyers has a unique ability to track and adjust to the throws. He has a big catch radius and the hands to make spectacular plays. He shows sufficient route-running ability; he doesn't always run the most precise routes. He shows some savvy in route running but is still learning the position, and how to stem routes and read defenders to find soft spots in zones. He had flashes of separation with quickness at the top of his routes but doesn't consistently run by defenders or use his off-hand. His balance and body control were inconsistent at times, but with the ball in the air, he shows that he can make the catch at its highest point. His release/ timing will also continue to develop as he grows.

Run Game

In the run game, he has sufficient blocking ability. He is willing to block with decent technique, but isn't the strongest at the POA.

Last Word

Meyers projects as a No. 4 receiver by his second season who fits best in the slot, but has the ability to play on the outside as well. On 3rd downs, he can use his hands and RAC ability out of the slot to move the chains. His speed and toughness suggest that he can be a contributor on most special teams units.

– Ian Riley

Strengths

- Tracking/adjustment
- Hands
- Playmaker

Weaknesses

- Inconsistent separation
- Route savvy
- Blocking ability

Critical Factors

Hands	Separation	Run After Catch
6	5	6

Positional Factors

Tracking / Adjust to Ball	Route Running	Route Savvy
7	5	5
Play Speed	**Playmaker**	**Balance / Body Control**
6	6	6
Clutch Performance	**Blocking**	**Ruggedness / Toughness**
6	5	6

Basic

	Receiving								
Year	Targets	Rec	Comp%	Yards	Air Yards	YAC	TD	Yds/Trgt	Drops
2016	19	13	68.4%	157	81	76	0	8.3	1
2017	96	63	65.6%	727	423	304	5	7.6	5
2018	121	92	76.0%	1047	666	381	4	8.7	3
	236	168	71.2%	1931	1170	761	9	8.2	9

Advanced

	Advanced Receiving					EPA	
Year	Catchable Catch %	YAC per Reception	Target Share	Avg Target Depth	Receiver Rating	Total	Per Target
2016	92.9%	5.9	4.4%	7.6	93.5	12	0.63
2017	84.0%	4.8	20.1%	9.2	101.3	33.2	0.35
2018	92.0%	4.1	25.0%	8.5	102.2	36	0.30
	88.9%	4.5	16.9%	8.7	101.1	81.3	0.34

Deep Dive

		Route Running				Positive Play %		Lined Up
Year	On-Target Catch %	Routes Run	Yards Per Route Run	Deep Percent	Unique Routes	vs. Man	vs. Zone	Slot%
2018	92.9%	365	2.9	33.2%	5	66.0%	56.4%	89.9%

Greg Dortch

Wake Forest Demon Deacons
Final Grade: 5.9 WR Rank: 28 of 35

Height	Weight	Year	Jersey #	Hometown
5085	170	3SO	3	Richmond, VA

One-Liner
Dortch is a quick, reliable receiver who profiles well as a rotational slot receiver and impactful return man, but his small size and durability are cause for concern at the next level.

Overall
Dortch was a slot receiver in Wake Forest's offense. He was a two-year starter, playing in 20 games. He has a very slight frame, but he is a very good athlete, with good quickness and elusiveness in the open field. Dortch is a tough competitor, but his lack of size is notable, and he has had some durability concerns already in his short career.

Pass Game
In the pass game, Dortch is a reliable option playing out of the slot. He has a good release and stutter step to fool defenders on quick-breaking routes with the speed to blow by them on deep balls. Dortch is a good route runner with experience in a diverse route tree who isn't afraid to go over the middle, despite his size. He uses his quickness to create separation on intermediate routes and has good tracking ability on deep routes and errant throws. Against zone, Dortch showed a consistent ability to exploit open areas and make himself available to the quarterback, displaying very good route savvy. He has shown the ability to pluck the ball outside his frame, while also knowing when to body catch and shield with his body. After the catch, Dortch is very elusive in the open field and he follows his blocks well, but often goes down on first contact and hasn't had great success on screen passes. Most of his post-catch production comes from outrunning defenders on deep routes.

Run Game
In the run game, he won't offer much in terms of blocking. He is willing to get in the path of defenders, but he's limited by his size and play strength. Dortch is a viable option on end-arounds and reverses, and he has the versatility to play out of the backfield. He has the speed to get to the edge and the elusiveness to avoid bigger opponents, but he doesn't have the strength or the contact balance to fight through tackles.

Last Word
Dortch was a very prolific returner at Wake Forest on both kickoffs and punts. He sets up his blocks well and does a good job of reading them correctly, while also displaying elusiveness in the open field. He can make an immediate contribution as a return man on any team. Dortch has the traits of a No. 3 NFL slot receiver, but there are reasonable size, toughness, and durability concerns that may keep him to a fourth option.

– Nick Aiello

Strengths	Weaknesses
• Separation with quickness	• Undersized
• Route savvy	• Blocking ability
• Return versatility	• Physicality

Critical Factors

Hands	Separation	Run After Catch
6	7	6

Positional Factors

Tracking / Adjust to Ball	Route Running	Route Savvy
6	6	7
Play Speed	**Playmaker**	**Balance / Body Control**
7	6	6
Clutch Performance	**Blocking**	**Ruggedness / Toughness**
6	4	4

Basic

	Receiving								
Year	Targets	Rec	Comp%	Yards	Air Yards	YAC	TD	Yds/Trgt	Drops
2017	74	53	71.6%	722	238	484	9	9.8	3
2018	132	89	67.4%	1078	595	483	8	8.2	3
	206	142	68.9%	1800	833	967	17	8.7	6

Advanced

	Advanced Receiving					EPA	
Year	Catchable Catch %	YAC per Reception	Target Share	Avg Target Depth	Receiver Rating	Total	Per Target
2017	86.9%	9.1	17.7%	8.5	136.4	19.3	0.26
2018	90.8%	5.4	30.6%	7.9	96.7	33.4	0.25
	89.3%	6.8	17.3%	8.1	111.3	52.8	0.26

Deep Dive

		Route Running				Positive Play %		Lined Up
Year	On-Target Catch %	Routes Run	Yards Per Route Run	Deep Percent	Unique Routes	vs. Man	vs. Zone	Slot%
2018	93.5%	499	2.2	33.3%	9	55.6%	51.4%	86.4%

Nyqwan Murray

Florida State Seminoles
Final Grade: 5.9 WR Rank: 29 of 35

Height	Weight	Year	Jersey #	Hometown
5105	192	4SR	8	Orlando, FL

One-Liner
Murray is a physical and smart route technician who will do most things well at the next level, but no one thing spectacularly.

Overall
Murray lined up in the slot, outside, and occasionally in the backfield for Florida State. He is a 4-year player and appeared in 41 games in his career, starting 18 of them. He has a slender frame and is a very good athlete who has good balance and body control. He is a tough competitor who plays on the edge.

Pass Game
In the pass game, Murray is a smart, physical player who uses his savvy to get open and his quickness in space to produce yards after the catch. He has a very good ability to find the open holes in a zone, as he runs crisp routes at ideal depths between defenders and breaks off routes in soft areas. Murray has a more difficult time getting open against man coverage. He tries to separate with physicality rather than shiftiness or savvy, which will be an issue at his size at the next level. His footwork off the line needs refinement, often false stepping into his route. He has fluid hips in and out of his breaks and can adjust to off-target throws in the air and along the sideline well with his body control. Murray has good, reliable hands but won't make many spectacular or tough catches. He needs to work on consistently catching the ball in traffic. Murray has good play speed but won't blow the top off a defense with an extra gear. Once the ball is in his hands, he makes yards after the catch by being a physical and elusive player who is difficult to bring down rather than just blowing by them with speed. He has good stop and start ability in and out of his breaks and can stay on his feet after initial contact with good balance. Ball security after the catch may be an issue as he runs with the ball loosely away from his body.

Run Game
In the run game, Murray is a willing blocker, but he is limited by his smaller size which will limit his effectiveness at the next level.

Last Word
Murray fits the profile of a slot receiver at the NFL level, but his size and separation skills should limit him to a fourth option. He can get open with savvy and make plays after the catch with toughness. His ability in space could make him a dangerous punt returner, as well, but his lack of breakaway speed may limit his ceiling

– Nick Aiello

Strengths	Weaknesses
• Intelligent route runner	• Undersized
• Physical for size	• Release footwork
• Complete skillset	• Blocking ability

Critical Factors

Hands	Separation	Run After Catch
6	6	6

Positional Factors

Tracking / Adjust to Ball	Route Running	Route Savvy
6	6	7
Play Speed	**Playmaker**	**Balance / Body Control**
6	6	6
Clutch Performance	**Blocking**	**Ruggedness / Toughness**
5	4	6

Basic

	Receiving								
Year	Targets	Rec	Comp%	Yards	Air Yards	YAC	TD	Yds/Trgt	Drops
2016	46	27	58.7%	441	291	150	5	9.6	1
2017	79	40	50.6%	604	386	218	4	7.6	6
2018	87	54	62.1%	744	368	376	3	8.6	3
	212	121	57.1%	1789	1045	744	12	8.4	10

Advanced

	Advanced Receiving					EPA	
Year	Catchable Catch %	YAC per Reception	Target Share	Avg Target Depth	Receiver Rating	Total	Per Target
2016	75.0%	5.6	11.1%	13.4	128.0	20	0.43
2017	76.9%	5.5	23.4%	12.6	66.6	-5.4	-0.07
2018	88.5%	7.0	19.6%	10.5	86.6	15.5	0.18
	81.2%	6.2	17.8%	11.9	88.1	30.1	0.14

Deep Dive

		Route Running				Positive Play %		Lined Up
Year	On-Target Catch %	Routes Run	Yards Per Route Run	Deep Percent	Unique Routes	vs. Man	vs. Zone	Slot%
2018	91.1%	321	2.3	48.3%	7	35.5%	43.3%	66.3%

Gary Jennings

West Virginia Mountaineers
Final Grade: 5.9 WR Rank: 30 of 35

Height	Weight	Year	Jersey #	Hometown
6010	213	4SR	12	Stafford, VA

One-Liner
Jennings has the speed and tracking ability to make plays at the next level, but needs to improve his route running to be a more consistent threat.

Overall
Jennings primarily played slot WR for West Virginia. He worked his way into the WR rotation as a true freshman and played as both a punt and kick returner. He played in 50 games over his career with the Mountaineers, starting in 22 of them. He's a solid athlete with good size and build.

Pass Game
In the passing game, he's a big, strong target with reliable hands. He tracks the ball in the air, high-pointing catches, and timing his jumps. It might not show up in his 40 time, but his play speed is very good and it shows on the field. He needs work on his release off the line and find a way to get more consistent separation instead of just relying on his speed. He will need to learn an NFL route tree, as he ran mostly screens, curls and fades at WVU. Along with learning to run new routes, he'll need to run them more crisply, and work on sinking his hips at the top of routes. He is very good in short spaces with short area-quickness, specifically in the red zone. His body control/ balance is very good. Jennings has the ability to track the ball in the air, turn his body, and box out a defender to catch the ball.

Run Game
In the run game, he plays tough, blocks hard, and uses his big frame when necessary, but doesn't have the strength at the POA to sustain blocks.

Last Word
He projects as a No. 3 slot receiver that can play inside and outside. On 3rd downs, he fits best inside where he can use his quickness and ability on short routes or hit the home run over the top. His speed and toughness should allow him to contribute as a gunner or returner on special teams.

– Ian Riley

Strengths	Weaknesses
• Hands	• Route savvy
• Explosive/speed	• Separation
• Body control	• RAC

Critical Factors

Hands	Separation	Run After Catch
6	5	6

Positional Factors

Tracking / Adjust to Ball	Route Running	Route Savvy
6	5	5
Play Speed	**Playmaker**	**Balance / Body Control**
7	6	7
Clutch Performance	**Blocking**	**Ruggedness / Toughness**
6	5	6

Basic

	Receiving								
Year	Targets	Rec	Comp%	Yards	Air Yards	YAC	TD	Yds/Trgt	Drops
2016	11	10	90.9%	165	66	99	2	15.0	0
2017	137	97	70.8%	1096	705	391	1	8.0	9
2018	74	54	73.0%	917	562	355	13	12.4	4
	222	161	72.5%	2178	1333	845	16	9.8	13

Advanced

	Advanced Receiving					EPA	
Year	Catchable Catch %	YAC per Reception	Target Share	Avg Target Depth	Receiver Rating	Total	Per Target
2016	100.0%	9.9	2.8%	8.5	158.3	11	1.00
2017	84.3%	4.0	28.8%	10.2	90.8	28.6	0.21
2018	84.4%	6.6	16.8%	13.1	142.8	56.7	0.77
	85.2%	5.3	16.9%	11.1	119.9	96.2	0.43

Deep Dive

		Route Running				Positive Play %		Lined Up
Year	On-Target Catch %	Routes Run	Yards Per Route Run	Deep Percent	Unique Routes	vs. Man	vs. Zone	Slot%
2018	85.5%	334	2.7	40.4%	8	66.7%	70.0%	80.6%

Papi White

Ohio Bobcats

Final Grade: 5.9 WR Rank: 31 of 35

Height	Weight	Year	Jersey #	Hometown
5085	177	5SR	4	Seminole, OK

One-Liner

White's ability to set up his routes and separate with speed should allow him to be a role-playing slot receiver at the next level, although he'll need to learn an NFL route tree and improve his ball security after the catch.

Overall

White played mainly in the slot for Ohio, and that is likely to be his primary position at the next level, but he also displayed some ability to line up out wide for the Bobcats. In his 43 career games he has played both RB and WR at OU, but he made the switch to receiver full time in 2017. He is a speedy playmaker that can take the top off the defense. He is undersized for the position, but his speed and playmaking ability make him a threat at all times.

Pass Game

White may be undersized, but he is not strictly a slot receiver as he shows the ability to line up wide and has great body control and tracking ability near the sideline. He shows the ability and control to catch the fade route. He is good at getting separation mainly due to his speed and quickness. That quickness allows him to gain valuable yards after the catch. He's an above average route runner, possesses very good route savvy and stems away from defenders sitting in zone coverage. White is also very good in short-yardage situations. He possesses very good short-area quickness and has the ability to beat a defender on short screen routes.

Run Game

In the run game, his size affects his ability to be an effective blocker, but he is not afraid to block. He's active as a run blocker and is willing to get in front of defenders.

Last Word

White projects as a solid No. 4 receiver playing almost exclusively out of the slot at the next level. He has college experience as a punt returner and could bring some value on special teams.

– Ian Riley

Strengths	**Weaknesses**
• Route savvy	• Route tree
• Separation with speed	• Ball security
• Playmaker	

Critical Factors

Hands	Separation	Run After Catch
6	6	5

Positional Factors

Tracking / Adjust to Ball	Route Running	Route Savvy
6	5	7
Play Speed	**Playmaker**	**Balance / Body Control**
6	6	6
Clutch Performance	**Blocking**	**Ruggedness / Toughness**
6	5	5

Basic

	Receiving								
Year	Targets	Rec	Comp%	Yards	Air Yards	YAC	TD	Yds/Trgt	Drops
2016	81	41	50.6%	672	274	398	6	8.3	5
2017	64	36	56.3%	631	422	209	3	9.9	4
2018	104	62	59.6%	987	605	382	9	9.5	4
	249	139	55.8%	2290	1301	989	18	9.2	13

Advanced

	Advanced Receiving					EPA	
Year	Catchable Catch %	YAC per Reception	Target Share	Avg Target Depth	Receiver Rating	Total	Per Target
2016	77.4%	9.7	18.1%	11.9	88.1	-5.5	-0.07
2017	81.8%	5.8	20.3%	15.6	99.2	10.9	0.17
2018	88.6%	6.2	34.0%	12.2	104.1	22.6	0.22
	83.2%	7.1	23.3%	13.0	97.6	28	0.11

Deep Dive

		Route Running				Positive Play %		Lined Up
Year	On-Target Catch %	Routes Run	Yards Per Route Run	Deep Percent	Unique Routes	vs. Man	vs. Zone	Slot%
2018	93.3%	333	3.0	50.8%	9	42.9%	51.5%	73.4%

Felton Davis III

Michigan State Spartans
Final Grade: 5.9 WR Rank: 32 of 35

Height	Weight	Year	Jersey #	Hometown
6032	200	4SR	18	Richmond, VA

One-Liner
Davis is a versatile and tough receiver who can run any route and play all over the field., who uses his size, but he doesn't separate on a consistent basis, and who is coming off of a tough injury.

Overall
Davis' primary position is WR. While at Michigan State, he lined up all over the field. Davis was a 4-year player and 2-year starter for the Spartans, playing in 38 games and starting 22 of them. Felton is a very good athlete but lacks the high-end speed to stretch the field. He runs the entire route tree but lacks precision and quickness in and out of his cuts. He shows good toughness as the majority of his catches came over the middle.

Pass Game
In the pass game, Davis makes up for his lack of elite speed with his size, length, ball skills and hands. He creates his separation using his size to body defenders out of the way and displays his balance and body control to make difficult catches look routine. Davis does a good job of using his hands to catch the ball but could improve on plucking the ball more frequently. He demonstrates knowledge of when to catch and shield with his body on catches in traffic and had a lot of goal line success using his size in posting up on curls or using his length on fades. He demonstrates very good clutch performance by making highlight-reel catches in the 4th quarter, on 3rd and long, or near the end-zone.

Run Game
In the run game, Davis is an ineffective blocker despite his size. He can contribute on rare occasions with end-arounds and reverses but isn't fast enough to consistently be a threat. He flashed his ability in a double reverse TD run against Northwestern.

Last Word
His speed and toughness suggest he could contribute on special teams. Davis has many positive traits of a No. 3 WR in the NFL. He can line up anywhere, run the entire route tree, and will thrive in the red zone. On 3rd downs, he can line up outside to use his size and post-up ability. However, his limited ability to separate with quickness will only be further hindered after his recent Achilles injury, and his ceiling at the moment may be closer to a fourth option.

– Evan Butler

Strengths	Weaknesses
• Clutch performance	• Inconsistent separation
• Catch in traffic	• Blocking
• Balance and body control	• Slight frame

Critical Factors

Hands	Separation	Run After Catch
6	5	6

Positional Factors

Tracking / Adjust to Ball	Route Running	Route Savvy
6	6	7
Play Speed	**Playmaker**	**Balance / Body Control**
6	6	6
Clutch Performance	**Blocking**	**Ruggedness / Toughness**
7	4	6

Basic

	Receiving								
Year	Targets	Rec	Comp%	Yards	Air Yards	YAC	TD	Yds/Trgt	Drops
2016	29	12	41.4%	150	121	29	1	5.2	0
2017	100	55	55.0%	774	582	192	9	7.7	3
2018	60	31	51.7%	474	347	127	4	7.9	4
	189	98	51.9%	1398	1050	348	14	7.4	7

Advanced

	Advanced Receiving					EPA	
Year	Catchable Catch %	YAC per Reception	Target Share	Avg Target Depth	Receiver Rating	Total	Per Target
2016	75.0%	2.4	8.0%	16.5	69.6	1	0.04
2017	78.6%	3.5	23.9%	13.7	101.8	23.5	0.23
2018	73.8%	4.1	12.4%	10.9	93.3	5.3	0.09
	76.6%	3.6	15.0%	13.3	94.2	29.8	0.16

Deep Dive

		Route Running				Positive Play %		Lined Up
Year	On-Target Catch %	Routes Run	Yards Per Route Run	Deep Percent	Unique Routes	vs. Man	vs. Zone	Slot%
2018	77.5%	240	2.0	58.8%	8	50.0%	45.0%	23.8%

Preston Williams

Colorado State Rams
Final Grade: 5.9 WR Rank: 33 of 35

Height	Weight	Year	Jersey #	Hometown
6031	210	4JR	11	Lovejoy, GA

One-Liner
Williams has the size and hands to become a matchup problem in the red zone, while his long strides give him the ability to stretch the field, but he'll need to be more savvy in his route running and get rid of the occasional focus drop at the next level.

Overall
Williams was an outside receiver in CSU's pro-style offense, but he slides inside on occasion. He played in 12 games with Tennessee as a freshman and sophomore before transferring to Colorado State. After sitting out 2017 due to transfer rules, he played in all 12 games in 2018 for the Rams, starting in 10 of them. Williams has long arms and is a good athlete with a track and field background. He was part of CSU's track team in 2017.

Pass Game
In the pass game, he possesses good balance and body control, which shows around the boundary with the ball in the air. He struggles to get off the line against press coverage. He was used as a screen target in the Rams' passing game quite a bit but didn't make as much out of those opportunities as he should have. Williams has enough speed to beat defenders over the top and is able to break off his routes well when running curls. He gets into and out of his routes quickly and is able to separate from defenders at the top of the route. His size and ability to box out defenders should help him become a threat near the red zone. Williams shows flashes of very good hands, but has also been inconsistent with his focus, dropping the occasional easy pass.

Run Game
In the run game, he is a willing blocker, but he can also be caught taking plays off. With his size and arm length, this is an area where he can improve quickly if he stays focused and takes to coaching.

Last Word
Due to still needing time to develop his all-around game, Williams projects as a No. 4 outside receiver at the next level, being used mainly in the red zone early on. On 3rd downs, he can use his size and speed on the outside to make plays to move the chains. He'll need to get tougher to be a solid contributor on special teams, but his speed suggests he could possibly play some as a gunner on punt and kickoff units.

– Kenny Kirkpatrick

Strengths	Weaknesses
• Athleticism	• Route running
• Hands	• Blocking
• High-point ability	• Catch in traffic

Critical Factors

Hands	Separation	Run After Catch
6	6	6

Positional Factors

Tracking / Adjust to Ball	Route Running	Route Savvy
6	6	5
Play Speed	**Playmaker**	**Balance / Body Control**
6	6	6
Clutch Performance	**Blocking**	**Ruggedness / Toughness**
6	4	5

Basic

	Receiving								
Year	Targets	Rec	Comp%	Yards	Air Yards	YAC	TD	Yds/Trgt	Drops
2016	13	9	69.2%	89	65	24	0	6.8	1
2018	176	96	54.5%	1340	969	371	14	7.6	10
	189	105	55.6%	1429	1034	395	14	7.6	11

Advanced

	Advanced Receiving					EPA	
Year	Catchable Catch %	YAC per Reception	Target Share	Avg Target Depth	Receiver Rating	Total	Per Target
2016	69.2%	2.7	3.5%	8.0	56.3	-0.7	-0.05
2018	75.6%	3.9	36.1%	13.4	91.6	11.4	0.06
	75.0%	3.8	14.4%	13.0	89.1	10.7	0.06

Deep Dive

		Route Running				Positive Play %		Lined Up
Year	On-Target Catch %	Routes Run	Yards Per Route Run	Deep Percent	Unique Routes	vs. Man	vs. Zone	Slot%
2018	81.7%	507	2.6	55.6%	7	47.1%	46.1%	18.1%

John Ursua

Hawaii Rainbow Warriors
Final Grade: 5.9 WR Rank: 34 of 35

Height	Weight	Year	Jersey #	Hometown
5091	175	4JR	5	Kailua-Kona, HI

One-Liner
Ursua is a quick receiver with good hands, but his frame and inconsistent route running and separation force him to being a reserve.

Overall
Ursua played slot receiver in a pass heavy spread offense. He played in 33 games and started in 32 for the Rainbow Warriors. He tore his ACL midway through the 2017 season and served a 2-year mission trip in Paris after graduating high school in 2012. He is very athletic, which is illustrated by the fact he was a three-sport athlete in high school. He has good speed and quickness and competes. He is a lot stronger than he looks, and plays with some toughness considering his size.

Pass Game
In the passing game, he gains separation with his speed and quickness off the line, but doesn't have the long speed or size to separate much down the field. He does a good job of hand fighting with defenders who press him at the line. He flashes good hands and the ability to control his body to make difficult catches, although he doesn't have the biggest catch radius. He catches the ball well with his hands more often than not. He struggles to make contested catches when defenders are in-phase. He doesn't run great routes and often runs them lazily, relying too much on his speed. He does a very good job of fighting through tackles. He fights for extra yards and isn't afraid to take on tacklers twice his size.

Run Game
In the run game, he is a willing blocker who is able to hold defenders in place long enough, although he doesn't have the size or strength to consistently sustain against larger DBs. He also was used as a rusher a handful of times and had some success, scoring 2 rushing touchdowns in his career.

Last Word
Ursua projects as a situational No.4 receiver with value on special teams and gadget plays. He has the ability to be an electric return man. He has playmaking qualities, but his value is limited.

– Austin Cochran

Strengths	Weaknesses
• Short-area quickness	• Often runs lazy routes
• Strong for his size	• Small catch radius
• Good hand-fighting ability	• Age concerns

Critical Factors

Hands	Separation	Run After Catch
6	5	6

Positional Factors

Tracking / Adjust to Ball	Route Running	Route Savvy
5	5	6
Play Speed	**Playmaker**	**Balance / Body Control**
6	6	5
Clutch Performance	**Blocking**	**Ruggedness / Toughness**
6	5	5

Basic

	Receiving								
Year	Targets	Rec	Comp%	Yards	Air Yards	YAC	TD	Yds/Trgt	Drops
2016	85	53	62.4%	652	401	251	3	7.7	7
2017	64	47	73.4%	667	277	390	5	10.4	2
2018	150	89	59.3%	1343	824	519	16	9.0	14
	299	189	63.2%	2662	1502	1160	24	8.9	23

Advanced

	Advanced Receiving					EPA	
Year	Catchable Catch %	YAC per Reception	Target Share	Avg Target Depth	Receiver Rating	Total	Per Target
2016	81.5%	4.7	20.4%	9.8	78.2	6.1	0.07
2017	94.0%	8.3	15.3%	8.4	132.7	29.3	0.46
2018	74.2%	5.8	27.9%	11.6	118.8	41.2	0.27
	80.4%	6.1	21.8%	10.4	110.2	76.6	0.26

Deep Dive

		Route Running				Positive Play %		Lined Up
Year	On-Target Catch %	Routes Run	Yards Per Route Run	Deep Percent	Unique Routes	vs. Man	vs. Zone	Slot%
2018	78.4%	563	2.4	45.5%	8	60.7%	43.5%	92.0%

DaMarkus Lodge

Ole Miss Rebels
Final Grade: 5.9 WR Rank: 35 of 35

Height	Weight	Year	Jersey #	Hometown
6017	202	4SR	5	Cedar Hill, TX

One-Liner
Lodge is a well-built receiver who has good body control and awareness along the sidelines, but lacks the physicality and route savvy to consistently create separation.

Overall
Lodge primarily played the Z receiver for Ole Miss in their Air Raid variant, and occasionally lined up at X or in the slot. He played in 42 games, making 24 starts. He is a good athlete with sufficient speed and good body control. He is well-built and has good footwork, particularly around the sideline. Once D.K. Metcalf was injured midway through the season, Lodge stepped in as the clear No. 2 WR for the team. His effort is suspect at times in both the running game and passing game. His physicality is also an issue; he doesn't always attack the ball or show a willingness to cross the middle of the field.

Pass Game
In the passing game, DaMarkus has a sufficient release off the line, and gains some separation due to his footwork and quickness at the top of the route. He can struggle against more physical defenders as he rarely uses his off hand to create separation, has only sufficient speed, and generally doesn't explode out of his cuts. He didn't run many routes and will need to learn an NFL route tree. He has good hands and is good at tracking the ball but lacks the physicality to always attack the ball and win through defenders. He is good at high-pointing the ball and times his jump well. He is particularly good along the sideline and has good body control and footwork to extend for catches and make plays. His has a wide catch radius as a result, but it is often needed as he doesn't possess the route savvy to always find the hole in the zone or keep moving to locate it. He shows some ability to get YAC, but it isn't a strength as he is unwilling to go down the middle of the field.

Run Game
In the run game, DaMarkus is a sufficient blocker, but lacks the consistency desired, and will not actively seek out blocks. He does possess good strength and is capable of holding a block when the effort is there.

Last Word
He will need to line up outside and his size and speed will allow him to play on special teams units at the next level.

– SIS Scouting Staff

Strengths	**Weaknesses**
• Hands	• Route savvy
• Tracking the ball	• Inconsistent in jump balls
• Body control near the sideline	• Physicality

Critical Factors

Hands	Separation	Run After Catch
6	5	5

Positional Factors

Tracking / Adjust to Ball	Route Running	Route Savvy
6	5	5
Play Speed	**Playmaker**	**Balance / Body Control**
5	6	6
Clutch Performance	**Blocking**	**Ruggedness / Toughness**
6	5	6

Basic

	Receiving								
Year	Targets	Rec	Comp%	Yards	Air Yards	YAC	TD	Yds/Trgt	Drops
2016	23	15	65.2%	203	147	56	2	8.8	0
2017	78	41	52.6%	698	553	145	7	8.9	9
2018	108	65	60.2%	877	558	319	4	8.1	6
	209	121	57.9%	1778	1258	520	13	8.5	15

Advanced

	Advanced Receiving					EPA	
Year	Catchable Catch %	YAC per Reception	Target Share	Avg Target Depth	Receiver Rating	Total	Per Target
2016	83.3%	3.7	4.8%	12.7	86.0	2.4	0.10
2017	75.9%	3.5	18.4%	16.9	86.4	1.1	0.01
2018	83.3%	4.9	25.3%	13.8	90.7	6.4	0.06
	80.7%	4.3	15.7%	14.8	88.6	10	0.05

Deep Dive

		Route Running				Positive Play %		Lined Up
Year	On-Target Catch %	Routes Run	Yards Per Route Run	Deep Percent	Unique Routes	vs. Man	vs. Zone	Slot%
2018	88.6%	388	2.3	58.0%	4	48.3%	55.3%	2.2%

Glossary

Air Yards
The number of yards the ball travels downfield from the line of scrimmage to where the receiver catches the ball

Catchable Catch%
Percentage of catchable targets to a receiver that resulted in completions

Comp%
Percentage of targets to a receiver that resulted in completions

Deep Percent
Percent of routes run by a receiver that have an average target depth of at least 15 yards

On-Target Catch%
Percentage of on-target, catchable throws to a receiver that resulted in completions

Positive Play %
Percentage of targets to the receiver with a positive Expected Points Added on the play

Receiver Rating
The quarterback's traditional Passer Rating on throws when targeting the receiver

Slot%
Percentage of plays on which the receiver lined up in the slot

Target Share
Percentage of a team's targets that went to the receiver

Unique Routes
Number of distinct routes that a receiver runs that make up at least five percent of his total routes run

YAC
Yards after catch, the amount of additional yards the receiver gains after catching the ball

Yds/Trgt
Receiving yards per pass attempt in which the receiver is targeted, including incompletions

Wide Receiver Leaderboards

Yards Per Target Leaders

Rank	Player	Team	Yds/Trgt
1	Emanuel Hall	Missouri	14.3
2	D.K. Metcalf	Ole Miss	13.9
3	Gary Jennings	West Virginia	12.4
4	Marquise Brown	Oklahoma	12.3
5	Hakeem Butler	Iowa State	11.8
6	Andy Isabella	UMASS	11.5
7	Antoine Wesley	Texas Tech	11.3
8	JJ Arcega-Whiteside	Stanford	11.1
9	A.J. Brown	Ole Miss	11.0
10	Terry Godwin	Georgia	10.7

Target Share Leaders

Rank	Player	Team	Target Share
1	Andy Isabella	UMASS	36.5%
2	Preston Williams	Colorado State	36.1%
3	Papi White	Ohio	34.0%
4	Hakeem Butler	Iowa State	31.6%
5	KeeSean Johnson	Fresno State	30.9%
6	Greg Dortch	Wake Forest	30.6%
7	N'Keal Harry	Arizona State	30.4%
8	Stanley Morgan Jr.	Nebraska	28.6%
9	A.J. Brown	Ole Miss	28.1%
10	John Ursua	Hawaii	27.9%

Catchable Catch Rate Leaders

Rank	Player	Team	Catchable Catch %
1	Parris Campbell	Ohio State	92.9%
2	Jakobi Meyers	NC State	92.0%
3	Terry Godwin	Georgia	91.7%
4	Riley Ridley	Georgia	91.7%
5	Stanley Morgan Jr.	Nebraska	90.9%
6	Greg Dortch	Wake Forest	90.8%
7	Andy Isabella	UMASS	90.3%
8	Antoine Wesley	Texas Tech	89.8%
9	Papi White	Ohio	88.6%
10	Nyqwan Murray	Florida State	88.5%

Receiving Expected Points Added Leaders

Rank	Player	Team	Receiving EPA
1	Kelvin Harmon	NC State	61.8
2	Andy Isabella	UMASS	61.7
3	Marquise Brown	Oklahoma	60.8
4	JJ Arcega-Whiteside	Stanford	60.7
5	Antoine Wesley	Texas Tech	58.7
6	Gary Jennings	West Virginia	56.7
7	Lil'Jordan Humphrey	Texas	55.2
8	KeeSean Johnson	Fresno State	54.3
9	Parris Campbell	Ohio State	53.0
10	Emanuel Hall	Missouri	46.6

Yards After Catch Per Reception Leaders

Rank	Player	Team	YAC per Reception
1	D.K. Metcalf	Ole Miss	10.1
2	Deebo Samuel	South Carolina	9.7
3	Parris Campbell	Ohio State	8.9
4	Marquise Brown	Oklahoma	8.7
5	Diontae Johnson	Toledo	8.5
6	Andy Isabella	UMASS	7.3
7	N'Keal Harry	Arizona State	7.1
8	Antoine Wesley	Texas Tech	7.1
9	Nyqwan Murray	Florida State	7.0
10	Lil'Jordan Humphrey	Texas	7.0

Yards Per Route Run Leaders

Rank	Player	Team	Yards Per Route Run
1	Andy Isabella	UMASS	4.2
2	Emanuel Hall	Missouri	3.9
3	Hakeem Butler	Iowa State	3.7
4	Marquise Brown	Oklahoma	3.6
5	Parris Campbell	Ohio State	3.5
6	Anthony Johnson	Buffalo	3.4
7	KeeSean Johnson	Fresno State	3.3
8	JJ Arcega-Whiteside	Stanford	3.1
9	A.J. Brown	Ole Miss	3.1
10	Papi White	Ohio	3.0

TIGHT END

Tight End Grading Scale

GRADE	DESCRIPTION
9.0 – 7.0	High-end 3 down starter. Pro Bowl level.
6.9 – 6.7	3 down starter with "Y" and "H" ability.
6.6 – 6.5	Lower-end starter with "Y" or "H" ability.
6.1 – 6.0	Developmental. Top traits but needs time.
5.9	Backup with "Y" and "H" ability.
5.8	Backup with "Y" or "H" ability.
5.7	3rd TE (special teams ability desired).

Tight End Rankings

Rank	Name	Grade	Page
1	T.J. Hockenson	7.0	190
2	Noah Fant	6.8	192
3	Josh Oliver	6.7	194
4	Drew Sample	6.7	196
5	Irv Smith Jr.	6.7	198
6	Caleb Wilson	6.6	200
7	Kaden Smith	6.6	202
8	Jace Sternberger	6.5	204
9	Tommy Sweeney	6.5	206
10	Keenen Brown	6.5	208
11	Donald Parham Jr.	6.1	210
12	Dawson Knox	6.0	212
13	Isaac Nauta	5.9	214
14	C.J. Conrad	5.9	216

T.J. Hockenson

Iowa Hawkeyes
Final Grade: 7.0 TE Rank: 1 of 14

Height	Weight	Year	Jersey #	Hometown
6041	250	3SO	38	Chariton, IA

One-Liner

Hockenson is a detail-oriented, high-IQ football player who shows speed, athleticism, blocking technique, and high effort to make for a complete next-level tight end.

Overall

Hockenson played as a Y-tight end and occasional slot receiver in Iowa's pro-style offense. The offense relied heavily on 12 and 21 personnel. After redshirting his first year with the Hawkeyes, he played in all 26 games since (starting 25), and worked his way into the team's two-tight end sets from the early going. He has very good size, an athletic build, and great overall movement and speed. He is aggressive at the point of attack, gives great effort in all areas, and takes the details of his assignments seriously.

Pass Game

Hockenson is very impressive off the line of scrimmage, using his high football intelligence, footwork, and athleticism, to get refined, smooth releases through traffic from the Y position. He is an excellent vertical route runner who uses his detailed footwork at the stem and great speed to separate downfield. He is a solid route runner in short and intermediate areas as well. He could stand to improve his short area quickness, and use it to separate more consistently on sharp cuts and breaks. He does use his size and strength at the stem to separate with savvy arm bars and elbow push offs. Hockenson is strong at the catch point with reliable hands in traffic. His basketball background allows for a high catch radius, but he is not consistent at hauling in difficult off-target throws. When given space after the catch, he has the ability to create yards with speed, athleticism, or physicality. He isn't used as a pass protector often, but shows the detailed positioning to be sufficient in this area, while losing some battles to experienced rushers due to power and hand use.

Run Game

In the run game, Hockenson is a very impressive blocker for his position. He shows very detailed footwork and a strong base to anchor with sound positioning. takes the details of his footwork and his positioning seriously. He shows a solid initial punch, and very good finishing ability at the second level. Hockenson is at his best sealing the edges on zone runs with sustained kickouts on the frontside, and strong effort cut blocks to seal the back. He occasionally has issues blocking head up defenders with superior hand use, but his intelligence, footwork and effort allow him to win a high percentage of his matchups, with flashes of excellence.

Last Word

Hockenson has the skill set of an impact special teams player, if needed. He profiles as a starting Y-tight end from day one. He has a complete set of physical tools to be both a speed mismatch downfield and a blocking mismatch in the box. Hockenson also possesses the mental capacity to excel at the nuances of the position.

– John Todd

Strengths	Weaknesses
• Football intelligence • Athleticism and speed • Blocking footwork	• Short area quickness • Receiving off target throws

Critical Factors

Blocking Ability	Receiving Ability	Football Intelligence
7	7	7

Positional Factors

Run Block	Pass Block	Mismatch	Play Speed
7	5	7	7
Catching Skills	**Run After Catch**	**Release**	**Separation**
6	7	7	6

Ruggedness / Toughness	Clutch	Special Teams Value
7	6	7

Basic

	Receiving								
Year	Targets	Rec	Comp%	Yards	Air Yards	YAC	TD	Yds/Trgt	Drops
2017	34	24	70.6%	320	187	133	3	9.4	1
2018	66	49	74.2%	745	387	358	6	11.3	2
	100	73	73.0%	1065	574	491	9	10.7	3

Advanced

	Advanced Receiving					EPA	
Year	Catchable Catch%	YAC per Reception	Target Share	Avg Target Depth	Receiver Rating	Total	Per Target
2017	82.8%	5.5	9.9%	9.2	117.3	20.6	0.61
2018	89.1%	7.3	16.6%	9.8	135.0	47.4	0.72
	86.9%	6.8	9.6%	9.6	129.0	68.1	0.68

Deep Dive

		Route Running		Blown Block %		Positive %		Lined Up
Year	On-Target Catch%	Routes Run	Yards Per Route Run	Run Plays	Pass Plays	vs. Man	vs. Zone	Split Out %
2018	92.2%	323	2.3	1.6%	2.6%	58.6%	70.4%	15.2%

Noah Fant

Iowa Hawkeyes
Final Grade: 6.8 TE Rank: 2 of 14

Height	Weight	Year	Jersey #	Hometown
6042	241	3JR	87	Omaha, NE

One-Liner
Fant is a fast, athletic tight end with fantastic size who will be a matchup nightmare for defenses in the NFL.

Overall
Fant has experience as a Y- and H-tight end and split out to the slot often for Iowa. He played in 35 career games and was a starter the past two seasons. He is a terrific athlete in a basketball player's frame, who poses a serious mismatch threat at any level. He isn't the most rugged football player, preferring to play in space, but he works hard on his blocking and finishes runs with strength.

Pass Game
Fant excels in the pass game. He's light on his feet and has good body control and balance. He has very impressive speed at his size and is a weapon on short, intermediate, and deep routes, and especially in the red zone. He can not only outsize defensive backs and blow past linebackers, but is also capable of the inverse, allowing him to separate in multiple ways. Fant uses his big frame to make tough catches with natural hands against safeties, and is simply too fast for linebackers to keep up with. He is fluid in space and does a good job of gaining extra yards after the catch.

Run Game
Iowa did not consistently employ Fant as a run blocker, and preferred to line him up on the back side or on the edge off the ball for his run-blocking snaps. However, when he is asked to block, he competes and is willing to get physical with defenders. He won't drive defenders off the ball, but he does a good job of sealing the ends and positioning himself to carry out his assignments. Especially with his size, he can be a capable blocker in the league.

Last Word
It's concerning Iowa took him off the field as much as they did, but his style of play is much better suited for modern NFL offenses than Iowa's. Fant profiles as a top-tier pass-catching tight end as either a Y or H in a vertical passing offensive scheme. He works hard through the whistle and has the athleticism and size to be a valuable weapon in versatile alignments.

– Jordan Edwards

Strengths	**Weaknesses**
• Mismatch ability • Size and speed • Catch point athleticism	• Front-side blocking • Playing time at Iowa

Critical Factors

Blocking Ability	Receiving Ability	Football Intelligence
6	7	7

Positional Factors

Run Block	Pass Block	Mismatch	Play Speed
6	5	8	7
Catching Skills	**Run After Catch**	**Release**	**Separation**
7	6	6	7

Ruggedness / Toughness	Clutch	Special Teams Value
5	6	5

Basic

	Receiving								
Year	Targets	Rec	Comp%	Yards	Air Yards	YAC	TD	Yds/Trgt	Drops
2016	17	9	52.9%	70	40	30	1	4.1	2
2017	60	30	50.0%	494	309	185	11	8.2	4
2018	61	39	63.9%	518	250	268	7	8.5	4
	138	78	56.5%	1082	599	483	19	7.8	10

Advanced

	Advanced Receiving					EPA	
Year	Catchable Catch%	YAC per Reception	Target Share	Avg Target Depth	Receiver Rating	Total	Per Target
2016	64.3%	3.3	5.6%	6.7	83.0	-1.6	-0.09
2017	69.8%	6.2	17.5%	12.3	103.8	10.3	0.17
2018	83.0%	6.9	15.3%	9.1	129.0	29.1	0.48
	75.0%	6.2	13.2%	10.2	115.4	37.8	0.27

Deep Dive

		Route Running		Blown Block %		Positive %		Lined Up
Year	On-Target Catch%	Routes Run	Yards Per Route Run	Run Plays	Pass Plays	vs. Man	vs. Zone	Split Out %
2018	88.1%	228	2.3	0.4%	0.0%	61.9%	51.6%	30.0%

Josh Oliver

San Jose State Spartans
Final Grade: 6.7 TE Rank: 3 of 14

Height	Weight	Year	Jersey #	Hometown
6045	246	4SR	89	Paso Robles, CA

One-Liner
Oliver is an impressive athlete with soft hands and a wide catch radius, as well as excellent toughness with and without the ball. He has a very high ceiling with more refinement to his game.

Overall
Oliver played both the Y- and H-tight end positions, as well as slot receiver, in San Jose State's RPO-based offense. He started in 36 of 49 career games, and was a consistent starter since his sophomore season. He was almost exclusively a blocking TE until his junior year. He has an ideal frame for the position and is a very fluid athlete. Oliver is a very tough football player who never misses a snap and shows high-end effort and tenacity with or without the ball.

Pass Game
As a pass catcher, he creates mismatches and can be used as a dominant weapon. He has the ability to release off the line from the slot or in-line and become a big target for his quarterback. He shows impressive route savvy to execute the details of his assignments, but he doesn't separate well on short area footwork alone. Oliver is adept at separating with physicality at the stem, but also uses his long speed and technique to easily shake defenders in trail. At the catch point, he has soft, natural hands, and offers a very wide catch radius. He doesn't have a problem with drops, but he does miss catchable balls at times. He makes up for those with the occasional athletic receptions over and through defenders near the sideline and end zone. Oliver's best receiving trait might be his ability to use his speed and athleticism to break tackles and finish runs after the catch. He is a solid target on third downs in traffic, and is a playmaker inside the 20.

Run Game
Oliver is a sufficient blocker in the run game. In-line, he lacks the technique to sustain and move defenders backward, but he uses his aggressive mentality and strong punch to do enough to win most battles. He occasionally misses assignments in pass protection, and his footwork needs refinement, but he has the willingness and athleticism to hold up. Oliver is a very good stalk and downfield blocker and makes an impact in this area every game.

Last Word
Oliver's speed and toughness will make for a strong special teamer in the NFL, if called upon. Oliver projects as a very good 3-down starter at the H-tight end position at the next level, with the ability to play Y as well. He has a very high ceiling due to his physical profile and rapid development over the last two years in San Jose State's offense.

– John Todd

Strengths	**Weaknesses**
• Toughness and effort • Size/ speed combination • Run after catch ability	• Blocking technique • Route sharpness

Critical Factors

Blocking Ability	Receiving Ability	Football Intelligence
5	7	7

Positional Factors

Run Block	Pass Block	Mismatch	Play Speed
5	5	7	7
Catching Skills	**Run After Catch**	**Release**	**Separation**
7	7	6	6

Ruggedness / Toughness	Clutch	Special Teams Value
8	6	7

Basic

	Receiving								
Year	Targets	Rec	Comp%	Yards	Air Yards	YAC	TD	Yds/Trgt	Drops
2016	8	3	37.5%	26	18	8	1	3.3	0
2017	61	36	59.0%	298	111	187	1	4.9	3
2018	103	56	54.4%	709	449	260	4	6.9	8
	172	95	55.2%	1033	578	455	6	6.0	11

Advanced

	Advanced Receiving					EPA	
Year	Catchable Catch%	YAC per Reception	Target Share	Avg Target Depth	Receiver Rating	Total	Per Target
2016	100.0%	2.7	2.4%	8.7	46.9	-7.5	-0.94
2017	80.0%	5.2	14.9%	3.8	56.6	-11.9	-0.19
2018	76.7%	4.6	23.3%	9.3	76.9	0.6	0.01
	78.5%	4.8	14.5%	7.3	67.8	-18.8	-0.11

Deep Dive

		Route Running		Blown Block %		Positive %		Lined Up
Year	On-Target Catch%	Routes Run	Yards Per Route Run	Run Plays	Pass Plays	vs. Man	vs. Zone	Split Out %
2018	83.9%	368	1.9	0.0%	2.4%	42.9%	44.4%	41.1%

Drew Sample

Washington Huskies
Final Grade: 6.7 TE Rank: 4 of 14

Height	Weight	Year	Jersey #	Hometown
6046	250	5SR	88	Bellevue, WA

One-Liner
Sample is a highly-intelligent blocking technician with the movement skills and hands to grow into a complete NFL tight end.

Overall
Sample was a tight end who occasionally lined up as a receiver in Washington's offense. He started in 40 of 51 career games. He has good size with a fairly athletic build. Sample is surprisingly fluid and has flexible mobility. He plays with a strong motor and gives very good effort through the whistle.

Pass Game
In the pass game, Sample releases very well off the line. He plays with high football intelligence and has sound footwork to beat press and sift through traffic off the snap into his route. He has never been a highly used receiving option, but he has the traits to be one moving forward. He isn't the quickest route runner, mostly running drags, check and releases, and underneath routes, but he can outrun some linebackers and he does a very good job of making himself available when the play breaks down. He has solid hands at the catch point, but he doesn't offer much after the catch and won't be considered a receiving mismatch in the league.

Run Game
In the run game, Sample is a blocking technician. He blocks with beautiful footwork and form, and he fits onto his assignments very well. He isn't the strongest drive blocker, but often he puts himself in such great positions that he can move defenders off the ball anyway. Sample does a very good job of washing down the line, while also having the quickness to flip his hips and seal.

Last Word
Sample should be a very good special teams contributor with his intelligence and blocking effort. He projects as a three down starting Y- or H-tight end, based on his blocking technique and toughness, as well as his movement skills and football intelligence. He is capable of growth as a receiver, but his blocking skills and smarts should allow him to see the field early.

– SIS Scouting Staff

Strengths	**Weaknesses**
• Blocking technique • Football intelligence • Fluidity in space	• Receiving volume • Athleticism after the catch

Critical Factors

Blocking Ability	Receiving Ability	Football Intelligence
7	6	7

Positional Factors

Run Block	Pass Block	Mismatch	Play Speed
7	6	5	6
Catching Skills	**Run After Catch**	**Release**	**Separation**
6	5	7	6

Ruggedness / Toughness	Clutch	Special Teams Value
7	6	7

Basic

	Receiving									
Year	Targets	Rec	Comp%	Yards	Air Yards	YAC	TD	Yds/Trgt	Drops
2016	12	9	75.0%	106	65	41	0	8.8	2
2017	9	7	77.8%	84	27	57	0	9.3	0
2018	36	25	69.4%	252	166	86	3	7.0	0
	57	41	71.9%	442	258	184	3	7.8	2

Advanced

	Advanced Receiving					EPA	
Year	Catchable Catch%	YAC per Reception	Target Share	Avg Target Depth	Receiver Rating	Total	Per Target
2016	75.0%	4.6	3.0%	7.1	101.4	10.9	0.91
2017	87.5%	8.1	2.7%	3.9	105.6	2.4	0.26
2018	92.6%	3.5	9.1%	7.5	105.3	11.7	0.32
	87.2%	4.5	5.0%	6.9	101.6	24.9	0.44

Deep Dive

		Route Running		Blown Block %		Positive %		Lined Up
Year	On-Target Catch%	Routes Run	Yards Per Route Run	Run Plays	Pass Plays	vs. Man	vs. Zone	Split Out %
2018	96.2%	250	1.0	0.4%	0.0%	50.0%	63.6%	16.3%

Irv Smith Jr.

Alabama Crimson Tide
Final Grade: 6.7 TE Rank: 5 of 14

Height	Weight	Year	Jersey #	Hometown
6033	241	3JR	82	New Orleans, LA

One-Liner
Smith is a smart, willing blocker who shows athleticism in his routes, very good speed, and chunk yardage creation after the catch.

Overall
Smith played on and off the ball as a tight end, as well as in the slot, for Alabama. He played in 38 career games, and did not become a full-time starter until his final season. He is a good athlete with very good straight-line speed and leaping ability. He has good size and a strong, athletic frame. He has good lateral quickness but needs to add lower-body strength. He competes well by blocking through the end of the play and always fighting for extra yards with the ball in his hands.

Pass Game
In the pass game, Smith's speed and route sharpness make him a good mismatch receiver. He can run past linebackers and box out defensive backs. He is a very quick accelerator off the line and uses good release techniques from in tight and the slot. He has good hands and possesses enough athleticism to make catches away from his body. He does a good job of turning into a running back with the ball in his hands, as he runs through arm tackles and finishes plays with aggression.

Run Game
In the run game, Smith shows good form and hand usage. Although he can get overpowered by larger defenders, he puts himself in the correct position and does enough to allow the runner to hit the hole. He needs to improve his lower-body strength, as he doesn't have the overall size to get by on size alone in the run game, but his technique is sound.

Last Word
By his second year, Smith should be a solid three-down starter, preferably as an H-tight end where he can be put in motion and schemed for mismatches. With some added strength, he will be able to sufficiently hold his own against NFL edge defenders when blocking. He will be a good receiving weapon early because of his speed and downfield athleticism. He profiles as a sufficient special teams player, who was used solely as a kick return lead blocker in college.

– Ben Hrkach

Strengths	**Weaknesses**
• Speed and acceleration • Detailed technique • Physicality	• Drive blocking • Lower-body strength

Critical Factors

Blocking Ability	Receiving Ability	Football Intelligence
5	6	7

Positional Factors

Run Block	Pass Block	Mismatch	Play Speed
5	6	6	7
Catching Skills	**Run After Catch**	**Release**	**Separation**
6	6	7	6

Ruggedness / Toughness	Clutch	Special Teams Value
6	6	5

Basic

	Receiving								
Year	**Targets**	**Rec**	**Comp%**	**Yards**	**Air Yards**	**YAC**	**TD**	**Yds/Trgt**	**Drops**
2017	17	14	82.4%	128	81	47	3	7.5	0
2018	60	44	73.3%	716	348	368	7	11.9	3
	77	58	75.3%	844	429	415	10	11.0	3

Advanced

	Advanced Receiving					EPA	
Year	**Catchable Catch%**	**YAC per Reception**	**Target Share**	**Avg Target Depth**	**Receiver Rating**	**Total**	**Per Target**
2017	93.3%	3.4	5.4%	6.4	137.6	7.8	0.46
2018	84.6%	8.2	13.9%	9.4	151.8	40	0.67
	86.6%	7.1	6.7%	8.7	150.1	47.8	0.62

Deep Dive

		Route Running		Blown Block %		Positive %		Lined Up
Year	**On-Target Catch%**	**Routes Run**	**Yards Per Route Run**	**Run Plays**	**Pass Plays**	**vs. Man**	**vs. Zone**	**Split Out %**
2018	93.6%	230	3.1	0.4%	2.7%	64.3%	55.6%	22.6%

Caleb Wilson

UCLA Bruins

Final Grade: 6.6 TE Rank: 6 of 14

Height	Weight	Year	Jersey #	Hometown
6045	235	4JR	81	Dallas, TX

One-Liner

Wilson has the hands and overall receiving ability to be a mismatch in the passing game, but lacks the consistent blocking ability to be an all-around top starter at the next level.

Overall

Wilson was primarily used as a move tight end in UCLA's hurry-up, pro-style offense. He started 17 of 29 games as a 3-year player and 2-year starter, though he only played five games in 2017 before suffering a broken foot that sidelined him for the remainder of that season. Wilson is a good athlete who shows good speed and runs smooth routes. He has good football intelligence, and is consistently aware of the situation in the moment, often making plays after they break down.

Pass Game

In the pass game, Caleb shows very good receiving ability. He runs very good routes and has strong hands at the catch point. After the catch, he can create yards on his own and make defenders miss. Off the line of scrimmage, he uses his athleticism to beat defenders, get a good release, and create good separation just before the catch point. Caleb's size and speed make him a mismatch for linebackers and defensive backs. When called to pass protect, he is a solid blocker and does enough to stay in front of his man.

Run Game

In the run game, he is just an average blocker who struggles to move his feet and play with strength at the POA. Wilson has a long frame and could stand to add some weight and muscle at the next level.

Last Word

He could play some special teams if needed, but needs to get more physical as a blocker to really be able to contribute on those units. Because he still needs time to develop as a blocker, he projects as a low-end H-tight end by his second season, and has potential to make a difference in the passing game.

– Dillon Josephsen

Strengths	Weaknesses
• Hands • Mismatch ability • Athleticism	• Run blocking • Spatial awareness

Critical Factors

Blocking Ability	Receiving Ability	Football Intelligence
5	7	6

Positional Factors

Run Block	Pass Block	Mismatch	Play Speed
4	6	6	6
Catching Skills	**Run After Catch**	**Release**	**Separation**
7	6	6	6
Ruggedness / Toughness	**Clutch**	**Special Teams Value**	
5	6	5	

Basic

	Receiving								
Year	Targets	Rec	Comp%	Yards	Air Yards	YAC	TD	Yds/Trgt	Drops
2016	23	16	69.6%	220	120	100	0	9.6	0
2017	50	38	76.0%	490	281	209	1	9.8	1
2018	97	60	61.9%	965	493	472	4	9.9	8
	170	114	67.1%	1675	894	781	5	9.9	9

Advanced

	Advanced Receiving					EPA	
Year	Catchable Catch%	YAC per Reception	Target Share	Avg Target Depth	Receiver Rating	Total	Per Target
2016	94.1%	6.3	4.8%	7.7	81.8	9.3	0.40
2017	90.5%	5.5	9.4%	7.4	104.6	21.6	0.43
2018	80.0%	7.9	24.9%	10.4	95.9	31.5	0.32
	85.1%	6.9	12.1%	9.1	96.6	62.4	0.37

Deep Dive

		Route Running		Blown Block %		Positive %		Lined Up
Year	On-Target Catch%	Routes Run	Yards Per Route Run	Run Plays	Pass Plays	vs. Man	vs. Zone	Split Out %
2018	85.7%	363	2.7	1.3%	4.5%	46.7%	64.3%	24.1%

Kaden Smith

Stanford Cardinal

Final Grade: 6.6 TE Rank: 7 of 14

Height	Weight	Year	Jersey #	Hometown
6036	252	3JR	82	Flower Mound, TX

One-Liner

Smith is an exceptional receiver, whose catch radius and strong hands allow him to win most contested situations, but his movement skills are lacking and his blocking technique needs refinement.

Overall

Smith was a Y- and H-tight end and frequent slot receiver in Stanford's pro-style offense. He started 10 of 25 games and was part of the Cardinal's two-deep tight end personnel since the start of 2017. He has a great frame and length for the position, but is an unspectacular athlete moving in space. He plays with good effort through the whistle in all areas.

Pass Game

In the pass game, Smith is an elite catcher of the football. He releases off the line from inline and the slot well, with good footwork to maneuver around box defenders. He doesn't create separation against man coverage with quickness or sharp route running, but rather relies on his size, strength, and catch radius to keep defenders away from the ball. This also makes him a good mismatch player at the next level, despite his mediocre movement skills. While he isn't quick, he is a savvy route runner, who uses detailed footwork to sell stems and find open zones. With the ball in the air, Smith can high point and pluck from all angles in traffic, along the sideline, and in the red zone, where he's a significant threat. He can adjust his body well and position himself between the ball and his defender, while almost always winning the battle at the catch point. He is a bit of a plodder and does not have good speed, but he can get rolling downhill with the ball in his hands and make himself difficult to tackle in one-on-one situations. He is a very reliable third down target in short areas, and has the size and catch radius advantage over most second-level players to win deep.

Run Game

In the run game, Smith has the size to hold his own against most defenders and has a bit of grit to his game, but his hand use at the point of attack needs development. His technique causes him to miss some assignments and backside seals. He has decent play strength but isn't much of a drive blocker. Smith is a decent blocker and can easily improve with refinement, as he has the toughness and size to move players when correctly engaged.

Last Word

He projects as a Y-tight end and early third down and red zone mismatch at the next level. He can develop into a solid starter with improved blocking technique and agility. His catching skills are excellent and difficult to find with his size, but the rest of his game needs to catch up as a supplement.

– SIS Scouting Staff

Strengths	Weaknesses
• Off-target receiving • Route savvy	• Separation with quickness • Speed • Blocking technique

Critical Factors

Blocking Ability	Receiving Ability	Football Intelligence
5	7	5

Positional Factors

Run Block	Pass Block	Mismatch	Play Speed
5	5	6	5
Catching Skills	**Run After Catch**	**Release**	**Separation**
8	5	6	5

Ruggedness / Toughness	Clutch	Special Teams Value
6	6	5

Basic

	Receiving								
Year	Targets	Rec	Comp%	Yards	Air Yards	YAC	TD	Yds/Trgt	Drops
2017	40	23	57.5%	414	313	101	5	10.4	4
2018	69	47	68.1%	635	471	164	2	9.2	3
	109	70	64.2%	1049	784	265	7	9.6	7

Advanced

	Advanced Receiving					EPA	
Year	Catchable Catch%	YAC per Reception	Target Share	Avg Target Depth	Receiver Rating	Total	Per Target
2017	76.7%	4.4	11.2%	13.9	122.3	28.4	0.71
2018	87.0%	3.5	16.6%	10.3	82.7	20.1	0.29
	83.3%	3.8	10.1%	11.6	98.0	48.5	0.44

Deep Dive

		Route Running		Blown Block %		Positive %		Lined Up
Year	On-Target Catch%	Routes Run	Yards Per Route Run	Run Plays	Pass Plays	vs. Man	vs. Zone	Split Out %
2018	90.2%	309	2.1	0.6%	0.0%	50.0%	60.0%	34.0%

Jace Sternberger

Texas A&M Aggies
Final Grade: 6.5 TE Rank: 8 of 14

Height	Weight	Year	Jersey #	Hometown
6041	250	4JR	81	Kingfisher, OK

One-Liner
Sternberger is something of a one-year wonder, but he has the natural athleticism and receiving ability to grow into a downfield weapon at the next level.

Overall
Sternberger is an H-tight end who received snaps at Y and in the slot in Texas A&M's spread offense. After transferring from junior college via Kansas, where he appeared in 10 games, he played in all 13 contests during his lone season for the Aggies, earning first team All-American honors. He has an athletic, slight build without much lower body strength, but is a smooth athlete with very good speed and athleticism.

Pass Game
Sternberger has a decent release off the line, but he can be easily rerouted by physical defenders. He is a quick and smooth route runner in and out of breaks, with the speed to blow past linebackers and some secondary players deep. He uses his body to box out defenders and his length to pluck the ball naturally. His hands are reliable and he has good leaping ability to extend his catch radius. Once the ball is in his hands, Sternberger shows good vision and contact balance to be difficult to tackle despite his frame. He positions himself well in pass protection and does a good job of helping with chips before entering his route, but can be overpowered and lose the hand battle.

Run Game
In the run game, Sternberger shows decent technique and a good attitude for blocking, but lacks the desired play strength. He shows a willingness to attack but his lower body strength keeps him from driving defenders inline. A&M put him in good positions to still have success on run plays by staggering him from the line in his H-tight end position and using him on wham blocks, inside pulls, and split zone plays, where he could get a head of steam behind him and build power at first contact. He doesn't sustain blocks well and can be put on the ground fairly easily.

Last Word
He should be useful on special teams because of his size, athleticism, and aggressiveness. Sternberger currently projects as a quality backup H-tight end but based on his one year of volume Power-5 usage resulting in great success, his best football may be ahead of him with further development. By year two in the NFL he could be a low-end starter and quality receiving threat from multiple alignments.

– SIS Scouting Staff

Strengths

- Play speed
- Athleticism
- Receiving threat potential

Weaknesses

- Inline drive blocking
- Play strength

Critical Factors

Blocking Ability	Receiving Ability	Football Intelligence
5	6	6

Positional Factors

Run Block	Pass Block	Mismatch	Play Speed
5	5	6	7
Catching Skills	**Run After Catch**	**Release**	**Separation**
6	6	5	6

Ruggedness / Toughness	Clutch	Special Teams Value
6	6	6

Basic

	Receiving								
Year	Targets	Rec	Comp%	Yards	Air Yards	YAC	TD	Yds/Trgt	Drops
2016	1	1	100.0%	5	5	0	0	5.0	0
2018	81	48	59.3%	832	424	408	10	10.3	2
	82	49	59.8%	837	429	408	10	10.2	2

Advanced

	Advanced Receiving					EPA	
Year	Catchable Catch%	YAC per Reception	Target Share	Avg Target Depth	Receiver Rating	Total	Per Target
2016	100.0%	0.0	0.2%	5.0	87.5	0.1	0.15
2018	94.1%	8.5	19.1%	10.0	113.3	25.1	0.31
	94.2%	8.3	9.3%	10.0	113.7	25.3	0.31

Deep Dive

		Route Running		Blown Block %		Positive %		Lined Up
Year	On-Target Catch%	Routes Run	Yards Per Route Run	Run Plays	Pass Plays	vs. Man	vs. Zone	Split Out %
2018	95.9%	389	2.1	0.9%	5.4%	52.5%	44.8%	16.8%

Tommy Sweeney

Boston College Eagles
Final Grade: 6.5 TE Rank: 9 of 14

Height	Weight	Year	Jersey #	Hometown
6046	253	5SR	89	Ramsey, NJ

One-Liner
Sweeney has a large catch radius, soft hands, and enough speed to result in a starting-caliber balanced in-line tight end combined with his great blocking skills.

Overall
Sweeney is a Y-tight end who took snaps at H and in the slot, in Boston College's run-heavy offense. He played in 50 career games and became a full-time starter in his sophomore season. He isn't a fluid space player and his body type isn't well defined or athletically built, but he brings size, toughness and blocking ability to his team, while still providing receiving reliability.

Pass Game
In the pass game, Sweeney is a sufficient contributor. He can catch well with big, soft hands in traffic and away from his frame. His movement skills are mediocre but his straight line speed is good. Sweeney mostly wins with length and catch radius, and doesn't separate himself with suddenness well. He doesn't bring much other than size to his run after catch skills, but he lowers his shoulder well and can be difficult to bring down for secondary players. He is a reliable target over the middle on crossers and on chip-flat routes, but he won't be considered a mismatch player at the next level.

Run Game
In the run game, Sweeney is a proficient blocker. He has a great deal of experience run blocking and he brings a strong initial punch and length. He will be able to hold his own against edge defenders and linebackers, and down blocks very well to the interior. His hand use could be improved, but he rarely misses assignments due to it.

Last Word
He should be a fine special teams player with his size and blocking ability. Sweeney projects to be a solid Y-TE in the NFL. His blocking ability will allow him to stay on the field and he can provide enough ability in the passing game as a short to intermediate option to require attention.

– SIS Scouting Staff

Strengths	Weaknesses
• Run blocking	• Athleticism in space
• Soft hands	• Route sharpness
• Football intelligence	• Block sustaining

Critical Factors

Blocking Ability	Receiving Ability	Football Intelligence
6	5	6

Positional Factors

Run Block	Pass Block	Mismatch	Play Speed
7	6	5	6
Catching Skills	**Run After Catch**	**Release**	**Separation**
6	5	5	5

Ruggedness / Toughness	Clutch	Special Teams Value
6	6	6

Basic

	Receiving								
Year	Targets	Rec	Comp%	Yards	Air Yards	YAC	TD	Yds/Trgt	Drops
2016	48	26	54.2%	353	259	94	3	7.4	4
2017	68	36	52.9%	512	208	304	4	7.5	5
2018	50	32	64.0%	348	216	132	3	7.0	1
	166	94	56.6%	1213	683	530	10	7.3	10

Advanced

	Advanced Receiving					EPA	
Year	Catchable Catch%	YAC per Reception	Target Share	Avg Target Depth	Receiver Rating	Total	Per Target
2016	74.3%	3.6	17.3%	11.0	90.0	0.9	0.02
2017	83.7%	8.4	18.8%	9.7	91.1	5.7	0.08
2018	91.4%	4.1	15.2%	7.6	87.8	4.3	0.09
	83.2%	5.6	17.1%	9.4	89.8	10.9	0.07

Deep Dive

		Route Running		Blown Block %		Positive %		Lined Up
Year	On-Target Catch%	Routes Run	Yards Per Route Run	Run Plays	Pass Plays	vs. Man	vs. Zone	Split Out %
2018	93.8%	244	1.4	1.0%	1.5%	44.4%	55.6%	16.1%

Keenen Brown

Texas State Bobcats
Final Grade: 6.5   TE Rank: 10 of 14

*

Height	Weight	Year	Jersey #	Hometown
6021	250	5SR	6	Houston, TX

One-Liner
Brown is an athletic former receiver with great size, ball skills, and starter upside with need for further technique development.

Overall
Brown was an off-ball H-tight end and frequent slot receiver in Texas State's shotgun spread offense. He played in 30 career games, which includes his time at Oklahoma State, where he only started once, and started throughout his final season after transferring to Texas State. He is a fantastic athlete for his size, which comes from his background as a receiver. (Brown switched positions after his freshman year). Brown gives good effort on all his assignments, but doesn't consistently work to the whistle when plays break down.

Pass Game
As a receiver, Brown has average acceleration off the line, but has learned sufficient release techniques from in tight. He has run a limited route tree consisting of mostly screens, seams, and flats and rarely requiring sharp breaks and cuts. Brown separates better with his size and speed than with short area quickness. At the catch point, he has big, soft hands, and uses his athleticism to high point the ball very well. He is very impressive after the catch and regularly breaks tackles with strength and elusiveness. For his size, he has great long speed to beat angles. Brown looks like a receiver with the ball in his hands, and that includes his ball security. He carries the ball very loosely in the open field, and will need to learn to tuck tighter when running through traffic and bracing for hits. Brown has experience blocking for screens outside, and he uses his size and length well in space. As a pass protector, he shows good footwork in his kick-slide, and a strong, sound base to anchor. However, he negates his length with wide, inaccurate hand use.

Run Game
In the run game, Brown needs to improve his technique as a blocker as he resorts to lunging shoulder charges too often, leaving him off balance and prone to whiffs. Usually his effort is high, and he has plenty of size and strength to develop into a solid blocker in all phases, including as a special teamer, but his overall technique needs improvement. A concerning note in this area is his habit of telegraphing his assignments. He noticeably looks at his target area pre-snap when lined up tight, whether it be down the line on split zone backside seals, linebackers on pulling plays and second level blocks, or straight ahead when blocking head up. It's a simple but important fix, and given his multiple years of development at the position, may be a sign of average football intelligence.

Last Word
Brown projects as a low end starting H-tight end. He possesses great size, athleticism, receiving traits, the versatility to split out as a receiver, and capable upside as a blocker inside.

– John Todd

Strengths	Weaknesses
• Natural receiving ability	• Run block technique
• Size and movement skills after catch	• Telegraphing assignments
• Mismatch potential	• Route tree experience

Critical Factors

Blocking Ability	Receiving Ability	Football Intelligence
5	7	4

Positional Factors

Run Block	Pass Block	Mismatch	Play Speed
4	5	7	6
Catching Skills	**Run After Catch**	**Release**	**Separation**
6	7	5	5
Ruggedness / Toughness	**Clutch**	**Special Teams Value**	
5	6	5	

Basic

	Receiving								
Year	Targets	Rec	Comp%	Yards	Air Yards	YAC	TD	Yds/Trgt	Drops
2016	2	2	100.0%	47	25	22	0	23.5	0
2017	7	4	57.1%	56	30	26	0	8.0	2
2018	75	52	69.3%	571	166	405	5	7.6	3
	84	58	69.0%	674	221	453	5	8.0	5

Advanced

	Advanced Receiving					EPA	
Year	Catchable Catch%	YAC per Reception	Target Share	Avg Target Depth	Receiver Rating	Total	Per Target
2016	100.0%	11.0	0.4%	12.5	118.8	4	2.02
2017	66.7%	6.5	1.4%	5.6	83.0	-0.2	-0.02
2018	88.1%	7.8	23.9%	4.1	108.3	11.4	0.15
	86.6%	7.8	6.7%	4.5	107.9	15.2	0.18

Deep Dive

		Route Running		Blown Block %		Positive %		Lined Up
Year	On-Target Catch%	Routes Run	Yards Per Route Run	Run Plays	Pass Plays	vs. Man	vs. Zone	Split Out %
2018	91.2%	203	2.8	0.4%	0.9%	47.4%	48.3%	40.4%

Donald Parham Jr.

Stetson Hatters

Final Grade: 6.1 TE Rank: 11 of 14

Height	Weight	Year	Jersey #	Hometown
6083	243	4SR	49	Lakeland, FL

One-Liner

Parham is an athletic H-tight end that brings solid mismatch and catching ability, but he may need some extra time to develop his frame, blocking ability, and to learn the overall intricacies of the game before he makes a large impact at the next level.

Overall

Parham is a tight end who played in Stetson's spread offense. He spent the majority of his time in the slot. He played about one third of his snaps as an in-line tight end. During his time on campus, he started 24 of the 34 games he played. He's still learning the intricacies of the game of football, as he only played one year of football in high school. He's a very good athlete who is long. Though he is a bit lanky, and could stand to gain some muscle and fill out his frame, especially in his lower body. He competes and works hard on the field, but needs to add some ruggedness and toughness to his game.

Pass Game

In the passing game, Parham possesses solid catching skills and the ability to create mismatches. His long frame gives him a large catch radius and allows him to make catches in traffic over defenders. He can use his body to box out defenders and not allow them to make a play on the ball. He has strong hands and makes contested catches, but there were times that he didn't put the ball away quick enough, forcing drops or fumbles. After the catch, he shows some burst and long speed to run away from defenders. He's an easy, long strider, and gains yards quickly. He's able to put moves on defenders and create a few extra YAC. As the season progressed, he looked more comfortable getting a clean release off the LOS. He didn't have to go against man coverage or press too often, but when he did, he showed that he could get off the line and separate. He does a good job avoiding contact, but in the middle of routes, there were too many times that he was getting re-routed. When he was re-routed during seam routes, he still stacked the defender, giving himself a better chance to make the catch uncontested. He'll need to learn an NFL route tree. A high majority of his routes were curls, flats, and seams. Playing a crucial role in the pass game, he rarely blocked in pass protection.

Run Game

In the run game, he showed a willingness to work and keep his legs driving. He wasn't always in the best position to make blocks, but he used good extension and leg drive to get defenders off the line. He comes in a bit out of control to the second level, but still tries to make a play. If he scrapes a defender and doesn't immediately have another to engage, he continues to look for ways to stay active in the play.

Last Word

Parham projects as a developmental H-tight end that has all the tools to be a mismatch at the next level. He needs to get stronger and learn more about the position and the NFL game. On 3rd downs, he will present a mismatch in the slot against smaller DBs and slower LBs. His competitiveness and speed should allow him to contribute on special teams.

– Nathan Cooper

Strengths	Weaknesses
• Mismatch ability	• Inconsistent blocking ability
• Catch radius	• Route running crispness
• Easy strider	• Route tree

Critical Factors

Blocking Ability	Receiving Ability	Football Intelligence
5	6	6

Positional Factors

Run Block	Pass Block	Mismatch	Play Speed
5	5	7	6
Catching Skills	**Run After Catch**	**Release**	**Separation**
7	6	6	6

Ruggedness / Toughness	Clutch	Special Teams Value
5	7	6

Parham's 6'8" frame and 84-inch wingspan made him a big target. He led all FCS receivers in receptions per game (9.4) and receiving yards per game (146.6) en route to being selected as a first-team All-American by AP, the AFCA and the Walter Camp Football Foundation among others. Parham leaves Stetson as the school's all-time leader in receptions, receiving yards and receiving touchdowns. He also left the school a winner. The Hatters won eight games, their most in a season since 1951.

It would be highly noteworthy if Parham were picked. Only two Stetson players have been selected in the NFL Draft. The last was guard Earl Looman in 1956.

Dawson Knox

Ole Miss Rebels
Final Grade: 6.0 TE Rank: 12 of 14

*

Height	Weight	Year	Jersey #	Hometown
6036	257	4JR	9	Brentwood, TN

One-Liner
Knox is a former quarterback who currently plays like a slot receiver in a tight end's body, and has flashed impressive speed and hands but lacks strength and run blocking ability at this stage.

Overall
Knox primarily played the H-tight end role and was a frequent slot receiver in Ole Miss' spread offense. He was a two-year starter, having enrolled as a walk-on quarterback before transitioning to tight end. Knox has a slim build and is a very good athlete, possessing very good fluidity and speed in space for his size. His competitiveness wavers at times and is quick to give up on blocks when he feels he is beat by the defender. However, he does come across the middle of the field without hesitation and makes plays in traffic.

Pass Game
In the passing game, Knox has very good speed and hands, and moves around comfortably as a slot receiver. These skills, along with his versatile alignment possibilities will make him a good mismatch at the next level. His route running isn't polished but he is intelligent and runs with savvy to maneuver into space well. His release from in tight is adequate but he is able to be rerouted by stronger defenders. His separation ability is good, and he can separate through speed, physicality, and shiftiness. Knox has natural hands, especially for someone with such a short receiving history. He attacks the ball and can pluck away from his body. He shows impressive, smooth footwork as a pass protector, and while he can lose against physicality, he has good technique moving backwards.

Run Game
In the run game, he lacks the desired initial punch aggression and functional play strength to move defenders off the ball. He is slow in progressing to his responsibility, and due to poor hip level, he is often out leveraged and overpowered. His ability to sustain engagement and drive on defenders often leads to blown blocks but he does show good reactive athleticism.

Last Word
Knox is a developmental prospect, due to his brief history at tight end and low receiving volume in an offense that should have allowed him to thrive. He moves like a slot receiver and blocks inside like one, too, and he will need increased play strength and run blocking technique in order to see the field and not key a defense to the play type. His speed, hands and combination of size and athleticism are appealing, but Knox needs time and reps to reach his potential.

– Aaron Gray

Strengths

- Speed and fluidity
- Natural receiving ability
- Pass-protection footwork

Weaknesses

- Run blocking technique and effort
- Play strength
- Tight end experience

Critical Factors

Blocking Ability	Receiving Ability	Football Intelligence
4	6	6

Positional Factors

Run Block	Pass Block	Mismatch	Play Speed
3	6	6	7
Catching Skills	**Run After Catch**	**Release**	**Separation**
7	6	5	6

Ruggedness / Toughness	Clutch	Special Teams Value
5	6	6

Basic

	Receiving								
Year	Targets	Rec	Comp%	Yards	Air Yards	YAC	TD	Yds/Trgt	Drops
2016	2	0	0.0%	0	0	0	0	0.0	1
2017	34	24	70.6%	321	169	152	0	9.4	2
2018	28	15	53.6%	284	154	130	0	10.1	1
	64	39	60.9%	605	323	282	0	9.5	4

Advanced

	Advanced Receiving					EPA	
Year	Catchable Catch%	YAC per Reception	Target Share	Avg Target Depth	Receiver Rating	Total	Per Target
2016	0.0%	-	0.4%	20.0	-	-1.9	-0.94
2017	88.9%	6.3	8.0%	8.8	88.0	4.2	0.12
2018	83.3%	8.7	6.6%	11.4	74.1	10.1	0.36
	83.0%	7.2	4.8%	10.3	79.2	12.4	0.19

Deep Dive

		Route Running		Blown Block %		Positive %		Lined Up
Year	On-Target Catch%	Routes Run	Yards Per Route Run	Run Plays	Pass Plays	vs. Man	vs. Zone	Split Out %
2018	93.8%	167	1.7	2.2%	2.1%	37.5%	50.0%	38.6%

Isaac Nauta

Georgia Bulldogs
Final Grade: 5.9 TE Rank: 13 of 14

Height	Weight	Year	Jersey #	Hometown
6035	240	3JR	18	Buford, GA

One-Liner
Nauta is a solid overall tight end with a downfield skillset and good mobility, but isn't exceptional enough in any one area to become a difference maker at the next level.

Overall
Nauta played primarily Y-tight end for Georgia and lined up frequently in the slot. He started 27 of 42 games in his career with the Bulldogs. He is a fluid athlete with good quickness and speed, and an athletic, slender build. He displays flashes of toughness but doesn't attack with ideal tenacity at a consistent level.

Pass Game
As a receiver, Nauta wins primarily with smooth movement skills in space and receiving savvy downfield. He gets off the line well and uses subtle, savvy footwork at the stem to get linebackers off balance. He has good body control and leaping ability to separate from defensive backs at the catch point, but he doesn't leave many secondary defenders behind with his route running ability. He has natural hands and plucks the ball out of the air. He has flashes of excellence as a receiver and lapses in concentration. After the catch, he has good speed and some tackle breaking ability, but doesn't have the massive size or elusiveness mismatch of some other tight ends.

Run Game
In the run game, Nauta is a willing blocker. He is limited by his slight frame and won't drive defenders off the ball, but he does a good job of fitting to his man. He doesn't have the foot speed to keep up with speed rushers in pass protection, but otherwise plays with sound technique. He works hard but will need to play with a stronger first punch and aggression to become anything beyond a serviceable blocker.

Last Word
He should be a decent special teams player, but is unlikely to become a difference maker. Nauta projects as a quality second tight end option, at either Y or H. He has enough quickness and savvy to get open against linebackers, size and catch-point athleticism to win against defensive backs, and blocking technique to be deployed in different ways. As a former top prep athlete, he never reached his full potential at Georgia, but still may in the NFL.

– Ben Hrkach

Strengths	Weaknesses
• Route savvy • Catch point separation • Fluidity	• Drive blocking • True mismatch traits

Critical Factors

Blocking Ability	Receiving Ability	Football Intelligence
5	6	6

Positional Factors

Run Block	Pass Block	Mismatch	Play Speed
5	5	5	6
Catching Skills	**Run After Catch**	**Release**	**Separation**
6	6	6	5

Ruggedness / Toughness	Clutch	Special Teams Value
5	6	5

Basic

	Receiving								
Year	Targets	Rec	Comp%	Yards	Air Yards	YAC	TD	Yds/Trgt	Drops
2016	46	29	63.0%	361	186	175	3	7.8	4
2017	20	9	45.0%	114	73	41	2	5.7	0
2018	35	30	85.7%	430	224	206	3	12.3	1
	101	68	67.3%	905	483	422	8	9.0	5

Advanced

	Advanced Receiving					EPA	
Year	Catchable Catch%	YAC per Reception	Target Share	Avg Target Depth	Receiver Rating	Total	Per Target
2016	78.4%	6.0	12.3%	8.1	100.0	12.1	0.26
2017	90.0%	4.6	6.6%	9.2	57.1	-8.1	-0.41
2018	96.8%	6.9	10.0%	7.8	146.4	20.2	0.58
	87.2%	6.2	9.9%	8.2	109.6	24.2	0.24

Deep Dive

		Route Running		Blown Block %		Positive %		Lined Up
Year	On-Target Catch%	Routes Run	Yards Per Route Run	Run Plays	Pass Plays	vs. Man	vs. Zone	Split Out %
2018	96.8%	187	2.3	0.3%	2.9%	71.4%	68.8%	27.3%

C.J. Conrad

Kentucky Wildcats
Final Grade: 5.9 TE Rank: 14 of 14

Height	Weight	Year	Jersey #	Hometown
6043	252	4SR	87	LaGrange, OH

One-Liner
Conrad will be an effective blocking tight end both in the run and the pass game and he can provide a threat as a receiver with growth and health.

Overall
Conrad is a Y-tight end who was moved around some in the multiple, pro-style offense at Kentucky. He was a 4-year starter at tight end for Kentucky. Conrad is an aggressive player with decent play speed and good toughness. He displays a willingness to be physical with linebackers, and defensive lineman while easily handling defensive backs.

Pass Game
Conrad is very good as a pass blocker. He does a good job of recognizing and picking up a blitz and he chips well before running routes. He has decent receiving ability. He has good catching skills but has a hard time getting open with decent releases and average separation. He rarely provides mismatches in the pass game due to his play speed. However, Conrad is sure handed and dependable when the ball is thrown his way. He is a clutch player on third down and can be a contributor as a run blocker, pass blocker or receiver.

Run Game
In the run game, Conrad is a good blocker that is able to block on all levels of the field and has the ability to get out in front and lead the ball carrier. He displays good football intelligence in the run game, finding the unblocked defender and creating holes.

Last Word
He displays the ability to play special teams with his production and strength. He was one of the personal protectors on the punt team and is willing to make tackles on special teams. Conrad projects to be a solid backup tight end with good Y-tight end ability and sufficient H-ability with upside in the pass game. He showed better athleticism before his injury and with improved health, can get back to that level. He can also have an impact on special teams with his toughness and blocking ability.

– Brian Rogers

Strengths

- Blocking ability
- Toughness
- Football intelligence

Weaknesses

- Run after catch
- Separation
- Health

Critical Factors

Blocking Ability	Receiving Ability	Football Intelligence
6	5	6

Positional Factors

Run Block	Pass Block	Mismatch	Play Speed
6	7	5	5
Catching Skills	**Run After Catch**	**Release**	**Separation**
6	4	5	4

Ruggedness / Toughness	Clutch	Special Teams Value
6	5	6

Basic

	Receiving								
Year	Targets	Rec	Comp%	Yards	Air Yards	YAC	TD	Yds/Trgt	Drops
2016	34	19	55.9%	262	74	188	4	7.7	6
2017	26	16	61.5%	286	85	201	4	11.0	1
2018	36	30	83.3%	318	159	159	3	8.8	1
	96	65	67.7%	866	318	548	11	9.0	8

Advanced

	Advanced Receiving					EPA	
Year	Catchable Catch%	YAC per Reception	Target Share	Avg Target Depth	Receiver Rating	Total	Per Target
2016	73.1%	9.1	11.1%	5.6	107.7	-1	-0.03
2017	84.2%	12.6	8.0%	7.8	122.8	8.7	0.33
2018	90.9%	5.3	12.6%	6.3	131.3	14.1	0.39
	83.3%	8.2	10.5%	6.4	125.6	21.8	0.23

Deep Dive

		Route Running		Blown Block %		Positive %		Lined Up
Year	On-Target Catch%	Routes Run	Yards Per Route Run	Run Plays	Pass Plays	vs. Man	vs. Zone	Split Out %
2018	93.8%	110	2.9	0.8%	2.3%	62.5%	56.3%	12.8%

Glossary

Air Yards
The number of yards the ball travels downfield from the line of scrimmage to where the receiver catches the ball

Blown Block%
Blown Block Rate, the percentage of blocking snaps that the player had a blown block

Catchable Catch%
Percentage of catchable targets to a receiver that resulted in completions

Comp%
Percentage of targets to a receiver that resulted in completions

On-Target Catch%
Percentage of on-target, catchable throws to a receiver that resulted in completions

Positive Play %
Percentage of targets to the receiver with a positive Expected Points Added on the play

Receiver Rating
The quarterback's traditional Passer Rating on throws when targeting the receiver

Split Out%
Percentage of plays on which the player lined up as a wide receiver

Target Share
Percentage of a team's targets that went to a receiver

YAC
Yards after catch, the amount of additional yards the receiver gains after catching the ball

Yds/Trgt
Receiving yards per pass attempt in which the receiver is targeted, including incompletions

Tight End Leaderboards

Yards Per Target Leaders			
Rank	**Player**	**Team**	**Yds/Trgt**
1	Isaac Nauta	Georgia	12.3
2	Irv Smith Jr.	Alabama	11.9
3	T.J. Hockenson	Iowa	11.3
4	Jace Sternberger	Texas A&M	10.3
5	Dawson Knox	Ole Miss	10.1
6	Caleb Wilson	UCLA	9.9
7	Kaden Smith	Stanford	9.2
8	C.J. Conrad	Kentucky	8.8
9	Noah Fant	Iowa	8.5
10	Keenen Brown	Texas State	7.6

Receiving Expected Points Added Leaders			
Rank	**Player**	**Team**	**Receiving EPA**
1	T.J. Hockenson	Iowa	47.4
2	Irv Smith Jr.	Alabama	40.0
3	Caleb Wilson	UCLA	31.5
4	Noah Fant	Iowa	29.1
5	Jace Sternberger	Texas A&M	25.1
6	Isaac Nauta	Georgia	20.2
7	Kaden Smith	Stanford	20.1
8	C.J. Conrad	Kentucky	14.1
9	Drew Sample	Washington	11.7
10	Keenen Brown	Texas State	11.4

Catchable Catch Rate Leaders			
Rank	**Player**	**Team**	**Catchable Catch%**
1	Isaac Nauta	Georgia	96.8%
2	Jace Sternberger	Texas A&M	94.1%
3	Drew Sample	Washington	92.6%
4	Tommy Sweeney	Boston College	91.4%
5	C.J. Conrad	Kentucky	90.9%
6	T.J. Hockenson	Iowa	89.1%
7	Keenen Brown	Texas State	88.1%
8	Kaden Smith	Stanford	87.0%
9	Irv Smith Jr.	Alabama	84.6%
10	Dawson Knox	Ole Miss	83.3%

Target Share Leaders			
Rank	**Player**	**Team**	**Target Share**
1	Caleb Wilson	UCLA	24.9%
2	Keenen Brown	Texas State	23.9%
3	Josh Oliver	San Jose State	23.3%
4	Jace Sternberger	Texas A&M	19.1%
5	T.J. Hockenson	Iowa	16.6%
6	Kaden Smith	Stanford	16.6%
7	Noah Fant	Iowa	15.3%
8	Tommy Sweeney	Boston College	15.2%
9	Irv Smith Jr.	Alabama	13.9%
10	C.J. Conrad	Kentucky	12.6%

Yards After Catch Per Reception Leaders			
Rank	**Player**	**Team**	**YAC per Reception**
1	Dawson Knox	Ole Miss	8.7
2	Jace Sternberger	Texas A&M	8.5
3	Irv Smith Jr.	Alabama	8.2
4	Caleb Wilson	UCLA	7.9
5	Keenen Brown	Texas State	7.8
6	T.J. Hockenson	Iowa	7.3
7	Isaac Nauta	Georgia	6.9
8	Noah Fant	Iowa	6.9
9	C.J. Conrad	Kentucky	5.3
10	Josh Oliver	San Jose State	4.6

Yards Per Route Run Leaders			
Rank	**Player**	**Team**	**Yards Per Route Run**
1	Irv Smith Jr.	Alabama	3.1
2	C.J. Conrad	Kentucky	2.9
3	Keenen Brown	Texas State	2.8
4	Caleb Wilson	UCLA	2.7
5	T.J. Hockenson	Iowa	2.3
6	Isaac Nauta	Georgia	2.3
7	Noah Fant	Iowa	2.3
8	Kaden Smith	Stanford	2.1
9	Jace Sternberger	Texas A&M	2.1
10	Josh Oliver	San Jose State	1.9

OFFENSIVE TACKLE

Offensive Tackle Grading Scale

GRADE	DESCRIPTION
9.0 – 7.0	High-end starter. Pro Bowl level.
6.9 – 6.7	Strong starter with 2 position flexibility.
6.6 – 6.5	Lower end starter who plays only 1 position.
6.3	3rd OT. Swing OT that plays RT and LT.
6.2	Multi-positional backup.
6.1 – 6.0	Developmental. Top traits but needs time.
5.9	Backup LT. 1 position player.
5.8	Backup RT. 1 position player.
5.7	4th OT. Functional depth level player.

Offensive Tackle Rankings

Greg Little

Ole Miss Rebels

Final Grade: 6.8 OT Rank: 1 of 16

Height	Weight	Year	Jersey #	Hometown
6051	325	3JR	74	Allen, TX

One-Liner

Little is an excellent pass protector who possesses great size, length and overall technique to grow into a very reliable blindside blocker.

Overall

Little was a left tackle in Ole Miss' Air Raid-influenced offense. He was a top high school recruit and started in 29 of his 36 career games. Little has great size and length for the position. He is a good athlete with decent movement skills and solid flexibility. He shows good competitive toughness and cares about his assignments.

Pass Game

Little is an excellent pass protector. His combination of technique and size makes him a very difficult matchup for speed and power rushers alike. His footwork is very good and he bends at the knees well to attack with sound form. He has power at first contact and rolls his hips into defenders beautifully. Little has very good anchoring flexibility to sit when defenders get into him up high. His hand use is benefitted by his length, as his placement can be inconsistent but typically doesn't give him issues. He is a very intelligent football player who understands his assignments and where defenders are moving. Little's reactive athleticism is good, as he can usually keep up and react to inside and outside moves, but he occasionally looks stiff when redirecting to mirror.

Run Game

In the run game, he comes off the snap with sound technique and leverage and uses his hip explosion to punch and lock out. When asked to pull, he exits his stance awkwardly instead of fluidly flipping his hips, but he comes down the line well with heavy feet and positions himself to kick out and seal. Little shows good leg drive and sustains better than he finishes to the ground, often content with executing his role and moving to the next play. He moves to the second level well and can win with superior size and strength there, but his overall athleticism limits his range outside the box.

Last Word

Little projects as a strong NFL starter at left tackle. He is solid in most areas but his excellent ability in pass protection and overall length and size give him a high ceiling. He has competed and won against elite talent, and has more room to grow.

– Walter Moore

Strengths	**Weaknesses**
• Pass protection	• Consistent hand placement
• Size and length	• Finishing blocks
• Anchoring flexibility	• Mirror quickness

Critical Factors

Reactive Athleticism	Anchor / Play Strength	Balance / Body Control
6	7	7

Positional Factors

Run Block	Pass Block	2nd Level	Awareness / Instincts
6	8	6	7

Hand Use	Range	Sustain / Finish
6	5	6
Power	**Flexibility**	**Ruggedness / Toughness**
6	7	6

Basic

			Blown Blocks			Penalties		Team
Year	G	GS	Total	Pass	Rush	Holding	False Starts	Opp Sacks
2016	12	5	11	7	4	0	1	27
2017	12	12	19	12	7	0	4	32
2018	12	12	10	6	4	0	1	33
	36	29	40	25	15	0	6	92

Team Stats

	Zone Run Blocking			Gap Run Blocking			Pass Block
Year	% of Runs	Y/A	Positive%	% of Runs	Y/A	Positive%	Pressure%
2016	51.4%	4.6	40.2%	36.1%	4.8	36.7%	31.8%
2017	39.0%	4.0	42.7%	45.2%	6.2	45.2%	31.9%
2018	31.7%	5.4	48.5%	45.2%	5.5	44.7%	25.9%
	40.8%	4.6	43.1%	42.0%	5.5	42.5%	29.9%

Deep Dive

	Blown Block %		When Running To His Gap				
Year	Pass	Run	Y/A	Yards Before Contact	Positive %	EPA	EPA Per Attempt
2018	1.31%	1.10%	5.2	2.8	47.6%	-3.5	-0.03

Jonah Williams

Alabama Crimson Tide
Final Grade: 6.8 OT Rank: 2 of 16

Height	Weight	Year	Jersey #	Hometown
6051	301	3JR	73	Folsom, CA

One-Liner
Williams doesn't possess ideal size or length to play tackle and could be moved inside, but his athletic skill set and overall technique project well as a blind-side protector.

Overall
Williams is primarily a left offensive tackle who has experience at right tackle in Alabama's balanced blocking scheme. He started all 44 games in his Crimson Tide career, 29 on the left side and 15 on the right. He is a good athlete and light on his feet, but is slightly undersized with less than ideal length for tackle. He has very good competitive toughness and works hard in all phases.

Pass Game
In the pass game, Williams is very technically sound with his upper body. His shuffle is smooth and natural off the line, and his hands are patient. He shows great, savvy hand techniques to win early. He plays too upright at times but has solid anchor strength to recover. He has agile feet to drop on vertical sets quickly and good mirror skills to counter. He has a tendency to play with a narrow base, which greatly affects his balance and negates some of his other strong form and technique.

Run Game
In the run game, Williams explodes off the ball and makes blocks with power. He can be dominant because of his very good upper- and lower-body strength, but his ability to sustain is limited due to his hand placement and arm length. He has a quick first step, initiates contact, and regularly keeps his feet moving to push the defender several yards back. His leverage is much improved moving forward and allows him to drive defenders well. He finishes with tenacity against compromised linemen. Williams flashes dominance on double teams and combination blocks to the second level. He moves upfield quickly, squares up defenders in space, and flips his hips to block off running lanes.

Last Word
Although undersized, Williams has the experience and athleticism to start early as a left tackle in the NFL. However, his body type and skill set translate very well to guard, and a team could certainly believe his more promising future is inside.

– Tony Shields

Strengths

- Mirror/match skills
- Hand use
- Combination/2nd-level blocking

Weaknesses

- Narrow base
- Length

Critical Factors

Reactive Athleticism	Anchor / Play Strength	Balance / Body Control
7	6	5

Positional Factors

Run Block	Pass Block	2nd Level	Awareness / Instincts
7	6	7	6

Hand Use	Range	Sustain / Finish
7	6	6
Power	**Flexibility**	**Ruggedness / Toughness**
7	6	7

Basic

			Blown Blocks			Penalties		Team
Year	G	GS	Total	Pass	Rush	Holding	False Starts	Opp Sacks
2016	15	15	14	9	5	0	4	24
2017	14	14	8	5	3	2	1	27
2018	15	15	14	6	8	1	2	15
	44	44	36	20	16	3	7	66

Team Stats

	Zone Run Blocking			Gap Run Blocking			Pass Block
Year	% of Runs	Y/A	Positive%	% of Runs	Y/A	Positive%	Pressure%
2016	64.0%	6.4	50.6%	26.5%	6.3	46.4%	29.3%
2017	55.9%	5.9	48.2%	30.6%	6.7	52.5%	35.8%
2018	62.8%	5.2	50.0%	29.1%	5.9	53.0%	30.5%
	60.9%	5.9	49.7%	28.7%	6.3	50.7%	31.6%

Deep Dive

	Blown Block %		When Running To His Gap				
Year	Pass	Run	Y/A	Yards Before Contact	Positive %	EPA	EPA Per Attempt
2018	1.39%	1.77%	5.3	2.3	48.5%	10.2	0.06

Cody Ford

Oklahoma Sooners

Final Grade: 6.7 OT Rank: 3 of 16

Height	Weight	Year	Jersey #	Hometown
6032	338	4JR	74	Pineville, LA

One-Liner

Ford is an enormous lineman with highly impressive athleticism and movement skills to match, but his hand use and consistent physicality need further development for him to reach his high ceiling.

Overall

Ford played right tackle in Oklahoma's spread offense, exclusively working out of a two-point stance. He has played in 29 career games with 21 starts, 7 of which came at left guard. He has massive size with a very thick lower half, but only average arm length. He is extremely athletic for his size and his movement skills are very impressive. He flashes a mean streak and dominant interior toughness, but he doesn't consistently bring an edge to the point of attack.

Pass Game

In the pass game, Ford has a beautiful vertical set. He is very quick moving backwards and keeps up with most speed rushers off the edge while maintaining great technique. He has some flexibility, but he doesn't consistently sit well in his stance, and defenders can beat him to the chest. Ford moves with good upper body technique, but his hand accuracy is inconsistent, and his grip strength seems to hold him back from manipulating and sustaining blocks. His lower body strength helps him anchor when his chest is exposed. He has excellent reactive athleticism for his size, but quicker pass rushers with fast hands give him trouble on short sets.

Run Game

In the run game, Ford is impressively fluid in open space. On pulls, he flips his hips with smooth footwork and builds momentum down the line. He is a load to anchor against when he has a head of steam, especially when he down blocks with good leverage and attacks with his shoulder. Too often, Ford attacks with his hands, which aren't heavy enough to shock. He has flashed the pure power to wash down lines and drive smaller defenders off the ball, but his aggression and power generation aren't consistent. He does a good job of positioning himself off the snap and adjusts to moving pieces very well. He moves to the second level well, but quicker linebackers can evade him, and he leaves his chest open on the move. His movement skills allow him to get out in front of screens and stretch plays with range, and he dominates secondary defenders. His hand use affects his ability to sustain blocks, but he finishes defenders in vulnerable positions well.

Last Word

Based on his size, athleticism, and high ceiling, Ford profiles as a solid starting caliber gap scheme right tackle at the next level. He has experience at guard, but his athleticism and pass-protection skills are best on the edge, and he would need to play with more power inside. He has the potential to grow into a blindside protector, as well. Ford's physical tools suggest a bright future, assuming he receives the necessary coaching and development.

– John Todd

Strengths	Weaknesses
• Vertical pass set	• Grip strength and hand use
• Movement skills for size	• Consistent first-punch power
• Positioning and footwork	• Chest exposure

Critical Factors

Reactive Athleticism	Anchor / Play Strength	Balance / Body Control
7	6	6

Positional Factors

Run Block	Pass Block	2nd Level	Awareness / Instincts
6	7	5	7

Hand Use	Range	Sustain / Finish
5	7	6
Power	**Flexibility**	**Ruggedness / Toughness**
7	5	6

Basic

			Blown Blocks			Penalties		Team
Year	G	GS	Total	Pass	Rush	Holding	False Starts	Opp Sacks
2016	3	3	2	2	0	1	0	20
2017	12	4	1	1	0	0	1	26
2018	14	14	15	2	13	6	2	19
	29	21	18	5	13	7	3	65

Team Stats

	Zone Run Blocking			Gap Run Blocking			Pass Block
Year	% of Runs	Y/A	Positive%	% of Runs	Y/A	Positive%	Pressure%
2016	49.4%	5.8	46.8%	43.2%	6.4	48.1%	27.8%
2017	50.6%	6.1	48.9%	38.7%	6.3	47.3%	27.0%
2018	43.1%	6.1	49.5%	45.1%	8.1	55.3%	22.6%
	47.8%	6.0	48.3%	42.3%	6.9	50.3%	25.8%

Deep Dive

	Blown Block %		When Running To His Gap				
Year	Pass	Run	Y/A	Yards Before Contact	Positive %	EPA	EPA Per Attempt
2018	0.48%	2.75%	7.4	4.4	56.3%	41.1	0.26

Andre Dillard

Washington State Cougars
Final Grade: 6.7 OT Rank: 4 of 16

Height	Weight	Year	Jersey #	Hometown
6047	310	5SR	60	Woodinville, WA

One-Liner
Dillard is a technically proficient, athletically gifted left tackle, but he needs to get stronger and gain experience as a run blocker.

Overall
Dillard is a left tackle who played in Mike Leach's four-wide Air Raid offense. He primarily used 45-degree and short sets while playing exclusively out of a 2-point stance. He played in 42 career games, starting 39 of them at left tackle. He is a very good athlete with an ideal frame and build for the position. He plays with good toughness and has not missed a start the past three seasons. Dillard possesses very good reactive athleticism with very good agility and change of direction quickness.

Pass Game
As a pass blocker, Dillard is very quick out of his stance and very smooth and fluid in his pass sets. He plays with good bend throughout his body. He has good length, demonstrates good timing and quickness with his punches, and has very good grip strength, which allows him to win the chest. His hand placement is inconsistent and needs refinement, but Dillard overall has a good set of tools with his upper body. He exhibits good mirror ability and redirects with ease in response to cross-face moves. He does a good job of diagnosing rush games up front and looks for work when unoccupied. Dillard plays with good pad level and a strong base and offers sufficient anchoring ability.

Run Game
Dillard has relatively limited reps as a run blocker, but flashes good quickness moving forward, has shown solid ability to reach as a zone blocker, and has the athletic traits to be effective in multiple NFL schemes. Dillard's ability to anchor run lanes is decent but could be improved, and he is unlikely to ever be a mauler in the run game. He doesn't have much experience as a combo blocker, and he has solid but unspectacular ability to get to the second level and finish. He is a good, fluid puller and was effective in space in Washington State's screen game.

Last Word
Dillard could start early depending on a team's comfort level with his run blocking, and he should be a solid left tackle starter by year two.

– Bryce Rossler

Strengths

- Reactive athleticism
- Footwork
- Body control

Weaknesses

- Drive blocking
- Consistent hand placement

Critical Factors

Reactive Athleticism	Anchor / Play Strength	Balance / Body Control
7	5	7

Positional Factors

Run Block	Pass Block	2nd Level	Awareness / Instincts
5	6	5	6

Hand Use	Range	Sustain / Finish
6	6	6
Power	**Flexibility**	**Ruggedness / Toughness**
5	6	6

Basic

			Blown Blocks			Penalties		Team
Year	G	GS	Total	Pass	Rush	Holding	False Starts	Opp Sacks
2016	13	13	10	7	3	1	10	31
2017	13	13	10	6	4	3	2	47
2018	13	13	6	3	3	0	4	13
	39	39	26	16	10	4	16	91

Team Stats

	Zone Run Blocking			Gap Run Blocking			Pass Block
Year	% of Runs	Y/A	Positive%	% of Runs	Y/A	Positive%	Pressure%
2016	72.5%	5.3	50.6%	8.1%	7.1	58.6%	22.9%
2017	66.9%	4.9	40.0%	7.4%	5.6	40.9%	24.1%
2018	56.9%	3.7	45.1%	20.1%	5.2	51.9%	23.0%
	66.2%	4.8	45.8%	11.4%	5.8	51.4%	23.3%

Deep Dive

	Blown Block %		When Running To His Gap				
Year	Pass	Run	Y/A	Yards Before Contact	Positive %	EPA	EPA Per Attempt
2018	0.44%	1.12%	4.7	2.1	54.5%	7.9	0.14

Bobby Evans

Oklahoma Sooners
Final Grade: 6.7 OT Rank: 5 of 16

Height	Weight	Year	Jersey #	Hometown
6042	301	4JR	71	Allen, TX

One-Liner
Evans is a college tackle who projects well outside or inside at the next level based on his frame, aggression, athleticism, and finishing ability.

Overall
Evans was a left tackle in Oklahoma's spread offense operating exclusively out of a two point stance. He started all 40 games in his career, spending his first two seasons at right tackle and moving over to left in 2018. He has a great frame and length for the tackle position. He is a very good athlete and moves smoothly in open space despite his length and size. Evans plays with tenacity every snap, constantly looking for extra blocks and throwing defenders to the ground whenever possible. He was very reliable and durable in his career in Norman.

Pass Game
In the pass game, Evans stands upright pre-snap and kick slides with impressive footwork and quickness. His length allows him to make first contact and he uses his hands well, but his grip strength is lacking. His ability to sustain blocks and adjust to counter moves is hindered when he can't latch on, but he is a good reactive athlete and often recovers well. Evans plays a bit high in pass protection and speed rushers can bend underneath him or attack his chest. He has a strong quick set, where he can punch quickly and not worry about getting vertical and playing high. His flexibility supplements his anchor, but he can be knocked off balance due to only sufficient lower body strength.

Run Game
Evans showed throughout his career that he is a very good athlete and can move naturally on pulling plays and screens. He flashes power moving forward and finishes vulnerable defenders with ferocity. When he uses proper technique, he is tough to disengage from, and his aggression is evident snap to snap. His second level blocking and range are solid because of his movement skills, but quicker second level defenders can dip and evade his hands occasionally.

Last Word
Evans projects as a solid, scheme-versatile starter at either guard or right tackle in the NFL. He has the length and athleticism to play tackle and should first get an opportunity there, but offers strong versatility at either position.

– Mark Johnson

Strengths

- Reactive athleticism
- Finishing tenacity
- Foot quickness

Weaknesses

- Grip strength
- Leverage
- Anchor strength

Critical Factors

Reactive Athleticism	Anchor / Play Strength	Balance / Body Control
7	5	6

Positional Factors

Run Block	Pass Block	2nd Level	Awareness / Instincts
6	6	6	6

Hand Use	Range	Sustain / Finish
5	6	7
Power	**Flexibility**	**Ruggedness / Toughness**
6	6	7

Basic

			Blown Blocks			Penalties		Team
Year	G	GS	Total	Pass	Rush	Holding	False Starts	Opp Sacks
2016	12	12	13	9	4	2	0	20
2017	14	14	11	7	4	2	1	26
2018	14	14	20	11	9	2	1	19
	40	40	44	27	17	6	2	65

Team Stats

	Zone Run Blocking			Gap Run Blocking			Pass Block
Year	% of Runs	Y/A	Positive%	% of Runs	Y/A	Positive%	Pressure%
2016	49.4%	5.8	46.8%	43.2%	6.4	48.1%	27.8%
2017	50.6%	6.1	48.9%	38.7%	6.3	47.3%	27.0%
2018	43.1%	6.1	49.5%	45.1%	8.1	55.3%	22.6%
	47.8%	6.0	48.3%	42.3%	6.9	50.3%	25.8%

Deep Dive

	Blown Block %		When Running To His Gap				
Year	Pass	Run	Y/A	Yards Before Contact	Positive %	EPA	EPA Per Attempt
2018	2.66%	1.90%	7.8	4.1	56.3%	48.1	0.30

Max Scharping

Northern Illinois Huskies
Final Grade: 6.6 OT Rank: 6 of 16

Height	Weight	Year	Jersey #	Hometown
6057	320	5SR	73	Green Bay, WI

One-Liner
Scharping has the strength, run blocking and athleticism to project as a starting tackle at the next level, but his quickness and hand use might prevent him from starting on the left side.

Overall
Scharping primarily played left tackle, but also has experience playing right tackle and right guard at NIU. He played in, and started, 53 games with the Huskies. He played the last two seasons at left tackle (27 games), while splitting his other 26 starts between right tackle and right guard during his first two years. He has the ability to get into his vertical set quickly to work against speed edge rushers, but can exhibit slow feet at times. Scharping flashes aggression and is not afraid to engage defenders with power, though he lacks consistency.

Pass Game
In the pass game, Scharping has the reactive athleticism to mirror defenders. He uses a combination of intelligence and body control to anticipate their moves and counter when defenders cross his face. He shows he can win with his hands and quickly locates the best way to beat his defender, though he does have a tendency to lunge from time to time. Even when he does get beat early by a speed rush, he has the ability to recover because he has the strength to push the defender out of the play, even from awkward positions. He also played at a high level against top competition last season.

Run Game
In the run game, Scharping does a good job of quickly getting into position to down block and anchor run lanes with his power. He uses hand placement in the run game to quickly turn defenders and remove them from the play, but he is inaccurate with his punch at times. When reaching the second level he often lunges against LBs and can whiff, removing himself from the play.

Last Word
Scharping projects as a solid starting right tackle by his second season, but he may not have the quickness needed to play on the left side.

– Zach Fernandez

Strengths	**Weaknesses**
• Strength	• Foot quickness
• Run blocking	• Hand accuracy
• Technique	• Use of his length

Critical Factors

Reactive Athleticism	Anchor / Play Strength	Balance / Body Control
6	7	6

Positional Factors

Run Block	Pass Block	2nd Level	Awareness / Instincts
7	6	5	6

Hand Use	Range	Sustain / Finish
5	5	6
Power	**Flexibility**	**Ruggedness / Toughness**
6	6	6

Basic

			Blown Blocks			Penalties		Team
Year	G	GS	Total	Pass	Rush	Holding	False Starts	Opp Sacks
2016	12	12	2	1	1	0	5	8
2017	13	13	13	6	7	1	1	27
2018	14	14	10	6	4	0	1	41
	39	39	25	13	12	1	7	76

Team Stats

	Zone Run Blocking			Gap Run Blocking			Pass Block
Year	% of Runs	Y/A	Positive%	% of Runs	Y/A	Positive%	Pressure%
2016	66.8%	5.4	45.5%	29.8%	6.1	44.9%	21.2%
2017	62.3%	5.2	45.9%	27.8%	4.0	35.5%	29.9%
2018	65.4%	4.7	43.2%	18.2%	4.5	36.4%	27.8%
	64.8%	5.1	44.8%	25.1%	4.9	39.3%	26.5%

Deep Dive

	Blown Block %		When Running To His Gap				
Year	Pass	Run	Y/A	Yards Before Contact	Positive %	EPA	EPA Per Attempt
2018	1.36%	0.72%	5.8	3.6	46.4%	2.0	0.01

Derwin Gray

Maryland Terrapins
Final Grade: 6.6 OT Rank: 7 of 16

Height	Weight	Year	Jersey #	Hometown
6045	330	5SR	55	Washington, DC

One-Liner
Gray possesses an ideal blend of technique and quickness to excel at the next level, but his length might cause issues.

Overall
Gray is a left tackle who played in Maryland's zone blocking scheme. He played in 37 career games, starting 25 of them, all as the left tackle. He is a very good athlete with a great combination of size and quickness. He does not possess ideal length or lower half thickness. He flashes a nasty mentality at times, but his overall effort can run hot and cold.

Pass Game
As a pass blocker, Gray shows some elite traits, specifically with his quick footwork and hand-fighting. He explodes back off the line and kick-slides with great technique and quick steps, allowing him to counter and mirror inside moves and keep pace with speed to the outside. Gray keeps his elbows tight, has good accuracy with his first punch and shows great skill with his ability to chop hands and displace rush moves. His lack of length however is an issue in this area. He struggles with long and strong edge rushers who can reach his chest before Gray can reach theirs. Additionally, he doesn't have great lower body strength to sit and anchor when conceding at the point of attack, but his ankle flexion, core strength and balance do help him recover against power.

Run Game
In the run game, Gray moves well laterally in zone and has the skills to be a factor at the second level. He doesn't explode into open space and hesitates to attack smaller defenders on the perimeter. He doesn't play with consistent leverage, and although he shows good leg drive, his limited length shows up when attempting to sustain blocks. While he flashes a mean streak to take defenders to the ground, it isn't a consistent part of his game. His heavy hands are evident on down blocks and slaps on screens.

Last Word
Gray commits a few too many penalties and doesn't always give consistent effort beyond executing his initial task, but he reads twists well and doesn't seem to be a liability from an assignment perspective. His talent and lack of length project him as a low end starter at left tackle in the NFL, with possible back up flexibility inside at guard.

– John Todd

Strengths	Weaknesses
• Footwork in pass protection	• Length
• Hand technique	• Lower body strength
• Reactive athleticism	• Leverage

Critical Factors

Reactive Athleticism	Anchor / Play Strength	Balance / Body Control
7	5	7

Positional Factors

Run Block	Pass Block	2nd Level	Awareness / Instincts
5	7	6	5

Hand Use	Range	Sustain / Finish
7	5	4
Power	**Flexibility**	**Ruggedness / Toughness**
6	6	5

Basic

			Blown Blocks			Penalties		Team
Year	G	GS	Total	Pass	Rush	Holding	False Starts	Opp Sacks
2016	13	3	6	2	4	1	1	50
2017	12	12	21	13	8	3	1	33
2018	10	10	9	2	7	3	4	29
	35	25	36	17	19	7	6	112

Team Stats

	Zone Run Blocking			Gap Run Blocking			Pass Block
Year	% of Runs	Y/A	Positive%	% of Runs	Y/A	Positive%	Pressure%
2016	34.0%	7.1	48.9%	50.1%	5.9	40.8%	36.2%
2017	59.4%	4.9	39.1%	26.8%	6.5	34.2%	31.8%
2018	70.9%	7.1	43.1%	20.7%	4.2	40.4%	36.2%
	54.0%	6.4	43.1%	33.3%	5.7	39.2%	34.7%

Deep Dive

	Blown Block %		When Running To His Gap				
Year	Pass	Run	Y/A	Yards Before Contact	Positive %	EPA	EPA Per Attempt
2018	1.14%	2.38%	6.6	3.9	47.0%	8.2	0.10

Kaleb McGary

Washington Huskies
Final Grade: 6.5 OT Rank: 8 of 16

Height	Weight	Year	Jersey #	Hometown
6067	321	5SR	58	Fife, WA

One-Liner
McGary is a big-bodied mauler who is strong at the point of attack with good feet, but his lack of reactive athleticism and flexibility may hold him back.

Overall
McGary was a right tackle for Washington in their pro-style, singleback, zone running scheme. He had 47 straight starts at RT and played in 53 games for the Huskies. He has elite size and is a powerful blocker who is also light on his feet, although he is a little stiff and upright with a long torso. He competes through the whistle and sets the tone for the entire offensive line, although he could be a little tougher during the play.

Pass Game
In the pass game, McGary shows inconsistent feet. In Washington's offense, they don't do many true kick slides, and he did a lot of short-setting in their quick passing game. He tends to play a little upright and on his heels which allows defenders to get into his chest and drive him back. When in the right position, he gets his hands on the defender and shuts him down. He does not get beat by power rushes and rarely gets beat by outside speed rushes. He has some trouble against counter moves and skilled hand-fighters.

Run Game
In the run game, McGary is a roadgrader and easily clears out DEs and plays with prime physicality. He has good range on outside runs and is sufficient on the second level. He has good hand placement on combo blocks and moves in-step with the entire line. He can be a little slow getting to the second level and has some trouble getting position on quicker LBs and DBs. He does, however, come in balanced and under control.

Last Word
He projects to start at RT and could make a move inside to guard and back up at the position.

– Kenneth Garron

Strengths	Weaknesses
• Dependability	• Pass block consistency
• Finish	• Reactive athleticism
• Run block strength	• Hand placement

Critical Factors

Reactive Athleticism	Anchor / Play Strength	Balance / Body Control
5	6	6

Positional Factors

Run Block	Pass Block	2nd Level	Awareness / Instincts
6	6	5	6

Hand Use	Range	Sustain / Finish
6	6	7
Power	**Flexibility**	**Ruggedness / Toughness**
7	5	6

Basic

			Blown Blocks			Penalties		Team
Year	G	GS	Total	Pass	Rush	Holding	False Starts	Opp Sacks
2016	14	14	7	3	4	2	0	28
2017	13	13	14	8	6	1	1	20
2018	14	14	7	2	5	5	3	24
	41	41	28	13	15	8	4	72

Team Stats

	Zone Run Blocking			Gap Run Blocking			Pass Block
Year	% of Runs	Y/A	Positive%	% of Runs	Y/A	Positive%	Pressure%
2016	41.2%	4.5	45.3%	49.3%	7.3	48.8%	30.3%
2017	48.9%	5.2	44.1%	41.2%	6.5	48.7%	30.7%
2018	57.2%	4.4	42.7%	31.1%	5.7	47.4%	37.5%
	49.3%	4.7	43.8%	40.3%	6.6	48.4%	32.9%

Deep Dive

	Blown Block %		When Running To His Gap				
Year	Pass	Run	Y/A	Yards Before Contact	Positive %	EPA	EPA Per Attempt
2018	0.47%	0.93%	5.3	2.1	47.9%	16.2	0.10

Yodny Cajuste

West Virginia Mountaineers
Final Grade: 6.5 OT Rank: 9 of 16

Height	Weight	Year	Jersey #	Hometown
6046	321	5SR	55	Miami, FL

One-Liner
Cajuste shows quickness, agility, and run-blocking prowess, but his shaky pass-blocking technique will need to improve or he will get exposed at the next level.

Overall
Cajuste is a left tackle who played in West Virginia's Air Raid offense. He's a four-year starter who started 31 of the 32 games he played at left tackle. His athletic ability is generally good but comes with significant questions. He has good agility and speed, but he cannot always utilize these qualities due to merely sufficient balance and body control. Cajuste shows sufficient competitiveness and toughness regularly but does flash moments of extra aggression which implies he is capable of being tougher than what he generally shows.

Pass Game
In the pass game, Cajuste has gotten good results, but has problems with his hand placement, and will often lunge at defenders. He overuses arm chops to try to knock defenders off-balance instead of focusing on squaring the defender up, landing his hands properly, and latching on. He is also regularly victimized against swim or rip moves because he does not use his hands to control defenders. However, Cajuste does show good awareness when pass blocking; he is quick to identify the most immediate threat to the QB, and handles stunts very well.

Run Game
As a run blocker, Cajuste is very good. He has a powerful first step and hit, and he shows a propensity for keeping his feet moving and driving his man downfield, especially in goal line situations. If he can get his hands placed correctly on a defender, which he does inconsistently, he wins more often than he loses. He has quick feet and good agility while pulling and getting to the second level, but has difficulty finishing because of what he lacks in body control. His inconsistent hand placement is worsened while he is on the move.

Last Word
Cajuste projects as a low-end starter at right tackle by his second season with some ability to back up at left tackle. He is better suited on the outside because he does not consistently exhibit the temperament necessary for an interior offensive lineman.

– Tony Shields

Strengths	**Weaknesses**
• Agility	• Hand-placement consistency
• Heavy hands	• Balance
• Run block strength	• Durability

Critical Factors

Reactive Athleticism	Anchor / Play Strength	Balance / Body Control
6	6	5

Positional Factors

Run Block	Pass Block	2nd Level	Awareness / Instincts
7	6	6	6

Hand Use	Range	Sustain / Finish
5	5	6
Power	**Flexibility**	**Ruggedness / Toughness**
6	6	5

Basic

			Blown Blocks			Penalties		Team
Year	G	GS	Total	Pass	Rush	Holding	False Starts	Opp Sacks
2016	1	1	0	0	0	0	0	26
2017	13	13	17	9	8	5	3	19
2018	11	11	7	5	2	5	2	29
	25	25	24	14	10	10	5	74

Team Stats

	Zone Run Blocking			Gap Run Blocking			Pass Block
Year	% of Runs	Y/A	Positive%	% of Runs	Y/A	Positive%	Pressure%
2016	74.4%	5.9	43.2%	15.7%	5.8	44.9%	24.0%
2017	56.6%	4.7	43.4%	31.1%	4.8	37.3%	24.4%
2018	66.3%	5.7	45.5%	18.8%	4.4	36.7%	22.7%
	66.4%	5.5	43.9%	21.5%	5.0	39.4%	23.7%

Deep Dive

	Blown Block %		When Running To His Gap				
Year	Pass	Run	Y/A	Yards Before Contact	Positive %	EPA	EPA Per Attempt
2018	1.28%	0.65%	5.5	2.7	47.9%	-3.7	-0.05

Tytus Howard

Alabama State Hornets

Final Grade: 6.3 OT Rank: 10 of 16

Height	Weight	Year	Jersey #	Hometown
6050	322	5SR	58	Monroeville, AL

One-Liner

Howard is a quick, reactive athlete that possesses footwork and lateral-movement skills for the next level, but his lack of experience at the position paired with his grabby hands and inconsistent finish make him a few years away.

Overall

Howard primarily played right tackle for the Hornets, mainly due to their primary quarterback being left-handed. Throughout games, they used him interchangeably at both right and left tackle, mainly based on the QB they have in the game. He showed up to ASU as a 200-pound QB/TE but grew in his first year and switched to offensive line as a redshirt freshman. He played in 37 games with 35 starts for Alabama State. As a former quarterback, he has the reactive athleticism needed to play the offensive line position. He competes and plays tough, although his aggression will hopefully come with time, considering he hasn't been a lineman for too long.

Pass Game

In the pass game, he has the footwork and quickness to play the left side. He possesses a quick kick slide and stays parallel to the line of scrimmage, waiting to meet defensive ends at the apex of their bend. He's athletic enough to re-direct and mirror rushers, while still being powerful enough to anchor. Most times he'll need to take a couple steps when engaged to sink his hips, but at that point he's able to anchor and keep away from the quarterback. He keeps good balance and body control at contact, and he rarely goes down to the ground. He doesn't use his length as much as he should. He has long arms and a strong upper body, but is grabby. He has fairly good hand placement, but seems to place his hands on defenders instead of giving a punch. He also waits too long to give an initial punch and allows good defenders to control his chest. He'll get beat on occasion against counters, but he recovers very quickly and easily. He also has the awareness to pass off and take on defenders without giving up much ground.

Run Game

In the run game, his athleticism and leg drive stand out. He has the athletic ability and quickness to reach block, while still having good lateral strength. He's not a mauler, mainly because he fails to use the full potential of his power. When he does latch on, he does a good job sustaining the block and driving his defender out of the play. He can also sustain at the POA and open up run lanes either in the B gap or to the edge. When climbing to the 2nd level, he is usually under control and squares himself to the defender.

Last Word

Howard projects as a backup swing tackle by his second season with the capability of becoming a full-time starter at left tackle once he becomes a more polished lineman. He fits best on the left side due to his quickness and athleticism, but he could play on the right side if needed.

– Nathan Cooper

Strengths	**Weaknesses**
• Raw athleticism	• Grabby with hands
• Footwork	• Doesn't always use his strength
• Lateral movement skills	• Inconsistent finish

Critical Factors

Reactive Athleticism	Anchor / Play Strength	Balance / Body Control
6	5	6

Positional Factors

Run Block	Pass Block	2nd Level	Awareness / Instincts
6	6	6	6

Hand Use	Range	Sustain / Finish
5	6	6
Power	**Flexibility**	**Ruggedness / Toughness**
5	7	6

The 300-plus pound Howard is a former high school quarterback who initially went to Alabama State as a tight end. Though he comes from a small school, he's made a big impact.

"I feel like I've got a chip on my shoulder to prove that I can play with the best of the best," Howard told reporters the week of the Senior Bowl.

Howard demonstrated that on multiple occasions that week, standing out in 1-on-1 drills against the likes of Montez Sweat. In the game, he drove All-ACC selection Zach Allen of Boston College back, clearing the way for a rushing touchdown.

Alabama State didn't have anyone drafted from 2008 to 2016, but Howard could join Jylan Ware as the second player picked from the school in three years. Ware went to the Raiders in the seventh round in 2017.

The highest drafted Alabama State player was defensive end Curtis Green, who was selected 46th overall by the Lions in 1981.

Jawaan Taylor

Florida Gators

Final Grade: 6.3 OT Rank: 11 of 16

Height	Weight	Year	Jersey #	Hometown
6045	328	3JR	65	Cocoa, FL

One-Liner

Taylor is a consistent run blocker and is capable of being an impressive pass protector because of his footwork, but his length and mirror skills should keep him from being a starter on the edges.

Overall

Taylor was a right tackle in Florida's offense, with previous experience starting on the left side as well. He played in 37 career games, starting all but two. He has a large, sturdy frame and average arm length. Taylor has solid athleticism and nimble feet. He plays with toughness and flashes violence in the run game.

Pass Game

As a pass protector, he plays with very good technique in his footwork. He has a good short set anchor and flashes a quick vertical set to keep up with speed, although it is inconsistent. He has quick feet, but doesn't mirror and change directions with sharpness against inside moves. He doesn't lose many battles due to power, but can be stood up and manipulated by longer defenders who beat him to his chest. Taylor's length is an issue on the edge, as he doesn't use it well and struggles to reach some lengthy edges.

Run Game

In the run game, he is strong enough to get a good initial push to open run lanes. He moves to the second level well and does a good job against linebackers, but his range beyond that is inconsistent. He is a much more consistent run blocker than pass protector, where he can have flashes of brilliance but noticeable lapses and limitations. He can be a punisher, attacking with tight elbows and proper form to sustain well. Taylor has had some awareness issues off the snap, not stepping in the correct direction and misidentifying moving parts at times. He was asked to pull inside his right guard often, and was able to flip his hips and fire upfield consistently.

Last Word

Taylor projects as a solid reserve swing tackle at the next level, offering versatility to guard because of his lack of length and strong run blocking abilities. His development at left tackle will need work, but he has a good, natural skillset and flashes of athletic pass protection prowess to hold up as a backup.

– Elijah Cornejo

Strengths	**Weaknesses**
• Run blocking consistency	• Use of length
• Footwork	• Awareness off snap
• Anchor ability	• Mirror skills

Critical Factors

Reactive Athleticism	Anchor / Play Strength	Balance / Body Control
5	6	6

Positional Factors

Run Block	Pass Block	2nd Level	Awareness / Instincts
6	6	6	5

Hand Use	Range	Sustain / Finish
5	5	6
Power	**Flexibility**	**Ruggedness / Toughness**
5	5	6

Basic

			Blown Blocks			Penalties		Team
Year	G	GS	Total	Pass	Rush	Holding	False Starts	Opp Sacks
2016	13	12	12	10	2	1	4	28
2017	11	11	26	14	12	3	3	37
2018	13	12	4	3	1	3	7	18
	37	35	42	27	15	7	14	83

Team Stats

	Zone Run Blocking			Gap Run Blocking			Pass Block
Year	% of Runs	Y/A	Positive%	% of Runs	Y/A	Positive%	Pressure%
2016	67.0%	4.7	43.3%	22.9%	4.3	40.2%	38.7%
2017	59.4%	5.5	42.2%	26.8%	5.0	42.1%	43.4%
2018	63.4%	5.7	48.0%	28.5%	6.1	49.7%	33.2%
	63.4%	5.3	44.8%	26.2%	5.2	44.7%	38.3%

Deep Dive

	Blown Block %		When Running To His Gap				
Year	Pass	Run	Y/A	Yards Before Contact	Positive %	EPA	EPA Per Attempt
2018	0.87%	0.23%	5.8	2.5	51.7%	30.9	0.18

David Edwards

Wisconsin Badgers
Final Grade: 6.3 OT Rank: 12 of 16

Height	Weight	Year	Jersey #	Hometown
6062	315	3JR	79	Downers Grove, IL

One-Liner
Edwards has all of the physical tools to be an athletic tackle on either side, but his instincts, motor and anchor strength will hold him back without development.

Overall
Edwards was a right offensive tackle for Wisconsin's power running scheme. All 31 of his starts came at right tackle, with 37 total games played. However, most of that time was spent protecting the blindside of a left-handed quarterback. Edwards is a good straight line athlete with decent lateral foot quickness and flexibility. He is a finesse lineman with only flashes of tenacity who often ends his play before the whistle. He has shown some competitiveness with having a short memory after blown blocks.

Pass Game
In the pass game, Edwards has a natural kick step. Combined with his get off and length, Edwards is very successful against speed rushes. Against power rushers, his height and lack of knee bend allow rushers to get into him and push him off of his spot. In the previous two seasons, his lack of strength was less noticeable. His lateral quickness makes him susceptible to quicker, more experienced pass rushers, as well. His inability to recover allows rushers to use moves to maneuver around him.

Run Game
In the run game, Edwards uses his size and length to wall off defenders. He has a very quick first step and is able to properly position himself to create running lanes. Once on the second level, he has the athletic ability to attack smaller defenders. His instincts often pop up as an issue, as he can lose track of his surroundings.

Last Word
Overall, Edwards has the size, length, and raw athleticism the NFL is looking for. He is able to get his body in the right position and could become a starting tackle if he can increase his strength. His current projection suggests he is best suited as a backup swing tackle.

– Ben Hrkach

Strengths	Weaknesses
• Size and length	• Anchor strength
• First step	• Lateral quickness
• Blocking in space	• Motor

Critical Factors

Reactive Athleticism	Anchor / Play Strength	Balance / Body Control
6	5	5

Positional Factors

Run Block	Pass Block	2nd Level	Awareness / Instincts
5	6	6	5

Hand Use	Range	Sustain / Finish
6	6	5
Power	**Flexibility**	**Ruggedness / Toughness**
5	5	5

Basic

			Blown Blocks			Penalties		Team
Year	G	GS	Total	Pass	Rush	Holding	False Starts	Opp Sacks
2016	13	7	6	4	2	1	3	24
2017	14	14	10	4	6	1	5	21
2018	10	10	11	7	4	2	2	25
	37	31	27	15	12	4	10	70

Team Stats

	Zone Run Blocking			Gap Run Blocking			Pass Block
Year	% of Runs	Y/A	Positive%	% of Runs	Y/A	Positive%	Pressure%
2016	53.3%	4.7	42.6%	40.5%	5.0	42.4%	32.6%
2017	64.1%	5.5	41.4%	31.4%	5.4	44.6%	37.0%
2018	63.3%	6.6	53.3%	29.3%	7.2	51.5%	28.6%
	60.0%	5.6	45.7%	34.0%	5.7	45.5%	32.8%

Deep Dive

	Blown Block %		When Running To His Gap				
Year	Pass	Run	Y/A	Yards Before Contact	Positive %	EPA	EPA Per Attempt
2018	2.81%	1.03%	6.2	2.8	49.4%	8.3	0.09

Calvin Anderson

Texas Longhorns
Final Grade: 6.3 OT Rank: 13 of 16

Height	Weight	Year	Jersey #	Hometown
6052	300	5SR	66	Austin, TX

One-Liner
Anderson is a strong, physical tackle who is an adept run blocker and has the tools to be a solid left tackle but needs to refine his pass blocking techniques.

Overall
Anderson was a left tackle for Texas after transferring from Rice as a graduate student. Anderson started all 36 games in his career at left tackle with the Owls, and all 14 in 2018 for the Longhorns. He has good size and length, with decent athleticism stemming from his background as a multi-sport athlete in high school. He plays with an edge and does a good job of keeping his head on a swivel looking for extra blocks.

Pass Game
In the pass game, Anderson has some waist bending tendencies. His technique is inconsistent and he plays on his toes with a wide base, which lead to difficulties anchoring at times. He is a physical player and has heavy hands to deliver a strong first punch with his length. His balance and footwork in pass protection need refinement, but he has some natural talent. Anderson recovers well and can redirect bigger and smaller linemen.

Run Game
He is a stronger player in the run game, where he can attack and drive with aggression. He moves to the second level well and stonewalls linebackers. Anderson is a strong finisher and latches on with good grip strength to sustain and take opponents to the ground.

Last Word
Despite some of his technical issues, Anderson is rarely a liability and has had sustained success at two programs. He has already proven he could make the jump from a smaller conference to the Big 12, and has the athletic profile, length and aggression of an NFL player, as well. Anderson projects as a right tackle with the necessary traits to swing to both sides at the next level, as he doesn't possess a significant strength nor an unfixable weaknesses.

– Gennady Gusak

Strengths	Weaknesses
• First punch power	• Pass protection technique
• Run blocking	• Flexibility
• Athletic tools	• Balance

Critical Factors

Reactive Athleticism	Anchor / Play Strength	Balance / Body Control
5	6	5

Positional Factors

Run Block	Pass Block	2nd Level	Awareness / Instincts
6	5	6	5

Hand Use	Range	Sustain / Finish
6	5	6
Power	**Flexibility**	**Ruggedness / Toughness**
6	5	6

Basic

			Blown Blocks			Penalties		Team
Year	G	GS	Total	Pass	Rush	Holding	False Starts	Opp Sacks
2016	12	12	16	11	5	4	4	33
2017	12	12	7	2	5	1	1	27
2018	14	14	18	13	5	4	2	28
	38	38	41	26	15	9	7	88

Team Stats

	Zone Run Blocking			Gap Run Blocking			Pass Block
Year	% of Runs	Y/A	Positive%	% of Runs	Y/A	Positive%	Pressure%
2016	69.5%	4.8	43.0%	14.0%	4.4	37.1%	32.4%
2017	73.8%	5.0	42.4%	13.6%	5.1	45.8%	37.3%
2018	62.0%	4.4	45.3%	24.0%	4.0	44.4%	32.2%
	67.9%	4.7	43.6%	17.7%	4.4	42.9%	33.4%

Deep Dive

	Blown Block %		When Running To His Gap				
Year	Pass	Run	Y/A	Yards Before Contact	Positive %	EPA	EPA Per Attempt
2018	2.57%	0.93%	5.0	2.2	46.4%	-6.3	-0.05

Mitch Hyatt

Clemson Tigers

Final Grade: 6.2 OT Rank: 14 of 16

Height	Weight	Year	Jersey #	Hometown
6052	310	4SR	75	Suwanee, GA

One-Liner

Hyatt had an illustrious career for the Tigers at left tackle, but his balance, ability to sustain blocks, and pass protect with sound technique suggest he's more of a versatile backup at the next level.

Overall

Hyatt played as an offensive tackle in Clemson's balanced offense, playing mostly out of a two-point stance. He has made 57 career starts for the Tigers. He has very good size and solid length. He has good athletic traits and decent movement skills. He is an aggressive player moving forward, and prefers to take the game to his opponents.

Pass Game

Hyatt is a sufficient pass protector who relies more on his reactive athleticism than strength and footwork. He pushes off the snap quickly and has good form with his vertical sets, but he often crosses his feet against speed. He has some waist-bending tendencies, which contribute to his occasional struggles with balance in all phases. He mirrors well and shows good awareness to pass off rushers. He is a decent hand fighter at the point of attack, but doesn't win many of those battles. Hyatt has difficulties anchoring against bull rushes, especially when he gives up his chest, and he does not have the ability to sit with flexibility to counter.

Run Game

In the run game, he attacks with aggression and very good leverage. He sticks his nose into defenders and generates good power from his hip explosion to knock players off the ball, especially on down blocks. He has a good base to drive, but finds himself on the ground quite a bit. His hand use and balance make it difficult for him to sustain blocks, and he rarely finishes to the ground. Hyatt puts himself in good position in the run game and doesn't often miss assignments. He moves well, and while he has some inconsistencies against quicker second level defenders, he can get out in front of screens with speed and handle defensive backs.

Last Word

Hyatt has done a sufficient job for the Tigers and has had a great deal of team success in his career, but despite his starting record, he projects best as a backup lineman at the next level. He profiles as a versatile backup, with experience on the blind side, but a skillset more suited for right tackle or even inside at guard.

– Cole Ratliff

Strengths	**Weaknesses**
• Run blocking	• Pass protection technique
• Range	• Balance and anchor
• Awareness	• Sustaining blocks

Critical Factors

Reactive Athleticism	Anchor / Play Strength	Balance / Body Control
6	5	5

Positional Factors

Run Block	Pass Block	2nd Level	Awareness / Instincts
7	5	5	6

Hand Use	Range	Sustain / Finish
5	6	4
Power	**Flexibility**	**Ruggedness / Toughness**
6	5	6

Basic

			Blown Blocks			Penalties		Team
Year	G	GS	Total	Pass	Rush	Holding	False Starts	Opp Sacks
2016	15	14	10	6	4	7	3	21
2017	13	13	15	12	3	2	1	31
2018	15	15	22	14	8	2	0	19
	43	42	47	32	15	11	4	71

Team Stats

	Zone Run Blocking			Gap Run Blocking			Pass Block
Year	% of Runs	Y/A	Positive%	% of Runs	Y/A	Positive%	Pressure%
2016	55.8%	4.6	42.0%	35.8%	5.0	48.1%	22.7%
2017	49.4%	4.9	47.5%	37.5%	5.5	44.4%	27.9%
2018	60.4%	7.1	50.9%	32.2%	7.1	53.8%	23.2%
	55.2%	5.6	46.8%	35.2%	5.8	48.5%	24.4%

Deep Dive

	Blown Block %		When Running To His Gap				
Year	Pass	Run	Y/A	Yards Before Contact	Positive %	EPA	EPA Per Attempt
2018	3.11%	1.94%	6.4	3.9	51.4%	13.2	0.12

Dennis Daley

South Carolina Gamecocks
Final Grade: 6.2 OT Rank: 15 of 16

Height	Weight	Year	Jersey #	Hometown
6050	304	4SR	74	Columbia, SC

One-Liner
Daley possesses the size, footwork, and strength to project as a solid right side backup with the potential to start at times, but he'll struggle with agile speed rushers.

Overall
Daley's primary college position was left offensive tackle. He was a two-year starter since transferring to South Carolina from junior college. Daley is a solid athlete for his size, with decent range, lateral agility, and good play strength. His awareness is sufficient, but he struggles with picking up on delayed blitzes and knowing when, and when not to, help his guard. Daley's hands are strong but a bit slow. He has a tendency to get both of his hands on the outside of his opponent's shoulder pads, which will likely result in a lot of holding calls at the next level if he doesn't break the habit.

Pass Game
As a pass blocker, Daley is sufficient. He can be beaten by straight speed rushes but his good anchor and flashes of power with good hip explosion help him to hold his own against most other types of rushes. He is at his best when in slide protection or screen blocking, as those help to showcase his lateral agility and movement skills.

Run Game
Daley's best phase is as a run blocker. He shows good play strength and range, and he is a good blocker when he gets to the second level.

Last Word
Daley's issues with pass protection awareness and inconsistent hand usage will likely prevent him from playing on the blind side at the NFL level, but he has the size, strength and athletic traits to be able to serve as a backup at right tackle and possibly guard in his first two seasons.

– Ronan Potts

Strengths	Weaknesses
• Hip explosion • Play strength • Lateral agility	• Speed rushers • Composure

Critical Factors

Reactive Athleticism	Anchor / Play Strength	Balance / Body Control
5	6	5

Positional Factors

Run Block	Pass Block	2nd Level	Awareness / Instincts
6	5	6	5

Hand Use	Range	Sustain / Finish
5	5	5
Power	**Flexibility**	**Ruggedness / Toughness**
5	6	5

Basic

			Blown Blocks			Penalties		Team
Year	G	GS	Total	Pass	Rush	Holding	False Starts	Opp Sacks
2017	12	11	22	18	4	0	2	29
2018	12	12	10	9	1	1	1	24
	24	23	32	27	5	1	3	53

Team Stats

	Zone Run Blocking			Gap Run Blocking			Pass Block
Year	% of Runs	Y/A	Positive%	% of Runs	Y/A	Positive%	Pressure%
2017	53.4%	4.4	43.1%	32.4%	5.4	43.0%	36.2%
2018	63.6%	5.2	39.6%	24.0%	5.4	45.7%	36.6%
	58.8%	4.9	41.1%	28.0%	5.4	44.2%	36.4%

Deep Dive

	Blown Block %		When Running To His Gap				
Year	Pass	Run	Y/A	Yards Before Contact	Positive %	EPA	EPA Per Attempt
2018	2.26%	0.31%	5.4	3.0	42.3%	0.6	0.01

Derrick Kelly II

Florida State Seminoles
Final Grade: 6.2 OT Rank: 16 of 16

Height	Weight	Year	Jersey #	Hometown
6046	320	5SR	74	Gretna, FL

One-Liner
Kelly is a smart, strong, and versatile player who uses his hands very well and adapts to his opponent throughout the game, but his lack of quickness and athleticism should keep him from starting in the NFL.

Overall
Kelly's primary position at Florida State was right tackle but he played left tackle and guard in his career, as well. He played in 34 games and started 28. Kelly is a below-average natural athlete with good anticipation and reaction skills. He is a tough player who demonstrates some nastiness in his blocks but struggles to stay healthy, as he missed time in two different seasons with the Seminoles.

Pass Game
In the pass game, Kelly makes very good use of his hands. He has a quick punch to engage defenders, followed by very good arm extension to keep them at bay. His hand placement is also very good and generally stays penalty-free. He has a very good anchor and won't be bull rushed due to his play strength. Kelly is a smart player and he adjusts well to his opponents in game, rarely getting beat by the same move twice. He also has the awareness and instincts to read blitzes well and react despite his limited athleticism. Kelly is most vulnerable to quicker edge rushers. He has a shallow first step off the ball and he doesn't have the quick footwork and movement skills to keep up with speed. In an attempt to make up for his lack of quickness, he tends to cross over and overcommit outside, leaving the inside open.

Run Game
In the run game, Kelly provides a physical presence on the offensive line and has demonstrated good power and good ability to hold his blocks to the whistle and finish them with authority. He has consistently demonstrated the ability to keep his feet moving and drive defenders after initial contact. However, he has average range due to his lack of athleticism. He is slow off the snap to reach, but he typically takes good angles and can use his size to wall and shield. He displays limited foot quickness and body control to pull and adjust at the second level.

Last Word
With his traits and his wealth of experience playing all over Florida State's line, Kelly projects to be a versatile backup offensive lineman. He should primarily play right tackle but has the size and strength to bump inside to guard.

– Nick Aiello

Strengths

- Physicality
- Hand use
- Versatility

Weaknesses

- Athleticism
- Range
- Second level ability

Critical Factors

Reactive Athleticism	Anchor / Play Strength	Balance / Body Control
4	7	5

Positional Factors

Run Block	Pass Block	2nd Level	Awareness / Instincts
5	6	4	6

Hand Use	Range	Sustain / Finish
7	4	6
Power	**Flexibility**	**Ruggedness / Toughness**
6	4	5

Basic

			Blown Blocks			Penalties		Team
Year	G	GS	Total	Pass	Rush	Holding	False Starts	Opp Sacks
2016	5	2	3	2	1	0	1	37
2017	13	13	28	13	15	0	3	32
2018	10	9	13	12	1	2	6	37
	28	24	44	27	17	2	10	106

Team Stats

	Zone Run Blocking			Gap Run Blocking			Pass Block
Year	% of Runs	Y/A	Positive%	% of Runs	Y/A	Positive%	Pressure%
2016	65.6%	5.9	48.0%	23.8%	7.4	51.2%	33.3%
2017	69.9%	5.4	46.4%	19.2%	4.4	31.8%	39.8%
2018	56.4%	4.4	31.8%	26.5%	2.0	24.5%	37.3%
	64.4%	5.3	43.4%	23.0%	4.8	37.0%	36.6%

Deep Dive

	Blown Block %		When Running To His Gap				
Year	Pass	Run	Y/A	Yards Before Contact	Positive %	EPA	EPA Per Attempt
2018	2.99%	0.39%	3.8	1.1	29.3%	-13.8	-0.17

OFFENSIVE GUARD

Offensive Guard Grading Scale

GRADE	DESCRIPTION
9.0 – 7.0	High-end starter. Pro Bowl level.
6.9 – 6.7	Strong starter with 2 position flexibility.
6.6 – 6.5	Lower end starter. Backup flexibility at OG or OC.
6.4	Starter with no position flexibility.
6.2	Multi-positional backup.
6.1 – 6.0	Developmental. Top traits but needs time.
5.7	Backup with no position flexibility. #4 OG or #3 OC.

Offensive Guard Rankings

Michael Deiter

Wisconsin Badgers

Final Grade: 6.8 OG Rank: 1 of 16

Height	Weight	Year	Jersey #	Hometown
6050	304	5SR	63	Curtice, OH

One-Liner

Deiter possesses an ideal combination of durability, toughness, versatility and experience to excel early at multiple positions across an offensive line.

Overall

Deiter played offensive guard in Wisconsin's pro-style offense. He has played and started in all 54 games of his record-breaking career, including 24 starts at left guard, 16 starts at center, and 14 starts at left tackle. He is a good athlete with very good movement skills, but lacks arm length. He's as durable as it gets and plays with a nasty disposition.

Pass Game

As a pass blocker, Deiter uses his strong core and lower half to anchor and stalemate interior rushers. He has very good ankle flexion to bend and uses great technique. He is a good reactive athlete but misses some punches against quicker rushers at the point of attack. He handled himself well against edge rushers at left tackle, but might struggle with speed at the next level. He's great at looking for work when unoccupied but has some misreads and can be slow to identify blitzes and stunts. Deiter takes the game to the defense, so his arm length is less of an issue inside.

Run Game

Deiter is a much more comfortable run blocker than pass protector. He fires off the ball quickly in both directions and has explosive heavy hands in the phone booth. He keeps his elbows tight and has excellent grip strength to manipulate defenders when kept close. Deiter is a load at first contact and a mauler at the whistle, usually winning one-on-one battles quickly and takes advantage of worn-down defenders. He has heavy feet as a drive blocker and a mean streak to finish for four quarters. His arm length hinders his ability to sustain blocks at a consistent high level and leads to some balance issues when being shed. He has the athleticism to get out in space and pulls very well, but second-level defenders can use their short-area quickness to avoid direct contact, which occasionally results in lunging. Deiter works very well with double teams, combo and down blocks, and has great hips to flip and seal run lanes.

Last Word

He's an extremely durable, reliable, and tough workhorse who will play from day one and for a long time in the NFL. He projects best as a guard in a power blocking scheme, but has the overall versatility to fill in at nearly every position across the offensive line and in various schemes. He could hold up at right tackle if necessary and has experience at center, but his lack of elite short-area quickness and anticipation suggest his best position is at guard.

– John Todd

Strengths

- Heavy hands and finishing
- Toughness/durability
- Versatility

Weaknesses

- Quickness at point of attack
- Pass protection awareness
- Length

Critical Factors

Reactive Athleticism	Anchor / Play Strength	Balance / Body Control
6	7	6

Positional Factors

Run Block	Pass Block	2nd Level	Awareness / Instincts
7	6	6	5

Hand Use	Range	Sustain / Finish
7	5	7
Power	**Flexibility**	**Ruggedness / Toughness**
7	7	8

Basic

			Blown Blocks			Penalties		Team
Year	G	GS	Total	Pass	Rush	Holding	False Starts	Opp Sacks
2016	14	14	16	9	7	0	0	24
2017	14	14	19	7	12	1	3	21
2018	13	13	11	2	9	5	1	25
	41	41	46	18	28	6	4	70

Team Stats

	Zone Run Blocking			Gap Run Blocking			Pass Block
Year	% of Runs	Y/A	Positive%	% of Runs	Y/A	Positive%	Pressure%
2016	53.3%	4.7	42.6%	40.5%	5.0	42.4%	32.6%
2017	64.1%	5.5	41.4%	31.4%	5.4	44.6%	37.0%
2018	63.3%	6.6	53.3%	29.3%	7.2	51.5%	28.6%
	60.0%	5.6	45.7%	34.0%	5.7	45.5%	32.8%

Deep Dive

	Blown Block %		When Running To His Gap				
Year	Pass	Run	Y/A	Yards Before Contact	Positive %	EPA	EPA Per Attempt
2018	0.61%	1.76%	6.5	3.1	53.1%	19.6	0.09

Nate Davis

Charlotte 49ers

Final Grade: 6.8 OG Rank: 2 of 16

Height	Weight	Year	Jersey #	Hometown
6033	317	5SR	64	Ashburn, VA

One-Liner

Davis is an impressively flexible and athletic offensive lineman who possesses the necessary technique and body composition to become a very solid NFL starting guard.

Overall

Davis was an offensive guard and tackle from Charlotte's zone-heavy blocking scheme. He played in 41 career games, with 30 starts coming at right guard and 7 at right tackle to finish his career after being suspended for the first four games of his senior season. He's an impressive athlete for his size, with very quick feet, good length, and excellent flexibility. He flashes a nasty streak, finishing opponents to the ground and extending blocks through the whistle.

Pass Game

In pass protection, Davis has great technique but can be undone by misreads and moving pieces at tackle. He has excellent footwork and shows high- quality hand usage inside to keep rushers off balance. He does a good job of passing off twists, but against quicker and longer edge rushers he can struggle with first contact and hand accuracy, leading to pressures via push-pull moves and speed around the arc. Davis has trouble when giving up his chest, but he has the strength and bend to sit and anchor, especially inside.

Run Game

In the run game, Davis has the strength and athleticism to move defenders at all levels. He blocks with excellent form, possessing an ideal blend of ankle flexion, upper body leverage, and balance. At the line of scrimmage, he looks like a tight end in his three point stance - it's rare to see someone his size sit so low in his stance and still have the explosion off the snap forwards and backwards. He's aggressive at the point of attack and has a very strong first punch downhill. Davis has great footwork and movement skills and plays with a fundamental base. He is very good in space and has quick, explosive hips to pull inside and out. He down blocks hard, but also has the hips, lateral movement, and combo-blocking skills to excel in zone. He keeps his elbows tight and drives well. Playing over his feet with his aggressive nature leads to occasional balance issues or lunges, but his form when engaged is very sound. He possesses good grip strength to sustain blocks and finishes very well when locked in.

Last Word

In the NFL, Davis projects as a very good starter at guard in any offense but primarily in gap-based schemes. With his tenacity, athleticism, flexibility, and technique, he can excel inside at the next level. While he has the footwork and athleticism to be a sufficient right tackle, his length against edge defenders and inconsistency diagnosing blitzes and stunts suggest his best position is at guard.

– John Todd

Strengths

- Bend/ankle flexion
- Pulling ability
- Footwork and base

Weaknesses

- Blitz and stunt reads
- Speed rushes off the edge

Critical Factors

Reactive Athleticism	Anchor / Play Strength	Balance / Body Control
7	6	6

Positional Factors

Run Block	Pass Block	2nd Level	Awareness / Instincts
7	6	6	4

Hand Use	Range	Sustain / Finish
7	7	7
Power	**Flexibility**	**Ruggedness / Toughness**
6	8	7

Basic

			Blown Blocks			Penalties		Team
Year	G	GS	Total	Pass	Rush	Holding	False Starts	Opp Sacks
2016	9	8	6	3	3	0	0	22
2017	12	12	11	7	4	0	3	22
2018	8	7	4	1	3	1	2	37
	29	27	21	11	10	1	5	81

Team Stats

	Zone Run Blocking			Gap Run Blocking			Pass Block
Year	% of Runs	Y/A	Positive%	% of Runs	Y/A	Positive%	Pressure%
2016	61.8%	4.7	40.9%	28.2%	5.2	45.9%	26.7%
2017	71.5%	5.3	35.6%	15.7%	4.4	25.4%	38.6%
2018	55.3%	4.5	39.7%	28.1%	4.5	34.2%	39.3%
	62.3%	4.8	38.7%	24.4%	4.8	37.0%	34.2%

Deep Dive

	Blown Block %		When Running To His Gap				
Year	Pass	Run	Y/A	Yards Before Contact	Positive %	EPA	EPA Per Attempt
2018	0.52%	1.11%	4.7	1.4	37.5%	-10.7	-0.10

Chris Lindstrom

Boston College Eagles

Final Grade: 6.8 OG Rank: 3 of 16

Height	Weight	Year	Jersey #	Hometown
6036	303	4SR	75	Dudley, MA

One-Liner

Lindstrom is a strong, mauling guard who shows the awareness and power to deliver a blow to defenders, but needs to use his hands more effectively.

Overall

Lindstrom played RG for Boston College's run-heavy, pro-style offense. He played in 50 career games, starting in 48 of them. He started most of his time at RG but played RT in the 2017 season. He has good size with a long torso and smallish chest. He's a good athlete who has some reactive athleticism and mirror ability. He has sufficient flexibility and doesn't sit incredibly low in his stance. He's a rugged player who plays hard and with toughness.

Pass Game

In the pass game, he has quick feet and moves well to stay with defenders. He has a very good anchor and very good play strength. He can short-set quickly and allow his QB time in the pocket. One of his best traits is his awareness. He is always looking for work and helps out his teammates when no one is rushing over him. He handles slant rushers and redirects them quickly and easily. He uses his hands well against interior rushers, although he will allow them to get into his chest on occasion.

Run Game

In the run game, he shows good range. He has the ability to pull, get to the second level, and block multiple defenders on a play. He combo-blocks very well and is quick to combo to the second level. He shows lateral strength and mobility in the run game and can get down the line with power. Lindstrom shows tendencies to rely on his strength in the run game and not use his hands as much as he should. He shows good body control and balance at the POA. His balance and footwork were evident when he played tackle in 2017. He has solid range and can reach defenders easily. He sustains his blocks and finishes through the whistle.

Last Word

Lindstrom projects as a starting right guard at the next level. He could fit in at left guard and center if he can snap the ball.

– Ian Riley

Strengths

- Looking for work in pass pro
- Run blocking
- Play strength

Weaknesses

- Inconsistent hand use
- Flexibility

Critical Factors

Reactive Athleticism	Anchor / Play Strength	Balance / Body Control
6	7	6

Positional Factors

Run Block	Pass Block	2nd Level	Awareness / Instincts
7	6	6	7

Hand Use	Range	Sustain / Finish
6	6	7
Power	**Flexibility**	**Ruggedness / Toughness**
7	5	6

Basic

			Blown Blocks			Penalties		Team
Year	G	GS	Total	Pass	Rush	Holding	False Starts	Opp Sacks
2016	13	13	12	6	6	0	0	29
2017	13	13	15	10	5	0	1	14
2018	12	12	5	0	5	1	0	24
	38	38	32	16	16	1	1	67

Team Stats

	Zone Run Blocking			Gap Run Blocking			Pass Block
Year	% of Runs	Y/A	Positive%	% of Runs	Y/A	Positive%	Pressure%
2016	53.2%	4.1	32.1%	37.1%	3.8	27.7%	32.0%
2017	59.8%	5.4	41.0%	30.6%	4.0	36.4%	34.2%
2018	64.3%	4.8	38.9%	28.7%	4.8	40.6%	30.2%
	59.1%	4.8	37.7%	32.1%	4.1	34.3%	32.2%

Deep Dive

	Blown Block %		When Running To His Gap				
Year	Pass	Run	Y/A	Yards Before Contact	Positive %	EPA	EPA Per Attempt
2018	0.00%	0.99%	3.5	1.3	35.9%	-34.2	-0.16

Beau Benzschawel

Wisconsin Badgers

Final Grade: 6.8 OG Rank: 4 of 16

Height	Weight	Year	Jersey #	Hometown
6062	307	5SR	66	Grafton, WI

One-Liner

Benzschawel is a very tall interior lineman with great strength, hands, and awareness to flash dominance in the run and pass game.

Overall

Benzschawel was an offensive guard in Wisconsin's run heavy offense, where he started 49 straight games, 43 at right guard. He is very tall for an interior lineman but has proportionally shorter arms, with a strong but undefined build. He is a decent athlete for his size but lacks the agility to hold up on the edge. He has proven durability and toughness, and plays with grit.

Pass Game

As a pass blocker, Benzschawel plays with a very good anchor and punch at the point of attack to seal a strong pocket. He plays with a wide base and doesn't allow his height to affect his leverage or chest exposure along the interior. Benzschawel has great, savvy hands to negate rush moves and keep arms out of passing lanes. His reactive athleticism is decent and can be masked inside a bit, but he makes up for it with very good pass protection awareness to pass off stunts and read moving pieces up front.

Run Game

As a run blocker, Benzschawel creates very good push with his play strength and heavy hands to wear down opponents. He works well on combo blocks to the second level but his range and athleticism in space is a weakness. He doesn't drive and chop his feet consistently, but his grip strength allows him to lock on and sustain and finish well.

Last Word

Benzschawel projects as a strong starting interior lineman with some flexibility to tackle. Despite being very tall for a guard, he has the strength and leverage ability to win inside at a consistent level in the run and pass game.

– SIS Scouting Staff

Strengths	Weaknesses
• Heavy hand use	• Lateral agility
• Anchor	• Range
• Pass pro awareness	• Foot quickness

Critical Factors

Reactive Athleticism	Anchor / Play Strength	Balance / Body Control
5	7	7

Positional Factors

Run Block	Pass Block	2nd Level	Awareness / Instincts
7	7	6	7

Hand Use	Range	Sustain / Finish
7	5	6
Power	**Flexibility**	**Ruggedness / Toughness**
6	6	7

Basic

			Blown Blocks			Penalties		Team
Year	G	GS	Total	Pass	Rush	Holding	False Starts	Opp Sacks
2016	14	14	23	15	8	0	1	24
2017	14	14	21	6	15	1	3	21
2018	13	13	8	2	6	0	3	25
	41	41	52	23	29	1	7	70

Team Stats

	Zone Run Blocking			Gap Run Blocking			Pass Block
Year	% of Runs	Y/A	Positive%	% of Runs	Y/A	Positive%	Pressure%
2016	53.3%	4.7	42.6%	40.5%	5.0	42.4%	32.6%
2017	64.1%	5.5	41.4%	31.4%	5.4	44.6%	37.0%
2018	63.3%	6.6	53.3%	29.3%	7.2	51.5%	28.6%
	60.0%	5.6	45.7%	34.0%	5.7	45.5%	32.8%

Deep Dive

	Blown Block %		When Running To His Gap				
Year	Pass	Run	Y/A	Yards Before Contact	Positive %	EPA	EPA Per Attempt
2018	0.62%	1.19%	7.5	2.9	51.1%	35.3	0.16

Connor McGovern

Penn State Nittany Lions
Final Grade: 6.7 OG Rank: 5 of 16

Height	Weight	Year	Jersey #	Hometown
6050	323	3JR	66	Larksville, PA

One-Liner
McGovern is a durable and versatile interior lineman whose intelligence and experience will allow him to succeed early at the next level, despite his tendency to concede first contact in the pass game.

Overall
McGovern was a right guard with significant experience at center in Penn State's mostly zone blocking scheme. He played in all 38 games in his career, and after becoming the full-time starter five games into his freshman year, he logged 20 starts at right guard and 14 at center. McGovern has a very good frame for the position with no bad weight and decent arm length. He is a good athlete with average foot quickness compensated by his intelligence and ability to anticipate and adjust to stunts and blitzes. He's a tough and durable competitor who takes the game to his opponents for four quarters.

Pass Game
In the pass game, McGovern plays with good footwork but an average initial punch and extension. He struggles with leverage and too often gives up his chest to first contact. However, his impressive core strength and ankle flexion allow him to recover and anchor against most interior rushers. He has shown the ability to kick slide along the arc to mirror speed from finesse rushers, as well as absorb contact at the point of attack and adjust against power. He combines his anticipation with his sound base to consistently handle counter moves. His awareness is only average at center, where he is a step late reacting to stunts while looking to help on both sides of the interior. At guard, where his reads are limited to half of the defensive front, he shows very good instincts to pass off twisting defenders and attack when looking for work.

Run Game
In the run game, McGovern shows very good leg drive and tenacity on down blocks, consistently moving defenders off the ball, especially from the guard position. He doesn't generate the same power or aggressiveness as a center, particularly against nose defenders. He has the athleticism to combo and make blocks at the second level, as well as pull and kick out edge defenders down the line of scrimmage, all while sustaining his technique with a very good base. He has flashed a nasty attitude to overpower and finish defenders.

Last Word
McGovern projects as an early starter at offensive guard in any blocking scheme with position flexibility to sufficiently handle the requirements at center if needed.

– John Todd

Strengths	Weaknesses
• Adjustments to twists and stunts • Leg drive and aggression • Durability	• Leverage in pass protection • Hand usage and extension

Critical Factors

Reactive Athleticism	Anchor / Play Strength	Balance / Body Control
6	6	7

Positional Factors

Run Block	Pass Block	2nd Level	Awareness / Instincts
7	6	6	7

Hand Use	Range	Sustain / Finish
5	6	6
Power	**Flexibility**	**Ruggedness / Toughness**
7	5	7

Basic

			Blown Blocks			Penalties		Team
Year	G	GS	Total	Pass	Rush	Holding	False Starts	Opp Sacks
2016	13	9	19	9	10	0	3	24
2017	13	13	23	14	9	2	0	29
2018	12	12	10	4	6	2	0	31
	38	34	52	27	25	4	3	84

Team Stats

	Zone Run Blocking			Gap Run Blocking			Pass Block
Year	% of Runs	Y/A	Positive%	% of Runs	Y/A	Positive%	Pressure%
2016	53.9%	4.3	35.2%	35.7%	6.6	49.5%	40.3%
2017	53.5%	5.3	45.8%	31.5%	6.3	51.8%	34.5%
2018	54.2%	5.6	48.0%	28.5%	5.6	43.5%	34.2%
	53.9%	5.0	42.8%	32.0%	6.2	48.3%	36.3%

Deep Dive

	Blown Block %		When Running To His Gap				
Year	Pass	Run	Y/A	Yards Before Contact	Positive %	EPA	EPA Per Attempt
2018	1.01%	1.33%	6.5	3.4	50.9%	31.4	0.14

BJ Autry

Jacksonville State Gamecocks
Final Grade: 6.6 OG Rank: 6 of 16

Height	Weight	Year	Jersey #	Hometown
6032	351	5SR	79	Eight Mile, AL

One-Liner
Autry is a massive, powerful lineman with surprising quickness and athleticism, but will be making a big leap from the FCS level, where his easy dominance and sufficient hands will take time to translate.

Overall
Autry was a left guard in Jacksonville State's balanced run scheme. He started at the junior college level where he was an All-American before transferring to Baylor and then to Jacksonville State, where he started all 25 games of his career. He is a massive human being who doesn't possess as much bad weight as expected, but needs to keep his weight under control. Despite his thick size, he doesn't have much of a backside. He is surprisingly agile and a good space player by any standards. He consistently plays through the whistle with a dominant mindset at his level of competition, imposing his will and finishing with regularity.

Pass Game
In the pass game, Autry is able to stop the power rush with ease at the FCS level. Stronger defenders have exposed his anchor technique on occasion, as he can be toppled up high when caught off guard not sitting with proper form. He is slow off the snap but sets with good, quick feet and a wide base. He shows good awareness to react to moving pieces up front. His hand accuracy is often an issue he gets away with. At the next level, he will need to punch with more consistent placement in order to sustain with consistency. Blitzers and smaller linemen are swallowed up at first contact when he locks on. He is very flexible for his size and can roll and explode his hips with good form, but playing at his weight has its limitations.

Run Game
In the run game, Autry uses his massive size and lower body strength to drive most defenders well off the ball. He doesn't merely lean into the defender and use his size to generate power - Autry engages his defender with sound positioning and keeps his feet moving. He is not limited schematically, as he can move laterally with solid block sustain, but is best in a power scheme where he can wash entire lines down and sufficiently flip his hips and move across the line. He gets to the second level well and has impressive range to the outside, wreaking havoc against corners and other smaller space players. Autry again gets by with inconsistent hand accuracy in the run game, where if he misses, his girth will often pass as a sufficient obstacle.

Last Word
In the NFL, Autry projects to be a strong contributor at the guard position, despite the jump in competition level. It may take him a year, but given his reactive athleticism and run blocking prowess, he profiles well to the next level, and could even fill in at right tackle if necessary. He will need to adjust to superior competition, improve his hand technique, and maintain his weight, but he has a high ceiling.

– Gennady Gusak

Strengths	Weaknesses
• Power	• Hand accuracy
• Athleticism for size	• Anchor technique
• Finishing tenacity	• Weight control

Critical Factors

Reactive Athleticism	Anchor / Play Strength	Balance / Body Control
6	7	6

Positional Factors

Run Block	Pass Block	2nd Level	Awareness / Instincts
7	6	6	6

Hand Use	Range	Sustain / Finish
5	6	7
Power	**Flexibility**	**Ruggedness / Toughness**
7	6	7

Michael Jordan

Ohio State Buckeyes
Final Grade: 6.6 OG Rank: 7 of 16

Height	Weight	Year	Jersey #	Hometown
6062	312	4JR	73	Canton, MI

One-Liner
Jordan is a position-versatile guard who has shown adaptability, excels in the phone booth, and has the athleticism to move laterally.

Overall
Jordan's primary position is offensive guard, where he made 27 starts in his career, though he also started 14 games at center in 2018. He is a good athlete with very good knee and hip flexion, good foot agility and lateral movement skills, and very good mirror/ match skills. He is a very aggressive blocker and often plays with a nasty attitude. Jordan's athleticism and competitiveness were not evident during the beginning stages of his transition to center, but became clearer as he became more comfortable.

Pass Game
In the pass game, Jordan plays with decent awareness and quick reactions. He regularly handles stunts smoothly, identifies and addresses inside rushing threats, and keeps his eyes out for delayed blitzes. Jordan showed significant instinctual lapses early in his junior season, but there were obvious improvements as he adapted to the position. He shows good short area play strength, and uses his violent hands and leverage to neutralize stronger interior rushers in pass protection.

Run Game
In the run game, Jordan can get significant push on combination blocks and will regularly finish his man to the ground. He is a powerful and aggressive zone blocker, and generates most of his strength from his lower body. He will not usually dominate defenders with his upper body alone, but he is able to drive back most linemen if he can latch on with leverage and drive forward with his legs. From time to time, he will lose balance when he leans too heavily into a defender and cannot sustain the block. Reach blocks, pulls, and slide blocks cause him the most problems. He has the athleticism to move laterally and get into space, as well as the body control to readjust on the move, but does not always land the block. There are instances where his athleticism is on full display and he makes high-difficulty moving blocks look easy, but he does not do this consistently.

Last Word
He should be viewed as a guard at the next level due to inconsistent shotgun snap placement, his personal statements that he feels more comfortable at guard, and the steep learning curve that he faced at center for the first half of the season. Jordan projects as a low-end starter with versatility to back up at center, but likely lacks the pass protection skills to regularly handle NFL edge rushers at tackle.

– Tony Shields

Strengths	Weaknesses
• Positional flexibility	• Slide blocks
• Recovery balance	• Snap accuracy
• Phone booth blocking	• Awareness at center

Critical Factors

Reactive Athleticism	Anchor / Play Strength	Balance / Body Control
7	6	6

Positional Factors

Run Block	Pass Block	2nd Level	Awareness / Instincts
7	6	6	5

Hand Use	Range	Sustain / Finish
6	6	6
Power	**Flexibility**	**Ruggedness / Toughness**
6	7	7

Basic

			Blown Blocks			Penalties		Team
Year	G	GS	Total	Pass	Rush	Holding	False Starts	Opp Sacks
2016	13	13	17	9	8	0	1	28
2017	14	14	13	6	7	3	3	22
2018	14	14	12	4	8	1	0	23
	41	41	42	19	23	4	4	73

Team Stats

	Zone Run Blocking			Gap Run Blocking			Pass Block
Year	% of Runs	Y/A	Positive%	% of Runs	Y/A	Positive%	Pressure%
2016	55.5%	6.2	59.4%	34.7%	6.3	47.7%	28.4%
2017	67.4%	6.5	52.6%	23.1%	5.5	51.1%	28.4%
2018	67.2%	5.1	47.2%	22.2%	3.8	45.9%	25.0%
	63.3%	5.9	52.7%	26.7%	5.4	48.2%	27.0%

Deep Dive

	Blown Block %		When Running To His Gap				
Year	Pass	Run	Y/A	Yards Before Contact	Positive %	EPA	EPA Per Attempt
2018	0.69%	1.51%	4.4	1.7	42.9%	-31.7	-0.11

Ben Powers

Oklahoma Sooners
Final Grade: 6.5 OG Rank: 8 of 16

Height	Weight	Year	Jersey #	Hometown
6037	310	4SR	72	Wichita, KS

One-Liner
Powers is a tough, physical interior blocker with quick feet, good range, and solid mirror skills in the pass game.

Overall
Powers lined up at left guard in Oklahoma's spread offense. After transferring in from community college he played in 38 games with 35 starts, nearly all on the left side. Powers has good size for an interior lineman, with good reactive athleticism, play strength, and body control. He's strong at the point of attack but doesn't consistently finish plays.

Pass Game
Powers is very good in pass protection. He is an above average knee bender who can stop bull rushes by interior defenders. He has a solid base to anchor and is very good at picking up blitzing defenders. His base gives him solid balance in pass protection, keeping his weight and pad level over his toes, and he consistently stays square against defenders.

Run Game
In the run game, Powers has good run blocking ability and is a solid second level competitor. He flashes but is inconsistent in sustaining and finishing. That said, he has good instincts and awareness to establish and sustain body position. Powers does well to push defensive linemen off the ball, but will occasionally end up on the ground in doing so. He has the ability to take the proper angles and get his head across on the backside backer in the box. He engages defenders with strong initial contact, but is inconsistent with his hand placement and may be susceptible to holding penalties at the next level. He's a smart football player who works well with teammates on combo blocks and double teams.

Last Word
Powers is a very tough lineman who plays with grit and will keep his eyes open for extra blocks, looking to try and take out defenders who do not keep their head on a swivel. He has some versatility, but mostly between the guard positions. His skills may translate to a tackle spot, but he should certainly be a solid starting guard at the next level with his size, strength, and movement skills.

– Brian Hammond

Strengths	**Weaknesses**
• Pass protection ability • Movement skills for size • Toughness	• Inconsistent hand placement • Finishing ability

Critical Factors

Reactive Athleticism	Anchor / Play Strength	Balance / Body Control
6	6	6

Positional Factors

Run Block	Pass Block	2nd Level	Awareness / Instincts
6	7	6	6

Hand Use	Range	Sustain / Finish
5	6	5
Power	**Flexibility**	**Ruggedness / Toughness**
6	6	7

Basic

			Blown Blocks			Penalties		Team
Year	G	GS	Total	Pass	Rush	Holding	False Starts	Opp Sacks
2016	11	10	8	3	5	0	1	20
2017	14	12	8	2	6	1	0	26
2018	13	13	6	2	4	2	0	19
	38	35	22	7	15	3	1	65

Team Stats

	Zone Run Blocking			Gap Run Blocking			Pass Block
Year	% of Runs	Y/A	Positive%	% of Runs	Y/A	Positive%	Pressure%
2016	49.4%	5.8	46.8%	43.2%	6.4	48.1%	27.8%
2017	50.6%	6.1	48.9%	38.7%	6.3	47.3%	27.0%
2018	43.1%	6.1	49.5%	45.1%	8.1	55.3%	22.6%
	47.8%	6.0	48.3%	42.3%	6.9	50.3%	25.8%

Deep Dive

	Blown Block %		When Running To His Gap				
Year	Pass	Run	Y/A	Yards Before Contact	Positive %	EPA	EPA Per Attempt
2018	0.48%	0.85%	7.3	4.1	48.5%	34.4	0.15

Bunchy Stallings

Kentucky Wildcats

Final Grade: 6.5 OG Rank: 9 of 16

Height	Weight	Year	Jersey #	Hometown
6026	317	5SR	65	McComb, MS

One-Liner

Stallings has experience at all three interior line positions and is a strong blocker in the run game, but his technique and anchor in pass protection, along with his awareness issues at center, should limit him to a low end starter at guard.

Overall

Stallings played multiple interior offensive line positions in Kentucky's run heavy offense, which frequently used zone blocking schemes. He started 32 games in his career, mostly at right guard with four at center his junior year. He frequently rotated between all three interior line positions mid-game. He has a round midsection with a strong lower body. He is a decent athlete for his size, with better lateral movement skills than speed and range. He finishes blocks with tenacity when locked in and lets his aggression boil over at times.

Pass Game

In the pass game, Stallings plays with good form. His strength and anchor are better moving forward than backwards, and he can be bull rushed when his technique wavers. His footwork needs improvement to help combat interior rushers, although he has good balance and flexibility in his hips to adjust. His hands are adequate but have some pop when accurate, and his grip is strong. Stallings' awareness and instincts, especially at center, are a weakness. He does not look for work well in both directions at center and passes off twists adequately at guard.

Run Game

In the run game, Stallings is a load and puts himself in good positions. He has enough power to wall off and move defenders one-on-one and shows good leg drive. He does a good job with combo blocks to engage quickly and move to his next target. He is a big body who can seal running lanes inside. Stallings' athleticism and movement skills in space are a weakness, and while he can flip his hips to pull, he doesn't do so with quickness. He attacks with pop but his hands occasionally miss. He flashes some finishing ability, but is a more consistent block sustainer.

Last Word

By his second year in the NFL, Stallings can grow into a low end starting guard, with enough experience at center to backup that position. He is a better fit on the left or right side, where he can drive off the ball and read one side of the field.

– SIS Scouting Staff

Strengths	**Weaknesses**
• Run blocking	• Pass pro assistance
• First punch pop	• Movement skills and range
• Block sustain moving forward	• Anchor inconsistency

Critical Factors

Reactive Athleticism	Anchor / Play Strength	Balance / Body Control
5	6	6

Positional Factors

Run Block	Pass Block	2nd Level	Awareness / Instincts
7	5	6	5

Hand Use	Range	Sustain / Finish
5	5	6
Power	**Flexibility**	**Ruggedness / Toughness**
6	6	7

Basic

			Blown Blocks			Penalties		Team
Year	G	GS	Total	Pass	Rush	Holding	False Starts	Opp Sacks
2016	12	7	5	2	3	2	1	28
2017	13	12	9	6	3	1	1	32
2018	13	13	12	7	5	0	1	30
	38	32	26	15	11	3	3	90

Team Stats

	Zone Run Blocking			Gap Run Blocking			Pass Block
Year	% of Runs	Y/A	Positive%	% of Runs	Y/A	Positive%	Pressure%
2016	60.5%	6.0	46.3%	30.7%	6.2	43.9%	33.2%
2017	56.5%	5.1	41.8%	31.9%	4.1	37.7%	33.8%
2018	61.4%	5.3	44.0%	27.8%	5.3	43.8%	33.4%
	59.6%	5.5	44.2%	30.1%	5.2	41.8%	33.5%

Deep Dive

	Blown Block %		When Running To His Gap				
Year	Pass	Run	Y/A	Yards Before Contact	Positive %	EPA	EPA Per Attempt
2018	2.57%	1.12%	4.9	1.6	44.1%	-5.7	-0.02

Deion Calhoun

Mississippi State Bulldogs
Final Grade: 6.4 OG Rank: 10 of 16

Height	Weight	Year	Jersey #	Hometown
6031	325	5SR	61	Pleasant Grove, AL

One-Liner
Calhoun is a thick and quick guard with good pulling ability and pass protection technique, but he needs to improve his consistency in terms of hand placement and balance at the point of attack.

Overall
Calhoun is an offensive guard who played in Mississippi State's RPO-heavy balanced blocking scheme. He played in 48 games with 36 starts, all of which came at right guard. He is a good athlete for his thick size with quick feet, long arms, and adequate body control. His extensive playing experience in the SEC shows solid ruggedness, but he isn't as nasty as preferred.

Pass Game
In the pass game, Calhoun plays with very good footwork and technique and rarely gets pushed back, more due to his lower body strength than ankle flexion. He can lose hand discipline on inside slant moves, but his reactive athleticism allows him to stay well positioned. He has the experience to be aware of stunts and different schemes, and has helped younger linemen next to him adjust, but he is prone to misread some blitzes. Calhoun has never played center and has little to no experience making line calls or adjustments.

Run Game
In the run game, Calhoun comes off slowly, but he is a very strong puller who uses his quick footwork to give himself momentum downhill and become a load at the point of attack. He is good at combo blocks getting to the second level, and he looks natural pulling inside or out. He has decent balance when engaged, but he is prone to look top heavy with whiffs on the move and doesn't generate as much power as he could because of it. Calhoun drives and sustains well when engaged, but his hand accuracy is sporadic. He has shown flashes of the nasty streak needed to finish blocks. He has the size and movement skills to excel in this area, but his play speed is generally a tick slow and results in a few more missed assignments than expected.

Last Word
Calhoun best projects as a guard in a power blocking scheme at the next level based on his pulling ability and initial punch power. He needs to improve his play speed and hand placement to maximize his strength, but he should be a sufficient starting caliber player by his second year.

– SIS Scouting Staff

Strengths	Weaknesses
• Pulling and second level ability	• Hand placement
• Footwork for size	• Power and finishing ability
• Upper and lower body strength	• Balance at contact

Critical Factors

Reactive Athleticism	Anchor / Play Strength	Balance / Body Control
6	6	5

Positional Factors

Run Block	Pass Block	2nd Level	Awareness / Instincts
6	6	6	5

Hand Use	Range	Sustain / Finish
5	6	5
Power	**Flexibility**	**Ruggedness / Toughness**
5	5	5

Basic

			Blown Blocks			Penalties		Team
Year	G	GS	Total	Pass	Rush	Holding	False Starts	Opp Sacks
2016	9	9	3	1	2	1	1	18
2017	13	13	29	13	16	1	2	13
2018	13	13	11	4	7	3	1	23
	35	35	43	18	25	5	4	54

Team Stats

	Zone Run Blocking			Gap Run Blocking			Pass Block
Year	% of Runs	Y/A	Positive%	% of Runs	Y/A	Positive%	Pressure%
2016	69.2%	5.8	46.2%	24.5%	7.7	51.2%	22.4%
2017	66.6%	5.4	47.5%	27.9%	5.3	44.8%	33.1%
2018	47.6%	6.0	49.8%	39.0%	6.1	51.3%	34.5%
	61.6%	5.7	47.6%	30.3%	6.2	49.0%	29.5%

Deep Dive

	Blown Block %		When Running To His Gap				
Year	Pass	Run	Y/A	Yards Before Contact	Positive %	EPA	EPA Per Attempt
2018	1.26%	1.67%	6.4	3.2	49.8%	31.2	0.14

Martez Ivey

Florida Gators

Final Grade: 6.2 OG Rank: 11 of 16

Height	Weight	Year	Jersey #	Hometown
6051	310	4SR	73	Apopka, FL

One-Liner

Ivey is a powerful, versatile lineman who is a very good run blocker, but his struggles with speed rushers and hand usage during pass blocking limit him to a backup his first two seasons.

Overall

Ivey played both left tackle and left guard, starting in 44 of 49 total games throughout his four-year career at Florida. He is a solid athlete who possesses good foot speed, above average balance and flexibility, and good height and weight. He is an aggressive player who competes at a high level, plays with good toughness and grit, and shows an ability to finish blocks with a mauler temperament.

Pass Game

As a pass blocker, he has good range and reactive athleticism to mirror movements from edge rushers. He displays good play strength to anchor defenders and neutralize the pass rush from stronger defenders. He has sufficient hand usage, displaying bad timing and poor placement, which results in him becoming off balance and not being able to latch onto defenders during the pass rush. He shows good awareness and processing skills with an ability to quickly diagnose situations, handle cross-face effectively and pick up loop/twist stunts and delayed blitzers.

Run Game

As a run blocker, he has very good vertical push power with the ability to walk defenders off the ball and generate movement with leg drive and strength. He has good pull quickness, displays the ability to locate defenders, and produces as a second level or combination blocker. He has good range to effectively reach block and get his head across defenders on backside blocks.

Last Word

He projects best as a backup guard at the next level due to his run block ability and temperament, as well as appearing more comfortable playing in a phone booth as opposed to handling edge rushers on an island. He could also play right tackle in a pinch given his experience playing left tackle in college.

– Nick Giella

Strengths	Weaknesses
• Range • Run blocking • Toughness	• Hand usage • Pass block consistency • Balance/body control

Critical Factors

Reactive Athleticism	Anchor / Play Strength	Balance / Body Control
6	6	5

Positional Factors

Run Block	Pass Block	2nd Level	Awareness / Instincts
7	5	6	6

Hand Use	Range	Sustain / Finish
5	6	6
Power	**Flexibility**	**Ruggedness / Toughness**
6	5	6

Basic

			Blown Blocks			Penalties		Team
Year	G	GS	Total	Pass	Rush	Holding	False Starts	Opp Sacks
2016	13	12	14	11	3	1	0	28
2017	11	11	33	22	11	3	5	37
2018	13	13	14	11	3	2	5	18
	37	36	61	44	17	6	10	83

Team Stats

	Zone Run Blocking			Gap Run Blocking			Pass Block
Year	% of Runs	Y/A	Positive%	% of Runs	Y/A	Positive%	Pressure%
2016	67.0%	4.7	43.3%	22.9%	4.3	40.2%	38.7%
2017	59.4%	5.5	42.2%	26.8%	5.0	42.1%	43.4%
2018	63.4%	5.7	48.0%	28.5%	6.1	49.7%	33.2%
	63.4%	5.3	44.8%	26.2%	5.2	44.7%	38.3%

Deep Dive

	Blown Block %		When Running To His Gap				
Year	Pass	Run	Y/A	Yards Before Contact	Positive %	EPA	EPA Per Attempt
2018	3.03%	0.66%	6.7	3.9	48.4%	13.1	0.10

Oli Udoh

Elon Phoenix

Final Grade: 6.2 OG Rank: 12 of 16

Height	Weight	Year	Jersey #	Hometown
6056	327	5SR	73	Fayetteville, NC

One-Liner

Udoh has the reactive athleticism and short-set anchor strength to play at the next level, but his inconsistent hand use and endurance concerns may hold him back early on.

Overall

Udoh is a right tackle who played for the Elon Phoenix. He's a four-year starter, starting in all 45 games he's played in at Elon. He's a solid athlete and moves well. His flexibility is noticeable and he shows the ankle flexion required to sit with power. He had some weight issues early in his career, but seems to have gotten it under control. He competes with toughness in his play. He finishes through the whistle and shows some nastiness in his game. His endurance is an issue, as he noticeably gets tired late in games.

Pass Game

In the pass game, Udoh shows the ability to anchor quickly and with strength when he short-sets. There are times where he will fall back on his heels or get his weight a little too far forward, stopping his feet, and making him susceptible to push-pull moves. He shows a quick kick-slide, but he isn't as powerful as when he short-sets. He has good reactive athleticism and is able to mirror defenders coming off the edge or stunting through the B gap. He shows good awareness to pick up defenders who are unaccounted for. He has good length and strong hands, but doesn't always use them. He worries more about getting into position than getting his hands up for an initial punch which allows the defender to get into his chest quickly and easily. His placement is only sufficient as he is inconsistent firing into the breast plate.

Run Game

In the run game, Udoh uses good leg drive to move defenders off the ball. He uses his flexibility to gain good leverage at the POA, and he uses his strength and power to move the LOS. When getting to the 2nd level, he shows good balance and comes in under control, although he rarely gets good enough position to sustain the block. He shows good range, as Elon had him pull from the right tackle position on numerous occasions. When going up against smaller defenders, he punishes them and takes them to the ground with regularity.

Last Word

Udoh projects as a versatile backup by his second season that would fit best at right guard, but he can also play at right tackle.

– Nathan Cooper

Strengths	Weaknesses
• Strong short-set anchor	• Inconsistent hand placement
• Finishes through the whistle	• Slow initial punch
• Reactive athleticism	• Endurance late in games

Critical Factors

Reactive Athleticism	Anchor / Play Strength	Balance / Body Control
6	6	6

Positional Factors

Run Block	Pass Block	2nd Level	Awareness / Instincts
6	5	5	6

Hand Use	Range	Sustain / Finish
5	6	6
Power	**Flexibility**	**Ruggedness / Toughness**
6	6	6

Udoh comes from a good family. His father is a doctor and his mother is a nurse and Udoh may eventually pursue a career in medicine himself. He told The Athletic that he weighed as much as 384 pounds before dropping to the 320s for the Shrine Game and Senior Bowl. His strong performance in the former netted him an invitation to the latter.

The last three players Elon has had drafted went 322nd, 251st and 238th, with the most recent of those being wide receiver Aaron Mellette in 2013. The last player from that school selected sooner than the seventh round was running back Jimmy Smith in 1984 (4th round).

Terronne Prescod

NC State Wolfpack

Final Grade: 6.2 OG Rank: 13 of 16

Height	Weight	Year	Jersey #	Hometown
6041	334	5SR	70	Decatur, GA

One-Liner
Prescod is a thick and powerful run blocking mauler, whose athleticism and movement skills are exploitable traits.

Overall
Prescod played right tackle and both guard positions or NC State. He played in 50 career games with 28 starts, 24 of which at left guard. He is a mauler with large size and a very thick lower half who flashes great power in short bursts. He has good toughness and is sufficient in sustaining blocks, and is a very strong finisher and regularly takes opponents to the ground through the whistle.

Pass Game
In the passing game, he possesses sufficient play strength and body control as he is able to set a short anchor with good, choppy footwork and control defenders with his hands. Prescod's limitations can be attributed to his sufficient reactive athleticism and average flexibility, where a more athletic and faster defender can beat him around the edge. He has very heavy hands to strike and anchors well against strength, despite his lack of true ankle flexion and bendability.

Run Game
Prescod is a very strong run blocker and plays with good awareness and instincts. He can use his power to run through opposing defenders and move people off the ball. He gave some top defensive linemen balance issues at contact with his pure power and striking ability. His athleticism and overall movement skills limit him greatly at the second level and outside the tackles. His speed is poor getting out in front of screens. He doesn't always fire out with explosion and lacks the short area quickness to handle smaller, faster second level defenders at the point of attack. His hips are sufficiently fluid to flip, reach and seal, but he struggles to pull and move down the line with effective quickness.

Last Word
Prescod showed position versatility throughout his career, but he is a natural guard with his load and run blocking skills. His athleticism won't hold up well at the next level, but he could fill in on the right side, if necessary. His movement skills will be difficult to overcome and will make him a position-versatile backup in the NFL, but his power and size are desirable assets.

– Cole Ratliff

Strengths	**Weaknesses**
• Powerful heavy hands	• Speed and range
• Anchor and run blocking	• Flexibility
• Toughness and finishing	• Second level ability

Critical Factors

Reactive Athleticism	Anchor / Play Strength	Balance / Body Control
5	6	5

Positional Factors

Run Block	Pass Block	2nd Level	Awareness / Instincts
5	6	5	6

Hand Use	Range	Sustain / Finish
6	5	5
Power	**Flexibility**	**Ruggedness / Toughness**
6	4	6

Basic

			Blown Blocks			Penalties		Team
Year	G	GS	Total	Pass	Rush	Holding	False Starts	Opp Sacks
2016	13	3	10	4	6	1	1	17
2017	13	13	17	6	11	2	0	15
2018	12	12	11	2	9	2	1	11
	38	28	38	12	26	5	2	43

Team Stats

	Zone Run Blocking			Gap Run Blocking			Pass Block
Year	% of Runs	Y/A	Positive%	% of Runs	Y/A	Positive%	Pressure%
2016	70.6%	4.2	38.3%	19.8%	5.1	51.0%	23.5%
2017	88.9%	5.1	43.5%	4.5%	5.4	36.4%	20.4%
2018	90.4%	4.2	40.6%	3.8%	3.5	44.4%	28.2%
	83.1%	4.5	41.0%	9.5%	4.9	47.8%	24.1%

Deep Dive

	Blown Block %		When Running To His Gap				
Year	Pass	Run	Y/A	Yards Before Contact	Positive %	EPA	EPA Per Attempt
2018	0.56%	2.68%	3.9	1.7	39.8%	-3.9	-0.04

Javon Patterson

Ole Miss Rebels

Final Grade: 6.2 OG Rank: 14 of 16

Height	Weight	Year	Jersey #	Hometown
6030	306	4SR	79	Petal, MS

One-Liner

Patterson is a solid all-around interior lineman with proven durability, versatility, and experience, but his communication and lower body strength will need improvement in order to make an impact in the NFL.

Overall

Patterson was a left guard in Ole Miss' Air Raid-influenced offense. He started in 42 of his 48 collegiate appearances, with three starts at center. He has good height and weight for the position, with solid reactive athleticism and flexibility for the interior. He is a very durable player who played with toughness in the SEC for four years.

Pass Game

In the pass game, Patterson is a sufficient reader of blitzes and stunts, but has some trouble with communicating and passing off rushers. He plays with good agility to react laterally and shows quick, accurate hands with tight elbows to mirror, punch, and lock in. He has sufficient strength but his anchor can be exposed against larger interior defenders. He usually shows good body control when adjusting and reacting laterally.

Run Game

In the run game, Patterson shows good strength and leverage to secure his gaps. He doesn't play with a powerful first punch, and will need improved leg drive going forward, but he can sufficiently pop linemen out of a gap. He keeps his hands in close and plays with sound upper body technique. He has experience in man and zone blocking. Patterson could communicate better on combination blocks, but individually, he moves with fluidity to the second level. He has flashed the ability to finish plays with tenacity, but is better suited to reach or seal and sustain.

Last Word

Patterson does a lot of things well, but nothing exceptionally. His versatility and durability are positives, and his experience at the highest level should translate well. He projects as a reliable interior backup with position flexibility at guard and center.

– SIS Scouting Staff

Strengths	**Weaknesses**
• Hand accuracy	• Communication
• Reactive athleticism	• Lower body strength
• Durability	• Finishing ability

Critical Factors

Reactive Athleticism	Anchor / Play Strength	Balance / Body Control
6	5	6

Positional Factors

Run Block	Pass Block	2nd Level	Awareness / Instincts
6	5	6	6

Hand Use	Range	Sustain / Finish
6	5	5
Power	**Flexibility**	**Ruggedness / Toughness**
5	6	6

Basic

			Blown Blocks			Penalties		Team
Year	G	GS	Total	Pass	Rush	Holding	False Starts	Opp Sacks
2016	12	12	10	7	3	0	2	27
2017	12	12	19	15	4	1	1	32
2018	12	12	11	1	10	0	3	33
	36	36	40	23	17	1	6	92

Team Stats

	Zone Run Blocking			Gap Run Blocking			Pass Block
Year	% of Runs	Y/A	Positive%	% of Runs	Y/A	Positive%	Pressure%
2016	51.4%	4.6	40.2%	36.1%	4.8	36.7%	31.8%
2017	39.0%	4.0	42.7%	45.2%	6.2	45.2%	31.9%
2018	31.7%	5.4	48.5%	45.2%	5.5	44.7%	25.9%
	40.8%	4.6	43.1%	42.0%	5.5	42.5%	29.9%

Deep Dive

	Blown Block %		When Running To His Gap				
Year	Pass	Run	Y/A	Yards Before Contact	Positive %	EPA	EPA Per Attempt
2018	0.21%	2.70%	5.8	2.8	45.4%	4.4	0.02

Malcolm Pridgeon

Ohio State Buckeyes
Final Grade: 6.2   OG Rank: 15 of 16

Height	Weight	Year	Jersey #	Hometown
6062	310	4SR	66	Central Islip, NY

One-Liner
Pridgeon is a versatile OL who has good reactive athleticism and anchor ability but needs to become more consistent with his hand use and toughness.

Overall
Pridgeon was a one year starter at left guard in Ohio State's spread offense that utilized a power running scheme. He played in 28 games for the Buckeyes, starting 14 of them. Pridgeon has a very good body type that directly correlates to his good play strength and anchor ability. Pridgeon brings versatility in that he can play offensive tackle as well due to his size, feet, hand usage, and length.

Pass Game
In the pass game, he does a good job of dropping anchor versus bull rushers and blitzes, stopping them in their tracks to set up a strong pocket for his QB. He flashes good hand use and has a strong initial punch but isn't consistent with his placement. Pridgeon struggles to recognize twisting stunts at times where he will be late to slide and pick it up, but his length allows him to at least get his hands on the defender to redirect them from the QB.

Run Game
In the run game, Pridgeon uses his quick feet to get into proper position and wall off defenders. His feet aren't stagnant and he has good drive once engaged. He is also quick and under control getting to the second level. He displays natural athleticism when attacking LBs or when pulling to lead on powers. When he gets his hands on the defender, he sustains the block and finishes them.

Last Word
Pridgeon projects to be a backup that can play both OG positions and can move to OT if necessary.

– Mark Johnson

Strengths

- Pass blocking
- Reactive athleticism
- Finish

Weaknesses

- Hand usage
- Range
- Experience

Critical Factors

Reactive Athleticism	Anchor / Play Strength	Balance / Body Control
6	6	5

Positional Factors

Run Block	Pass Block	2nd Level	Awareness / Instincts
6	6	6	5

Hand Use	Range	Sustain / Finish
5	5	6
Power	**Flexibility**	**Ruggedness / Toughness**
5	5	5

Basic

			Blown Blocks			Penalties		Team
Year	G	GS	Total	Pass	Rush	Holding	False Starts	Opp Sacks
2016			0	0	0	0	0	28
2017	14	0	0	0	0	0	0	22
2018	14	14	13	5	8	4	4	23
	28	14	13	5	8	4	4	73

Team Stats

	Zone Run Blocking			Gap Run Blocking			Pass Block
Year	% of Runs	Y/A	Positive%	% of Runs	Y/A	Positive%	Pressure%
2016	55.5%	6.2	59.4%	34.7%	6.3	47.7%	28.4%
2017	67.4%	6.5	52.6%	23.1%	5.5	51.1%	28.4%
2018	67.2%	5.1	47.2%	22.2%	3.8	45.9%	25.0%
	63.3%	5.9	52.7%	26.7%	5.4	48.2%	27.0%

Deep Dive

	Blown Block %		When Running To His Gap				
Year	Pass	Run	Y/A	Yards Before Contact	Positive %	EPA	EPA Per Attempt
2018	0.87%	1.51%	4.2	1.7	42.5%	-28.7	-0.13

Dru Samia

Oklahoma Sooners

Final Grade: 6.2 OG Rank: 16 of 16

Height	Weight	Year	Jersey #	Hometown
6050	304	4SR	75	Sacramento, CA

One-Liner

Samia has experience at both right guard and tackle and plays with good hand use, much more finesse than power and struggles in open space.

Overall

Samia was a RG in Oklahoma's spread offense. He played 52 games for the Sooners, starting in 48 of them. During Samia's freshman year, he started nine games at right tackle and proceeded to start at right tackle during his sophomore year for the first game of the season. He was then moved to right guard and started there from that point forward. Samia's flexion is a concern as it seems he doesn't have good ankle bend and looks extremely stiff at times. He always plays hard through the whistle and does not take plays off. His tenacity is noticeable. Samia shows his ability with his good hands in controlling defenders, being able to move them when warranted. He doesn't have the reactive athleticism to always react quickly enough to redirect defenders slanting to or away from him.

Pass Game

In the passing game, Samia's anchor and play strength are major question marks when translating to the next level. Samia lacks the strength to play against the bigger defensive tackles. He gets pushed back into the QB too often and doesn't move defenders like a right guard should.

Run Game

In the run game, Samia is a solid athlete with good feet to be pulled in run blocking concepts. While he is a little slow, Samia is excellent when pulling but gets lost when a target is not immediately present. This also shows in the zone scheme, where Samia can get lost looking for people to block and his lack of athleticism shows when in the open field. He uses his feet to his advantage by taking short and choppy steps to make sure he is in good position when eyeing up a block. Samia's body control is sufficient, but when off balance, he doesn't show the ability to stay balanced when moving and trying to execute a block.

Last Word

While Samia does show that he is versatile, he projects best at right guard. He could fill in at LG, and it's not out of the question that he could move into center.

– Drew Schweitzer

Strengths	Weaknesses
• Ruggedness	• Anchor and play strength
• Hand usage	• Flexion
• Versatility	• Range

Critical Factors

Reactive Athleticism	Anchor / Play Strength	Balance / Body Control
5	5	5

Positional Factors

Run Block	Pass Block	2nd Level	Awareness / Instincts
6	5	5	6

Hand Use	Range	Sustain / Finish
6	5	5
Power	**Flexibility**	**Ruggedness / Toughness**
5	5	6

Basic

			Blown Blocks			Penalties		Team
Year	G	GS	Total	Pass	Rush	Holding	False Starts	Opp Sacks
2016	13	13	15	6	9	1	2	20
2017	13	12	20	8	12	1	1	26
2018	14	14	12	3	9	2	1	19
	40	39	47	17	30	4	4	65

Team Stats

	Zone Run Blocking			Gap Run Blocking			Pass Block
Year	% of Runs	Y/A	Positive%	% of Runs	Y/A	Positive%	Pressure%
2016	49.4%	5.8	46.8%	43.2%	6.4	48.1%	27.8%
2017	50.6%	6.1	48.9%	38.7%	6.3	47.3%	27.0%
2018	43.1%	6.1	49.5%	45.1%	8.1	55.3%	22.6%
	47.8%	6.0	48.3%	42.3%	6.9	50.3%	25.8%

Deep Dive

	Blown Block %		When Running To His Gap				
Year	Pass	Run	Y/A	Yards Before Contact	Positive %	EPA	EPA Per Attempt
2018	0.73%	1.90%	7.5	3.5	53.8%	47.2	0.20

CENTER

Center Grading Scale

GRADE	DESCRIPTION
9.0 – 7.0	High-end starter. Pro Bowl level.
6.9 – 6.7	Strong starter with 2 position flexibility.
6.6 – 6.5	Lower end starter. Backup flexibility at OG or OC.
6.4	Starter with no position flexibility.
6.2	Multi-positional backup.
6.1 – 6.0	Developmental. Top traits but needs time.
5.7	Backup with no position flexibility. #4 OG or #3 OC.

Center Rankings

Rank	Name	Grade	Page
1	Garrett Bradbury	6.9	290
2	Dalton Risner	6.9	292
3	Elgton Jenkins	6.8	294
4	Erik McCoy	6.7	296
5	Ross Pierschbacher	6.5	298
6	Justin Falcinelli	6.5	300
7	Lamont Gaillard	6.4	302
8	Alec Eberle	6.4	304
9	Ryan Anderson	6.2	306

Garrett Bradbury

NC State Wolfpack

Final Grade: 6.9 OC Rank: 1 of 9

Height	Weight	Year	Jersey #	Hometown
6027	304	6SR	65	Charlotte, NC

One-Liner

Bradbury is an outstanding athlete who wins with explosiveness, angles, and leverage, but could stand to get stronger and play with more balance.

Overall

Bradbury played center his junior and senior seasons in an offense which frequently employed 1- and 3-step drops in the passing game and wide zone in the rushing game. He also played guard his redshirt sophomore season. He is an active pre-snap communicator. He demonstrates excellent quickness out of his stance and plays with good pad level and base as a pass protector. However, at times his base will get wide, forcing him to lose some of his strength at the POA.

Pass Game

In the pass game, he plays with active eyes and shows the ability to process blitzes and line games, and has very good re-direct quickness to pick up his assignments. Bradbury is a very good reactive athlete with high-end mirroring ability. He possesses good hand quickness and sufficient snatch ability as a pass protector. He often deadens his feet when shooting his hands in pass protection, which occasionally results in him playing top-heavy. His hand placement and punch are both solid, although he often concedes his chest when he fits his hands wide, compromising his ability to anchor.

Run Game

His lateral explosion is excellent in the wide zone gap. He was asked to reach and seal playside 2i- and 3-techniques without guard help and did so with consistency and ease. He does a sufficient job of anchoring the run lane once he has worked into seal position. He generates power through athletic explosion and leverage and may struggle to vertically displace high-caliber nose tackles on man/gap concepts at the NFL level. He shows good timing off zone combos and takes very good angles to the second level, reaching LBs with excellent quickness, and has very good flexibility to contour his body and adjust to targets on the fly. He occasionally lowers his hat into second-level blocks whiffing on some defenders, and must eliminate this habit to maximize effectiveness at the second level. While he was not asked to pull in NC State's zone scheme, his athletic traits, 2nd-level ability, and effectiveness in the screen game suggest he should be very good in this facet. There were quite a few times where his feet kept getting stepped on and fell off-balance, although he shows the ability to recover from awkward positions and regain it.

Last Word

Bradbury plays with a good understanding of torque and is an aggressive finisher at all levels who looks for work when he's uncovered. He performed well against top competition as a senior. Bradbury projects as a high-end starting center at the next level, who could fill in as a guard if needed.

– Bryce Rossler

Strengths	**Weaknesses**
• Pass blocking • Reach blocking/range • Technically sound	• Inconsistent base • Power/leg drive

Critical Factors

Reactive Athleticism	Anchor / Play Strength	Balance / Body Control
7	6	6

Positional Factors

Run Block	Pass Block	2nd Level	Awareness / Instincts
6	7	6	7

Hand Use	Range	Sustain / Finish
6	7	6
Power	**Flexibility**	**Ruggedness / Toughness**
5	7	6

Basic

			Blown Blocks			Penalties		Team
Year	G	GS	Total	Pass	Rush	Holding	False Starts	Opp Sacks
2016	13	13	13	7	6	1	2	17
2017	13	13	14	4	10	2	0	15
2018	13	13	16	4	12	2	0	11
	39	39	43	15	28	5	2	43

Team Stats

	Zone Run Blocking			Gap Run Blocking			Pass Block
Year	% of Runs	Y/A	Positive%	% of Runs	Y/A	Positive%	Pressure%
2016	70.6%	4.2	38.3%	19.8%	5.1	51.0%	23.5%
2017	88.9%	5.1	43.5%	4.5%	5.4	36.4%	20.4%
2018	90.4%	4.2	40.6%	3.8%	3.5	44.4%	28.2%
	83.1%	4.5	41.0%	9.5%	4.9	47.8%	24.1%

Deep Dive

	Blown Block %		When Running To His Gap				
Year	Pass	Run	Y/A	Yards Before Contact	Positive %	EPA	EPA Per Attempt
2018	0.80%	2.70%	3.2	1.4	43.0%	-12.8	-0.14

Dalton Risner

Kansas State Wildcats
Final Grade: 6.9 OC Rank: 2 of 9

Height	Weight	Year	Jersey #	Hometown
6045	308	5SR	71	Wiggins, CO

One-Liner
Risner is a starting caliber offensive lineman wherever he's needed, using his athleticism, strength, quickness, leadership, and intelligence to lead a line and impact the game in both phases.

Overall
Risner's primary position at Kansas State was right tackle. He was a four-year starter. Risner started 13 games at center in 2015, then moved to right tackle for his final 37 career starts. He has a history of injuries, but only missed one game during his collegiate career. Risner is very athletic with fluid movement and quick feet. He has moments where his hips don't sink and appear stiff, but he is able to compensate with strength and quickness. Risner plays nasty, as he always hustles and routinely punishes defenders, finishes blocks through the whistle. He possesses excellent football intelligence and awareness, and was responsbile for line calls during his Wildcats career.

Pass Game
As a pass blocker, Risner displays good balance, the body control required to recover from undesirable positions, and very good reactive athleticism to change direction quickly and nullify stunts. He has good strength and hand placement, using them to stonewall rushers and anchor his short sets at ideal depth. In pass sets, he can occasionally get sloppy with his footwork and establish a narrow base, attributing to instances where balance becomes an issue. He uses communication to direct the line's actions and is effective at orchestrating movements post-snap to account for twists and stunts.

Run Game
As a run blocker, Risner has very good drive off the line and is adept at sealing run lanes through isolation or combination blocks. He has very good pull quickness and is skilled at progressing to the second level and supplying impactful blocks in space. He shows good ability to latch onto defenders and sustain blocks, keeping consistent leg drive to win the positioning battle.

Last Word
Risner has the rare combination of tools to be an immediate starter at numerous positions in the NFL. However, the position his skillset best translates to is center due to his intelligence and leadership, ability to get to the second level, reactive quickness, and anchor ability. His versatility will be a desired commodity at the next level.

– Aaron Gray

Strengths	Weaknesses
• Positional flexibility • Leadership and intelligence • Athleticism	• Flexibility • Pass protection footwork

Critical Factors

Reactive Athleticism	Anchor / Play Strength	Balance / Body Control
7	6	6

Positional Factors

Run Block	Pass Block	2nd Level	Awareness / Instincts
7	6	7	7

Hand Use	Range	Sustain / Finish
6	7	7
Power	**Flexibility**	**Ruggedness / Toughness**
6	6	7

Basic

			Blown Blocks			Penalties		Team
Year	G	GS	Total	Pass	Rush	Holding	False Starts	Opp Sacks
2016	13	13	15	5	10	2	4	27
2017	12	12	3	0	3	0	2	25
2018	12	12	13	1	12	0	0	32
	37	37	31	6	25	2	6	84

Team Stats

	Zone Run Blocking			Gap Run Blocking			Pass Block
Year	% of Runs	Y/A	Positive%	% of Runs	Y/A	Positive%	Pressure%
2016	63.0%	5.3	47.2%	26.5%	6.2	54.4%	28.1%
2017	48.3%	5.1	46.4%	37.6%	6.0	41.5%	27.8%
2018	43.3%	4.8	39.0%	40.8%	5.1	42.0%	32.5%
	52.0%	5.1	44.8%	34.7%	5.7	45.2%	29.5%

Deep Dive

	Blown Block %		When Running To His Gap				
Year	Pass	Run	Y/A	Yards Before Contact	Positive %	EPA	EPA Per Attempt
2018	0.31%	2.59%	5.8	3.7	41.9%	6.9	0.04

Elgton Jenkins

Mississippi State Bulldogs
Final Grade: 6.8 OC Rank: 3 of 9

Height	Weight	Year	Jersey #	Hometown
6043	314	5SR	74	Clarksdale, MS

One-Liner

Jenkins is a long, strong and versatile lineman with impressive pass protection instincts and anchor ability in the interior.

Overall

Jenkins is a center who played in Mississippi State's RPO based run-heavy offense. He has previous starting experience at both tackle and guard, and played center his final two seasons with the Bulldogs. He has played in 49 career games and started 34 of them, with 26 coming at center. He has strong size and very good length, with a fairly athletic cut, but little backside. He is a good competitor, shows aggression at the point of attack, flashes tenacity with his finishing ability, and has handled multiple position changes very well.

Pass Game

In the pass game, Jenkins is versatile and long. He establishes a great anchor with a sound base and great ankle flexion. He sustains blocks with good hand use to lock out. His reactive athleticism is sufficient, but his mirror ability is inconsistent and can be masked inside at center. Jenkins shows impressive instincts to look for help and deliver blows to both sides of the line. He recognizes and picks up stunts very well. He sits a bit upright, but is rarely knocked off balance.

Run Game

In the run game, Jenkins can generate leg drive and move defenders, especially on combination blocks. He works well with his teammates and blocks well at the second level with his length. He plays with leverage and intelligence. Jenkins flashes a mean streak and has very impressive upper-body strength to throw defenders to the ground and finish.

Last Word

Jenkins profiles as an early starter at the next level, with the experience and versatility to fill in at multiple positions, but his best fit is at center. His overall athleticism suits him better inside, and his instincts and length are great assets for the interior.

– Jordan Edwards

Strengths	Weaknesses
• Upper-body strength	• Lateral athleticism
• Instincts	• Initial-punch power
• Pass protection anchor	

Critical Factors

Reactive Athleticism	Anchor / Play Strength	Balance / Body Control
5	7	7

Positional Factors

Run Block	Pass Block	2nd Level	Awareness / Instincts
6	7	6	7

Hand Use	Range	Sustain / Finish
6	6	6
Power	**Flexibility**	**Ruggedness / Toughness**
6	7	6

Basic

			Blown Blocks			Penalties		Team
Year	G	GS	Total	Pass	Rush	Holding	False Starts	Opp Sacks
2016	12	5	3	1	2	1	1	18
2017	13	13	15	2	13	2	0	13
2018	13	13	7	4	3	1	0	23
	38	31	25	7	18	4	1	54

Team Stats

	Zone Run Blocking			Gap Run Blocking			Pass Block
Year	% of Runs	Y/A	Positive%	% of Runs	Y/A	Positive%	Pressure%
2016	69.2%	5.8	46.2%	24.5%	7.7	51.2%	22.4%
2017	66.6%	5.4	47.5%	27.9%	5.3	44.8%	33.1%
2018	47.6%	6.0	49.8%	39.0%	6.1	51.3%	34.5%
	61.6%	5.7	47.6%	30.3%	6.2	49.0%	29.5%

Deep Dive

	Blown Block %		When Running To His Gap				
Year	Pass	Run	Y/A	Yards Before Contact	Positive %	EPA	EPA Per Attempt
2018	1.22%	0.69%	6.3	3.1	50.5%	23.4	0.12

Erik McCoy

Texas A&M Aggies

Final Grade: 6.7 OC Rank: 4 of 9

Height	Weight	Year	Jersey #	Hometown
6036	310	4JR	64	Lufkin, TX

One-Liner

McCoy is a very fluid and mobile center prospect with the pop and flexibility to succeed at different levels of the defense, but his ability to sustain blocks and move linemen off the ball could be improved.

Overall

McCoy lined up at center in Texas A&M's shotgun RPO-based offense. He played and started in all 38 games in his career. He has average arm length but has a fairly athletic build and a thick and strong lower half. McCoy is a good reactive athlete who is light on his feet and moves very well in space. He is a tough, aggressive player at contact and flashes some finishing nastiness.

Pass Game

In the pass game, he has a good short set and anchors well with his lower body strength and flexibility. His balance and body control are very good, showing the ability to bend at the knees and brace for surprise rushers and stunts. He is intelligent inside and does a good job of looking for work. His hands have pop, but his accuracy is an issue. He doesn't fit to rushers with consistency, and struggles to sustain as a result. He gets his hands up quickly off his snap, but brings them wide instead of keeping his elbows tight, limiting his punch and leaving him in vulnerable positions. McCoy shows the ability to win against nose tackles and odd techniques alike.

Run Game

In the run game, he stalemates well but doesn't always generate a push off the line. His body control and flexibility allow him to explode through his hips and flash a powerful punch occasionally, especially when down blocking. His aggression at the point of attack results in solid finishing ability. He works very well with combination blocks and is a great second level blocker. His movement skills in open space are very fluid, and his agility and reactive athleticism allow him to engage and lock onto linebackers and cornerbacks. He is very quick out ahead of screens.

Last Word

McCoy has all the physical, athletic tools to be a solid starting center early in his career. His mobility and body control are NFL traits, but his hand technique will need improvement to limit mistakes.

– Jordan Edwards

Strengths	**Weaknesses**
• Body control	• Hand accuracy
• Fluidity in space	• Leg drive
• Pop and finish	• Sustaining blocks

Critical Factors

Reactive Athleticism	Anchor / Play Strength	Balance / Body Control
6	6	7

Positional Factors

Run Block	Pass Block	2nd Level	Awareness / Instincts
6	6	7	6

Hand Use	Range	Sustain / Finish
5	7	6
Power	**Flexibility**	**Ruggedness / Toughness**
5	6	6

Basic

			Blown Blocks			Penalties		Team
Year	G	GS	Total	Pass	Rush	Holding	False Starts	Opp Sacks
2016	13	13	10	6	4	2	0	21
2017	13	13	12	3	9	0	2	30
2018	12	12	6	2	4	1	1	34
	38	38	28	11	17	3	3	85

Team Stats

	Zone Run Blocking			Gap Run Blocking			Pass Block
Year	% of Runs	Y/A	Positive%	% of Runs	Y/A	Positive%	Pressure%
2016	62.2%	6.1	45.0%	27.3%	6.9	48.1%	26.5%
2017	62.9%	3.8	35.6%	27.1%	6.5	33.8%	34.7%
2018	58.9%	6.0	49.5%	30.3%	6.0	41.6%	41.2%
	61.3%	5.3	43.3%	28.3%	6.4	41.1%	34.1%

Deep Dive

	Blown Block %		When Running To His Gap				
Year	Pass	Run	Y/A	Yards Before Contact	Positive %	EPA	EPA Per Attempt
2018	0.44%	0.86%	5.2	1.6	43.2%	-5.5	-0.04

Ross Pierschbacher

Alabama Crimson Tide
Final Grade: 6.5 OC Rank: 5 of 9

Height	Weight	Year	Jersey #	Hometown
6034	306	5SR	71	Cedar Falls, IA

One-Liner

Pierschbacher is a smart, versatile, low-end starting center with good athleticism and sufficient power, but doesn't dominate in the run game and will occasionally struggles to short-set against stronger defensive tackles.

Overall

Pierschbacher played center for Alabama. He played in 58 career games for the Tide and was mostly a LG before switching to center in 2018. He shows good reactive athleticism, allowing him to mirror the pass rush moves of interior defensive linemen. He has good flexibility and can effectively bend his hips and ankles instead of leaning too far forward. He shows good balance and body control, but falls down in traffic from time to time. He has good toughness and has played through pain.

Pass Game

In the pass game, he is a good blocker, but can get pushed back a yard or two too far when setting the depth of the pocket in short sets. He also shows very good awareness and instincts and is great at communicating with his teammates and reacting in order to pick up blitzes and stunts. His play strength and ability to anchor are good, although he gets pushed back several yards in pass protection too often. Ross shows very good hand use and engages defenders well.

Run Game

In the run game, he is very good because of his ability to engage with defenders and position himself, which helps create run lanes, but usually only creates significant push with combo blocks due to his merely sufficient power. He has good range, is an effective puller, and lands difficult reach blocks; he will not explode through his target but he will get to his spot quickly and not allow the defender to make the play. He shows good second level ability and takes good angles to defenders down the field. His ability to sustain/finish is good, but he hardly ever puts defenders in the dirt by himself. He can regularly neutralize defenders in the run game but does not consistently push defenders back.

Last Word

By his second year, Ross projects as a low-end starting center due to his intelligence, size, and limited power, but his versatility and experience at guard suggest he can also play either guard spot in the NFL if his team needs him to.

– Jeremy Percy

Strengths

- Awareness and instincts
- Reach blocks
- Recovery

Weaknesses

- Leg drive
- Pass anchor consistency
- Finish ability

Critical Factors

Reactive Athleticism	Anchor / Play Strength	Balance / Body Control
6	6	6

Positional Factors

Run Block	Pass Block	2nd Level	Awareness / Instincts
7	6	6	7

Hand Use	Range	Sustain / Finish
6	6	6
Power	**Flexibility**	**Ruggedness / Toughness**
5	6	6

Basic

			Blown Blocks			Penalties		Team
Year	G	GS	Total	Pass	Rush	Holding	False Starts	Opp Sacks
2016	15	15	15	6	9	0	1	24
2017	13	12	13	1	12	0	1	27
2018	15	15	14	7	7	1	1	15
	43	42	42	14	28	1	3	66

Team Stats

	Zone Run Blocking			Gap Run Blocking			Pass Block
Year	% of Runs	Y/A	Positive%	% of Runs	Y/A	Positive%	Pressure%
2016	64.0%	6.4	50.6%	26.5%	6.3	46.4%	29.3%
2017	55.9%	5.9	48.2%	30.6%	6.7	52.5%	35.8%
2018	62.8%	5.2	50.0%	29.1%	5.9	53.0%	30.5%
	60.9%	5.9	49.7%	28.7%	6.3	50.7%	31.6%

Deep Dive

	Blown Block %		When Running To His Gap				
Year	Pass	Run	Y/A	Yards Before Contact	Positive %	EPA	EPA Per Attempt
2018	1.58%	1.44%	6.4	2.7	60.2%	42.7	0.24

Justin Falcinelli

Clemson Tigers

Final Grade: 6.5 OC Rank: 6 of 9

Height	Weight	Year	Jersey #	Hometown
6032	315	5SR	50	Middletown, MD

One-Liner

Falcinelli has potential to be a starting-caliber center because of his base, hips, and movement skills, but he shows inconsistency and is limited by his anchor strength in pass protection.

Overall

Falcinelli was a two-year starter at center for Clemson. After a redshirt season in 2014, he played in 52 career games with 28 starts. Falcinelli is a dependable center who plays with good anticipation and awareness. He doesn't stand out as a mauler or a very quick player, but he finishes run blocks and is athletic enough to be a consistent pass blocker. Falcinelli is tough, has consistently played well against good competition, and doesn't take plays off.

Pass Game

In the pass game, Falcinelli diagnoses stunts and blitzes well and is rarely beat on initial contact or hand use. His short-area quickness and strength are good enough against ACC teams, but he may struggle versus NFL talent. He has been a solid player for Clemson who rarely allows quarterback pressures, but he does get pushed back relatively easily. He is a team-first solid contributor and teammate but won't dominate the man across from him.

Run Game

In the run game, Falcinelli is a versatile player. He is asked to pull and perform combo blocks at the second level and rarely blows an assignment. He doesn't have a huge impact in these roles but he gets his job done. He looks most comfortable blocking backside on gap-scheme plays. He rarely drives defenders back but he gives the ball carrier a chance. His strength doesn't stand out on the ACC level and is one of his weaknesses, especially when anchoring.

Last Word

By year two, Falcinelli projects as a low-end starting center, with possible backup guard flexibility based on his sound base, hips, and pulling ability. He will need to improve his quickness and anchor strength to reach a higher ceiling, but he is a player you can win with.

– Pat Dougherty

Strengths	Weaknesses
• Pulling ability and range	• Anchor strength
• Footwork and base	• Lateral agility
• Flexibility	

Critical Factors

Reactive Athleticism	Anchor / Play Strength	Balance / Body Control
6	5	6

Positional Factors

Run Block	Pass Block	2nd Level	Awareness / Instincts
6	5	5	5

Hand Use	Range	Sustain / Finish
5	7	5
Power	**Flexibility**	**Ruggedness / Toughness**
6	6	6

Basic

			Blown Blocks			Penalties		Team
Year	G	GS	Total	Pass	Rush	Holding	False Starts	Opp Sacks
2016	11	0	2	1	1	0	0	21
2017	14	14	14	8	6	0	1	31
2018	14	14	6	4	2	0	2	19
	39	28	22	13	9	0	3	71

Team Stats

	Zone Run Blocking			Gap Run Blocking			Pass Block
Year	% of Runs	Y/A	Positive%	% of Runs	Y/A	Positive%	Pressure%
2016	55.8%	4.6	42.0%	35.8%	5.0	48.1%	22.7%
2017	49.4%	4.9	47.5%	37.5%	5.5	44.4%	27.9%
2018	60.4%	7.1	50.9%	32.2%	7.1	53.8%	23.2%
	55.2%	5.6	46.8%	35.2%	5.8	48.5%	24.4%

Deep Dive

	Blown Block %		When Running To His Gap				
Year	Pass	Run	Y/A	Yards Before Contact	Positive %	EPA	EPA Per Attempt
2018	0.94%	0.51%	6.1	2.7	48.4%	11.3	0.06

Lamont Gaillard

Georgia Bulldogs
Final Grade: 6.4 OC Rank: 7 of 9

Height	Weight	Year	Jersey #	Hometown
6024	303	5SR	53	Fayetteville, NC

One-Liner
Gaillard's anchor ability, play strength, and ability to sustain and finish blocks should allow him to start at center at the next level, but his hand use and range could use improving.

Overall
Gaillard is a center who played in Georgia's pro-style offense. He played in 44 games, making starts in 42 of them at center for the Bulldogs. He is a good athlete for the position and competes and shows toughness on each play. He not only plays to the whistle but through the whistle with regularity.

Pass Game
In the pass game, Gaillard possesses good anchor and play strength as he is able to negate his opponent's strength with force and drop anchor quickly. He has good reactive athleticism and body control as he is able to mirror defender movements. He is able to keep his pad level and weight balanced in order to both sustain leverage and stay square to the line of scrimmage. He is a good pass blocker, but his hand use is just sufficient and his hand placement could use refining. At times, his hands can get outside of the shoulder pads and his initial punch can be beaten by a defender with stronger hands. He communicates well with his fellow offensive linemen and has demonstrated the ability to make line calls.

Run Game
In the run game, Gaillard shows power and leg drive to push defenders back on their heels. He can sustain and finish blocks through the whistle. His range and 2nd level ability are above average as he is able to pull effectively, but he doesn't always get himself into good position on the 2nd level. At times, he plays with a high pad level in space.

Last Word
Gaillard has good awareness and instincts, as he is able to read and react to the defense and pick up stunts effectively. He plays with a good level of ruggedness and toughness as he finishes blocks, drives defenders into the ground, and plays with an edge. His small frame and lack of range suggest he will be limited to playing center at the next level, where he projects to be a starter by his second season.

– Cole Ratliff

Strengths	Weaknesses
• Anchor	• Hand use
• Pass blocking	• Range
• Body control	• 2nd level ability

Critical Factors

Reactive Athleticism	Anchor / Play Strength	Balance / Body Control
6	6	6

Positional Factors

Run Block	Pass Block	2nd Level	Awareness / Instincts
6	6	5	6

Hand Use	Range	Sustain / Finish
5	5	6
Power	**Flexibility**	**Ruggedness / Toughness**
6	6	6

Basic

			Blown Blocks			Penalties		Team
Year	G	GS	Total	Pass	Rush	Holding	False Starts	Opp Sacks
2016	13	13	8	3	5	0	1	24
2017	15	15	18	8	10	1	2	22
2018	14	14	8	4	4	0	1	20
	42	42	34	15	19	1	4	66

Team Stats

	Zone Run Blocking			Gap Run Blocking			Pass Block
Year	% of Runs	Y/A	Positive%	% of Runs	Y/A	Positive%	Pressure%
2016	39.5%	5.1	44.6%	52.5%	5.5	44.3%	24.6%
2017	82.9%	6.6	47.2%	9.4%	4.7	36.1%	29.7%
2018	85.7%	6.5	46.8%	2.9%	5.4	43.8%	23.1%
	70.7%	6.3	46.6%	20.3%	5.4	42.8%	25.6%

Deep Dive

	Blown Block %		When Running To His Gap				
Year	Pass	Run	Y/A	Yards Before Contact	Positive %	EPA	EPA Per Attempt
2018	1.16%	0.91%	5.7	2.1	45.7%	8.5	0.03

Alec Eberle

Florida State Seminoles
Final Grade: 6.4 OC Rank: 8 of 9

*

Height	Weight	Year	Jersey #	Hometown
6032	295	5SR	54	Mechanicsville, VA

One-Liner
Eberle shows the toughness, aggression, and leadership to be an NFL center, but as a one-position player, he will need improved strength in order to become a starting-caliber player.

Overall
Eberle's primary position is center. He played in 48 career games, including 44 consecutive starts. He has decent size for the position but has short arms. Eberle is an average athlete with heavy feet and he needs to get stronger in all areas. He is an extremely tough player who has played through injuries and pain in his career.

Pass Game
In the pass game, Eberle displays good overall pass blocking ability. He has good instincts and shows the ability to recognize stunts and blitzes. He does a good job of assisting his guards when he doesn't have anyone to block. His hand usage needs to be more consistent, and he can get grabby, leading to holding calls, but overall he is sufficient in this area. He had some noticeable miscommunications in pass protection which led to free hits on the quarterback. He is usually quick to anchor against bull rushes but has trouble against powerful defensive linemen. His reactive athleticism is sufficient but his lateral agility is limited, which make it tough for him to slide and recover.

Run Game
In the run game, Eberle is a sufficient run blocker. He is quick out of his stance and very aggressive at the point of attack. He can sustain blocks and seal running lanes at the line of scrimmage, but will need better leg drive to do so consistently. Eberle has a good feel for combo blocks to the second level. He isn't strong enough to be a true mauler, but he flashes the ability to finish blocks. His power is just average and he won't move many guys on the next level, as he struggles against bigger and stronger defensive linemen. He has sufficient range and enough movement skills in space to pull. He is sufficient at getting to the second level, but more athletic linebackers will give him trouble. Eberle's balance and body control are sufficient. He ends up on the ground a little too often, but this can be improved with improved strength. He can lose leverage and get driven off the ball. He best fits a zone blocking scheme.

Last Word
Eberle is a smart player that can handle making calls for the offensive line and possesses top leadership traits and a team-first attitude. He is a center-only prospect due to his lack of arm length and inability to generate movement in the run game.

– Alex O'Brien

Strengths	Weaknesses
• Toughness and leadership	• Overall strength
• Aggression at point of attack	• Leg drive
	• Durability

Critical Factors

Reactive Athleticism	Anchor / Play Strength	Balance / Body Control
6	4	5

Positional Factors

Run Block	Pass Block	2nd Level	Awareness / Instincts
5	5	6	5

Hand Use	Range	Sustain / Finish
5	6	6
Power	**Flexibility**	**Ruggedness / Toughness**
5	5	8

Basic

			Blown Blocks			Penalties		Team
Year	G	GS	Total	Pass	Rush	Holding	False Starts	Opp Sacks
2016	13	13	16	9	7	2	3	37
2017	13	13	23	14	9	2	3	32
2018	12	12	7	5	2	2	1	37
	38	38	46	28	18	6	7	106

Team Stats

	Zone Run Blocking			Gap Run Blocking			Pass Block
Year	% of Runs	Y/A	Positive%	% of Runs	Y/A	Positive%	Pressure%
2016	65.6%	5.9	48.0%	23.8%	7.4	51.2%	33.3%
2017	69.9%	5.4	46.4%	19.2%	4.4	31.8%	39.8%
2018	56.4%	4.4	31.8%	26.5%	2.0	24.5%	37.3%
	64.4%	5.3	43.4%	23.0%	4.8	37.0%	36.6%

Deep Dive

	Blown Block %		When Running To His Gap				
Year	Pass	Run	Y/A	Yards Before Contact	Positive %	EPA	EPA Per Attempt
2018	1.02%	0.57%	3.9	0.7	32.8%	-36.0	-0.20

Ryan Anderson

Wake Forest Demon Deacons
Final Grade: 6.2 OC Rank: 9 of 9

Height	Weight	Year	Jersey #	Hometown
6052	305	5SR	70	Raleigh, NC

One-Liner
Anderson is a versatile interior offensive lineman who has a quality combination of athleticism, movement skills, and instincts, but he may struggle at the next level against stronger defensive linemen.

Overall
Anderson was a versatile offensive lineman for Wake Forest. He played right tackle and right guard but was predominantly a center, which is where he started 42 of 46 games throughout his playing career. He is a good athlete and possesses good foot speed, decent balance and flexibility, and very good height and frame. Anderson is a strong competitor, playing with an aggressive temperament, and flashing some grit to finish blocks and attack defenders consistently.

Pass Game
Anderson is sufficient in the pass game, displaying a decent anchor with flashes of the necessary ability to neutralize the pass rush and use his long arms to lock out defenders, negating their strength. He plays with his head on a swivel and displays good reactive athleticism and instincts, showing a good feel for the pass rush and good lateral agility to mirror movements from defenders and keep his shoulders square while engaging physically. He has good hand usage, utilizing smart timing and placement to establish inside control and win leverage on defenders in pass protection. He struggles with stronger defensive linemen on bull rushes, showing a tendency to give up ground and get pushed back. He has a tendency to play with a high pad level, but shows sufficient flexibility in pass protection to recover from awkward positions.

Run Game
In the run game, Anderson is a good blocker, showing effectiveness on backside blocks with a quick first step and strong punch. He wins with positioning and is able to reach defenders with good pull quickness and range in space, consistently getting his head across defenders. He is able to consistently sustain the line of scrimmage during zone schemes, and is effective on double teams and combination blocks. Anderson generates good movement in power situations, using his leg drive and a strong base while staying upright. He works up to the second level well with quickness and athleticism while taking smart angles on linebackers. He struggles to adjust and locate targets while on the move, and has difficulty staying on quicker linebackers.

Last Word
Anderson can be a contributing backup at multiple positions across the line due to his length and balanced overall skillset. He is most experienced and the cleanest fit at center, where he can best utilize his instincts and second level movement skills.

– Nick Giella

Strengths	**Weaknesses**
• Size and length	• Anchor and play strength
• Second level skills	• Finishing ability
• Experienced versatility	• Flexibility

Critical Factors

Reactive Athleticism	Anchor / Play Strength	Balance / Body Control
6	5	5

Positional Factors

Run Block	Pass Block	2nd Level	Awareness / Instincts
6	5	6	6

Hand Use	Range	Sustain / Finish
6	6	5
Power	**Flexibility**	**Ruggedness / Toughness**
6	5	6

Basic

			Blown Blocks			Penalties		Team
Year	G	GS	Total	Pass	Rush	Holding	False Starts	Opp Sacks
2016	13	13	23	14	9	0	8	39
2017	13	13	7	0	7	0	3	19
2018	13	13	4	2	2	1	0	34
	39	39	34	16	18	1	11	92

Team Stats

	Zone Run Blocking			Gap Run Blocking			Pass Block
Year	% of Runs	Y/A	Positive%	% of Runs	Y/A	Positive%	Pressure%
2016	43.8%	3.9	41.4%	43.6%	4.6	28.8%	42.1%
2017	58.7%	4.5	38.8%	31.9%	5.5	39.3%	29.4%
2018	56.3%	5.0	41.3%	33.2%	5.2	37.9%	31.2%
	53.2%	4.6	40.5%	36.1%	5.0	34.8%	33.8%

Deep Dive

	Blown Block %		When Running To His Gap				
Year	Pass	Run	Y/A	Yards Before Contact	Positive %	EPA	EPA Per Attempt
2018	0.43%	0.37%	5.2	2.4	43.2%	-7.7	-0.03

Glossary

Blown Block %
Blown Block Rate, the percentage of blocking snaps that the player had a blown block

Positive% (Runs To Gap split)
Percentage of carries by the running back with a positive Expected Points Added

Pressure%
Percentage of plays where a defensive player recorded a quarterback hurry, hit, knockdown or sack

Y/A (Runs To Gap split)
Yards per rush attempt

Offensive Lineman Leaderboards

Pass Blown Block Rate Leaders			
Rank	Player	Team	Pass BB%
1	Chris Lindstrom	Boston College	0.00%
2	Javon Patterson	Ole Miss	0.21%
3	Dalton Risner	Kansas State	0.31%
4	Ryan Anderson	Wake Forest	0.43%
5	Andre Dillard	Washington State	0.44%
6	Erik McCoy	Texas A&M	0.44%
7	Kaleb McGary	Washington	0.47%
8	Cody Ford	Oklahoma	0.48%
9	Ben Powers	Oklahoma	0.48%
10	Nate Davis	Charlotte	0.52%

Runs to Gap: Positive Play Percentage Leaders			
Rank	Player	Team	Positive %
1	Ross Pierschbacher	Alabama	60.2%
2	Cody Ford	Oklahoma	56.3%
3	Bobby Evans	Oklahoma	56.3%
4	Andre Dillard	Washington State	54.5%
5	Dru Samia	Oklahoma	53.8%
6	Michael Deiter	Wisconsin	53.1%
7	Jawaan Taylor	Florida	51.7%
8	Mitch Hyatt	Clemson	51.4%
9	Beau Benzschawel	Wisconsin	51.1%
10	Connor McGovern	Penn State	50.9%

Run Blown Block Rate Leaders			
Rank	Player	Team	Run BB%
1	Jawaan Taylor	Florida	0.23%
2	Dennis Daley	South Carolina	0.31%
3	Ryan Anderson	Wake Forest	0.37%
4	Derrick Kelly II	Florida State	0.39%
5	Justin Falcinelli	Clemson	0.51%
6	Alec Eberle	Florida State	0.57%
7	Yodny Cajuste	West Virginia	0.65%
8	Martez Ivey	Florida	0.66%
9	Elgton Jenkins	Mississippi State	0.69%
10	Max Scharping	Northern Illinois	0.72%

Runs to Gap: Rushing EPA Leaders			
Rank	Player	Team	EPA
1	Bobby Evans	Oklahoma	48.1
2	Dru Samia	Oklahoma	47.2
3	Ross Pierschbacher	Alabama	42.7
4	Cody Ford	Oklahoma	41.1
5	Beau Benzschawel	Wisconsin	35.3
6	Ben Powers	Oklahoma	34.4
7	Connor McGovern	Penn State	31.4
8	Deion Calhoun	Mississippi State	31.2
9	Jawaan Taylor	Florida	30.9
10	Elgton Jenkins	Mississippi State	23.4

Runs to Gap: Yards Before Contact Leaders			
Rank	Player	Team	Yards Before Contact
1	Cody Ford	Oklahoma	4.4
2	Bobby Evans	Oklahoma	4.1
3	Ben Powers	Oklahoma	4.1
4	Derwin Gray	Maryland	3.9
5	Mitch Hyatt	Clemson	3.9
6	Martez Ivey	Florida	3.9
7	Dalton Risner	Kansas State	3.7
8	Max Scharping	Northern Illinois	3.6
9	Dru Samia	Oklahoma	3.5
10	Connor McGovern	Penn State	3.4

Runs to Gap: Rushing EPA Per Attempt Leaders			
Rank	Player	Team	EPA Per Attempt
1	Bobby Evans	Oklahoma	0.30
2	Cody Ford	Oklahoma	0.26
3	Ross Pierschbacher	Alabama	0.24
4	Dru Samia	Oklahoma	0.20
5	Jawaan Taylor	Florida	0.18
6	Beau Benzschawel	Wisconsin	0.16
7	Ben Powers	Oklahoma	0.15
8	Andre Dillard	Washington State	0.14
9	Connor McGovern	Penn State	0.14
10	Deion Calhoun	Mississippi State	0.14

NOSE TACKLE

Nose Tackle Grading Scale

GRADE	DESCRIPTION
9.0 – 7.0	High-end 3 down starter. Pro Bowl level.
6.9 – 6.7	Strong starter who plays on all 3 downs.
6.3	Solid 2 down starter. Run only player.
6.2	Versatile backup with positional flexibility.
6.1 – 6.0	Developmental. Top traits but needs time.
5.9	Top backup NT. Only 1 position player.
5.8	Average backup NT. Only 1 position player.
5.7	Low-end backup NT with growable upside.

Nose Tackle Rankings

Rank	Name	Grade	Page
1	Dexter Lawrence	6.9	312
2	Daylon Mack	6.3	314
3	Khalen Saunders	6.2	316
4	Dontavius Russell	6.2	318
5	Kenny Bigelow Jr.	6.2	320
6	Greg Gaines	5.9	322
7	Ed Alexander	5.9	324
8	Shy Tuttle	5.7	326

Dexter Lawrence

Clemson Tigers
Final Grade: 6.9 NT Rank: 1 of 8

Height	Weight	Year	Jersey #	Hometown
6032	350	3JR	90	Wake Forest, NC

One-Liner
Lawrence is a strong interior defensive lineman who has the hand use, body control and mismatch ability to be a solid starter at the next level, but he'll need to improve his endurance to make sure he sees the field to make the most of his skill set.

Overall
Lawrence primarily played NT for Clemson's base 4-3 defense, but lined up anywhere from 0- to 5-technique and sometimes slid outside when they played a 3-man front on pass rush situations. He played in 40 games with 36 starts during his time with the Tigers. As a basketball player in high school, he has good reactive athleticism for the interior defensive line position. He also brings ruggedness and toughness in his play. His stamina/endurance is a question, as he's only able to be full-go for about 2-3 plays at a time.

Run Game
In the run game, he's a player that offenses should want to double team, although he's able to eat them up most of the time. He beats up centers and guards one-on-one and makes plays around the line of scrimmage. He has good lateral strength and mobility to get down the line and make plays on the ball carrier. He has good range that allows him to successfully make all plays within the tackle box. He has very good balance and body control at the POA. Offensive linemen have a tough time getting him to the ground. He has a thick lower-half and stays upright with good leverage to play his gaps and eat up space. When he gets to the ball carrier, he brings them down and doesn't miss very many tackles.

Pass Game
He brings some pass-rush ability, mostly as a bull rusher. He has the heavy hands and strength at the POA to control the lineman in front of him and drive him back into the quarterback. He wins the leverage battle most plays and is disruptive by creating pressures more often than generating raw stats. He brings mismatch ability when he's able to go up against a lineman one-on-one to use his bull rush ability, strength and power.

Last Word
Lawrence projects best as a 4-3 nose tackle that can interchangeably play the 3-technique as well. He could play nose in a 3-4, but his skillset would be better utilized in a 4-3. Although he doesn't have elite endurance to stay on the field for sustained drives, he's a three-down player that will contribute in the run game and as a pass rusher on 3rd downs.

– Nathan Cooper

Strengths	Weaknesses
• Play strength at POA	• Endurance questions
• Body control	• Sufficient pass rush
• Heavy hands	

Critical Factors

Play Strength	Mismatch	Balance / Body Control
7	6	7

Positional Factors

Pass Rush	Hand Use	Range
5	6	6
Stamina	**Ruggedness / Toughness**	**Football Intelligence**
5	6	6
Production	**Tackling**	
6	6	

Basic

	Tackling			Pass Rush					
Year	Tackles	TFL	FF	Sacks	Hurries	Hits	Knockdowns	Pressures	Passes Batted
2016	59	9.0	0	6.5	33	21	6	43	0
2017	36	3.5	1	3.0	13	5	2	20	0
2018	34	7.0	0	1.5	23	16	6	25	0
	129	19.5	1	11.0	69	42	14	88	0

Advanced

	Tackling				Per Game			Impact	
Year	Broken Tackles	BT%	Tackle Share	Avg Depth of Tackle	Tackles	TFL	Pressures	Pressure Share	EPA on Sacks/TFL
2016	5	7.9%	5.2%	1.6	3.9	0.6	2.9	16.8%	-12.8
2017	2	5.4%	3.1%	1.9	2.9	0.3	1.7	7.2%	-6.9
2018	0	0.0%	3.1%	1.0	2.6	0.5	1.9	8.1%	-13.2
	7	5.2%	3.8%	1.5	3.2	0.5	2.2	10.4%	-32.9

Deep Dive

	Total Snaps		Pass Rush		When Run At			Lined Up		
Year	Pass	Run	Pressure%	Sack%	RunAt%	Bounce%	Pos%	NT%	DT%	DE%
2018	240	199	10.3%	0.6%	18.4%	41.7%	19.4%	48.1%	48.7%	2.1%

Daylon Mack

Texas A&M Aggies
Final Grade: 6.3 NT Rank: 2 of 8

Height	Weight	Year	Jersey #	Hometown
6010	327	4SR	34	Gladewater, TX

One-Liner
Mack is a powerful, tough NT who has the ability to collapse the pocket in the pass game, but needs to add pass-rush moves, consistent hand use and endurance to become a factor on all three downs.

Overall
Mack was a nose tackle in Texas A&M's 3-4, playing 0-3 techniques. He was primarily a backup at Texas A&M until 2018, starting 14 of 52 games played. He is very good in the run game and does not play on 3rd down most of the time. He is a big body who is athletic, strong and moves well for 320 pounds. An issue is that he noticeably gets tired and less explosive throughout the game.

Run Game
In the run game, he takes on multiple defenders and plugs the gaps very well. He can make tackles behind the line of scrimmage. He is extremely explosive off the ball, as his first step is noticeably quicker than most DTs. He is laterally strong and is rangy enough to get down the line to make plays. He shows good mismatch ability and will work over offensive linemen when in 1-on-1 situations. He shows some stamina and endurance issues and will only make it a few plays at a time.

Pass Game
Against the pass, his explosion and strength allow him to get good push off the ball. He has the ability to drive an OL back into the QB with his strength at the POA. He shows good balance and body control. His technique is clean, and he looks comfortable and balanced exploding off the ball. His hand use is inconsistent and needs improvement. He does a good job of getting his hands up in the passing game and using them to drive the OL with a bull rush. However, he almost exclusively uses the bull rush. He did not use his hands to get much leverage or separation. He shows a tendency to give up on some plays, especially once he stalls out or gets beat at the POA.

Last Word
Mack projects as a two-down NT that fits best in a 3-4, but could also fit into a 4-3 defensive scheme. His explosion and strength at the POA should prove well on early downs, but he needs to improve his pass rush repertoire to be more effective in the pass game.

– SIS Scouting Staff

Strengths	**Weaknesses**
• First-step explosion	• Overaggressiveness in run game
• Collapses the pocket	• Inconsistent hand use
• Athleticism	• Play recognition

Critical Factors

Play Strength	Mismatch	Balance / Body Control
6	6	6

Positional Factors

Pass Rush	Hand Use	Range
5	5	6
Stamina	**Ruggedness / Toughness**	**Football Intelligence**
5	5	5
Production	**Tackling**	
5	6	

Basic

	Tackling			Pass Rush					
Year	Tackles	TFL	FF	Sacks	Hurries	Hits	Knockdowns	Pressures	Passes Batted
2016	25	3.5	1	1.5	5	2	0	7	0
2017	20	4.5	1	1.0	13	6	1	15	0
2018	30	10.0	0	5.5	23	10	4	29	1
	75	18.0	2	8.0	41	18	5	51	1

Advanced

	Tackling				Per Game			Impact	
Year	Broken Tackles	BT%	Tackle Share	Avg Depth of Tackle	Tackles	TFL	Pressures	Pressure Share	EPA on Sacks/TFL
2016	3	10.7%	2.1%	2.1	1.9	0.3	0.5	3.0%	-7.5
2017	0	0.0%	2.0%	2.1	1.5	0.3	1.2	6.6%	-7.6
2018	2	6.3%	4.1%	0.9	2.3	0.8	2.2	15.3%	-17.3
	5	6.3%	2.6%	1.6	1.9	0.5	1.3	7.9%	-32.4

Deep Dive

	Total Snaps		Pass Rush		When Run At			Lined Up		
Year	Pass	Run	Pressure%	Sack%	RunAt%	Bounce%	Pos%	NT%	DT%	DE%
2018	258	217	10.3%	2.1%	19.1%	47.5%	35.0%	44.2%	51.8%	3.6%

Khalen Saunders

Western Illinois Leathernecks
Final Grade: 6.2 NT Rank: 3 of 8

Height	Weight	Year	Jersey #	Hometown
6005	320	4SR	99	St. Louis, MO

One-Liner
Saunders was a dominant interior lineman at the FCS level, where he utilized high-end athleticism and agility to disrupt backfields with finesse, but will need to improve his physicality and lower body strength to become a complete three-down NFL competitor.

Overall
Saunders was a defensive lineman in Western Illinois' base 3-4 defensive front, mostly lining up as a 0, 1 or 3-technique, with occasional pass rushing snaps as a stand-up edge. He played 47 games in his decorated career for the Leathernecks, making two All-Conference teams and being named a Second Team FCS All-American in 2018. He is a fantastic athlete for his size, and his gymnastics background is apparent in his open-field speed and agility. Saunders shows great hustle sideline to sideline and can get on impressive hot streaks, but his snap-to-snap physical motor needs consistency.

Run Game
Against the run, he comes off the ball with good leverage and explosive hips, flashing a quick strike and ability to use his length to bench press and read. He does a great job of feeling down blocks and sitting with good core strength and interior contact balance while keeping his eyes in the backfield to stack and shed. Saunders has dominant quickness to knife through outside zone runs and disrupt behind the line, but at the next level he will need to play with more lane discipline. He often jumps behind reaching linemen, which results in tackles for loss as well as open alleys for backs. He does not anchor well vertically, especially with lower-body strength against double teams. Saunders is a very finesse nose, winning with quick hands and a heavily-used juke-swim move, but needs to improve as a stout physical interior presence. He's tough to handle laterally with his quickness and body control, and has very impressive range downfield and outside the tackles, but can be moved backwards.

Pass Game
As a pass rusher, he dances too much at the line of scrimmage and is content to spy. Saunders needs to become a better pocket collapser using bull rushes, as his one-trick agility that dominated FCS opponents won't be as advantageous in the NFL. He flashed better power and physical leverage in Mobile at the Senior Bowl, competing well against top D-I talent. If he can bring that level of upfield push to games, he will round into a more complete player.

Last Word
Saunders projects as a one-gapping rotational backup along a defensive line, whose quickness, hand use, and athleticism will translate well, but will have a ceiling if he doesn't improve his lower-body strength and ability to consistently stalemate and drive with physicality.

– John Todd

Strengths	Weaknesses
• Quick hands	• Anchor strength
• Speed and hustle in open field	• Lane discipline
• Stack and shed awareness	• Interior physicality and pocket push

Critical Factors

Play Strength	Mismatch	Balance / Body Control
5	5	6

Positional Factors

Pass Rush	Hand Use	Range
5	7	7
Stamina	**Ruggedness / Toughness**	**Football Intelligence**
6	5	6

Production	Tackling
6	5

Khalen Saunders comes from a school with a pretty good football pedigree. Alums include linebacker Bryan Cox and defensive back Rodney Harrison. But if selected, Saunders would be the first player from the school to be drafted this decade.

"I've gotta earn everything I get," Saunders said at the Senior Bowl.

Saunders is best known for a viral video in which he shows off that he can do backflips, which is all the more impressive when you consider he weighs 320 pounds. Saunders learned how to do backflips growing up in St. Louis.

"Once you learn how to do it, you don't forget how to do it," he said. "I take pride in being above-average in my athleticism."

Saunders was a three-year starter, who ranked third on the team in tackles and second in sacks his senior season. For that, he earned AP All-American honors.

And by the way, Saunders has a collegiate rushing and receiving touchdown to his credit. Perhaps we'll see his backflip as an NFL touchdown celebration.

Dontavius Russell

Auburn Tigers
Final Grade: 6.2 NT Rank: 4 of 8

Height	Weight	Year	Jersey #	Hometown
6031	319	4SR	95	Carrollton, GA

One-Liner
Russell has the balance and play recognition to be a versatile reserve player, but lacks the play strength and mismatch ability to be a consistent threat as a starter on the defensive line at the next level.

Overall
Russell is a DT who lined up on the right side of the line at Auburn, primarily as a 3-technique, but has reduced down to the nose on occasion. They would also stand him up and have him rush the edge on a few plays. He was a mainstay on Auburn's defensive line, starting in 49 of the 52 games he played in. Russell is a good athlete for his size with good play speed, balance, and quickness. He has sufficient strength, but attacks slower linemen before they are able to engage him. He always gets his hands on the lineman first and will battle through the whistle. He gives good chase when he's on the field, but doesn't have the endurance to run more than three plays at a time.

Run Game
Against the run, Russell's first-step quickness and hands allow him to control the lineman, then diagnose the play quickly and cut off the runner. He can get overpowered on double teams. His hands and balance allow him to evade scrape blocks. He has enough quickness and technique to beat doubles and can win on pass downs against an OC.

Pass Game
Against the pass, Russell uses his get-off and hands to win. He is adept at feeling screens and is able to use his athleticism to blow them up.

Last Word
Overall, he's a solid player against the run and pass, but doesn't possess much mismatch ability to be targeted by offensive coaches. By his second year, Russell projects to be a versatile reserve on the defensive interior. He has the pass rush ability to move around on the line and should improve his strength once in an NFL weight room. On special teams, he will most likely only play on FG units due to his size.

– Ben Hrkach

Strengths	**Weaknesses**
• Balance	• Play strength
• Pass rush ability	• Mismatch ability
• Football intelligence	• Range

Critical Factors

Play Strength	Mismatch	Balance / Body Control
5	5	6

Positional Factors

Pass Rush	Hand Use	Range
6	6	5
Stamina	**Ruggedness / Toughness**	**Football Intelligence**
5	5	6

Production	Tackling
4	5

Basic

	Tackling			Pass Rush					
Year	Tackles	TFL	FF	Sacks	Hurries	Hits	Knockdowns	Pressures	Passes Batted
2016	28	0.0	0	0.0	9	7	1	11	0
2017	45	7.5	1	4.0	13	10	8	18	0
2018	35	6.0	0	0.5	10	7	2	11	0
	108	13.5	1	4.5	32	24	11	40	0

Advanced

	Tackling				Per Game			Impact	
Year	Broken Tackles	BT%	Tackle Share	Avg Depth of Tackle	Tackles	TFL	Pressures	Pressure Share	EPA on Sacks/TFL
2016	5	15.2%	2.6%	2.8	2.2	0.0	0.8	5.3%	0.0
2017	5	10.0%	4.6%	2.2	3.2	0.5	1.3	7.5%	-9.2
2018	3	7.9%	3.4%	1.6	2.7	0.5	0.8	5.7%	-8.9
	13	10.7%	3.6%	2.2	2.7	0.3	1.0	6.3%	-18.1

Deep Dive

	Total Snaps		Pass Rush		When Run At			Lined Up		
Year	Pass	Run	Pressure%	Sack%	RunAt%	Bounce%	Pos%	NT%	DT%	DE%
2018	293	265	3.7%	0.2%	14.7%	34.2%	23.7%	11.8%	74.4%	11.5%

Kenny Bigelow Jr.

West Virginia Mountaineers
Final Grade: 6.2 NT Rank: 5 of 8

✱

Height	Weight	Year	Jersey #	Hometown
6025	307	5SR	40	Wilmington, DE

One-Liner
Bigelow has had a difficult injury history, but has quick hands and plenty of explosiveness and athleticism left to make an impact as a rotational interior pass rusher at the next level.

Overall
Bigelow played primarily as a nose tackle for West Virginia in 2018 and played sparingly as a 1- and a 3-technique previously at Southern California. Before transferring, he played in 19 career games for USC, plagued by knee injuries, and then started all 12 games for the Mountaineers. He is a quick-twitch athlete with very good first-step explosion. He has average strength and balance for the NFL. Bigelow has worked hard to return from serious injury, but on the field, he needs to improve his effort away from the ball.

Run Game
Against the run, he gets his hands on opposing linemen quickly. Due to his first step, he can often get in the backfield before the line can react. He relies on a swim move very often and can expose his chest too much to smarter, quicker opponents. He works down the line well with his athleticism and range. When facing doubles, Bigelow rarely holds his position with lower body strength and gets washed out easily.

Pass Game
Against the pass, Bigelow uses his get-off and hand use to win against solo blockers. Once in the backfield, his lack of lateral movement limits his ability to close and finish at the quarterback.

Last Word
In the NFL, Bigelow projects to fit across a line's interior based on the front as a one-gapper, offering more of a contribution on passing downs. His lack of strength and stamina limits his ability to play all three downs as a nose tackle. His injury history is troublesome, but he has a pedigree as a former top prep athlete and has still shown enough athleticism and explosiveness to make an impact.

– Ben Hrkach

Strengths	**Weaknesses**
• First-step explosion	• Lower-body strength
• Quick hands	• Motor
• Pass rush upside	• Injury history

Critical Factors

Play Strength	Mismatch	Balance / Body Control
5	6	5

Positional Factors

Pass Rush	Hand Use	Range
6	5	6
Stamina	**Ruggedness / Toughness**	**Football Intelligence**
5	6	4

Production	Tackling
4	4

Basic

	Tackling			Pass Rush					
Year	Tackles	TFL	FF	Sacks	Hurries	Hits	Knockdowns	Pressures	Passes Batted
2017	1	0.0	0	0.0	1	1	1	1	0
2018	21	5.0	1	2.0	11	6	2	13	0
	22	5.0	1	2.0	12	7	3	14	0

Advanced

	Tackling				Per Game			Impact	
Year	Broken Tackles	BT%	Tackle Share	Avg Depth of Tackle	Tackles	TFL	Pressures	Pressure Share	EPA on Sacks/TFL
2017	0	0.0%	0.1%	0.0	0.2	0.0	0.2	0.4%	0.0
2018	2	8.7%	2.8%	1.1	1.8	0.4	1.1	7.3%	-6.8
	2	8.3%	1.4%	1.0	1.2	0.3	0.8	3.1%	-6.8

Deep Dive

	Total Snaps		Pass Rush		When Run At			Lined Up		
Year	Pass	Run	Pressure%	Sack%	RunAt%	Bounce%	Pos%	NT%	DT%	DE%
2018	223	231	6.2%	1.0%	36.1%	34.1%	46.3%	96.9%	0.4%	0.2%

Greg Gaines

Washington Huskies
Final Grade: 5.9 NT Rank: 6 of 8

Height	Weight	Year	Jersey #	Hometown
6011	307	5SR	99	La Habra, CA

One-Liner
Gaines is a stout interior defender who is strong at occupying double teams, but will be limited outside of his range and motor.

Overall
Gaines was primarily a nose tackle in Washington's base three-man front, but often shifted out to 3- and even 5-technique. He played 54 career games, starting 47 of them. Built like a fire hydrant, Gaines has a stout lower body and thick but short arms, with a fairly lean core for his size. His change of direction is understandably poor, but he has a high motor. His extensive playing history and lack of games missed for the Huskies, despite injury, proves a high level of competitive toughness and accountability.

Run Game
Against the run, Gaines is strong at the point of attack and excels at eating up blockers at the line of scrimmage. He is asked to balance between one- and two-gapping, but offers more value to his team in a two-gapping role. He regularly stalemates double teams and occupies the interior of the offensive line, freeing up teammates such as 2017 first-round pick Vita Vea to rush one on one. His inconsistent leverage and lack of elite play strength will keep him from fighting through double teams. He shows very good range against zone schemes and often chases down ball carriers with aggression well outside the tackle box. His hand usage is stronger and more accurate against the run than in the pass game, but his short arms make it difficult for him to shed blocks.

Pass Game
As a pass rusher, his hand usage is erratic and undisciplined. Gaines is usually taken off the field in obvious 3rd down situations, but when asked, he has shown some ability to be a contributor in this area. Most of his positive rushes need to be manufactured, however. Specifically, Washington uses him in a number of twists and stunts, and he does a good job of attacking angles to utilize his strength to get pressure, despite a lack of rush moves and technique.

Last Word
Gaines projects as a two-down backup nose tackle with minimal positional flexibility, and the ability to capably fill in a starting role.

– John Todd

Strengths	Weaknesses
• Stalemating double teams	• Upfield disruption
• Range outside the tackles	• Pass rush technique
• Durability and team-first attitude	• Arm length

Critical Factors

Play Strength	Mismatch	Balance / Body Control
6	5	5

Positional Factors

Pass Rush	Hand Use	Range
5	5	7
Stamina	**Ruggedness / Toughness**	**Football Intelligence**
6	7	6

Production	Tackling
6	6

Basic

	Tackling			Pass Rush					
Year	Tackles	TFL	FF	Sacks	Hurries	Hits	Knockdowns	Pressures	Passes Batted
2016	35	9.0	0	4.0	15	5	2	20	0
2017	31	5.5	0	2.5	13	9	4	18	3
2018	54	5.5	0	3.5	29	14	6	37	0
	120	20.0	0	10.0	57	28	12	75	3

Advanced

	Tackling				Per Game			Impact	
Year	Broken Tackles	BT%	Tackle Share	Avg Depth of Tackle	Tackles	TFL	Pressures	Pressure Share	EPA on Sacks/TFL
2016	9	20.5%	3.9%	0.9	2.5	0.6	1.4	8.1%	-8.1
2017	2	6.1%	3.2%	1.6	2.4	0.4	1.4	9.5%	-9.5
2018	1	1.8%	5.7%	1.9	3.9	0.4	2.6	16.5%	-11.1
	12	9.1%	4.3%	1.5	2.9	0.5	1.8	11.4%	-28.7

Deep Dive

	Total Snaps		Pass Rush		When Run At			Lined Up		
Year	Pass	Run	Pressure%	Sack%	RunAt%	Bounce%	Pos%	NT%	DT%	DE%
2018	376	293	9.6%	0.7%	30.0%	52.9%	32.2%	39.9%	52.0%	7.5%

Ed Alexander

LSU Tigers
Final Grade: 5.9 NT Rank: 7 of 8

Height	Weight	Year	Jersey #	Hometown
6021	331	3JR	99	Hammond, LA

One-Liner

Alexander is a very strong nose tackle with some playmaking ability against the run, but he is raw as a pass rusher and will need improved technique to become more than a space eater in the league.

Overall

Alexander is a nose tackle who played in 32 games in his three years at LSU. He has very good size and strength. Alexander has good arm length, balance, and flexibility. He has good bend in his knees and ankles. He fires out with good leverage and strikes well with a good first step. He routinely uses his play strength to beat his opponents. He uses his very strong lower body to anchor and hold his ground. Alexander shows sufficient strength in the upper body, with decent shed skills. He is a good mismatch against weaker competition and won his fair share of reps against the top competition in his conference. Teams often accounted for Alexander with double teams, and he was adept at occupying and stalemating at the line.

Run Game

Alexander shows good range when moving laterally against off-tackle and outside runs, tracking the ballcarrier naturally. He runs well and is a frequent contributor in backside pursuit. His football intelligence is sufficient, as he shows the ability to diagnose runs and screens but can be caught being too aggressive attacking upfield.

Pass Game

Alexander's ability to rush the passer mostly comes from his strength to bull rush and push the pocket. He does not show a wide repertoire of pass rush moves. Alexander has good hand use, often getting his hands inside and on the chest plate of offensive linemen to win with leverage. When he was healthy, he played a majority of snaps without showing fatigue.

Last Word

Alexander's production is underwhelming but he was accounted for by opposing offenses regularly. Alexander projects to be a rotational first-and-second-down nose tackle with limited pass rush ability in the NFL.

– Jake Schwanitz

Strengths	Weaknesses
• Play strength	• Pass rushing
• Range and lateral movement	• Production
• Stamina	• Play diagnosis

Critical Factors

Play Strength	Mismatch	Balance / Body Control
7	5	6

Positional Factors

Pass Rush	Hand Use	Range
4	5	6
Stamina	**Ruggedness / Toughness**	**Football Intelligence**
6	6	5

Production	Tackling
5	5

Basic

	Tackling			Pass Rush					
Year	Tackles	TFL	FF	Sacks	Hurries	Hits	Knockdowns	Pressures	Passes Batted
2016	13	0.5	0	0.0	2	1	0	2	0
2017	18	1.0	0	1.0	7	4	2	8	0
2018	27	3.0	0	1.0	13	9	5	15	0
	58	4.5	0	2.0	22	14	7	25	0

Advanced

	Tackling				Per Game			Impact	
Year	Broken Tackles	BT%	Tackle Share	Avg Depth of Tackle	Tackles	TFL	Pressures	Pressure Share	EPA on Sacks/TFL
2016	0	0.0%	1.6%	2.9	1.2	0.0	0.2	1.2%	-0.9
2017	2	10.0%	1.7%	1.9	1.8	0.1	0.8	3.4%	-1.5
2018	2	6.9%	2.4%	1.6	2.5	0.3	1.4	6.8%	-3.5
	4	6.5%	1.9%	2.0	1.8	0.1	0.8	4.0%	5.9

Deep Dive

	Total Snaps		Pass Rush		When Run At			Lined Up		
Year	Pass	Run	Pressure%	Sack%	RunAt%	Bounce%	Pos%	NT%	DT%	DE%
2018	175	195	7.5%	0.6%	30.0%	24.6%	56.1%	94.3%	5.4%	0.3%

Shy Tuttle

Tennessee Volunteers
Final Grade: 5.7 NT Rank: 8 of 8

Height	Weight	Year	Jersey #	Hometown
6021	300	4SR	2	Midway, NC

One-Liner
Tuttle lacks interior strength and toughness, but he may be able to further develop his quickness, athleticism, and hands to become a rotational piece.

Overall
Tuttle typically lined up as a 0- or 3-technique for Tennessee. His first two years on campus were shortened due to season-ending injuries, but he stayed relatively healthy during his junior and senior years. Tuttle shows good burst off the line and pursues plays well from sideline to sideline. He doesn't have outstanding strength, stoutness or shed ability but he controls his gap and penetrates well when asked to do so.

Run Game
In the run game, Tuttle usually is a two-gap defender. He plays with good discipline and shows his athleticism in pursuit. He has the ability to stalemate run blockers and consistently keep himself in the play but doesn't have great strength. When asked to one-gap, he has flashed but rarely blows anybody off the ball. Tuttle diagnoses plays well, and in one-on-one situations, he stacks, reads and redirects the ballcarrier well. He has struggled against double teams and is limited by his shed ability and overall strength.

Pass Game
In the pass game, Tuttle shows good athleticism but didn't have a huge impact for Tennessee. He mainly tries to power his way to the quarterback but has had average production, largely due to injury. He has quick hands and has flashed agility and motor but doesn't get to the quarterback consistently.

Last Word
Tuttle had some good moments and was a solid nose guard for the Vols but can't be relied upon to step into this role in the NFL. He best projects as a depth backup interior player, who will need to further prove his durability and show consistent athleticism to be given a rotational role on a defense.

– Pat Dougherty

Strengths	Weaknesses
• Quick hands	• Double-team anchor
• Agility/ body control	• Upfield disruption
• Interior athleticism	• Durability

Critical Factors

Play Strength	Mismatch	Balance / Body Control
4	5	6

Positional Factors

Pass Rush	Hand Use	Range
4	6	6
Stamina	**Ruggedness / Toughness**	**Football Intelligence**
5	4	5

Production	Tackling
4	5

Basic

	Tackling			Pass Rush					
Year	Tackles	TFL	FF	Sacks	Hurries	Hits	Knockdowns	Pressures	Passes Batted
2016	9	1.0	0	0.0	4	1	0	4	0
2017	27	2.5	0	0.0	1	0	0	1	0
2018	30	2.0	0	1.0	9	3	0	10	0
	66	5.5	0	1.0	14	4	0	15	0

Advanced

	Tackling				Per Game			Impact	
Year	Broken Tackles	BT%	Tackle Share	Avg Depth of Tackle	Tackles	TFL	Pressures	Pressure Share	EPA on Sacks/TFL
2016	1	10.0%	0.8%	3.5	1.3	0.1	0.6	1.9%	-1.9
2017	0	0.0%	2.7%	2.3	2.7	0.3	0.1	0.7%	-5.4
2018	6	16.7%	3.6%	2.8	2.5	0.2	0.8	6.3%	-3.4
	7	9.6%	2.2%	2.7	2.3	0.2	0.5	2.9%	-10.6

Deep Dive

	Total Snaps		Pass Rush		When Run At			Lined Up		
Year	Pass	Run	Pressure%	Sack%	RunAt%	Bounce%	Pos%	NT%	DT%	DE%
2018	261	284	3.6%	0.0%	33.3%	39.4%	37.2%	44.4%	51.0%	4.6%

DEFENSIVE TACKLE / 5-TECH

Defensive Tackle / 5-Tech Grading Scale

GRADE	DESCRIPTION
9.0 – 7.0	High-end 3 down starter. Pro Bowl level.
6.9 – 6.7	Strong starter who plays on all 3 downs.
6.6 – 6.5	Lower-end starter. 2 down player or plus pass rusher.
6.2	Versatile backup with positional flexibility.
6.1 – 6.0	Developmental. Top traits but needs time.
5.9	Top backup. 3 down, 1 position player.
5.8	Role playing backup. Base or 3rd down role.
5.7	Low-end backup.

Defensive Tackle / 5-Tech Rankings

Quinnen Williams

Alabama Crimson Tide
Final Grade: 7.4 DT Rank: 1 of 24

Height	Weight	Year	Jersey #	Hometown
6026	295	3SO	92	Birmingham, AL

One-Liner
Williams is an explosively powerful defensive talent, whose rare interior contact balance creates consistent overwhelming backfield chaos, resulting in a next-level force for years to come.

Overall
Williams played multiple positions along Alabama's interior defensive line, typically starting as a 1-technique in their base three-man front. His 15 starts in 29 career games all came in 2018. He is a very good athlete and a phenomenal physical presence, who is solidly thick throughout with good length. He plays with a high motor when his stamina isn't depleted and brings an energy to their defense.

Run Game
As a run defender, Williams is a wrecking ball. He is consistently first off the snap with great leverage and fast hands. His lateral explosion and footwork are exceptional, as he regularly lines up in one gap and has fired into the next before the line can react, creating leverage mismatches. Williams possesses rare contact balance and body control, and his core strength is elite. His quickness keeps linemen from getting consistent clean and square target areas, and he is unaffected by chips and interior help that isn't head on. Combined with his motor and range, he continually creates backfield disruption against zone. Williams' heavy hands and initial punch power shock opponents, and he has explosive hips to keep lines off balance. He stacks and sheds single blocks very well and plays with his eyes in the backfield with good awareness. He stalemates double teams but does not split well and dies on them when tired.

Pass Game
As a pass rusher, he works very well with his teammates on twists and stunts, and bench presses shorter armed linemen with his length. Williams plays with very good hand use and can win with quick swims over the top or powerful rips underneath, nullifying blockers latched to his hip. His combination of power and agility keeps linemen guessing, and he mixes up his pass rush plan for four quarters. He has shown some bend and decent ankle flexion when rushing the arc from outside. He attacks ball carriers with good closing speed and makes plays well outside his range.

Last Word
Williams projects as an elite NFL player early, who is scheme versatile but best fits in a four-man front as a 1- and 3-technique one-gapper. He is football young, especially at his current playing weight, and there is reason to question his lack of playing time in 2017, but his one year of dominance was special.

– John Todd

Strengths	Weaknesses
• Interior contact balance • Hip and lateral explosion • Initial punch power	• Could barely get on field in 2017 • Stamina

Critical Factors

1st Step Explosion	Play Strength	Pass Rush Ability
8	8	7

Positional Factors

Shed Ability	Hand Use	Agility / Body Control
7	7	9
Motor	**Football Intelligence**	**Discipline**
7	7	7
Tackling	**Ruggedness / Toughness**	
6	6	

Basic

	Tackling			Pass Rush					
Year	Tackles	TFL	FF	Sacks	Hurries	Hits	Knockdowns	Pressures	Passes Batted
2017	20	5.5	0	2.0	5	2	0	7	0
2018	68	18.0	0	7.0	43	30	15	57	0
	88	23.5	0	9.0	48	32	15	64	0

Advanced

	Tackling				Per Game			Impact	
Year	Broken Tackles	BT%	Tackle Share	Avg Depth of Tackle	Tackles	TFL	Pressures	Pressure Share	EPA on Sacks/TFL
2017	1	4.8%	2.1%	0.5	1.4	0.4	0.5	2.5%	-6.3
2018	3	4.2%	7.7%	0.9	4.5	1.2	3.8	19.2%	-31.7
	4	4.3%	4.9%	0.8	3.0	0.8	2.2	11.1%	-38.0

Deep Dive

	Total Snaps		Pass Rush		When Run At			Lined Up		
Year	Pass	Run	Pressure%	Sack%	RunAt%	Bounce%	Pos%	NT%	DT%	DE%
2018	327	296	17.6%	2.2%	23.5%	44.9%	29.0%	29.2%	67.4%	2.9%

Ed Oliver

Houston Cougars
Final Grade: 7.1 DT Rank: 2 of 24

Height	Weight	Year	Jersey #	Hometown
6015	292	3JR	10	Houston, TX

One-Liner
Oliver is a disruptive, penetrating 3-technique DT who lacks ideal size but is a pass-rushing difference-maker who wins with first-step explosion, quickness, and athleticism.

Overall
Oliver lined up between the guards, usually as a single-gapping 0- or 1-technique in Houston's three-man front. He is a very athletic DT who plays out of a very low three-point stance. He shows excellent explosiveness off the ball and is a natural ankle bender who creates a small angle between his shin and the turf. Oliver lacks ideal size and is not suited to play in a two-gapping system. He is a penetrator and disruptor who best projects as an under tackle in an even front. He shows competitiveness and flashes a nasty streak in his play.

Run Game
Oliver is not as strong against the run as he is against the pass, but while he is not well-suited to be a two-gap space-eater, he has good strength for his size and compensates for what he lacks with excellent quickness. He makes himself skinny and shows very good hand use to shed blocks. He hustles to the ball from the backside and shows elite speed for the position. Oliver struggles to anchor vs the double-team but has quickness to split it. He does a good job of reading blocks and fighting pressure, and he uses his get-off to reset the line of scrimmage in the backfield. On the NFL level, expect teams to attack Oliver by running at him; he can get swallowed up by larger OLs from time to time and is on the ground too much. That said, he shows other traits that allow him to be productive behind the line of scrimmage both penetrating and finishing.

Pass Game
Oliver's best value comes as an interior pass rusher. His get-off makes him very difficult for OLs to deal with him, and he shows the ability to create an edge and live in the backfield. He shows quick hands to win the battle for hand placement, and he relentlessly works counters until the play is dead. If the ball does get off before he gets home, you see his rare speed for the position as he hustles out of the stack. His explosion, athleticism, and quickness make him a tough matchup for any pass protection scheme to deal with.

Last Word
It's hard to compare anybody to what Aaron Donald has been doing in the NFL recently, but Oliver's college film is the probably the closest thing we have seen to Donald, since he came out of Pitt, in terms of athleticism from the defensive tackle position. Oliver jumps off the field compared to AAC competition with top flexibility, explosiveness, and speed. He lacks position flexibility and is best suited as a 3-technique in an under front.

– Matt Manocherian

Strengths

- Get-off explosion
- Athleticism
- Pass rush productivity

Weaknesses

- Lacks ideal size
- 3-technique only
- Anchor strength

Critical Factors

1st Step Explosion	Play Strength	Pass Rush Ability
8	6	7

Positional Factors

Shed Ability	Hand Use	Agility / Body Control
7	7	7
Motor	**Football Intelligence**	**Discipline**
7	6	6
Tackling	**Ruggedness / Toughness**	
7	6	

Basic

	Tackling			Pass Rush					
Year	Tackles	TFL	FF	Sacks	Hurries	Hits	Knockdowns	Pressures	Passes Batted
2016	61	20.5	4	5.0	19	9	5	25	3
2017	66	14.5	2	5.5	22	14	4	29	1
2018	50	14.5	1	3.0	27	6	4	30	0
	177	49.5	7	13.5	68	29	13	84	4

Advanced

	Tackling				Per Game			Impact	
Year	Broken Tackles	BT%	Tackle Share	Avg Depth of Tackle	Tackles	TFL	Pressures	Pressure Share	EPA on Sacks/TFL
2016	7	10.3%	7.9%	2.1	4.7	1.6	1.9	13.1%	-30.3
2017	4	5.7%	7.3%	2.0	5.5	1.2	2.4	19.5%	-21.5
2018	2	3.8%	4.9%	1.6	6.3	1.8	3.8	17.3%	-15.3
	13	6.8%	6.6%	1.9	5.4	1.5	2.5	16.4%	-67.1

Deep Dive

	Total Snaps		Pass Rush		When Run At			Lined Up		
Year	Pass	Run	Pressure%	Sack%	RunAt%	Bounce%	Pos%	NT%	DT%	DE%
2018	256	239	11.7%	1.2%	30.0%	33.8%	25.4%	64.2%	24.4%	8.7%

Jeffery Simmons

Mississippi State Bulldogs
Final Grade: 6.9 DT Rank: 3 of 24

*

Height	Weight	Year	Jersey #	Hometown
6026	300	3JR	94	Macon, MS

One-Liner
Simmons has a strong blend of size, technique, raw power and versatility, which add up to a gifted next-level starter.

Overall
Simmons played from nose guard to 3-tech on either side of the line in Mississippi State's four-man defensive front. He played in 38 career games, only missing the first game of his career due to suspension. He has an ideal frame for an interior lineman, with solid athleticism and natural power. He is a four-quarter competitor who rarely takes snaps off and gives effort through the whistle.

Run Game
Simmons is a stalwart run defender who comes off with good leverage and great hip explosion. He does a great job of getting his hands on linemen quickly and using his length and heavy hands to shock, find the ball and shed. Simmons can win with easy strength and initial punch power, as well as with upper-body quickness and hand technique on swim moves, taking advantage of off-balance linemen in multiple ways. He moves well laterally to make plays along the line but is a standout double-team defender. Despite his athletic frame, he plays with the technique, core strength and raw power needed to occupy multiple blockers, split double teams and fight through combo blocks. Simmons feels moving pieces well and plays with awareness and quick reactions to brace and adjust to slanting linemen. He occasionally stops his feet and allows himself to get sealed, but he is rarely blown back.

Pass Game
As a pass rusher, while he hasn't had the tangible sack production in his career, he works well with his linemates and gets solid pressure up the middle. He pushes the pocket well and allows the edges to work one on one. Simmons could improve his counter move pool and drive, as well as his closing speed, to become a more complete player, but the upside and tools are there. He reads screens very quickly and plays with very good football intelligence.

Last Word
Simmons projects as a high-end, three-down, starting level talent in either a 4-3 or 3-4 scheme, but is probably at his most valuable two-gapping in a three-man front. He has the position flexibility, body type and skill set to succeed from multiple alignments and schemes.

– John Todd

Strengths	Weaknesses
• Easy strength and power	• Counters/secondary moves
• Anchor and fight through double teams	• Pass rush production
• Alignment flexibility	

Critical Factors

1st Step Explosion	Play Strength	Pass Rush Ability
6	7	5

Positional Factors

Shed Ability	Hand Use	Agility / Body Control
7	7	6
Motor	**Football Intelligence**	**Discipline**
7	7	6
Tackling	**Ruggedness / Toughness**	
6	7	

Basic

	Tackling			Pass Rush					
Year	Tackles	TFL	FF	Sacks	Hurries	Hits	Knockdowns	Pressures	Passes Batted
2016	38	2.0	2	0.0	14	3	2	14	1
2017	62	12.5	2	5.5	29	24	8	41	0
2018	60	14.5	1	2.0	22	15	6	28	1
	160	29.0	5	7.5	65	42	16	83	2

Advanced

	Tackling				Per Game			Impact	
Year	Broken Tackles	BT%	Tackle Share	Avg Depth of Tackle	Tackles	TFL	Pressures	Pressure Share	EPA on Sacks/TFL
2016	1	2.6%	3.3%	2.5	3.2	0.2	1.2	7.9%	-6.3
2017	11	15.1%	6.7%	1.4	4.8	1.0	3.2	18.3%	-25.3
2018	5	7.7%	6.5%	0.9	4.6	1.1	2.2	12.5%	-23.8
	17	9.6%	5.4%	1.4	4.2	0.8	2.2	13.3%	-55.5

Deep Dive

	Total Snaps		Pass Rush		When Run At			Lined Up		
Year	Pass	Run	Pressure%	Sack%	RunAt%	Bounce%	Pos%	NT%	DT%	DE%
2018	332	250	8.9%	0.6%	18.6%	43.5%	30.4%	55.7%	42.1%	2.2%

Christian Wilkins

Clemson Tigers
Final Grade: 6.8 DT Rank: 4 of 24

Height	Weight	Year	Jersey #	Hometown
6032	315	5SR	42	Springfield, MA

One-Liner
Wilkins is a high energy, versatile, athletic interior defensive lineman with good run stop ability and play strength who needs to improve against double teams.

Overall
Wilkins lined up everywhere on the defensive line for the Tigers, but primarily lined up at 3-Tech in their 4-3 base defense. In an odd front, he would occasionally reduce down to a 0 or out to a 5. He played in 59 games for Clemson, starting in 45 of them. He's a very good athlete for the position and has good hip flexibility. In the 2018 game against Florida State, he lined up at running back and scored his first career TD. Wilkins is a high-energy player with a big on-field personality and a certain swagger to his game. He is a tough competitor with a good motor, but goes periods throughout games where it feels like he disappears. He's most effective when lined up over the center at a 0 or 1 technique.

Run Game
In the run game, he's disruptive by creating penetration and clogging run lanes. He's a very good tackler around the LOS and his production over 4 years speaks for itself. He has solid hand placement when run fitting, but struggles to get off double teams. He has good range and lateral mobility to get down the line and either make the play on the ball carrier or force cutbacks. He's more of a one-gapper than two-gapper, but his power allows him to take on OL at the POA.

Pass Game
Against the pass, Wilkins gets penetration and creates a smaller pocket for opposing QBs. He is quick off the line, but his line play derives more from his power. He likes to bull rush offensive linemen and use rip moves to slither through gaps, but overall his counter-move repertoire is limited.

Last Word
Wilkins projects as a 3-Tech in a 4-3 defensive scheme, but has the versatility to play anywhere in the interior of the defensive line. With his athleticism and strength, he should take a starting spot no later than his second season. On 3rd down, allowing him to penetrate as a one-gapping 3-Tech or reducing him down to 1-Tech would be the best fit for him with his pass rush ability. At Clemson, Wilkins was a personal protector on the punt unit, and was also on the field goal unit, so with his experience and skill set he could contribute on some special teams units.

– Jordan Edwards

Strengths	Weaknesses
• Disruptive in the run game • Athleticism • Versatility	• Splitting/holding up against double teams • Disappears during games at times

Critical Factors

1st Step Explosion	Play Strength	Pass Rush Ability
6	7	6

Positional Factors

Shed Ability	Hand Use	Agility / Body Control
6	6	7
Motor	**Football Intelligence**	**Discipline**
6	6	6

Tackling	Ruggedness / Toughness
7	7

Basic

	Tackling			Pass Rush					
Year	Tackles	TFL	FF	Sacks	Hurries	Hits	Knockdowns	Pressures	Passes Batted
2016	49	12.0	0	3.5	24	15	7	34	3
2017	62	8.5	0	4.5	22	17	5	30	1
2018	49	13.0	1	5.5	28	21	10	42	1
	160	33.5	1	13.5	74	53	22	106	5

Advanced

	Tackling				Per Game			Impact	
Year	Broken Tackles	BT%	Tackle Share	Avg Depth of Tackle	Tackles	TFL	Pressures	Pressure Share	EPA on Sacks/TFL
2016	13	21.0%	4.8%	1.6	3.3	0.8	2.3	13.3%	-11.8
2017	3	4.8%	5.6%	2.2	4.3	0.6	2.1	10.8%	-13.6
2018	3	5.8%	4.6%	0.8	3.3	0.9	2.8	13.6%	-27.0
	19	10.7%	5.0%	1.6	3.6	0.8	2.4	12.6%	-52.5

Deep Dive

	Total Snaps		Pass Rush		When Run At			Lined Up		
Year	Pass	Run	Pressure%	Sack%	RunAt%	Bounce%	Pos%	NT%	DT%	DE%
2018	351	252	12.2%	1.6%	18.9%	27.7%	25.5%	44.1%	53.2%	1.5%

Charles Omenihu

Texas Longhorns

Final Grade: 6.8 DT Rank: 5 of 24

Height	Weight	Year	Jersey #	Hometown
6055	274	4SR	90	Rowlett, TX

One-Liner

Omenihu has very good length and strength with good pass rush moves that will create interior pressure at the next level, but needs to improve his motor and consistent tackling ability.

Overall

Omenihu is a DE that played primarily with his hand in the dirt as an odd front WDE for Texas. He would occasionally line up on an OG in a 2-3 technique as well as a stand-up OLB. He started 33 of 51 career games in his four years at Texas. Omenihu is a strong and explosive athlete with good balance and bend. He gets his hands on opposing linemen before they are able to attack him. He has shown the tenacity to fight through doubles and clean up plays away from him, though his motor is inconsistent.

Run Game

In the run game, Omenihu is stout at the POA. His first step allows him to get into position and set the edge. He can easily control linemen with his long arms and is adept at shedding blocks. When being blocked by a single TE, he quickly dispatches them and makes the tackle.

Pass Game

Against the pass, Omenihu shows the ability to use multiple moves to win. He sets up linemen and utilizes effective counter moves. He has very good functional length that can neutralize a long-armed OT. His pass rush was as effective whether he was standing or had his hand in the dirt. In coverage, he is noticeably raw. He does show the athleticism and football intelligence to become functional in the flat.

Last Word

By his second year, Omenihu projects as a three-down starter as a 3-5 technique. On third down, he will be a very good pass rusher against interior linemen. His skill set suggests he'll be a sufficient ST player, due to his size, strength and athleticism.

– Ben Hrkach

Strengths	**Weaknesses**
• Strength	• Lateral athleticism
• Length	• Consistency
• Agility/body control	• Motor

Critical Factors

1st Step Explosion	Play Strength	Pass Rush Ability
6	7	6

Positional Factors

Shed Ability	Hand Use	Agility / Body Control
6	6	7
Motor	**Football Intelligence**	**Discipline**
5	6	7

Tackling	Ruggedness / Toughness
5	6

Basic

	Tackling			Pass Rush					
Year	Tackles	TFL	FF	Sacks	Hurries	Hits	Knockdowns	Pressures	Passes Batted
2016	26	4.5	0	3.5	14	6	1	20	0
2017	28	7.0	2	4.0	13	10	6	19	0
2018	48	17.0	1	9.5	22	18	5	37	0
	102	28.5	3	17.0	49	34	12	76	0

Advanced

	Tackling				Per Game			Impact	
Year	Broken Tackles	BT%	Tackle Share	Avg Depth of Tackle	Tackles	TFL	Pressures	Pressure Share	EPA on Sacks/TFL
2016	5	16.1%	2.8%	2.1	2.2	0.4	1.7	9.9%	-7.2
2017	4	12.5%	3.5%	1.8	2.2	0.5	1.5	9.9%	-15.4
2018	6	11.1%	5.8%	0.6	3.4	1.2	2.6	18.9%	-23.6
	15	12.8%	4.0%	1.3	2.6	0.7	1.9	12.9%	-46.2

Deep Dive

	Total Snaps		Pass Rush		When Run At			Lined Up		
Year	Pass	Run	Pressure%	Sack%	RunAt%	Bounce%	Pos%	NT%	DT%	DE%
2018	462	324	8.5%	2.2%	8.7%	42.9%	21.4%	0.6%	16.0%	79.5%

Jerry Tillery

Notre Dame Fighting Irish
Final Grade: 6.7 DT Rank: 6 of 24

Height	Weight	Year	Jersey #	Hometown
6056	305	4SR	99	Shreveport, LA

One-Liner
Tillery has the range, play strength and powerful hand-strike ability to be a solid starter at the next level, although he needs to improve his motor and endurance for the entirety of games.

Overall
Tillery primarily lined up as a 3-Tech for the Irish, and occasionally lined up as a 1-Tech and out on the edge. He played in 50 games during his four years at Notre Dame. Tillery has a long frame and uses it extremely well. He has quick hands and a violent first strike against offensive lineman. His motor and stamina can be inconsistent at times, but has shown to still be productive at the end of games. When he's tired, he starts to raise his pad level. Tillery is a good competitor and knows when he needs to turn his intensity up, as he has had some of his best games against high-level competition this year against Michigan and Stanford.

Run Game
Versus the run, Tillery uses his length and powerful hand strike to create space between him and the lineman to read and react to the play. He has quick hands and uses them well when shedding blocks. He has really good range and lateral mobility from inside the tackle box, and even shows flashes of running plays down towards the sidelines.

Pass Game
Versus the pass, Tillery's quick first step and violent punch forces penetration to create pressure in the pocket. He shows the ability to use his power to bull rush defenders and also counters with moves on occasion. There are times versus both the pass and run game where Tillery fails to finish the play after forcing the initial pressure.

Last Word
With Tillery's long frame and skillset, he projects to be a solid starter as a 5-Tech in a base 3-4 defensive scheme. On 3rd downs, he has the versatility to line up inside and out on the edge.

– Jordan Edwards

Strengths	**Weaknesses**
• Hand use	• Stamina/motor
• Striking power	• Finishing plays
• Range	• Pad level

Critical Factors

1st Step Explosion	Play Strength	Pass Rush Ability
6	7	6

Positional Factors

Shed Ability	Hand Use	Agility / Body Control
6	7	6
Motor	**Football Intelligence**	**Discipline**
5	6	6
Tackling	**Ruggedness / Toughness**	
6	7	

Basic

	Tackling			Pass Rush					
Year	Tackles	TFL	FF	Sacks	Hurries	Hits	Knockdowns	Pressures	Passes Batted
2016	36	3.0	0	0.0	11	1	1	11	0
2017	53	8.0	1	4.5	30	24	9	38	0
2018	31	9.0	2	7.0	28	17	5	38	0
	120	20.0	3	11.5	69	42	15	87	0

Advanced

	Tackling				Per Game			Impact	
Year	Broken Tackles	BT%	Tackle Share	Avg Depth of Tackle	Tackles	TFL	Pressures	Pressure Share	EPA on Sacks/TFL
2016	4	10.0%	4.0%	2.4	3.0	0.3	0.9	11.1%	-3.0
2017	3	5.4%	5.2%	3.0	4.1	0.6	2.9	17.8%	-14.4
2018	3	8.8%	3.4%	1.4	2.4	0.7	2.9	15.4%	-13.5
	10	7.7%	4.2%	2.4	3.2	0.5	2.3	15.6%	-30.9

Deep Dive

	Total Snaps		Pass Rush		When Run At			Lined Up		
Year	Pass	Run	Pressure%	Sack%	RunAt%	Bounce%	Pos%	NT%	DT%	DE%
2018	398	257	9.4%	1.8%	11.8%	26.7%	33.3%	10.5%	82.0%	7.3%

Gerald Willis III

Miami FL Hurricanes
Final Grade: 6.7 DT Rank: 7 of 24

Height	Weight	Year	Jersey #	Hometown
6032	300	5SR	9	New Orleans, LA

One-Liner
Willis is an explosive, agile, and versatile defensive tackle, who can generate pressure and impact games from multiple alignments, but has some off-field concerns and needs to play with more consistency.

Overall
Willis played primarily 3-technique in a 4-3 defensive front, but also saw time as a nose tackle this season. He was a one-year starter, starting in 12 of 21 games for the Hurricanes throughout his career. He is a very good athlete who has a great frame for the position and displays a strong combination of quickness, explosiveness, and lateral agility. He plays with an inconsistent but often impactful motor and effort; he is a competitive player when engaged.

Run Game
Against the run, Willis possesses good play strength at the point of attack, showing an ability to negate his opponent's strength, neutralize blockers, and consistently play behind the line of scrimmage. He struggles to fight through double teams and tends to give up ground and get pushed back. He shows very good explosion off the snap, with the initial quickness to close the cushion and the ability to penetrate with explosiveness and power.

Pass Game
In the pass game, Willis shows good pass rush ability to generate pressure, using an array of moves, including a swim and rip. He also has the power to collapse the pocket and walk linemen back, using proper leverage and solid leg drive. He displays good, technical hand usage, usually winning the hand fighting battle and establishing control at the line of scrimmage. Willis has good shed ability, displaying an ability to consistently disengage blockers with a good hand punch, placement, and strength. He displays good short-area quickness and lateral agility, demonstrating balance and flexion while working in traffic and space. Willis is effective while running stunts, using his body control and timing to avoid blockers and generate pressure while working off his teammates, but he has a tendency to lose gap discipline and not stay square. He demonstrates good football intelligence, with an ability to key and diagnose plays, showing good timing to deflect passes at the line of scrimmage and process information quickly.

Last Word
Willis plays with decent ruggedness, occasionally playing with violence and grit while attacking and engaging the offensive linemen with physicality, but also takes too many plays off and doesn't dominate as much as he should. Willis is a good tackler, showing good striking ability, technique, and efficiency, but does not always finish the play behind the line when he has a chance. Willis projects as a scheme and alignment versatile one-gapping defender at the next level.

– Nick Giella

Strengths	Weaknesses
• Explosion off the snap	• Consistency
• Hand use	• Discipline
• Interior agility	• Off-field concerns

Critical Factors

1st Step Explosion	Play Strength	Pass Rush Ability
7	6	6

Positional Factors

Shed Ability	Hand Use	Agility / Body Control
6	7	6
Motor	**Football Intelligence**	**Discipline**
5	6	5

Tackling	Ruggedness / Toughness
6	5

Basic

	Tackling			Pass Rush					
Year	Tackles	TFL	FF	Sacks	Hurries	Hits	Knockdowns	Pressures	Passes Batted
2016	19	5.5	0	1.5	4	1	1	6	2
2018	56	18.0	0	4.0	16	12	5	23	1
	75	23.5	0	5.5	20	13	6	29	3

Advanced

	Tackling				Per Game			Impact	
Year	Broken Tackles	BT%	Tackle Share	Avg Depth of Tackle	Tackles	TFL	Pressures	Pressure Share	EPA on Sacks/TFL
2016	1	5.0%	2.1%	1.3	2.1	0.6	0.7	2.8%	-10.4
2018	9	13.8%	6.6%	0.9	4.7	1.5	1.9	11.1%	-25.9
	10	11.8%	4.3%	1.0	3.6	1.1	1.4	6.9%	-36.3

Deep Dive

	Total Snaps		Pass Rush		When Run At			Lined Up		
Year	Pass	Run	Pressure%	Sack%	RunAt%	Bounce%	Pos%	NT%	DT%	DE%
2018	290	315	7.7%	1.4%	13.1%	53.7%	24.4%	22.5%	76.0%	1.5%

Zach Allen

Boston College Eagles
Final Grade: 6.7 DT Rank: 8 of 24

Height	Weight	Year	Jersey #	Hometown
6043	280	4SR	2	New Canaan, CT

One-Liner
Allen is a good run defender who uses his size and technique to disrupt plays with the strength to get to the QB, but needs to improve his consistency and explosion off the line.

Overall
Allen's primary position was 5- or 7-Tech in Boston College's 4-2-5 defensive scheme. He played in 50 career games and was a two-year starter having started in 26 of them. Allen is a good athlete who uses his size to his advantage. He's a former basketball player and it shows throughout his play. However, he looks to have gained some weight and gotten a step slower in 2018 compared to his 2017 film. He is a player who competes every play and attacks his opponent head on.

Run Game
In the run game, he plays with strength and mobility. He uses his strength and size to stack and shed opposing linemen and make his way to the ball carrier. He possesses the lateral mobility needed to get down the LOS and make plays. He is very good at maneuvering through traffic and not getting out of position. He's not incredibly explosive off the line, but he's powerful and shows it with strong hands. His heavy hands allow him to shed blocks and make plays not just in the run game, but also in the pass game.

Pass Game
In the pass game, he is a consistent threat, but does not have a lot of moves in his arsenal. His ability to attack the offensive line and bull rush makes him a constant threat, and if he could find some counter moves to add to it, he could make an even bigger impact. During his college career he produced as a pass rusher, wreaking havoc on quarterbacks.

Last Word
Allen projects as a 5-Tech in a 3-4 defense at the next level. He could slide down to 3-Tech or out to 7 in even fronts, especially to rush the passer.

– SIS Scouting Staff

Strengths	**Weaknesses**
• Pass rush ability • Strength • Run stopping	• Explosiveness • Speed

Critical Factors

1st Step Explosion	Play Strength	Pass Rush Ability
5	6	7

Positional Factors

Shed Ability	Hand Use	Agility / Body Control
6	7	6
Motor	**Football Intelligence**	**Discipline**
7	6	6

Tackling	Ruggedness / Toughness
6	7

Basic

	Tackling			Pass Rush					
Year	Tackles	TFL	FF	Sacks	Hurries	Hits	Knockdowns	Pressures	Passes Batted
2016	36	12.0	0	6.5	13	8	6	21	3
2017	100	14.0	0	4.0	33	27	9	49	2
2018	61	14.5	1	5.5	40	25	15	54	2
	197	40.5	1	16.0	86	60	30	124	7

Advanced

	Tackling				Per Game			Impact	
Year	Broken Tackles	BT%	Tackle Share	Avg Depth of Tackle	Tackles	TFL	Pressures	Pressure Share	EPA on Sacks/TFL
2016	5	12.2%	4.8%	1.7	2.8	0.9	1.6	11.8%	-12.8
2017	9	8.3%	9.9%	1.7	7.7	1.1	3.8	24.4%	-19.1
2018	9	12.9%	6.3%	1.2	5.1	1.2	4.5	26.2%	-26.3
	23	10.5%	7.1%	1.5	5.2	1.1	3.3	21.2%	-58.3

Deep Dive

	Total Snaps		Pass Rush		When Run At			Lined Up		
Year	Pass	Run	Pressure%	Sack%	RunAt%	Bounce%	Pos%	NT%	DT%	DE%
2018	444	343	12.4%	1.3%	10.7%	36.1%	36.1%	0.0%	4.7%	90.3%

Dre'Mont Jones

Ohio State Buckeyes
Final Grade: 6.7 DT Rank: 9 of 24

Height	Weight	Year	Jersey #	Hometown
6021	286	4JR	86	Cleveland, OH

One-Liner
Jones is a disruptive pass rusher with quick hands and impressive interior agility, who will need improved strength and block shedding ability to become a more complete football player.

Overall
Jones lined up mostly as a 3-technique for Ohio State, and occasionally bumped outside in pass rushing situations. He started in 37 of 39 career games, having earned a starting role early in his freshman season. He only played two years of high school football and quickly became a top prospect. Jones has a long, thin frame for an interior defender that he's still growing into, with natural raw athleticism. He has very good lateral agility, and a quick first step off the snap of the ball. Jones is a fluid athlete at his size and has very good speed as an interior defensive lineman. Jones is a good competitor with a good motor who turns on an extra gear in pass rush situations.

Run Game
Against the run, Jones relies on his speed to fit. He lacks lower body strength to shock and drive linemen at the point of attack and create disruption. He shows the ability to stalemate linemen at the line of scrimmage, but struggles closing down run gaps and getting off blocks. Jones plays with great lateral quickness and agility but doesn't possess great body control to balance, as he gets washed down the line too easily. Jones needs to improve his gap discipline versus the run.

Pass Game
He excels at rushing the passer. He uses his hands very well to create separation from offensive lineman and win the hand battle. His speed, quickness, and range are mismatches against interior blockers and he has shown an array of rush moves. Jones needs to improve his ability to create pressure via pushing the pocket from the interior with strength.

Last Word
He projects as a solid starter as a 4-3 scheme 3-tech, or possibly a 5-tech in a 3-4. His pass rush ability will get him on the field early, but his body still needs to develop and strengthen to become a more impactful run defender at the next level. On third downs, Jones can offer alignment flexibility, as he has the frame and traits to come off the edge, but is best suited as an agility mismatch inside.

– Jordan Edwards

Strengths	Weaknesses
• Quick hand use	• Play strength
• Lateral agility	• Block shedding
• Interior pass rush	• Balance and toughness

Critical Factors

1st Step Explosion	Play Strength	Pass Rush Ability
6	5	7

Positional Factors

Shed Ability	Hand Use	Agility / Body Control
5	7	6
Motor	**Football Intelligence**	**Discipline**
6	5	5
Tackling	**Ruggedness / Toughness**	
6	5	

Basic

	Tackling			Pass Rush					
Year	Tackles	TFL	FF	Sacks	Hurries	Hits	Knockdowns	Pressures	Passes Batted
2016	49	4.0	0	0.0	9	6	4	11	0
2017	18	5.0	0	1.0	20	16	6	24	2
2018	47	12.5	1	8.0	31	26	11	46	1
	114	21.5	1	9.0	60	48	21	81	3

Advanced

	Tackling				Per Game			Impact	
Year	Broken Tackles	BT%	Tackle Share	Avg Depth of Tackle	Tackles	TFL	Pressures	Pressure Share	EPA on Sacks/TFL
2016	0	0.0%	5.4%	2.6	3.8	0.3	0.8	5.8%	-4.6
2017	0	0.0%	1.9%	1.0	1.5	0.4	2.0	8.3%	-5.6
2018	4	7.8%	5.2%	3.0	3.4	0.9	3.3	16.8%	-22.5
	4	3.4%	4.1%	2.5	2.9	0.6	2.1	10.8%	-32.7

Deep Dive

	Total Snaps		Pass Rush		When Run At			Lined Up		
Year	Pass	Run	Pressure%	Sack%	RunAt%	Bounce%	Pos%	NT%	DT%	DE%
2018	462	321	9.9%	1.8%	9.4%	40.0%	33.3%	8.3%	80.5%	10.9%

Isaiah Buggs

Alabama Crimson Tide
Final Grade: 6.6 DT Rank: 10 of 24

Height	Weight	Year	Jersey #	Hometown
6025	295	4SR	49	Ruston, LA

One-Liner

Buggs is a very strong and scheme-versatile athlete whose coachability, toughness and leadership will help him become a non-flashy but reliable starter at the next level.

Overall

Buggs primarily played as a two-gapping strongside 4i-6 tech for Alabama, although he occasionally lined up at 3- and 7-tech. The Tide would either spell him on rush downs or reduce him inside. He played in 29 career games for Alabama. Buggs is slow off the snap often, but then flashes good upfield burst in obvious passing situations.

Run Game

He anchors his gap well against man/gap concepts and honors his contain responsibilities. He has a good feel for pulls in his periphery and diagnoses reach blocks quickly to flow laterally against zone with good range. He exhibits the ability to anchor and split double teams. Buggs has good length and is capable of jostling opposing linemen with a quick and violent initial punch. He does not consistently stuff cut blocks effectively. He takes some plays off in backside pursuit but plays with optimal extension and does a good job of setting the edge. He has powerful hands to shed suddenly and he finishes tackles consistently.

Pass Game

He demonstrates the ability to win pass rush reps with long-arm, bull rush, club, rip, and spin moves. He is a fluid mover and was an effective looper in the stunt game as both an interior rusher and an end. His pass-rush plan is nonexistent on most reps. His rush often stalls if his initial move is foiled, and he hasn't shown a go-to counter move. He has very good closing speed to the quarterback for a 290-pounder and finishes at a high rate. Buggs does a good job of getting his hands into passing lanes when he can't get home.

Last Word

He demonstrates good aggressiveness, toughness and versatility as a 5-tech, but is best suited further inside at 3.

– Bryce Rossler

Strengths	**Weaknesses**
• Upper- and lower-body strength	• Quickness off the snap
• Scheme versatility	• Consistent motor
• Intangibles	• Pass rush plan

Critical Factors

1st Step Explosion	Play Strength	Pass Rush Ability
4	7	5

Positional Factors

Shed Ability	Hand Use	Agility / Body Control
6	7	6
Motor	**Football Intelligence**	**Discipline**
5	6	7
Tackling	**Ruggedness / Toughness**	
6	7	

Basic

	Tackling			Pass Rush					
Year	Tackles	TFL	FF	Sacks	Hurries	Hits	Knockdowns	Pressures	Passes Batted
2017	52	2.5	0	1.5	31	21	11	34	0
2018	50	13.5	2	10.0	26	20	4	40	0
	102	16.0	2	11.5	57	41	15	74	0

Advanced

	Tackling				Per Game			Impact	
Year	Broken Tackles	BT%	Tackle Share	Avg Depth of Tackle	Tackles	TFL	Pressures	Pressure Share	EPA on Sacks/TFL
2017	5	8.8%	5.1%	2.3	3.7	0.2	2.4	12.3%	-4.7
2018	7	12.3%	5.0%	1.6	3.3	0.9	2.7	13.5%	-28.7
	12	10.5%	5.1%	2.0	3.5	0.6	2.6	12.9%	-33.4

Deep Dive

	Total Snaps		Pass Rush		When Run At			Lined Up		
Year	Pass	Run	Pressure%	Sack%	RunAt%	Bounce%	Pos%	NT%	DT%	DE%
2018	382	274	10.3%	2.6%	12.5%	55.9%	35.3%	0.0%	20.6%	75.2%

L.J. Collier

TCU Horned Frogs
Final Grade: 6.6 DT Rank: 11 of 24

Height	Weight	Year	Jersey #	Hometown
6022	280	5SR	91	Munday, TX

One-Liner
Collier is a long run defender capable of controlling the line of scrimmage and contributing as a pass rusher, but will need improved athleticism and explosive traits to be a true edge rusher.

Overall
Collier played as a hybrid edge, splitting time between 5 tech and stand up outside linebacker. He played in 42 career games and was at least a rotational player for three seasons. He has long arms but is not well cut and has some midsection thickness. He is strong, has good bend and flexibility, and flashes explosion off the snap and at the point of attack. He plays with a high motor and does a good job of taking his game to his opponents before they can attack him.

Run Game
Against the run, Collier shocks blockers with his hands and controls the line of scrimmage. He has some two gap ability with his length and anchor. He has sufficient speed to corral backs trying to bounce outside. Collier plays with a high motor and works hard to find himself around the ball often. He doesn't finish tackles consistently and his athleticism makes it tough for him to play in space often.

Pass Game
Against the pass, Collier has a very good bull rush. He uses his hands and length to beat linemen to first contact, allowing him to manipulate them from the snap. He plays with awareness and keeps quarterbacks well contained. He has good flexibility to bend around the edge and with better explosion could develop a nice speed rush.

Last Word
Collier profiles best as a 5-tech in the NFL, where he can play with his hand in the dirt and use his length but still be able to showcase some of his pass rush on the edge. He is a strong run defender with good pass rushing upside.

– Ben Hrkach

Strengths	Weaknesses
• Length and hand use	• Lateral agility
• Motor	• Closing speed
• Pass rushing upside	• Finishing plays

Critical Factors

1st Step Explosion	Play Strength	Pass Rush Ability
6	6	6

Positional Factors

Shed Ability	Hand Use	Agility / Body Control
6	7	5
Motor	**Football Intelligence**	**Discipline**
7	6	6

Tackling	Ruggedness / Toughness
5	7

Basic

	Tackling			Pass Rush					
Year	Tackles	TFL	FF	Sacks	Hurries	Hits	Knockdowns	Pressures	Passes Batted
2016	19	4.5	0	4.5	6	1	0	11	0
2017	19	4.5	0	4.0	23	13	5	28	0
2018	43	11.5	0	6.0	35	21	11	46	0
	81	20.5	0	14.5	64	35	16	85	0

Advanced

	Tackling				Per Game			Impact	
Year	Broken Tackles	BT%	Tackle Share	Avg Depth of Tackle	Tackles	TFL	Pressures	Pressure Share	EPA on Sacks/TFL
2016	2	9.5%	1.7%	2.4	1.5	0.3	0.8	6.8%	-9.3
2017	1	5.0%	1.9%	2.4	1.4	0.3	2.0	11.3%	-6.8
2018	5	10.4%	5.1%	2.5	3.9	1.0	4.2	22.3%	-13.7
	8	9.0%	2.8%	2.5	2.1	0.5	2.2	13.8%	-29.7

Deep Dive

	Total Snaps		Pass Rush		When Run At			Lined Up		
Year	Pass	Run	Pressure%	Sack%	RunAt%	Bounce%	Pos%	NT%	DT%	DE%
2018	358	297	14.6%	1.9%	6.7%	50.0%	45.0%	0.3%	2.3%	37.6%

Kingsley Keke

Texas A&M Aggies
Final Grade: 6.5 DT Rank: 12 of 24

Height	Weight	Year	Jersey #	Hometown
6025	286	4SR	8	Richmond, TX

One-Liner
Keke possesses the play strength, football intelligence and agility to start at the next level, but his motor and shed ability could be improved.

Overall
Keke played 5-tech in Texas A&M's 3-4 defense. He played in 52 career games, starting in 35. He is thick and has good size and strength for the position. He possesses a big base and strong upper body to absorb double teams and protect linebackers. He's a good athlete who moves well and competes with toughness.

Run Game
In the run game, he has good hand use but will need to improve to shed blockers and disengage more regularly. He has very good agility and body control, moving with ease and flexibility for an interior defensive lineman. He moves well laterally while still keeping strength at the POA. He's explosive with good short-area quickness for his size. He is a good tackler, tough in the trenches and plays with intent. He has very good football intelligence which allows him to diagnose the play, read and react to locate the ball and close gaps. He has very good discipline as he knows his responsibilities to set the edge, keep leverage and hold ground and stay square, but that can also take away some of his aggressiveness at times.

Pass Game
Against the pass, he shows solid pass rush ability. He uses a strong bull rush, but can play high at times and lose leverage, causing him not to create the pressure he could given his play strength. He has decent first step explosion to get off the line and anticipate, but his motor is just sufficient given the position he plays and the power he shows.

Last Word
Keke projects best as a one-gapping 3-tech at the next level. He shows some ability to rush the passer on 3rd down, but possesses enough play strength at the POA to play on 1st and 2nd.

– Cole Ratliff

Strengths	Weaknesses
• Play strength	• Motor
• Football intelligence	• Shed ability
• Agility	• Awareness

Critical Factors

1st Step Explosion	Play Strength	Pass Rush Ability
5	6	6

Positional Factors

Shed Ability	Hand Use	Agility / Body Control
5	6	6
Motor	**Football Intelligence**	**Discipline**
5	7	7

Tackling	Ruggedness / Toughness
6	6

Basic

	Tackling			Pass Rush					
Year	Tackles	TFL	FF	Sacks	Hurries	Hits	Knockdowns	Pressures	Passes Batted
2016	32	6.0	0	4.0	8	2	1	12	2
2017	53	2.5	0	1.0	14	4	1	17	2
2018	50	11.0	1	7.0	18	9	4	26	1
	135	19.5	1	12.0	40	15	6	55	5

Advanced

	Tackling				Per Game			Impact	
Year	Broken Tackles	BT%	Tackle Share	Avg Depth of Tackle	Tackles	TFL	Pressures	Pressure Share	EPA on Sacks/TFL
2016	4	11.1%	3.0%	1.8	2.5	0.5	0.9	5.2%	-9.0
2017	3	5.4%	4.8%	6.0	4.1	0.2	1.3	7.5%	-3.9
2018	2	3.8%	5.9%	1.2	3.8	0.8	2.0	13.7%	-22.9
	9	6.3%	4.4%	3.2	3.5	0.5	1.4	8.5%	-35.8

Deep Dive

	Total Snaps		Pass Rush		When Run At			Lined Up		
Year	Pass	Run	Pressure%	Sack%	RunAt%	Bounce%	Pos%	NT%	DT%	DE%
2018	408	267	6.1%	1.7%	15.0%	38.5%	35.9%	15.3%	20.4%	63.7%

Byron Cowart

Maryland Terrapins
Final Grade: 6.5 DT Rank: 13 of 24

Height	Weight	Year	Jersey #	Hometown
6033	297	3JR	9	Tampa, FL

One-Liner
With coaching in the film room to help better diagnose plays, and on the field to help piece together his complete set of tools, Cowart has a chance to reach his lofty prep career potential at the next level.

Overall
Cowart was a lineman on Maryland's defense, after transferring from community college via Auburn. He played in 23 games for the Tigers and 12 for the Terrapins in 2018. He has a solid size and frame, with thick thighs and good length, and has shown to be a good, agile athlete.

Run Game
Against the run, Cowart shows good mobility, but his best traits are his play strength and his powerful hands. His hand use is very good, but he needs to improve on translating that into consistent block shedding at the point of attack. He has the innate natural athleticism and agility, but he doesn't diagnose run directions and play designs in front of him well enough to produce at a consistent level. He flashes a desired motor, but too often he doesn't pursue from the back side or noticeably takes plays off. Cowart has shown the ability to be able to play on all three downs due to his good hand usage at the point of attack to create separation between himself and the offensive linemen. However, he will need to improve on translating that separation into finding the ball and beating blockers to make sure he can stay on the field for third downs.

Pass Game
In the pass game, Cowart has the ability to make an impact due to his power and hand usage to create space and collapse the pocket. He has proven that he needs to be accounted for whenever he is on the field. His first step off the ball is inconsistent but has flashes of a difference-making trait. His pass rushing ability can improve with coaching and development, as he has the tools but needs to play with better effort and desire.

Last Word
Based on his pedigree, he has a high ceiling to make an impact at the next level in multiple fronts and schemes. He fits best as a 5-technique defensive lineman who can ideally reduce down and rush from the inside in passing situations.

– Mark Johnson

Strengths	Weaknesses
• Blend of size and athleticism	• Play diagnosis
• Play strength	• Motor
• Hand use	• Production

Critical Factors

1st Step Explosion	Play Strength	Pass Rush Ability
5	6	6

Positional Factors

Shed Ability	Hand Use	Agility / Body Control
6	7	6
Motor	**Football Intelligence**	**Discipline**
5	5	5
Tackling	**Ruggedness / Toughness**	
5	6	

Basic

	Tackling			Pass Rush					
Year	Tackles	TFL	FF	Sacks	Hurries	Hits	Knockdowns	Pressures	Passes Batted
2016	6	1.0	1	0.0	2	2	2	3	0
2017	3	0.5	0	0.0	2	1	0	2	0
2018	40	5.5	1	4.0	17	8	3	23	0
	49	7.0	2	4.0	21	11	5	28	0

Advanced

	Tackling				Per Game			Impact	
Year	Broken Tackles	BT%	Tackle Share	Avg Depth of Tackle	Tackles	TFL	Pressures	Pressure Share	EPA on Sacks/TFL
2016	1	14.3%	0.7%	0.6	0.6	0.1	0.3	1.4%	-1.7
2017	0	0.0%	0.3%	0.2	1.5	0.3	1.0	0.8%	-1.2
2018	4	9.1%	4.5%	2.1	3.3	0.5	1.9	16.0%	-11.9
	5	9.3%	1.8%	1.8	2.2	0.3	1.3	4.7%	-14.8

Deep Dive

	Total Snaps		Pass Rush		When Run At			Lined Up		
Year	Pass	Run	Pressure%	Sack%	RunAt%	Bounce%	Pos%	NT%	DT%	DE%
2018	250	277	9.4%	1.6%	5.1%	14.3%	71.4%	0.9%	17.8%	81.2%

DeMarcus Christmas

Florida State Seminoles
Final Grade: 6.2 DT Rank: 14 of 24

Height	Weight	Year	Jersey #	Hometown
6037	302	5SR	90	Sarasota, FL

One-Liner
Christmas has the first-step explosion and hands to get in the backfield, as well as the strength and balance to hold up against double teams, but needs to become a more polished pass rusher and improve his motor and durability at the next level.

Overall
Christmas is a DT who lined up primarily as a 3-technique in a 4-3 scheme for the Seminoles. He became a full-time starter in his second full season, accumulating 50 games played and 38 starts during his career. He has good size and is built thick from the bottom up. He is agile and able to maintain his very good strength while moving around blocks due to his very good balance. He also shows good range and pursuit by chasing down runs away from him. His toughness is evident by the way he competes against double teams, easily holding his position and occasionally breaking through doubles. However, he needs to play with a more consistent motor from play to play.

Run Game
Against the run is where Christmas shines. His good first step allows him to engage quickly with the OL and his good hand technique sets him up to use his strength to control the OL. Once engaged, Christmas is good at diagnosing the play and moving the OL either direction to fill the intended run gap. His agility and balance give him the ability to get off the block and attack the runner.

Pass Game
Against the pass, Christmas primarily uses a bull rush to collapse the pocket. He keeps his balance well and rarely allows the QB to escape via open lanes up the middle. At FSU, he was rarely on the field for third downs and will be limited in that aspect at the next level. However, he does flash the ability to rush the passer from the interior with good hands and first-step explosion.

Last Word
Christmas projects to be a quality rotational lineman at the next level that can play both the 1-technique and the 3-technique.

– Ben Hrkach

Strengths	Weaknesses
• Play strength	• Pass rush moves
• Balance	• Durability
• Play recognition	• Motor

Critical Factors

1st Step Explosion	Play Strength	Pass Rush Ability
6	7	5

Positional Factors

Shed Ability	Hand Use	Agility / Body Control
6	5	6
Motor	**Football Intelligence**	**Discipline**
5	5	6
Tackling	**Ruggedness / Toughness**	
5	6	

Basic

	Tackling			Pass Rush					
Year	Tackles	TFL	FF	Sacks	Hurries	Hits	Knockdowns	Pressures	Passes Batted
2016	22	3.5	1	3.0	2	1	1	7	3
2017	34	4.5	0	1.0	14	2	1	15	2
2018	30	2.5	0	0.0	6	3	0	6	2
	86	10.5	1	4.0	22	6	2	28	7

Advanced

	Tackling				Per Game			Impact	
Year	Broken Tackles	BT%	Tackle Share	Avg Depth of Tackle	Tackles	TFL	Pressures	Pressure Share	EPA on Sacks/TFL
2016	1	4.3%	2.6%	2.9	1.7	0.3	0.5	3.4%	-5.8
2017	1	2.9%	3.7%	1.9	2.6	0.3	1.2	7.4%	-7.5
2018	1	3.4%	3.0%	1.6	2.5	0.2	0.5	2.8%	-4.0
	3	3.4%	3.1%	2.1	2.3	0.3	0.8	4.5%	-17.3

Deep Dive

	Total Snaps		Pass Rush		When Run At			Lined Up		
Year	Pass	Run	Pressure%	Sack%	RunAt%	Bounce%	Pos%	NT%	DT%	DE%
2018	215	236	2.9%	0.0%	14.4%	35.3%	41.2%	8.6%	88.0%	2.9%

Jonathan Ledbetter

Georgia Bulldogs
Final Grade: 6.2 DT Rank: 15 of 24

Height	Weight	Year	Jersey #	Hometown
6034	271	4SR	13	Tucker, GA

One-Liner
Ledbetter is a stout run stopper with great strength and shed ability, but will need to improve his 1st step/speed to have an impact as a pass rusher.

Overall
Ledbetter primarily lined up as 4-5-Tech for Georgia and occasionally slid down into the interior. He played in 43 games during his four years on campus, starting 28. He's a good athlete for his size and competes with toughness.

Run Game
In the run game, he shows outstanding strength, discipline and shed ability. He typically is a two-gap player, as he controls the man in front of him on a consistent basis. Ledbetter works hard at the point of attack, but doesn't have great range or a consistent motor. His strength is his best asset, as he is hardly ever taken completely out of a play by a block. He shuts down most runs his direction by stacking and shedding with savvy hand use and overall strength. He shows good discipline. Ledbetter depends on these skills, as he lacks some first-step speed/quickness. He is a sure tackler, but doesn't make many plays in pursuit. He's a dependable player, but his lack of range limits his production. Some of these issues may be due to injuries, as he looked hurt against Auburn this year.

Pass Game
In the pass game, he can work his way to the QB with strength and hand use, but his first-step speed keeps him from having a consistent impact. On longer developing plays, he doesn't always generate sacks, but does get some pressure on the quarterback. He uses a few different moves, but likes to use speed around the edge and will bull when reduced down.

Last Word
Ledbetter projects as a versatile backup that can play along most areas of the defensive line. He fits best as a 5-Tech, but has the ability to reduce down on 3rd downs occasionally.

– Pat Dougherty

Strengths	Weaknesses
• Strength	• Get-off quickness
• Shed ability	• Range
• Discipline	• Motor

Critical Factors

1st Step Explosion	Play Strength	Pass Rush Ability
5	7	5

Positional Factors

Shed Ability	Hand Use	Agility / Body Control
6	6	5
Motor	**Football Intelligence**	**Discipline**
5	6	6

Tackling	Ruggedness / Toughness
6	6

Basic

	Tackling			Pass Rush					
Year	Tackles	TFL	FF	Sacks	Hurries	Hits	Knockdowns	Pressures	Passes Batted
2016	23	2.0	0	1.0	4	4	1	7	0
2017	35	4.5	0	2.5	27	15	8	33	0
2018	56	6.5	2	1.0	12	11	3	18	0
	114	13.0	2	4.5	43	30	12	58	0

Advanced

	Tackling				Per Game			Impact	
Year	Broken Tackles	BT%	Tackle Share	Avg Depth of Tackle	Tackles	TFL	Pressures	Pressure Share	EPA on Sacks/TFL
2016	2	8.0%	2.6%	3.5	3.3	0.3	1.0	5.3%	-0.8
2017	3	7.9%	3.5%	3.0	2.3	0.3	2.2	13.1%	-10.0
2018	1	1.8%	5.0%	2.4	4.0	0.5	1.3	10.0%	-10.2
	6	5.0%	3.7%	2.9	3.2	0.4	1.6	10.3%	-21.0

Deep Dive

	Total Snaps		Pass Rush		When Run At			Lined Up		
Year	Pass	Run	Pressure%	Sack%	RunAt%	Bounce%	Pos%	NT%	DT%	DE%
2018	235	188	8.0%	0.4%	10.6%	45.0%	40.0%	0.7%	23.4%	74.7%

Kevin Givens

Penn State Nittany Lions
Final Grade: 6.2 DT Rank: 16 of 24

Height	Weight	Year	Jersey #	Hometown
6005	285	4JR	30	Altoona, PA

One-Liner
Givens has the explosiveness and agility to become a rotational penetrator, but needs improved hand use and gap integrity to become a reliable starter.

Overall
Givens' primary position was as a one gap 3-technique in a 4-3 defense. He has previous experience as an edge defender in the same scheme. He played in 50 career games with 33 starts. He is slightly undersized but has good lower body thickness. Givens is an explosive athlete who gets off the ball quickly with good flexibility and body control. He takes plays off occasionally and does not always chase after plays from the backside or behind.

Run Game
Against the run, Givens penetrates the line by getting into the blocker's chest before they can get their hands on him. Once in the backfield, his agility allows him to break down in front of the ball carrier and chase in either direction. He can penetrate too far upfield and wash himself out of plays, leaving wide running lanes. Givens holds his own against doubles and is rarely overpowered to the ground. He stalemates well against strength but is not a two gapping player.

Pass Game
Against the pass, Givens' explosion allows him to win against single blockers. His go-to move is the rip. He wins with his first step. Givens also flashes a good deke move for blockers who overstep to account for his quickness. He does not show the ability to win with hand fighting.

Last Word
He best projects as a rotational one-gap 3-technique penetrator who can flash on third downs. He explodes off the snap and can be a disruptive player in the backfield, but will need a better motor, gap discipline, and hand use to become a more complete football player.

– Ben Hrkach

Strengths	**Weaknesses**
• 1st-step explosion	• Gap discipline
• Penetration skills	• Motor
• Agility	• Hand use

Critical Factors

1st Step Explosion	Play Strength	Pass Rush Ability
7	6	5

Positional Factors

Shed Ability	Hand Use	Agility / Body Control
5	5	6
Motor	**Football Intelligence**	**Discipline**
5	6	5

Tackling	Ruggedness / Toughness
5	6

Basic

	Tackling			Pass Rush					
Year	Tackles	TFL	FF	Sacks	Hurries	Hits	Knockdowns	Pressures	Passes Batted
2016	28	6.5	0	4.0	11	9	2	20	1
2017	21	4.0	1	3.5	21	8	1	25	2
2018	34	9.5	0	5.0	15	9	1	21	0
	83	20.0	1	12.5	47	26	4	66	3

Advanced

	Tackling				Per Game			Impact	
Year	Broken Tackles	BT%	Tackle Share	Avg Depth of Tackle	Tackles	TFL	Pressures	Pressure Share	EPA on Sacks/TFL
2016	7	20.0%	2.5%	1.9	2.2	0.5	1.5	8.2%	-13.3
2017	3	12.5%	2.1%	1.7	1.9	0.4	2.3	8.8%	-6.3
2018	4	10.5%	3.6%	0.7	2.8	0.8	1.8	9.5%	-13.4
	14	14.4%	2.7%	1.3	2.3	0.6	1.8	8.8%	-33.0

Deep Dive

	Total Snaps		Pass Rush		When Run At			Lined Up		
Year	Pass	Run	Pressure%	Sack%	RunAt%	Bounce%	Pos%	NT%	DT%	DE%
2018	319	302	6.8%	1.6%	15.9%	31.3%	43.8%	12.6%	84.2%	3.2%

Trysten Hill

UCF Knights

Final Grade: 6.2 DT Rank: 17 of 24

Height	Weight	Year	Jersey #	Hometown
6010	315	3JR	9	Lee, FL

One-Liner

Hill is a versatile, athletic lineman with a high motor and a very good first step, and although he's shown flashes of dominant play strength, he needs to be more consistent with it before he can be considered a starter.

Overall

Hill is a versatile defensive lineman who played DE and DT in both a 3-4 scheme and a 4-3 scheme at UCF. He was a 3-year player and 2-year starter, playing in 37 games and starting 27 of them. Despite starting as a freshman, Hill came off the bench his junior season in all but one game after a coaching change that saw their scheme switch from a 3-4 to a 4-3. Hill is a good athlete with above-average play strength allowing him to flex between DE and DT. Hill is a rugged, nasty player with a high-motor always looking to get after the ball.

Run Game

In the run game, Hill only shows above-average gap discipline which allows for lanes to open up and for linemen to take him where they want. His instincts and hand use need improvement as he finds himself out of position often and he rarely uses his hands to control opposing blockers. He doesn't demonstrate good play strength or anchor ability as he can be manipulated by solo blockers, but his quick first step allows him to get into the backfield almost untouched at times.

Pass Game

In the pass game, Hill only has adequate ability to get to the quarterback despite his very good 1st step. He struggles to consistently find the strength to go through offensive linemen and often finds himself stonewalled at the line of scrimmage. He does a good job a of extending his arms and combining it with a swim move, but doesn't show enough consistency or enough variety in his pass rush repertoire to be a real threat to the quarterback.

Last Word

Hill needs to become more consistent in every area of his game before he can be used as a starter at the next level. He projects to be a backup defensive lineman with the ability to flex between DE and DT by his second season.

– SIS Scouting Staff

Strengths	Weaknesses
• 1st-step explosion	• Play strength at POA
• Athleticism	• Inconsistency
• High motor	• Shed ability

Critical Factors

1st Step Explosion	Play Strength	Pass Rush Ability
7	5	5

Positional Factors

Shed Ability	Hand Use	Agility / Body Control
5	5	6
Motor	**Football Intelligence**	**Discipline**
6	5	5

Tackling	Ruggedness / Toughness
6	6

Basic

	Tackling			Pass Rush					
Year	Tackles	TFL	FF	Sacks	Hurries	Hits	Knockdowns	Pressures	Passes Batted
2016	15	4.5	1	1.0	5	2	0	6	0
2017	22	4.5	0	2.0	12	4	1	14	0
2018	36	9.5	0	3.0	13	8	4	18	0
	73	18.5	1	6.0	30	14	5	38	0

Advanced

	Tackling				Per Game			Impact	
Year	Broken Tackles	BT%	Tackle Share	Avg Depth of Tackle	Tackles	TFL	Pressures	Pressure Share	EPA on Sacks/TFL
2016	7	31.8%	1.8%	0.2	1.2	0.3	0.5	3.6%	-9.5
2017	3	12.0%	2.2%	1.9	1.7	0.3	1.1	6.3%	-7.4
2018	7	16.3%	3.6%	2.1	3.3	0.9	1.6	8.3%	-12.5
	17	18.9%	2.6%	1.6	2.0	0.5	1.0	6.3%	-29.4

Deep Dive

	Total Snaps		Pass Rush		When Run At			Lined Up		
Year	Pass	Run	Pressure%	Sack%	RunAt%	Bounce%	Pos%	NT%	DT%	DE%
2018	222	233	7.7%	1.4%	12.2%	32.1%	46.4%	46.4%	49.0%	4.6%

Corbin Kaufusi

BYU Cougars

Final Grade: 6.2 DT Rank: 18 of 24

Height	Weight	Year	Jersey #	Hometown
6075	275	5SR	90	Provo, UT

One-Liner

Kaufusi is a very long, thick and versatile defensive front seven player who will need improved lower body strength and instincts to see more snaps.

Overall

Kaufusi played as an edge rusher and Sam linebacker in BYU's 4-3 defense. He played in 37 games and started in 28. He is a good athlete, especially for his size, with a sufficient first-step. He wins with his size and length. He is a fierce competitor and a leader out on the field. He has a very high motor and stamina level, never taking a play off and consistently finishing to the whistle.

Run Game

In the run game, Kaufusi has good overall play strength, but to be successful at the next level he will need to get stronger in his lower body. Due to his size, he will almost always lose the leverage battle. Improved anchor and drive ability will assist his chances of staying on the field inside. He does a good job of setting the edge when playing outside, but his play diagnosis is inconsistent. He has great range and motor and can make plays all over the field. Kaufusi regularly would chase and cover plays from the opposite side of the field and get home. He was able to spy Khalil Tate against Arizona, displaying his athleticism and sideline to sideline mobility.

Pass Game

In the pass game, he has the ability to hurt you in many ways. Kaufusi does a good job of using his length to beat blockers, but he has very strong hands and does a very good job of taking away blockers' strength. He has a good swim and push-pull move. Occasionally defenders can get into his body and he struggles to shed. It's hard for him to keep his chest from being exposed with his size. He is surprisingly sufficient in coverage, but standing him up doesn't use him to the best of his abilities.

Last Word

Kaufusi should be a versatile reserve defensive lineman by his second year, with the ability to play inside or outside and even stand up, if necessary. He offers length and size, and is a good, balanced defender against the run and pass. Kaufusi will also be an impactful special teams player. His mobility allows him to play on multiple units, and his size has made him a specialist at blocking kicks.

– SIS Scouting Staff

Strengths

- Motor
- Length and size
- Versatility

Weaknesses

- Lower body strength
- Instincts
- Chest exposure

Critical Factors

1st Step Explosion	Play Strength	Pass Rush Ability
5	6	5

Positional Factors

Shed Ability	Hand Use	Agility / Body Control
5	7	5
Motor	**Football Intelligence**	**Discipline**
7	5	5
Tackling	**Ruggedness / Toughness**	
6	6	

Basic

	Tackling			Pass Rush					
Year	Tackles	TFL	FF	Sacks	Hurries	Hits	Knockdowns	Pressures	Passes Batted
2016	34	3.0	0	2.5	21	8	5	25	1
2017	71	6.5	2	6.0	18	9	4	24	1
2018	57	9.0	0	8.5	23	14	6	35	0
	162	18.5	2	17.0	62	31	15	84	2

Advanced

	Tackling				Per Game			Impact	
Year	Broken Tackles	BT%	Tackle Share	Avg Depth of Tackle	Tackles	TFL	Pressures	Pressure Share	EPA on Sacks/TFL
2016	5	12.8%	3.8%	3.9	2.6	0.2	1.9	12.3%	-6.6
2017	4	5.3%	7.3%	3.3	5.5	0.5	1.8	19.4%	-17.8
2018	6	9.5%	7.2%	3.4	5.2	0.8	3.2	21.6%	-17.6
	15	8.5%	6.1%	3.4	4.4	0.5	2.3	17.2%	-42.0

Deep Dive

	Total Snaps		Pass Rush		When Run At			Lined Up		
Year	Pass	Run	Pressure%	Sack%	RunAt%	Bounce%	Pos%	NT%	DT%	DE%
2018	311	279	13.6%	3.1%	8.6%	50.0%	41.7%	0.2%	0.3%	62.5%

Renell Wren

Arizona State Sun Devils
Final Grade: 6.2 DT Rank: 19 of 24

Height	Weight	Year	Jersey #	Hometown
6044	315	5SR	95	St. Louis, MO

One-Liner
Wren is a strong, highly-athletic, and versatile DT who can potentially play all over the line one day, but is too raw to make an impact early in his career.

Overall
Wren played as a 1- or 2-gapping nose tackle in Arizona's 3-4 scheme and almost always lined up as a 0, 1, 2i, or 2 technique. He started 13 of 42 career games for the Sun Devils. Wren is a very good athlete with a much leaner build than a typical NT. Although it is not always exhibited, Wren shows flashes of both very good speed and quickness. He plays balanced and agile, and is light on his feet. He appears to keep getting better as the game progresses; when other players get tired, Wren gets stronger. He is an impressive and willing competitor, but his toughness is questionable; he is more likely to chase a ballcarrier downfield than he is to fight through a double team.

Run Game
Versus the run, Wren shows good upper body strength, but almost never wins with strength alone. Wren plays too upright and his hands are inactive, which causes his raw power to be ineffective. If a blocker can get both hands on Wren at the beginning of a play, there is a low chance Wren will fight free. For Wren to disrupt a run play, he needs to beat the OG or OC with a quick first step and lateral quickness, which he does inconsistently. He is able to hold the point of attack from time to time, even against double teams, but rarely gets penetration. He is a sure tackler when he get his hands on a ballcarrier, but that is more likely to occur downfield than in the backfield. Wren does a good job of keeping his head up to locate the ballcarrier quickly and track him throughout the play.

Pass Game
Versus the pass, Wren has the same issues; he consistently gets little or no penetration and is largely not a disruptor, despite looking fast and strong. He isn't incredibly productive as a rusher and doesn't possess many different pass rush moves.

Last Word
Given his height, weight, and overall build, Wren has potential to play anywhere on the line, but projects as a better fit as a 5-tech in the NFL. His athleticism and strength are evident, but his results and production are poor due to his technique and the fact that he was playing out of position for his entire SR season. Given his competitive nature, high motor, and athleticism, Wren will be able to play on any of the four core special teams units immediately.

– Tony Shields

Strengths	Weaknesses
• Athleticism	• Functional power
• Motor/stamina	• Shedding blockers
• Raw power	• Impact/production

Critical Factors

1st Step Explosion	Play Strength	Pass Rush Ability
5	5	5

Positional Factors

Shed Ability	Hand Use	Agility / Body Control
5	5	6
Motor	**Football Intelligence**	**Discipline**
7	5	6
Tackling	**Ruggedness / Toughness**	
6	5	

Basic

	Tackling			Pass Rush					
Year	Tackles	TFL	FF	Sacks	Hurries	Hits	Knockdowns	Pressures	Passes Batted
2016	16	6.0	1	1.5	5	2	1	7	1
2017	20	2.0	0	0.5	13	2	0	15	0
2018	39	4.5	0	1.0	8	1	0	9	1
	75	12.5	1	3.0	26	5	1	31	2

Advanced

	Tackling				Per Game			Impact	
Year	Broken Tackles	BT%	Tackle Share	Avg Depth of Tackle	Tackles	TFL	Pressures	Pressure Share	EPA on Sacks/TFL
2016	4	20.0%	2.1%	0.1	1.3	0.5	0.6	3.3%	-8.9
2017	1	4.8%	2.2%	5.8	1.5	0.2	1.2	8.2%	-5.4
2018	1	2.5%	4.5%	2.2	3.0	0.3	0.7	5.7%	-6.4
	6	7.4%	2.9%	2.6	2.0	0.3	0.8	5.6%	-20.6

Deep Dive

	Total Snaps		Pass Rush		When Run At			Lined Up		
Year	Pass	Run	Pressure%	Sack%	RunAt%	Bounce%	Pos%	NT%	DT%	DE%
2018	277	321	3.5%	0.4%	28.4%	37.8%	46.7%	78.6%	18.6%	2.8%

Ricky Walker

Virginia Tech Hokies
Final Grade: 6.2 DT Rank: 20 of 24

Height	Weight	Year	Jersey #	Hometown
6017	297	5SR	8	Hampton, VA

One-Liner
Walker is a versatile DT who wins with his quickness and explosion, has good range and is stout versus the run, but struggles to impact the passing attack due to strength and technique issues.

Overall
Walker played both 1- and 3-Tech in Virginia Tech's base 4-3 defense, as well as the 0 and the 5 when the defense shifted to an odd front. He started 30 of the 51 games that he played in for the Hokies. Walker is a good athlete for his size, showing good explosiveness, reactive athleticism and body control as an interior lineman. He has sufficient strength, and questionable arm-length, leading to his struggles in pass rush and disengaging from blockers. He shows good competitiveness, motor, and toughness, with the occasional instance of giving up on a play early due to being worn down.

Run Game
In the run game, Walker is quick off the ball and is good at handling both one- and two-gap responsibilities depending on the scheme. His strength is sufficient, forcing him to use a quick first step to cross defenders as a 3-tech and establish his presence in a gap. He is stout in the run game, handling wash-down blocks and lead backs without ceding much ground. He shows good range on plays that move the line, having the ability to stay with his responsibility and minimize cutback opportunities, as well as get involved on tackle opportunities. He will occasionally play high, giving up leverage to the blocker and losing the ability to make an impact on the play.

Pass Game
In the pass game, Walker is sufficient enough, but struggles if his first step is matched by the blocker or is slow off the ball. He wins off the line with quickness and speed to compensate for his lack of multiple pass- rushing moves and ideal strength. He can get past blockers without his speed and quickness, but at a very inconsistent rate, and usually too late for him to make an impact on the QB. The combination of inconsistent hand violence, dependence on a single move, and his inability to force consistent separation from himself and the blocker lead to his pass rushing rating as merely sufficient rather than good. This could limit his 3rd down usage, but if on the field, he would be effective on 3rd down at either the 3- or 1-technique position, relying on quickness and explosion off the line to collapse the pocket from the inside.

Last Word
Walker offers positional versatility with experience playing across all positions on the defensive line, but is limited in his ability to make consistent impacts on plays, making him a backup with flexion. Walker's ability to play both the 3- and 1-technique in an even front gives him valuable versatility, and his explosiveness allows for him to have an impact, but his consistency, play strength, and pass rush suggests that he projects best in backup role.

– Aaron Gray

Strengths	**Weaknesses**
• Quickness	• Pass rush moves
• Agile for his size	• Separation from blocker
• Versatility	• Inconsistent hand use

Critical Factors

1st Step Explosion	Play Strength	Pass Rush Ability
6	5	5

Positional Factors

Shed Ability	Hand Use	Agility / Body Control
5	5	6
Motor	**Football Intelligence**	**Discipline**
6	6	6

Tackling	Ruggedness / Toughness
6	6

Basic

	Tackling			Pass Rush					
Year	Tackles	TFL	FF	Sacks	Hurries	Hits	Knockdowns	Pressures	Passes Batted
2016	28	7.0	0	1.5	12	6	2	15	3
2017	40	12.0	0	4.5	14	10	3	22	1
2018	47	10.0	2	2.0	17	9	0	23	0
	115	29.0	2	8.0	43	25	5	60	4

Advanced

	Tackling				Per Game			Impact	
Year	Broken Tackles	BT%	Tackle Share	Avg Depth of Tackle	Tackles	TFL	Pressures	Pressure Share	EPA on Sacks/TFL
2016	5	15.6%	2.5%	1.3	1.9	0.5	1.1	6.8%	-11.3
2017	4	9.1%	4.7%	0.8	3.1	0.9	1.7	9.2%	-17.6
2018	3	6.0%	5.0%	2.3	3.6	0.8	1.8	12.1%	-21.7
	12	9.5%	4.0%	1.5	2.9	0.7	1.5	9.2%	-50.6

Deep Dive

	Total Snaps		Pass Rush		When Run At			Lined Up		
Year	Pass	Run	Pressure%	Sack%	RunAt%	Bounce%	Pos%	NT%	DT%	DE%
2018	322	322	7.4%	0.6%	18.1%	43.1%	31.0%	33.9%	56.5%	8.1%

Daniel Wise

Kansas Jayhawks

Final Grade: 6.2 DT Rank: 21 of 24

Height	Weight	Year	Jersey #	Hometown
6024	283	4SR	96	Lewisville, TX

One-Liner

Wise does not flash his talents consistently enough in both the passing and run games and while he has the explosiveness, hands, and strength to make an impact, he'll most likely be a versatile backup at the next level.

Overall

Wise primary played the 5-Tech in Kansas's 3-3-5 defense. He played at every position along the defensive line during the course of each game. He was a 3.5 year starter, starting in 42 of the 47 games he played in for the Jayhawks. He is a good athlete who shows burst off the line, good strength and quickness with above-average stop-and-start ability. He is a tough player who looks to make his mark on every game. He makes big plays when his team needs him to and often wears down the offensive line by the 4th quarter.

Run Game

In the run game, he is very good at disrupting the play, especially when he slants inside. He has some lateral strength and mobility, but isn't likely to run down speedier backs on the edge. He is above-average at the point of attack, but can struggle against quicker lineman. He has strong, active hands to keep blockers' hands off of him.

Pass Game

In the pass game, he has good pass rushing ability and uses a variety of moves, but primarily uses a bull rush and swim move. He has been very effective against the pass and capitalizes on the chances he gets. He has a good motor combined with several counter moves to make him more dangerous the longer the hold needs.

Last Word

He projects as a rotational DL primarily on passing downs with some position flexibility. He can play the 5-Tech on 1st and 2nd down and reduce down inside on 3rd if needed.

– SIS Scouting Staff

Strengths	Weaknesses
• Quick first step	• Lacks discipline
• Strong, active hands	• Maintaining gap assignment
• Tough, physical throughout game	• Can be too aggressive at times

Critical Factors

1st Step Explosion	Play Strength	Pass Rush Ability
6	6	6

Positional Factors

Shed Ability	Hand Use	Agility / Body Control
5	6	5
Motor	**Football Intelligence**	**Discipline**
6	5	5

Tackling	Ruggedness / Toughness
6	6

Basic

	Tackling			Pass Rush					
Year	Tackles	TFL	FF	Sacks	Hurries	Hits	Knockdowns	Pressures	Passes Batted
2016	38	9.5	0	3.0	13	9	4	18	0
2017	52	13.5	0	6.0	29	29	10	42	1
2018	36	10.5	0	5.0	12	7	3	20	0
	126	33.5	0	14.0	54	45	17	80	1

Advanced

	Tackling				Per Game			Impact	
Year	Broken Tackles	BT%	Tackle Share	Avg Depth of Tackle	Tackles	TFL	Pressures	Pressure Share	EPA on Sacks/TFL
2016	4	9.5%	4.7%	1.3	3.5	0.9	1.6	13.4%	-11.3
2017	4	7.3%	5.6%	1.6	4.3	1.1	3.5	27.8%	-24.0
2018	3	7.7%	4.8%	1.4	3.0	0.9	1.7	14.1%	-16.5
	11	8.1%	5.0%	1.5	3.6	1.0	2.3	18.7%	-51.7

Deep Dive

	Total Snaps		Pass Rush		When Run At			Lined Up		
Year	Pass	Run	Pressure%	Sack%	RunAt%	Bounce%	Pos%	NT%	DT%	DE%
2018	346	317	6.1%	1.5%	10.4%	51.5%	42.4%	1.7%	37.6%	60.0%

Amani Bledsoe

Oklahoma Sooners

Final Grade: 6.2 DT Rank: 22 of 24

Height	Weight	Year	Jersey #	Hometown
6050	287	3JR	72	Lawrence, KS

One-Liner

Bledsoe is a versatile, reserve-caliber defensive lineman who offers adequate pass rush ability through burst or strength, the ability to defend the interior run effectively, and high competitiveness and motor, but is best suited for sub-packages or depth

Overall

Bledsoe played primarily a 3-technique in Oklahoma's hybrid 3-4, but was used in a versatile role in which he aligned in the 5-technique and the 1-technique depending on situation and sub-package deployment. He started 22 of 30 career games for the Sooners. Oklahoma relied on his athletic ability to fill the versatile role, as he possesses good quickness and footwork for his size, as well as the ability to move fluidly and without wasted motion. He is a competitive player with good motor and consistently plays through the end of the play.

Run Game

Versus the run, Bledsoe is effective at single-gap responsibilities. He has ability to absorb the initial block and sink his hips to establish position. He is susceptible to being washed down by larger blockers who are exceptionally physical, or through combo blocks, but is effective at restricting the secondary blocker from progressing to the linebacker level, opening lanes for scrapes and gap fills. He has the tendency to pop up at the snap, raising his pad level and offering his chest to blockers, which make it difficult for him to fight through the block, extend his arms, or shed to make plays. When asked to set the edge or keep contain, he shows the ability to sit and absorb pulls/lead blocks, creating the desired logjam and allowing for gang tackles.

Pass Game

Versus the pass, Bledsoe is sufficient at generating a rush from both the inside and outside. He relies on strength and lockout as an inside rusher and uses more speed and late burst on the outside to win. He doesn't possess a large pass-rush repertoire.

Last Word

With his versatility to play both 3-tech and 5-tech and inconsistent ability to defend the run, Bledsoe projects as a reserve lineman who can provide key depth in multiple roles along the defensive line. His overall pass rush ability will allow for him to see the field on 3rd down, either in a sub package predicated on speed rush or through other means. His athleticism and versatility make him a good candidate to fill a special teams role across multiple units.

– Aaron Gray

Strengths

- Versatility
- Body control

Weaknesses

- Inconsistent explosion
- Can be engulfed by larger OL
- Inconsistent hand use

Critical Factors

1st Step Explosion	Play Strength	Pass Rush Ability
5	6	5

Positional Factors

Shed Ability	Hand Use	Agility / Body Control
5	5	6
Motor	**Football Intelligence**	**Discipline**
6	5	6
Tackling	**Ruggedness / Toughness**	
5	6	

Basic

	Tackling			Pass Rush					
Year	Tackles	TFL	FF	Sacks	Hurries	Hits	Knockdowns	Pressures	Passes Batted
2016	2	0.0	0	0.0	3	1	1	3	0
2017	20	2.5	0	2.0	5	3	1	7	0
2018	35	3.0	0	2.0	18	8	6	21	4
	57	5.5	0	4.0	26	12	8	31	4

Advanced

	Tackling				Per Game			Impact	
Year	Broken Tackles	BT%	Tackle Share	Avg Depth of Tackle	Tackles	TFL	Pressures	Pressure Share	EPA on Sacks/TFL
2016	0	0.0%	0.1%	1.5	0.3	0.0	0.5	1.4%	0.0
2017	4	16.7%	2.2%	1.9	2.0	0.3	0.7	4.2%	-3.8
2018	7	16.7%	3.3%	2.6	2.5	0.2	1.5	10.7%	-4.0
	11	16.2%	2.0%	2.3	1.9	0.2	1.0	5.4%	-7.8

Deep Dive

	Total Snaps		Pass Rush		When Run At			Lined Up		
Year	Pass	Run	Pressure%	Sack%	RunAt%	Bounce%	Pos%	NT%	DT%	DE%
2018	399	393	5.6%	0.6%	10.3%	37.5%	40.0%	3.9%	54.9%	40.3%

Terry Beckner Jr.

Missouri Tigers

Final Grade: 5.9 DT Rank: 23 of 24

Height	Weight	Year	Jersey #	Hometown
6032	295	4SR	5	East St. Louis, MO

One-Liner

Beckner is a one-gap, penetrating 3-tech who has good explosion off the ball with good strength and hand use, but lacks the consistent pass rush and shedding abilities to be a quality starter in the league.

Overall

Beckner primarily played 1- or 3-technique in a 4-3 and nose tackle when the defense shifted into a 3-4. Beckner is a 4-year player, but only a two-year starter with knee injuries ending his freshman and sophomore seasons. He started 31 of the 43 games he played for the Tigers. Beckner is a good athlete who moves well in the trenches and in the open field.

Run Game

In the run game, he displays good lateral strength and mobility. He is able to take on double teams and stand his ground while protecting his gap. He has good explosiveness off the line and his play strength allows him to disrupt plays. Beckner shows a willingness to be involved in the run game and has the range to track down rushers across the line of scrimmage. He has the ability to handle offensive guards and centers but guesses too often in the run game and allows himself to get blocked. He possesses some mismatch ability inside but is more effective when penetrating quickly through the line.

Pass Game

In the pass game, he displays a decent pass rush against top talent which allows him to play on 3rd downs. He gets to the quarterback using power and body control. He uses a swim move most often and even when it is stopped by the offensive linemen, he remains balanced and can still be disruptive in the backfield. In his senior year, Beckner's raw production was limited compared to his junior season when he recorded seven sacks.

Last Word

By year two, Beckner projects to be a top depth-level defensive tackle where he can use his quickness and play strength to one-gap upfield.

– Brian Rogers

Strengths	**Weaknesses**
• Tackling	• Pass rush ability
• Play strength	• Shed ability
• Hand use	• Agility/short-area quickness

Critical Factors

1st Step Explosion	Play Strength	Pass Rush Ability
6	6	5

Positional Factors

Shed Ability	Hand Use	Agility / Body Control
5	6	5
Motor	**Football Intelligence**	**Discipline**
6	6	6
Tackling	**Ruggedness / Toughness**	
6	6	

Basic

	Tackling			Pass Rush					
Year	Tackles	TFL	FF	Sacks	Hurries	Hits	Knockdowns	Pressures	Passes Batted
2016	23	2.0	0	0.0	4	5	3	6	1
2017	41	10.5	0	7.0	24	20	10	34	2
2018	34	10.0	1	3.5	19	11	5	25	0
	98	22.5	1	10.5	47	36	18	65	3

Advanced

	Tackling				Per Game			Impact	
Year	Broken Tackles	BT%	Tackle Share	Avg Depth of Tackle	Tackles	TFL	Pressures	Pressure Share	EPA on Sacks/TFL
2016	1	4.2%	2.7%	2.3	3.3	0.3	0.9	3.5%	-2.6
2017	8	16.3%	4.1%	0.8	3.2	0.8	2.6	15.0%	-15.1
2018	2	5.6%	4.5%	1.1	2.6	0.8	1.9	12.6%	-13.4
	11	10.1%	3.7%	1.3	3.0	0.7	2.0	10.9%	-31.1

Deep Dive

	Total Snaps		Pass Rush		When Run At			Lined Up		
Year	Pass	Run	Pressure%	Sack%	RunAt%	Bounce%	Pos%	NT%	DT%	DE%
2018	337	219	7.7%	1.1%	18.4%	52.5%	27.5%	47.3%	50.0%	1.1%

Cortez Broughton

Cincinnati Bearcats
Final Grade: 5.9 DT Rank: 24 of 24

Height	Weight	Year	Jersey #	Hometown
6021	291	4SR	96	Warner Robins, GA

One-Liner

Broughton has the 1st-step explosion and production in the run game to be a disruptive interior defensive lineman, but his motor, discipline and lack of consistent pass rush will limit him to a backup role.

Overall

Broughton primarily played the 3-Tech in Cincinnati, but played some other techniques in a one-gapping scheme where they used him all over the defensive line. He started 37 of 50 games with the Bearcats. He is slightly undersized for the position, but can work with what he has due to his initial quickness. He shows flashes of power, but needs to get up to speed to utilize it, as it doesn't stick out. He has a very hot-and-cold motor which could be attributed to his stamina and lack of endurance. His range and play speed are very limited and it hurts his ability to make plays when he has a chance to. He is very raw with talent and ability, but needs to work on technique and discipline.

Run Game

Against the run, he lives in the backfield. He is very explosive and tends to blow right through gaps in zone blocking. Broughton has an ability to see gaps and explode through them by combining his quick first step with getting skinny to make a play. He shows the ability to find the ball and shed blockers, but can get hung up on blocks. He is inconsistent against double teams, as he has been able to stalemate or even make a push, but often gets pushed backwards. He often gets washed down the line when he shoots gaps.

Pass Game

Against the pass is where Broughton seems to struggle the most, as he lacks a high motor and drive to get to the quarterback. He's a quick one-gapper, but doesn't seem to show much in the way of a pass rush. He has a wide variety of rush moves he likes to use including a swim, bull, and long arm. His bull rush is his most impressive move when he plays with leverage to beat his opponent. He often rushes standing straight up with poor leverage and loses his leg drive to be effective, which leads to him being stonewalled and he often gives up. He can generate pocket push at times, but doesn't show an ability to disengage the OL to attack the QB.

Last Word

Broughton projects as a backup one-gapping 3-tech who will most likely see time on run downs early on.

– Zach Fernandez

Strengths	**Weaknesses**
• 1st-step explosion	• Play speed
• Tackle/finish	• Range
• Versus the run	• Back side discipline

Critical Factors

1st Step Explosion	Play Strength	Pass Rush Ability
7	5	5

Positional Factors

Shed Ability	Hand Use	Agility / Body Control
5	5	5
Motor	**Football Intelligence**	**Discipline**
4	6	4

Tackling	Ruggedness / Toughness
6	5

Basic

	Tackling			Pass Rush					
Year	Tackles	TFL	FF	Sacks	Hurries	Hits	Knockdowns	Pressures	Passes Batted
2016	43	5.5	0	2.5	16	9	2	22	1
2017	35	3.5	0	1.0	17	10	6	21	1
2018	49	16.0	2	6.5	22	16	5	32	2
	127	25.0	2	10.0	55	35	13	75	4

Advanced

	Tackling				Per Game			Impact	
Year	Broken Tackles	BT%	Tackle Share	Avg Depth of Tackle	Tackles	TFL	Pressures	Pressure Share	EPA on Sacks/TFL
2016	2	4.4%	4.5%	3.6	3.6	0.5	1.8	18.2%	-8.7
2017	3	7.9%	3.3%	1.7	2.9	0.3	1.8	13.7%	-4.2
2018	7	12.5%	6.5%	1.3	3.8	1.2	2.5	14.0%	-24.2
	12	8.6%	4.7%	2.2	3.4	0.7	2.0	14.9%	-37.1

Deep Dive

	Total Snaps		Pass Rush		When Run At			Lined Up		
Year	Pass	Run	Pressure%	Sack%	RunAt%	Bounce%	Pos%	NT%	DT%	DE%
2018	339	277	8.9%	1.9%	13.5%	27.0%	40.5%	5.5%	51.8%	42.0%

Glossary

Avg Tackle Depth
Average number of yards away from the line of scrimmage that the defender made his tackles

Bounce% (When Run At split)
Percentage of runs that didn't go through the designed gap

Broken Tackles
Tackle attempts where the defender failed to bring down the ballcarrier. Counts both broken tackles (physical) and missed tackles (elusive)

BT%
Percentage of tackle attempts where the defender failed to bring down the ballcarrier. Counts both broken tackles (physical) and missed tackles (elusive)

Hits
Plays with meaningful contact made by the defender on the quarterback before or as he releases the football

Hurries
Plays where the defender forces the quarterback to rush a throw before he may have otherwise thrown it

Knockdowns
Plays where the quarterback gets knocked down to the ground by the defender

Passes Batted
Plays where the defender knocked a pass down at the line of scrimmage

Pos% (When Run At split)
The percentage of plays that resulted in a positive EPA (a successful play for the offense)

Pressures
Plays in which there is a quarterback hurry, hit, knockdown or sack

Pressure%
Percentage of pass rushes that resulted in a pressure

Pressure Share
Percentage of a team's pressures made by the defender

RunAt%
Percentage of carries where the defender was positioned in the designed gap

Sack%
Percentage of pass rushes that resulted in a sack

Tackle Share
Percentage of a team's tackles made by the defender

Nose Tackle / Defensive Tackle Leaderboards

Pressures Leaders

Rank	Player	Team	Pressures
1	Quinnen Williams	Alabama	57
2	Zach Allen	Boston College	54
3	Dre'Mont Jones	Ohio State	46
4	L.J. Collier	TCU	46
5	Christian Wilkins	Clemson	42
6	Isaiah Buggs	Alabama	40
7	Jerry Tillery	Notre Dame	38
8	Greg Gaines	Washington	37
9	Charles Omenihu	Texas	37
10	Corbin Kaufusi	BYU	35

Expected Points Added on Sacks/TFL Leaders

Rank	Player	Team	EPA
1	Quinnen Williams	Alabama	-31.7
2	Isaiah Buggs	Alabama	-28.7
3	Christian Wilkins	Clemson	-27.0
4	Zach Allen	Boston College	-26.3
5	Gerald Willis III	Miami FL	-25.9
6	Cortez Broughton	Cincinnati	-24.2
7	Jeffery Simmons	Mississippi State	-23.8
8	Charles Omenihu	Texas	-23.6
9	Kingsley Keke	Texas A&M	-22.9
10	Dre'Mont Jones	Ohio State	-22.5

Tackle Share Leaders

Rank	Player	Team	Tackle Share
1	Khalen Saunders	Western Illinois	9.6%
2	Quinnen Williams	Alabama	7.7%
3	Corbin Kaufusi	BYU	7.2%
4	Gerald Willis III	Miami FL	6.6%
5	Jeffery Simmons	Mississippi State	6.5%
6	Cortez Broughton	Cincinnati	6.5%
7	Zach Allen	Boston College	6.3%
8	Kingsley Keke	Texas A&M	5.9%
9	Charles Omenihu	Texas	5.8%
10	Greg Gaines	Washington	5.7%

Bounce % When Run At Leaders

Rank	Player	Team	Bounce%
1	Isaiah Buggs	Alabama	55.9%
2	Gerald Willis III	Miami FL	53.7%
3	Greg Gaines	Washington	52.9%
4	Terry Beckner Jr.	Missouri	52.5%
5	Daniel Wise	Kansas	51.5%
6	Corbin Kaufusi	BYU	50.0%
7	L.J. Collier	TCU	50.0%
8	Daylon Mack	Texas A&M	47.5%
9	Jonathan Ledbetter	Georgia	45.0%
10	Quinnen Williams	Alabama	44.9%

Average Depth of Tackle Leaders

Rank	Player	Team	Avg Tackle Depth
1	Charles Omenihu	Texas	0.6
2	Kevin Givens	Penn State	0.7
3	Christian Wilkins	Clemson	0.8
4	Daylon Mack	Texas A&M	0.9
4	Quinnen Williams	Alabama	0.9
4	Jeffery Simmons	Mississippi State	0.9
4	Gerald Willis III	Miami FL	0.9
8	Dexter Lawrence	Clemson	1.0
9	Kenny Bigelow Jr.	West Virginia	1.1
9	Terry Beckner Jr.	Missouri	1.1

Pressure % Leaders

Rank	Player	Team	Pressure%
1	Quinnen Williams	Alabama	17.6%
2	L.J. Collier	TCU	14.6%
3	Corbin Kaufusi	BYU	13.6%
4	Zach Allen	Boston College	12.4%
5	Christian Wilkins	Clemson	12.2%
6	Ed Oliver	Houston	11.7%
7	Dexter Lawrence	Clemson	10.3%
8	Daylon Mack	Texas A&M	10.3%
9	Isaiah Buggs	Alabama	10.3%
10	Dre'Mont Jones	Ohio State	9.9%

EDGE RUSHER

Edge Rusher Grading Scale

GRADE	DESCRIPTION
9.0 – 7.0	High-end 3 down starter. Pro Bowl level.
6.9 – 6.7	Strong starter who plays on all 3 downs.
6.6 – 6.5	Low-end starter. 2 down player or plus pass rusher.
6.2	Versatile backup with positional flexibility.
6.1 – 6.0	Developmental. Top traits but needs time.
5.9	Top backup. 3rd LB. Quality special teamer.
5.8	Average backup. 4th LB. Quality special teamer.

Edge Rusher Rankings

Nick Bosa

Ohio State Buckeyes
Final Grade: 7.0 Edge Rusher Rank: 1 of 23

Height	Weight	Year	Jersey #	Hometown
6036	263	3JR	97	Fort Lauderdale, FL

One-Liner

Bosa projects to be an immediate, difference-making starter with potential to become a Pro Bowler based on his ability to impact both the pass and the run game, along with his technical proficiency and lack of significant weaknesses.

Overall

Bosa usually lined up as a 5-technique DE in Ohio State's four-man defensive front, though he would occasionally widen in obvious passing situations or slide into the B gap for short yardage. He was a dominant college player who stood out even amongst Ohio State's talented defense. While he doesn't have the elite athleticism of a Khalil Mack, he is very good across the board in terms of his size, build, play strength, and explosiveness. His game is refined, as he shows excellent balance and technique, and he has a very similar style of play to that of his older brother, Joey.

Pass Game

Bosa has an excellent pass rush repertoire. He consistently shows a very good get-off, and he is effective attacking an inside or outside edge, using the bull rush, converting speed to power, and with counters. He shows both functional strength and technical proficiency in his hand use. He is effective on stunts and a mismatch for all TEs and RBs, as well as many OTs when matched up one-on-one. He is a powerful hitter when he gets to the quarterback, and he is very productive in the opponent's backfield and creating turnovers. He projects to be an immediate-impact pass rusher at the next level.

Run Game

Bosa is also a strong run defender. He does a very good job of setting an edge on the front-side of run plays. While he isn't as rangy as some of the top athletes on the edge, he consistently shortens the field with his ability to anchor and maintain outside leverage. He shows intelligence and instinctiveness as he reads and reacts to blocking schemes. He is also an effective penetrator, using his explosive 1st step to slant into gaps and engage linemen before they can set. In short-yardage situations, Ohio State used him to slide inside and he showed the ability to anchor like a DT.

Last Word

Bosa projects to be an immediate starter who fits best as a DE in a 4-3 scheme, but he shows versatility to play in any system. As a top-edge prospect, he is not as explosive as Myles Garrett was coming out a few years ago, but Bosa is much more polished than Garrett was at the time, shows a consistently relentless motor, and has very few weaknesses. The best comparison for Nick Bosa is his brother Joey, and if he can stay healthy, Nick has a chance to make an even larger, faster impact.

– Matt Manocherian

Strengths	Weaknesses
• Pass rush variety • Hand use and technique • Explosive get-off	• Lacks elite athleticism • Injury concerns

Critical Factors

Pass Rush Ability	1st Step Explosion	Point Of Attack / Set Edge
7	7	7

Positional Factors

Pass Rush Repertoire	Bend	Hand Use	Play Strength
8	6	7	7
Range	**Flat Coverage**	**Motor**	**Football Intelligence**
6	5	7	7
Discipline	**Tackling**	**Ruggedness**	**Special Teams Value**
6	7	7	6

Basic

	Tackling			Pass Rush					
Year	Tackles	TFL	FF	Sacks	Hurries	Hits	Knockdowns	Pressures	Passes Batted
2016	28	7.0	0	5.0	21	11	5	26	0
2017	35	16.0	0	8.5	39	34	13	57	1
2018	15	5.5	1	4.0	7	8	2	13	0
	78	28.5	1	17.5	67	53	20	96	1

Advanced

	Tackling				Coverage			Impact	
Year	Broken Tackles	BT%	Tackle Share	Avg Depth of Tackle	Targets	Int	Y/Trgt	Pressure Share	EPA on Sacks/TFL
2016	1	3.4%	3.3%	1.1	0	0	-	13.7%	-12.4
2017	5	12.5%	3.5%	0.6	0	0	-	19.7%	-28.2
2018	0	0.0%	1.8%	1.9	0	0	-	4.7%	-14.0
	6	7.1%	2.9%	1.0	0	0	-	12.7%	-54.6

Deep Dive

	Total Snaps			Lined Up	Pass Rush			When Run At		
Year	Pass Rush	Pass Cov	Run	3-Point Stance%	Rush%	Pressure%	Sack%	Bounce%	Pos%	EPA Per Attempt
2018	64	1	44	100.0%	98.5%	19.7%	6.1%	0.0%	0.0%	-0.74

Montez Sweat

Mississippi State Bulldogs
Final Grade: 6.9 Edge Rusher Rank: 2 of 23

Height	Weight	Year	Jersey #	Hometown
6060	252	4SR	9	Stone Mountain, GA

One-Liner
Sweat has an ideal frame, and his length and hand use contribute to a physical set of tools that profile as an impact edge rusher at the next level.

Overall
Sweat lined up in the 5-technique for Mississippi State on either side of center. He started 25 of 26 career games for the Bulldogs after transferring in from community college via Michigan State due to suspension. He has an ideal, long frame and very good athletic ability. He plays hard and attacks with aggression but his pursuit away from the ball is inconsistent.

Pass Game
Sweat is a very good pass rusher. His impressive balance and ankle flexion allow him to bend very well and get below the pad level of offensive lineman, despite his own size. He shows very good speed and change of direction with his rushes. He can dominate offensive linemen with his combination of balance, power, speed, and length. His tools make for a natural pass rusher, and his repertoire of moves, while good, can be improved upon. He moves well in space and is sufficient in flat coverage, although he will need coaching and reps to become natural.

Run Game
While he's more impactful getting after the quarterback, Sweat also uses his skill set to be a solid run defender, which will keep him on the field for three downs. He does a good job of using his length and core strength to bench press inferior blockers in the run game and shed on the edge. He sets a good edge against all competition and offensive opponents, but his lower-body strength needs development to become a better inline anchor. He does do a good job of using his hands and change-of - direction elusiveness to avoid pulling blocks. Sweat shows good intelligence and discipline with his assignments, usually reading his keys and quickly diagnosing the play in front of him. He displays a solid motor and range, along with his speed and length, to make tackles sideline to sideline. Sweat could be a more diligent pursuer from the backside to pinch cutback lanes and make extra effort plays for his team.

Last Word
Sweat projects as a three-down edge defender, ideally with his hand in the dirt, but he has shown enough athleticism and tools to be capable standing up in a 3-4. He should be an impact edge rusher, especially if his technique and snap-to-whistle drive can match his gifted toolset. His size, toughness, and range suggest he could be a solid special teams contributor if necessary.

– Ian Berg

Strengths	Weaknesses
• Length and hand use • First-step explosion • Pass rush ability	• Anchor against the run • Inconsistent pursuit

Critical Factors

Pass Rush Ability	1st Step Explosion	Point Of Attack / Set Edge
7	7	6

Positional Factors

Pass Rush Repertoire	Bend	Hand Use	Play Strength
6	7	7	6
Range	**Flat Coverage**	**Motor**	**Football Intelligence**
6	5	6	6
Discipline	**Tackling**	**Ruggedness**	**Special Teams Value**
6	6	6	6

Basic

	Tackling			Pass Rush					
Year	Tackles	TFL	FF	Sacks	Hurries	Hits	Knockdowns	Pressures	Passes Batted
2017	45	15.0	0	10.0	28	24	12	48	0
2018	52	13.5	1	11.5	30	26	8	46	0
	97	28.5	1	21.5	58	50	20	94	0

Advanced

	Tackling				Coverage			Impact	
Year	Broken Tackles	BT%	Tackle Share	Avg Depth of Tackle	Targets	Int	Y/Trgt	Pressure Share	EPA on Sacks/TFL
2017	5	10.0%	5.3%	1.6	0	0	-	21.4%	-27.0
2018	2	3.7%	6.3%	2.3	2	0	5.5	20.5%	-25.5
	7	6.7%	5.8%	2.0	2	0	5.5	21.0%	-52.5

Deep Dive

	Total Snaps			Lined Up	Pass Rush			When Run At		
Year	Pass Rush	Pass Cov	Run	3-Point Stance%	Rush%	Pressure%	Sack%	Bounce%	Pos%	EPA Per Attempt
2018	258	19	167	97.1%	93.1%	17.3%	4.0%	50.0%	31.3%	-0.36

Josh Allen

Kentucky Wildcats

Final Grade: 6.9 Edge Rusher Rank: 3 of 23

Height	Weight	Year	Jersey #	Hometown
6041	258	4SR	41	Montclair, NJ

One-Liner

Allen has the explosive pass rush ability, strength in the run game and sufficient-enough coverage skills to be a major contributor as a three-down edge rusher at the next level.

Overall

Allen played short-side OLB for Kentucky in its 3-3-5 defensive scheme. He started 35 of his 51 games as a Wildcat over the past four years. He's a quick-twitch, reactive athlete that has a high motor and good pursuit to the football. Toughness shows up in his play throughout each game.

Pass Game

In the passing game, he shows very good pass rush ability in all situations. He mostly rushes with his hand off the ground but will occasionally rush from a 3-point stance. He's very explosive off the ball and knows how to time and set up his moves. He uses a variety of pass-rush moves, including a bull rush, push-pull and rips. He has the power and extension to bull and drive into offensive linemen and the flexibility to be able to bend around the edge and get low to the ground underneath the blockers. Not only can he produce with sacks, but he's able to consistently pressure the QB and force turnovers in the backfield. When he doesn't rush, he's able to play the flat and man up with receivers. He's better as a zone defender but has shown that he can stay with tight ends in man coverage down the field. However, he's a bit stiff in his change of direction when out in space as a cover defender. On screens, he shows the ability to read and react quickly enough to blow them up.

Run Game

Against the run, he produces with tackle numbers. He shows sufficient tackling ability, but he doesn't finish enough around the line of scrimmage. He's a disciplined player on the backside and is strong enough at the point of attack to set the edge play-side. He possesses heavy hands and does a good job using them against tight ends to stack and shed. He has the lateral quickness and range to get down the LOS and make plays from the backside.

Last Word

Allen projects as a 3-down starter that fits best as a strong-side OLB in a 3-4 and has the traits to also fit into a 4-3 as a SAM LB. He can rush the passer on all downs, play the run when needed and drop into coverage when asked. Although not an ideal situation for him, he could contribute some on special teams.

– Nathan Cooper

Strengths	**Weaknesses**
• Pass rush ability	• Stiff in coverage
• Explosive off the ball	• Inconsistent tackler
• Range	

Critical Factors

Pass Rush Ability	1st Step Explosion	Point Of Attack / Set Edge
7	7	6

Positional Factors

Pass Rush Repertoire	Bend	Hand Use	Play Strength
7	7	7	7
Range	**Flat Coverage**	**Motor**	**Football Intelligence**
7	5	6	7
Discipline	**Tackling**	**Ruggedness**	**Special Teams Value**
6	5	6	6

Basic

	Tackling			Pass Rush					
Year	Tackles	TFL	FF	Sacks	Hurries	Hits	Knockdowns	Pressures	Passes Batted
2016	60	6.5	3	7.0	11	5	4	20	0
2017	66	9.0	1	7.0	31	26	13	42	1
2018	87	21.0	5	17.0	43	30	10	67	0
	213	36.5	9	31.0	85	61	27	129	1

Advanced

	Tackling				Coverage			Impact	
Year	Broken Tackles	BT%	Tackle Share	Avg Depth of Tackle	Targets	Int	Y/Trgt	Pressure Share	EPA on Sacks/TFL
2016	3	4.8%	6.2%	4.4	4	0	3.5	17.5%	-14.6
2017	12	15.4%	6.7%	4.7	16	1	3.1	22.7%	-18.5
2018	7	7.4%	10.8%	3.3	8	0	6.6	31.6%	-45.0
	22	9.4%	7.8%	4.0	28	1	4.1	25.2%	-78.1

Deep Dive

	Total Snaps			Lined Up	Pass Rush			When Run At		
Year	Pass Rush	Pass Cov	Run	3-Point Stance%	Rush%	Pressure%	Sack%	Bounce%	Pos%	EPA Per Attempt
2018	234	158	344	3.7%	59.7%	26.8%	7.2%	24.0%	44.0%	0.09

Clelin Ferrell

Clemson Tigers

Final Grade: 6.8 Edge Rusher Rank: 4 of 23

Height	Weight	Year	Jersey #	Hometown
6041	265	4JR	99	Richmond, VA

One-Liner

Ferrell has the explosive get-off, pass rush ability and leverage at the POA to be a starting edge player at the next level, but his stiff hips and inconsistent motor may give him problems early on.

Overall

Ferrell was primarily the right defensive end for the National Champion Clemson Tigers in their 4-3 base defense. He played in 44 games during college career, starting in every single one of them. He will split his time between having his hand in the ground and standing up on the edge. He is a very good athlete with good length who competes and shows toughness in his play. His motor is inconsistent, mainly in regards to his backside and downfield pursuit.

Pass Game

Against the pass, he's disruptive in a variety of ways. His get-off is extremely quick and explosive, and he's normally one of the first players off the ball. He shows a very good pass rush repertoire that consists of swim, spin, rip, speed and bull-rushes. He does a good job setting up his moves. He likes to primarily use speed and then counter by starting with speed to get the offensive tackle upfield and then dip back inside with a swim or spin move. He has sufficient bend, but is a little stiff and doesn't have the elite flexibility to bend seamlessly around the edge. When he uses power to bull rush, he has good length and strength at the POA to get some movement into the backfield. He uses his hands well and knows where to place them during his rush to get the best leverage. He dropped into flat coverage on occasion, but doesn't have the COD skills to be a great coverage defender.

Run Game

In the run game, he shows good strength at the POA to set the edge. Against tight ends, he is able to get hands on with good placement to control the edge. He's got heavy hands and delivers a strong initial punch. Although he's a bit stiff, he shows good lateral movement and range down the line. He makes tackles all over the field, but misses some chances to make plays in the backfield.

Last Word

Ferrell fits best as a starting 4-3 defensive end, but is scheme-versatile and could play 3-4 OLB. He shows more explosion with his hand in the ground, but is still disruptive standing up on the edge. His motor may make it tough for him to want to contribute on special teams, but his traits suggest that he could be successful on some units.

– Nathan Cooper

Strengths

- Very quick get-off
- Uses an array of pass rush moves
- Lateral range

Weaknesses

- Hot & cold motor
- Doesn't finish tackles
- A little stiff in the hips

Critical Factors

Pass Rush Ability	1st Step Explosion	Point Of Attack / Set Edge
6	7	6

Positional Factors

Pass Rush Repertoire	Bend	Hand Use	Play Strength
7	5	6	6
Range	**Flat Coverage**	**Motor**	**Football Intelligence**
7	5	5	6
Discipline	**Tackling**	**Ruggedness**	**Special Teams Value**
6	5	6	6

Basic

	Tackling			Pass Rush					
Year	Tackles	TFL	FF	Sacks	Hurries	Hits	Knockdowns	Pressures	Passes Batted
2016	41	11.5	0	5.5	23	25	12	38	0
2017	62	15.5	2	9.0	36	29	14	56	0
2018	52	19.5	3	11.5	39	26	10	59	1
	155	46.5	5	26.0	98	80	36	153	1

Advanced

	Tackling				Coverage			Impact	
Year	Broken Tackles	BT%	Tackle Share	Avg Depth of Tackle	Targets	Int	Y/Trgt	Pressure Share	EPA on Sacks/TFL
2016	8	16.3%	4.1%	1.3	3	0	2.3	14.8%	-17.1
2017	6	8.8%	6.1%	1.7	3	0	11.7	20.1%	-21.9
2018	6	10.3%	5.0%	1.2	0	0	-	19.2%	-38.1
	20	11.4%	5.0%	1.4	6	0	7.0	18.1%	-77.2

Deep Dive

	Total Snaps			Lined Up	Pass Rush			When Run At		
Year	Pass Rush	Pass Cov	Run	3-Point Stance%	Rush%	Pressure%	Sack%	Bounce%	Pos%	EPA Per Attempt
2018	314	60	294	75.4%	84.0%	17.4%	3.6%	31.3%	37.5%	-0.21

D'Andre Walker

Georgia Bulldogs
Final Grade: 6.7 Edge Rusher Rank: 5 of 23

Height	Weight	Year	Jersey #	Hometown
6021	245	4SR	15	Fairburn, GA

One-Liner

Walker is an explosive, athletic, versatile edge rusher with the pass rush ability, bend and range to be a solid starter at the next level, but ultimately needs to get stronger and more powerful.

Overall

Walker primarily played as a 3-4 outside linebacker for the Bulldogs, but also put his hand in the ground as a 4-3 defensive end. He played in 54 games over his four-year career at Georgia. He is a good athlete who possesses the balance, flexibility, short area quickness and explosiveness needed, but has average height and weight for the position. He's a highly-competitive player who plays with a high motor, is relentless in the pass rush and has good physical toughness. He has good stamina as a pass rusher, displaying an ability to be productive late in games and consistently bring energy and effort to each drive.

Pass Game

In the pass game, Walker has good first-step explosion, showing the initial quickness to close the cushion and penetrate his assigned gap. He has good pass rush ability with the versatility both from a two-point stance as an OLB and a three-point stance as a DE. He consistently generates pressure on the quarterback while keeping a low pad level and uses an array of moves, including a rip, swim, club and chop. He has enough play strength and power to effectively bull rush opponents and is effective while taking on double teams. D'Andre has very good bend around the edge, possessing ankle flexion to cut the corner and get past tackles, while maintaining good quickness and explosiveness. He uses his hands well, showing solid hand placement and timing to win hand-to-hand combat battles, lock out on blockers and easily disengage and shed blocks. He possesses good processing skills and displays good reactive athleticism, showing an ability to quickly diagnose and anticipate plays, while being able to locate the ball and take sharp pursuit angles. He is good in flat coverage and has the range to play in space and quickly get to his assignment, while also displaying the ability to play man coverage against tight ends and running backs.

Run Game

In the run game, D'Andre can set the edge and displays sufficient play strength at the POA to negate his opponents' strength with force, but occasionally will lose contain when he does not play with discipline and initiate contact with his shoulders. He is a solid tackler who can bring runners down with good technique, leg drive and efficiency.

Last Word

D'Andre projects best as a 3-4 outside linebacker, who can play on all three downs due to his ability to play well against the run and be productive as a pass rusher. He certainly has special teams value at the next level due to his combination of speed, size and aggression.

– Nick Giella

Strengths	**Weaknesses**
• Pass rush ability	• Discipline
• Bend	• Overall strength
• Range	

Critical Factors

Pass Rush Ability	1st Step Explosion	Point Of Attack / Set Edge
6	6	6

Positional Factors

Pass Rush Repertoire	Bend	Hand Use	Play Strength
6	7	6	5
Range	**Flat Coverage**	**Motor**	**Football Intelligence**
7	6	6	6
Discipline	**Tackling**	**Ruggedness**	**Special Teams Value**
5	6	6	6

Basic

	Tackling			Pass Rush					
Year	Tackles	TFL	FF	Sacks	Hurries	Hits	Knockdowns	Pressures	Passes Batted
2016	18	2.5	0	0.0	8	1	1	8	0
2017	38	11.5	1	5.5	20	15	5	28	0
2018	44	9.0	4	7.5	16	16	9	29	1
	100	23.0	5	13.0	44	32	15	65	1

Advanced

	Tackling				Coverage			Impact	
Year	Broken Tackles	BT%	Tackle Share	Avg Depth of Tackle	Targets	Int	Y/Trgt	Pressure Share	EPA on Sacks/TFL
2016	1	6.7%	1.6%	1.7	0	0	-	6.0%	-3.7
2017	5	12.5%	4.0%	2.0	4	0	0.0	11.2%	-15.2
2018	3	6.4%	4.7%	2.4	5	0	1.0	16.1%	-15.2
	9	8.8%	3.5%	2.1	9	0	0.6	11.5%	34.1

Deep Dive

	Total Snaps			Lined Up	Pass Rush			When Run At		
Year	Pass Rush	Pass Cov	Run	3-Point Stance%	Rush%	Pressure%	Sack%	Bounce%	Pos%	EPA Per Attempt
2018	221	45	214	42.9%	83.1%	11.7%	2.9%	25.0%	31.3%	-0.40

Jaylon Ferguson

Louisiana Tech Bulldogs
Final Grade: 6.7 Edge Rusher Rank: 6 of 23

Height	Weight	Year	Jersey #	Hometown
6043	256	5SR	45	St. Francisville, LA

One-Liner
Ferguson is a balanced pass rusher who can win outside, inside and through tackles, but fails to make a significant impact against the run.

Overall
Ferguson primarily played as a one-gapping weakside defensive end for Louisiana Tech, playing out of both 2- and 3-point stances. He was a fifth-year senior who started 43 of 51 career games. He is a good athlete and possesses good quickness, acceleration, COD and flexibility. Ferguson gives good effort as a pass rusher but shows average motor versus the run.

Pass Game
As a pass rusher, he demonstrates good explosive quickness out of both 2-point and 3-point stances. He sets up his rushes with first step/speed; his primary moves are speed-to-power, chop-rip, and inside redirects off of speed. Ferguson has good bend and accentuates it with stutter moves and good hand use to crease the edge to corner. His overall production ceiling as a pass rusher is dependent on improving his ability to finish. He was not tasked with dropping into coverage at Louisiana Tech and his athleticism doesn't project favorably to be a consistently productive zone or man defender.

Run Game
As a run defender, he honors backside contain and does a good job of diagnosing blocking concepts and sensing pulls in his periphery. He plays with good hand use and extension but does not control the POA versus TEs. He is a good down-the-line and face-up tackler and average tackler in space due to suboptimal pursuit angles.

Last Word
Ferguson exhibits very good play strength, but average pad level will limit his effectiveness at setting the edge against the run in the NFL. He can line up in multiple techniques on 3rd down and pin his ears back to rush the passer. He projects as a starter at weakside defensive end due to his first step explosiveness, hand usage, and pass rush ability and could stand to improve stoutness versus the run at the POA.

– SIS Scouting Staff

Strengths	Weaknesses
• Strength	• Motor
• Hand use in pass rush	• Run defense
• Speed to power	• Bend consistency

Critical Factors

Pass Rush Ability	1st Step Explosion	Point Of Attack / Set Edge
7	6	6

Positional Factors

Pass Rush Repertoire	Bend	Hand Use	Play Strength
6	6	6	7
Range	**Flat Coverage**	**Motor**	**Football Intelligence**
5	5	5	6
Discipline	**Tackling**	**Ruggedness**	**Special Teams Value**
6	6	6	5

Basic

	Tackling			Pass Rush					
Year	Tackles	TFL	FF	Sacks	Hurries	Hits	Knockdowns	Pressures	Passes Batted
2016	45	12.5	3	12.0	30	15	9	44	0
2017	37	9.0	0	6.0	30	22	11	41	0
2018	63	24.0	1	17.5	39	18	13	63	1
	145	45.5	4	35.5	99	55	33	148	1

Advanced

	Tackling				Coverage			Impact	
Year	Broken Tackles	BT%	Tackle Share	Avg Depth of Tackle	Targets	Int	Y/Trgt	Pressure Share	EPA on Sacks/TFL
2016	5	10.0%	4.6%	2.7	3	0	1.3	23.9%	-19.8
2017	5	11.9%	4.4%	2.7	0	0	-	21.9%	-14.0
2018	3	4.5%	7.4%	1.0	1	0	0.0	34.4%	-48.1
	13	8.2%	5.4%	2.0	4	0	1.0	26.7%	-82.0

Deep Dive

	Total Snaps			Lined Up	Pass Rush			When Run At		
Year	Pass Rush	Pass Cov	Run	3-Point Stance%	Rush%	Pressure%	Sack%	Bounce%	Pos%	EPA Per Attempt
2018	297	13	299	44.3%	95.8%	19.4%	5.4%	43.6%	35.9%	-0.15

Joe Jackson

Miami FL Hurricanes

Final Grade: 6.6 Edge Rusher Rank: 7 of 23

Height	Weight	Year	Jersey #	Hometown
6046	265	3JR	99	Homestead, FL

One-Liner

Jackson is a talented pass rusher who can also hold his own in the run game, but needs to improve his hand usage and add some counter moves to be a more well-rounded player at the next level.

Overall

Jackson's primary position is 4-3 right defensive end; he will occasionally stand up on the edge. He was a 3-year player and a 2-year starter at defensive end, starting in 26 of the 39 games he played. Jackson is a very good athlete with a quick first step. He is an intelligent player with a high motor. He has very good stamina and sustains his effort throughout the game.

Pass Game

As a pass rusher, Jackson produces from both up and down positions. He often has an extra blocker sent to his side and still does a very good job at piling up pressures and sacks. He has sufficient hands and doesn't use them enough. This leaves him to rely mostly on his speed and power as a pass rusher, though he does have good spin and rip moves when he uses them. He uses good leverage and leg drive when bull rushing and is able to create pressure in the backfield. He predetermines most of his rush moves and doesn't have many counters. He tends to play with high pad level, which forces him to get washed out of the play.

Run Game

Jackson is also a good player against the run. His play speed and strength allow him to effectively set the edge, and his high motor and good range keep him from quitting in backside pursuit. He's shown on multiple occasions the pursuit ability from the backside to make a play on a ballcarrier down the field. He doesn't always use good hand placement against OL in order to stack and shed. Going up against TEs, he bullies them with his physicality.

Last Word

Jackson projects as a low-end starter at defensive end in a 4-3 defensive scheme, though his ability and athleticism could be used at OLB in odd fronts. On 3rd downs, he can rush from the edge standing up or with his hand in the ground. He could reduce down on occasion, but he was neutralized by larger, stronger OGs when he did so in college.

– Ronan Potts

Strengths	**Weaknesses**
• Explosiveness • Play strength • Toughness	• Inconsistent hand usage • Counter moves

Critical Factors

Pass Rush Ability	1st Step Explosion	Point Of Attack / Set Edge
6	6	6

Positional Factors

Pass Rush Repertoire	Bend	Hand Use	Play Strength
5	6	5	6
Range	**Flat Coverage**	**Motor**	**Football Intelligence**
6	5	6	6
Discipline	**Tackling**	**Ruggedness**	**Special Teams Value**
6	6	7	6

Basic

	Tackling			Pass Rush					
Year	Tackles	TFL	FF	Sacks	Hurries	Hits	Knockdowns	Pressures	Passes Batted
2016	32	11.0	2	7.5	20	12	7	30	0
2017	49	9.0	1	6.5	28	19	6	39	0
2018	45	15.5	2	9.0	29	19	9	43	0
	126	35.5	5	23.0	77	50	22	112	0

Advanced

	Tackling				Coverage			Impact	
Year	Broken Tackles	BT%	Tackle Share	Avg Depth of Tackle	Targets	Int	Y/Trgt	Pressure Share	EPA on Sacks/TFL
2016	3	8.6%	3.4%	1.6	0	0	-	14.2%	-17.5
2017	7	12.5%	5.0%	2.0	0	0	-	15.7%	-16.6
2018	7	13.5%	4.8%	1.2	0	1	-	20.7%	-26.0
	17	11.9%	4.4%	1.6	0	1	-	16.7%	-60.1

Deep Dive

	Total Snaps			Lined Up	Pass Rush			When Run At		
Year	Pass Rush	Pass Cov	Run	3-Point Stance%	Rush%	Pressure%	Sack%	Bounce%	Pos%	EPA Per Attempt
2018	278	26	283	87.2%	91.4%	14.9%	3.2%	33.3%	36.7%	0.04

Rashan Gary

Michigan Wolverines
Final Grade: 6.6 Edge Rusher Rank: 8 of 23

Height	Weight	Year	Jersey #	Hometown
6042	283	3JR	3	Plainfield, NJ

One-Liner
Gary is a former top recruit who never reached his full potential in college, but has shown raw talent, quickness, and versatile mismatch ability to become a successful next-level player.

Overall
Gary was a defensive end in Michigan's hybrid 4-2-5 defensive scheme, where he almost exclusively played with his hand in the dirt and lined up anywhere from 9- to 3-tech in 2018. He appeared in 34 career games with 21 starts after signing with the Wolverines as the top recruit in the nation, according to some services. He has good length and size for the edge after slimming down and moving from further inside in high school. He is a decent athlete who moves well for his size. Gary has played with a very high motor throughout his career, although his energy and stamina ran hot and cold in 2018, possibly due to injuries. He isn't an overly tough and physical player but has flashed aggression.

Pass Game
As a pass rusher, he has strong upside. Gary has a very limited pass rush repertoire, as he currently relies on either his explosion off the snap or beating a lineman to his chest with length and bull rushing. He uses his hands well but needs quicker technique and a diverse move set to reach his pass-rushing potential. He doesn't have tremendous strength against offensive linemen, but he dominates tight ends and has the frame to grow. He has some bend and flexibility along the arc, but mostly explodes off and speeds around the corner cleanly or has to convert to power. He is raw off the edge but can be reduced inside on third downs to create quickness mismatches.

Run Game
Gary is currently a much stronger player in the run game. He fires off and wins first contact consistently, and while he doesn't overpower linemen, he sets a strong edge. He reads plays well at the stack but needs improved shed ability, as he struggles to shake grip strength and power. He wins against the run with his quickness and ability to get skinny through holes. He plays with a very high motor to pursue from the backside and has made numerous hustle plays to all areas of the field throughout his career. However, in 2018, he was substituted more often after missing time and seemed to tire more frequently.

Last Word
He never compiled the elite production expected of him, but he flashed dominance at times and is still a raw football player. Gary projects as a very versatile edge defender at the next level, who is raw on the edge but has a high upside with improved technique and lower-body strength. He can be moved around on passing downs in the future but is currently already a strong run defender. He should be a fine special teams player if needed but won't be impactful.

– SIS Scouting Staff

Strengths	**Weaknesses**
• Explosion off the snap	• Pass rush repertoire
• Run defense and motor	• Bend and flexibility
• Pass rush upside	• Play strength

Critical Factors

Pass Rush Ability	1st Step Explosion	Point Of Attack / Set Edge
6	7	6

Positional Factors

Pass Rush Repertoire	Bend	Hand Use	Play Strength
4	5	6	5
Range	**Flat Coverage**	**Motor**	**Football Intelligence**
6	4	7	6
Discipline	**Tackling**	**Ruggedness**	**Special Teams Value**
6	6	5	5

Basic

	Tackling			Pass Rush					
Year	Tackles	TFL	FF	Sacks	Hurries	Hits	Knockdowns	Pressures	Passes Batted
2016	26	5.5	0	0.5	13	11	7	17	0
2017	65	10.5	1	5.5	35	27	12	51	0
2018	40	7.5	0	3.5	16	13	6	21	0
	131	23.5	1	9.5	64	51	25	89	0

Advanced

	Tackling				Coverage			Impact	
Year	Broken Tackles	BT%	Tackle Share	Avg Depth of Tackle	Targets	Int	Y/Trgt	Pressure Share	EPA on Sacks/TFL
2016	2	7.1%	3.2%	2.0	0	0	-	8.2%	-9.4
2017	5	7.1%	7.0%	1.9	1	0	3.0	19.2%	-18.5
2018	4	9.1%	5.2%	1.7	0	0	-	11.0%	-13.2
	11	7.7%	5.2%	1.9	1	0	3.0	13.4%	-41.1

Deep Dive

	Total Snaps			Lined Up	Pass Rush			When Run At		
Year	Pass Rush	Pass Cov	Run	3-Point Stance%	Rush%	Pressure%	Sack%	Bounce%	Pos%	EPA Per Attempt
2018	164	5	168	99.1%	97.0%	12.5%	2.1%	37.5%	25.0%	-0.38

Oshane Ximines

Old Dominion Monarchs

Final Grade: 6.5 Edge Rusher Rank: 9 of 23

Height	Weight	Year	Jersey #	Hometown
6034	241	5SR	7	Ahoskie, NC

One-Liner

Ximines has raw strength and athleticism off the edge and possesses the pass rush ability needed to create consistent pressure on the QB, but needs to improve his play strength at the POA to be more than a 3rd down player.

Overall

Ximines played defensive end for Old Dominion's 4-2-5 defense. He played in 49 career games, starting in all but one of them, as he was spelled for a senior on Senior Day in 2016. Ximines is a good athlete who has good physical toughness and competitiveness. He's built for the position with a long torso and solid frame. He played a lot of lesser competition, but even when he faced Virginia Tech, he showed that he was the best player on the field.

Pass Game

He displays a good pass rush repertoire which features a push-pull, swim, and a bull rush. Ximines plays with sufficient strength which he uses in his bull rush, both one- and two-handed, as well as when setting the edge. He prefers to use power over speed. He isn't the most flexible player, and it shows with his only sufficient bend as he runs the loop. He didn't get asked to drop into coverage too often, and when he did, he showed average ability. He is an unorthodox long strider who struggles to change directions with RBs and TEs.

Run Game

Against the run, he does a sufficient job of setting the edge against linemen. He needs to maintain discipline and gap integrity more consistently. He also shows good reactive athleticism when facing read option plays. He is quick to diagnose and is a good tackler with a lot of production over his career, although most of his production comes in the pass rush.

Last Word

Ximines projects as a high-end 3rd down pass rusher with the possibility that he can play some on 1st and 2nd down as a 3-4 OLB or a 4-3 DE. On 3rd downs, he can come off the edge standing up or with his hand on the ground.

– Mark Johnson

Strengths

- Relentless pursuit
- Clutch performer
- Pass rush repertoire

Weaknesses

- Change of direction ability
- Coverage experience
- Setting the edge

Critical Factors

Pass Rush Ability	1st Step Explosion	Point Of Attack / Set Edge
6	6	5

Positional Factors

Pass Rush Repertoire	Bend	Hand Use	Play Strength
6	5	6	5
Range	Flat Coverage	Motor	Football Intelligence
5	4	7	5
Discipline	Tackling	Ruggedness	Special Teams Value
5	6	6	5

Basic

	Tackling			Pass Rush					
Year	Tackles	TFL	FF	Sacks	Hurries	Hits	Knockdowns	Pressures	Passes Batted
2016	44	11.5	3	7.5	17	20	10	33	3
2017	42	13.0	4	9.0	37	25	12	49	1
2018	60	18.5	4	11.5	31	18	8	46	0
	146	43.0	11	28.0	85	63	30	128	4

Advanced

	Tackling				Coverage			Impact	
Year	Broken Tackles	BT%	Tackle Share	Avg Depth of Tackle	Targets	Int	Y/Trgt	Pressure Share	EPA on Sacks/TFL
2016	5	10.4%	4.6%	3.5	1	0	0.0	18.1%	-24.4
2017	4	8.7%	4.9%	2.3	0	0	-	30.2%	-27.3
2018	3	4.8%	6.9%	1.0	1	1	0.0	31.7%	-35.9
	12	7.7%	5.5%	2.1	2	1	0.0	26.2%	-87.6

Deep Dive

	Total Snaps			Lined Up	Pass Rush			When Run At		
Year	Pass Rush	Pass Cov	Run	3-Point Stance%	Rush%	Pressure%	Sack%	Bounce%	Pos%	EPA Per Attempt
2018	305	27	303	78.6%	91.9%	14.4%	3.4%	37.9%	55.2%	0.10

Brian Burns

Florida State Seminoles

Final Grade: 6.5 Edge Rusher Rank: 10 of 23

Height	Weight	Year	Jersey #	Hometown
6042	235	3JR	99	Fort Lauderdale, FL

One-Liner

Burns has the length and explosive athletic traits that profile much better than his actual play, due to his non-physical play style and lack of a counter rush.

Overall

Burns is an edge defender who rushed from the left and right side 5- to 9-tech in Florida State's four-man defensive front, while also standing up on occasion. He played in 38 career games, starting in 25, and made an impact since he stepped on campus with 9.5 sacks in his true freshman All-American season. He is an explosive, flexible athlete with very good length and a solid frame to add strength and weight. Burns rarely leaves the field and plays with a decent motor but isn't aggressive or a snap to whistle competitor.

Pass Game

As a pass rusher, he has ideal athletic traits and size to become a specialist at the next level. He comes out of his stance like a track athlete out of the blocks with great leverage and a long first step. However, Burns shies from contact and does not play with physicality. His repertoire consists of finesse moves only and good footwork on swims, speed around the arc, and the occasional spin. He is very elusive and evades slow hands and feet with ease. Burns lacks the strength for bull rushes, speed-to-power, or other utilization of his size and length. He shows great ankle flexion and shoulder dip to bend around the corner and very good closing speed around the quarterback. He lacks secondary moves to continue working after a failed initial rush. His hand use is sufficient, but not heavy and too frequently relied upon, as he often sits back and hand fights instead of attacking. In the open field, his athleticism is evident as he chases after the ball well behind the line but doesn't offer much hustle downfield. Burns has shown comfortability on rare coverage snaps and has the natural spatial athleticism to succeed in the flats.

Run Game

Against the run, he struggles to make an impact against physical linemen and has a tough time shedding heavy hands. He has the length to keep contain, but Burns' rush-lane discipline is subpar. On passing downs, he occasionally finds himself stunting into his interior teammates, and especially on run plays he often fires off the snap too far upfield thinking pass, leaving large running lanes for the offense. He is a better chase-down tackler than stout head-on run stuffer.

Last Word

Burns projects better as a 3-4 stand up situational pass rusher rather than playing with his hand down, based on his athletic makeup and movement skills but lack of physicality. His upside is high as he has all the desired tools of an impact edge rusher, but he needs improved strength and toughness to reach a higher ceiling.

– John Todd

Strengths	Weaknesses
• Upfield explosion	• Physicality and use of length
• Athleticism and flexibility	• Rush lane discipline
• Length and frame	• Counter moves

Critical Factors

Pass Rush Ability	1st Step Explosion	Point Of Attack / Set Edge
6	7	4

Positional Factors

Pass Rush Repertoire	Bend	Hand Use	Play Strength
6	7	5	4
Range	**Flat Coverage**	**Motor**	**Football Intelligence**
6	6	5	5
Discipline	**Tackling**	**Ruggedness**	**Special Teams Value**
4	5	3	5

Basic

	Tackling			Pass Rush					
Year	Tackles	TFL	FF	Sacks	Hurries	Hits	Knockdowns	Pressures	Passes Batted
2016	26	10.0	1	9.0	19	9	2	30	0
2017	47	12.0	3	4.5	22	23	6	35	2
2018	55	16.0	2	10.0	46	26	8	65	1
	128	38.0	6	23.5	87	58	16	130	3

Advanced

	Tackling				Coverage			Impact	
Year	Broken Tackles	BT%	Tackle Share	Avg Depth of Tackle	Targets	Int	Y/Trgt	Pressure Share	EPA on Sacks/TFL
2016	4	13.3%	3.3%	2.5	3	0	3.3	14.7%	-14.9
2017	5	9.6%	5.3%	3.1	3	0	8.0	17.3%	-27.5
2018	3	5.2%	6.3%	2.7	2	0	8.0	30.2%	-33.0
	12	8.6%	5.0%	2.8	8	0	6.3	20.9%	-75.3

Deep Dive

	Total Snaps			Lined Up	Pass Rush			When Run At		
Year	Pass Rush	Pass Cov	Run	3-Point Stance%	Rush%	Pressure%	Sack%	Bounce%	Pos%	EPA Per Attempt
2018	400	47	364	73.4%	89.5%	16.2%	2.5%	20.0%	40.0%	-0.25

Maxx Crosby

Eastern Michigan Eagles
Final Grade: 6.5 Edge Rusher Rank: 11 of 23

Height	Weight	Year	Jersey #	Hometown
6041	247	4JR	92	Colleyville, TX

One-Liner
Crosby has the explosiveness, length and high motor to win around the edge at the next level but lacks the strength at the POA to play much on run downs.

Overall
Crosby lined up primarily as a strongside defensive end in a 4-3 at EMU. He played almost exclusively in a four-point stance, though occasionally he would stand up. He played in 37 games during his college career, starting in 24 of them the past two seasons. Crosby is an explosive athlete with a very good first step and functional length. He plays with a very high motor, always chases plays away from him, and consistently gets his hands on the blocker before they can engage him.

Pass Game
Against the pass, Crosby is at his best. His quickness off the ball allows him to get behind most linemen and his bend is sufficient enough to flatten quickly at the top of his rush. He utilizes his length for a good speed-to-power rush to counter linemen who are overstepping to match his quickness. His hand fighting is good, and he can keep larger blockers from swallowing him up.

Run Game
Against the run, Crosby uses his length and hands to shed blockers and make plays in the backfield. He is adequate at taking on doubles and stronger blockers directly because of his frame. His quickness and bend allow him to evade plodding linemen while keeping his balance to attack the ballcarrier. He is reliable at bringing the ballcarrier to the ground.

Last Word
By his second year, Crosby projects as a pass rush specialist off the edge. His current frame fits best as a 3-4 OLB, but if he fills out and puts on some muscle, he could put his hand in the ground for a 4-3 defense. He has the physical ability and mindset to come in on third down and be a menace to the QB. He can be used on special teams as well because of his athleticism, motor, and tackling ability.

– Ben Hrkach

Strengths	**Weaknesses**
• Explosive first step	• POA/set edge
• Toughness	• Play strength
• Hand usage	• Flat coverage

Critical Factors

Pass Rush Ability	1st Step Explosion	Point Of Attack / Set Edge
6	7	4

Positional Factors

Pass Rush Repertoire	Bend	Hand Use	Play Strength
6	5	7	5
Range	**Flat Coverage**	**Motor**	**Football Intelligence**
7	5	7	6
Discipline	**Tackling**	**Ruggedness**	**Special Teams Value**
6	6	6	6

Basic

	Tackling			Pass Rush					
Year	Tackles	TFL	FF	Sacks	Hurries	Hits	Knockdowns	Pressures	Passes Batted
2016	31	5.0	0	1.5	13	7	4	15	0
2017	59	17.5	5	11.0	31	18	12	44	0
2018	64	15.5	4	7.5	37	22	10	48	0
	154	38.0	9	20.0	81	47	26	107	0

Advanced

	Tackling				Coverage			Impact	
Year	Broken Tackles	BT%	Tackle Share	Avg Depth of Tackle	Targets	Int	Y/Trgt	Pressure Share	EPA on Sacks/TFL
2016	4	11.4%	2.6%	1.8	0	0	-	10.8%	-8.6
2017	4	6.3%	6.8%	2.0	0	0	-	28.9%	-41.3
2018	11	14.7%	6.3%	1.2	0	1	-	38.4%	-32.6
	19	11.0%	5.2%	1.6	0	1	-	25.7%	-82.4

Deep Dive

	Total Snaps			Lined Up	Pass Rush			When Run At		
Year	Pass Rush	Pass Cov	Run	3-Point Stance%	Rush%	Pressure%	Sack%	Bounce%	Pos%	EPA Per Attempt
2018	281	21	407	93.1%	93.0%	16.2%	2.3%	29.2%	43.8%	-0.10

Chase Winovich

Michigan Wolverines
Final Grade: 6.5 Edge Rusher Rank: 12 of 23

Height	Weight	Year	Jersey #	Hometown
6026	255	5SR	15	Jefferson Hills, PA

One-Liner
Winovich is a relentless, high-motor player who wins with effort and hand use, despite his athletic limitations.

Overall
Winovich primarily lined up at weakside defensive end. He played in 45 career games at Michigan. He is slightly undersized for a hand-in-the-dirt player and isn't a great athlete with tight hips. His aggression and hustle are exceptional, as he works from sideline to sideline and from snap to whistle. He plays with a very good motor and a blue-collar attitude, consistently looking to outwork the man in front of him.

Pass Game
Against the pass, he lacks the desired quick twitch of other edge rushers. Winovich has a sufficient first step and comes off with good leverage but isn't an explosive athlete. He attacks with violent hands and shows solid technique with his rush moves. He often uses a strong rip move, has good speed-to-power, and has enough athleticism to evade lunging blockers. Winovich doesn't have the flexibility to bend around the edge fluidly, but he chases the quarterback relentlessly and wins with his effort and motor. He has experience both standing up and with his hand down but will need to stand up at the next level. He has not been asked to drop into coverage often but has flashed comfortability on his few reps.

Run Game
Against the run, Winovich often chases ballcarriers well downfield. He plays with good football intelligence, as he diagnoses what is in front of him and follows his keys to the ball. He usually plays disciplined with his run gaps and sets the edge to force plays from the front side, but his motor can lead to overpursuit outside his assignments. He plays with good hand use in the run game to stack and shed at the point of attack. He is a sound tackler but could improve his play strength to better attack and anchor larger opponents.

Last Word
Winovich projects as a low-end starter and rotational edge rusher, whose motor and tenacity against the run and pass can provide a spark and energize a unit. He should be a good special teams contributor in the league.

– Alex O'Brien

Strengths	**Weaknesses**
• High motor	• First step explosion
• Sideline to sideline range	• Fluid athleticism
• Hand use	• Play strength and flexion

Critical Factors

Pass Rush Ability	1st Step Explosion	Point Of Attack / Set Edge
6	5	6

Positional Factors

Pass Rush Repertoire	Bend	Hand Use	Play Strength
6	5	6	5
Range	**Flat Coverage**	**Motor**	**Football Intelligence**
6	5	7	6
Discipline	**Tackling**	**Ruggedness**	**Special Teams Value**
5	6	6	6

Basic

	Tackling			Pass Rush					
Year	Tackles	TFL	FF	Sacks	Hurries	Hits	Knockdowns	Pressures	Passes Batted
2016	32	9.5	1	5.0	6	6	3	14	0
2017	76	17.5	2	7.5	37	30	19	59	0
2018	57	15.0	0	5.0	30	20	12	37	0
	165	42.0	3	17.5	73	56	34	110	0

Advanced

	Tackling				Coverage			Impact	
Year	Broken Tackles	BT%	Tackle Share	Avg Depth of Tackle	Targets	Int	Y/Trgt	Pressure Share	EPA on Sacks/TFL
2016	0	0.0%	3.8%	1.3	0	0	-	6.7%	-18.3
2017	3	3.8%	8.5%	2.8	0	0	-	22.3%	-30.9
2018	4	6.6%	7.5%	1.2	0	0	-	19.4%	-21.5
	7	4.1%	6.6%	1.9	0	0	-	16.6%	-70.7

Deep Dive

	Total Snaps			Lined Up	Pass Rush			When Run At		
Year	Pass Rush	Pass Cov	Run	3-Point Stance%	Rush%	Pressure%	Sack%	Bounce%	Pos%	EPA Per Attempt
2018	301	11	292	92.7%	96.5%	11.8%	1.6%	23.5%	44.1%	0.00

Jachai Polite

Florida Gators

Final Grade: 6.5 Edge Rusher Rank: 13 of 23

Height	Weight	Year	Jersey #	Hometown
6016	242	3JR	99	Daytona Beach, FL

One-Liner

Polite is a raw pass rusher with the athleticism and explosiveness to be a force on third downs, but his inconsistency and lack of power setting the edge in the run game will keep him from contributing on all three downs early on.

Overall

Polite primarily played off the edge as a stand-up rusher in Florida's hybrid 3-3-5 defensive scheme. He played in 32 games, starting 9 of them for the Gators. Jachai is very athletic and has good explosiveness off the line. Aside from his athleticism and overall ability, his motor runs hot with solid toughness. He is a good competitor and plays hard but needs to be more consistent with his play.

Pass Game

In the pass game, his explosiveness off the ball is what stands out. He has good bend and flexibility, allowing him to get around the tackle and to the quarterback. He also has the COD ability to start outside then hit inside to get through the line. He has a plan coming into the play and will counter if need be, with speed-to-power and spin being effective for him. He's not always productive in terms of raw statistics, although he puts up big numbers in the backfield. He also generates pressure on the quarterback.

Run Game

In the run game, Polite is very disciplined as a backside defender, but needs to get stronger at the POA to set the edge. He is very reliable in doing his job and to keep outside contain. Polite is also a good tackler who can make plays all over the field. He possesses the strength and lateral mobility to come off the edge from the back side down the line and make the play. He needs to use more consistent hand placement but fires off and gets into the blocker quickly.

Last Word

Polite projects as a low-end starter as a 3-4 OLB by his second season. His skill set would be best utilized on 3rd downs when he can pin his ears back and rush the passer. He could be an effective special teams player because of his motor, drive, size, and athleticism.

– Walter Moore

Strengths	Weaknesses
• Athleticism	• Overall inconsistency
• Discipline	• Hand use
• Explosiveness	• Setting the edge

Critical Factors

Pass Rush Ability	1st Step Explosion	Point Of Attack / Set Edge
6	6	5

Positional Factors

Pass Rush Repertoire	Bend	Hand Use	Play Strength
6	6	5	5
Range	**Flat Coverage**	**Motor**	**Football Intelligence**
6	5	6	5
Discipline	**Tackling**	**Ruggedness**	**Special Teams Value**
5	6	5	6

Basic

	Tackling			Pass Rush					
Year	Tackles	TFL	FF	Sacks	Hurries	Hits	Knockdowns	Pressures	Passes Batted
2016	12	3.5	1	2.0	4	2	0	6	0
2017	22	5.5	1	2.0	13	13	3	19	0
2018	45	16.5	5	10.0	23	15	4	38	0
	79	25.5	7	14.0	40	30	7	63	0

Advanced

	Tackling				Coverage			Impact	
Year	Broken Tackles	BT%	Tackle Share	Avg Depth of Tackle	Targets	Int	Y/Trgt	Pressure Share	EPA on Sacks/TFL
2016	1	7.7%	1.5%	0.0	0	0	-	2.8%	-8.0
2017	7	24.1%	3.2%	6.7	0	0	-	12.0%	-7.1
2018	2	4.3%	5.2%	1.0	0	0	-	19.7%	-36.8
	10	11.4%	3.3%	2.5	0	0	-	11.2%	-51.9

Deep Dive

	Total Snaps			Lined Up	Pass Rush			When Run At		
Year	Pass Rush	Pass Cov	Run	3-Point Stance%	Rush%	Pressure%	Sack%	Bounce%	Pos%	EPA Per Attempt
2018	246	41	214	0.4%	85.7%	14.1%	3.8%	33.3%	38.9%	-0.42

Anthony Nelson

Iowa Hawkeyes

Final Grade: 6.5 Edge Rusher Rank: 14 of 23

Height	Weight	Year	Jersey #	Hometown
6067	272	4JR	98	Urbandale, IA

One-Liner

Nelson is an edge defender who offers good strength and edge-setting at the POA in the run game with his length, as well as some pass rushing alignment versatility, but he has notable athletic limitations.

Overall

Nelson primarily played left defensive end in Iowa's 4-3 scheme. He started 27 of 39 career games. He has a tall, strong, athletic cut with very good length. He is stronger than he appears, but he could still use some added bulk and thickness. He is an average athlete in space with tight hips and mediocre change-of-direction skills. He plays with good grit and toughness, which shines when he plays behind his pads and gets physical. He displays a good motor.

Pass Game

Against the pass, Nelson flashes effectiveness despite his athletic limitations. He can convert his limited speed to power, walking offensive lineman into the quarterback's lap with ease when timed correctly. He does not eat up much ground with his first step and won't beat many linemen around the corner from the jump. He flashes a good repertoire of moves, but mostly shows a reliable bull rush. He also displayed some counter moves to alter his plan mid-play. He has powerful hands, showing that he is capable of delivering a jolt that knocks linemen off balance. He is unable to consistently bend and dip at the top of his pass rush arc and struggles to get his hips turned toward the quarterback. He has some ankle flexibility, but not enough to consistently tilt around the edge. He has the power and versatility to line up and rush inside or outside.

Run Game

Against the run, he does a good job of setting the edge and holding his own at the point of attack. He keeps a good pad level despite his tall frame. He possesses good play strength moving forward but can also anchor against power one-on-one. His hand placement against the run is very good. He uses his long arms to extend and keep his frame clean. He can stack and shed blockers with ease and has also shown some two-gapping potential when reduced inside, although his lower body strength and anchor against double teams could be improved. He is a good overall tackler and has a large radius due to his length. The added bulk would help him from getting overpowered by better run blockers in the NFL. He plays with good discipline and football intelligence, feeling and adjusting to blocking schemes with his hands and diagnosing quickly. His range is limited because of his lateral agility and movement skills in space, but he has a high motor to chase.

Last Word

Nelson adds no real value in coverage beyond his height to disrupt passing lanes, which projects him as a 4-3 defensive end or a 3-4 5-technique, with the versatility to bump inside in some scenarios.

– Alex O'Brien

Strengths	**Weaknesses**
• Ability to set the edge	• Explosion off snap
• Hand use	• Bendability
• Bull rush	• Stand up versatility

Critical Factors

Pass Rush Ability	1st Step Explosion	Point Of Attack / Set Edge
6	4	6

Positional Factors

Pass Rush Repertoire	Bend	Hand Use	Play Strength
6	5	7	6
Range	**Flat Coverage**	**Motor**	**Football Intelligence**
5	3	6	6
Discipline	**Tackling**	**Ruggedness**	**Special Teams Value**
6	6	6	5

Basic

	Tackling			Pass Rush					
Year	Tackles	TFL	FF	Sacks	Hurries	Hits	Knockdowns	Pressures	Passes Batted
2016	30	7.0	2	6.0	30	25	10	41	0
2017	37	7.5	1	6.0	34	32	13	53	3
2018	49	14.0	0	10.5	26	22	10	45	0
	116	28.5	3	22.5	90	79	33	139	3

Advanced

	Tackling				Coverage			Impact	
Year	Broken Tackles	BT%	Tackle Share	Avg Depth of Tackle	Targets	Int	Y/Trgt	Pressure Share	EPA on Sacks/TFL
2016	4	11.8%	3.2%	1.9	0	0	-	23.0%	-16.0
2017	7	15.9%	4.0%	1.8	2	0	0.0	26.0%	-16.6
2018	1	2.0%	5.6%	2.3	0	0	-	27.1%	-20.6
	12	9.4%	4.2%	2.1	2	0	0.0	25.4%	-53.2

Deep Dive

	Total Snaps			Lined Up	Pass Rush			When Run At		
Year	Pass Rush	Pass Cov	Run	3-Point Stance%	Rush%	Pressure%	Sack%	Bounce%	Pos%	EPA Per Attempt
2018	275	69	236	96.7%	79.9%	13.0%	3.4%	40.0%	40.0%	0.02

Austin Bryant

Clemson Tigers

Final Grade: 6.2 Edge Rusher Rank: 15 of 23

Height	Weight	Year	Jersey #	Hometown
6045	280	4SR	7	Pavo, GA

One-Liner

Bryant has the athleticism, raw pass rush ability, and range to be a solid edge rusher but needs to build upon his consistency in multiple areas to become a starter.

Overall

At Clemson, Bryant saw time as a 3-technique and out with his hand in the ground, as well as on the edge as a stand-up OLB in their base 4-3 defense. He played in 51 games with 29 starts for the Tigers. He's a long athlete who competes and plays with toughness. However, Bryant will go long periods of games making no impact, getting off the ball slowly and showing less twitch than he is capable of. On too many plays, he gets easily handled by a lone lineman or at times even a solo TE, as he struggles with his hand use.

Pass Game

In the passing game, with a hand in the ground, Bryant is often slow off the line, showing no real plan of attack on the rush. He gets too upright and shows little bend, causing him to be easily contained. He shows more pass rush success when standing up, using his speed around the edge. When standing, he often drops into zone coverage in the flat with effectiveness, especially making tackles in the open field. Bryant shows his speed, tackling, and pass rush ability in flashes, which begs for more consistency. His best pass rush move is speed, using bend around the edge. He could use development of other options.

Run Game

In the run game, his strength lies in his length and speed. He uses his length to create separation from blockers to maintain the edge, keeping his outside arm free and forcing the play inside. Bryant's speed allows him to make plays off the edge or disrupt plays by shooting the B gap. His speed and length allow him room to read plays, contain, and run ballcarriers down from the back side, showing his very good range. His weaknesses include shedding blockers with hand use, his FBI in reading the play, and strength. He can get lost in the play without reacting or being able to shed blockers as he does get pushed off the LOS, while very rarely forcing a blocker back into the backfield.

Last Word

Bryant projects best as a 3-4 OLB at the next level. His first step explosiveness and pass rush are consistent when standing. Bryant shows so much more athleticism, bend, and leverage when rushing from an OLB position. He is able to use his speed more effectively from the outside than when his hand is in the ground. He could also see time as a weakside defensive end, though he gets too vertical at the snap, leaving himself open and losing leverage. His athleticism suggests he could provide some help on special teams, but his lack of consistent toughness may suggest otherwise.

– Evan Butler

Strengths	Weaknesses
• Speed around the edge	• Strength
• Length	• Hand use
• Athleticism	• Play recognition

Critical Factors

Pass Rush Ability	1st Step Explosion	Point Of Attack / Set Edge
6	6	6

Positional Factors

Pass Rush Repertoire	Bend	Hand Use	Play Strength
4	6	6	6
Range	**Flat Coverage**	**Motor**	**Football Intelligence**
7	6	6	5
Discipline	**Tackling**	**Ruggedness**	**Special Teams Value**
6	6	5	5

Basic

	Tackling			Pass Rush					
Year	Tackles	TFL	FF	Sacks	Hurries	Hits	Knockdowns	Pressures	Passes Batted
2016	11	3.0	0	2.5	7	6	2	14	0
2017	49	12.5	2	7.5	35	17	5	46	1
2018	42	13.5	0	8.5	20	15	8	31	0
	102	29.0	2	18.5	62	38	15	91	1

Advanced

	Tackling				Coverage			Impact	
Year	Broken Tackles	BT%	Tackle Share	Avg Depth of Tackle	Targets	Int	Y/Trgt	Pressure Share	EPA on Sacks/TFL
2016	1	8.3%	1.1%	2.4	1	0	0.0	5.5%	-4.3
2017	6	10.9%	5.2%	1.9	4	1	0.3	16.5%	-17.3
2018	2	4.5%	3.6%	0.6	0	0	-	10.1%	-22.9
	9	8.1%	3.3%	1.4	5	1	0.2	10.8%	-44.5

Deep Dive

	Total Snaps			Lined Up	Pass Rush			When Run At		
Year	Pass Rush	Pass Cov	Run	3-Point Stance%	Rush%	Pressure%	Sack%	Bounce%	Pos%	EPA Per Attempt
2018	306	56	281	70.1%	84.5%	9.7%	2.8%	21.1%	39.5%	-0.14

Jalen Jelks

Oregon Ducks

Final Grade: 6.2 Edge Rusher Rank: 16 of 23

Height	Weight	Year	Jersey #	Hometown
6054	250	5SR	97	Phoenix, AZ

One-Liner

Jelks shows good pursuit to the football with raw pass rush ability, but needs to get stronger at the POA on the edge to be consistent at the next level.

Overall

Jelks mainly played 3-4 OLB coming off the left side for Oregon. Some games they played him as a 5-technique in their 3-3-5 and reduced down when they went to two-man fronts. He played in 44 games and has started 25 of them. He's a very good athlete with good length. He shows toughness in his game but is not as physical as a DL should be. He plays with a good motor and is always going full-speed. He shows good range and pursuit to the football when he's away from the play.

Pass Game

In the pass game, he shows flashes, but is ultimately raw in his pass rush ability. He's explosive at the snap and tries to use a few different pass rush moves, but is slow with his punch and usually allows blockers to get into his chest. When using swim moves, he gets too tall at the POA and is easily washed by offensive linemen. He doesn't show the bend needed by a speed rusher, as he usually just gets washed out when trying to come around the edge. He doesn't have the thickest frame and could stand to put on more muscle, but when he bull rushes, he seems to get penetration into the backfield with good extension and leg drive. He can be disruptive but needs to finish plays more often in the backfield. He shows an equal amount of efficiency when rushing from an up or down position, as his counter moves usually dictate his production. He was rarely asked to cover, but did cover the flats on a few occasions. He seems to have the athleticism to be rangy in coverage, but didn't look comfortable when doing it.

Run Game

In the run game, he missed a lot of tackles in space. When he'd finally get into position to make a play, he was out of control more often than not and would fail to bring down the ball carrier. He doesn't show the ability to set the edge as he is unable to hold his ground and easily gets washed out by offensive tackles. Even going up against TEs he struggles to consistently win and set the edge. He's also rarely able to stand his ground against doubles. He doesn't show great strength to move laterally down the LOS while taking on blockers.

Last Word

Jelks projects best as a stand-up edge rusher in a 3-4 scheme, but could also fit into a 4-3 as a Sam linebacker. He has the ability to reduce down on 3rd downs and use his pass rush ability against interior OL. His athleticism, motor and pursuit skills suggest he could be a solid special teams player.

– Nathan Cooper

Strengths	**Weaknesses**
• Explosive first step • Good extension on bull rush	• Lacks strength to set the edge • Slow initial punch • Plays high at the POA

Critical Factors

Pass Rush Ability	1st Step Explosion	Point Of Attack / Set Edge
6	6	4

Positional Factors

Pass Rush Repertoire	Bend	Hand Use	Play Strength
6	5	5	5
Range	**Flat Coverage**	**Motor**	**Football Intelligence**
6	5	6	6
Discipline	**Tackling**	**Ruggedness**	**Special Teams Value**
6	5	6	6

Basic

	Tackling			Pass Rush					
Year	Tackles	TFL	FF	Sacks	Hurries	Hits	Knockdowns	Pressures	Passes Batted
2016	31	6.0	0	3.0	6	2	1	10	1
2017	59	14.5	0	6.5	39	25	10	47	6
2018	55	7.5	0	3.5	30	26	8	43	0
	145	28.0	0	13.0	75	53	19	100	7

Advanced

	Tackling				Coverage			Impact	
Year	Broken Tackles	BT%	Tackle Share	Avg Depth of Tackle	Targets	Int	Y/Trgt	Pressure Share	EPA on Sacks/TFL
2016	5	13.9%	3.6%	5.1	1	1	5.0	7.5%	-8.0
2017	7	10.6%	6.8%	1.5	1	0	0.0	20.6%	-19.7
2018	6	9.8%	5.8%	2.4	0	0	-	18.6%	-12.6
	18	11.0%	5.4%	2.7	2	1	2.5	16.9%	-40.4

Deep Dive

	Total Snaps			Lined Up	Pass Rush			When Run At		
Year	Pass Rush	Pass Cov	Run	3-Point Stance%	Rush%	Pressure%	Sack%	Bounce%	Pos%	EPA Per Attempt
2018	351	26	279	64.6%	93.1%	11.7%	1.0%	32.4%	37.8%	-0.03

Jordan Brailford

Oklahoma State Cowboys
Final Grade: 6.2 Edge Rusher Rank: 17 of 23

Height	Weight	Year	Jersey #	Hometown
6025	241	4JR	94	Tulsa, OK

One-Liner
Brailford has the explosion off the line and pass rush ability to make an impact at the next level, yet his lack of strength at the POA in the run game will most likely limit him to 3rd downs early in his career.

Overall
Brailford is an explosive pass rusher who lined up at DE and OLB in Oklahoma State's base 4-3. When they moved to an odd front, he even stood up in the A gaps and as an off-ball LB. He played in 36 games for the Cowboys and started in 19 of them. Brailford is a solid athlete and plays with very good play speed. He has good size for his position with his length but has only sufficient play strength. He operates with a hot and cold motor, which may be due to him wearing down late in games.

Pass Game
He is most effective in the pass game, but he does have the ability to play all three downs. He has the ability to beat his man at DE or OLB with pure athleticism and speed. He has a quick first step with explosion and a pass rush repertoire that consists of speed off the edge, bull rush, and spin. He uses his hands well in order to keep linemen at arm's length. He doesn't look to be comfortable covering the flat and doesn't show much range in overall pass coverage.

Run Game
In the run game, Brailford has shown to be adequate. He has good FBI and position discipline and the tackle production to back it up. Brailford has flashed the ability to be disruptive in the backfield. He has some lateral quickness, but his play strength has shown to be a concern in the run game. He struggles to set the edge and gets washed out of plays easily.

Last Word
Brailford projects as a versatile backup rusher who fits best standing up on the edge in a 3-4 but could slide inside or put his hand in the ground. Early on, he will most likely see most of his time on 3rd downs until he develops more strength at the POA in the run game. He should provide some help on special teams as well.

– Ian Riley

Strengths	**Weaknesses**
• Explosive first step	• Setting the edge
• Pass rush ability	• Coverage ability
• Athleticism	• Play strength

Critical Factors

Pass Rush Ability	1st Step Explosion	Point Of Attack / Set Edge
6	6	5

Positional Factors

Pass Rush Repertoire	Bend	Hand Use	Play Strength
6	6	6	5
Range	**Flat Coverage**	**Motor**	**Football Intelligence**
5	5	5	5
Discipline	**Tackling**	**Ruggedness**	**Special Teams Value**
6	6	6	6

Basic

	Tackling			Pass Rush					
Year	Tackles	TFL	FF	Sacks	Hurries	Hits	Knockdowns	Pressures	Passes Batted
2016	3	0.0	0	0.0	0	0	0	0	0
2017	54	11.0	1	4.0	12	5	3	18	0
2018	53	16.0	1	9.0	36	20	9	46	0
	110	27.0	2	13.0	48	25	12	64	0

Advanced

	Tackling				Coverage			Impact	
Year	Broken Tackles	BT%	Tackle Share	Avg Depth of Tackle	Targets	Int	Y/Trgt	Pressure Share	EPA on Sacks/TFL
2016	0	0.0%	0.4%	4.0	0	0	-	0.0%	0.0
2017	6	10.0%	5.8%	3.8	4	1	1.8	8.8%	-27.0
2018	11	17.2%	5.8%	2.6	1	0	0.0	22.4%	-26.5
	17	13.4%	4.0%	3.2	5	1	1.4	10.6%	-53.4

Deep Dive

	Total Snaps			Lined Up	Pass Rush			When Run At		
Year	Pass Rush	Pass Cov	Run	3-Point Stance%	Rush%	Pressure%	Sack%	Bounce%	Pos%	EPA Per Attempt
2018	333	57	308	45.0%	85.4%	13.1%	2.7%	15.0%	55.0%	0.13

Porter Gustin

USC Trojans

Final Grade: 6.2 Edge Rusher Rank: 18 of 23

Height	Weight	Year	Jersey #	Hometown
6042	260	4SR	45	Elk Ridge, UT

One-Liner

Gustin is a strong, intelligent, and detail-oriented linebacker with a high motor, whose injury history and stiffness may keep him from becoming a starting-level player.

Overall

Gustin played as an edge linebacker on both sides of the ball in USC's base nickel defense. He also played off the ball in certain packages. He played in 37 career games as a three-year starter but was hampered by multiple serious injuries his final two seasons with the Trojans. He is very well-cut and has decent arm length. He is a stiff athlete but plays with a relentless motor and competes every snap.

Pass Game

In the pass game, Gustin is a sufficient edge rusher. His repertoire of successful moves consists of bull rushes and push-pull techniques, as he struggles athletically winning with finesse. His jump off the snap is more powerful than fast, and he uses his hands and length well at the point of attack. He looks unnatural bending around the edge but flashes the ability to dip and reduce an offensive lineman's target zone on him. Gustin does a good job of driving his outside leg into the ground and pushing the pocket with length and lower body power. He has been asked to spy the quarterback from off the ball and he does a good job of keeping contain and tracking eyes. He isn't asked to drop into coverage often, but he isn't fluid in space and could at most be sufficient in the flats due to his intelligence and awareness.

Run Game

In the run game, Gustin is a highly intelligent and detailed football player. What he lacks in athleticism and physical tools, he makes up for with intangibles, assignment detail, and motor. He does a very good job of sticking to the hip of down blocks, squeezing down the back side, and pinching split-zone blocks and other pulls. He stays home and rarely overpursues, while setting the edge with good form and discipline. Gustin plays with a high motor and regularly chases after plays well downfield and outside his expected area.

Last Word

Gustin's skill set should add up to a reliable core special teams contributor. If he can fully recover and remain healthy going forward, he could be a low-end two-down starter as a 3-4 edge rusher or 4-3 Sam linebacker. Currently, Gustin best projects as a quality versatile reserve linebacker, capable of bringing leadership and energy to a second unit and fourth downs. His injury history may limit an already-limited athlete, but his intangibles suggest he can overcome that.

– SIS Scouting Staff

Strengths	**Weaknesses**
• Football intelligence	• Flexibility and finesse
• Motor	• Spatial athleticism
• Ability to set the edge	• Injury history

Critical Factors

Pass Rush Ability	1st Step Explosion	Point Of Attack / Set Edge
5	5	6

Positional Factors

Pass Rush Repertoire	Bend	Hand Use	Play Strength
5	5	6	6
Range	**Flat Coverage**	**Motor**	**Football Intelligence**
5	5	7	7
Discipline	**Tackling**	**Ruggedness**	**Special Teams Value**
7	6	6	7

Basic

	Tackling			Pass Rush					
Year	Tackles	TFL	FF	Sacks	Hurries	Hits	Knockdowns	Pressures	Passes Batted
2016	68	12.0	0	5.5	46	21	7	56	2
2017	17	4.0	0	4.0	5	3	1	9	0
2018	26	7.5	0	7.0	14	8	4	25	0
	111	23.5	0	16.5	65	32	12	90	2

Advanced

	Tackling				Coverage			Impact	
Year	Broken Tackles	BT%	Tackle Share	Avg Depth of Tackle	Targets	Int	Y/Trgt	Pressure Share	EPA on Sacks/TFL
2016	9	11.8%	8.3%	3.2	0	0	-	27.9%	-18.0
2017	1	5.6%	1.8%	2.6	0	0	-	3.3%	-5.8
2018	2	7.1%	3.2%	2.2	1	0	14.0	12.7%	-14.1
	12	9.8%	4.4%	2.9	1	0	14.0	13.4%	-37.9

Deep Dive

	Total Snaps			Lined Up	Pass Rush			When Run At		
Year	Pass Rush	Pass Cov	Run	3-Point Stance%	Rush%	Pressure%	Sack%	Bounce%	Pos%	EPA Per Attempt
2018	150	24	123	0.0%	86.2%	15.2%	4.3%	20.0%	50.0%	0.21

Sutton Smith

Northern Illinois Huskies
Final Grade: 6.2 Edge Rusher Rank: 19 of 23

Height	Weight	Year	Jersey #	Hometown
6003	234	4JR	15	St. Charles, MO

One-Liner
Smith is too undersized to become a starting edge defender and may be better served moving off the ball, but his motor, athleticism, and mentality suggest he can back up multiple linebacker positions and contribute on fourth downs.

Overall
Smith was an edge defender for Northern Illinois, where he was used strictly as a pass and run stuffer with very little experience dropping into coverage. He played in 37 career games after being recruited as a running back. He is undersized and lacks desired length but has a thick backside and strong arms.

Pass Game
As a pass rusher, Smith possesses solid athletic traits which translate to a strong first step off the ball. He shows quick hands and a decent repertoire of moves to win with leverage against bigger and longer blockers, but his lack of length is often his biggest weakness off the edge and will be more of an issue at the next level. He works hard and plays with a strong motor through the whistle. He bends well and closes fast to the quarterback. Smith plays with a lot of passion and competitiveness on the field and is a galvanizing presence for his defense.

Run Game
Against the run, he works hard but will struggle due to his size and play strength. He can set the edge sufficiently with quickness and effort, not length, but he has issues anchoring and shedding against in-line blockers.

Last Word
Smith might best fit further off the ball, where he can play more in space and not have his length and play strength hold him back. He should still offer enough pass rush ability and motor to assist a team in a rotational third down edge role, as he doesn't project well as a run defender. However, his athleticism, frame, and movement skills suggest he could back up an off-ball linebacker position as well with reps and coaching in coverage. Smith will also be a solid special teams contributor because of his toughness, aggression, and mentality.

– Mark Johnson

Strengths	Weaknesses
• First-step explosion	• Play strength
• Motor	• Height and length
• Bend	• Coverage experience

Critical Factors

Pass Rush Ability	1st Step Explosion	Point Of Attack / Set Edge
6	6	5

Positional Factors

Pass Rush Repertoire	Bend	Hand Use	Play Strength
5	6	5	4
Range	**Flat Coverage**	**Motor**	**Football Intelligence**
6	5	6	5
Discipline	**Tackling**	**Ruggedness**	**Special Teams Value**
6	5	6	6

Basic

	Tackling			Pass Rush					
Year	Tackles	TFL	FF	Sacks	Hurries	Hits	Knockdowns	Pressures	Passes Batted
2016	13	2.0	0	1.0	7	7	1	9	0
2017	66	30.5	2	14.0	62	48	15	86	3
2018	62	27.0	4	15.0	40	26	7	60	0
	141	59.5	6	30.0	109	81	23	155	3

Advanced

	Tackling				Coverage			Impact	
Year	Broken Tackles	BT%	Tackle Share	Avg Depth of Tackle	Targets	Int	Y/Trgt	Pressure Share	EPA on Sacks/TFL
2016	3	30.0%	0.8%	2.5	0	0	-	6.7%	-2.8
2017	4	5.7%	7.0%	0.8	0	0	-	32.8%	-52.9
2018	8	11.4%	6.6%	1.5	1	0	12.0	27.6%	-46.1
	15	10.0%	5.0%	1.2	1	0	12.0	25.3%	-101.8

Deep Dive

	Total Snaps			Lined Up	Pass Rush			When Run At		
Year	Pass Rush	Pass Cov	Run	3-Point Stance%	Rush%	Pressure%	Sack%	Bounce%	Pos%	EPA Per Attempt
2018	455	21	361	16.1%	95.6%	12.3%	3.3%	46.7%	33.3%	-0.38

Malik Reed

Nevada Wolf Pack

Final Grade: 5.9 Edge Rusher Rank: 20 of 23

Height	Weight	Year	Jersey #	Hometown
6006	235	5SR	90	Dothan, AL

One-Liner

Reed shines as an edge rusher in the pass game due to his repertoire, first step explosiveness and motor, but needs to build his coverage skills and get stronger at the POA against the run to play on all three downs at the next level.

Overall

Reed lined up at outside linebacker for Nevada and showed the versatility to play wide in a three-point and four-point stance. He played defensive end up until his senior season when he moved to strongside linebacker. He played in 50 career games for the Wolfpack. He shows quick first-step explosion with good length. Reed has a high motor and consistently pursues the ballcarrier or passer outside of the pocket.

Pass Game

In the pass game, he shows a high motor and solid pass rush repertoire, but only sufficient skills in pass coverage. He favors a speed rush and is able to bend around the corner. He also possesses a swim move in his arsenal, which he uses predetermined or as a counter move. When he doesn't pressure the passer, he often puts his hand in the air to minimize passing angles. He often lined up in a wide 9-technique with his hand down in the dirt on third downs.

In coverage, he gets lost in space but has the speed to stay with backs and tight ends. He is new to the position, but he can use his speed and athleticism to improve his coverage skills to be a consistent player in the passing game.

Run Game

In the run game, he lacks the ability to shed blocks and has only adequate FBI when recognizing run play designs. He's sufficient at using his hands in the trenches, using his length to keep OL away from his body. However, he needs to get stronger in the upper body.

Last Word

At the NFL level, Reed projects as a backup 3-4 edge rusher. He will be successful as a pass rusher on 3rd downs early on. Reed has the length, motor and ability to help contribute some on special teams.

– Jonny Guerra

Strengths	Weaknesses
• Pass rush ability	• Block shedding
• First step explosion	• Pass coverage
• Motor	• Upper body strength

Critical Factors

Pass Rush Ability	1st Step Explosion	Point Of Attack / Set Edge
6	6	5

Positional Factors

Pass Rush Repertoire	Bend	Hand Use	Play Strength
6	6	5	5
Range	**Flat Coverage**	**Motor**	**Football Intelligence**
5	5	6	5
Discipline	**Tackling**	**Ruggedness**	**Special Teams Value**
6	6	5	6

Basic

	Tackling			Pass Rush					
Year	Tackles	TFL	FF	Sacks	Hurries	Hits	Knockdowns	Pressures	Passes Batted
2016	56	9.5	3	5.0	27	9	3	32	0
2017	47	10.0	3	9.0	31	21	11	44	0
2018	70	14.5	4	8.0	35	16	7	44	0
	173	34.0	10	22.0	93	46	21	120	0

Advanced

	Tackling				Coverage			Impact	
Year	Broken Tackles	BT%	Tackle Share	Avg Depth of Tackle	Targets	Int	Y/Trgt	Pressure Share	EPA on Sacks/TFL
2016	11	16.9%	6.8%	3.8	1	0	10.0	27.6%	-10.3
2017	6	11.3%	4.6%	2.9	0	0	-	25.1%	-22.1
2018	7	9.1%	8.0%	3.4	5	0	11.2	20.1%	-25.5
	24	12.3%	6.4%	3.4	6	0	11.0	23.5%	-57.9

Deep Dive

	Total Snaps			Lined Up	Pass Rush			When Run At		
Year	Pass Rush	Pass Cov	Run	3-Point Stance%	Rush%	Pressure%	Sack%	Bounce%	Pos%	EPA Per Attempt
2018	225	216	366	17.8%	51.0%	15.8%	3.1%	43.8%	43.8%	-0.20

Ben Banogu

TCU Horned Frogs

Final Grade: 5.9 Edge Rusher Rank: 21 of 23

Height	Weight	Year	Jersey #	Hometown
6034	247	5SR	15	McKinney, TX

One-Liner

Banogu can contribute as a backup pass rusher due to his frame and his repertoire, but he needs to find more consistency in defending the run before he can be a 3-down contributor.

Overall

Banogu lined up as a defensive end and on-ball linebacker for the Horned Frogs. He is a 2-year player and 2-year starter for TCU, and started all 27 games he played in after transferring from Louisiana-Monroe, where he started all 13 games in 2015. He is a strong, physical athlete with a long, thick frame and a decent first step who has played from both a 2-point and 3-point stance, although he looks uncomfortable with his hand in the dirt. He has a good motor and is always competing in both the pass and run game.

Pass Game

As a pass rusher, he tends to rely on his strength rather than his technique at times. He has a decent burst off the snap of the ball, but he has shown to be inconsistent with it. He sets his moves up well and loves to set up the offensive tackle on an outside rush then cut back inside He's inconsistent at setting the edge in pass rush situations, because he likes to dip inside too often. He has a good repertoire of moves using his speed, a bull rush, a club and rip a majority of the time. Banogu has average bend as he struggles rushing around the edge, preferring to win inside.

Run Game

In the run game, he is disruptive and doesn't get moved easily at the POA. He does a sufficient job of setting the edge and is able to make tackles at or near the LOS. He tends to lose gap discipline and move inside when he needs to contain, allowing for running backs to bounce outside and convert bigger gains.

Last Word

He needs better, more consistent hand use to go up against larger NFL offensive tackles. By year two, Banogu projects to be a top backup who can contribute on passing downs, but he needs to refine how he plays against the run and learn to stay disciplined before he can contribute on all three downs.

– Jordan Edwards

Strengths	Weaknesses
• Play strength • Pass rush ability • High motor	• Breaks contain too often • Play recognition • Relies on strength/athleticism over technique

Critical Factors

Pass Rush Ability	1st Step Explosion	Point Of Attack / Set Edge
6	5	5

Positional Factors

Pass Rush Repertoire	Bend	Hand Use	Play Strength
6	4	5	6
Range	**Flat Coverage**	**Motor**	**Football Intelligence**
5	5	6	5
Discipline	**Tackling**	**Ruggedness**	**Special Teams Value**
5	6	6	5

Basic

	Tackling			Pass Rush					
Year	Tackles	TFL	FF	Sacks	Hurries	Hits	Knockdowns	Pressures	Passes Batted
2017	49	15.5	3	8.5	33	22	9	44	1
2018	56	16.5	1	8.5	50	30	12	63	0
	105	32.0	4	17.0	83	52	21	107	1

Advanced

	Tackling				Coverage			Impact	
Year	Broken Tackles	BT%	Tackle Share	Avg Depth of Tackle	Targets	Int	Y/Trgt	Pressure Share	EPA on Sacks/TFL
2017	6	10.9%	5.7%	2.1	1	0	0.0	17.7%	-24.7
2018	13	18.8%	7.3%	2.0	1	0	4.0	30.6%	-15.9
	19	15.3%	4.1%	2.0	2	0	2.0	17.4%	-40.6

Deep Dive

	Total Snaps			Lined Up	Pass Rush			When Run At		
Year	Pass Rush	Pass Cov	Run	3-Point Stance%	Rush%	Pressure%	Sack%	Bounce%	Pos%	EPA Per Attempt
2018	405	47	357	30.8%	89.6%	14.3%	2.1%	60.0%	40.0%	-0.09

Cece Jefferson

Florida Gators
Final Grade: 5.9 Edge Rusher Rank: 22 of 23

*

Height	Weight	Year	Jersey #	Hometown
6010	252	4SR	96	Glen St. Mary, FL

One-Liner
Jefferson has the raw pass rush ability to contribute on passing downs early at the next level but needs refinement and must get stronger to be an effective three-down player.

Overall
Jefferson primarily played as an edge rusher in Florida's hybrid 3-3-5 defense, coming off the edge both standing up and with his hand in the dirt. He played in 48 games with 26 starts for the Gators. He is a very aggressive player who plays with a high motor and toughness on each play. He is a solid athlete who has decent range within the tackle box. He is disciplined with sufficient FBI but will lose contain at times.

Pass Game
Against the pass, he shows promise but inconsistency. He is an adequate pass rusher with pass rush moves that rely on his strength or speed. He has little bend and doesn't have a plan when he is pass rushing. He usually comes in out of control and doesn't have great balance when contacting blockers. He has a tendency to get tangled up with linemen and gets taken out of plays because he loses his feet.

Run Game
Against the run, Jefferson shows solid strength at the POA, yet he doesn't have the ability to hold the edge against bigger linemen. He has a quick first step off the line and uses his lateral mobility to run down plays from the back side. He is a very good tackler as he attempts to deliver a blow on each tackle. Due to Florida's scheme, he didn't drop much into coverage; however, he could be an average flat defender with his athleticism.

Last Word
Jefferson projects as a backup 4-3 DE beginning mainly on 3rd downs as a pass rusher, with the ability to stand up on the edge. He could see some time on early downs once he gets stronger and stouter at the POA.

– SIS Scouting Staff

Strengths

- Raw pass rush skill
- First step quickness
- Hand use

Weaknesses

- Play strength at POA
- Pass coverage
- Pass rush repertoire

Critical Factors

Pass Rush Ability	1st Step Explosion	Point Of Attack / Set Edge
5	6	5

Positional Factors

Pass Rush Repertoire	Bend	Hand Use	Play Strength
5	4	6	6
Range	**Flat Coverage**	**Motor**	**Football Intelligence**
5	4	6	5
Discipline	**Tackling**	**Ruggedness**	**Special Teams Value**
5	6	6	6

Basic

	Tackling			Pass Rush					
Year	Tackles	TFL	FF	Sacks	Hurries	Hits	Knockdowns	Pressures	Passes Batted
2016	30	6.5	0	1.5	13	8	4	16	0
2017	47	13.0	0	4.0	14	11	6	20	1
2018	16	6.0	0	1.0	11	7	2	14	1
	93	25.5	0	6.5	38	26	12	50	2

Advanced

	Tackling				Coverage			Impact	
Year	Broken Tackles	BT%	Tackle Share	Avg Depth of Tackle	Targets	Int	Y/Trgt	Pressure Share	EPA on Sacks/TFL
2016	6	16.7%	3.5%	1.0	0	0	-	7.5%	-9.5
2017	11	19.0%	6.4%	2.1	1	0	10.0	12.7%	-18.5
2018	2	11.1%	1.8%	0.1	1	0	1.0	7.3%	-8.5
	19	17.0%	3.7%	1.4	2	0	5.5	8.8%	-36.5

Deep Dive

	Total Snaps			Lined Up	Pass Rush			When Run At		
Year	Pass Rush	Pass Cov	Run	3-Point Stance%	Rush%	Pressure%	Sack%	Bounce%	Pos%	EPA Per Attempt
2018	186	27	165	40.2%	87.3%	5.9%	0.5%	41.7%	50.0%	0.30

Justin Hollins

Oregon Ducks

Final Grade: 5.9 Edge Rusher Rank: 23 of 23

Height	Weight	Year	Jersey #	Hometown
6052	245	5SR	11	Arlington, TX

One-Liner

Hollins flashes as a pass rusher with good tackling and coverage ability, but is ultimately limited due to his pass rush repertoire and lack of strength on the edge at the POA.

Overall

Hollins primarily served as an odd-front edge rusher while occasionally dropping into zone coverage. He has the athleticism to play as a 4-3 SAM. He played in 52 games for the Ducks, starting 37. He's a good, long athlete that competes, although he needs to get tougher in the trenches.

Pass Game

In the pass game, Hollins is passive at the LOS and doesn't optimize his size and power. Hollins rushes from a two-point stance and has sufficient first step explosiveness. He shows flashes of good pass rush ability, but his pass rush arsenal is limited and he's overly reliant on his bull rush and swipe/swim moves. He demonstrates power in his bull rush to jostle tackles, but does so inconsistently. Hollins flashes the ability to use his hands effectively, but is generally not very active as a hand fighter. Overall, he has sufficient cover skills. As a man defender, he has the strength, size, and ability to cover tight ends at a sufficient level, but he struggles against fast, shifty running backs. In zone, he struggles to maintain proper eye discipline and often bites on play action or gets manipulated by the quarterback's eyes. When Hollins sticks in his zone, he does an adequate job of defending against crossing receivers.

Run Game

In the run game, he does a sufficient job of setting the edge. However, Hollins is not an aggressive defender, and he often struggles to disengage and affect the ball carrier, especially when he concedes his chest early in the rep. When he does have to make the tackle, he has good tackling skills and rarely has any missed or broken tackles. If the ballcarrier does break a run, he's athletic enough and uses adequate range and pursuit to make the tackle deep down the field.

Last Word

At the next level, Hollins projects as a depth rusher off the edge, especially on 3rd downs, who can also contribute some in pass coverage. He has the athleticism and tackling ability that suggests he could be effective on some special teams units.

– Elijah Cornejo

Strengths	**Weaknesses**
• Containment on the edge • Athleticism	• Aggressiveness • Lack of pass rush moves • Play strength at POA

Critical Factors

Pass Rush Ability	1st Step Explosion	Point Of Attack / Set Edge
5	5	5

Positional Factors

Pass Rush Repertoire	Bend	Hand Use	Play Strength
4	4	5	5
Range	**Flat Coverage**	**Motor**	**Football Intelligence**
5	5	5	5
Discipline	**Tackling**	**Ruggedness**	**Special Teams Value**
5	6	5	6

Basic

	Tackling			Pass Rush					
Year	Tackles	TFL	FF	Sacks	Hurries	Hits	Knockdowns	Pressures	Passes Batted
2016	46	7.0	0	2.0	7	8	3	11	1
2017	59	9.0	3	3.5	22	19	4	31	0
2018	69	14.5	5	7.5	33	18	6	44	1
	174	30.5	8	13.0	62	45	13	86	2

Advanced

	Tackling				Coverage			Impact	
Year	Broken Tackles	BT%	Tackle Share	Avg Depth of Tackle	Targets	Int	Y/Trgt	Pressure Share	EPA on Sacks/TFL
2016	5	9.8%	4.6%	4.1	4	0	3.5	8.2%	-11.4
2017	3	4.8%	6.1%	2.8	7	1	3.1	13.6%	-18.1
2018	5	6.8%	7.4%	3.3	7	1	4.0	19.0%	-32.6
	13	7.0%	6.0%	3.4	18	2	3.6	14.5%	-62.1

Deep Dive

	Total Snaps			Lined Up	Pass Rush			When Run At		
Year	Pass Rush	Pass Cov	Run	3-Point Stance%	Rush%	Pressure%	Sack%	Bounce%	Pos%	EPA Per Attempt
2018	309	194	397	0.4%	61.4%	12.3%	2.1%	45.5%	33.3%	-0.33

Glossary

3-Point Stance %
Percentage of plays where the defender was lined up with one hand on the ground

Avg Depth of Tackle
Average number of yards away from the line of scrimmage that the defender made his tackles

Bounce% (When Run At split)
Percentage of runs that didn't go through the designed gap

Broken Tackles
Tackle attempts where the defender failed to bring down the ballcarrier. Counts both broken tackles (physical) and missed tackles (elusive)

BT%
Percentage of tackle attempts where the defender failed to bring down the ballcarrier. Counts both broken tackles (physical) and missed tackles (elusive)

Hits
Plays with meaningful contact made by the defender on the quarterback before or as he releases the football

Hurries
Plays where the defender forces the quarterback to rush a throw before he may have otherwise thrown it

Knockdowns
Plays where the quarterback gets knocked down to the ground by the defender

Passes Batted
Plays where the defender knocked a pass down at the line of scrimmage

Pos% (When Run At split)
The percentage of plays that resulted in a positive EPA (a successful play for the offense)

Pressures
Plays in which there is a quarterback hurry, hit, knockdown or sack

Pressure%
Percentage of pass rushes that resulted in a pressure

Pressure Share
Percentage of a team's pressures made by the defender

Rush%
Percentage of quarterback dropbacks where the defender rushed the quarterback

Sack%
Percentage of pass rushes that resulted in a sack

Tackle Share
Percentage of a team's tackles made by the defender

Edge Rusher Leaderboards

Pressure Leaders			
Rank	Player	Team	Pressures
1	Josh Allen	Kentucky	67
2	Brian Burns	Florida State	65
3	Jaylon Ferguson	Louisiana Tech	63
4	Ben Banogu	TCU	63
5	Sutton Smith	Northern Illinois	60
6	Clelin Ferrell	Clemson	59
7	Maxx Crosby	Eastern Michigan	48
8	Montez Sweat	Mississippi State	46
9	Oshane Ximines	Old Dominion	46
10	Jordan Brailford	Oklahoma State	46

Expected Points Added on Sacks/TFL Leaders			
Rank	Player	Team	EPA
1	Jaylon Ferguson	Louisiana Tech	-48.1
2	Sutton Smith	Northern Illinois	-46.1
3	Josh Allen	Kentucky	-45.0
4	Clelin Ferrell	Clemson	-38.1
5	Jachai Polite	Florida	-36.8
6	Oshane Ximines	Old Dominion	-35.9
7	Brian Burns	Florida State	-33.0
8	Maxx Crosby	Eastern Michigan	-32.6
9	Justin Hollins	Oregon	-32.6
10	Jordan Brailford	Oklahoma State	-26.5

Average Depth of Tackle Leaders			
Rank	Player	Team	Avg Depth of Tackle
1	Cece Jefferson	Florida	0.1
2	Austin Bryant	Clemson	0.6
3	Oshane Ximines	Old Dominion	1.0
4	Jachai Polite	Florida	1.0
5	Jaylon Ferguson	Louisiana Tech	1.0
6	Clelin Ferrell	Clemson	1.2
7	Maxx Crosby	Eastern Michigan	1.2
8	Chase Winovich	Michigan	1.2
9	Joe Jackson	Miami FL	1.2
10	Sutton Smith	Northern Illinois	1.5

Pressure Rate Leaders			
Rank	Player	Team	Pressure%
1	Josh Allen	Kentucky	26.8%
2	Nick Bosa	Ohio State	19.7%
3	Jaylon Ferguson	Louisiana Tech	19.4%
4	Clelin Ferrell	Clemson	17.4%
5	Montez Sweat	Mississippi State	17.3%
6	Brian Burns	Florida State	16.2%
7	Maxx Crosby	Eastern Michigan	16.2%
8	Malik Reed	Nevada	15.8%
9	Porter Gustin	USC	15.2%
10	Joe Jackson	Miami FL	14.9%

Pressure Share Leaders			
Rank	Player	Team	Pressure Share
1	Maxx Crosby	Eastern Michigan	38.4%
2	Jaylon Ferguson	Louisiana Tech	34.4%
3	Oshane Ximines	Old Dominion	31.7%
4	Josh Allen	Kentucky	31.6%
5	Ben Banogu	TCU	30.6%
6	Brian Burns	Florida State	30.2%
7	Sutton Smith	Northern Illinois	27.6%
8	Anthony Nelson	Iowa	27.1%
9	Jordan Brailford	Oklahoma State	22.4%
10	Joe Jackson	Miami FL	20.7%

Sack Percentage Leaders			
Rank	Player	Team	Sack%
1	Josh Allen	Kentucky	7.2%
2	Nick Bosa	Ohio State	6.1%
3	Jaylon Ferguson	Louisiana Tech	5.4%
4	Porter Gustin	USC	4.3%
5	Montez Sweat	Mississippi State	4.0%
6	Jachai Polite	Florida	3.8%
7	Clelin Ferrell	Clemson	3.6%
8	Oshane Ximines	Old Dominion	3.4%
9	Anthony Nelson	Iowa	3.4%
10	Sutton Smith	Northern Illinois	3.3%

LINEBACKER

Linebacker Grading Scale

GRADE	DESCRIPTION
9.0 – 7.0	High-end 3 down starter. Pro Bowl level.
6.9 – 6.7	Strong starter who plays on all 3 downs.
6.6 – 6.5	Low-end starter. 3rd down coverage LB.
6.2	Versatile backup with positional flexibility.
6.1 – 6.0	Developmental. Top traits but needs time.
5.9	Top backup. 3rd LB. Quality special teamer.
5.8	Average backup. 4th LB. Quality special teamer.
5.7	Low-end backup LB with growable upside.

Linebacker Rankings

Rank	Name	Grade	Page
1	Devin White	7.0	432
2	Devin Bush	6.8	454
3	Mack Wilson	6.8	434
4	Germaine Pratt	6.8	456
5	Terrill Hanks	6.6	458
6	Kendall Joseph	6.5	436
7	Chase Hansen	6.5	460
8	Ryan Connelly	6.5	462
9	Cameron Smith	6.5	438
10	Dakota Allen	6.5	464
11	Vosean Joseph	6.5	466
12	David Long Jr.	6.2	468
13	Joey Alfieri	6.2	470
14	Tyrel Dodson	6.2	440
15	Joe Giles-Harris	6.2	442
16	Drue Tranquill	6.2	472
17	Andrew Van Ginkel	6.0	474
18	Ben Burr-Kirven	5.9	476
19	Te'von Coney	5.9	444
20	Khalil Hodge	5.9	446
21	Otaro Alaka	5.9	448
22	Tre Lamar	5.9	450
23	Terez Hall	5.9	478
24	Jahlani Tavai	5.9	452
25	Dre Greenlaw	5.9	480

Devin White

LSU Tigers
Final Grade: 7.0 LB Rank: 1 of 25

Height	Weight	Year	Jersey #	Hometown
6002	240	3JR	40	Springhill, LA

One-Liner
White is a sideline-to-sideline, 3-down Mike that possesses very good instincts and play speed, but he'll need to be more consistent as a tackler at the next level.

Overall
White played Mike linebacker for LSU's 3-3-5 defense. He is a good straight-line athlete, but a little stiff in his movements. He plays hard and shows a high level of competitiveness and toughness.

Run Game
Against the run, he makes the calls and is the QB of the defense. He possesses very good instincts and can read and react to flow very well. More times than not he notices false pulls and will anticipate the true direction of the run. He's a somewhat inconsistent block-shedder who primarily struggles against larger offensive linemen. He can stack and shed fairly consistently against smaller linemen and tight ends. His range is his defining trait. He's able to play with lateral speed from sideline to sideline. As a tackler, he lets a lot of tackle opportunities out of his grasp. He takes pretty good angles but needs to play with more control in order to not overrun ballcarriers. He tries to deliver a blow and tends to not wrap up by just throwing a shoulder into the ball carrier. He'll also miss some tackles in the backfield. He's able to slither through the trash to find the ball, but will occasionally fall to his knees and let him out of his grasp. His production shows in the raw statistics but he left tackles on the field. When he breaks down and wraps up, he's able to make tackles near or behind the LOS, out on the edge and even run some guys down from behind in the 2nd level. He's a stout player but doesn't always use his hands as much as he should at the POA.

Pass Game
Against the pass, he brings the communication ability that is required from a Mike. He knows the calls and makes sure guys are where they need to be. He's able to drop comfortably into zone coverage and possesses good awareness to receivers running in and out of his zone. LSU ran Tampa 2 a few times where he dropped into deep middle coverage and didn't look out of place. He's not incredibly disruptive in zones, but can make some plays on the ball and force QB's to look elsewhere. In man coverage, he's not incredibly fluid, so it's tough for him to stick with and change directions against quicker receivers. He brings some blitz ability, but overall isn't too productive when he does. He's able to find some gaps and get pressure on the QB occasionally, but he's better served in pass defense as a zone defender.

Last Word
White projects as a 3-down Mike in a 4-3 or 3-4 scheme. His traits suggest he'd also be a solid contributor on all special teams units.

– Nathan Cooper

Strengths	Weaknesses
• Sideline-to-sideline range • Instinctual read-react ability • Slithers through the trash	• Misses too many tackle opportunities • Not fluid enough in man coverage

Critical Factors

3-Down Value	Intelligence / Instincts	Play Speed
6	7	6

Positional Factors

QB Defense	Stoutness	Navigate Trash	Shed Ability
6	6	6	6
Ruggedness	**Range**	**Man Coverage**	**Zone Coverage**
6	8	5	6
Tackling / Productivity	**Blitz**	**Special Teams Value**	
5	5	7	

Basic

	Tackling			Pass Rush		Coverage					
Year	Tackles	TFL	FF	Sacks	Pressures	Trgt	Comp	Comp%	Int	Yds	Yds/Trgt
2016	26	2.5	1	1.0	2	2	2	100.0%	0	33	16.5
2017	131	13.5	0	4.5	36	18	8	44.4%	1	98	5.4
2018	123	11.0	3	3.0	30	23	16	69.6%	0	169	7.3
	280	27.0	4	8.5	68	43	26	60.5%	1	300	7.0

Advanced

	Tackling				Coverage					
Year	Broken Tackles	BT%	Tackle Share	Avg Depth of Tackle	Passes Defensed	Pos%	Deserved Catch%	YAC	Rating	EPA
2016	3	16.7%	1.9%	3.5	0	100.0%	100.0%	17	118.8	3.1
2017	17	11.5%	13.6%	4.6	0	27.8%	90.9%	41	61.8	-2.1
2018	11	8.2%	14.0%	5.3	2	52.2%	94.4%	86	54.4	0.2
	31	10.3%	9.9%	4.9	2	44.2%	93.5%	144	62.2	1.1

Deep Dive

	Total Snaps		Pass Rush			Man Coverage			Zone Coverage		
Year	Pass	Run	Blitz%	Pressure%	Sack%	Man%	Yds/ Snap	Pos%	Zone%	Yds/ Snap	Pos%
2018	450	344	22.7%	24.8%	3.0%	66.9%	4.6	32.0%	33.1%	5.8	31.3%

Mack Wilson

Alabama Crimson Tide
Final Grade: 6.8 LB Rank: 3 of 25

Height	Weight	Year	Jersey #	Hometown
6005	239	3JR	30	Montgomery, AL

One-Liner
Wilson is a rangy, explosive off-ball linebacker whose coverage instincts and leadership are high-quality NFL traits.

Overall
Wilson was primarily a Mike linebacker in Alabama's 3-4 and 3-3-5 defenses, who has moved all over their defensive front. He played in 42 career games and started since late in his sophomore season. He is a bit undersized but has an athletic cut with good lower-body thickness. Wilson is a great athlete at the linebacker position, with good speed and explosive striking ability at contact. He has good reaction skills and a sudden burst. He is a violent football player who doesn't shy from contact, but his motor behind plays is inconsistent. Wilson excels in coverage for the Crimson Tide. He is the leader of the defense and is a constant communicator pre- and post-snap.

Run Game
Against the run, Wilson is a good tackler in close spaces, but can overpursue and fail to break down outside the box. He has great range sideline to sideline to get to plays but needs to improve his ability to finish them. He follows his keys very well and is rarely misdirected. In the box, Wilson struggles with his play strength and shedding ability against power and length, and he doesn't anchor well. However, he compensates inside with his explosive striking ability at the point of attack against blockers and ball carriers. He can be knocked off-balance navigating through trash but his athleticism and instincts help. He has experience playing on multiple special teams units and could be a high-impact player on fourth downs.

Pass Game
He is a very good zone defender who gets great depth on his drops. Wilson is very comfortable in space and plays with great instincts to feel routes and jump into passing lanes. He is a good man defender on tight ends and backs with his short area quickness but has struggled when matched up with slot receivers. Wilson has impressive ball skills and athleticism at the catch point for a linebacker. He isn't a frequent blitzer, and doesn't have the strength to overpower blockers, but has flashed effectiveness with his speed on twists and delayed rushes, and is a strong quarterback spy.

Last Word
Wilson projects well as a very good three-down talent in the NFL as a middle or weakside linebacker. He is a quick, fluid athlete, which helps him navigate in tight areas, and has great leadership and communication qualities, but his play strength and ability to stack and shed need to be developed.

– Jordan Edwards

Strengths	**Weaknesses**
• Communication and instincts	• Overpursuit and finishing
• Range and zone coverage	• Block shedding
• Striking ability	• Play strength

Critical Factors

3-Down Value	Intelligence / Instincts	Play Speed
6	7	6

Positional Factors

QB Defense	Stoutness	Navigate Trash	Shed Ability
7	5	5	5
Ruggedness	**Range**	**Man Coverage**	**Zone Coverage**
6	7	6	7

Tackling / Productivity	Blitz	Special Teams Value
6	5	7

Basic

	Tackling			Pass Rush		Coverage					
Year	Tackles	TFL	FF	Sacks	Pressures	Trgt	Comp	Comp%	Int	Yds	Yds/Trgt
2016	8	0.0	0	0.0	1	0	0	-	0	0	-
2017	39	2.5	0	0.0	12	10	3	30.0%	4	34	3.4
2018	67	1.5	0	1.0	21	25	14	56.0%	2	132	5.3
	114	4.0	0	1.0	34	35	17	48.6%	6	166	4.7

Advanced

	Tackling				Coverage					
Year	Broken Tackles	BT%	Tackle Share	Avg Depth of Tackle	Passes Defensed	Pos%	Deserved Catch%	YAC	Rating	EPA
2016	0	0.0%	0.3%	2.0	0	-	-	0	0.0	0.0
2017	3	7.9%	3.8%	5.8	1	30.0%	66.7%	25	1.7	-8.2
2018	14	17.3%	6.9%	4.8	3	32.0%	76.2%	57	37.4	-8.4
	17	13.8%	3.7%	5.1	4	31.4%	74.1%	82	26.6	-16.6

Deep Dive

	Total Snaps		Pass Rush			Man Coverage			Zone Coverage		
Year	Pass	Run	Blitz%	Pressure%	Sack%	Man%	Yds/ Snap	Pos%	Zone%	Yds/ Snap	Pos%
2018	491	375	11.9%	27.6%	1.7%	61.5%	5.7	38.8%	38.5%	6.2	32.1%

Kendall Joseph

Clemson Tigers
Final Grade: 6.5 LB Rank: 6 of 25

Height	Weight	Year	Jersey #	Hometown
5111	235	6SR	34	Belton, SC

One-Liner
Joseph is a tough, instinctive linebacker who is a reliable tackler and can play all three downs due to his ability to play well in both man and zone coverage, but needs to get more stout at the POA.

Overall
Joseph played Mike linebacker in Clemson's 4-3 defense. He started 40 out of the 48 games that he appeared in throughout his career with the Tigers. He is a solid athlete with slightly below-average height and weight. He possesses good change of direction, short area burst, lateral agility, and reactive athleticism. He is a very competitive player who demonstrates very good ruggedness, playing with grit and engaging with violence while taking on blockers and working to the football. He shows very good ability to lead the defense: calling signals for the unit, making sure his teammates are aligned in the correct position, constantly communicating to his secondary before the snap and making the correct adjustments.

Run Game
In the run game, Joseph has good processing skills and instincts, quickly diagnosing the play and reading his keys to be one step ahead. He recognizes blocking schemes and has a good ability to flow to the play with good play speed, taking good angles and maintaining the correct leverage. He has sufficient stoutness but is able to stack offensive linemen and other blockers at the point of attack, while staying square and maintaining gap integrity. He demonstrates the ability to shed, using good hand usage and play strength to effectively get off blockers. He displays solid ability to navigate trash, showing he can scrape and flow, locate the ball carrier through traffic and make plays around the ball. He is a good tackler with the ability to strike an opponent with force, has good technique, consistently wraps, brings his hips, and can finish plays.

Pass Game
In the pass game, Joseph is good in man coverage with the ability to mirror tight ends and running backs, displaying good hip fluidity to turn and run to stay in phase. He is good in zone coverage and gets depth quickly, while showing very good recognition of route concepts. He also displays solid range, with the ability to play from sideline to sideline and play in space, demonstrating good play speed while in pursuit of the ballcarrier. He can get to tough spots in zone coverage and has the versatility to play outside of his immediate area, showing his value as a three-down linebacker. He is sufficient as a blitzer, showing some burst and timing off the edge and up the middle to generate pressure. He does not have the production as a pass rusher to be a true difference maker in this area at the next level and struggled to finish due to his lack of pass rush moves and bend.

Last Word
Joseph projects as a low-end starting Mike LB playing on all three downs by his second season at the next level. He can play special teams due to his combination of speed, strength, aggression, athleticism and overall tackling production.

– Nick Giella

Strengths	Weaknesses
• Trash navigation	• Blitzing ability
• Command of defense	• Block shedding
• Ruggedness	• Stoutness at point of attack

Critical Factors

3-Down Value	Intelligence / Instincts	Play Speed
6	6	6

Positional Factors

QB Defense	Stoutness	Navigate Trash	Shed Ability
7	5	6	6
Ruggedness	**Range**	**Man Coverage**	**Zone Coverage**
7	6	6	6

Tackling / Productivity	Blitz	Special Teams Value
6	5	6

Basic

	Tackling			Pass Rush		Coverage					
Year	Tackles	TFL	FF	Sacks	Pressures	Trgt	Comp	Comp%	Int	Yds	Yds/Trgt
2016	103	11.0	2	3.5	16	14	7	50.0%	1	64	4.6
2017	89	3.0	1	0.5	17	12	9	75.0%	1	45	3.8
2018	71	6.0	0	3.5	26	15	11	73.3%	0	122	8.1
	263	20.0	3	7.5	59	41	27	65.9%	2	231	5.6

Advanced

	Tackling				Coverage					
Year	Broken Tackles	BT%	Tackle Share	Avg Depth of Tackle	Passes Defensed	Pos%	Deserved Catch%	YAC	Rating	EPA
2016	17	14.2%	10.5%	4.1	1	42.9%	100.0%	30	86.6	2.0
2017	11	11.0%	8.0%	4.3	0	41.7%	100.0%	27	80.2	-4.5
2018	12	14.5%	6.7%	4.7	1	60.0%	84.6%	33	69.3	0.8
	40	13.2%	8.4%	4.3	2	48.8%	94.4%	90	78.4	-1.7

Deep Dive

	Total Snaps		Pass Rush			Man Coverage			Zone Coverage		
Year	Pass	Run	Blitz%	Pressure%	Sack%	Man%	Yds/ Snap	Pos%	Zone%	Yds/ Snap	Pos%
2018	424	305	24.4%	22.0%	3.5%	41.5%	5.9	45.0%	58.5%	4.6	32.6%

Cameron Smith

USC Trojans
Final Grade: 6.5 LB Rank: 9 of 25

Height	Weight	Year	Jersey #	Hometown
6020	230	4SR	35	Roseville, CA

One-Liner
Smith is an experienced leader with a good overall skillset combined with a high level of instinctual mental processing to make plays in the middle of a defense.

Overall
Smith was a Mike linebacker in USC's 3-3-5 defensive scheme. He was a 4-year player, starting in 45 of his 47 games played throughout his playing career. He has good size and is well cut, with big hands and solid arm length. Smith is a good athlete, with a combination of balance, short area quickness, and change of direction in the middle of the field. Smith is a very competitive player with good physical and mental toughness.

Run Game
He has sufficient range sideline to sideline, as well as decent stack and shed ability on linemen at the second level. He can improve in this area, but he can hold up playing between the tackles. He should be a strong special teams player early.

Pass Game
In the pass game, Smith is good in man coverage against tight ends and running backs, showing an ability to turn and run as well as mirror. He is an instinctual zone defender, showing good spatial awareness and a good understanding of route concepts. He drops quickly and communicates well in the pass game to pass off receivers through his area. Smith is a sufficient blitzer, as he doesn't win often against linemen but has shown the ability to beat running backs one on one.

Last Word
Smith can play on all three downs, but he doesn't do any one thing exceptionally well. He is a solid overall middle linebacker who projects well inside within a 3-4 or 4-3 scheme. He has a lot of experience at a major program and has proven leadership as a two-time captain.

– Brian Rogers

Strengths	Weaknesses
• Instincts	• Anchor stoutness
• Production and leadership	• Range
• Three-down value	• Blitz mismatch

Critical Factors

3-Down Value	Intelligence / Instincts	Play Speed
6	7	6

Positional Factors

QB Defense	Stoutness	Navigate Trash	Shed Ability
6	5	6	5
Ruggedness	**Range**	**Man Coverage**	**Zone Coverage**
6	5	6	6

Tackling / Productivity	Blitz	Special Teams Value
6	5	6

Basic

	Tackling			Pass Rush		Coverage					
Year	Tackles	TFL	FF	Sacks	Pressures	Trgt	Comp	Comp%	Int	Yds	Yds/Trgt
2016	81	5.5	1	1.0	11	17	13	76.5%	0	63	3.7
2017	113	8.5	0	0.5	12	27	17	63.0%	1	163	6.0
2018	80	4.5	0	1.0	10	18	14	77.8%	0	120	6.7
	274	18.5	1	2.5	33	62	44	71.0%	1	346	5.6

Advanced

	Tackling				Coverage					
Year	Broken Tackles	BT%	Tackle Share	Avg Depth of Tackle	Passes Defensed	Pos%	Deserved Catch%	YAC	Rating	EPA
2016	8	9.0%	8.7%	4.1	2	35.3%	87.5%	49	100.9	-3.3
2017	10	8.1%	11.6%	3.8	2	44.4%	95.2%	76	89.0	3.7
2018	4	4.8%	10.4%	4.8	2	55.6%	93.3%	88	131.5	10.6
	22	7.4%	10.3%	4.2	6	45.2%	92.3%	213	104.6	11.0

Deep Dive

	Total Snaps		Pass Rush			Man Coverage			Zone Coverage		
Year	Pass	Run	Blitz%	Pressure%	Sack%	Man%	Yds/ Snap	Pos%	Zone%	Yds/ Snap	Pos%
2018	357	274	20.6%	11.4%	1.4%	61.2%	5.2	40.9%	38.8%	6.8	50.6%

Tyrel Dodson

Texas A&M Aggies
Final Grade: 6.2 LB Rank: 14 of 25

Height	Weight	Year	Jersey #	Hometown
6012	242	3JR	25	Franklin, TN

One-Liner
Dodson is an athletic linebacker who has inside/outside flexion and read-and-react abilities that profile as a capable backup in multiple areas.

Overall
Dodson is a versatile linebacker having seen game action at both inside and outside linebacker for Texas A&M over his 3-year collegiate career. He served as a starter for two seasons, while playing a reserve and special teams role as a true freshman. He has a long-armed, athletic build. Dodson is a good athlete, moving fluidly and quickly for his size and showing the ability to make impactful plays with his length and quickness. He is a solid competitor but has shown an inconsistent motor on plays away from him.

Run Game
Versus the run, he has adequate stoutness at the point of attack and an inconsistent shed ability against larger, quicker, and more physical opponents. He relies on his strong read-and-react skills to position himself to make plays. He is an accomplished tackler and has solid production, but much of it comes from cleaning up piles, reinforcement, or getting just enough of the ballcarrier to knock them off balance.

Pass Game
Versus the pass, Dodson shows solid coverage ability in both man and zone responsibilities. He is better in man, as it gives him a specific responsibility and doesn't allow for him to get flat footed and establish tunnel vision on the quarterback. He has a tendency to get lost in zone when he keys to the backfield more than feeling his surroundings. Despite this, he shows good spatial awareness and ability to read and anticipate. He has the athleticism and speed to carry running backs and tight ends downfield in man coverage. As a blitzer, Dodson shows good explosion off the line but lacks a refined repertoire of tools to consistently beat linemen. He finds much of his success as a blitzer when other defenders get pressure, allowing for him to disengage from his blocker and chase the quarterback on a second effort. Dodson shows adequate communicative ability but isn't the primary leader on the defensive side of the ball. He isn't called upon enough to align the defense or make adjustment calls to be deemed better than sufficient.

Last Word
Based on his versatility and ability to defend the pass in both zone and man coverage, Dodson is capable of remaining on the field across all three downs in either an inside or outside linebacker role.

– Aaron Gray

Strengths	Weaknesses
• Versatility	• Taking angles
• Read and react	• Zone coverage
• Athleticism for size	• Communication

Critical Factors

3-Down Value	Intelligence / Instincts	Play Speed
6	6	6

Positional Factors

QB Defense	Stoutness	Navigate Trash	Shed Ability
5	5	5	5
Ruggedness	**Range**	**Man Coverage**	**Zone Coverage**
5	6	6	6

Tackling / Productivity	Blitz	Special Teams Value
5	6	5

Basic

	Tackling			Pass Rush		Coverage					
Year	Tackles	TFL	FF	Sacks	Pressures	Trgt	Comp	Comp%	Int	Yds	Yds/Trgt
2016	31	1.5	0	0.0	1	3	3	100.0%	0	40	13.3
2017	108	9.5	0	5.5	22	25	16	64.0%	3	192	7.7
2018	71	6.0	0	0.5	8	21	11	52.4%	1	150	7.1
	210	17.0	0	6.0	31	49	30	61.2%	4	382	7.8

Advanced

	Tackling				Coverage					
Year	Broken Tackles	BT%	Tackle Share	Avg Depth of Tackle	Passes Defensed	Pos%	Deserved Catch%	YAC	Rating	EPA
2016	2	6.3%	2.8%	5.0	0	66.7%	100.0%	20	118.8	2.0
2017	21	16.3%	10.6%	3.9	4	40.0%	77.3%	128	54.1	-5.2
2018	10	12.7%	9.7%	4.7	2	33.3%	83.3%	71	55.7	-8.7
	33	13.8%	7.4%	4.4	6	38.8%	81.4%	219	60.1	-12.0

Deep Dive

	Total Snaps		Pass Rush			Man Coverage			Zone Coverage		
Year	Pass	Run	Blitz%	Pressure%	Sack%	Man%	Yds/ Snap	Pos%	Zone%	Yds/ Snap	Pos%
2018	436	294	13.8%	8.5%	0.0%	48.7%	5.6	36.0%	51.3%	7.9	47.5%

Joe Giles-Harris

Duke Blue Devils
Final Grade: 6.2 LB Rank: 15 of 25

Height	Weight	Year	Jersey #	Hometown
6006	240	4JR	44	Nyack, NY

One-Liner
Giles-Harris has the instincts and coverage ability to play LB at the next level, but doesn't have the speed or range to be a starter.

Overall
Giles-Harris played all LB spots for Duke, mostly lining up as a Mike. He played and started in 34 straight games the last three seasons before suffering an MCL injury vs. Miami that cut his 2018 season short. He plays with a sufficient level of athleticism, but seems to rely more on his intelligence and instincts to get in correct position. Giles-Harris competes with toughness and consistently plays hard.

Run Game
Versus the run, Giles-Harris produces as a tackler. He's able to make tackles at and near the LOS. He's good at picking his way through the trash to fill his gap. He's inconsistent shedding blockers; he can stack and shed tight ends and backs, but has trouble taking on linemen. He's powerful and plays stout but has ineffective hand usage at the POA.

Pass Game
Versus the pass, he shows good communication skills to make sure everyone is lined up where they need to be and make any calls that should be made. He uses his reactive athleticism to stay with tight ends in man coverage. He doesn't have the speed to stay with many quick receivers. In zone, he has decent drop range, but is more effective coming downhill or toward the sideline to close on receivers. He plays with good instincts and processing skills to quickly diagnose screen plays. He shows some ability to blitz off the edge, but only seems to be effective when he's clean.

Last Word
By Giles-Harris' second season, he projects to be a backup Mike that can prove versatile along all LB positions. On 3rd downs, he can be used in coverage, mainly zone, where he can come up and make plays in front of him. His toughness should allow him to contribute on some special teams units.

– SIS Scouting Staff

Strengths	**Weaknesses**
• Instincts	• Play speed
• Zone coverage ability	• Range
• Navigating through trash	• Stoutness

Critical Factors

3-Down Value	Intelligence / Instincts	Play Speed
6	6	5

Positional Factors

QB Defense	Stoutness	Navigate Trash	Shed Ability
6	5	6	5
Ruggedness	**Range**	**Man Coverage**	**Zone Coverage**
6	5	5	6

Tackling / Productivity	Blitz	Special Teams Value
6	5	7

Basic

	Tackling			Pass Rush		Coverage					
Year	Tackles	TFL	FF	Sacks	Pressures	Trgt	Comp	Comp%	Int	Yds	Yds/Trgt
2016	111	9.5	0	4.0	14	10	6	60.0%	1	107	10.7
2017	120	13.0	1	3.5	27	16	13	81.3%	1	108	6.8
2018	80	6.0	0	2.0	14	17	13	76.5%	0	92	5.4
	311	28.5	1	9.5	55	43	32	74.4%	2	307	7.1

Advanced

	Tackling				Coverage					
Year	Broken Tackles	BT%	Tackle Share	Avg Depth of Tackle	Passes Defensed	Pos%	Deserved Catch%	YAC	Rating	EPA
2016	15	12.0%	13.5%	4.5	2	50.0%	75.0%	43	130.0	4.1
2017	11	8.4%	13.3%	3.0	1	56.3%	92.9%	103	94.8	6.4
2018	11	12.1%	7.9%	4.0	1	47.1%	88.2%	72	88.4	0.0
	37	10.7%	11.3%	3.8	4	51.2%	87.2%	218	101.6	10.5

Deep Dive

	Total Snaps		Pass Rush			Man Coverage			Zone Coverage		
Year	Pass	Run	Blitz%	Pressure%	Sack%	Man%	Yds/ Snap	Pos%	Zone%	Yds/ Snap	Pos%
2018	283	315	29.7%	14.1%	1.3%	60.7%	4.7	34.1%	39.3%	4.6	50.8%

Te'von Coney

Notre Dame Fighting Irish
Final Grade: 5.9 LB Rank: 19 of 25

Height	Weight	Year	Jersey #	Hometown
6007	244	4SR	4	Palm Beach Gardens, FL

One-Liner
Coney is a good overall run defender with long speed and instincts but needs to be more effective in coverage and become the leader of a defense at the next level.

Overall
Coney played Mike linebacker for the Irish. He started in 28 of his 49 career games. He is a good athlete, but not explosive or twitchy. He possesses solid long speed and has good size and length for the position. His frame is well-muscled, with potentially some room to grow if he needs to add more weight. He can be a little lanky in his movements. He's not a consistent tone-setter, yet his grit and toughness are good. His motor runs hot and cold.

Run Game
Against the run, he displays good range and can play from sideline to sideline. His overall instincts against the run are good, but he will have some lapses in play recognition. Generally, he does a sufficient job of working through trash to get to the ballcarrier. He's a very good form tackler with plenty of production. Coney's not a traditional stack-and-shed linebacker, but he does a sufficient job of using his length to keep himself clean from blockers. His stoutness is effective, but he needs to be more aggressive taking on blocks at the point of attack. He will occasionally take bad angles to the football. He appears to communicate with his teammates, but he doesn't seem to be the guy that knits the group together.

Pass Game
Against the pass, he is not given many man coverage responsibilities. He has enough athleticism to be at least sufficient in this area when on the right matchup. He doesn't show much anticipation in zone coverage but is adequate in this area. He made some flash plays in coverage but overall is inconsistent. Inconsistency in coverage limits his three-down ability. He doesn't try to reroute receivers very often. As a blitzer, he has some closing burst that could help him become more effective. He needs to improve his timing when rushing the passer.

Last Word
Coney projects as a top backup at Mike LB who has the experience and traits to be a good special teams player. Early on, he may be a two-down player, coming off the field on 3rd downs.

– Alex O'Brien

Strengths	Weaknesses
• Instincts	• Overall coverage ability
• Tackling ability	• Three-down ability
• Range	• Shedding at the POA

Critical Factors

3-Down Value	Intelligence / Instincts	Play Speed
5	6	6

Positional Factors

QB Defense	Stoutness	Navigate Trash	Shed Ability
5	6	5	5
Ruggedness	**Range**	**Man Coverage**	**Zone Coverage**
6	6	5	5

Tackling / Productivity	Blitz	Special Teams Value
7	5	6

Basic

	Tackling			Pass Rush		Coverage					
Year	Tackles	TFL	FF	Sacks	Pressures	Trgt	Comp	Comp%	Int	Yds	Yds/Trgt
2016	64	1.5	0	0.0	4	6	6	100.0%	0	49	8.2
2017	116	12.5	1	3.0	10	10	9	90.0%	0	44	4.4
2018	125	9.5	0	5.0	28	19	10	52.6%	1	62	3.3
	305	23.5	1	8.0	42	35	25	71.4%	1	155	4.4

Advanced

	Tackling				Coverage					
Year	Broken Tackles	BT%	Tackle Share	Avg Depth of Tackle	Passes Defensed	Pos%	Deserved Catch%	YAC	Rating	EPA
2016	2	3.2%	6.6%	4.8	0	50.0%	100.0%	33	100.7	0.8
2017	4	3.5%	11.2%	3.7	0	50.0%	100.0%	30	118.3	0.0
2018	4	3.1%	13.0%	4.4	3	26.3%	76.5%	43	20.0	-16.6
	10	3.3%	10.3%	4.2	3	37.1%	87.9%	106	65.8	-15.7

Deep Dive

	Total Snaps		Pass Rush			Man Coverage			Zone Coverage		
Year	Pass	Run	Blitz%	Pressure%	Sack%	Man%	Yds/ Snap	Pos%	Zone%	Yds/ Snap	Pos%
2018	512	381	18.4%	14.9%	1.1%	60.7%	5.7	36.3%	39.3%	4.8	35.6%

Khalil Hodge

Buffalo Bulls
Final Grade: 5.9 LB Rank: 20 of 25

Height	Weight	Year	Jersey #	Hometown
6011	255	4SR	4	Stockton, CA

One-Liner
Hodge is a productive inside backer that has the instincts and communication skills to make it at the next level, though his sufficient play speed and inability to consistently shed blocks will limit him early on.

Overall
Hodge was the primary Mike in Buffalo's 4-3 defense, occasionally kicking outside. He played 37 games in three years for the Bulls, making starts in 36 of them. He's a solid athlete but isn't a quick-twitch guy. He plays with toughness and competes from the Mike position.

Run Game
Against the run, he is a very productive tackler, but lacks consistency. He racked up over 400 tackles in three years at Buffalo but had a chance to get even more. There are times where he slips off some easy tackles and his lack of burst makes him just a step too slow in bringing down even more. When he meets ball carriers in the hole, he delivers a blow, but will fall to his knees many times to bring them down. He'll allow ball carriers to fall forward occasionally when he makes tackles but is able to make tackles near the line of scrimmage. He will use his hands to stack blockers but doesn't possess the size or enough strength to shed on a consistent basis or be stout at the POA. If going up against smaller blockers, he does a good job fighting through. He's able to navigate through the trash and find the ball and make plays. He plays rangy, but his lack of speed limits him making many plays at the sideline. He plays with good instincts and read-and-react ability, but his speed doesn't allow him to always get there. Although he plays fast, he lacks a burst and the 2nd gear to catch speedier ball carriers.

Pass Game
In the pass game, he shows that he's the QB of the defense. He makes all the calls and gets his teammates lined up where they need to be. In zone coverage, he shows the spatial awareness and instincts to track receivers in and out of his zones and jump on routes to make a play on the ball. He's able to drop into the 3rd level of the defense and be effective as a cover defender. In man coverage, he's stiff in the hips and doesn't possess the short-area quickness or change-of-direction skills to effectively and consistently stay with receivers. He can turn and run with them down the field, but has a tough time breaking in or out with them at the top of their routes. As a blitzer, he shows that he can come off the edge, but needs open run lanes to get pressure on the QB.

Last Word
Hodge projects as a 4-3 Mike at the next level. Early on, he would excel more as a 2-down player. His physicality and production should allow him to be a solid contributor on most special teams units.

– Nathan Cooper

Strengths	Weaknesses
• Instincts	• Play speed
• Communication skills	• Shed ability
• Navigating through trash	• Short-area quickness/change of direction skills

Critical Factors

3-Down Value	Intelligence / Instincts	Play Speed
5	6	5

Positional Factors

QB Defense	Stoutness	Navigate Trash	Shed Ability
6	5	6	5
Ruggedness	**Range**	**Man Coverage**	**Zone Coverage**
6	5	5	6

Tackling / Productivity	Blitz	Special Teams Value
6	5	6

Basic

	Tackling			Pass Rush		Coverage					
Year	Tackles	TFL	FF	Sacks	Pressures	Trgt	Comp	Comp%	Int	Yds	Yds/Trgt
2016	124	7.0	0	1.0	1	4	2	50.0%	0	38	9.5
2017	154	6.0	2	3.0	13	14	9	64.3%	2	114	8.1
2018	140	6.0	1	3.0	11	12	5	41.7%	1	53	4.4
	418	19.0	3	7.0	25	30	16	53.3%	3	205	6.8

Advanced

	Tackling				Coverage					
Year	Broken Tackles	BT%	Tackle Share	Avg Depth of Tackle	Passes Defensed	Pos%	Deserved Catch%	YAC	Rating	EPA
2016	16	11.6%	12.0%	4.4	0	50.0%	100.0%	24	122.9	2.8
2017	10	6.1%	15.1%	5.2	0	50.0%	83.3%	60	50.0	-1.2
2018	6	4.1%	13.3%	3.7	1	16.7%	88.9%	13	55.2	-10.6
	32	7.2%	13.5%	4.5	1	36.7%	87.0%	97	58.3	-9.0

Deep Dive

	Total Snaps		Pass Rush			Man Coverage			Zone Coverage		
Year	Pass	Run	Blitz%	Pressure%	Sack%	Man%	Yds/ Snap	Pos%	Zone%	Yds/ Snap	Pos%
2018	428	384	11.9%	12.2%	3.1%	37.7%	5.5	37.3%	62.3%	5.7	35.2%

Otaro Alaka

Texas A&M Aggies
Final Grade: 5.9 LB Rank: 21 of 25

Height	Weight	Year	Jersey #	Hometown
6030	240	5SR	42	Houston, TX

One-Liner
Alaka is a very tough linebacker who excels at stopping the run and has some solid coverage ability, but his inability to consistently shed blocks and play in man coverage will force him to be a backup.

Overall
Alaka lines up at the Mike linebacker position. He played in 53 total games. He's an above-average athlete whose strength is stopping the run. He plays the position with good instincts, speed, and very good toughness.

Run Game
Versus the run, he has good instincts to read the play and react to the ballcarrier. He's a solid but inconsistent tackler and does not break down in open space. He can be easily avoided by ballcarriers with very good elusiveness and instincts. He has the ability to navigate through trash and his ability to fight off blocks is sufficient. He's good at taking proper angles and pursuing the football, but sometimes gets sucked into traffic and taken out of the play. He's a stout defender and is strong with a willingness to meet blockers in the hole at the point of attack. He's not very good with his hands and relies on strength, power, and leverage to shed blocks. He also has good range and ability to hustle to the ball from sideline to sideline.

Pass Game
Versus the pass, he is an adequate QB of the defense who is capable of being a signal caller and adjusting the formations. He's a good blitzer and can generate pressure on the QB. He uses power and leverage against blockers and is better at blitzing the inside gaps than the outside. He's good in zone coverage and above average in man. He can cover ground and play in the hook zone but struggles to cover tight ends or running backs in one-on-one situations. He often has his eyes in the backfield looking to make a play against the run and will bite on play action. He's very tough and gritty, and blockers with bad technique have a difficult time with him. He rarely ends up on his back by getting run over or pancaked.

Last Word
Overall, Alaka is a very tough linebacker who excels at stopping the run, but he's not a playmaker at the position. He projects as a 3-down backup linebacker in the NFL with the ability to be productive on special teams. He can play in a 4-3 scheme or a 3-4 but is better in a 2-point stance than a 3-point.

– Brian Hammond

Strengths	**Weaknesses**
• Run defense	• QB defense
• Competitive toughness	• Man coverage
• Stoutness	• Shed ability

Critical Factors

3-Down Value	Intelligence / Instincts	Play Speed
5	6	6

Positional Factors

QB Defense	Stoutness	Navigate Trash	Shed Ability
5	6	6	5
Ruggedness	**Range**	**Man Coverage**	**Zone Coverage**
7	6	5	6

Tackling / Productivity	Blitz	Special Teams Value
6	6	6

Basic

	Tackling			Pass Rush		Coverage					
Year	Tackles	TFL	FF	Sacks	Pressures	Trgt	Comp	Comp%	Int	Yds	Yds/Trgt
2016	72	8.0	0	2.0	11	13	10	76.9%	0	108	8.3
2017	86	11.0	1	5.5	18	18	13	72.2%	1	101	5.6
2018	79	13.0	2	4.0	21	13	7	53.8%	0	90	6.9
	237	32.0	3	11.5	50	44	30	68.2%	1	299	6.8

Advanced

	Tackling				Coverage					
Year	Broken Tackles	BT%	Tackle Share	Avg Depth of Tackle	Passes Defensed	Pos%	Deserved Catch%	YAC	Rating	EPA
2016	4	5.3%	6.5%	4.9	1	69.2%	100.0%	53	126.4	6.3
2017	12	12.4%	8.3%	3.9	1	44.4%	92.9%	31	122.7	-4.0
2018	15	16.1%	10.2%	4.0	0	46.2%	100.0%	79	69.4	-1.8
	31	11.7%	8.1%	4.2	2	52.3%	97.0%	163	108.0	0.5

Deep Dive

	Total Snaps		Pass Rush			Man Coverage			Zone Coverage		
Year	Pass	Run	Blitz%	Pressure%	Sack%	Man%	Yds/Snap	Pos%	Zone%	Yds/Snap	Pos%
2018	352	254	26.0%	11.0%	2.7%	41.9%	7.8	45.5%	58.1%	8.7	49.2%

Tre Lamar

Clemson Tigers
Final Grade: 5.9 LB Rank: 22 of 25

Height	Weight	Year	Jersey #	Hometown
6022	255	3JR	57	Roswell, GA

One-Liner
Lamar is an inside linebacker with good strength and power to shed blockers in the run game and plug the gaps between the tackles, but his sideline-to-sideline range and coverage skills will suffer against top competition.

Overall
Lamar played off-ball LB for Clemson's 4-3 defense, occasionally coming off the edge. He played in 39 career games and started 22 of them. He started 14 of 15 games in 2018, missing one due to an ankle injury. He's a good athlete who has some length. He is a tough, physical player who lacks some range.

Run Game
Between the tackles in the run game, he is difficult to block and consistently plugs gaps and navigates through the trash. He sheds blockers and shows some strike ability with his hands, stacking and shedding offensive linemen. His ability to use his hands, strength and power is where he thrives. He has the range to make plays outside the tackle box, but not sideline to sideline. Outside the tackles is where he misses the most opportunities to make a tackle. His ability to anticipate and diagnose a play before it happens isn't fully developed. He tends to take bad angles which gets him caught up in traffic.

Pass Game
Against the pass, he lacks zone coverage skills and tends to get beat in man coverage, especially against dynamic players. He is uncomfortable when tasked to cover a shallow zone in Cover 3 or a deeper zone in Cover 2. He is a good communicator and tries to be involved on every play. He offers some blitz ability when there is a clear path to the target but doesn't have the necessary rush skills to consistently disrupt the quarterback.

Last Word
Lamar projects as a backup inside linebacker who can play on any down but will do his best in the run game early on. He may not be quick enough to make an impact on special teams but possesses the speed and toughness to be given an opportunity on some units.

– Dan Foehrenbach

Strengths	Weaknesses
• Navigating the trash	• Sideline-to-sideline range
• Downhill tackling	• Man coverage
• Play speed	• Angles in reaction to play

Critical Factors

3-Down Value	Intelligence / Instincts	Play Speed
5	5	6

Positional Factors

QB Defense	Stoutness	Navigate Trash	Shed Ability
6	5	6	5
Ruggedness	**Range**	**Man Coverage**	**Zone Coverage**
6	5	4	5

Tackling / Productivity	Blitz	Special Teams Value
5	5	5

Basic

	Tackling			Pass Rush		Coverage					
Year	Tackles	TFL	FF	Sacks	Pressures	Trgt	Comp	Comp%	Int	Yds	Yds/Trgt
2016	16	2.0	0	0.0	1	3	2	66.7%	0	21	7.0
2017	49	4.5	1	4.0	11	4	4	100.0%	0	25	6.3
2018	79	5.5	1	3.0	19	8	6	75.0%	1	44	5.5
	144	12.0	2	7.0	31	15	12	80.0%	1	90	6.0

Advanced

	Tackling				Coverage					
Year	Broken Tackles	BT%	Tackle Share	Avg Depth of Tackle	Passes Defensed	Pos%	Deserved Catch%	YAC	Rating	EPA
2016	1	10.0%	0.8%	1.2	0	33.3%	100.0%	18	86.8	0.7
2017	7	13.7%	4.0%	2.3	0	50.0%	100.0%	15	132.3	3.9
2018	7	8.2%	7.3%	3.0	0	37.5%	87.5%	26	47.9	-4.0
	15	10.3%	4.1%	2.7	0	40.0%	93.3%	59	86.1	0.6

Deep Dive

	Total Snaps		Pass Rush			Man Coverage			Zone Coverage		
Year	Pass	Run	Blitz%	Pressure%	Sack%	Man%	Yds/ Snap	Pos%	Zone%	Yds/ Snap	Pos%
2018	275	251	27.5%	22.7%	4.0%	45.9%	6.6	41.7%	54.1%	4.5	34.1%

Jahlani Tavai

Hawaii Rainbow Warriors
Final Grade: 5.9 LB Rank: 24 of 25

Height	Weight	Year	Jersey #	Hometown
6026	245	5SR	31	Inglewood, CA

One-Liner
Tavai is a strong LB that has the instincts to be productive at the next level, but his lack of playing speed and coverage skills may hold him back.

Overall
Tavai is a versatile athlete who plays OLB in a 3-4. He played in 47 games for Hawaii, starting in 45 of them. He has average size and length. He has average play speed and his motor is a concern. He is a very tough, instinctive tackler. He has the ability to set the edge and make tackles at all three levels of the field.

Run Game
Tavai is effective in the run game, as well. He plays very close to the line of scrimmage and uses his athletic ability and play strength to disrupt the backfield. He is good at shedding blockers and does not get taken out of a play very easily. He doesn't play very aggressively. His pursuit angles tend to get less sharp as the game goes on, as his first step also gets noticeably less explosive.

Pass Game
Against the pass, he is effective rushing the QB using his instincts and strength, although he isn't the most agile pass rusher. He doesn't show good bend while rushing around the edge but does show good hand use with moves such as bull rush and swim. He will show flashes of an elite pass rusher, but it is not consistent. Tavai never looks to be comfortable in coverage, although he does have the athleticism to improve. He has very discipline for zone, but his lack of speed and quickness hurts him in man coverage.

Last Word
Tavai is a tough, strong, LB who has the ability to rush the passer and stop the run. He engages with his hands and finishes plays, but it is not consistent. He has the skills to be a backup/ depth Mike LB at the next level.

– SIS Scouting Staff

Strengths	**Weaknesses**
• Shed ability	• Play speed
• Pass rush	• Coverage skils
• Versatility	• Poor judgement/angles

Critical Factors

3-Down Value	Intelligence / Instincts	Play Speed
5	6	4

Positional Factors

QB Defense	Stoutness	Navigate Trash	Shed Ability
6	5	6	6
Ruggedness	**Range**	**Man Coverage**	**Zone Coverage**
5	5	5	5

Tackling / Productivity	Blitz	Special Teams Value
6	6	6

Basic

	Tackling			Pass Rush		Coverage					
Year	Tackles	TFL	FF	Sacks	Pressures	Trgt	Comp	Comp%	Int	Yds	Yds/Trgt
2016	128	20.0	2	7.0	25	12	11	91.7%	1	127	10.6
2017	121	11.0	0	5.5	27	14	8	57.1%	1	118	8.4
2018	86	5.0	1	2.0	14	14	7	50.0%	0	43	3.1
	335	36.0	3	14.5	66	40	26	65.0%	2	288	7.2

Advanced

	Tackling				Coverage					
Year	Broken Tackles	BT%	Tackle Share	Avg Depth of Tackle	Passes Defensed	Pos%	Deserved Catch%	YAC	Rating	EPA
2016	17	11.7%	12.8%	4.9	2	83.3%	100.0%	42	115.6	9.5
2017	13	9.7%	14.3%	4.6	2	42.9%	69.2%	48	108.6	4.3
2018	4	4.5%	8.0%	5.0	3	21.4%	72.7%	24	56.5	-5.0
	34	9.2%	11.6%	4.8	7	47.5%	80.6%	114	100.8	8.8

Deep Dive

	Total Snaps		Pass Rush			Man Coverage			Zone Coverage		
Year	Pass	Run	Blitz%	Pressure%	Sack%	Man%	Yds/ Snap	Pos%	Zone%	Yds/ Snap	Pos%
2018	193	244	38.2%	14.7%	2.9%	43.4%	6.8	38.9%	56.6%	7.8	46.8%

Devin Bush

Michigan Wolverines
Final Grade: 6.8 LB Rank: 2 of 25

Height	Weight	Year	Jersey #	Hometown
5111	233	3JR	10	Pembroke Pines, FL

One-Liner
Bush is an undersized off-ball linebacker with excellent speed, range, and hitting ability who projects to develop into a strong three-down starter on the next level.

Overall
Bush lined up at inside linebacker for Michigan in their hybrid defense. He lacks ideal height and length for a linebacker on the NFL level, but he has a sturdy build and shows very good speed, athleticism, and versatility to fit as a modern Will, slotting in as a WLB for a 4-3 team or a WILB in a 3-4. He is a twitchy athlete and a big hitter, and he makes plays all over the football field. His lack of length may cause him problems in terms of matching up with TEs and disengaging from OLs, so his effectiveness will be maximized in a chase LB role to the open side of the formation.

Run Game
As a run defender, Bush shows good play strength and is a very good tackler. He has great range and will add speed to any defense. He does a good job of reading and reacting, showing discipline in tending to his responsibilities before chasing plays. He brings toughness to the defense, establishing himself as the hammer and not the nail when he comes to hit. That said, he is not ideally suited for a role where he has to take on OLs in the run game due to his lack of length.

Pass Game
In man coverage, Bush is a very good matchup against RBs. He shows the ability to travel with backs into the slot or even out wide. He can be grabby in coverage and will need to learn better technique, but he will always be limited in his ability to match up against bigger targets. In zone, he shows very good range but limited awareness. He has the speed to carry vertical routes up the seam and can become a very good zone defender if he develops this skill. Additionally, Bush is a dangerous blitzer who is shot out of a cannon, can bend the edge, and easily defeats backs in pass protection. He creates pressures and lays big hits on the QB. He shows excellent blitz timing and a knack for disguising his rushes pre-snap.

Last Word
Bush is a good communicator pre-snap who shows leadership on the field. While his lack of length might've been a fatal flaw in a different era or on a lesser athlete, Bush has a role in the modern NFL. His speed and versatility are coveted traits, and he brings the wood as a hitter. He projects as an eventual three-down starter who at a minimum should be an immediate difference-maker on sub downs and special teams. He compares to a smaller version of Jaylon Smith as a prospect.

– Matt Manocherian

Strengths

- Play speed
- Sideline-to-sideline range
- Blitz ability

Weaknesses

- Height/length
- Take-on blocks
- Covering TEs

Critical Factors

Pass Coverage	Play Speed	Intelligence / Instincts
6	8	6

Positional Factors

3-Down Value	Man Coverage	Zone Coverage	QB Defense
7	6	6	6
Range	**Blitz**	**Tackling / Productivity**	**Stoutness**
8	7	7	5
Navigate Trash	**Shed Ability**	**Ruggedness**	**Special Teams Value**
7	6	7	7

Basic

	Tackling			Pass Rush		Coverage					
Year	Tackles	TFL	FF	Sacks	Pressures	Trgt	Comp	Comp%	Int	Yds	Yds/Trgt
2016	12	0.0	0	0.0	0	2	1	50.0%	0	39	19.5
2017	102	10.0	0	5.5	26	19	8	42.1%	1	100	5.3
2018	66	5.5	0	4.5	17	21	9	42.9%	0	124	5.9
	180	15.5	0	10.0	43	42	18	42.9%	1	263	6.3

Advanced

	Tackling				Coverage					
Year	Broken Tackles	BT%	Tackle Share	Avg Depth of Tackle	Passes Defensed	Pos%	Deserved Catch%	YAC	Rating	EPA
2016	0	0.0%	0.9%	9.4	0	50.0%	50.0%	20	95.8	3.4
2017	5	4.7%	11.5%	4.5	3	21.1%	75.0%	70	37.2	-5.3
2018	6	8.3%	8.8%	4.0	4	33.3%	69.2%	80	42.6	-5.5
	11	5.9%	7.1%	4.5	7	28.6%	70.4%	170	44.0	-7.4

Deep Dive

	Total Snaps		Pass Rush			Man Coverage			Zone Coverage		
Year	Pass	Run	Blitz%	Pressure%	Sack%	Man%	Yds/ Snap	Pos%	Zone%	Yds/ Snap	Pos%
2018	333	286	19.7%	20.3%	5.5%	87.1%	4.1	32.8%	12.9%	5.8	35.7%

Germaine Pratt

NC State Wolfpack
Final Grade: 6.8 LB Rank: 4 of 25

Height	Weight	Year	Jersey #	Hometown
6025	240	6SR	3	High Point, NC

One-Liner
Pratt is a rangy backer with the size and movement skills, coupled with the play speed and instincts to be a high-end solid starter at the next level.

Overall
Pratt played off-ball linebacker for NC State's 4-3 defensive scheme. He was recruited as a safety and served as the backup free safety at NC State for his first two years. Pratt played in 46 games at NC State, starting in 11 of them. He underwent shoulder surgery in 2016 and sat out the season. During this time, he was moved from safety to linebacker. He is a very good athlete with very good speed and awareness. He has good coverage ability and the range to play sideline to sideline. Pratt plays with a very high motor and is almost always around the ball at the end of plays, even if he isn't the one making the play.

Run Game
Versus the run, he reads the play well, adjusts the defense, and often correctly points out which direction the play will go. He sheds blocks well, keeping blockers at arm's length and maintaining his vision on the ball, and nearly always shedding in the correct direction. He stays disciplined on counters and play fakes, adjusting and changing directions quickly to make the play, although he doesn't always break down quickly enough to change directions with explosion. When a runner gets past the second level, Pratt takes very good angles and uses his speed to chase him down.

Pass Game
Versus the pass, Pratt is solid in both coverages. He never looks lost in coverage, but can be beat when covering quick, twitchy slot receivers, as he is a bit stiff in the hips and struggles to change directions. He does a good job of reading the QB's eyes and then putting himself in position to make the play. When rushing the passer, Pratt can efficiently navigate through the middle of the offensive line or use his speed and acceleration off the edge.

Last Word
Germaine Pratt projects to be Will linebacker in the NFL, given his athleticism and coverage skills. He is a 3-down linebacker, staying on the field to cover or blitz on 3rd down. Pratt can and has effectively played safety, but is best used closer to the line of scrimmage, where he can make plays. Pratt's speed, tackling ability, and range will make him, at the least, a key contributor on special teams immediately.

– Gennady Gusak

Strengths	Weaknesses
• Play speed	• Stoutness
• Instincts	• Shed ability
• Production	• Change of direction

Critical Factors

Pass Coverage	Play Speed	Intelligence / Instincts
6	7	7

Positional Factors

3-Down Value	Man Coverage	Zone Coverage	QB Defense
6	5	6	7
Range	**Blitz**	**Tackling / Productivity**	**Stoutness**
7	6	7	5
Navigate Trash	**Shed Ability**	**Ruggedness**	**Special Teams Value**
6	5	6	7

Basic

	Tackling			Pass Rush		Coverage					
Year	Tackles	TFL	FF	Sacks	Pressures	Trgt	Comp	Comp%	Int	Yds	Yds/Trgt
2017	68	5.0	0	0.0	11	19	10	52.6%	2	132	6.9
2018	98	8.0	2	6.0	27	22	19	86.4%	0	150	6.8
	166	13.0	2	6.0	38	41	29	70.7%	2	282	6.9

Advanced

	Tackling				Coverage					
Year	Broken Tackles	BT%	Tackle Share	Avg Depth of Tackle	Passes Defensed	Pos%	Deserved Catch%	YAC	Rating	EPA
2017	8	10.8%	7.4%	5.9	3	42.1%	66.7%	99	70.5	-3.1
2018	6	5.8%	12.1%	5.2	1	59.1%	90.9%	79	95.1	4.4
	14	7.9%	6.4%	5.5	4	51.2%	81.1%	178	87.7	1.3

Deep Dive

	Total Snaps		Pass Rush			Man Coverage			Zone Coverage		
Year	Pass	Run	Blitz%	Pressure%	Sack%	Man%	Yds/ Snap	Pos%	Zone%	Yds/ Snap	Pos%
2018	415	239	19.4%	26.0%	6.5%	58.8%	6.7	40.0%	41.2%	7.2	52.7%

Terrill Hanks

New Mexico State Aggies
Final Grade: 6.6 LB Rank: 5 of 25

Height	Weight	Year	Jersey #	Hometown
6020	234	4SR	2	Miami, FL

One-Liner
Hanks fits the mold as a modern coverage linebacker who, despite his take-on run defense in the box, has the necessary sideline-to-sideline speed and athleticism to make an impact on third downs and beyond.

Overall
Hanks was a first-year starter as a 3-4 weakside linebacker in New Mexico State's defense. Hanks converted from safety to linebacker prior to his sophomore season. He played in 46 career games. He has solid height and length but is extremely well built physically and very in shape.

Run Game
Against the run, Hanks' range is a strength, but his speed can sometimes get him in trouble with over-pursuing sideline to sideline and not breaking down. His instincts are decent, but he needs to work on diagnosing runs and beating plays to the spot. He struggles to take on and sift through traffic inside the box on screens and lateral runs with linemen to the second level, and he bites on too many fakes. Hanks doesn't shed blocks from bigger linemen well and is much better suited navigating a clean box. He arrives at the ball with physicality and is capable of big hits but needs to consistently wrap up with more sound technique.

Pass Game
Versus the pass, Hanks shows sound comfortability covering running backs and tight ends. He shows good hip flexibility, puts his foot in the ground and goes as soon as the ball leaves the quarterback's hands. He has very good speed to stay with slot receivers and shows the versatility inside and outside the box that weakside linebackers need to succeed in the NFL. Hanks possesses natural fluid movements when in man and in zone coverage, but his spatial awareness is a better asset than his change-of-direction ability in man. He can still transition like a safety and closes well to the flats. Hanks can rush the passer as a blitzer and wins with quickness and initial burst, but he is more comfortable at the second and third levels of the defense.

Last Word
Hanks best projects as a 4-3 weakside linebacker, where he can utilize his coverage skills and range as well as limit his need to navigate through trash and shed blocks from interior linemen. Hanks would be a natural fit on special teams with his skill set in space.

– Drew Schweitzer

Strengths	Weaknesses
• Play speed	• Overpursuit
• Comfort in coverage	• Navigating within box
• Range	• Run diagnosis

Critical Factors

Pass Coverage	Play Speed	Intelligence / Instincts
6	7	5

Positional Factors

3-Down Value	Man Coverage	Zone Coverage	QB Defense
5	5	6	5
Range	**Blitz**	**Tackling / Productivity**	**Stoutness**
7	5	5	5
Navigate Trash	**Shed Ability**	**Ruggedness**	**Special Teams Value**
4	4	5	6

Basic

	Tackling			Pass Rush		Coverage					
Year	Tackles	TFL	FF	Sacks	Pressures	Trgt	Comp	Comp%	Int	Yds	Yds/Trgt
2016	97	9.0	2	2.0	12	26	13	50.0%	2	110	4.2
2017	105	12.5	2	7.0	25	35	18	51.4%	2	201	5.7
2018	92	6.5	1	1.0	13	15	9	60.0%	1	90	6.0
	294	28.0	5	10.0	50	76	40	52.6%	5	401	5.3

Advanced

	Tackling				Coverage					
Year	Broken Tackles	BT%	Tackle Share	Avg Depth of Tackle	Passes Defensed	Pos%	Deserved Catch%	YAC	Rating	EPA
2016	15	14.0%	8.7%	4.3	5	34.6%	75.0%	80	42.1	-15.2
2017	15	12.6%	10.4%	4.6	3	40.0%	80.8%	86	54.6	-5.9
2018	13	12.4%	8.4%	4.5	0	33.3%	85.7%	42	99.3	3.0
	43	13.0%	9.2%	4.5	8	36.8%	80.0%	208	59.2	-18.1

Deep Dive

	Total Snaps		Pass Rush			Man Coverage			Zone Coverage		
Year	Pass	Run	Blitz%	Pressure%	Sack%	Man%	Yds/ Snap	Pos%	Zone%	Yds/ Snap	Pos%
2018	266	424	19.7%	20.4%	2.0%	37.3%	3.9	35.7%	62.7%	8.0	50.0%

Chase Hansen

Utah Utes

Final Grade: 6.5 LB Rank: 7 of 25

Height	Weight	Year	Jersey #	Hometown
6021	230	5SR	22	Highland, UT

One-Liner

Hansen can become a starter at the next level with his play speed, intelligence and range and will contribute on special teams, but his ability to blitz and shed blockers needs improvement.

Overall

Hansen is a 4-3 Will linebacker with good size/ build and very good playing speed and athleticism for the position. He played in 43 games in his career with 35 starts. Hansen plays sideline to sideline and possesses a good motor and competitive demeanor. He possesses very good football intelligence, as he knows both his and his teammates' responsibilities and also has the ability to switch positions.

Run Game

Versus the run, he has very good technique as a tackler and is very good at cutting off run lanes, but gets in trouble if he is slow to react and waits in the hole. He struggles to navigate through trash and shed blocks. He shows good acceleration and pursuit after diagnosing the play and good eyes to process quickly against zone-read and play action.

Pass Game

In the pass game, he doesn't possess short area quickness, which can cause him trouble in man coverage. He has good zone coverage ability as he is able to respond to crossing routes in his zone and react. He has very good range allowing him to cover sideline to sideline, which he showed playing safety before making the move to linebacker. He has good three-level ability and doesn't need to come off the field in any situation, but his stoutness is just sufficient and he needs to play with a lower pad level to gain leverage and deliver at the point of attack against blockers. His blitz ability is above average as he has speed to come off the edge, but he needs to develop his blitz technique as he has done little of it.

Last Word

Hansen projects as a low-end two-down starter as a weakside linebacker by his second year.

– Cole Ratliff

Strengths	Weaknesses
• Play speed	• Blitzing ability
• Instincts	• Shedding blocks
• Range	• Trash navigation

Critical Factors

Pass Coverage	Play Speed	Intelligence / Instincts
6	7	7

Positional Factors

3-Down Value	Man Coverage	Zone Coverage	QB Defense
6	6	6	6
Range	**Blitz**	**Tackling / Productivity**	**Stoutness**
7	5	7	5
Navigate Trash	**Shed Ability**	**Ruggedness**	**Special Teams Value**
5	5	6	7

Basic

	Tackling			Pass Rush		Coverage					
Year	Tackles	TFL	FF	Sacks	Pressures	Trgt	Comp	Comp%	Int	Yds	Yds/Trgt
2016	88	5.5	3	1.0	13	32	11	34.4%	3	140	4.4
2017	50	2.5	0	1.0	6	19	11	57.9%	1	75	3.9
2018	113	22.0	0	4.0	22	18	10	55.6%	2	107	5.9
	251	30.0	3	6.0	41	69	32	46.4%	6	322	4.7

Advanced

	Tackling				Coverage					
Year	Broken Tackles	BT%	Tackle Share	Avg Depth of Tackle	Passes Defensed	Pos%	Deserved Catch%	YAC	Rating	EPA
2016	16	15.4%	11.1%	7.6	4	28.1%	61.9%	48	9.4	-19.7
2017	7	12.3%	6.2%	6.5	1	36.8%	93.8%	39	84.3	0.7
2018	13	10.3%	13.2%	3.3	3	50.0%	80.0%	53	50.0	-4.4
	36	12.5%	10.2%	5.5	8	36.2%	76.9%	140	34.8	-23.4

Deep Dive

	Total Snaps		Pass Rush			Man Coverage			Zone Coverage		
Year	Pass	Run	Blitz%	Pressure%	Sack%	Man%	Yds/ Snap	Pos%	Zone%	Yds/ Snap	Pos%
2018	442	319	24.2%	21.4%	3.9%	47.6%	5.7	40.0%	52.4%	6.7	49.0%

Ryan Connelly

Wisconsin Badgers
Final Grade: 6.5 LB Rank: 8 of 25

Height	Weight	Year	Jersey #	Hometown
6021	237	4SR	43	Eden Prairie, MN

One-Liner
Connelly is an instinctual, athletic LB with long arms and a natural ability to evade blockers, but he needs to get more stout in the run game and improve his tackling at the next level.

Overall
Connelly played primarily as an ILB in Wisconsin's 3-4 defense. He lined up occasionally as an edge rusher. He started 26 games and played in 52 in total. He has ideal size and long arms. He has good athleticism and is explosive when attacking downhill. He has a thick lower body and is a little stiff. His motor runs hot all the time and he pursues the football all over the field. He gets his hands on blockers and always hits the hole at full speed.

Run Game
Against the run, Connelly relies on his instincts and ability to beat blockers. He is quick to shoot the gap which can lead to him taking himself out of the play. He has the instincts to read plays quickly, although he will guess wrong on occasion. Once he gets to the play, he has trouble consistently bringing down the ballcarrier. He often overruns the ball and slips off too many tackles.

Pass Game
Against the pass, Connelly is effective in coverage and as a blitzer. He has the size and speed to match up with TEs and RBs. He also has good instincts when dropping in a zone and will jump on routes that settle in front of him. He's a little stiff in his change of direction and has some trouble in man coverage against speedier receivers. When blitzing, he has very good timing, subtle evasive moves, and strong, natural hands to win against blockers. He also shows some ability to rush off the edge, using counter moves such as a swim against bigger OTs.

Last Word
Connelly is a high-effort player and will be able to play on all four special teams units. He projects as low-end starting Will LB in either a 4-3 or 3-4 base scheme. He should play his best on 3rd downs when he can sit in coverage and use his speed and range

– SIS Scouting Staff

Strengths	Weaknesses
• Instincts	• Inconsistent tackling
• Block shedding	• Stoutness
• Blitz ability	• Stiff in his movements

Critical Factors

Pass Coverage	Play Speed	Intelligence / Instincts
6	6	6

Positional Factors

3-Down Value	Man Coverage	Zone Coverage	QB Defense
6	5	6	6
Range	**Blitz**	**Tackling / Productivity**	**Stoutness**
6	6	4	5
Navigate Trash	**Shed Ability**	**Ruggedness**	**Special Teams Value**
6	6	7	7

Basic

	Tackling			Pass Rush		Coverage					
Year	Tackles	TFL	FF	Sacks	Pressures	Trgt	Comp	Comp%	Int	Yds	Yds/Trgt
2016	57	7.0	0	0.0	4	6	4	66.7%	1	33	5.5
2017	85	11.0	1	3.0	16	31	16	51.6%	1	105	3.4
2018	92	10.0	1	3.0	20	14	10	71.4%	0	54	3.9
	234	28.0	2	6.0	40	51	30	58.8%	2	192	3.8

Advanced

	Tackling				Coverage					
Year	Broken Tackles	BT%	Tackle Share	Avg Depth of Tackle	Passes Defensed	Pos%	Deserved Catch%	YAC	Rating	EPA
2016	8	13.1%	6.8%	4.8	1	33.3%	80.0%	24	80.6	-0.7
2017	7	7.7%	11.0%	3.2	1	35.5%	95.5%	35	30.4	-17.9
2018	13	12.6%	11.4%	3.8	0	14.3%	100.0%	19	77.7	-5.3
	28	11.0%	9.7%	3.8	2	29.4%	94.7%	78	40.6	-24.0

Deep Dive

	Total Snaps		Pass Rush			Man Coverage			Zone Coverage		
Year	Pass	Run	Blitz%	Pressure%	Sack%	Man%	Yds/Snap	Pos%	Zone%	Yds/Snap	Pos%
2018	340	331	22.5%	21.6%	4.1%	42.9%	6.1	35.6%	57.1%	5.1	37.9%

Dakota Allen

Texas Tech Red Raiders
Final Grade: 6.5 LB Rank: 10 of 25

Height	Weight	Year	Jersey #	Hometown
6005	235	5SR	40	Humble, TX

One-Liner
Allen has had great production in his career due to his instincts, range and toughness, and he should find a role at the next level despite his size and hand use.

Overall
Allen played mostly Will linebacker and some Mike in Texas Tech's 3-3-5 defensive scheme. He played in 36 games in his Texas Tech career, starting in 24. He left the program for East Mississippi Community College in 2016, started 12 games there, and returned a year later. He is slightly undersized for the position, but very athletic and versatile with sideline-to-sideline range. He gives good effort on all three downs and is relentless in pursuit.

Run Game
In the run game, he makes a lot of plays in the box and near the line of scrimmage because of his toughness and low pad level. His range and motor are great assets outside the tackles and result in great production numbers. He has flashed pop to blow up blocks, but his size limits him often. He needs to improve his ability to shed blocks with his hands and navigate through the box cleaner.

Pass Game
In the passing game, Allen could work better to track and pass off crossing defenders in zone. He reads the quarterback's eyes very well and can run and chase underneath. His short area quickness is sufficient in man, but he can be shaken by third-down backs and outsized by mismatch tight ends. He does a good job of anticipating routes, however, and can be a solid man defender. He is a good blitzer who plays fast and can disrupt with his motor but doesn't offer much of a move set or hand use to beat linemen with technique. Allen does a good job of working hard to always find himself around the ball, and he finishes plays well. His production dropped at the end of the season due to playing with a broken hand, but his effort did not.

Last Word
Allen projects as a low-end starting Will linebacker, based on his traits in space and toughness. His motor and leadership will give him plenty of opportunities to carve out a role for himself within a defense that should allow him to range with a clean box and make tackles. Given his speed and tackling ability, he can be a solid contributor on special teams.

– Cole Ratliff

Strengths	Weaknesses
• Read-and-react ability	• Stoutness
• Toughness	• Hand use
• Range	• Block shedding

Critical Factors

Pass Coverage	Play Speed	Intelligence / Instincts
5	6	7

Positional Factors

3-Down Value	Man Coverage	Zone Coverage	QB Defense
6	6	5	6
Range	**Blitz**	**Tackling / Productivity**	**Stoutness**
6	6	7	5
Navigate Trash	**Shed Ability**	**Ruggedness**	**Special Teams Value**
5	5	7	6

Basic

	Tackling			Pass Rush		Coverage					
Year	Tackles	TFL	FF	Sacks	Pressures	Trgt	Comp	Comp%	Int	Yds	Yds/Trgt
2017	101	5.0	1	2.0	20	15	9	60.0%	2	61	4.1
2018	77	6.5	0	0.5	12	17	14	82.4%	0	157	9.2
	178	11.5	1	2.5	32	32	23	71.9%	2	218	6.8

Advanced

	Tackling				Coverage					
Year	Broken Tackles	BT%	Tackle Share	Avg Depth of Tackle	Passes Defensed	Pos%	Deserved Catch%	YAC	Rating	EPA
2017	9	8.3%	10.2%	4.9	2	26.7%	69.2%	18	29.4	-14.6
2018	6	7.2%	8.3%	3.7	1	64.7%	93.3%	88	105.1	7.8
	15	7.9%	9.3%	4.4	3	46.9%	82.1%	106	64.3	-6.9

Deep Dive

	Total Snaps		Pass Rush			Man Coverage			Zone Coverage		
Year	Pass	Run	Blitz%	Pressure%	Sack%	Man%	Yds/ Snap	Pos%	Zone%	Yds/ Snap	Pos%
2018	350	235	9.6%	31.3%	1.6%	49.4%	7.0	43.8%	50.6%	6.7	44.3%

Vosean Joseph

Florida Gators

Final Grade: 6.5 LB Rank: 11 of 25

Height	Weight	Year	Jersey #	Hometown
6002	226	3JR	11	Miami, FL

One-Liner

Joseph has the speed, athleticism, range and instincts to be a solid low-end starter at the next level, but his size and inability to play much between the tackles will limit him.

Overall

Joseph primarily played weakside linebacker in Florida's hybrid 3-3-5 defense. He played in 37 games with 22 starts during his three years. He is a very good athlete who plays extremely fast. He plays decently tough but competes on each play.

Run Game

In the run game, he possesses great speed and range, allowing him to make plays from sideline to sideline as well as in the backfield. His burst from the linebacker position allows him to make a play anywhere on the field once he diagnoses the play, as his instincts and ability to read and react are solid. However, he sometimes lacks discipline and doesn't break down at the tackle point which causes some missed tackles. He has poor stoutness and just average shedding ability, as he relies on his speed and quickness to get around offensive lineman. If OL contact him, most times he'll get swallowed up. His lack of size also affects his ability to tackle larger running backs, as seen in the Georgia game, when he fell off a few tackles in the backfield. If a lineman gets his hands on him, he is unable to stack and shed most times.

Pass Game

In the pass game, his speed and physicality allow him to run with slot receivers and TEs in man coverage. However, he doesn't have the COD skills to stay with quicker receivers. Although he tends to get lost trying to drop to proper depths to cover crossing routes, he's instinctual and flies toward the LOS to players in his zone. He lacks some discipline and often gets stuck in no man's land near the line of scrimmage, not dropping into the hook/curl zone after play-action fakes. He is a good blitzer off the edge and delayed blitzer up the middle thanks to his great speed and excellent acceleration but needs to come almost completely clean to be effective. He doesn't seem to communicate much or call out defensive schemes often out on the field.

Last Word

Joseph projects best as a Will LB in a 4-3 defensive scheme. He will need to get bigger to be consistently productive in the run game, but his speed and athleticism will allow for him to make plays on the edge and in the passing game. Those traits should also translate over to most special teams units.

– Ian Berg

Strengths	**Weaknesses**
• Play speed	• Misses some tackles
• Motor	• Stoutness in the box
• Range	• Lost in coverage at times

Critical Factors

Pass Coverage	Play Speed	Intelligence / Instincts
5	7	6

Positional Factors

3-Down Value	Man Coverage	Zone Coverage	QB Defense
5	5	5	4
Range	**Blitz**	**Tackling / Productivity**	**Stoutness**
7	6	6	3
Navigate Trash	**Shed Ability**	**Ruggedness**	**Special Teams Value**
5	4	5	7

Basic

	Tackling			Pass Rush		Coverage					
Year	Tackles	TFL	FF	Sacks	Pressures	Trgt	Comp	Comp%	Int	Yds	Yds/Trgt
2016	14	0.0	0	0.0	2	3	1	33.3%	0	18	6.0
2017	53	4.0	1	0.0	3	22	16	72.7%	1	169	7.7
2018	97	9.0	0	4.0	11	21	14	66.7%	0	121	5.8
	164	13.0	1	4.0	16	46	31	67.4%	1	308	6.7

Advanced

	Tackling				Coverage					
Year	Broken Tackles	BT%	Tackle Share	Avg Depth of Tackle	Passes Defensed	Pos%	Deserved Catch%	YAC	Rating	EPA
2016	9	42.9%	1.5%	4.3	1	33.3%	66.7%	4	54.9	0.0
2017	16	23.2%	7.2%	4.0	1	50.0%	84.2%	161	75.8	3.5
2018	16	14.4%	10.2%	4.0	5	42.9%	83.3%	60	81.6	0.3
	41	20.4%	6.3%	4.0	7	45.7%	82.5%	225	77.1	3.8

Deep Dive

	Total Snaps		Pass Rush			Man Coverage			Zone Coverage		
Year	Pass	Run	Blitz%	Pressure%	Sack%	Man%	Yds/ Snap	Pos%	Zone%	Yds/ Snap	Pos%
2018	336	306	13.7%	21.7%	6.5%	53.6%	5.2	36.7%	46.4%	5.7	31.7%

David Long Jr.

West Virginia Mountaineers
Final Grade: 6.2 LB Rank: 12 of 25

Height	Weight	Year	Jersey #	Hometown
5112	230	4JR	11	Cincinnati, OH

One-Liner
Long has range, blitzing versatility, and the ability to turn and run downfield, but without better stoutness inside, his usage is limited.

Overall
Long played primarily as a Will linebacker at West Virginia behind a three-man line. He also lined up as an on-ball edge rusher at times. He had 32 starts in 34 total games played. He has an athletic build with average arm length. He is an explosive athlete with aggression and vision to see a play and attack.

Run Game
Against the run, Long can be very disruptive in the backfield. When he diagnoses the play correctly, he can easily shoot gaps before backs and linemen can react. He also has good hand use and agility to maneuver blocks and keep linemen off him. On the second level, Long can get engulfed by linemen who are able to reach him before he makes his move. He also shows difficulties reading backfield designs and can take himself out of plays.

Pass Game
In coverage, Long is better in man than zone. He has the ability to turn and run with running backs and tight ends and mirror out of the backfield. In zone, he too often looks lost and can seem uncertain of his responsibilities. He can run and chase with range, however, and is comfortable in space. Long is a great blitzer, timing his blitzes well. He creates mismatches against linemen with his superior and quickness and against running backs with his strength. He flashes good hands when rushing from the edge and a good side step against heavy-footed tackles.

Last Word
Long projects to be a quality backup Will linebacker with edge-rusher flexibility at the next level, based on his solid three-level ability and play speed. He will need to improve his lower body strength and ability to play within the box in order to start consistently.

– Ben Hrkach

Strengths	Weaknesses
• Ability to turn and run	• Size and length
• Blitzing mismatch	• Stoutness
• Tackling production	• Zone coverage awareness

Critical Factors

Pass Coverage	Play Speed	Intelligence / Instincts
5	7	6

Positional Factors

3-Down Value	Man Coverage	Zone Coverage	QB Defense
6	6	5	6
Range	**Blitz**	**Tackling / Productivity**	**Stoutness**
6	7	6	5
Navigate Trash	**Shed Ability**	**Ruggedness**	**Special Teams Value**
6	6	7	7

Basic

	Tackling			Pass Rush		Coverage					
Year	Tackles	TFL	FF	Sacks	Pressures	Trgt	Comp	Comp%	Int	Yds	Yds/Trgt
2016	61	5.0	0	2.0	9	2	2	100.0%	0	5	2.5
2017	77	15.5	0	4.0	22	11	7	63.6%	0	58	5.3
2018	110	19.5	2	6.5	22	11	10	90.9%	0	110	10.0
	248	40.0	2	12.5	53	24	19	79.2%	0	173	7.2

Advanced

	Tackling				Coverage					
Year	Broken Tackles	BT%	Tackle Share	Avg Depth of Tackle	Passes Defensed	Pos%	Deserved Catch%	YAC	Rating	EPA
2016	10	14.7%	6.2%	3.4	0	50.0%	100.0%	5	118.8	0.2
2017	17	18.1%	8.8%	1.7	2	27.3%	87.5%	37	77.1	-2.8
2018	19	15.4%	13.8%	2.6	1	72.7%	100.0%	47	108.3	5.6
	46	16.1%	9.4%	2.5	3	50.0%	95.0%	89	110.6	3.0

Deep Dive

	Total Snaps		Pass Rush			Man Coverage			Zone Coverage		
Year	Pass	Run	Blitz%	Pressure%	Sack%	Man%	Yds/ Snap	Pos%	Zone%	Yds/ Snap	Pos%
2018	422	349	43.8%	10.9%	3.2%	27.6%	6.1	48.9%	72.4%	7.4	48.8%

Joey Alfieri

Stanford Cardinal

Final Grade: 6.2 LB Rank: 13 of 25

Height	Weight	Year	Jersey #	Hometown
6021	239	5SR	32	Portland, OR

One-Liner

Alfieri possesses the speed, pass rushing ability and coverage skills to be a solid Will at the next level, but needs to improve his shed ability and gain additional coverage experience.

Overall

Alfieri is a Will linebacker who played in a base 3-4 at Stanford. He played in 50 career collegiate games with 40 starts. He's a good athlete with very good speed and size for the position. He shows good competitive drive and toughness as he plays effectively in the box and can navigate the trash with regularity to make plays.

Run Game

In the run game, he is a good tackler and possesses sufficient football intelligence and instincts to read the play, diagnose it, and react to fill gaps and make plays. However, his strength and shed ability could use improvement as he is prone to getting stuck in blocks and unable to shed which takes him out of the play. He isn't incredibly stout and relies on his ability to navigate through the trash to make plays.

Pass Game

In the passing game, he has shown good pass coverage skills, using his speed and a good understanding of route concepts to drop in coverage effectively. His pass rushing ability and ability to play either with his hand in the ground or standing up are his biggest assets. He has an ability to effectively blitz and rush the quarterback and disrupt the play coming off the edge or through the middle. Despite taking regular snaps while lined up in the slot, Alfieri may be held back by his lack of man coverage experience at the next level, although he looked good when he got the chance in college.

Last Word

With his combination of skills, Alfieri could contribute immediately on all big four core special teams. Based on his size, speed, and ability to play in coverage as well as blitz, Alfieri projects as a versatile backup with inside and outside flexibility by his second year.

– Cole Ratliff

Strengths	Weaknesses
• Play speed	• Shed ability
• Blitz ability	• Stoutness
• 3-down/level	• FBI/Instincts

Critical Factors

Pass Coverage	Play Speed	Intelligence / Instincts
6	7	5

Positional Factors

3-Down Value	Man Coverage	Zone Coverage	QB Defense
6	6	6	5
Range	**Blitz**	**Tackling / Productivity**	**Stoutness**
6	6	6	5
Navigate Trash	**Shed Ability**	**Ruggedness**	**Special Teams Value**
6	5	6	6

Basic

	Tackling			Pass Rush		Coverage					
Year	Tackles	TFL	FF	Sacks	Pressures	Trgt	Comp	Comp%	Int	Yds	Yds/Trgt
2016	52	10.0	1	5.0	36	11	5	45.5%	2	22	2.0
2017	35	4.0	0	2.0	9	8	2	25.0%	0	7	0.9
2018	36	4.0	1	3.5	16	6	3	50.0%	0	46	7.7
	123	18.0	2	10.5	61	25	10	40.0%	2	75	3.0

Advanced

	Tackling				Coverage					
Year	Broken Tackles	BT%	Tackle Share	Avg Depth of Tackle	Passes Defensed	Pos%	Deserved Catch%	YAC	Rating	EPA
2016	9	15.0%	6.3%	3.4	0	9.1%	66.7%	9	12.9	-11.7
2017	10	22.7%	3.1%	4.5	0	12.5%	100.0%	4	39.6	-6.2
2018	5	12.2%	3.7%	4.7	1	50.0%	75.0%	17	75.7	1.5
	24	16.6%	4.3%	4.1	1	20.0%	76.5%	30	14.6	-16.5

Deep Dive

	Total Snaps		Pass Rush			Man Coverage			Zone Coverage		
Year	Pass	Run	Blitz%	Pressure%	Sack%	Man%	Yds/ Snap	Pos%	Zone%	Yds/ Snap	Pos%
2018	257	251	52.5%	8.6%	1.7%	54.3%	6.8	43.1%	45.7%	6.6	53.5%

Drue Tranquill

Notre Dame Fighting Irish
Final Grade: 6.2 LB Rank: 16 of 25

Height	Weight	Year	Jersey #	Hometown
6020	228	5SR	23	Fort Wayne, IN

One-Liner
Tranquill is an undersized off-ball linebacker who can contribute on passing downs and special teams, but his physicality and injury history will limit his effectiveness.

Overall
Tranquill played off-ball linebacker in Notre Dame's six-man box defense. He played in 51 career games and started 40, around recoveries from multiple ACL tears. He switched to full-time linebacker before the 2017 season, after playing a safety-hybrid role in his first few years for the Irish. He is a bit undersized for the position with good athleticism. Tranquill has shown great toughness in his career to fight back from injury, but is more of an effort space player than physical thumper on the field.

Run Game
Tranquill is a good tackler who doesn't strike particularly hard but does not miss or allow many broken tackles. He has adequate stoutness and stands his ground against pulling linemen and fullbacks well. Tranquill is decent at navigating through trash with his athleticism but gets caught up often when engaged.

Pass Game
Tranquill is good in pass coverage and is often used to cover tight ends due to his athletic ability and safety experience. He shows good play speed and range from sideline to sideline. He has solid football intelligence and linebacker instincts. Tranquill is sufficient at all three levels as he has skills and reps all over the field, but isn't the healthy safety he once was and also isn't much of an impact player at and behind the line of scrimmage. He is an average blitzer and doesn't shed blocks with physicality consistently. He is very good at being the quarterback of the defense, having been a two-time captain and shown good communication skills pre-snap.

Last Word
Tranquill has played through and fought back from injury without letting it affect his play. He best projects as a backup off-ball Will linebacker, with some Mike traits as well, in a defense that will ask him to move backward more than forward. He has the profile of a future core special teams player.

– Jeremy Percy

Strengths

- Pass coverage
- Instincts
- Leadership

Weaknesses

- Shed ability
- Blitzing impact
- Trash navigation

Critical Factors

Pass Coverage	Play Speed	Intelligence / Instincts
6	5	6

Positional Factors

3-Down Value	Man Coverage	Zone Coverage	QB Defense
5	6	6	7
Range	**Blitz**	**Tackling / Productivity**	**Stoutness**
6	4	5	5
Navigate Trash	**Shed Ability**	**Ruggedness**	**Special Teams Value**
5	4	6	7

Basic

	Tackling			Pass Rush		Coverage					
Year	Tackles	TFL	FF	Sacks	Pressures	Trgt	Comp	Comp%	Int	Yds	Yds/Trgt
2016	77	1.0	0	0.0	4	17	10	58.8%	1	134	7.9
2017	88	7.0	1	1.5	16	25	13	52.0%	1	109	4.4
2018	59	6.0	0	3.5	9	17	8	47.1%	0	52	3.1
	224	14.0	1	5.0	29	59	31	52.5%	2	295	5.0

Advanced

	Tackling				Coverage					
Year	Broken Tackles	BT%	Tackle Share	Avg Depth of Tackle	Passes Defensed	Pos%	Deserved Catch%	YAC	Rating	EPA
2016	16	17.2%	9.3%	7.5	2	35.3%	84.6%	86	103.6	1.5
2017	9	10.0%	8.6%	4.9	2	44.0%	71.4%	32	46.9	-7.8
2018	12	16.9%	7.1%	4.2	4	23.5%	69.2%	12	29.5	-11.2
	37	14.6%	8.3%	5.6	8	35.6%	74.5%	130	58.2	-17.6

Deep Dive

	Total Snaps		Pass Rush			Man Coverage			Zone Coverage		
Year	Pass	Run	Blitz%	Pressure%	Sack%	Man%	Yds/ Snap	Pos%	Zone%	Yds/ Snap	Pos%
2018	466	304	14.4%	10.6%	3.8%	62.0%	5.7	39.3%	38.0%	5.2	38.3%

Andrew Van Ginkel

Wisconsin Badgers
Final Grade: 6.0 LB Rank: 17 of 25

Height	Weight	Year	Jersey #	Hometown
6026	230	5SR	17	Rock Valley, IA

One-Liner
Van Ginkel is a very fast, quick, and high-motor edge defender whose play strength will be difficult to transition to the same position in the NFL, so a developmental move away from the ball may best suit his skill set.

Overall
Van Ginkel played outside linebacker in Wisconsin's base 3-4 defense. He started in all 26 games of his career as a Badger, after spending his first three collegiate years between South Dakota and Iowa Western Community College. He is a lanky and thin edge defender with impressive speed, quickness, and overall athleticism in space. He plays hard but has thickness and strength limitations that keep him from being a physically-imposing football player. His hustle and speed outside the tackles is noticeable, however.

Run Game
Against the run, Van Ginkel works hard in the box, but his play strength is below average for the edge position and he stalemates at the line at best against tight ends and some linemen. He has the length and aggression to set the edge sufficiently but can get washed out too easily against power. He plays with a very high motor and hustles to the ball from all areas of the field.

Pass Game
In the pass game, Van Ginkel is an elusive edge rusher. He explodes off the snap from his typical on-ball position and can easily beat linemen with speed inside and outside. He flashes excellent burst and bend around the arc and makes it very difficult for even the quickest of blockers to keep up vertically. He has an array of finesse moves in his repertoire. The issue with Van Ginkel as an edge rusher is his play strength. His size and power hold him back significantly, and his rush is often over whenever he can be contacted. However, he is often dropped into flat coverages and has shown natural spatial athleticism to backpedal and feel receivers around him. He will need a lot of development in this area, but he plays with intelligence and good awareness, and he has the athleticism and range to cover. He wasn't asked to cover often in man, and while he has the short area quickness and speed to match up with tight ends and running backs, he will naturally need work on his technique. He is already a sufficient zone defender and can grow into something more with his awareness and range. However, a move away from the ball will require processing of a wider area, which can be a difficult transition. His blitzing ability at the next level from an off-ball position will be excellent when he can be sent situationally and schemed up for speed mismatches.

Last Word
Van Ginkel projects as a developmental Will linebacker at the next level. His strength and size in the trenches won't hold up in the NFL. He can become a rangy, versatile coverage linebacker with reps and experience, and his pass rushing ability will still be a coveted asset.

– SIS Scouting Staff

Strengths	Weaknesses
• Finesse pass rush	• Play strength
• Speed, range, and motor	• Stoutness
• Spatial athleticism	• Experience in coverage

Critical Factors

Pass Coverage	Play Speed	Intelligence / Instincts
5	6	5

Positional Factors

3-Down Value	Man Coverage	Zone Coverage	QB Defense
6	4	5	4
Range	**Blitz**	**Tackling / Productivity**	**Stoutness**
7	8	6	4
Navigate Trash	**Shed Ability**	**Ruggedness**	**Special Teams Value**
5	4	5	6

Basic

	Tackling			Pass Rush		Coverage					
Year	Tackles	TFL	FF	Sacks	Pressures	Trgt	Comp	Comp%	Int	Yds	Yds/Trgt
2017	39	10.0	1	6.5	32	7	3	42.9%	2	87	12.4
2018	57	7.0	2	5.5	25	5	3	60.0%	0	18	3.6
	96	17.0	3	12.0	57	12	6	50.0%	2	105	8.8

Advanced

	Tackling				Coverage					
Year	Broken Tackles	BT%	Tackle Share	Avg Depth of Tackle	Passes Defensed	Pos%	Deserved Catch%	YAC	Rating	EPA
2017	4	10.8%	4.1%	2.2	1	28.6%	60.0%	57	89.6	-6.3
2018	3	5.3%	6.9%	4.2	2	40.0%	75.0%	9	67.1	-0.4
	7	7.4%	5.5%	3.5	3	33.3%	66.7%	66	68.4	-6.7

Deep Dive

	Total Snaps		Pass Rush			Man Coverage			Zone Coverage		
Year	Pass	Run	Blitz%	Pressure%	Sack%	Man%	Yds/ Snap	Pos%	Zone%	Yds/ Snap	Pos%
2018	290	283	63.5%	12.7%	2.5%	36.3%	4.5	31.0%	63.8%	6.3	41.2%

Ben Burr-Kirven

Washington Huskies
Final Grade: 5.9 LB Rank: 18 of 25

Height	Weight	Year	Jersey #	Hometown
5115	221	4SR	25	Menlo Park, CA

One-Liner
Burr-Kirven is a sideline-to-sideline player who excels in space and will thrive on special teams but is limited by his size and stoutness.

Overall
Burr-Kirven primarily played Will linebacker in Washington's 3-3-5 base defense. He was a 4-year player and 2-year starter at linebacker, appearing in 47 career games and starting 18 of them. Although he is very undersized for the position, Burr-Kirven is a very good athlete with a background in track. He has a tremendously high motor and will play sideline to sideline on each snap.

Run Game
In the run game, Burr-Kirven has very good speed and range to move laterally across the field and fill gaps. Despite his size, he sheds blocks against bigger, more powerful linemen very well, but he also tends to put all his effort into the shed and doesn't find the ball consistently. His aggressive nature and inability to fight straight through blocks allow him to be washed out of plays and lose gap integrity in the box. Burr-Kirven is slow to diagnose plays and he doesn't anticipate well along the interior. This causes him to get caught in trash. However, his movement skills and agility help him navigate well most of the time. He should be an outstanding special teams player at the next level. Due to his size, Burr-Kirven isn't a prototypical form tackler despite his production. He tends to catch and drag to tackle and rarely stands up players, which could lead to missed and broken tackles in the league. On his tackles, he consistently attacks the ball with a strong punch and good technique, which has led to multiple forced fumbles throughout his career.

Pass Game
In the pass game, Burr-Kirven primarily played zone at Washington. He has a good ability to read and react to the routes around him while keeping his eyes in the backfield to make a play on the ball. He has good hips which allow for fluid change of direction and transition from his backpedal, and he will chase down any crossers who catch the ball near his zone. While he didn't play man coverage very often at Washington, Burr-Kirven has the speed to keep up with backs out of the backfield or receivers out of the slot, as well as the ability to spy on more mobile quarterbacks. Burr-Kirven is average in blitz scenarios as he doesn't have the size to blow up running backs or the pass rushing moves to get around offensive linemen. He is better off sitting back in the second level and using his range in space than mixing it up behind the line.

Last Word
Burr-Kirven projects to be a quality backup Will linebacker in a 4-3 scheme, where defensive linemen can keep him clean to move laterally. He could play a major role on all special teams units due to his speed and nose for the ball.

– Nick Aiello

Strengths	Weaknesses
• High motor	• Undersized
• Straight-line speed	• Stoutness
• Production	• Tackling form

Critical Factors

Pass Coverage	Play Speed	Intelligence / Instincts
6	7	6

Positional Factors

3-Down Value	Man Coverage	Zone Coverage	QB Defense
5	6	6	6
Range	**Blitz**	**Tackling / Productivity**	**Stoutness**
7	4	7	4
Navigate Trash	**Shed Ability**	**Ruggedness**	**Special Teams Value**
5	6	5	8

Basic

	Tackling			Pass Rush		Coverage					
Year	Tackles	TFL	FF	Sacks	Pressures	Trgt	Comp	Comp%	Int	Yds	Yds/Trgt
2016	45	2.0	0	0.0	9	10	6	60.0%	1	85	8.5
2017	90	4.0	2	1.0	9	26	20	76.9%	1	145	5.6
2018	172	4.0	3	2.0	16	40	30	75.0%	2	280	7.0
	307	10.0	5	3.0	34	76	56	73.7%	4	510	6.7

Advanced

	Tackling				Coverage					
Year	Broken Tackles	BT%	Tackle Share	Avg Depth of Tackle	Passes Defensed	Pos%	Deserved Catch%	YAC	Rating	EPA
2016	8	15.1%	4.8%	4.8	1	50.0%	87.5%	43	47.9	-0.2
2017	10	10.2%	9.3%	4.9	3	57.7%	84.0%	63	57.4	-7.2
2018	11	6.1%	18.6%	5.0	1	55.0%	91.7%	139	72.9	-1.8
	29	8.8%	10.8%	5.0	5	55.3%	88.4%	245	64.0	-9.2

Deep Dive

	Total Snaps		Pass Rush			Man Coverage			Zone Coverage		
Year	Pass	Run	Blitz%	Pressure%	Sack%	Man%	Yds/ Snap	Pos%	Zone%	Yds/ Snap	Pos%
2018	491	374	11.4%	24.1%	3.7%	26.7%	5.0	38.0%	73.3%	5.2	41.5%

Terez Hall

Missouri Tigers
Final Grade: 5.9 LB Rank: 23 of 25

Height	Weight	Year	Jersey #	Hometown
6010	230	4SR	24	Lithonia, GA

One-Liner
Hall is a decent linebacker with traits to play on and off the ball, but should fit as a weakside defender with his intelligence and movement skills in space.

Overall
Hall is an outside linebacker who played primarily on the weakside in 4-2-5 and 3-3-5 schemes while at Missouri. In his Missouri career, he played in 47 games, starting in 24 of them. He is a good athlete who is able stay on the field on all three downs, as he is able to be an effective playmaker against the pass. He is a leader on the field, showing good communication pre-snap and when dropping in coverage.

Run Game
In the run game, he sets a strong edge to get into a lineman's chest and bench him as a contain player, then shed with length and awareness to make a play. He has struggled against top competition in this area, but he has the tools to develop further in this area. He hasn't had the production of some other Will defenders due to his movement all over the defense and his tweener qualities. He doesn't navigate through a heavy box cleanly when playing off the ball. His speed and range can be improved but are solid traits combined with his pop at the point of attack and pass rushing skills.

Pass Game
In the passing game, he was able to show decent range and speed. His zone instincts need improvement as he was inconsistent with his depth and moving with receivers across the zone as players crossed his face. He rarely lines up in man-to-man but when he does, he has shown the ability to transition and drive on backs and tight ends in underneath coverage. He is a good pass rusher and is a natural edge player. He can win with savvy speed and with some explosive pop at first punch, and displays strong hand use close to the line. Hall will need development in his pass coverage, but his movement skills in space and inconsistent anchor stoutness suit him best on the weak side off the ball, not as consistently battling in the trenches.

Last Word
Hall best projects as a reserve player with versatile alignment possibilities. He should be a good special teams player and will have to make his mark in this area while he develops in pass coverage.

– Ian Berg

Strengths	**Weaknesses**
• Pass rushing ability	• Pass coverage
• Intelligence	• Anchor stoutness
• Block shedding	• Trash navigation

Critical Factors

Pass Coverage	Play Speed	Intelligence / Instincts
5	5	6

Positional Factors

3-Down Value	Man Coverage	Zone Coverage	QB Defense
5	5	5	5
Range	**Blitz**	**Tackling / Productivity**	**Stoutness**
5	6	5	5
Navigate Trash	**Shed Ability**	**Ruggedness**	**Special Teams Value**
5	6	5	6

Basic

	Tackling			Pass Rush		Coverage					
Year	Tackles	TFL	FF	Sacks	Pressures	Trgt	Comp	Comp%	Int	Yds	Yds/Trgt
2016	21	0.0	0	0.0	4	4	3	75.0%	0	29	7.3
2017	84	9.5	0	1.0	12	22	15	68.2%	0	126	5.7
2018	70	9.5	1	5.0	20	12	3	25.0%	1	22	1.8
	175	19.0	1	6.0	36	38	21	55.3%	1	177	4.7

Advanced

	Tackling				Coverage					
Year	Broken Tackles	BT%	Tackle Share	Avg Depth of Tackle	Passes Defensed	Pos%	Deserved Catch%	YAC	Rating	EPA
2016	2	9.1%	2.1%	8.8	0	50.0%	75.0%	17	94.8	-0.4
2017	9	9.7%	9.1%	4.5	2	40.9%	94.7%	105	63.8	-5.6
2018	7	9.1%	9.1%	4.0	1	8.3%	71.4%	4	4.9	-11.1
	18	9.4%	6.6%	4.8	3	31.6%	86.7%	126	45.6	-17.1

Deep Dive

	Total Snaps		Pass Rush			Man Coverage			Zone Coverage		
Year	Pass	Run	Blitz%	Pressure%	Sack%	Man%	Yds/ Snap	Pos%	Zone%	Yds/ Snap	Pos%
2018	431	326	20.0%	14.5%	3.6%	57.3%	8.1	43.2%	42.7%	7.3	39.4%

Dre Greenlaw

Arkansas Razorbacks
Final Grade: 5.9 LB Rank: 25 of 25

Height	Weight	Year	Jersey #	Hometown
5114	230	4SR	23	Fayetteville, AR

One-Liner
Greenlaw is an undersized WLB who uses his quickness, football intelligence and coverage ability to make impactful plays in pass defense, and his read & react and speed to make plays against the run; he will need to get bigger and stronger at the POA to w

Overall
Greenlaw played Will linebacker in Arkansas' base 3-4 scheme and aligned on the weak side of the defense in both 3-3-5 or 4-2-5 defensive schemes. Greenlaw played 42 games for Arkansas, starting 38 of them. He is a very good athlete, having transitioned from safety to LB in college. He is undersized for his position, making him susceptible to being swallowed up by offensive linemen or heavy congestion, but allows for him to display good range and quickness to attack gaps or cover the hook/curl area of the field. Greenlaw's motor is inconsistent, as he will flash a high motor in some situations and other times give up on plays where an impact could have been made.

Run Game
In the run game, Greenlaw is good at recognizing the play development and using lateral quickness to position himself to make plays. Much of his collegiate production comes from his ability to quickly identify the weakness in the blocking scheme and attack the opening to make the play. Greenlaw's positioning and football intelligence are the biggest reasons why he has good production, routinely finding his way to the ball all over the field. He is susceptible to getting lost in the congestion of 2nd-level blocks and is consistently outmuscled by offensive linemen. He wins in these situations with his quickness and savvy but could face difficulty at the pro level with bigger, faster, stronger competitors. Greenlaw serves as a key communicator on the defensive side of the ball, routinely communicating both forward and backward with the various levels of the scheme.

Pass Game
In the pass game, Greenlaw is much more effective in coverage responsibility than blitz responsibility, although in coverage he is sufficient overall. He is rarely called upon to pressure the passer, and when he is, he struggles to get off blocks or impact the pocket due to lack of strength and moves. He shows more in zone than man, using his skills as a former safety to make impact plays. He shows good range in coverage and holds his own when covering backs out of the backfield and tight ends. He is better in zone, giving him the ability to read the QB's eyes to undercut/jump routes or defense the pass, but occasionally gets lazy with his footwork, standing flat footed, and being slow to react because of it. In man, he is susceptible to physical receivers, but uses good ball skills to play the pass and limit the ability for completion.

Last Word
Because of inadequate size for the position and a skill set uniquely geared toward defending the pass game, Greenlaw projects best as a top backup Will linebacker. He shows enough toughness and competitiveness to contribute on some special teams units.

– Aaron Gray

Strengths	**Weaknesses**
• Play speed • Read-react	• Play strength at POA • Aggression • Overall coverage ability

Critical Factors

Pass Coverage	Play Speed	Intelligence / Instincts
5	6	6

Positional Factors

3-Down Value	Man Coverage	Zone Coverage	QB Defense
6	5	6	6
Range	**Blitz**	**Tackling / Productivity**	**Stoutness**
6	4	6	4
Navigate Trash	**Shed Ability**	**Ruggedness**	**Special Teams Value**
4	4	5	6

Basic

	Tackling			Pass Rush		Coverage					
Year	Tackles	TFL	FF	Sacks	Pressures	Trgt	Comp	Comp%	Int	Yds	Yds/Trgt
2016	42	0.5	0	0.0	2	5	3	60.0%	1	41	8.2
2017	106	1.5	1	1.0	7	9	5	55.6%	0	119	13.2
2018	82	5.5	1	2.0	6	11	8	72.7%	2	100	9.1
	230	7.5	2	3.0	15	25	16	64.0%	3	260	10.4

Advanced

	Tackling				Coverage					
Year	Broken Tackles	BT%	Tackle Share	Avg Depth of Tackle	Passes Defensed	Pos%	Deserved Catch%	YAC	Rating	EPA
2016	4	8.7%	5.3%	6.7	0	40.0%	80.0%	24	46.7	-1.9
2017	14	11.7%	12.1%	6.4	1	55.6%	83.3%	64	137.5	5.5
2018	8	8.9%	9.3%	6.0	0	45.5%	80.0%	54	91.3	-3.3
	26	10.2%	8.9%	6.3	1	48.0%	81.0%	142	85.8	0.2

Deep Dive

	Total Snaps		Pass Rush			Man Coverage			Zone Coverage		
Year	Pass	Run	Blitz%	Pressure%	Sack%	Man%	Yds/ Snap	Pos%	Zone%	Yds/ Snap	Pos%
2018	200	248	20.2%	5.1%	0.0%	45.2%	9.6	40.4%	54.8%	7.8	52.2%

Glossary

Avg Depth of Tackle
Average number of yards away from the line of scrimmage that the defender made his tackles

Broken Tackles
Tackle attempts where the defender failed to bring down the ballcarrier. Counts both broken tackles (physical) and missed tackles (elusive)

BT%
Percentage of tackle attempts where the defender failed to bring down the ballcarrier. Counts both broken tackles (physical) and missed tackles (elusive)

Deserved Catch%
The percentage of targets as the primary defender that the receiver either caught or dropped the ball when the pass was catchable.

Passes Defensed
The number of times the defender broke up a throw at the catch point. This can be done by either knocking the ball away or hitting the receiver as the ball reaches them to disrupt the catch.

Pos% (Coverage split)
The percentage of plays where the defender was targeted that resulted in a positive EPA (a successful play for the offense)

Pressure%
Percentage of pass rushes that resulted in a quarterback hurry, hit, knockdown, or sack

Rating (Coverage split)
Traditional QB Rating on passes where the defender was targeted

Rush%
Percentage of quarterback dropbacks where the defender rushed the quarterback

Sack%
Percentage of pass rushes that resulted in a sack

Tackle Share
Percentage of a team's tackles made by the defender

Linebacker Leaderboards

Average Tackle Depth Leaders			
Rank	Player	Team	Avg Tackle Depth
1	David Long Jr.	West Virginia	2.6
2	Tre Lamar	Clemson	3.0
3	Chase Hansen	Utah	3.3
4	Dakota Allen	Texas Tech	3.7
5	Khalil Hodge	Buffalo	3.7
6	Ryan Connelly	Wisconsin	3.8
7	Joe Giles-Harris	Duke	4.0
8	Otaro Alaka	Texas A&M	4.0
9	Terez Hall	Missouri	4.0
10	Vosean Joseph	Florida	4.0

Passer Rating Allowed Leaders			
Rank	Player	Team	Passer Rating Allowed
1	Te'von Coney	Notre Dame	20.0
2	Drue Tranquill	Notre Dame	29.5
3	Mack Wilson	Alabama	37.4
4	Devin Bush	Michigan	42.6
5	Chase Hansen	Utah	50.0
6	Devin White	LSU	54.4
7	Tyrel Dodson	Texas A&M	55.7
8	Kendall Joseph	Clemson	69.3
9	Ben Burr-Kirven	Washington	72.9
10	Vosean Joseph	Florida	81.6

Tackle Share Leaders			
Rank	Player	Team	Tackle Share
1	Ben Burr-Kirven	Washington	18.6%
2	Devin White	LSU	14.0%
3	David Long Jr.	West Virginia	13.8%
4	Khalil Hodge	Buffalo	13.3%
5	Chase Hansen	Utah	13.2%
6	Te'von Coney	Notre Dame	13.0%
7	Germaine Pratt	NC State	12.1%
8	Ryan Connelly	Wisconsin	11.4%
9	Cameron Smith	USC	10.4%
10	Vosean Joseph	Florida	10.2%

Yards Per Man Coverage Snap Leaders			
Rank	Player	Team	Yds/Snap
1	Terrill Hanks	New Mexico State	3.9
2	Devin Bush	Michigan	4.1
3	Devin White	LSU	4.6
4	Joe Giles-Harris	Duke	4.7
5	Ben Burr-Kirven	Washington	5.0
6	Cameron Smith	USC	5.2
7	Vosean Joseph	Florida	5.2
8	Tyrel Dodson	Texas A&M	5.6
9	Drue Tranquill	Notre Dame	5.7
10	Chase Hansen	Utah	5.7

Broken Tackle Percentage Leaders			
Rank	Player	Team	Broken Tackle %
1	Te'von Coney	Notre Dame	3.1%
2	Khalil Hodge	Buffalo	4.1%
3	Jahlani Tavai	Hawaii	4.5%
4	Cameron Smith	Hawaii	4.5%
5	Andrew Van Ginkel	Wisconsin	5.3%
6	Germaine Pratt	NC State	5.8%
7	Ben Burr-Kirven	Washington	6.1%
8	Dakota Allen	Texas Tech	7.2%
9	Devin White	LSU	8.2%
10	Tre Lamar	Clemson	8.2%

Yards Per Zone Coverage Snap Leaders			
Rank	Player	Team	Yds/Snap
1	Joe Giles-Harris	Duke	4.6
2	Kendall Joseph	Clemson	4.6
3	Te'von Coney	Notre Dame	4.8
4	Ben Burr-Kirven	Washington	5.2
5	Drue Tranquill	Notre Dame	5.2
6	Vosean Joseph	Florida	5.7
7	Devin White	LSU	5.8
8	Devin Bush	Michigan	5.8
9	Mack Wilson	Alabama	6.2
10	Chase Hansen	Utah	6.7

CORNERBACK

Cornerback Grading Scale

GRADE	DESCRIPTION
9.0 – 7.0	High-end 3 down starter. Pro Bowl level.
6.9 – 6.7	Strong starter who plays on all 3 downs.
6.6 – 6.5	3rd CB. Capable starter with inside/outside flexibility.
6.4	3rd CB. Role-player. Lacks inside/outside flexibility
6.2	Versatile backup with CB/DS flexibility.
6.1 – 6.0	Developmental. Top traits but needs time.
5.9	Top backup. 4th CB. Quality special teamer.
5.8	4th CB w/o special teams ability. 5th CB w/ SPT.
5.7	Low-end backup CB with growable upside.

Cornerback Rankings

Rank	Name	Grade	Page
1	Deandre Baker	7.0	486
2	Greedy Williams	7.0	488
3	Byron Murphy	6.9	490
4	Nik Needham	6.8	492
5	Kendall Sheffield	6.7	494
6	Jamel Dean	6.7	496
7	Rock Ya-Sin	6.7	498
8	Duke Shelley	6.6	500
9	Julian Love	6.6	502
10	Trayvon Mullen	6.6	504
11	Iman Marshall	6.6	506
12	Hamp Cheevers	6.5	508
13	Joejuan Williams	6.5	510
14	Kris Boyd	6.5	512
15	Michael Jackson	6.4	514
16	Amani Oruwariye	6.4	516
17	Jordan Miller	6.4	518
18	Nate Brooks	6.4	520
19	Lonnie Johnson Jr.	6.4	522
20	Ugochukwu Amadi	6.2	524
21	Jamal Peters	6.2	526
22	Nate Meadors	6.2	528
23	Saivion Smith	6.2	530
24	Blessuan Austin	6.2	532
25	Isaiah Johnson	6.0	534
26	Montre Hartage	5.9	536

Deandre Baker

Georgia Bulldogs
Final Grade: 7.0 CB Rank: 1 of 26

Height	Weight	Year	Jersey #	Hometown
5111	185	4SR	18	Miami, FL

One-Liner
Baker is a physical, reactive athlete with great length that possesses excellent closing speed, very good ball skills and instincts, but his hip fluidity and short-area transition may be an issue.

Overall
Baker lined up primarily at outside corner for Georgia, only sliding into the slot or across formation in certain circumstances. He appeared in 11 games as a true freshman and was an impact player for the Bulldogs since, starting in 34 of 51 games he played. He has good size with very good arm length. Baker plays with tremendous confidence, communicates on the field and shows an edge when antagonizing receivers.

Pass Game
Baker doesn't seem to lose confidence when beat in pass coverage, but will find himself in staredown and shoving matches with receivers on run plays, sometimes losing track of the ball and play. His FBI is solid, as the ball seems to find him. Closing speed is one of Baker's greatest traits. His speed plays a large part in what makes him a solid man to man and very good zone cornerback. He shows good transition skills, but mainly uses his speed to make up for any deficiencies. He has the ability to mirror and run the route for the receiver often. Baker possesses great flexibility with quick feet and fluid hips, rarely crossing over his body and wins with technique regularly. He has matched up and shadowed some of the best receivers the nation has had to offer and is a consistent winner in those matchups. He plays with very good strength overall, especially in pass coverage being physical with receivers. He was used as a blitzer more often earlier in his career.

Run Game
In the run game, he doesn't always put his speed to use. He doesn't show much urgency in run support and does not deliver a blow or try to be the first man to the ball. He's an inconsistent tackler and isn't reliable 1-on-1 in space.

Last Word
Baker projects as an instant starter and contributor as an outside corner at the next level. He fits best outside on 3rd downs and has the traits to be a very good contributor on special teams as a gunner, jammer and possibly as a returner.

– Jake Schwanitz

Strengths	Weaknesses
• Closing speed	• Run support
• Ball skills	• Hip fluidity/transition
• Very reliable in coverage	

Critical Factors

Reactive Athleticism	Play Speed	Ball Skills
7	7	7

Positional Factors

Off-Man	Press Man	Zone Coverage	Slot Coverage
7	6	7	5
Transition	**Closing Speed**	**Football Intelligence**	**Mental Toughness**
6	8	6	6
Open-Field Tackling	**Play Strength**	**Run Support**	**Special Teams Value**
6	7	5	7

Basic

	Coverage								Tackling	
Year	Trgt	Comp	Comp%	Yards	Yds/Trgt	Int	Int Drops	TD Allowed	Tackles	TFL
2016	23	12	52.2%	198	8.6	2	1	1	27	1.0
2017	19	5	26.3%	104	5.5	1	1	0	13	0.0
2018	43	19	44.2%	176	4.1	2	2	0	40	1.0
	85	36	42.4%	478	5.6	5	4	1	80	2.0

Advanced

	Coverage							Tackling	
Year	Pass Breakups	Pos%	Deserved Catch%	YAC	Rating	EPA	EPA/ Trgt	Broken Tackles	BT%
2016	8	39.1%	66.7%	16	59.7	-10.6	-0.46	3	10.0%
2017	6	15.8%	54.5%	32	28.0	-4.9	-0.26	3	18.8%
2018	13	34.9%	60.6%	9	46.3	-19.7	-0.46	1	2.4%
	27	31.8%	61.5%	57	45.1	-35.2	-0.41	7	8.0%

Deep Dive

	Total Snaps		Lined Up	Man Coverage			Zone Coverage			Blitz
Year	Pass	Run	Slot%	Man%	Yds/ Snap	Pos%	Zone%	Yds/ Snap	Pos%	Blitz%
2018	365	318	13.6%	54.4%	4.3	33.1%	45.6%	5.9	45.5%	1.6%

Greedy Williams

LSU Tigers

Final Grade: 7.0 CB Rank: 2 of 26

Height	Weight	Year	Jersey #	Hometown
6021	185	3SO	29	Shreveport, LA

One-Liner

Williams is a long, smooth athlete in transition, who projects to be a top cover corner in the NFL with his impressive press mirror ability and ball skills.

Overall

Williams played outside press cornerback for LSU, with experience playing both sides of the field. He started all 25 games in his career, but skipped his final bowl game to focus on draft prep. He is a long and extremely smooth athlete with easy speed and decent foot quickness. Williams is a physical corner but lacks strength, relying on his length to disrupt route runners more than forcefully rerouting. He doesn't show much hustle or intensity in the run game or chasing after ballcarriers.

Pass Game

As a cover corner, Williams often lines up in press man and mirrors in a direct backpedal off the line of scrimmage, with natural hip turn transitions. He does not often jam but has the length to do so. He has impressive patience and stays calm through jab step releases and double moves. He never panics and shows very good reactive athleticism and an excellent transition from his backpedal to break quickly when his receiver finally sells out for his route. His mirror ability is best in a trail technique after bailing from press. He has some experience in the slot, but his lack of suddenness and short-area explosion suit him better outside. Williams' best attribute in coverage is his vision. He has excellent vision and instincts to be able to match his assignment in man while still tracking the quarterback's load. Much of his turnover production can be attributed to his eyes and anticipation. He shows an innate feel for passing off crossing receivers in man and pulling off his assignments to jump underneath routes. His vision and communication are assets in zone, but he is best used in more active schemes. In addition to his high football IQ, he also has naturally very good ball skills. Williams is great at using his length to attack the ball at the catch point, as well as tracking and matching his receiver's eyes and hands on deep routes with his back turned. Despite his high interception production, his catching skill is good but not elite. While he likes to hand fight and disrupt with his arms downfield, he can be manipulated at the top of routes by receivers who separate with strength.

Run Game

In the run game, Williams isn't aggressive attacking stalk blockers and pressing the edge. He misses some tackles due to his technique, usually by simply diving at ballcarriers' legs with his head down. His intelligence does show up in run support, as he does a good job of keeping contain to force runners back inside.

Last Word

Williams projects as a high-end outside press corner at the next level, who can step in immediately and contribute in multiple schemes. His vision and smooth downhill transition ability will translate quickly.

– John Todd

Strengths	Weaknesses
• Eyes and QB vision • Patience and transition • Length and ball skills	• Tackling technique • Covering physicality

Critical Factors

Reactive Athleticism	Play Speed	Ball Skills
7	7	7

Positional Factors

Off-Man	Press Man	Zone Coverage	Slot Coverage
6	7	6	5
Transition	**Closing Speed**	**Football Intelligence**	**Mental Toughness**
8	6	8	7
Open-Field Tackling	**Play Strength**	**Run Support**	**Special Teams Value**
4	5	4	6

Basic

	Coverage								Tackling	
Year	Trgt	Comp	Comp%	Yards	Yds/Trgt	Int	Int Drops	TD Allowed	Tackles	TFL
2016	0		-	0	-	0	0		1	0.0
2017	64	21	32.8%	284	4.4	6	0	1	37	1.5
2018	68	23	33.8%	373	5.5	2	1	3	34	0.0
	132	44	33.3%	657	5.0	8	1	4	72	1.5

Advanced

	Coverage							Tackling	
Year	Pass Breakups	Pos%	Deserved Catch%	YAC	Rating	EPA	EPA/ Trgt	Broken Tackles	BT%
2016	0	-	-	0	-	0.0	-	0	0.0%
2017	19	26.6%	51.0%	22	13.5	-37.8	-0.59	5	11.9%
2018	16	30.9%	60.0%	41	43.3	-16.8	-0.25	6	15.0%
	35	28.8%	55.2%	63	26.0	-54.6	-0.41	11	13.3%

Deep Dive

	Total Snaps		Lined Up	Man Coverage			Zone Coverage			Blitz
Year	Pass	Run	Slot%	Man%	Yds/ Snap	Pos%	Zone%	Yds/ Snap	Pos%	Blitz%
2018	416	367	20.4%	62.7%	4.9	33.8%	37.3%	5.5	32.1%	1.6%

Byron Murphy

Washington Huskies

Final Grade: 6.9 CB Rank: 3 of 26

Height	Weight	Year	Jersey #	Hometown
5112	182	3SO	1	Scottsdale, AZ

One-Liner

Murphy is a complete cover corner who excels in press-man and zone with great instincts and football intelligence, but needs to improve his off-man ability and run support.

Overall

Murphy's primary position is LCB, where he played exclusively at Washington in their base Cover 3 scheme. He was a 2-year player and starter, starting all 20 of the games he played in. Murphy is an outstanding athlete who possesses good hip fluidity and change-of-direction skill. He is a tough competitor and consistently plays bigger than his size, demonstrating multiple times that he can dislodge the ball from the receiver with big hits and pure physicality.

Pass Game

In the pass game, Murphy is most comfortable playing zone or press-man coverage. He is an instinctive, ball-hawking corner with very good change-of-direction and ball skills. He has fluid hips to keep up with receivers in and out of their breaks and he has the reactive athleticism to stay in receivers' pockets throughout their routes. His closing speed and ball skills are consistently on display as he meets receivers at the catch point and puts his hands directly on the ball to force it out. In zone coverage, Murphy is a very good read-and-react player who can recognize where the QB is going with the ball and close in a hurry to that spot. He tends to try to bait quarterbacks into shallow throws to make a game-changing play rather than play the receiver, which leads to easy dump-off completions. In press coverage, Murphy has surprising strength for his size and good length to redirect receivers at the line of scrimmage. He also plays with very good body control and a low center of gravity, so he won't get pushed off the top of the route by stronger, more physical receivers looking for separation. In off-man, Murphy looks to be at his least comfortable. He is a very aggressive player, so he will fly up and close in a hurry, but he tends to be out of control, leading to some missed tackles and allowing bigger plays after the catch.

Run Game

In the run game, Murphy plays aggressively and he's not afraid to come up and challenge at the LOS. He has the ability to tackle in the open field, although he occasionally will dive at the legs of receivers. Murphy has shown that he has some issues with shedding the blocks of bigger, more physical receivers. Despite this, he does a good job of maintaining outside leverage and forcing plays back towards his help on runs to the outside.

Last Word

Murphy is best suited to play outside and he rarely played in the slot at Washington, but his change-of-direction and reactive athleticism would translate very well against quick, shifty receivers. Due to his instincts, ability to stay glued to receivers, and ball skills, Murphy projects as a solid starter and fringe No. 1 CB.

– Nick Aiello

Strengths	**Weaknesses**
• Eye discipline/field awareness	• Off-man ability
• Closing speed	• Inconsistent run support
• Smooth COD skills	• Over-aggressive at times

Critical Factors

Reactive Athleticism	Play Speed	Ball Skills
7	7	7

Positional Factors

Off-Man	Press Man	Zone Coverage	Slot Coverage
6	7	7	7
Transition	**Closing Speed**	**Football Intelligence**	**Mental Toughness**
6	7	7	6
Open-Field Tackling	**Play Strength**	**Run Support**	**Special Teams Value**
5	6	5	6

Basic

	Coverage								Tackling	
Year	Trgt	Comp	Comp%	Yards	Yds/Trgt	Int	Int Drops	TD Allowed	Tackles	TFL
2017	24	12	50.0%	169	7.0	3	0	2	17	2.0
2018	62	30	48.4%	335	5.4	4	1	3	56	3.0
	86	42	48.8%	504	5.9	7	1	5	73	5.0

Advanced

	Coverage							Tackling	
Year	Pass Breakups	Pos%	Deserved Catch%	YAC	Rating	EPA	EPA/ Trgt	Broken Tackles	BT%
2017	9	45.8%	68.4%	33	66.1	1.0	0.04	2	10.5%
2018	17	40.3%	70.8%	24	54.2	-17.3	-0.28	5	8.2%
	26	41.9%	70.1%	57	57.5	-16.3	-0.19	7	8.8%

Deep Dive

	Total Snaps		Lined Up	Man Coverage			Zone Coverage			Blitz
Year	Pass	Run	Slot%	Man%	Yds/ Snap	Pos%	Zone%	Yds/ Snap	Pos%	Blitz%
2018	466	408	16.8%	31.8%	4.8	36.6%	68.2%	5.2	40.9%	2.4%

Nik Needham

UTEP Miners

Final Grade: 6.8 CB Rank: 4 of 26

Height	Weight	Year	Jersey #	Hometown
5112	203	4SR	5	Buena Park, CA

One-Liner

Needham is a physical competitor with strong coverage skills across the board, who will prove to be a more highly-regarded talent in the NFL than he was in college.

Overall

Needham primarily played outside cornerback in UTEP's base nickel scheme, playing a mix of off-man and press-bail techniques. He was a 4-year starter at UTEP, playing in 47 games and starting 41. He is a very good athlete who plays with balance, flexible hips, and explosive burst. Needham is very physically and mentally tough, as he seeks contact and battles on the perimeter, while also being a tenacious, competitive nuisance to receivers. He is often seen making checks to his secondary and is a galvanizing and passionate leader after big plays.

Pass Game

In the pass game, Needham is sticky in man coverage and shows awareness in zone. In off-man, Needham shows quick footwork in his backpedal, keeps his hips low, and has a fluid transition with few, if any, extra steps. He is solid in press-bail and does well in trail techniques, but his hand accuracy and reroute ability when in true press assignments is inconsistent. He projects very well to the slot with his reactive change-of-direction skills and physicality near the line. After his transition, he has solid closing speed and eyes to find the ball. At the catch point, Needham has very good body control to play big and high point. He has a knack for getting his hands on the ball, but despite his high number of passes defensed in his career, has logged only three interceptions. In zone coverage, Needham plays with very good eyes and awareness to key on the quarterback's load and anticipate routes. He regularly jumps and blows up screen plays.

Run Game

Against the run, he is a very willing participant. He has difficulty shedding blockers but gives great effort to keep contain and fight. He is a violent open-field tackler and attacks with sound technique, although he drops his head and lunges at times.

Last Word

Needham is a high-level athlete and physical competitor, with a versatile skill set that will allow him to play in multiple alignments. He best projects as a solid starter in base who moves inside to the slot in nickel, where his change-of-direction skills and quick transitions, as well as his run support, can be put on display.

– Tony Shields

Strengths	Weaknesses
• Transition • Competitiveness and mental toughness • Run support	• Consistent press • Shedding blocks

Critical Factors

Reactive Athleticism	Play Speed	Ball Skills
7	6	6

Positional Factors

Off-Man	Press Man	Zone Coverage	Slot Coverage
6	6	6	7
Transition	**Closing Speed**	**Football Intelligence**	**Mental Toughness**
7	6	7	7
Open-Field Tackling	**Play Strength**	**Run Support**	**Special Teams Value**
6	5	7	7

Basic

	Coverage								Tackling	
Year	Trgt	Comp	Comp%	Yards	Yds/Trgt	Int	Int Drops	TD Allowed	Tackles	TFL
2016	47	22	46.8%	245	5.2	0	0	1	51	1.0
2017	39	13	33.3%	242	6.2	1	0	2	58	2.5
2018	40	20	50.0%	234	5.9	1	0	3	59	1.0
	126	55	43.7%	721	5.7	2	0	6	168	4.5

Advanced

	Coverage							Tackling	
Year	Pass Breakups	Pos%	Deserved Catch%	YAC	Rating	EPA	EPA/ Trgt	Broken Tackles	BT%
2016	13	36.2%	66.7%	42	69.9	-4.7	-0.10	8	13.6%
2017	9	25.6%	64.0%	39	62.1	-7.7	-0.20	4	6.5%
2018	10	37.5%	66.7%	16	82.7	-4.6	-0.12	11	15.7%
	32	33.3%	66.0%	97	71.6	-17.0	-0.14	23	12.0%

Deep Dive

	Total Snaps		Lined Up	Man Coverage			Zone Coverage			Blitz
Year	Pass	Run	Slot%	Man%	Yds/ Snap	Pos%	Zone%	Yds/ Snap	Pos%	Blitz%
2018	332	422	12.6%	41.4%	4.9	34.0%	58.6%	7.0	41.8%	1.4%

Kendall Sheffield

Ohio State Buckeyes
Final Grade: 6.7 CB Rank: 5 of 26

Height	Weight	Year	Jersey #	Hometown
5106	193	3JR	8	Missouri City, TX

One-Liner
Sheffield is a speedy corner with very good reactive athleticism and coverage ability, but needs to work on being physical at the line more consistently.

Overall
Sheffield lined up as the field CB for the Buckeyes and played a lot of Cover 2 and Cover 3 schemes, while also sliding into the slot on occasion. He played in 28 games at Ohio State, starting in 17 of them. Sheffield has very good speed and quick feet at the corner position. He has the reactive athleticism to mirror receivers quickly and easily. He competes every play but would like to see him show more aggressiveness and physicality on a more consistent basis.

Pass Game
Versus the pass, Sheffield shows great ability to run the receiver's route and stay with the receiver step-for-step. He shows good ball skills when thrown to but would like to see him make more of his opportunities. He doesn't get his hands on receivers often enough in press and usually falls flat-footed when waiting for the WR to dance and release off the line. He shows the ability to quickly transition out of his backpedal and use his closing speed to break on the ball. Sometimes he will flip his hips a little too early when WRs start eating up his cushion. He uses a lot of press-bail technique and seems to lose track of out-breaking routes when doing so. In zone, he can use his vision to survey the QB and the area around him to seek out receivers coming to him.

Run Game
Versus the run, Sheffield doesn't show great ability to shed blockers on the outside. He uses his speed to chase down runs. Although he doesn't support the run incredibly well, he is a good open-field form tackler.

Last Word
Sheffield projects as a No. 2 CB, with the ability to work both inside and out. On 3rd down, he fits best on the outside in man coverage. Due to his ability to run step-for-step with receivers, Sheffield could add versatility and play in the slot at the next level. With his speed, he could add special teams value as a gunner or even a return specialist.

– Jordan Edwards

Strengths	Weaknesses
• Speed • Mirror-match movements • Transition	• Physicality • Support in the run game

Critical Factors

Reactive Athleticism	Play Speed	Ball Skills
7	7	6

Positional Factors

Off-Man	Press Man	Zone Coverage	Slot Coverage
6	6	6	6
Transition	**Closing Speed**	**Football Intelligence**	**Mental Toughness**
6	7	6	6
Open-Field Tackling	**Play Strength**	**Run Support**	**Special Teams Value**
6	5	5	6

Basic

	Coverage								Tackling	
Year	Trgt	Comp	Comp%	Yards	Yds/Trgt	Int	Int Drops	TD Allowed	Tackles	TFL
2017	46	29	63.0%	384	8.3	0	0	0	39	1.0
2018	56	24	42.9%	478	8.5	2	1	5	37	1.0
	102	53	52.0%	862	8.5	2	1	5	76	2.0

Advanced

	Coverage							Tackling	
Year	Pass Breakups	Pos%	Deserved Catch%	YAC	Rating	EPA	EPA/ Trgt	Broken Tackles	BT%
2017	8	47.8%	84.2%	51	89.4	7.8	0.17	2	4.9%
2018	8	39.3%	63.9%	18	95.7	7.4	0.13	1	2.6%
	16	43.1%	74.3%	69	92.9	15.2	0.15	3	3.8%

Deep Dive

	Total Snaps		Lined Up	Man Coverage			Zone Coverage			Blitz
Year	Pass	Run	Slot%	Man%	Yds/ Snap	Pos%	Zone%	Yds/ Snap	Pos%	Blitz%
2018	420	342	10.7%	65.9%	5.5	33.6%	34.1%	7.6	46.0%	0.0%

Jamel Dean

Auburn Tigers
Final Grade: 6.7 CB Rank: 6 of 26

Height	Weight	Year	Jersey #	Hometown
6005	208	3JR	12	Cocoa, FL

One-Liner
Dean has the coverage ball skills to make big-time plays at the next level but needs to become more aware and raise his motor with more consistency at the next level.

Overall
Dean's primary position is CB, where he played on both sides of the field at Auburn with rare rotations to a single-high position. After transferring from Ohio State due to his extensive injury history, Dean became a 2-year player and a 2-year starter at Auburn, playing in 26 games and starting 22 of them. He is a good athlete with good hips and good transition. He isn't a very tough competitor and is hesitant to get involved in plays outside of him being the primary defender.

Pass Game
In the pass game, Dean is a very good press defender. He has the size and strength to affect the release and timing of the route, and the speed and hip fluidity to turn and run with the receiver after the initial press. He excels defending quick routes as he has good lateral agility to help keep up with receivers and the length and ball skills to knock the ball away. His closing speed and transition ability allow him to play off-man well when defending intermediate routes, and his play speed allows him to run with most receivers down the field on deep routes. He can get fooled by stutter steps off the line from quicker, shiftier receivers which translates poorly to playing as an inside corner. In zone coverage, he can recognize when players enter and leave his zone and does a good job of denying his area and staying behind receivers. He has very limited awareness outside of his responsibilities in the run and pass game. Although he is susceptible to double moves, Dean generally does a good job of recognizing routes in either zone or man and getting his head around to look for the ball on deep throws. He has trouble diagnosing plays from the snap and struggles to adapt to improvised plays.

Run Game
In the run game, Dean prefers to not get involved, although he will make a last-ditch effort if he is the last line of defense. He has difficulty shedding blocks and gets overpowered by tight ends and bigger receivers despite his size.

Last Word
On 3rd downs, he'll fit best outside in press. Due to his hesitations when getting involved in the run game, he may not be a viable starter on special teams, but his size and speed will allow him to act as a fill-in in a pinch.

– Nick Aiello

Strengths	Weaknesses
• Man coverage • Ball skills • Play speed	• Awareness • Run support • Inside/outside flex

Critical Factors

Reactive Athleticism	Play Speed	Ball Skills
6	7	7

Positional Factors

Off-Man	Press Man	Zone Coverage	Slot Coverage
6	7	6	5
Transition	**Closing Speed**	**Football Intelligence**	**Mental Toughness**
6	6	6	5
Open-Field Tackling	**Play Strength**	**Run Support**	**Special Teams Value**
5	6	4	5

Basic

	Coverage								Tackling	
Year	Trgt	Comp	Comp%	Yards	Yds/Trgt	Int	Int Drops	TD Allowed	Tackles	TFL
2016	1	0	0.0%	0	0.0	0	0	0	0	0.0
2017	40	14	35.0%	220	5.5	0	0	4	42	2.5
2018	47	15	31.9%	230	4.9	2	1	2	28	2.0
	88	29	33.0%	450	5.1	2	1	6	70	4.5

Advanced

	Coverage							Tackling	
Year	Pass Breakups	Pos%	Deserved Catch%	YAC	Rating	EPA	EPA/ Trgt	Broken Tackles	BT%
2016	0	0.0%	0.0%	0	39.6	-0.6	-0.62	0	-
2017	9	25.0%	58.3%	12	89.7	-9.5	-0.24	5	10.6%
2018	10	21.3%	59.3%	20	45.5	-20.0	-0.42	8	22.2%
	19	22.7%	57.7%	32	64.8	-30.1	-0.34	13	15.7%

Deep Dive

	Total Snaps		Lined Up	Man Coverage			Zone Coverage			Blitz
Year	Pass	Run	Slot%	Man%	Yds/ Snap	Pos%	Zone%	Yds/ Snap	Pos%	Blitz%
2018	283	274	15.3%	64.8%	4.6	28.8%	35.2%	7.6	41.2%	1.0%

Rock Ya-Sin

Temple Owls
Final Grade: 6.7 CB Rank: 7 of 26

Height	Weight	Year	Jersey #	Hometown
5116	189	4SR	6	Decatur, GA

One-Liner
Ya-Sin is a well-built corner who has flashed the ball skills, reactive athleticism, and man-cover ability to be a solid starter in the NFL, but he needs to improve his off-man and zone coverage ability.

Overall
Ya-Sin primarily lined up at left cornerback in Temple's 4-3 defensive scheme. He started in 36 of his 45 career games played between his time at Presbyterian and Temple. He possesses good size and length with a high-cut build. He has good play speed and burst. He has loose and fluid hips, but he isn't incredibly twitchy or explosive when changing direction. He possesses good body control and balance. He's a tough player who is willing to be physical and mentally tough, showing the ability to recover after down moments.

Pass Game
Versus the pass, he shows solid press-man coverage ability. Ya-Sin possesses patient feet and does a good job of reading the receiver off his release. He flashes good mirror-and-match ability. His smooth hip mobility allows him to stay in phase with receivers. He plays in the receiver's hip pocket with some consistency. When in press, he is too handsy and penalty-prone but is physical off the line. He often opens his hips early to run downfield, leaving him susceptible to short, out-breaking routes. He has some inconsistency with measuring his footwork and needs to further develop his technique. He has the ability to be sufficient in zone, as he shows good route recognition, but he needs to improve his footwork and learn to re-route more. He shows good transition, but improved footwork would help him be more consistent. He flashes ball skills by putting his body in good position to use his length to disrupt the catch point. However, his ball tracking and location could use some work, and he dropped some easy interceptions. He'll play the receiver more than the ball and could get more breakups if he played the ball. He's a smart player that displays good reactive athleticism. He lacks a bit of closing burst, but he has the instincts and ability to at least be sufficient in off-man coverage. He wasn't asked to cover from the slot but should be sufficient in this area.

Run Game
Versus the run, he offers sufficient run support. He'll tend to pick and choose which tackles to get in on, although he will attack ballcarriers with physical strikes when he decides to hit. He usually plays with good leverage and has the play strength to hold his own against stalk blocks, but has some trouble shedding them with consistency. He can occasionally be late to recognize run plays. He tends to take some bad angles to the ball and is an average open field tackler.

Last Word
Ya-Sin projects as a No. 2 CB on the outside by his second season at the next level. He should offer good special teams ability due to his physical and competitive nature.

– Alex O'Brien

Strengths	Weaknesses
• Press-man coverage	• Open-field tackling
• Ball skills	• Off-man coverage
• Reactive athleticism	• Footwork

Critical Factors

Reactive Athleticism	Play Speed	Ball Skills
7	6	6

Positional Factors

Off-Man	Press Man	Zone Coverage	Slot Coverage
5	7	5	5
Transition	**Closing Speed**	**Football Intelligence**	**Mental Toughness**
6	5	6	6
Open-Field Tackling	**Play Strength**	**Run Support**	**Special Teams Value**
4	6	5	6

Basic

	Coverage								Tackling	
Year	Trgt	Comp	Comp%	Yards	Yds/Trgt	Int	Int Drops	TD Allowed	Tackles	TFL
2016	5	1	20.0%	8	1.6	0	0	0	1	0.0
2017	9	5	55.6%	62	6.9	1	0	2	6	1.0
2018	61	32	52.5%	252	4.1	2	1	1	49	2.0
	75	38	50.7%	322	4.3	3	1	3	56	3.0

Advanced

	Coverage							Tackling	
Year	Pass Breakups	Pos%	Deserved Catch%	YAC	Rating	EPA	EPA/ Trgt	Broken Tackles	BT%
2016	3	20.0%	25.0%	0	39.6	-3.2	-0.64	3	75.0%
2017	1	44.4%	85.7%	3	77.1	-0.3	-0.03	0	0.0%
2018	13	39.3%	73.5%	25	54.8	-3.9	-0.06	2	3.9%
	17	38.7%	71.7%	28	58.9	-7.4	-0.10	5	8.2%

Deep Dive

	Total Snaps		Lined Up	Man Coverage			Zone Coverage			Blitz
Year	Pass	Run	Slot%	Man%	Yds/ Snap	Pos%	Zone%	Yds/ Snap	Pos%	Blitz%
2018	359	453	18.6%	72.5%	4.9	39.3%	27.5%	4.4	31.3%	0.5%

Duke Shelley

Kansas State Wildcats
Final Grade: 6.6 CB Rank: 8 of 26

Height	Weight	Year	Jersey #	Hometown
5085	180	4SR	8	Tucker, GA

One-Liner
Shelley is very undersized, but his speed, elite leaping ability, and impressive transition skills will still make for an impact third cornerback.

Overall
Shelley was primarily an outside corner on both sides of the field in Kansas State's defense, with a number of snaps in the slot as well. He played in 38 career games before missing the second half of 2018 with a leg injury. He is undersized, but a very good athlete with very good speed and extremely impressive leaping ability, which helps make up for his lack of height. He lacks play strength but compensates with aggression and physicality.

Pass Game
In the passing game, Shelley uses his top-end athleticism to backpedal, turn and run stride for stride with most receivers downfield. He runs effortlessly and has very good transition and fluid hips. He has natural ball skills at the catch point, as he gets his head around and locates the ball well, then uses his leaping ability and great hands to make plays on the ball well outside his frame. Shelley can stop and close well and comes downhill quickly and with physicality. He is better in off-man as an outside corner, but he is sufficient in press despite his length and strength due to his recovery speed and compact frame to disrupt receivers. Shelley is also solid in zone coverage, feeling for receivers in space and having the leaping ability to surprise quarterbacks throwing into Cover 2 holes. He has the athletic ability and hips to play in the slot, but is more natural outside with better long speed than short area quickness.

Run Game
In the run game, Shelley is very physical coming up to the line and is good at squaring up his hips and wrapping up with sound technique. He is a very good open-field tackler, but his lack of size and strength give him trouble against larger ballcarriers. He shows solid football intelligence to diagnose and read plays.

Last Word
Shelley best projects as a third cornerback with inside/outside flexibility in multiple schemes, whose natural athletic ability and innate ball skills will compensate for his lack of size more often than not. He should be a solid special teams player with his physicality and return versatility.

– SIS Scouting Staff

Strengths	Weaknesses
• Ball skills • Athleticism and play speed • Run support and physicality	• Play strength • Size and length

Critical Factors

Reactive Athleticism	Play Speed	Ball Skills
6	7	7

Positional Factors

Off-Man	Press Man	Zone Coverage	Slot Coverage
6	5	6	6
Transition	**Closing Speed**	**Football Intelligence**	**Mental Toughness**
6	6	6	6
Open-Field Tackling	**Play Strength**	**Run Support**	**Special Teams Value**
6	4	6	6

Basic

	Coverage								Tackling	
Year	Trgt	Comp	Comp%	Yards	Yds/Trgt	Int	Int Drops	TD Allowed	Tackles	TFL
2016	52	30	57.7%	442	8.5	3	0	4	46	1.0
2017	94	49	52.1%	661	7.0	2	0	4	57	1.0
2018	53	24	45.3%	232	4.4	3	0	2	32	1.0
	199	103	51.8%	1335	6.7	8	0	10	135	3.0

Advanced

	Coverage							Tackling	
Year	Pass Breakups	Pos%	Deserved Catch%	YAC	Rating	EPA	EPA/ Trgt	Broken Tackles	BT%
2016	7	50.0%	82.5%	27	87.2	-12.3	-0.24	4	8.0%
2017	12	44.7%	82.2%	62	84.6	-1.7	-0.02	10	14.9%
2018	14	39.6%	64.3%	4	47.1	-16.8	-0.32	4	11.1%
	33	44.7%	77.4%	93	75.3	-30.8	-0.15	18	11.8%

Deep Dive

	Total Snaps		Lined Up	Man Coverage			Zone Coverage			Blitz
Year	Pass	Run	Slot%	Man%	Yds/ Snap	Pos%	Zone%	Yds/ Snap	Pos%	Blitz%
2018	261	207	12.5%	48.1%	5.7	50.0%	51.9%	5.2	37.2%	0.7%

Julian Love

Notre Dame Fighting Irish
Final Grade: 6.6   CB Rank: 9 of 26

Height	Weight	Year	Jersey #	Hometown
5106	193	3JR	27	Westchester, IL

One-Liner
Love is a very sound CB who has fluid hips and good instincts and ball skills, but lacks the physicality at the line in press coverage.

Overall
Love's primary position is slot corner, with the flexibility to play outside or in the safety role. Love was a three-year starter for the Irish with 38 games played and 34 starts. He has a prototypical build for the position, smooth hips, and quick feet. While his long speed is a concern, he is a very competitive player with a high football IQ who brings it to the field for his team on every play. It seems as if he lacks confidence in his speed which might hold him back from being an even better player.

Pass Game
Against the pass, he uses his instincts to read the receiver's hips and puts his foot in the ground to close. He possesses good closing speed to prevent YAC but does not break on the ball cleanly in many situations. He primarily played an off-man role for ND in which he liked to read and react to the WR and QB. He does a nice job of layering his eyes on the quarterback and receiver when he makes his break. In press-man, he allows too many free releases due to lack of hand use at the LOS. He plays flat-footed in press and tends to occasionally get beat. He shows a lack of discipline in technique by turning his hips too early instead of staying square, which could be attributed to long speed issues. Throughout the route, he uses his hands to feel the WR to stay in phase, although he has a tendency to get too physical at times. He plays conservatively and does not overpursue or take himself out of a position to make a play. He has very good ball skills and always has his hands actively trying to jar the ball loose at the catch point.

Run Game
Against the run, Love possesses a good understanding of stacking blockers and forcing the runner inside. He struggles to disengage against bigger blockers but does a nice job of keeping his eyes in the backfield to find the ball. He's a physical player who will not shy away from making tackles but will avoid piles.

Last Word
Love's play speed and tackling ability will translate well to special teams and he could be a contributor right away on punts or kickoffs. By year two, Love projects to be a starting nickel corner with the ability to flex outside or to a safety position.

– Zach Fernandez

Strengths	Weaknesses
• Very fluid hips and movements • Instincts • Ball skills	• Discipline in technique • Tendency to play on heels • Hand usage

Critical Factors

Reactive Athleticism	Play Speed	Ball Skills
6	6	7

Positional Factors

Off-Man	Press Man	Zone Coverage	Slot Coverage
7	5	6	6
Transition	**Closing Speed**	**Football Intelligence**	**Mental Toughness**
6	6	7	6
Open-Field Tackling	**Play Strength**	**Run Support**	**Special Teams Value**
6	5	6	6

Basic

	Coverage								Tackling	
Year	Trgt	Comp	Comp%	Yards	Yds/Trgt	Int	Int Drops	TD Allowed	Tackles	TFL
2016	40	22	55.0%	283	7.1	1	0	3	43	2.0
2017	82	33	40.2%	421	5.1	3	2	6	70	1.0
2018	74	34	45.9%	394	5.3	1	1	1	63	1.0
	196	89	45.4%	1098	5.6	5	3	10	176	4.0

Advanced

	Coverage							Tackling	
Year	Pass Breakups	Pos%	Deserved Catch%	YAC	Rating	EPA	EPA/ Trgt	Broken Tackles	BT%
2016	4	50.0%	82.1%	45	102.4	7.6	0.19	6	12.2%
2017	23	36.6%	62.1%	35	66.2	-28.2	-0.34	4	5.4%
2018	16	36.5%	64.3%	37	55.8	-14.8	-0.20	6	8.7%
	43	39.3%	66.9%	117	69.6	-35.3	-0.18	16	8.3%

Deep Dive

	Total Snaps		Lined Up	Man Coverage			Zone Coverage			Blitz
Year	Pass	Run	Slot%	Man%	Yds/ Snap	Pos%	Zone%	Yds/ Snap	Pos%	Blitz%
2018	463	381	25.4%	65.8%	5.2	36.2%	34.2%	4.2	32.6%	2.7%

Trayvon Mullen

Clemson Tigers
Final Grade: 6.6 CB Rank: 10 of 26

Height	Weight	Year	Jersey #	Hometown
6012	195	3JR	1	Fort Lauderdale, FL

One-Liner
Mullen has the reactive athleticism and closing speed to be a solid nickel corner early on despite his off-man and transition deficiencies.

Overall
Mullen started at CB for Clemson, playing the left or right side depending on the matchup. He would go a few drives on one side before switching over to the other. He played in 41 games, starting in 26 of them for the Tigers during his three years. He is quick and agile with very good mirroring skills and reactive athleticism. He is a long and rangy corner and is extremely competitive, frustrating his opponents by talking trash.

Pass Game
In the pass game, he shows good press-man skills. He is aggressive at the line and will oftentimes bully the receiver. Since he is aggressive at the line so much, he can lose the receiver, but is able to recover with his closing speed. When playing press-man, he often uses a trail technique to bait the QB and make a play on the ball using his speed. When a receiver uses his off-hand to create a throwing window, Mullen struggles to recover and close the gap. He shows good play strength at the line jamming receivers, but he is easily pushed around by stronger receivers down the field. Using his closing speed and play recognition skills, he's able to make up for his transition ability in off-man. When he uses press bail or off-man, he has a tough time transitioning and staying with the receiver when he breaks his route. When backpedaling, he plays high and on his heels. Mullen does a very good job of recognizing the play, making a play on the ball, but not over-committing in case it is a double move. In zone, Mullen is good, but can get lost watching the quarterback too much and lose track of the receiver in his zone. His ball skills are solid, as he does a good job high-pointing the ball and finding the most opportune time to jump the route. When the receiver has his hands on the ball, Mullen does a good job of battling the receiver's hands to knock the ball loose.

Run Game
In the run game, Mullen is not very aggressive and can allow a few extra yards. When he needs to, he makes the plays and does not have many broken or missed tackles. If he becomes more aggressive and follows his run assignments better, he could be a very good run support corner.

Last Word
Mullen projects as a No. 3 CB who can play on all three downs by his second season. He would fit best in the slot, especially on 3rd downs, where he can use his reactive athleticism and press ability against smaller receivers. He could also play on the outside. At Clemson, Mullen was used as a gunner and could become a decent contributor on special teams at the next level.

– Elijah Cornejo

Strengths	**Weaknesses**
• Mirroring	• Eye discipline
• Closing speed	• Lacks aggressiveness
• Physicality at the line	• Transition out of press-bail

Critical Factors

Reactive Athleticism	Play Speed	Ball Skills
7	6	6

Positional Factors

Off-Man	Press Man	Zone Coverage	Slot Coverage
5	6	6	6
Transition	**Closing Speed**	**Football Intelligence**	**Mental Toughness**
5	7	6	6
Open-Field Tackling	**Play Strength**	**Run Support**	**Special Teams Value**
5	6	5	6

Basic

	Coverage								Tackling	
Year	Trgt	Comp	Comp%	Yards	Yds/Trgt	Int	Int Drops	TD Allowed	Tackles	TFL
2016	7	4	57.1%	19	2.7	0	0	0	17	0.5
2017	51	25	49.0%	251	4.9	3	0	0	40	0.0
2018	40	18	45.0%	219	5.5	1	0	0	36	3.0
	98	47	48.0%	489	5.0	4	0	0	93	3.5

Advanced

	Coverage							Tackling	
Year	Pass Breakups	Pos%	Deserved Catch%	YAC	Rating	EPA	EPA/ Trgt	Broken Tackles	BT%
2016	1	28.6%	66.7%	3	62.2	-2.5	-0.35	0	0.0%
2017	9	39.2%	75.0%	43	38.9	-9.9	-0.19	4	9.1%
2018	3	35.0%	84.6%	41	52.0	-8.7	-0.22	3	7.7%
	13	36.7%	77.8%	87	45.8	-21.1	-0.21	7	7.0%

Deep Dive

	Total Snaps		Lined Up	Man Coverage			Zone Coverage			Blitz
Year	Pass	Run	Slot%	Man%	Yds/ Snap	Pos%	Zone%	Yds/ Snap	Pos%	Blitz%
2018	351	335	23.2%	47.6%	4.6	32.6%	52.4%	4.8	32.2%	1.3%

Iman Marshall

USC Trojans
Final Grade: 6.6 CB Rank: 11 of 26

Height	Weight	Year	Jersey #	Hometown
6010	203	4SR	8	Long Beach, CA

One-Liner
Marshall has the speed and reactive athleticism to make early contributions at the next level, but needs to improve his strength and true backpedal to become a starter.

Overall
Marshall primarily played the right CB position for the Trojans, but occasionally slid inside to the slot or played matchups on certain receivers. He played in 50 games at USC, starting 48. He is a very good reactive athlete that is built well, although he plays a bit smaller than he truly is. He possesses good straight-line speed but is stiff laterally.

Pass Game
In the passing game, he shows good ball-tracking skills and is consistently able to make a play on the ball. He is able to change directions quickly and fluidly, as well as stop almost immediately from a sprint. Marshall also shows good anticipation of where the receiver and the ball will be. He has very good mirror/match ability; in press-man coverage, he does a good job of jamming his man at the line, although he could be more consistent. He then mirrors him step-for-step, even while looking back at the QB. In off-man, he is able to turn and run with his receiver and maintain coverage. However, he tends to turn a bit early to not get caught flat-footed once the WR eats up his cushion. In zone, Marshall has good anticipation and is good at reading the QB's eyes without getting manipulated. He plays a lot of bail technique off the line and is susceptible to out-breaking routes, although he is fluid in his transition toward in-breaking ones.

Run Game
In the run game, Marshall doesn't aggressively pursue ballcarriers, and his tackling isn't a strength. He won't pursue much from the backside and when he does get tackle opportunities, he wraps and drags most times. He'll get chippy at times, as evidenced against N'Keal Harry and Arizona State, as they had some battles on the perimeter.

Last Word
Marshall projects as a No. 3 CB by his second season, playing both outside and inside. On 3rd downs, he can use his press ability and reactive athleticism to oppose speedy slot receivers. Marshall has the speed and awareness to play special teams, but his aggressiveness and tackling need work.

– Gennady Gusak

Strengths	Weaknesses
• Reactive athleticism	• Run support
• Man coverage abiity	• Aggressiveness
• Ball tracking	• Lateral agility

Critical Factors

Reactive Athleticism	Play Speed	Ball Skills
7	6	6

Positional Factors

Off-Man	Press Man	Zone Coverage	Slot Coverage
6	6	6	6
Transition	**Closing Speed**	**Football Intelligence**	**Mental Toughness**
6	7	6	7
Open-Field Tackling	**Play Strength**	**Run Support**	**Special Teams Value**
5	5	4	6

Basic

	Coverage								Tackling	
Year	Trgt	Comp	Comp%	Yards	Yds/Trgt	Int	Int Drops	TD Allowed	Tackles	TFL
2016	60	30	50.0%	439	7.3	3	2	2	52	2.0
2017	52	28	53.8%	402	7.7	0	3	1	51	0.5
2018	46	20	43.5%	258	5.6	0	1	1	49	4.5
	158	78	49.4%	1099	7.0	3	6	4	152	7.0

Advanced

	Coverage							Tackling	
Year	Pass Breakups	Pos%	Deserved Catch%	YAC	Rating	EPA	EPA/ Trgt	Broken Tackles	BT%
2016	9	36.7%	75.0%	24	64.5	-4.9	-0.08	5	8.8%
2017	10	46.2%	73.2%	49	85.6	13.6	0.26	4	7.3%
2018	7	37.0%	73.3%	15	68.9	-2.1	-0.05	4	7.5%
	26	39.9%	73.9%	88	72.7	6.6	0.04	13	7.9%

Deep Dive

	Total Snaps		Lined Up	Man Coverage			Zone Coverage			Blitz
Year	Pass	Run	Slot%	Man%	Yds/ Snap	Pos%	Zone%	Yds/ Snap	Pos%	Blitz%
2018	401	395	18.3%	66.2%	6.8	43.1%	33.8%	6.3	47.8%	0.7%

Hamp Cheevers

Boston College Eagles
Final Grade: 6.5 CB Rank: 12 of 26

Height	Weight	Year	Jersey #	Hometown
5096	180	3JR	4	Trenton, FL

One-Liner
Cheevers has the ball skills and COD ability to succeed as a slot corner and his experience will allow him to play outside in a pinch, but he'll get bullied by bigger, more physcial X/Z receivers due to his size and play strength.

Overall
Cheevers primarily played right outside corner at Boston College. He was a 3-year player and 1-year starter with 30 games played and 15 starts. Cheevers is a very good athlete with solid play speed and fluid hips which allow him to transition and change direction with ease. He is a tough competitor with a nonstop motor who will chase down a play from anywhere on the field.

Pass Game
In the pass game, Cheevers has the speed to keep up with most receivers and the ball skills to create turnovers and make plays. In press coverage, he struggles getting his hands on receivers and mirroring their moves off the line of scrimmage. Due to his size, he is susceptible to being boxed out on inside-breaking routes. He lacks the play strength to affect the release and spends a lot of his time in recovery mode off press. His lack of play strength is also apparent when contesting jump balls as receivers can out-muscle him. He is both more comfortable and more effective in off-man and zone, which is what he played at BC. In off-man, Cheevers has very good transition out of his backpedal and the ability to track the ball in the air, allowing him to easily keep up with deep routes and make a play when the ball arrives. His change of direction and good closing speed allow him to react to the ball being thrown short and make a tackle in the open-field. Cheevers needs to improve his route recognition as he can get caught flat-footed on double moves causing separation. In zone coverage, he has good awareness and instincts to fall off his receivers and jump on the intended route. This knack for being in the right place at the right time allowed Hamp to lead the FBS in interceptions for the 2018 season. Although he didn't play slot corner at BC, his change of direction, transition, and closing speed all translate nicely to the position.

Run Game
In the run game, Cheevers is eager to come up to the line of scrimmage and challenge ballcarriers, although he is limited by his size. He is a physical player against the run and can shed blocks of bigger receivers in order to get to the ballcarrier. Hamp is a willing tackler in the open field but he has been prone to broken tackles from more physical backs.

Last Word
By his second year, Cheevers projects to be a No. 3 slot cornerback who can play outside in a pinch. On 3rd downs, his speed and mirror ability should allow him to stick with speedy slot receivers. Hamp can also be a day-one contributor as a gunner on special teams due to his play speed and ability to shed blocks.

– Nick Aiello

Strengths	Weaknesses
• Play speed	• Play strength
• Transition	• Press-man ability
• Ball skills	• Undersized

Critical Factors

Reactive Athleticism	Play Speed	Ball Skills
5	7	7

Positional Factors

Off-Man	Press Man	Zone Coverage	Slot Coverage
6	5	7	6
Transition	**Closing Speed**	**Football Intelligence**	**Mental Toughness**
7	6	6	6
Open-Field Tackling	**Play Strength**	**Run Support**	**Special Teams Value**
5	4	5	6

Basic

	Coverage								Tackling	
Year	Trgt	Comp	Comp%	Yards	Yds/Trgt	Int	Int Drops	TD Allowed	Tackles	TFL
2017	20	7	35.0%	117	5.9	2	0	0	15	2.0
2018	65	29	44.6%	400	6.2	7	2	3	42	1.0
	85	36	42.4%	517	6.1	9	2	3	57	3.0

Advanced

	Coverage							Tackling	
Year	Pass Breakups	Pos%	Deserved Catch%	YAC	Rating	EPA	EPA/ Trgt	Broken Tackles	BT%
2017	8	25.0%	50.0%	4	16.0	-24.3	-1.22	1	6.3%
2018	15	40.0%	69.4%	62	48.2	-18.2	-0.28	11	20.8%
	23	36.5%	64.6%	66	34.9	-42.5	-0.50	12	17.4%

Deep Dive

	Total Snaps		Lined Up	Man Coverage			Zone Coverage			Blitz
Year	Pass	Run	Slot%	Man%	Yds/ Snap	Pos%	Zone%	Yds/ Snap	Pos%	Blitz%
2018	447	416	13.0%	52.4%	7.3	47.0%	47.6%	5.6	36.1%	1.0%

Joejuan Williams

Vanderbilt Commodores
Final Grade: 6.5 CB Rank: 13 of 26

Height	Weight	Year	Jersey #	Hometown
6021	208	3JR	8	Nashville, TN

One-Liner
Williams has all of the physical tools to be an exceptional player at the next level, but too many inconsistencies in ball skills and coverage and lacking top-end speed suggests he may merely be a backup.

Overall
At Vanderbilt, Williams played all over the field as a CB, mainly in a press-man technique. He played in 36 games for the Commodores. He's a good, reactive athlete who competes and shows toughness both mentally and physically. He shows good football intelligence on every play.

Pass Game
In the pass game, he shows that he can cover all over the field at any position, best shown against Notre Dame when he consistently picked up the TE. His best assets are his size and length, which he uses in press-man and displays with his ball skills. Williams is best in press-man as his athleticism shines with his mirror ability. He consistently stays on the receiver's hip throughout the route. He struggles with top-end speed on any inside or deep vertical routes. However, he still uses his length to make up for these few separation issues. At the LOS, he needs to show more patience as he can get beat with a bad jam, opening early, or by getting crossed up. Again, he almost always makes up for this with his other tools. When in off man or zone, he consistently shows slow transition from backpedal to break allowing catches in front of him. In zone coverages, he sometimes gets stuck in transition, losing players entering and leaving his area. When not in press-man, he can be a little more tight-hipped than usual. He likes to play against the tough competition and raised his game when he faced A.J. Brown, DaMarkus Lodge, and Riley Ridley.

Run Game
In the run game, Williams is a good tackler but can dive at ballcarriers while leaving his feet. He doesn't show the aggressiveness to stick his nose in the play and never piles on to help make tackles. He shows little strength once engaged to shed defenders.

Last Word
At the next level, Williams projects as a 3rd corner by his second season, providing depth outside and inside with a strong possibility of becoming a starter with consistent play. He will be best in a primarily man scheme but can play all over the field. His speed and toughness should allow him to be a solid contributor on special teams.

– Evan Butler

Strengths	Weaknesses
• Press man ability • Size and length • Ball skills	• Inconsistent hip transition from back-pedal • Not an aggressive tackler • Top-end speed

Critical Factors

Reactive Athleticism	Play Speed	Ball Skills
6	6	6

Positional Factors

Off-Man	Press Man	Zone Coverage	Slot Coverage
6	7	6	6
Transition	**Closing Speed**	**Football Intelligence**	**Mental Toughness**
5	5	6	6
Open-Field Tackling	**Play Strength**	**Run Support**	**Special Teams Value**
6	5	5	6

Basic

	Coverage								Tackling	
Year	Trgt	Comp	Comp%	Yards	Yds/Trgt	Int	Int Drops	TD Allowed	Tackles	TFL
2016	18	12	66.7%	142	7.9	0	0	0	18	1.5
2017	51	24	47.1%	229	4.5	0	0	2	39	1.5
2018	68	28	41.2%	387	5.7	4	0	5	66	3.0
	137	64	46.7%	758	5.5	4	0	7	123	6.0

Advanced

	Coverage							Tackling	
Year	Pass Breakups	Pos%	Deserved Catch%	YAC	Rating	EPA	EPA/ Trgt	Broken Tackles	BT%
2016	2	55.6%	85.7%	22	90.5	6.9	0.38	7	28.0%
2017	7	35.3%	78.4%	9	64.9	-6.7	-0.13	6	13.3%
2018	16	36.8%	68.8%	40	47.9	-26.6	-0.39	5	7.0%
	25	38.7%	74.7%	71	59.8	-26.4	-0.19	18	12.8%

Deep Dive

	Total Snaps		Lined Up	Man Coverage			Zone Coverage			Blitz
Year	Pass	Run	Slot%	Man%	Yds/ Snap	Pos%	Zone%	Yds/ Snap	Pos%	Blitz%
2018	413	453	16.0%	63.9%	7.1	46.2%	36.1%	6.7	41.6%	1.1%

Kris Boyd

Texas Longhorns

Final Grade: 6.5 CB Rank: 14 of 26

Height	Weight	Year	Jersey #	Hometown
5114	195	4SR	2	Gilmer, TX

One-Liner

Boyd is a solid reactive athlete who has the physicality and ball skills of a starting CB, but his play in off-man and sufficient closing speed down the field may set him back.

Overall

Boyd played the left CB spot in Texas's secondary, with the exception of playing the boundary against USC. They like to mix up man and zone and will cycle between press and off-coverage. He started 33 of his 51 games played for the Longhorns. He has good athleticism and shows quick-twitch ability. He plays with toughness, physicality and competes in his play.

Pass Game

In the pass game, Boyd has the reactive athleticism to mirror and stick with receivers down the field. He has good ball skills at the catch point and knows how to read the body language of the receiver. He tends to get boxed out by bigger receivers, but does a good job making plays on the ball for being slightly undersized. He tends to be a little high in his backpedal and will sometimes be playing on his heels. That, in turn, will force him to be slightly slower in his transition. He shows good ability in press man and zone coverage but struggles at times in off-man. In off-man, he turns his hips too early in fear of getting beat downfield and usually is too slow to transition quickly enough to break on curl, comeback and out routes. He plays fast, but only shows sufficient closing speed down the field, which is why he turns out of his backpedal too quickly. He'll get beat on double-moves early in the game but possesses the football intelligence to recognize it later in the game. Against TCU, he was beat on a sluggo early in the game, but in the 4th quarter, recognized it and reacted quick enough to run the route for the receiver.

Run Game

In the run game, he's not afraid to come down into the box and make a play. He's physical with receivers and shows the ability to tackle in the open-field and around the LOS. Against USC, when there wasn't a receiver to the boundary, he played at the back-end of the box essentially as an extra linebacker. His physicality and tackling ability suggests he'd be a solid contributor on special teams.

Last Word

Boyd projects as a 3rd CB by year two with the ability to play outside or inside, mainly in a press man or zone scheme. His tackling ability and range could allow him to fill in at safety for a short-term stint. He fits better on the outside on 3rd downs, due to his size possibly being an issue going up against larger tight ends in the slot.

– Nathan Cooper

Strengths
- Physicality
- Ball skills
- Reactive athleticism

Weaknesses
- Transition ability
- Off-man coverage
- Closing speed

Critical Factors

Reactive Athleticism	Play Speed	Ball Skills
6	6	6

Positional Factors

Off-Man	Press Man	Zone Coverage	Slot Coverage
5	6	6	6
Transition	**Closing Speed**	**Football Intelligence**	**Mental Toughness**
5	5	6	6
Open-Field Tackling	**Play Strength**	**Run Support**	**Special Teams Value**
6	6	6	7

Basic

	Coverage								Tackling	
Year	Trgt	Comp	Comp%	Yards	Yds/Trgt	Int	Int Drops	TD Allowed	Tackles	TFL
2016	50	31	62.0%	459	9.2	0	4	3	50	0.0
2017	59	21	35.6%	409	6.9	2	2	3	53	0.5
2018	88	41	46.6%	637	7.2	1	3	5	65	3.5
	197	93	47.2%	1505	7.6	3	9	11	168	4.0

Advanced

	Coverage							Tackling	
Year	Pass Breakups	Pos%	Deserved Catch%	YAC	Rating	EPA	EPA/ Trgt	Broken Tackles	BT%
2016	4	52.0%	87.5%	51	103.7	11.7	0.23	11	18.0%
2017	17	28.8%	54.8%	43	70.5	-4.2	-0.07	5	8.6%
2018	16	42.0%	71.6%	117	80.5	5.1	0.06	9	12.2%
	37	40.6%	71.1%	211	83.4	12.6	0.06	25	13.0%

Deep Dive

	Total Snaps		Lined Up	Man Coverage			Zone Coverage			Blitz
Year	Pass	Run	Slot%	Man%	Yds/ Snap	Pos%	Zone%	Yds/ Snap	Pos%	Blitz%
2018	518	434	10.3%	47.1%	6.8	43.4%	52.9%	6.9	42.3%	1.4%

Michael Jackson

Miami FL Hurricanes
Final Grade: 6.4 CB Rank: 15 of 26

Height	Weight	Year	Jersey #	Hometown
6006	207	4SR	28	Birmingham, AL

One-Liner
Jackson is a physical, press-man corner that tackles well and will contribute as a 4-down player, but needs to improve his off-man ability with better transition at the next level.

Overall
Jackson lined up primarily at outside corner at Miami and would occasionally line up in the slot against tight ends and at safety. Jackson played in 51 games, including 4 bowl games, starting 23 of them. He was named a starter in 2017 and went on to have the best year of his career, culminating with All-ACC Second Team honors. Jackson is a physical player who always engages the receiver when the ball is snapped. He plays with effort on every play and communicates with teammates.

Pass Game
Versus the pass, Jackson is best at press-man. He engages his receiver early and likes to be physical at the LOS, but would benefit from more consistent hand work.. He can get caught flat-footed and loses the WR while looking in the backfield. When beat, Jackson recovers well with good closing speed and takes good angles in catching up to receivers. Jackson is not thrown at often, but when targeted, he has displayed good ball skills.

Run Game
Versus the run, Jackson is an aggressive, hard-hitting tackler with good instincts. When the ball is handed off, he is quick to react and maintains responsibility.

Last Word
Jackson projects to be a reliable 3rd corner that can only play on the outside. On 3rd downs, he fits best on the outside. He has the base size and athleticism to cover NFL receivers and would benefit from improved technique. Jackson was a primary contributor on special teams early in his career.

– SIS Scouting Staff

Strengths	**Weaknesses**
• Press man	• Change of direction
• Aggressiveness/Physicality	• Off-man
• Recovery	• Anticipation

Critical Factors

Reactive Athleticism	Play Speed	Ball Skills
6	6	6

Positional Factors

Off-Man	Press Man	Zone Coverage	Slot Coverage
5	7	6	5
Transition	**Closing Speed**	**Football Intelligence**	**Mental Toughness**
6	6	6	6
Open-Field Tackling	**Play Strength**	**Run Support**	**Special Teams Value**
7	7	6	7

Basic

	Coverage								Tackling	
Year	Trgt	Comp	Comp%	Yards	Yds/Trgt	Int	Int Drops	TD Allowed	Tackles	TFL
2016	3	2	66.7%	18	6.0	0	0	0	6	0.0
2017	50	20	40.0%	227	4.5	4	0	1	48	2.0
2018	43	16	37.2%	232	5.4	0	0	1	40	2.5
	96	38	39.6%	477	5.0	4	0	2	94	4.5

Advanced

	Coverage							Tackling	
Year	Pass Breakups	Pos%	Deserved Catch%	YAC	Rating	EPA	EPA/ Trgt	Broken Tackles	BT%
2016	1	33.3%	100.0%	0	82.6	-2.0	-0.65	1	14.3%
2017	10	30.0%	71.9%	24	21.4	-29.7	-0.59	6	11.1%
2018	7	32.6%	63.0%	31	34.3	-8.1	-0.19	4	9.1%
	18	31.3%	69.4%	55	23.1	-39.8	-0.41	11	10.5%

Deep Dive

	Total Snaps		Lined Up	Man Coverage			Zone Coverage			Blitz
Year	Pass	Run	Slot%	Man%	Yds/ Snap	Pos%	Zone%	Yds/ Snap	Pos%	Blitz%
2018	308	397	26.1%	58.3%	4.2	29.1%	41.7%	5.4	45.5%	1.8%

Amani Oruwariye

Penn State Nittany Lions
Final Grade: 6.4 CB Rank: 16 of 26

Height	Weight	Year	Jersey #	Hometown
6016	204	5SR	21	Tampa, FL

One-Liner
Oruwariye has good length, athleticism, and ball skills, but needs to improve his FBI and willingness in the run game to be more than a rotational CB.

Overall
Oruwariye primarily lined up at outside cornerback for Penn State, where they played a mix of press-man, off-man, and zone. He was a one-year starter with 12 total starts in 48 games played during his four years. He possesses very good size and length for the position. He's a twitchy athlete for being a tall corner. His effort can be questioned when the play isn't directed towards him, but when it is, he is sure to be involved.

Pass Game
Against the pass, Oruwariye excels in off-man because of his good reactive athleticism, balance, and body control. He also possesses good play speed along with a smooth transition which allows him to be more aggressive and recover if he gets beat early. His footwork is inconsistent and at times he looks stiff in his backpedal which can cause trouble when mirroring receivers in man coverage. He also doesn't effectively get his hands on the receiver at the LOS. He has quick reactive athleticism skills to react to the receiver's movements almost instantly with a burst of short-area quickness. He does a good job of tracking the ball for the most part, although sometimes he doesn't get his head around. When he's in position to make a play on the ball, most of the time he's able to take advantage of it with interceptions or pass breakups.

Run Game
Against the run, Oruwariye can tend to shy away from contact at times. He will eat up blocks or make the tackle, but he can get overly aggressive and lunge, causing missed tackles.

Last Word
Oruwariye projects to be a rotational starting corner who is limited to the outside at the next level. He'll be able to use his speed and athleticism on most special teams units.

– Zach Fernandez

Strengths	**Weaknesses**
• Length	• Closing speed
• Reactive athleticism	• Press-man ability
• Ball skills	• Football intelligence

Critical Factors

Reactive Athleticism	Play Speed	Ball Skills
6	6	6

Positional Factors

Off-Man	Press Man	Zone Coverage	Slot Coverage
6	6	6	5
Transition	**Closing Speed**	**Football Intelligence**	**Mental Toughness**
6	5	5	6
Open-Field Tackling	**Play Strength**	**Run Support**	**Special Teams Value**
5	6	5	7

Basic

	Coverage								Tackling	
Year	Trgt	Comp	Comp%	Yards	Yds/Trgt	Int	Int Drops	TD Allowed	Tackles	TFL
2016	14	7	50.0%	114	8.1	1	0	2	22	0.0
2017	40	20	50.0%	247	6.2	4	0	2	30	0.0
2018	69	30	43.5%	410	5.9	3	1	4	47	1.0
	123	57	46.3%	771	6.3	8	1	8	99	1.0

Advanced

	Coverage							Tackling	
Year	Pass Breakups	Pos%	Deserved Catch%	YAC	Rating	EPA	EPA/ Trgt	Broken Tackles	BT%
2016	1	42.9%	88.9%	4	117.3	3.2	0.23	1	4.3%
2017	11	30.0%	71.4%	29	46.6	-3.6	-0.09	8	21.1%
2018	14	34.8%	71.4%	78	58.2	-19.1	-0.28	10	17.5%
	26	34.1%	73.1%	111	61.4	-19.5	-0.16	19	16.1%

Deep Dive

	Total Snaps		Lined Up	Man Coverage			Zone Coverage			Blitz
Year	Pass	Run	Slot%	Man%	Yds/ Snap	Pos%	Zone%	Yds/ Snap	Pos%	Blitz%
2018	393	351	19.6%	42.9%	4.0	33.3%	57.1%	5.3	36.2%	3.1%

Jordan Miller

Washington Huskies
Final Grade: 6.4 CB Rank: 17 of 26

Height	Weight	Year	Jersey #	Hometown
6005	181	4SR	23	Oceanside, CA

One-Liner
Miller has the reactive athleticism to stay with receivers in man coverage and ball skills to create turnovers, but needs to become more well-rounded at the next level.

Overall
Miller primarily plays outside cornerback, having played a Cover 3 man/zone blend for the Huskies. He was a starter for two seasons, starting in 19 of the 46 games he played in. He is a good athlete with easy long speed. He does have a tendency to take it easy when the play isn't directly at him. He responds well to bad plays by fighting for the ball if beat in coverage and increasing focus after allowing a catch.

Pass Game
In the pass game, Jordan plays predominantly in a 3/4 turn technique. He excels in man coverage. His quick feet and reactive athleticism allow him to mirror receivers. His good closing speed and length make press coverage his best skill. He gets to his top speed quickly and his long strides afford him control and balance to find the ball and play it in the air. He has very good ball skills and rarely drops any pass he can get his hands on. Occasionally in off-man and often in zone coverage, he can find himself in no man's land.

Run Game
In the run game, he does just enough to get by, often getting taken out of the play by blockers. From time to time, he will show the ability to hold the proper position and shed poor blocks. He is a sufficient tackler for a CB. He prefers to throw his body at a runner as opposed to wrapping up.

Last Word
Miller projects to be a rotational starter by his second year and has the ball skills and athletic ability to create turnovers at the next level. On 3rd downs, he'll fit best on the outside where he can use his length. He has the size and speed to be an immediate contributor on punt and punt return teams.

– Ben Hrkach

Strengths	**Weaknesses**
• Press man	• Strength
• Ball skills	• Run support/tackling
• Length	• Football intelligence

Critical Factors

Reactive Athleticism	Play Speed	Ball Skills
6	6	7

Positional Factors

Off-Man	Press Man	Zone Coverage	Slot Coverage
6	7	5	5
Transition	**Closing Speed**	**Football Intelligence**	**Mental Toughness**
5	6	5	6
Open-Field Tackling	**Play Strength**	**Run Support**	**Special Teams Value**
5	5	5	6

Basic

	Coverage								Tackling	
Year	Trgt	Comp	Comp%	Yards	Yds/Trgt	Int	Int Drops	TD Allowed	Tackles	TFL
2016	9	5	55.6%	47	5.2	1	0	0	7	0.0
2017	25	10	40.0%	102	4.1	2	0	0	22	0.0
2018	37	21	56.8%	260	7.0	2	1	2	26	1.0
	71	36	50.7%	409	5.8	5	1	2	55	1.0

Advanced

	Coverage							Tackling	
Year	Pass Breakups	Pos%	Deserved Catch%	YAC	Rating	EPA	EPA/ Trgt	Broken Tackles	BT%
2016	2	33.3%	83.3%	10	70.1	-1.4	-0.15	0	0.0%
2017	8	32.0%	50.0%	20	19.1	-10.7	-0.43	2	8.3%
2018	6	37.8%	80.0%	16	74.2	-5.1	-0.14	11	29.7%
	16	35.2%	69.6%	46	54.3	-17.2	-0.24	13	19.1%

Deep Dive

	Total Snaps		Lined Up	Man Coverage			Zone Coverage			Blitz
Year	Pass	Run	Slot%	Man%	Yds/ Snap	Pos%	Zone%	Yds/ Snap	Pos%	Blitz%
2018	301	260	13.9%	25.7%	4.9	30.6%	74.3%	5.1	36.3%	3.1%

Nate Brooks

North Texas Mean Green
Final Grade: 6.4 CB Rank: 18 of 26

Height	Weight	Year	Jersey #	Hometown
5115	180	4SR	9	Whitehouse, TX

One-Liner
Brooks operates better out of off-man/zone schemes, and uses his good play speed, ball skills and physicality to be a role-playing starter, but needs to improve his play strength at the line of scrimmage to be an all-around contributor.

Overall
Brooks is a cornerback who played primarily on the outside of defensive alignments in off-man and zone coverages. He started in 45 of 48 games for North Texas. He is a good athlete who can stick with receivers downfield and anticipate movements, although he will struggle on occasion. He has good play speed and fluid hips, making for easy transition to turn and run. Brooks uses his athleticism to make plays on the ball and receiver, and often relies on it to cover any lapses in coverage. He is a good competitor, willing to mix it up with the opposition and demonstrates the desired mentality of a cornerback.

Pass Game
Versus the pass, Brooks is sufficient in press man coverage, but is good in both off-man and zone coverage. He uses the spacing to his advantage, giving him time to diagnose and anticipate the receivers route and/or read the quarterback's eyes and progression. However, the cushion Brooks typically employs makes him susceptible to quick-hitting passes and heightens the importance of his ability to read/react/redirect/drive to the ball and catch point. He is physical with receivers once the cushion is reduced, and he applies pressure to them throughout their route. He is eager to establish inside leverage, regardless of coverage scheme, making him susceptible to passes toward the boundary such as fades, corners and outs. He shows good transition ability, making it difficult for receivers to run past or beat him on contested balls. Brooks' ball skills are solid, as he uses his athleticism, speed and anticipation to disrupt the pass or intercept the ball down the field.

Run Game
Versus the run, Brooks shows good recognition and block shed ability. He positions himself well and fights off downfield blocks to either tackle the rusher or redirect ballcarriers to his help. He is a solid tackler, willing to come up and stick ballcarriers, but occasionally opts to dive and swipe instead of form tackle.

Last Word
Based on his overall coverage ability, play speed, reactive athleticism, ball skills, anticipation and limitation to the outside of defensive schemes, Nate Brooks projects as a role-playing No. 3 cornerback in the NFL by year two. His ability in off-man and zone, his ability to read the passer and anticipate the play, and his physical style make him an ideal fit for the outside corner role in the modern defense. He has only played corner in his college career but shows potential as a safety due to his communication, play identification, and zone coverage skills. His skill set suggests that he could contribute on some special teams units

– Aaron Gray

Strengths	Weaknesses
• Communication	• Press/bump and run coverage
• Anticipation/read-react	• Play strength
• Ball skills	• Reactive athleticism

Critical Factors

Reactive Athleticism	Play Speed	Ball Skills
5	6	7

Positional Factors

Off-Man	Press Man	Zone Coverage	Slot Coverage
6	5	6	5
Transition	**Closing Speed**	**Football Intelligence**	**Mental Toughness**
6	6	6	6
Open-Field Tackling	**Play Strength**	**Run Support**	**Special Teams Value**
5	5	6	6

Basic

	Coverage								Tackling	
Year	Trgt	Comp	Comp%	Yards	Yds/Trgt	Int	Int Drops	TD Allowed	Tackles	TFL
2016	58	27	46.6%	501	8.6	4	0	6	56	2.0
2017	26	16	61.5%	312	12.0	0	1	4	33	0.0
2018	113	55	48.7%	669	5.9	6	0	2	69	1.5
	197	98	49.7%	1482	7.5	10	1	12	158	3.5

Advanced

	Coverage							Tackling	
Year	Pass Breakups	Pos%	Deserved Catch%	YAC	Rating	EPA	EPA/ Trgt	Broken Tackles	BT%
2016	12	39.7%	75.0%	100	82.6	3.4	0.06	12	17.6%
2017	2	42.3%	80.0%	8	142.9	13.1	0.51	5	13.2%
2018	19	41.6%	73.2%	113	51.1	-29.2	-0.26	7	9.2%
	33	41.1%	74.6%	221	74.0	-12.7	-0.06	24	13.2%

Deep Dive

	Total Snaps		Lined Up	Man Coverage			Zone Coverage			Blitz
Year	Pass	Run	Slot%	Man%	Yds/ Snap	Pos%	Zone%	Yds/ Snap	Pos%	Blitz%
2018	471	379	7.3%	48.7%	7.5	41.2%	51.3%	5.9	38.1%	0.4%

Lonnie Johnson Jr.

Kentucky Wildcats

Final Grade: 6.4 CB Rank: 19 of 26

Height	Weight	Year	Jersey #	Hometown
6022	210	4SR	6	Gary, IN

One-Liner

Johnson is a long corner with great size and good speed to be a contributor on the perimeter, but he lacks the quick change-of-direction skills to stick tight to slot receivers.

Overall

Johnson was an outside cornerback in Kentucky's defense, playing a mix of man and zone schemes. He played in 22 games for the Wildcats and started 14 of them after transferring in from community college. He is a long, tall, and well-built athlete who has good speed, but he struggles with short area quickness. He is a good, physical competitor who only comes out of games due to Kentucky's heavy secondary rotations.

Pass Game

Johnson is very good in zone coverage and has a firm grasp of his responsibilities. Despite his lack of production, he has good ball skills and does a good job of getting his head around on deep throws. He should be limited to an outside cornerback position due to his limited foot quickness to keep up with shiftier players in the slot. He doesn't get beat deep often due to his speed but struggles to minimize separation out of breaks. In press-man, his length is an asset, but he struggles to consistently get his hands on receivers. If he can refine his technique, he can be an effective press-corner at the next level. His physicality is inconsistent at times and he can seem passive when attacking the ball at the catchpoint.

Run Game

In the run game, Johnson is a willing contributor and can make plays due to his high football intelligence and size but can struggle to disengage from blocks. He is rarely out of position and can hit with force but doesn't look to press up and attack the line.

Last Word

He has very good special teams value due to his physical traits and ability to make tackles in the open field with his long arms. He projects as an early-depth cornerback who is a special teams staple. By his second year, Johnson profiles as a third corner on the outside with ideal length and zone coverage skills, which will be coveted by some teams based on scheme.

– SIS Scouting Staff

Strengths	**Weaknesses**
• Length	• Change of direction
• Fluid hips	• Slot coverage
• Football intelligence	• Production

Critical Factors

Reactive Athleticism	Play Speed	Ball Skills
5	6	6

Positional Factors

Off-Man	Press Man	Zone Coverage	Slot Coverage
6	6	7	4
Transition	**Closing Speed**	**Football Intelligence**	**Mental Toughness**
5	6	6	6
Open-Field Tackling	**Play Strength**	**Run Support**	**Special Teams Value**
6	6	5	7

Basic

	Coverage								Tackling	
Year	Trgt	Comp	Comp%	Yards	Yds/Trgt	Int	Int Drops	TD Allowed	Tackles	TFL
2017	52	37	71.2%	456	8.8	0	1	4	40	1.0
2018	33	18	54.5%	228	6.9	1	0	3	23	0.0
	85	55	64.7%	684	8.0	1	1	7	63	1.0

Advanced

	Coverage							Tackling	
Year	Pass Breakups	Pos%	Deserved Catch%	YAC	Rating	EPA	EPA/ Trgt	Broken Tackles	BT%
2017	6	59.6%	84.8%	32	115.5	13.7	0.26	3	7.0%
2018	5	39.4%	75.0%	13	81.4	4.7	0.14	6	20.7%
	11	51.8%	81.1%	45	102.3	18.5	0.22	9	12.5%

Deep Dive

	Total Snaps		Lined Up	Man Coverage			Zone Coverage			Blitz
Year	Pass	Run	Slot%	Man%	Yds/ Snap	Pos%	Zone%	Yds/ Snap	Pos%	Blitz%
2018	317	325	17.9%	34.5%	4.4	34.0%	65.5%	5.0	31.5%	0.9%

Ugochukwu Amadi

Oregon Ducks

Final Grade: 6.2 CB Rank: 20 of 26

Height	Weight	Year	Jersey #	Hometown
5095	201	4SR	7	Nashville, TN

One-Liner

Amadi is a thick, short, versatile corner who plays with good reactive athleticism and ball skills, but lacks physicality in the run game and the ability to reliably tackle in the open field.

Overall

Amadi was listed as a free safety for Oregon, but mostly played in the slot in an off-man role. He was a cornerback recruit out of high school and played there during his first two seasons with the Ducks. He played 51 career games with 34 starts. Amadi is slightly undersized but sufficiently thick for his hybrid role. He has good reactive athleticism, speed, and hips, which allow him to match receivers. He plays hard but lacks aggression and has occasional lapses in mental toughness.

Pass Game

In coverage, he shows that he can blanket receivers with his mirror ability and recovery speed. He turns and runs well with slot receivers deep. His reaction quickness is solid in short areas, and he recognizes and anticipates routes very well. He almost never presses receivers, preferring to sit and react away from the line. He has good ability to transition downhill and good closing speed to contest catches and limit yards after the catch. Amadi has good hands and ball skills and tracks well in the air when he gets his head around. However, he has occasional issues with mistiming his ability to high-point, which is crucial at his height. He is a dangerous returner with the ball in his hands, both on interceptions and punt returns. His size and open-field tackling suggest he would only be a sufficient special teams player on other units.

Run Game

Against the run, he lacks physicality. He is mediocre in run support and tackling, and his aggression to the ball shows questionable competitive toughness.

Last Word

Amadi profiles as a versatile reserve defensive back, capable of sufficiently filling in as a slot cornerback or free safety. He has some outside corner flexibility but is limited by his size, and his lack of proficiency in run support will keep him from a box safety role.

– Ian Berg

Strengths	Weaknesses
• Short area quickness	• Physicality
• Natural ball skills	• Size and length
• Slot coverage and versatility	• Run support

Critical Factors

Reactive Athleticism	Play Speed	Ball Skills
6	6	6

Positional Factors

Off-Man	Press Man	Zone Coverage	Slot Coverage
5	5	5	6
Transition	**Closing Speed**	**Football Intelligence**	**Mental Toughness**
6	6	7	5
Open-Field Tackling	**Play Strength**	**Run Support**	**Special Teams Value**
4	4	4	6

Basic

	Coverage								Tackling	
Year	Trgt	Comp	Comp%	Yards	Yds/Trgt	Int	Int Drops	TD Allowed	Tackles	TFL
2016	46	26	56.5%	324	7.0	0	0	2	40	0.0
2017	50	26	52.0%	372	7.4	3	0	2	44	1.5
2018	61	27	44.3%	362	5.9	3	1	2	57	4.0
	157	79	50.3%	1058	6.7	6	1	6	141	5.5

Advanced

	Coverage							Tackling	
Year	Pass Breakups	Pos%	Deserved Catch%	YAC	Rating	EPA	EPA/ Trgt	Broken Tackles	BT%
2016	6	50.0%	82.4%	28	93.0	7.9	0.17	4	9.1%
2017	10	42.0%	72.2%	43	73.1	-5.3	-0.11	3	6.4%
2018	10	34.4%	69.0%	36	61.0	-5.7	-0.09	9	13.6%
	26	41.4%	74.1%	107	74.2	-3.1	-0.02	16	10.2%

Deep Dive

	Total Snaps		Lined Up	Man Coverage			Zone Coverage			Blitz
Year	Pass	Run	Slot%	Man%	Yds/ Snap	Pos%	Zone%	Yds/ Snap	Pos%	Blitz%
2018	443	388	73.5%	52.1%	5.2	35.4%	47.9%	6.8	45.3%	7.5%

Jamal Peters

Mississippi State Bulldogs
Final Grade: 6.2 CB Rank: 21 of 26

Height	Weight	Year	Jersey #	Hometown
6012	220	4SR	2	Bassfield, MS

One-Liner
Peters is a long and strong outside cornerback with extended history at safety, whose traits may not add up to an eventual starting player, but rather a versatile secondary reserve.

Overall
Peters' primarily played outside corner in Mississippi State's base nickel defense. He played in 46 career games, with sporadic starts his first three years before becoming a full-time starting corner in 2018. He was recruited as a top safety and moved between safety and corner for much of his career. Peters is a good athlete with passable play speed, especially for someone his size. He is a physical player with good play strength and mental toughness.

Pass Game
Versus the pass, Peters is solid in both man and zone coverage, with good, smooth transitions out of his backpedal. He is sufficient in press but doesn't use it enough for someone with his physical attributes. He is unable to consistently close the cushion on quick cuts & double moves, which will likely keep him from being anything more than sufficient in the slot at the next level. Peters is a smart football player who reads well in zone and uses his length to disrupt routes and make plays on the ball at the catch point.

Run Game
Against the run, he is aggressive when the play is coming in his direction and makes good, clean open-field tackles. He uses his length to keep himself clean against stalk blocks on the edge and is a sound force defender outside.

Last Word
Peters' mobility, tackling, and length should lead him to be a good special teams contributor at the next level. He best projects as a position-flexible backup at outside cornerback and safety, due to his playing experience and football intelligence, and he also lacks short area quickness to play in the slot, length, strength and physicality.

– Ronan Potts

Strengths	Weaknesses
• Size and length	• Short area quickness
• Run defense	• Long speed
• Back-end flexibility	• Slot versatility

Critical Factors

Reactive Athleticism	Play Speed	Ball Skills
5	5	6

Positional Factors

Off-Man	Press Man	Zone Coverage	Slot Coverage
5	5	6	5
Transition	**Closing Speed**	**Football Intelligence**	**Mental Toughness**
6	5	6	6
Open-Field Tackling	**Play Strength**	**Run Support**	**Special Teams Value**
6	6	6	6

Basic

	Coverage								Tackling	
Year	Trgt	Comp	Comp%	Yards	Yds/Trgt	Int	Int Drops	TD Allowed	Tackles	TFL
2016	23	14	60.9%	180	7.8	2	0	3	17	1.0
2017	19	10	52.6%	182	9.6	1	1	1	25	0.0
2018	24	12	50.0%	139	5.8	0	0	0	32	0.0
	66	36	54.5%	501	7.6	3	1	4	74	1.0

Advanced

	Coverage							Tackling	
Year	Pass Breakups	Pos%	Deserved Catch%	YAC	Rating	EPA	EPA/ Trgt	Broken Tackles	BT%
2016	6	43.5%	77.3%	5	88.8	-6.6	-0.29	5	22.7%
2017	3	42.1%	80.0%	14	63.8	-5.0	-0.26	0	0.0%
2018	5	45.8%	75.0%	10	67.9	5.7	0.24	6	15.8%
	14	43.9%	77.2%	29	74.1	-5.9	-0.09	11	12.9%

Deep Dive

	Total Snaps		Lined Up	Man Coverage			Zone Coverage			Blitz
Year	Pass	Run	Slot%	Man%	Yds/ Snap	Pos%	Zone%	Yds/ Snap	Pos%	Blitz%
2018	216	175	18.2%	44.8%	5.5	31.1%	55.2%	5.2	35.2%	3.6%

Nate Meadors

UCLA Bruins

Final Grade: 6.2 CB Rank: 22 of 26

Height	Weight	Year	Jersey #	Hometown
5112	195	4SR	22	San Bernadino, CA

One-Liner

Meadors is a versatile player with solid speed and man coverage skills, but needs to improve his reactive athleticism and ball skills to prove worthy of being called upon as a rotational player in the secondary.

Overall

Meadors primarily played outside cornerback in a 3-4 defense, but also spent a lot of time in the slot on both the left and right side of the field. He has also played safety in the past. He played in 42 games and started in 30 at both safety and corner for the Bruins. He's a good all-around athlete with the speed to keep up with most receivers, although he did get burned a few times against Oklahoma's speedier receivers. He's long and does a good job using his length to stay in-phase with receivers.

Pass Game

In the passing game, he does a good job in man coverage. He uses his hands well to stay on the receiver's hip and is always in a good position. He lacks the reactive athleticism to mirror receivers and be effective in zone. He plays his best in the slot and has good play strength to cover TEs. He has solid footwork and does a good job of coming out of his breaks with fluid hips and transition ability. He competes hard in the pass game and is not afraid to come downhill and stick his nose into a run play from time to time.

Run Game

In the run game, he is a good tackler. He does a good job of setting the edge. He doesn't mind coming up and supporting the run. He can play three or four positions effectively in the secondary and his versatility will allow him to be an asset.

Last Word

Meadors projects as a versatile backup defensive back who fits best in the slot and could slide back to safety. He would likely be playing as a nickel defender in the slot on 3rd down. He's a three-down player who can play outside corner, slot corner, free safety and possibly strong safety in a pinch. His skill set will allow him to be a solid contributor on special teams.

– Austin Cochran

Strengths	**Weaknesses**
• Length	• Ball skills/production
• Transition	• Reactive athleticism
• Versatility	• Zone awareness

Critical Factors

Reactive Athleticism	Play Speed	Ball Skills
5	6	5

Positional Factors

Off-Man	Press Man	Zone Coverage	Slot Coverage
7	6	5	6
Transition	**Closing Speed**	**Football Intelligence**	**Mental Toughness**
6	6	6	6
Open-Field Tackling	**Play Strength**	**Run Support**	**Special Teams Value**
6	6	6	6

Basic

	Coverage								Tackling	
Year	Trgt	Comp	Comp%	Yards	Yds/Trgt	Int	Int Drops	TD Allowed	Tackles	TFL
2016	34	16	47.1%	155	4.6	0	1	1	35	0.0
2017	57	26	45.6%	289	5.1	1	0	1	53	1.5
2018	37	22	59.5%	389	10.5	1	1	4	37	1.0
	128	64	50.0%	833	6.5	2	2	6	125	2.5

Advanced

	Coverage							Tackling	
Year	Pass Breakups	Pos%	Deserved Catch%	YAC	Rating	EPA	EPA/ Trgt	Broken Tackles	BT%
2016	5	32.4%	66.7%	11	57.8	-7.4	-0.22	1	2.8%
2017	10	35.1%	77.8%	49	59.8	-7.7	-0.13	5	8.6%
2018	3	54.1%	79.3%	61	120.2	15.0	0.41	0	0.0%
	18	39.8%	75.3%	121	76.7	-0.1	0.00	6	4.6%

Deep Dive

	Total Snaps		Lined Up	Man Coverage			Zone Coverage			Blitz
Year	Pass	Run	Slot%	Man%	Yds/ Snap	Pos%	Zone%	Yds/ Snap	Pos%	Blitz%
2018	226	279	56.6%	58.0%	7.5	45.0%	42.0%	5.8	49.4%	2.0%

Saivion Smith

Alabama Crimson Tide

Final Grade: 6.2 CB Rank: 23 of 26

Height	Weight	Year	Jersey #	Hometown
6005	200	3JR	4	Tampa, FL

One-Liner

Smith is a long, physical corner who has the skill set to succeed at corner or safety, but his change-of-direction deficiency and inability to lock down opposing receivers will make him a rotational defensive back.

Overall

Smith primarily played outside corner in a man-to-man scheme at Alabama. He was a one-year player and one-year starter, playing in 15 games and starting 12 of them. He's a solid athlete with good play speed, but he struggles with flipping his hips and changing direction against quicker receivers. He is a tough competitor who fought to reclaim his starting job after three games on the bench midseason.

Pass Game

In the pass game, Saivion excels in man coverage, primarily being used in press-man. He likes to use a stab technique with his inside arm that occasionally leads to overextensions and a free release for the receiver if he misses. He also struggles against in-breaking routes due to a tendency to open his hips outside once the ball is snapped. His aggressive nature leaves him susceptible to double moves and head fakes, which can freeze him and allow receivers to gain separation. When Smith does get his hands on a receiver, he does a good job of keeping up with them on deep routes and using the sideline as an extra defender. He has the play strength to stay with the bigger, more physical receivers as he won't get pushed off the top of the route. In off-man, Smith is quick to open his hips while bailing, which can turn him around and leave receivers wide open on short-intermediate routes. While he has good closing speed, his change-of-direction deficiency won't allow him to react in time to the ball arriving. In zone coverage, Smith struggles to identify his responsibility, allowing a lot of room for receivers to work in his area. However, once he does identify his responsibility, he does a good job of closing to the ball and making the tackle. While the ball is in the air, Smith does a good job of getting his head around and looking for it when he's not in recovery mode off the line of scrimmage. He has good instincts and ball skills to adjust on poorly thrown balls in order to create for his team.

Run Game

In the run game, Smith is a very good open-field tackler who seems to consistently finish on contact, even on diving tackle attempts. He has the ability to shed blocks and come up in run support at the line of scrimmage.

Last Word

Due to his size, physicality, and speed, Smith should be a contributor on special teams from day one, while his instincts and ball skills will allow him to play safety if needed. By his second season in the NFL, Smith should be a backup outside corner who can flex to FS in a pinch. On 3rd downs, he can use his length and man coverage ability on the outside.

– Nick Aiello

Strengths	Weaknesses
• Physicality	• Slot coverage
• Length	• Transition
• Man coverage	• Reactive athleticism

Critical Factors

Reactive Athleticism	Play Speed	Ball Skills
5	6	6

Positional Factors

Off-Man	Press Man	Zone Coverage	Slot Coverage
6	6	5	4
Transition	**Closing Speed**	**Football Intelligence**	**Mental Toughness**
5	6	6	6
Open-Field Tackling	**Play Strength**	**Run Support**	**Special Teams Value**
7	6	6	6

Basic

	Coverage								Tackling	
Year	Trgt	Comp	Comp%	Yards	Yds/Trgt	Int	Int Drops	TD Allowed	Tackles	TFL
2016	6	3	50.0%	60	10.0	0	0	0	3	0.0
2018	56	32	57.1%	612	10.9	3	1	6	56	0.0
	62	35	56.5%	672	10.8	3	1	6	59	0.0

Advanced

	Coverage							Tackling	
Year	Pass Breakups	Pos%	Deserved Catch%	YAC	Rating	EPA	EPA/ Trgt	Broken Tackles	BT%
2016	2	50.0%	66.7%	18	85.4	2.3	0.38	0	0.0%
2018	7	46.4%	81.8%	68	116.1	24.0	0.43	5	8.2%
	9	46.8%	80.0%	86	113.1	26.3	0.42	5	7.8%

Deep Dive

	Total Snaps		Lined Up	Man Coverage			Zone Coverage			Blitz
Year	Pass	Run	Slot%	Man%	Yds/ Snap	Pos%	Zone%	Yds/ Snap	Pos%	Blitz%
2018	389	339	22.9%	63.7%	5.9	38.8%	36.3%	6.5	36.1%	1.0%

Blessuan Austin

Rutgers Scarlet Knights
Final Grade: 6.2 CB Rank: 24 of 26

Height	Weight	Year	Jersey #	Hometown
6002	195	4SR	1	Queens, NY

One-Liner
Austin possesses the natural talent to eventually become a starting outside cornerback in the NFL if he can return to full health after another knee surgery, but for now conservatively projects as a versatile secondary reserve.

Overall
Austin played outside corner at Rutgers on both the left and right side of the field, primarily in a press-coverage scheme. He was a four-year starter for the Scarlet Knights, although his 2017 and 2018 campaigns were both cut short due to a torn ACL in his right knee. He competed in 27 games, starting all but one of those. Austin is an above-average, physical athlete with good shadow ability and decent recovery speed. Austin brought the same physicality to every play, always engaging the receiver at the snap.

Pass Game
Against the pass, Austin is a long corner who likes to play in his receiver's face off the line. He is a good press corner who jams and trails well. His ball skills and length allow him to make plays and compete at the catch point, and he has flashed the ability to make highlight reel catches. While Austin generally maintains coverage of his receiver, he can struggle to transition if his receiver breaks inside. He does have good recovery speed, however, and is generally well positioned to make immediate tackles. He reads quarterbacks well in zone and demonstrates good route anticipation.

Run Game
Against the run, Austin does a good job of filling run lanes and making tackles in the open field, but he struggles to disengage from receivers at times. He is a sufficient participant in run support but won't go out of his way to attack downhill.

Last Word
With health, Austin projects well as a solid, versatile reserve defensive back at the next level. By his second year, he has the potential to become a starting outside corner in the NFL, but it will depend heavily on how his athleticism and cutting ability remain affected from his serious knee injuries. His length, speed, awareness, and injury history (which possibly contributed to impaired change-of-direction skills) might make him a good candidate for free safety. He should be a fine special teams player.

– Gennady Gusak

Strengths	Weaknesses
• Man coverage	• Injury history
• Awareness	• Change of direction
• Ball skills and length	• Slot coverage

Critical Factors

Reactive Athleticism	Play Speed	Ball Skills
5	6	6

Positional Factors

Off-Man	Press Man	Zone Coverage	Slot Coverage
6	6	6	5
Transition	**Closing Speed**	**Football Intelligence**	**Mental Toughness**
5	5	5	6
Open-Field Tackling	**Play Strength**	**Run Support**	**Special Teams Value**
6	5	5	6

Basic

	Coverage									Tackling	
Year	Trgt	Comp	Comp%	Yards	Yds/Trgt	Int	Int Drops	TD Allowed	Tackles	TFL
2016	42	20	47.6%	317	7.5	1	1	2	41	1.0
2017	11	5	45.5%	82	7.5	1	0	0	11	0.0
2018	2	0	0.0%	0	0.0	1	0	0	3	2.0
	55	25	45.5%	399	7.3	3	1	2	55	3.0

Advanced

	Coverage							Tackling	
Year	Pass Breakups	Pos%	Deserved Catch%	YAC	Rating	EPA	EPA/ Trgt	Broken Tackles	BT%
2016	14	47.6%	58.8%	42	69.2	6.3	0.15	8	16.3%
2017	2	45.5%	87.5%	3	33.1	2.2	0.20	1	8.3%
2018	1	0.0%	0.0%	0	0.0	-4.1	-2.06	0	0.0%
	17	45.5%	62.8%	45	52.0	4.3	0.08	9	14.1%

Deep Dive

	Total Snaps		Lined Up	Man Coverage			Zone Coverage			Blitz
Year	Pass	Run	Slot%	Man%	Yds/ Snap	Pos%	Zone%	Yds/ Snap	Pos%	Blitz%
2018	8	9	0.0%	80.0%	0.0	0.0%	20.0%	4.0	0.0%	12.5%

Isaiah Johnson

Houston Cougars
Final Grade: 6.0 CB Rank: 25 of 26

Height	Weight	Year	Jersey #	Hometown
6022	207	5SR	14	Bryan, TX

One-Liner
Johnson is a cornerback with great size and the athleticism worthy of development due to his lack of experience playing the position.

Overall
Johnson is a cornerback who has primarily played out wide. In his sophomore season, Johnson appeared in 11 games as a wide receiver for the Cougars. As a junior, he played in all 12 games as a cornerback, starting 5, and then went on to become the full-time starter as a senior. Johnson is a great athlete. As a former track star and wide receiver, he has great speed and a fluid motion in and out of cuts. He showed toughness taking this position switch in stride and learning enough to become their leading corner.

Pass Game
In the pass game, Johnson is solid in man coverage tracking his receiver. He has fluid hips and solid speed, allowing him to stay in line with his man. In zone, he has shown impressive read-and-react ability for someone new to the position. His experience as a receiver lends itself to very good ball skills.

Run Game
In the run game, Johnson simply needs to be more physical and willing to set the edge when necessary. He is the frequent target of screens due to not physically engaging the lead blocker in a sufficient way. Can make the tackle when in position but doesn't do enough to get himself there.

Last Word
Johnson projects as a developmental corner, and a worthwhile one at that due to his size and athleticism. He has shown surprising comfortability making the position change, and he has the physical tools to become a solid outside press corner with his length and potential, given the right developmental environment.

– Conor Dickinson

Strengths	Weaknesses
• Length	• Transition
• Ball skills	• Short area quickness
• Read-and-react in zone	• Position inexperience

Critical Factors

Reactive Athleticism	Play Speed	Ball Skills
5	6	7

Positional Factors

Off-Man	Press Man	Zone Coverage	Slot Coverage
5	5	6	4
Transition	**Closing Speed**	**Football Intelligence**	**Mental Toughness**
4	6	6	6
Open-Field Tackling	**Play Strength**	**Run Support**	**Special Teams Value**
5	5	4	6

Basic

	Coverage								Tackling	
Year	Trgt	Comp	Comp%	Yards	Yds/Trgt	Int	Int Drops	TD Allowed	Tackles	TFL
2016	0		-	0	-	0	0		5	0.0
2017	45	24	53.3%	238	5.3	2	1	1	45	0.0
2018	69	39	56.5%	559	8.1	2	0	3	66	0.5
	114	63	55.3%	797	7.0	4	1	4	116	0.5

Advanced

	Coverage							Tackling	
Year	Pass Breakups	Pos%	Deserved Catch%	YAC	Rating	EPA	EPA/ Trgt	Broken Tackles	BT%
2016	0	-	-	0	-	0.0	-	0	0.0%
2017	10	44.4%	74.3%	32	68.2	-3.7	-0.08	4	8.2%
2018	9	52.2%	84.9%	76	73.3	2.2	0.03	10	13.2%
	19	49.1%	80.7%	108	71.3	-1.6	-0.01	14	10.8%

Deep Dive

	Total Snaps		Lined Up	Man Coverage			Zone Coverage			Blitz
Year	Pass	Run	Slot%	Man%	Yds/ Snap	Pos%	Zone%	Yds/ Snap	Pos%	Blitz%
2018	360	371	5.3%	27.8%	6.1	44.0%	72.2%	6.7	41.7%	1.6%

Montre Hartage

Northwestern Wildcats
Final Grade: 5.9 CB Rank: 26 of 26

Height	Weight	Year	Jersey #	Hometown
5110	187	4SR	24	Cordele, GA

One-Liner
Hartage is a long-armed, physical corner with very good ball skills, but he needs some time and proper coaching to get rid of some bad habits he learned in college.

Overall
Hartage played cornerback in a base 4-3 defense that primarily played Cover 3 zone. He usually shadowed the offense's number one receiver and played both sides of the field. He was a 4-year player and 3-year starter, appearing in 51 games. He is a solid athlete with good footwork and long arms, which help him stay with defenders well in man coverage.

Pass Game
In the passing game, he shows very good ball skills and does a great job of tracking the ball in the air and is very physical at the point of attack contesting passes. He struggles in zone coverage for many reasons. He has a tough time reading plays and seems to break late on the ball. He has stiff hips, which make it tough for him to transition fluidly. He gets beat on 10-yard digs and curls with ease because of his stiff hips and difficult transition. He does a good job in man coverage. He is never really asked to press, but has long arms and plays physical, so he shows the ability. Montre is a ballhawk with a high number of pass breakups and interceptions in his career.

Run Game
In the run game, he is a good tackler who gets the job done, but he is not very physical and always receives the hit instead of giving it. He very rarely sticks his nose in the line of scrimmage to make a tackle. He shows flashes that he can be aggressive in the run game but does not do it consistently. He is a tough, physical corner who brings it on every pass play, but he sometimes seems unwilling and uninterested to engage in the run game.

Last Word
Hartage projects as a No. 4 CB who can play in dime situations. On 3rd downs, he fits best outside. He possesses the skill set to contribute in some capacity on special teams.

– Austin Cochran

Strengths	Weaknesses
• Ball skills	• Top-end speed
• Press man ability	• Struggles to read plays
• Good tackler	• Unbalanced in backpedal

Critical Factors

Reactive Athleticism	Play Speed	Ball Skills
6	6	7

Positional Factors

Off-Man	Press Man	Zone Coverage	Slot Coverage
6	6	5	5
Transition	**Closing Speed**	**Football Intelligence**	**Mental Toughness**
5	6	5	6
Open-Field Tackling	**Play Strength**	**Run Support**	**Special Teams Value**
6	6	5	6

Basic

	Coverage								Tackling	
Year	Trgt	Comp	Comp%	Yards	Yds/Trgt	Int	Int Drops	TD Allowed	Tackles	TFL
2016	61	30	49.2%	464	7.6	5	0	1	62	0.0
2017	92	46	50.0%	540	5.9	3	0	1	58	1.5
2018	75	34	45.3%	525	7.0	2	0	2	54	1.0
	228	110	48.2%	1529	6.7	10	0	4	174	2.5

Advanced

	Coverage							Tackling	
Year	Pass Breakups	Pos%	Deserved Catch%	YAC	Rating	EPA	EPA/ Trgt	Broken Tackles	BT%
2016	12	45.9%	72.3%	56	52.9	-3.2	-0.05	6	8.8%
2017	12	41.3%	72.3%	45	53.7	-12.8	-0.14	5	7.9%
2018	14	42.7%	60.0%	61	72.4	2.2	0.03	4	6.9%
	38	43.0%	68.3%	162	59.6	-13.7	-0.06	15	7.9%

Deep Dive

	Total Snaps		Lined Up	Man Coverage			Zone Coverage			Blitz
Year	Pass	Run	Slot%	Man%	Yds/ Snap	Pos%	Zone%	Yds/ Snap	Pos%	Blitz%
2018	359	320	26.9%	32.5%	5.1	30.7%	67.5%	7.6	46.7%	0.3%

Glossary

Broken Tackles
Tackle attempts where the defender failed to bring down the ballcarrier. Counts both broken tackles (physical) and missed tackles (elusive)

BT%
Percentage of tackle attempts where the defender failed to bring down the ballcarrier. Counts both broken tackles (physical) and missed tackles (elusive)

Deserved Catch%
The percentage of targets as the primary defender that the receiver either caught or dropped the ball when the pass was catchable

Pass Breakups
The number of times the defender batted, deflected or defensed a pass

Pos% (Coverage split)
The percentage of plays where the defender was targeted that resulted in a positive EPA (a successful play for the offense)

Rating (Coverage split)
Traditional Passer Rating on passes where the defender was targeted

Rush%
Percentage of quarterback dropbacks where the defender rushed the quarterback

Slot%
Percentage of plays the defender lined up across from a slot receiver

Cornerback Leaderboards

Deserved Catch Percentage Leaders

Rank	Player	Team	Deserved Catch%
1	Jamel Dean	Auburn	59.3%
2	Greedy Williams	LSU	60.0%
3	Montre Hartage	Northwestern	60.0%
4	Deandre Baker	Georgia	60.6%
5	Michael Jackson	Miami FL	63.0%
6	Kendall Sheffield	Ohio State	63.9%
7	Duke Shelley	Kansas State	64.3%
8	Julian Love	Notre Dame	64.3%
9	Nik Needham	UTEP	66.7%
10	Joejuan Williams	Vanderbilt	68.8%

Broken Tackle Percentage Leaders

Rank	Player	Team	BT%
1	Nate Meadors	UCLA	0.0%
2	Deandre Baker	Georgia	2.4%
3	Kendall Sheffield	Ohio State	2.6%
4	Rock Ya-Sin	Temple	3.9%
5	Montre Hartage	Northwestern	6.9%
6	Joejuan Williams	Vanderbilt	7.0%
7	Iman Marshall	USC	7.5%
8	Trayvon Mullen	Clemson	7.7%
9	Byron Murphy	Washington	8.2%
10	Saivion Smith	Alabama	8.2%

Passer Rating Allowed Leaders

Rank	Player	Team	Rating
1	Michael Jackson	Miami FL	34.3
2	Greedy Williams	LSU	43.3
3	Jamel Dean	Auburn	45.5
4	Deandre Baker	Georgia	46.3
5	Duke Shelley	Kansas State	47.1
6	Joejuan Williams	Vanderbilt	47.9
7	Hamp Cheevers	Boston College	48.2
8	Nate Brooks	North Texas	51.1
9	Trayvon Mullen	Clemson	52.0
10	Byron Murphy	Washington	54.2

Yards Per Man Coverage Snap Leaders

Rank	Player	Team	Yds/Snap
1	Amani Oruwariye	Penn State	4.0
2	Michael Jackson	Miami FL	4.2
3	Deandre Baker	Georgia	4.3
4	Lonnie Johnson Jr.	Kentucky	4.4
5	Trayvon Mullen	Clemson	4.6
6	Jamel Dean	Auburn	4.6
7	Byron Murphy	Washington	4.8
8	Greedy Williams	LSU	4.9
9	Rock Ya-Sin	Temple	4.9
10	Jordan Miller	Washington	4.9

Tackles Leaders

Rank	Player	Team	Tackles
1	Nate Brooks	North Texas	69
2	Joejuan Williams	Vanderbilt	66
3	Isaiah Johnson	Houston	66
4	Kris Boyd	Texas	65
5	Julian Love	Notre Dame	63
6	Nik Needham	UTEP	59
7	Ugochukwu Amadi	Oregon	57
8	Byron Murphy	Washington	56
9	Saivion Smith	Alabama	56
10	Montre Hartage	Northwestern	54

Yards Per Zone Coverage Snap Leaders

Rank	Player	Team	Yds/Snap
1	Julian Love	Notre Dame	4.2
2	Rock Ya-Sin	Temple	4.4
3	Trayvon Mullen	Clemson	4.9
4	Lonnie Johnson Jr.	Kentucky	5.0
5	Jordan Miller	Washington	5.1
6	Duke Shelley	Kansas State	5.2
7	Jamal Peters	Mississippi State	5.2
8	Byron Murphy	Washington	5.2
9	Amani Oruwariye	Penn State	5.3
10	Michael Jackson	Miami FL	5.4

SAFETY

Safety Grading Scale

GRADE	DESCRIPTION
9.0 – 7.0	High-end 3 down starter. Pro Bowl level.
6.9 – 6.7	Strong starter who plays on all 3 downs.
6.4	3rd safety. Low-end starter.
6.2	Versatile backup with CB/DS flexibility.
6.1 – 6.0	Developmental. Top traits but needs time.
5.9	2 down starter. Box safety only.
5.8	Average backup. 4th DS. Quality special teamer.
5.7	Low-end backup DS with growable upside.

Safety Rankings

Rank	Name	Grade	Page
1	Taylor Rapp	7.0	542
2	Deionte Thompson	6.9	544
3	Johnathan Abram	6.8	546
4	Chauncey Gardner-Johnson	6.8	548
5	Nasir Adderley	6.7	550
6	Jaquan Johnson	6.7	552
7	Marvell Tell III	6.4	554
8	Amani Hooker	6.4	556
9	Darnell Savage Jr.	6.4	558
10	Mike Edwards	6.4	560
11	Mark McLaurin	6.4	562
12	Juan Thornhill	6.4	564
13	Andrew Wingard	6.4	566
14	Khari Willis	6.4	568
15	Sheldrick Redwine	6.4	570
16	Jalen Young	6.2	572
17	Demetrius Flannigan-Fowles	6.2	574
18	Lukas Denis	6.2	576
19	McKinley Whitfield	5.9	578
20	Zedrick Woods	5.9	580

Taylor Rapp

Washington Huskies
Final Grade: 7.0 S Rank: 1 of 20

Height	Weight	Year	Jersey #	Hometown
5116	200	3JR	7	Bellingham, WA

One-Liner
Rapp is an instinctive, rangy safety with an extremely high motor, who makes plays from all over the field and arrives at the ball with aggression.

Overall
Rapp lined up all over the field in Washington's base nickel defense, mostly as a strong safety but also with snaps as a two- or single-high safety. He can often be found in and around the box, either starting or finishing a play there. He started in 35 of 40 career games. He has a good, long body for the position, but is a bit thin for his style of play. He is an explosive athlete with great burst and fluid movement skills in space. Rapp is a leader in the secondary with his communication skills, and plays with an extremely high motor, flying to the ball on every play and finishing with aggression.

Pass Game
Against the pass, he plays smart and disciplined football. He has the ability to drop into his zones quickly from all over the field and doesn't sell out on runs when playing in the box. Rapp is comfortable in zone and flies to the ball with smooth downhill transitions. He isn't often used in man but has the change-of-direction ability and recovery speed to be successful. He does a good job as a single-high safety and his range allows him to defend the middle of the field, but his reading abilities are better used closer to the line. He isn't a natural ball hawk and plays his man more often than the ball in coverage. Rapp is an excellent blitzer near the line. He is very impactful with his closing speed and physicality to work with the front seven on stunts and disrupt backfields.

Run Game
In the run game, he has a good feel for run-game flow and his range against the run is elite. Rapp plays with good leverage and is a strong force player on the edges. His strength when playing as a true extra linebacker is limited and he struggles to win inside with anything other than physicality and aggression. Rapp noticeably plays with the highest motor on the field at all times, as he makes plays from the backside with regularity and always finds himself around the ball. He is an impressive, under control open-field tackler, who does a great job of breaking down and strafing like a basketball player near the point of attack. He takes great angles to the ball from all levels of the field and has the speed to get there. He explodes at contact and makes up for his stoutness well.

Last Word
Rapp should be an excellent special teams player at the next level. He projects as a very physical and versatile high-end starting safety, who best fits near the box and slot at strong safety, but has the back-end comfortability and range to be interchangeable. His effort and motor are elite traits that should translate immediately.

– Alex O'Brien

Strengths	Weaknesses
• Instincts and anticipation • Range and motor • Physicality	• Ball-hawking traits • Strength in box

Critical Factors

3-Level Impact	Intelligence / Instincts	Play Speed
6	7	7

Positional Factors

Man Coverage	Zone Coverage	Ball Skills / Tracking
6	6	5
Range	**Tackling**	**Toughness / Physicality**
8	7	7

Leadership	Special Teams Value
7	8

Basic

	Coverage								Tackling	
Year	Trgt	Comp	Comp%	Yards	Yds/Trgt	Int	Int Drops	TD Allowed	Tackles	TFL
2016	16	11	68.8%	82	5.1	4	0	0	55	0.5
2017	18	11	61.1%	86	4.8	1	0	0	60	3.5
2018	12	5	41.7%	39	3.3	2	2	0	57	6.0
	46	27	58.7%	207	4.5	7	2	0	172	10.0

Advanced

	Coverage					Tackling			
Year	Pass Breakups	Pos%	Deserved Catch%	EPA	EPA/ Trgt	Broken Tackles	BT%	Tackle Share	Avg Depth of Tackle
2016	6	37.5%	78.6%	-7.5	-0.47	3	5.7%	5.5%	10.5
2017	1	38.9%	100.0%	-5.6	-0.31	6	9.7%	6.5%	8.4
2018	7	16.7%	58.3%	-6.5	-0.54	2	3.6%	5.8%	8.6
	14	32.6%	80.0%	-19.6	-0.43	11	6.5%	5.9%	9.1

Deep Dive

	Total Snaps		Lined Up		Man Coverage			Blitz		
Year	Pass	Run	Slot%	Box%	Trgt	Yds/Trgt	Pos%	Blitz%	Pressure%	Sack%
2018	422	377	14.4%	14.3%	5	1.2	0.0%	9.4%	29.3%	12.2%

Deionte Thompson

Alabama Crimson Tide
Final Grade: 6.9 S Rank: 2 of 20

Height	Weight	Year	Jersey #	Hometown
6012	196	4JR	14	Orange, TX

One-Liner
Thompson possesses length, range, aggression, and athleticism at the catch point, and he profiles as an immediate NFL starter in the middle of a secondary.

Overall
Thompson played free safety in Alabama's base nickel defense. He played in 43 career games with 17 starts, nearly all coming his final season. He is thin, but tall and very long. He is an excellent athlete with great leaping ability, fluid hips, and very good speed, aided by his long strides. He moves very easily and occasionally can seem to take some plays off, but Thompson is aggressive downhill and compensates for his lack of play strength by arriving at the ball with force.

Pass Game
In coverage, Thompson lines up mostly as the deep safety in Cover 1 or 3, while occasionally lining up over the slot or rolling into underneath zones. Thompson is an extremely rangy deep safety who is very comfortable in his role as a center fielder. His instincts, ability to eat up grass sideline-to-sideline, and athleticism at the catch point allow him to make plays all over the third level of the field. He is smooth in his backpedal and transitions with flexible hips. Thompson can cover a ton of ground with his long legs and speed, but his easy movement skills sometimes turn into taking it easy. He has the potential to reach more balls than he does, but after the first few weeks of the season, teams stopped throwing near him down the seams. His feel for short zones is good and he has decent man coverage abilities, but his long limbs can look out of place in quick change-of-direction slot situations. Thompson also has experience playing wide receiver earlier in his college career, and it shows in his ball skills and high-pointing ability. He drives on the ball and undercuts receivers well. He will also roll into blitzes, and he uses his speed and length to come off the edge and disrupt.

Run Game
Against the run, Thompson is a physical presence despite his lanky, slender frame. He flies downhill and does a good job of attacking the outside leg. To make up for his relative lack of play strength, he throws his body around with physicality and puts his all into his hits. He misses a number of tackles, however, due to his poor form and inability to wrap up with sound, strong technique. He is a good force defender and his aggression allows him to play in the box when needed.

Last Word
Thompson had to wait his turn at Alabama but proved himself this year. He profiles as an immediate free safety starter at the next level, with range and ball skills to quickly make an impact. He has the ability to play at all three levels of the field, as well as on multiple special teams units, but he best fits in the middle of the field reading the quarterback's eyes and negating the seams.

– John Todd

Strengths

- Athletic ball skills
- Length and range
- Downhill aggression

Weaknesses

- Form tackling
- Quickness in slot

Critical Factors

3-Level Impact	Intelligence / Instincts	Play Speed
7	7	7

Positional Factors

Man Coverage	Zone Coverage	Ball Skills / Tracking
5	6	8
Range	**Tackling**	**Toughness / Physicality**
8	5	7
Leadership	**Special Teams Value**	
5	7	

Basic

	Coverage								Tackling	
Year	Trgt	Comp	Comp%	Yards	Yds/Trgt	Int	Int Drops	TD Allowed	Tackles	TFL
2016	0	0	-	0	-	0	0	0	8	0.0
2017	5	3	60.0%	36	7.2	1	0	0	26	1.0
2018	27	13	48.1%	149	5.5	2	1	3	80	3.0
	32	16	50.0%	185	5.8	3	1	3	114	4.0

Advanced

	Coverage					Tackling			
Year	Pass Breakups	Pos%	Deserved Catch%	EPA	EPA/ Trgt	Broken Tackles	BT%	Tackle Share	Avg Depth of Tackle
2016	0	-	-	0.0	-	2	50.0%	0.2%	7.3
2017	2	40.0%	100.0%	-6.3	-1.27	3	12.5%	2.5%	7.4
2018	8	29.6%	71.4%	0.3	0.01	17	17.9%	8.6%	9.3
	10	31.3%	75.0%	-6.1	-0.19	22	17.9%	3.7%	8.8

Deep Dive

	Total Snaps		Lined Up		Man Coverage			Blitz		
Year	Pass	Run	Slot%	Box%	Trgt	Yds/Trgt	Pos%	Blitz%	Pressure%	Sack%
2018	480	407	8.2%	2.0%	20	4.7	35.0%	1.4%	14.3%	7.1%

Johnathan Abram

Mississippi State Bulldogs
Final Grade: 6.8 S Rank: 3 of 20

Height	Weight	Year	Jersey #	Hometown
5112	215	4SR	38	Columbia, MS

One-Liner
Abram is a competitor who has the instincts and physicality to play in the box as well as the speed and range to play deep, but needs to improve his overall coverage ability at the next level.

Overall
Abram played SS, FS and Star at Mississippi State, playing deep, around the box, and in the slot. He was a 2-year starter at Mississippi State, appearnig in 26 games after coming over from Georgia (2015) and Jones County CC (2016). Abram is a very good athlete who plays fast and with good hip fluidity. He is a fierce competitor who is willing to challenge any opponent.

Pass Game
In the pass game, Abram needs to develop both his man coverage and zone coverage skills. In man coverage, he displays fluid hips, but does lose some speed when transitioning from his backpedal. Abram needs to react quickly to receivers' breaks as he can get caught flat-footed which allows for separation. He can get beat in a straight line down the seam and doesn't have the closing speed to catch up, but has enough speed to keep up with most slot receivers. He has some issues with tracking the ball as he struggles to get his head around on deep throws. He is a very physical player and isn't afraid to jam receivers on their routes, at times getting a little too handsy. In off-man, he has the speed to close and get to the ball in a hurry, making a tackle at the point of the catch or breaking up the pass. In zone coverage, he does a very good job of reading the quarterback while sitting in shallow zones, ready to close on any pass-catchers in the area and make a play on the ball. As a single-high, he has the speed to be very rangy and cover a lot of ground. He communicates well with his teammates on the back end.

Run Game
In the run game, Abram can succeed anywhere on the field. In the box, he is a very active player who can fill gaps with authority. He runs alleys well with good angles and pursuit to come down and make plays around the LOS. He is a very physical player who is always looking to deliver a big hit. His aggression comes at the cost of good tackling technique and he is prone to putting his head down and missing tackles, but he has an excellent ability to finish on contact. Abram's play strength makes him a nightmare to block for tight ends and receivers, as he has shown an ability to throw blockers aside in the open field on his way to the ball.

Last Word
Abram projects as a starting SS at the next level, but can interchangeably play FS and in the slot. On 3rd downs, he fits best around the box where he can use his range and physicality. His speed, aggression, and tackling ability translate very well to special teams and will make for an immediate contributor in that area.

– Nick Aiello

Strengths	**Weaknesses**
• Play speed • Leadership • Physicality	• Pass coverage • Over-aggressive

Critical Factors

3-Level Impact	Intelligence / Instincts	Play Speed
6	7	7

Positional Factors

Man Coverage	Zone Coverage	Ball Skills / Tracking
5	6	6
Range	**Tackling**	**Toughness / Physicality**
7	7	7
Leadership	**Special Teams Value**	
7	8	

Basic

	Coverage								Tackling	
Year	Trgt	Comp	Comp%	Yards	Yds/Trgt	Int	Int Drops	TD Allowed	Tackles	TFL
2017	24	13	54.2%	153	6.4	0	1	1	73	4.0
2018	38	18	47.4%	259	6.8	2	1	1	95	6.5
	62	31	50.0%	412	6.6	2	2	2	168	10.5

Advanced

	Coverage					Tackling			
Year	Pass Breakups	Pos%	Deserved Catch%	EPA	EPA/ Trgt	Broken Tackles	BT%	Tackle Share	Avg Depth of Tackle
2017	5	37.5%	73.7%	2.0	0.08	13	15.7%	9.0%	10.8
2018	6	31.6%	80.0%	-5.3	-0.14	13	12.5%	10.8%	8.6
	11	33.9%	77.3%	-3.3	-0.05	26	13.9%	10.0%	9.6

Deep Dive

	Total Snaps		Lined Up		Man Coverage			Blitz		
Year	Pass	Run	Slot%	Box%	Trgt	Yds/Trgt	Pos%	Blitz%	Pressure%	Sack%
2018	394	347	30.1%	11.5%	22	7.0	27.3%	12.4%	37.3%	5.9%

Chauncey Gardner-Johnson

Florida Gators
Final Grade: 6.8 S Rank: 4 of 20

Height	Weight	Year	Jersey #	Hometown
6000	205	3JR	23	Cocoa, FL

One-Liner
Gardner-Johnson is a versatile defender who has the play speed, range, and toughness to be a successful 3-level defender at the next level.

Overall
Gardner-Johnson's primary position was slot CB in Florida's hybrid 3-3-5 defense and rarely played in the deep third of the field. He'll line up around the LOS whether he's in coverage or in the box playing the run. He played in 37 games for the Gators, starting in 24 of them. He is a very good athlete with quick feet and good body control. He is very shifty with his movements. He plays fast, quick and aggressive with good balance and flexibility. He's rugged, competitive and plays tough.

Pass Game
Against the pass, he's physical at the line of scrimmage, engaging with his hands, and has the length and play speed to guard a WR or TE in the slot. He is good in man and zone coverage. In man, he displays good transition ability, but peeks in the backfield at times and loses track of his man. He's also susceptible to double moves. He tracks the ball well, possesses ball skills and has the instincts to jump routes. In zone, he's able to keep his eyes in the backfield and find receivers crossing into his zone. He's used to blitzing from the CB position on occasion and makes plays in the backfield.

Run Game
In the run game, he can tackle at all levels of the field. He's not afraid to take on blockers and likes to be physical. He can play in the box and make tackles at the line of scrimmage. He can play in center field, make open-field tackles and has the speed to make touchdown saving tackles. He has a tendency to play over-aggressive and run past some tackle opportunities. His pursuit angles will get less sharp as the game progresses and his play speed decreases. His stamina noticeably dips late in games, having essentially played in the slot and around the box for the entirety.

Last Word
Gardner-Johnson projects as a SS at the next level who can interchange at FS and also be the Nickel CB. Although he didn't play much on the back end in college, his range, instincts and ball skills will allow him to succeed in that role. His versatility will allow defensive coaches to place him just about anywhere in any scheme. On 3rd down, he should play closer to the line to use his physicality against slot receivers. His speed and toughness make for a heavy contribution on special teams at the next level.

– Ian Riley

Strengths	**Weaknesses**
• Versatility	• Stamina
• Play speed	• Over-pursuit
• Range	

Critical Factors

3-Level Impact	Intelligence / Instincts	Play Speed
6	6	7

Positional Factors

Man Coverage	Zone Coverage	Ball Skills / Tracking
6	6	6
Range	**Tackling**	**Toughness / Physicality**
7	6	7

Leadership	Special Teams Value
7	7

Basic

	Coverage								Tackling	
Year	Trgt	Comp	Comp%	Yards	Yds/Trgt	Int	Int Drops	TD Allowed	Tackles	TFL
2016	9	6	66.7%	107	11.9	3	1	1	32	0.5
2017	19	9	47.4%	128	6.7	2	0	0	57	6.0
2018	51	21	41.2%	226	4.4	4	0	0	70	6.5
	79	36	45.6%	461	5.8	9	1	1	159	13.0

Advanced

	Coverage					Tackling			
Year	Pass Breakups	Pos%	Deserved Catch%	EPA	EPA/ Trgt	Broken Tackles	BT%	Tackle Share	Avg Depth of Tackle
2016	5	55.6%	75.0%	7.6	0.84	10	29.4%	3.0%	12.0
2017	8	36.8%	66.7%	-5.2	-0.28	20	26.0%	8.6%	9.5
2018	7	23.5%	71.0%	-32.8	-0.64	9	12.3%	7.5%	7.2
	20	30.4%	70.2%	-30.5	-0.39	39	21.2%	6.3%	8.9

Deep Dive

	Total Snaps		Lined Up		Man Coverage			Blitz		
Year	Pass	Run	Slot%	Box%	Trgt	Yds/Trgt	Pos%	Blitz%	Pressure%	Sack%
2018	333	297	91.9%	4.0%	31	4.2	22.6%	4.5%	37.5%	12.5%

Nasir Adderley

Delaware Fightin' Blue Hens
Final Grade: 6.7 S Rank: 5 of 20

Height	Weight	Year	Jersey #	Hometown
5117	195	4SR	23	Philadelphia, PA

One-Liner
Adderley has the instincts, speed, and ball skills to start at safety at the next level, but he'll need to improve his pursuit angles to produce more against the run.

Overall
Adderley played FS for Delaware, which primarily uses zone concepts out of both 1- and 2-high looks. He started all 45 games he played in for the Blue Hens. He's a twitchy athlete who has fluid hips and very good play speed. He competes from down to down and plays with toughness and physicality. He played CB his first two seasons before switching to safety his last two. He plays with instincts, but there are times when he looks lost.

Pass Game
In the pass game, he shows the tracking ability to make plays on the ball. His ball skills show up not only in defending passes but also in interceptions. He made some highlight-reel interceptions against Richmond. His 3-level ability shows up in the intermediate and deep levels in the passing game. His range is good enough that he's able to fly around from the middle of the field to the sideline in either a 1-high or 2-high look. He has the closing speed to make up a lot of ground quickly whether it be toward the sideline or down the field. His speed and instincts allow him to be successful in deep zone coverage. He can play man coverage on tight ends and backs out of the backfield as a slot corner. He has experience at corner, but struggles to transition quickly enough on the outside. He didn't show a ton of communication but did get some guys lined up on occasion.

Run Game
In the run game, he isn't afraid to be physical. He's aggressive in run support and flies downhill and to the edge. The biggest issue for him is figuring out his angles. He pursues the ball extremely well and quickly, but takes poor angles, missing out on a lot of opportunities to make plays. When he does meet a ballcarrier, his tackling is good enough to bring them down with consistency, but he does tend to throw shoulders instead of wrapping up. He'll make tackles all over the field.

Last Word
Adderley projects as a starting FS in any scheme and is versatile enough to play SS and slot CB as well. On 3rd downs, he fits best as a deep defender where he can use his range against the pass. His playing style, speed, and physicality suggest that he should be a core special teams contributor.

– Nathan Cooper

Strengths	Weaknesses
• Ball skills • Rangy • Play speed	• Takes poor angles • Looks lost at times

Critical Factors

3-Level Impact	Intelligence / Instincts	Play Speed
6	6	7

Positional Factors

Man Coverage	Zone Coverage	Ball Skills / Tracking
5	6	6
Range	**Tackling**	**Toughness / Physicality**
6	6	6

Leadership	Special Teams Value
6	7

Adderley has one of the more impressive mentors of anyone in this year's draft class. His grandfather's cousin Herb Adderley was a Hall of Fame defensive back who won three Super Bowls with the Packers and Cowboys.

Nasir Adderley had a career-high 87 tackles for the Blue Hens as a senior. He also led the team with four interceptions. Delaware has a good NFL draft history, with defensive tackle Bilal Nichols being the most recent selection by the Bears last season. But Adderley will be the first defensive back selected from the school since George Schmitt in 1983.

Adderley has said he wants to be an "interchangeable" player. Versatility was a part of Herb Adderley's repertoire as well. Herb was a running back at Michigan State before converting to defensive back.

Jaquan Johnson

Miami FL Hurricanes
Final Grade: 6.7 S Rank: 6 of 20

Height	Weight	Year	Jersey #	Hometown
5103	186	4SR	4	Miami, FL

One-Liner
Johnson is a slightly undersized, but very instinctual and high-motor box safety who can also play free, with the physicality and intangibles that suggest he can start in the NFL.

Overall
Johnson's primary position is SS, but due to Miami's scheme, Johnson also frequently lined up at FS and OLB. He was a 4-year player and 2-year starter at SS, appearing in 50 games. He is a good athlete with good play speed and range. He is a very intelligent player with very good football instincts and plays with a high motor. Johnson doesn't give up on a play and he hasn't met someone that he doesn't want to hit. He was the heart and soul of the Miami defense and there was a noticeable difference when he was not on the field. He is very talkative and is usually the one responsible for lining up the defensive backs based on what the offense is showing.

Pass Game
Against the pass, Johnson is solid in man coverage. He can run with most receivers but will tend to get a bit grabby when matched up against bigger, more physical opponents due to his size limitations. Johnson is good in zone coverage and fully capable of playing a center fielder role. He also showcases good ball skills when opponents throw his way.

Run Game
Against the run, Johnson plays with very good toughness, especially for someone of his size. He takes very good angles and can tackle at all levels of the field. He has good power, especially when he gets going downfield, and he loves to come in with a big hit on a cleanup tackle.

Last Word
His size may cause some concern, but he certainly plays bigger than his measurements and hasn't had any significant durability concerns. Due to his leadership, intelligence, and his ability against both the run and pass, Johnson projects as a starting strong safety by his second season at the next level but has the instincts and ability to also play FS if asked or if the scheme warrants. His playing style suggests that he could potentially be a special teams captain and contribute on nearly every unit.

– Ronan Potts

Strengths
- FBI/Instincts/Intangibles
- Clutch tackling
- Run support/hustle

Weaknesses
- Timed speed
- Lower-body strength/size

Critical Factors

3-Level Impact	Intelligence / Instincts	Play Speed
6	7	6

Positional Factors

Man Coverage	Zone Coverage	Ball Skills / Tracking
6	6	6
Range	**Tackling**	**Toughness / Physicality**
6	7	7

Leadership	Special Teams Value
8	7

Basic

	Coverage								Tackling	
Year	Trgt	Comp	Comp%	Yards	Yds/Trgt	Int	Int Drops	TD Allowed	Tackles	TFL
2016	15	7	46.7%	73	4.9	1	2	2	43	3.0
2017	19	13	68.4%	149	7.8	4	1	2	100	3.5
2018	14	9	64.3%	104	7.4	2	0	0	91	1.0
	48	29	60.4%	326	6.8	7	3	4	234	7.5

Advanced

	Coverage					Tackling			
Year	Pass Breakups	Pos%	Deserved Catch%	EPA	EPA/ Trgt	Broken Tackles	BT%	Tackle Share	Avg Depth of Tackle
2016	5	33.3%	72.7%	-0.3	-0.02	4	9.1%	4.7%	8.2
2017	8	63.2%	76.5%	8.2	0.43	7	6.7%	9.7%	10.8
2018	4	57.1%	90.0%	1.8	0.13	3	3.3%	9.4%	8.2
	17	52.1%	78.9%	9.7	0.20	14	5.9%	8.0%	9.3

Deep Dive

	Total Snaps		Lined Up		Man Coverage			Blitz		
Year	Pass	Run	Slot%	Box%	Trgt	Yds/Trgt	Pos%	Blitz%	Pressure%	Sack%
2018	262	365	17.2%	18.8%	8	6.8	37.5%	5.1%	14.3%	0.0%

Marvell Tell III

USC Trojans

Final Grade: 6.4 S Rank: 7 of 20

Height	Weight	Year	Jersey #	Hometown
6021	195	4SR	7	Pasadena, CA

One-Liner
Tell has the athletic traits of a starting-caliber safety, but his technical issues as a man defender, his mediocre deep zone instincts, and his lack of stoutness may hurt him.

Overall
Tell's primary position is FS and he mainly played as a split and MOF safety for USC, although he occasionally played off-man on slot receivers. He has good height and length, but he has a slight build for a safety with spindly legs, and he may struggle to handle routine box duties or man coverage responsibilities against tight ends and larger WRs in the pros. He has very good athleticism for the position.

Pass Game
He's very fluid in his backpedal and quickly transitions both to the sideline and downhill. He does a good job of covering ground when he triggers downhill. Tell demonstrates good route recognition in underneath zone coverage. He has the athletic traits to develop into a good man defender. Tell flashes good recovery speed when beaten in man and has the ability to cut crossing routes. He occasionally becomes flat-footed as route runners erase his cushion from off coverage and he loses a step at the breakpoint as a result. Tell lacks experience in press-man, but his length and athleticism suggest he may be able to develop the ability to press slot WRs at a good level in the pros. He lacks sufficient anticipation as a deep safety and is slow to react to the quarterback loading to throw. He's a former receiver who does a good job of tracking and adjusting to the ball when working forward, laterally, and with his back to the quarterback. He's good at playing the catchpoint and creating PBUs, and extends to attack the ball in the air.

Run Game
Tell takes good pursuit angles in run support and is a willing tackler. He does a sufficient job of keeping his outside shoulder clean when playing inside-out. He is not a form tackler and offers just mediocre hitting power, as he relies on dragging runners down.

Last Word
Tell played special teams for USC as a senior and was honored as a Pac-12 special teams player of the week in 2018. He has the speed, aggression, and pursuit instincts to be a good special teams player in the pros.

– Bryce Rossler

Strengths	Weaknesses
• Ball skills	• Stoutness
• Range	• Man coverage
• Play speed	• Deep zone instincts

Critical Factors

3-Level Impact	Intelligence / Instincts	Play Speed
5	4	6

Positional Factors

Man Coverage	Zone Coverage	Ball Skills / Tracking
5	5	6
Range	**Tackling**	**Toughness / Physicality**
5	5	5
Leadership	**Special Teams Value**	
6	6	

Basic

	Coverage								Tackling	
Year	Trgt	Comp	Comp%	Yards	Yds/Trgt	Int	Int Drops	TD Allowed	Tackles	TFL
2016	11	6	54.5%	110	10.0	1	1	1	41	1.0
2017	27	15	55.6%	164	6.1	3	0	1	89	2.0
2018	37	18	48.6%	183	4.9	1	0	1	59	1.0
	75	39	52.0%	457	6.1	5	1	3	189	4.0

Advanced

	Coverage					Tackling			
Year	Pass Breakups	Pos%	Deserved Catch%	EPA	EPA/ Trgt	Broken Tackles	BT%	Tackle Share	Avg Depth of Tackle
2016	3	45.5%	60.0%	0.3	0.03	8	16.7%	4.7%	8.8
2017	4	37.0%	85.0%	-4.2	-0.16	11	11.1%	8.8%	9.3
2018	5	32.4%	77.8%	-5.5	-0.15	11	15.7%	7.4%	7.2
	12	36.0%	77.2%	-9.4	-0.13	30	13.8%	7.0%	8.5

Deep Dive

	Total Snaps		Lined Up		Man Coverage			Blitz		
Year	Pass	Run	Slot%	Box%	Trgt	Yds/Trgt	Pos%	Blitz%	Pressure%	Sack%
2018	366	345	16.0%	9.4%	22	5.6	31.8%	5.5%	33.3%	0.0%

Amani Hooker

Iowa Hawkeyes
Final Grade: 6.4 S Rank: 8 of 20

Height	Weight	Year	Jersey #	Hometown
5112	210	3JR	27	Minneapolis, MN

One-Liner
Hooker is a highly-intelligent zone defender with great intangibles, but his shortcomings in range and third-level athleticism may keep him from a full-time deep safety role.

Overall
Hooker played strong safety and nickel defensive back in Iowa's zone-heavy defense. He moved from safety to a hybrid nickel role after the fourth game of 2018, as the Hawkeyes transitioned from a base 4-3 to a 4-2-5 defense for the rest of the season. He played in 36 career games and began starting early in his sophomore season. He has average height but good overall size with an athletic build and decent lower body thickness. Hooker has good play speed but is only a decent athlete with flashes of tight hips and sufficient change-of-direction skills. He is a very aggressive player who is always around the ball and attacks with physicality.

Pass Game
In pass coverage, Hooker is a much better zone defender than man, especially from his natural safety position. At strong safety, he was mostly responsible for Cover 2 deep zones and Cover 1 and 3 short robber, hook and flat zones underneath. Hooker is a highly intelligent football player. He is an excellent communicator before, during and after plays, regularly jumping assignments based on his pre-snap reads. He disguises coverages well and has a smooth transition from his backpedal to driving on the ball. He passes off receivers and shows great instincts for his zones. He has sufficient range underneath but couldn't get to some playable balls from two-high. Hooker has good ball skills and natural hands, and has often anticipated throws before the quarterback's load based on his reads and eyes, resulting in pulled passes and extended plays. From his nickel role, he was more responsible for one side of the field, which limited his impact. Hooker is an average man defender who can turn and run well in a straight line but struggles with change of direction and flipping his hips. He was also assigned more disguised blitzes from nickel, where he made an impact jumping into screen passing lanes and offering some pass rush with his motor.

Run Game
Against the run, Hooker is an aggressive, downhill defender. He usually wraps up well and can bring a big hit, but he can overpursue flying to the ball. He is an intelligent pre-snap run blitzer based on motions. He is a very strong force player, taking smart angles to drive his slot blockers outside to keep contain.

Last Word
Hooker projects best as a high-quality third safety at strong and capable starter. He also should be a very good special teams contributor at the next level. He has all the intelligence, leadership, aggression, and motor necessary to succeed, but he is zone dependent and lacks some of the athletic, rangy tools to consistently get to his spots.

– John Todd

Strengths	Weaknesses
• Intelligence and communication	• Deep safety range
• Zone instincts	• Short area quickness
• Physicality and aggression	• Scheme dependent

Critical Factors

3-Level Impact	Intelligence / Instincts	Play Speed
5	8	6

Positional Factors

Man Coverage	Zone Coverage	Ball Skills / Tracking
4	7	6
Range	**Tackling**	**Toughness / Physicality**
5	6	7
Leadership	**Special Teams Value**	
7	7	

Basic

	Coverage								Tackling	
Year	Trgt	Comp	Comp%	Yards	Yds/Trgt	Int	Int Drops	TD Allowed	Tackles	TFL
2016	1	0	0.0%	0	0.0	0	0	0	3	0.0
2017	23	11	47.8%	160	7.0	2	0	3	57	0.0
2018	43	22	51.2%	220	5.1	4	0	2	65	3.5
	67	33	49.3%	380	5.7	6	0	5	125	3.5

Advanced

	Coverage					Tackling			
Year	Pass Breakups	Pos%	Deserved Catch%	EPA	EPA/ Trgt	Broken Tackles	BT%	Tackle Share	Avg Depth of Tackle
2016	0	0.0%	-	-1.2	-1.17	0	-	0.0%	-
2017	6	43.5%	73.3%	2.8	0.12	8	12.5%	6.9%	14.1
2018	11	37.2%	69.7%	-14.2	-0.33	4	6.1%	7.4%	6.1
	17	38.8%	70.8%	-12.6	-0.19	12	9.2%	4.7%	10.1

Deep Dive

	Total Snaps		Lined Up		Man Coverage			Blitz		
Year	Pass	Run	Slot%	Box%	Trgt	Yds/Trgt	Pos%	Blitz%	Pressure%	Sack%
2018	416	381	69.9%	2.5%	19	6.8	42.1%	5.6%	9.5%	4.8%

Darnell Savage Jr.

Maryland Terrapins
Final Grade: 6.4 S Rank: 9 of 20

Height	Weight	Year	Jersey #	Hometown
5110	199	4SR	4	Newark, DE

One-Liner
Savage has the physicality, play speed, and instincts around the short and intermediate levels to be a quality backup and core special teamer at the next level.

Overall
Savage mainly played strong safety in a hybrid 3-4/3-3-5 scheme. The secondary mostly played in a 1-high scheme and Savage usually dropped down around the box on most plays. He played in 45 career games for the Terps. He's a really good athlete with quick-twitch ability. He plays incredibly physical and aggressive from play to play.

Pass Game
In the passing game, he doesn't show much ability to be a deep safety on the back-end. He has good ball skills and tracking ability, but he's more productive in the short and intermediate levels. He plays sufficient man coverage to stick with slot receivers. He plays well in zone coverage and shows good read-and-react ability and instincts to take on crossers and jump routes, although play action will catch him being a bit too aggressive at times. He likes to keep his eyes in the backfield to jump on the first look the offense gives. He also likes to catch receivers at the top of their routes and get hands on them, not letting them cleanly get into their route. What he lacks in range on the back-end, he's able to make up with his play speed. He also shows the ability to be a leader on the field and communicate with his teammates.

Run Game
Against the run, he shows good physicality and run support. Once he sees the handoff, he's flying toward the LOS to make a play on the ballcarrier. However, he will take some bad angles to the ball on occasion. With how aggressive he plays and how quickly he comes up to support the run, most of his tackles happen within a few yards of the LOS.

Last Word
He projects as a No. 3 safety that fits best as a SS, but could play some FS and slot corner on occasion. On 3rd downs, he will be best utilized to play close to the line and use his physicality against the run in 3rd-and-short. He could also play some in the slot on 3rd down to use his physicality against tight ends and his speed against backs. Due to his skill set, he will be a core special teams player that will undoubtedly contribute on all units.

– Nathan Cooper

Strengths	**Weaknesses**
• Physicality • Play speed • Instincts	• Deep-level ability • Consistent man coverage

Critical Factors

3-Level Impact	Intelligence / Instincts	Play Speed
5	6	7

Positional Factors

Man Coverage	Zone Coverage	Ball Skills / Tracking
5	6	6
Range	**Tackling**	**Toughness / Physicality**
6	6	7
Leadership	**Special Teams Value**	
6	7	

Basic

	Coverage								Tackling	
Year	Trgt	Comp	Comp%	Yards	Yds/Trgt	Int	Int Drops	TD Allowed	Tackles	TFL
2016	26	13	50.0%	112	4.3	1	2	1	65	3.5
2017	42	23	54.8%	289	6.9	3	2	0	62	0.0
2018	37	18	48.6%	161	4.4	4	0	0	54	2.5
	105	54	51.4%	562	5.4	8	4	1	181	6.0

Advanced

	Coverage					Tackling			
Year	Pass Breakups	Pos%	Deserved Catch%	EPA	EPA/ Trgt	Broken Tackles	BT%	Tackle Share	Avg Depth of Tackle
2016	4	46.2%	90.0%	-1.7	-0.06	10	13.7%	7.0%	9.9
2017	12	45.2%	70.6%	-1.1	-0.03	22	26.2%	7.5%	14.4
2018	9	37.8%	77.8%	-9.0	-0.24	8	12.9%	6.9%	7.5
	25	42.9%	77.8%	-11.7	-0.11	40	18.3%	7.1%	10.7

Deep Dive

	Total Snaps		Lined Up		Man Coverage			Blitz		
Year	Pass	Run	Slot%	Box%	Trgt	Yds/Trgt	Pos%	Blitz%	Pressure%	Sack%
2018	296	353	22.2%	7.6%	20	3.4	35.0%	0.7%	0.0%	0.0%

Mike Edwards

Kentucky Wildcats
Final Grade: 6.4   S Rank: 10 of 20

Height	Weight	Year	Jersey #	Hometown
5106	204	4SR	7	Cincinnati, OH

One-Liner
Edwards is a slightly undersized but tough safety with value at all three levels of a defense, but his zone awareness and tackling angles could hold him back from starting for some teams.

Overall
Edwards was a strong safety for Kentucky who lined up primarily in the slot and near the line of scrimmage. He occasionally was asked to play single-high deep safety. He started 44 out of 51 games throughout his playing career. Edwards is a good athlete with adequate height and weight, with a good combination of balance, change of direction, and short area quickness. He has good play speed and hip fluidity. Edwards is a very competitive player, showing good mental and physical toughness throughout the game and never shying away from contact.

Pass Game
In the pass game, he demonstrates good ball skills to track the ball in the air and has the leaping ability to compete at the catch point with taller receivers. He has the foot quickness and man coverage skills to mirror opposing slot receivers. He blitzes well with smart timing and can beat backs and tight ends in pass protection. As a deep middle safety, Edwards' range is more limited than when he plays closer to the line. His mental processing slows the further he gets from the ball, and his instincts are better in two high with help, and in short-to-intermediate areas. Edwards tends to keep his eyes in the back field and can allow receivers to sit down behind him in open spots.

Run Game
Against the run, Edwards is a good force player, keeping outside contain and overpowering stalk blocks. He tackles well near the line with physicality and a strong strike. Downfield, he doesn't take ideal angles in space and can miss some tackles or not catch up to plays he should be able to reach. He plays downhill and pursues well.

Last Word
Edwards profiles as an immediate contributor on multiple special teams units based on his toughness and ability to break down. He projects to be a quality backup by his second year and a versatile contributor. His man coverage skills will allow him to attack short completions and his physicality and downhill nature offer assistance in the box.

– Ben Hrkach

Strengths	Weaknesses
• Three-level value	• Zone coverage
• Man coverage	• Angles
• Tackling aggression	• Range

Critical Factors

3-Level Impact	Intelligence / Instincts	Play Speed
7	5	6

Positional Factors

Man Coverage	Zone Coverage	Ball Skills / Tracking
6	5	6
Range	**Tackling**	**Toughness / Physicality**
5	5	6

Leadership	Special Teams Value
6	6

Basic

	Coverage								Tackling	
Year	Trgt	Comp	Comp%	Yards	Yds/Trgt	Int	Int Drops	TD Allowed	Tackles	TFL
2016	35	12	34.3%	201	5.7	3	0	2	94	2.5
2017	38	19	50.0%	237	6.2	5	0	2	100	2.5
2018	42	20	47.6%	328	7.8	2	2	1	86	7.0
	115	51	44.3%	766	6.7	10	2	5	280	12.0

Advanced

	Coverage					Tackling			
Year	Pass Breakups	Pos%	Deserved Catch%	EPA	EPA/ Trgt	Broken Tackles	BT%	Tackle Share	Avg Depth of Tackle
2016	8	25.7%	69.6%	-12.7	-0.36	8	7.8%	10.2%	11.1
2017	12	42.1%	67.7%	-11.4	-0.30	21	17.4%	11.0%	8.1
2018	8	38.1%	83.9%	-3.5	-0.08	11	11.3%	11.3%	9.5
	28	35.7%	74.1%	-27.5	-0.24	40	12.5%	10.8%	9.6

Deep Dive

	Total Snaps		Lined Up		Man Coverage			Blitz		
Year	Pass	Run	Slot%	Box%	Trgt	Yds/Trgt	Pos%	Blitz%	Pressure%	Sack%
2018	386	402	46.6%	3.3%	16	5.1	31.3%	5.5%	27.3%	0.0%

Mark McLaurin

Mississippi State Bulldogs
Final Grade: 6.4 S Rank: 11 of 20

Height	Weight	Year	Jersey #	Hometown
6012	215	4SR	41	Collins, MS

One-Liner
McLaurin has the instincts, speed, and tackling ability to contribute at the next level, but lacks some overall coverage ability to be a starter.

Overall
McLaurin's primary position is FS, but he also played SS, lined up in the slot, and down in the box as a linebacker for Mississippi State. He started 31 of the 51 games he appeared in. McLaurin is a good athlete who competes with toughness and aggression. He has good speed attacking the LOS and uses his long arms to his advantage in tackling and pass coverage.

Pass Game
In the passing game, McLaurin played both zone and man coverage at MSU. He regularly communicates with his teammates on defense. He showed good ball skills with 3 INTs against Louisville in 2017. He is productive with interceptions, as well as breaking up passes and preventing YAC. He is athletic enough to run with any receiver in man, but occasionally struggles against quick receivers coming out of their breaks. He doesn't blow many coverage assignments but will get caught with his eyes in the backfield on occasion. He understands coverages and who to cover in different route concepts.

Run Game
In the run game, he's a fearless tackler. He consistently produces all over the field. He does a great job attacking the LOS and running the alleys, striking through from the back side. He is quick to identify run plays and quickly turns his backpedal into pursuit toward the LOS. He shows good downhill range and gets to the LOS quickly and under control with aggression and long strides. He missed two tackles in space against Lamar Jackson 1-on-1 in 2017, but rarely ever misses tackles near the LOS or against other players in space.

Last Word
McLaurin projects as a No. 3 SS by his second season who can also play FS and in the slot. On 3rd downs, he would fit best near the LOS where he can play in the slot or the box. He can immediately contribute on special teams due to his very good tackling, aggressive play style, and speed.

– Dan Davis

Strengths	Weaknesses
• Tackling	• Zone coverage range
• Run support	• Man coverage vs. quick WRs
• FBI	• Eye discipline

Critical Factors

3-Level Impact	Intelligence / Instincts	Play Speed
6	6	6

Positional Factors

Man Coverage	Zone Coverage	Ball Skills / Tracking
5	6	6
Range	**Tackling**	**Toughness / Physicality**
6	7	6
Leadership	**Special Teams Value**	
6	7	

Basic

	Coverage								Tackling	
Year	Trgt	Comp	Comp%	Yards	Yds/Trgt	Int	Int Drops	TD Allowed	Tackles	TFL
2016	13	6	46.2%	153	11.8	2	1	0	51	2.0
2017	31	13	41.9%	360	11.6	6	0	3	81	3.5
2018	27	19	70.4%	279	10.3	0	0	0	77	3.5
	71	38	53.5%	792	11.2	8	1	3	209	9.0

Advanced

	Coverage					Tackling			
Year	Pass Breakups	Pos%	Deserved Catch%	EPA	EPA/ Trgt	Broken Tackles	BT%	Tackle Share	Avg Depth of Tackle
2016	5	46.2%	87.5%	-0.6	-0.05	5	9.3%	5.1%	13.6
2017	10	38.7%	84.2%	11.1	0.36	12	13.3%	9.5%	8.7
2018	4	59.3%	82.6%	10.6	0.39	9	10.7%	9.1%	10.0
	19	47.9%	84.0%	21.1	0.30	26	11.4%	7.7%	10.4

Deep Dive

	Total Snaps		Lined Up		Man Coverage			Blitz		
Year	Pass	Run	Slot%	Box%	Trgt	Yds/Trgt	Pos%	Blitz%	Pressure%	Sack%
2018	420	370	8.2%	5.4%	11	7.2	54.5%	2.3%	30.0%	0.0%

Juan Thornhill

Virginia Cavaliers
Final Grade: 6.4 S Rank: 12 of 20

Height	Weight	Year	Jersey #	Hometown
6006	202	4SR	21	Altavista, VA

One-Liner
Thornhill is a rangy, deep-zone safety who has the speed and ball skills to make it at the next level, but his lack of overall physicality and sufficient instincts make him a better depth player and special teamer than starter.

Overall
Thornhill played a good mix of FS and SS in Virginia's 3-3-5 defense, while also playing in the box as an extra linebacker for stretches in some games. He played in 46 career games and was a primary starter starting in his sophomore season. He's a good athlete with length for the safety position, having been a solid basketball player in high school. He's got some toughness and competes on every down.

Pass Game
In the passing game, he has very good ball skills and tracking ability. He knows how to play the receiver and when to turn around and look for the football. Not only is he able to break up passes, but he's able to convert a high percentage of those into interceptions. He has good speed and range from the back-end and takes good angles to get to the ball. He's a better zone defender than man defender. In zone, he's able to read the eyes of the quarterback and does a good job picking up receivers running through his zone. His stiff hips and high backpedal make it tough for him to transition and stay completely in phase when in man coverage. Precise route-runners are able to create separation at the top of their routes against him. His leadership and communication ability are shown from the back end throughout games.

Run Game
Against the run, he shows good tackling production, but doesn't have the best technique. He likes to dive at the legs and feet of ballcarriers, and while this proves effective most times, he will go spurts where he misses multiple tackle attempts. He does a good job filling running lanes, but doesn't always take the best angles toward the line of scrimmage and will have to use his speed to make tackles further down the field than they should be. His aggression in run support is hot and cold, as he shows flashes of flying down, but doesn't show much initiative to help when he's on the backside. He plays very disciplined, although he lacks instincts in the run game and will stand flat-footed against play action and zone reads.

Last Word
Thornhill projects as a No. 3 FS who has the ability to start on occasion. On 3rd downs, he would be better served to play deep safety and use his range and ball skills in the passing game. He won't be a standout special teams player but should contribute on multiple units.

– Nathan Cooper

Strengths	**Weaknesses**
• Ball skills	• Read-and-react quickness
• Range	• Tackling technique
• Leadership	• Physicality

Critical Factors

3-Level Impact	Intelligence / Instincts	Play Speed
6	5	6

Positional Factors

Man Coverage	Zone Coverage	Ball Skills / Tracking
5	6	7
Range	**Tackling**	**Toughness / Physicality**
6	6	5

Leadership	Special Teams Value
6	6

Basic

	Coverage								Tackling	
Year	Trgt	Comp	Comp%	Yards	Yds/Trgt	Int	Int Drops	TD Allowed	Tackles	TFL
2016	46	24	52.2%	527	11.5	2	0	6	49	3.0
2017	57	23	40.4%	417	7.3	4	2	5	58	4.5
2018	43	15	34.9%	213	5.0	6	3	2	101	4.5
	146	62	42.5%	1157	7.9	12	5	13	208	12.0

Advanced

	Coverage					Tackling			
Year	Pass Breakups	Pos%	Deserved Catch%	EPA	EPA/ Trgt	Broken Tackles	BT%	Tackle Share	Avg Depth of Tackle
2016	9	50.0%	70.3%	17.6	0.38	4	7.8%	5.9%	11.0
2017	18	35.1%	55.8%	-7.2	-0.13	4	7.1%	6.3%	10.1
2018	11	25.6%	60.0%	-35.0	-0.81	11	10.0%	12.5%	8.4
	38	37.0%	61.8%	-24.6	-0.17	19	8.8%	8.2%	9.5

Deep Dive

	Total Snaps		Lined Up		Man Coverage			Blitz		
Year	Pass	Run	Slot%	Box%	Trgt	Yds/Trgt	Pos%	Blitz%	Pressure%	Sack%
2018	379	387	23.8%	2.9%	19	6.6	26.3%	3.5%	33.3%	0.0%

Andrew Wingard

Wyoming Cowboys
Final Grade: 6.4 S Rank: 13 of 20

Height	Weight	Year	Jersey #	Hometown
6000	205	4SR	28	Arvada, CO

One-Liner
Wingard provides very good run support at the LOS with his tackling and high football intelligence, but will struggle in coverage especially with more athletic counterparts.

Overall
Wingard played SS for Wyoming, which runs a base 4-3 on defense. He played mostly around the box, but also played in some 1-high and 2-high looks on the backend. He played in all 51 games in his four seasons. He's a solid athlete and relies on his toughness and competitive edge during games. He shows a high football intelligence and good instincts at reading plays, while maintaining solid positioning and not over-pursuing.

Pass Game
He does a sufficient job in the passing game. He struggles with speedy receivers and backs in man and lacks the range when playing 1-high. He shows the ability to transition out of his backpedal which puts him in good positions to make tackles. In zone coverage, he can get lost in space, with his eyes caught in the backfield and losing receivers. Also, he's not always fluid and plays hesitant. He doesn't show great flexibility in his hips in coverage. When in the box, he plays well in flat and curl zones. He'll blitz from the edge or through the A gaps with speed and achieves success with QB pressures.

Run Game
Against the run, he shows his toughness by welcoming contact and sticking his nose in the play. He's a very good tackler, with few missed tackles, if any. He very rarely gets tied up with a blocker, sheds well and keeps his distance to remain elusive to make a play. He's good at continually setting the edge when playing at the LOS against TEs. He can still support the run game from his deep safety spot, contains the run with second-level help and runs to the pylon when on the opposite side of the play.

Last Word
Wingard projects as a No. 3 SS at the next level. Similar to his time at Wyoming, he will be most successful playing in the box and making plays around the LOS, where he fits on 3rd downs. He'll be a very good special teams player due to his play speed and physicality.

– Evan Butler

Strengths	**Weaknesses**
• Very good tackler	• Struggles with top-end speed
• Good run support at LOS	• Eyes stuck in backfield in zone
• Very tough and physical	• Limited range

Critical Factors

3-Level Impact	Intelligence / Instincts	Play Speed
5	6	6

Positional Factors

Man Coverage	Zone Coverage	Ball Skills / Tracking
5	5	6
Range	**Tackling**	**Toughness / Physicality**
5	7	7
Leadership	**Special Teams Value**	
7	7	

Basic

	Coverage								Tackling	
Year	Trgt	Comp	Comp%	Yards	Yds/Trgt	Int	Int Drops	TD Allowed	Tackles	TFL
2016	27	8	29.6%	167	6.2	2	2	1	124	8.5
2017	21	9	42.9%	104	5.0	5	0	1	109	8.0
2018	17	9	52.9%	89	5.2	2	0	0	88	2.0
	65	26	40.0%	360	5.5	9	2	2	321	18.5

Advanced

	Coverage					Tackling			
Year	Pass Breakups	Pos%	Deserved Catch%	EPA	EPA/ Trgt	Broken Tackles	BT%	Tackle Share	Avg Depth of Tackle
2016	7	29.6%	55.6%	-6.2	-0.23	25	16.8%	14.1%	7.8
2017	8	33.3%	62.5%	-10.0	-0.48	15	12.2%	11.3%	6.0
2018	4	35.3%	64.3%	-12.5	-0.73	12	12.0%	10.5%	6.3
	19	32.3%	60.4%	-28.7	-0.44	52	14.0%	12.0%	6.8

Deep Dive

	Total Snaps		Lined Up		Man Coverage			Blitz		
Year	Pass	Run	Slot%	Box%	Trgt	Yds/Trgt	Pos%	Blitz%	Pressure%	Sack%
2018	395	389	20.3%	24.4%	6	5.7	50.0%	8.1%	39.4%	3.0%

Khari Willis

Michigan State Spartans
Final Grade: 6.4   S Rank: 14 of 20

Height	Weight	Year	Jersey #	Hometown
5112	215	4SR	27	Jackson, MI

One-Liner
Willis has 3-level talent, good play speed and sure tackling ability, but his overall coverage skills are just sufficient which could hold him back from starting.

Overall
Willis is a strong safety who played both in the box and as a single-high at MSU. He was a 4-year player and 2-year starter, appearing in 46 games . He is a good athlete who plays fast. He is a tough competitor with a high motor who will make plays anywhere on the field.

Pass Game
In the pass game, Willis is sufficient in man coverage as he can be stiff at times in his movement and have trouble with faster receivers. He has good zone coverage skills as he is able to diagnose routes and read the QB, and his range allows him to make plays from sideline to sideline. He has sufficient ball skills as he is able to defend and catch the ball with ease being a former running back, but occasionally takes poor angles. Pre-snap, he has shown good leadership skills in controlling the defense and putting everyone in the right spot, but his play speed is only good for the position he plays and the responsibilities and ground he has to cover.

Run Game
In the run game, Willis possesses good size for the position and plays with high football intelligence and instincts to diagnose and react to the play. He is a very good tackler and plays with toughness and physicality, which allows him to play close to the line of scrimmage, navigate the trash and make the stop. He has good 3-level talent as he is effective both against the run and the pass.

Last Word
Willis projects as a No. 3 SS at the next level where he can make plays across the field. On 3rd downs, he fits best near the LOS where he can use his physicality in the run game or against receivers. His special teams value is an asset, as his skill set would allow him to be very good on coverage units.

– Cole Ratliff

Strengths	**Weaknesses**
• Tackling	• Man coverage
• High-motor	• Consistent ball skills
• Toughness	• Reactive athleticism

Critical Factors

3-Level Impact	Intelligence / Instincts	Play Speed
6	6	6

Positional Factors

Man Coverage	Zone Coverage	Ball Skills / Tracking
5	6	5
Range	**Tackling**	**Toughness / Physicality**
6	7	7
Leadership	**Special Teams Value**	
6	7	

Basic

	Coverage								Tackling	
Year	Trgt	Comp	Comp%	Yards	Yds/Trgt	Int	Int Drops	TD Allowed	Tackles	TFL
2016	5	4	80.0%	41	8.2	0	0	0	26	0.0
2017	33	19	57.6%	237	7.2	2	0	0	71	3.5
2018	50	30	60.0%	366	7.3	2	2	1	83	1.0
	88	53	60.2%	644	7.3	4	2	1	180	4.5

Advanced

	Coverage					Tackling			
Year	Pass Breakups	Pos%	Deserved Catch%	EPA	EPA/ Trgt	Broken Tackles	BT%	Tackle Share	Avg Depth of Tackle
2016	1	80.0%	80.0%	3.4	0.68	3	13.0%	2.4%	11.3
2017	6	48.5%	85.2%	-0.5	-0.01	9	11.4%	9.2%	8.6
2018	10	48.0%	80.0%	15.4	0.31	11	11.7%	9.7%	9.5
	17	50.0%	81.9%	18.4	0.21	23	11.7%	7.1%	9.3

Deep Dive

	Total Snaps		Lined Up		Man Coverage			Blitz		
Year	Pass	Run	Slot%	Box%	Trgt	Yds/Trgt	Pos%	Blitz%	Pressure%	Sack%
2018	497	350	24.9%	1.2%	24	7.3	54.2%	2.3%	16.7%	0.0%

Sheldrick Redwine

Miami FL Hurricanes
Final Grade: 6.4 S Rank: 15 of 20

Height	Weight	Year	Jersey #	Hometown
6003	202	4SR	22	Miami, FL

One-Liner
Redwine is a safety with good ball skills and instincts but needs to improve his tackle form and man coverage ability at the next level.

Overall
Redwine lined up at FS for the Hurricanes and interchanged at SS from time to time as well. He played in 49 games during his career and started 30. Redwine is a solid athlete with a long frame and has good flexibility, quick feet, and good closing speed. He has good balance and displays fluid hip movement. Redwine is a tough competitor and a willing tackler on all three levels. He is a vocal leader, calling out coverages on the back end.

Pass Game
Versus the pass, Redwine shows good range as a single-high safety. He is an intelligent defender and can recognize plays developing in front of him with the ability to read and react quickly. He has good ball skills when he has the chance to make a play on the ball. His closing speed and body control allow him to take passing lanes away. Redwine struggles at times against the pass in man coverage as he doesn't always have the ability or speed to stay with some receivers. However, he is physical and engages defenders down the field.

Run Game
Versus the run, Redwine shows the ability to run the alley and make tackles near the LOS. He's aggressive and isn't afraid to come down and make a play. His form could be better, as he ducks his head often and doesn't look at his target all the way through the tackle.

Last Word
Redwine projects as a No. 3 who can back up both safety spots. On third down, he would be best lining up at FS and roaming the middle of the field. He has special teams ability and experience and should contribute on all units at the next level.

– Jordan Edwards

Strengths	**Weaknesses**
• Ball skills	• Man coverage
• Instincts	• Tackling technique
• Range	• Inconsistent physicality

Critical Factors

3-Level Impact	Intelligence / Instincts	Play Speed
6	6	6

Positional Factors

Man Coverage	Zone Coverage	Ball Skills / Tracking
5	6	6
Range	**Tackling**	**Toughness / Physicality**
6	5	5

Leadership	Special Teams Value
6	7

Basic

	Coverage								Tackling	
Year	Trgt	Comp	Comp%	Yards	Yds/Trgt	Int	Int Drops	TD Allowed	Tackles	TFL
2016	37	22	59.5%	346	9.4	0	1	1	31	0.0
2017	40	23	57.5%	372	9.3	2	2	3	61	1.0
2018	26	13	50.0%	177	6.8	3	0	2	71	4.0
	103	58	56.3%	895	8.7	5	3	6	163	5.0

Advanced

	Coverage					Tackling			
Year	Pass Breakups	Pos%	Deserved Catch%	EPA	EPA/ Trgt	Broken Tackles	BT%	Tackle Share	Avg Depth of Tackle
2016	5	54.1%	83.3%	16.7	0.45	7	18.9%	3.5%	13.4
2017	8	45.0%	78.8%	-2.8	-0.07	12	16.4%	6.3%	10.2
2018	5	42.3%	83.3%	-0.6	-0.02	11	13.6%	8.1%	11.6
	18	47.6%	81.5%	13.3	0.13	30	15.7%	6.0%	11.4

Deep Dive

	Total Snaps		Lined Up		Man Coverage			Blitz		
Year	Pass	Run	Slot%	Box%	Trgt	Yds/Trgt	Pos%	Blitz%	Pressure%	Sack%
2018	318	419	20.5%	6.4%	10	2.7	30.0%	6.3%	23.8%	14.3%

Jalen Young

Florida Atlantic Owls
Final Grade: 6.2 S Rank: 16 of 20

Height	Weight	Year	Jersey #	Hometown
5105	185	4SR	18	Belle Glade, FL

One-Liner
Young is a small, hybrid safety with very good speed and tracking who can be a ball hawk in the secondary, but needs to improve at all three levels and become a more consistent tackler.

Overall
Young primarily lined up as a free safety, but occasionally lined up in the box as a strong safety. He played in 48 total games at FAU and was a four-year starter. He plays with very good speed and good competitiveness/ aggression, and he can contribute sufficient skills at all levels on the field.

Pass Game
Versus the pass, he shows good man and zone coverage skills. In man, he has good off-man techniques being able to mirror receivers and tight ends while keeping over-the-top leverage. He also has the ability to press but lacks sufficient skills to jam and disrupt the timing. In zone, he displays very good reactive athleticism and proper deep leverage. He stays low in his backpedal and is very smooth in and out of his breaks and flipping his hips to turn and run. His ability to track the ball in the air is very good. He's a playmaker in the secondary and is a threat to take it for six if he comes down with an INT. His overall coverage skills are good enough to play the role of a 3rd corner but not replace one.

Run Game
Versus the run, he shows above-average tackling ability. He can make tackles in the 2nd level without breaking down, but can be inconsistent at tackling bigger, stronger ballcarriers such as tight ends and power backs. He runs the alley to make plays but needs to be more consistent in the run game. On 3rd down, he will primarily line up as a deep safety. Young can play the FS position with good toughness and physicality. He is not afraid to deliver a big hit to his opponent while maintaining consistent durability. He also shows adequate leadership on the field most times, making sure everyone in the secondary understands what the coverage is.

Last Word
Young projects as a backup safety in the NFL with starter upside if he is able to put on more weight. He can also play in the slot if needed and has some value as a returner on special teams.

– Brian Hammond

Strengths	**Weaknesses**
• Reactive athleticism	• Inconsistent tackler
• Ball skills	• Physicality in press
• Play speed	• Size

Critical Factors

3-Level Impact	Intelligence / Instincts	Play Speed
5	6	7

Positional Factors

Man Coverage	Zone Coverage	Ball Skills / Tracking
6	6	7
Range	**Tackling**	**Toughness / Physicality**
6	5	6
Leadership	**Special Teams Value**	
5	6	

Basic

	Coverage								Tackling	
Year	Trgt	Comp	Comp%	Yards	Yds/Trgt	Int	Int Drops	TD Allowed	Tackles	TFL
2016	29	21	72.4%	311	10.7	2	0	2	90	1.5
2017	30	17	56.7%	290	9.7	7	1	1	77	2.5
2018	12	6	50.0%	90	7.5	1	0	1	62	1.5
	71	44	62.0%	691	9.7	10	1	4	229	5.5

Advanced

	Coverage					Tackling			
Year	Pass Breakups	Pos%	Deserved Catch%	EPA	EPA/ Trgt	Broken Tackles	BT%	Tackle Share	Avg Depth of Tackle
2016	4	55.2%	91.7%	6.6	0.23	12	11.9%	11.0%	10.1
2017	8	56.7%	73.9%	5.2	0.17	16	17.2%	7.4%	8.4
2018	3	50.0%	60.0%	-0.8	-0.06	7	10.3%	7.0%	7.1
	15	54.9%	78.9%	11.0	0.16	35	13.4%	8.4%	8.7

Deep Dive

	Total Snaps		Lined Up		Man Coverage			Blitz		
Year	Pass	Run	Slot%	Box%	Trgt	Yds/Trgt	Pos%	Blitz%	Pressure%	Sack%
2018	254	247	4.4%	10.4%	2	4.0	50.0%	3.4%	22.2%	0.0%

Demetrius Flannigan-Fowles

Arizona Wildcats
Final Grade: 6.2   S Rank: 17 of 20

Height	Weight	Year	Jersey #	Hometown
6012	209	4SR	6	Tucson, AZ

One-Liner
Flannigan-Fowles is a back-end safety/slot defender who has good play speed and coverage skills, but his slow reactive instincts and questionable physicality may limit him at the next level.

Overall
Flannigan-Fowles' primary position is FS, and his secondary position is SS. He was a 4-year player and a 3-year starter. He appeared in 50 career games and officially moved to FS late in 2017. He is a good athlete with good speed. He can keep up with receivers out of their breaks and mirrors their movements well. He uses his speed well and flips his hips with ease. He has a long frame that has room for more size, and his frame allows him to cover ground quickly. He is not afraid to get involved in tackles or go against bigger players.

Pass Game
Against the pass, he has good footwork and can mirror receivers. He is very good at communicating with the defense pre-snap. He has the range to play deep zone, but his instincts slow down his play speed. He is good at dropping into his zone and picking up receivers as they come. He uses his long arms to break up passes, and he has good hands to make interceptions.

Run Game
In the running game, he is willing to do the dirty work. Demetrius makes an impact without always showing up on the stat sheet. He is good at making tackles near the line of scrimmage but is an inconsistent open-field tackler overall. He will throw his body instead of wrapping with his arms and misses tackles. He has the length and strength to shed blockers, but struggles against pulling lineman and TEs. Demetrius lacks the instincts to anticipate a play. He was easily fooled by play action and trick plays and struggled to find the ball, specifically against BYU. This also allows receivers to get behind him in pass coverage.

Last Word
He has the size and athleticism to play either FS or SS. He can be a contributor on special teams. He can play deep or close to the LOS on 3rd downs. He has most of the physical traits needed to play at the NFL level, but his ceiling will be determined by how much he can improve his reactive awareness and instincts. He has the tools to be a starting safety, but his instincts keep him from being a 3-down starter.

– Dan Davis

Strengths	**Weaknesses**
• Communication ability	• Slow to read-react
• Ball skills	• Inconsistent physicality
• Closing speed	• Backpedal and transition ability

Critical Factors

3-Level Impact	Intelligence / Instincts	Play Speed
5	5	6

Positional Factors

Man Coverage	Zone Coverage	Ball Skills / Tracking
6	6	6
Range	**Tackling**	**Toughness / Physicality**
5	5	5
Leadership	**Special Teams Value**	
6	6	

Basic

	Coverage								Tackling	
Year	Trgt	Comp	Comp%	Yards	Yds/Trgt	Int	Int Drops	TD Allowed	Tackles	TFL
2016	23	11	47.8%	156	6.8	2	0	2	77	3.0
2017	34	22	64.7%	423	12.4	3	0	3	87	1.0
2018	28	14	50.0%	210	7.5	0	1	1	51	2.0
	85	47	55.3%	789	9.3	5	1	6	215	6.0

Advanced

	Coverage					Tackling			
Year	Pass Breakups	Pos%	Deserved Catch%	EPA	EPA/ Trgt	Broken Tackles	BT%	Tackle Share	Avg Depth of Tackle
2016	8	34.8%	60.0%	-1.7	-0.07	19	19.8%	9.5%	8.8
2017	7	58.8%	82.1%	20.3	0.60	16	15.5%	9.1%	11.8
2018	7	39.3%	68.2%	-4.3	-0.15	9	15.0%	6.1%	8.3
	22	45.9%	71.4%	14.3	0.17	44	17.0%	8.3%	9.8

Deep Dive

	Total Snaps		Lined Up		Man Coverage			Blitz		
Year	Pass	Run	Slot%	Box%	Trgt	Yds/Trgt	Pos%	Blitz%	Pressure%	Sack%
2018	417	384	17.1%	9.0%	13	5.0	38.5%	0.2%	0.0%	0.0%

Lukas Denis

Boston College Eagles
Final Grade: 6.2 S Rank: 18 of 20

Height	Weight	Year	Jersey #	Hometown
5113	184	4SR	21	Everett, MA

One-Liner
Denis could be a productive single-high due to his range and ball skills, but he lacks the size or physicality to play near the line of scrimmage.

Overall
Denis is a FS who primarily plays as a single-high, although he also played corner prior to switching to safety full-time after the 2016 season. He is a 3-year player and 2-year starter with 40 games played in his career. Denis is a solid athlete with good play speed and range but has a slighter frame than a prototypical safety. He is a good competitor but could stand to improve his leadership ability and be more of an active communicator in the secondary.

Pass Game
In the pass game, Denis is a rangy player with good ball skills. He plays with good position discipline and rarely allows a receiver to get behind him in coverage. He's good in zone coverage as the deep man but lacks the instincts to play closer to the line of scrimmage and jump intermediate routes. He plays fast with quick feet and good hip fluidity. In man-coverage, Denis has shown an inability to fight for position against bigger receivers due to his physicality and lack of play strength, although he can play corner in a pinch in the right matchup.

Run Game
In the run game, Denis struggles to contribute much. He plays deep off the line and tends to overcommit when playing downhill, taking poor angles to the ball and putting himself out of position as the last line of defense. While he has demonstrated the ability to shed blocks when coming up in run support, he is a grab-and-drag tackler and doesn't always finish on contact which could lead to problems with his size at the next level.

Last Word
Denis can be a good special teams contributor due to his good play speed and ability to shed blocks. By year two, he projects to be a backup safety with corner flex due to his playing experience. On 3rd downs, he would fit best on the back end to use his range and ball skills.

– SIS Scouting Staff

Strengths	Weaknesses
• Zone coverage • Ball skills • Range	• Man coverage • Physicality • Run support

Critical Factors

3-Level Impact	Intelligence / Instincts	Play Speed
5	5	6

Positional Factors

Man Coverage	Zone Coverage	Ball Skills / Tracking
5	6	6
Range	**Tackling**	**Toughness / Physicality**
6	5	4

Leadership	Special Teams Value
5	6

Basic

	Coverage								Tackling	
Year	Trgt	Comp	Comp%	Yards	Yds/Trgt	Int	Int Drops	TD Allowed	Tackles	TFL
2016	15	7	46.7%	81	5.4	1	0	1	8	0.0
2017	45	21	46.7%	238	5.3	7	3	4	85	0.5
2018	25	16	64.0%	217	8.7	1	3	3	58	2.0
	85	44	51.8%	536	6.3	9	6	8	151	2.5

Advanced

	Coverage					Tackling			
Year	Pass Breakups	Pos%	Deserved Catch%	EPA	EPA/ Trgt	Broken Tackles	BT%	Tackle Share	Avg Depth of Tackle
2016	5	46.7%	61.5%	0.4	0.03	1	14.3%	0.9%	9.5
2017	18	37.8%	66.7%	-15.8	-0.35	16	15.8%	8.9%	9.2
2018	4	56.0%	85.7%	10.7	0.43	13	18.3%	6.3%	10.9
	27	44.7%	71.4%	-4.7	-0.06	30	16.8%	5.7%	9.9

Deep Dive

	Total Snaps		Lined Up		Man Coverage			Blitz		
Year	Pass	Run	Slot%	Box%	Trgt	Yds/Trgt	Pos%	Blitz%	Pressure%	Sack%
2018	379	367	8.7%	3.2%	16	9.8	62.5%	2.6%	20.0%	5.0%

McKinley Whitfield

Tulsa Golden Hurricane
Final Grade: 5.9 S Rank: 19 of 20

Height	Weight	Year	Jersey #	Hometown
6022	214	4SR	5	Spiro, OK

One-Liner
Whitfield has the length, raw athleticism, and a physical, aggressive mindset to contribute in some capacity at the next level, but will need to improve his overall instincts with consistent tackling ability to see much time outside of ST.

Overall
Whitfield played SS for Tulsa. He played in 50 career games for the Golden Hurricane. He is a long athlete who is put together well with good build and explosiveness. He is a long strider and has good play speed. He shows very good toughness and does not shy away from contact.

Pass Game
Against the pass, he plays fast but has a tough time transitioning out of his backpedal, especially when he's in off-man. Due to his size, he struggles to drop his weight and transition cleanly. He is proficient at dropping deep and using his length and speed to eliminate anything over top. He also does well at diagnosing and blowing up screens when playing near the LOS. In man coverage, he is most effective when using a bump and run, although he's a little stiff and doesn't have great lateral quickness. He has the potential to be a successful blitzer due to his quick first step, but he was not asked to do so at Tulsa.

Run Game
Against the run, Whitfield is good at coming downhill and attacking the play. He runs the alleys and isn't afraid to put his body on the line. He has strong hands and uses his length to keep blockers off him. His tackling is inconsistent, mostly due to inefficient angles and his physicality, wanting to deliver a large blow on each tackle attempt.

Last Word
By his second year, he will be a backup SS and a very productive ST player because of his size, athleticism, and physicality. On 3rd downs, he should be used close to the line where he can use his toughness and physicality. Whitfield has the body andathleticism to become a versatile player with a very raw feel for the game.

– Ben Hrkach

Strengths	Weaknesses
• Physicality	• Lateral quickness
• Play speed	• Range
• Length	• FBI

Critical Factors

3-Level Impact	Intelligence / Instincts	Play Speed
5	5	6

Positional Factors

Man Coverage	Zone Coverage	Ball Skills / Tracking
5	5	6
Range	**Tackling**	**Toughness / Physicality**
5	5	7
Leadership	**Special Teams Value**	
5	7	

Basic

	Coverage								Tackling	
Year	Trgt	Comp	Comp%	Yards	Yds/Trgt	Int	Int Drops	TD Allowed	Tackles	TFL
2016	16	7	43.8%	146	9.1	2	0	1	50	2.5
2017	18	12	66.7%	299	16.6	1	0	1	112	2.5
2018	35	12	34.3%	156	4.5	2	0	0	72	1.5
	69	31	44.9%	601	8.7	5	0	2	234	6.5

Advanced

	Coverage					Tackling			
Year	Pass Breakups	Pos%	Deserved Catch%	EPA	EPA/ Trgt	Broken Tackles	BT%	Tackle Share	Avg Depth of Tackle
2016	6	43.8%	61.5%	0.2	0.01	1	2.1%	5.2%	8.5
2017	5	55.6%	81.3%	9.3	0.52	14	11.2%	12.3%	10.0
2018	8	28.6%	56.0%	-19.6	-0.56	16	18.2%	7.9%	8.3
	19	39.1%	64.8%	-10.1	-0.15	31	11.9%	8.4%	9.1

Deep Dive

	Total Snaps		Lined Up		Man Coverage			Blitz		
Year	Pass	Run	Slot%	Box%	Trgt	Yds/Trgt	Pos%	Blitz%	Pressure%	Sack%
2018	270	443	65.2%	8.8%	19	5.5	36.8%	0.0%	-	-

Zedrick Woods

Ole Miss Rebels

Final Grade: 5.9 S Rank: 20 of 20

Height	Weight	Year	Jersey #	Hometown
5110	201	4SR	36	Lake City, FL

One-Liner

Woods is a tough, in-the-box strong safety who isn't afraid of contact but will prove to be a liability in pass coverage.

Overall

Woods played strong safety for Ole Miss, often used as an extra box defender and occasionally at single-high. He was a 4-year player and 3-year starter. He has proven to be very durable throughout his career. He is an above-average athlete with good play speed and a background in track. Woods is a tough player who always looks to make the big hit. He is very physical with route runners and thrives when playing in the box near the line of scrimmage.

Pass Game

In the pass game, Woods struggles to make a big impact. In man coverage, he is physical at the line but allows separation at the top of the route and doesn't have the recovery speed to make up for it. When playing as a single-high, Woods plays with a high motor, actively going after deep balls outside of the numbers in an attempt to help his corners. He has good hip-fluidity to change direction quickly and track the ball while it's in the air, but he doesn't demonstrate the closing speed to get to the ball before it reaches its target. Woods has short strides, including in his backpedal, which he tends to stay in for too long. This and his reading ability limit his range. He has difficulty diagnosing plays and struggles reading the quarterback's eyes as a single-high. He doesn't get the breaks he should on the ball, and he has shown a lack of awareness for routes being run around him.

Run Game

In the run game, Woods possesses a very good ability to finish tackles. However, he does play very upright and demonstrates average form, tackling players high around the shoulder pads. His play strength allows him to finish most tackles, but better form will increase his reliability. Woods is willing to take on blockers and fill in run lanes without hesitation, although he struggles at times to shed those blockers and occasionally plays out of position. Woods is never one to shy away from a head-on collision and has the strength to stand-up ballcarriers who try to run him over. He doesn't demonstrate good backside pursuit as he takes himself out of the play if he deems it is too far away.

Last Word

Due to his play speed and tackling prowess, Woods will be a good special teams contributor. As a senior, Woods proved to be a leader on the field with his constant communication, and his passion was notably contagious to his teammates. By his second year, Woods projects to be a backup box safety, who will struggle in pass defense but offers quality intangibles.

– Nick Aiello

Strengths	**Weaknesses**
• Strong tackler	• Limited range
• Leadership	• Man coverage
• Physicality	• Reading and awareness

Critical Factors

3-Level Impact	Intelligence / Instincts	Play Speed
5	5	6

Positional Factors

Man Coverage	Zone Coverage	Ball Skills / Tracking
5	5	6
Range	**Tackling**	**Toughness / Physicality**
5	7	6
Leadership	**Special Teams Value**	
6	6	

Basic

	Coverage								Tackling	
Year	Trgt	Comp	Comp%	Yards	Yds/Trgt	Int	Int Drops	TD Allowed	Tackles	TFL
2016	17	10	58.8%	169	9.9	3	1	0	63	1.5
2017	19	10	52.6%	178	9.4	0	0	0	63	2.0
2018	27	13	48.1%	179	6.6	2	0	2	79	0.5
	63	33	52.4%	526	8.3	5	1	2	205	4.0

Advanced

	Coverage					Tackling			
Year	Pass Breakups	Pos%	Deserved Catch%	EPA	EPA/ Trgt	Broken Tackles	BT%	Tackle Share	Avg Depth of Tackle
2016	5	47.1%	84.6%	2.3	0.14	1	1.7%	6.1%	9.4
2017	5	36.8%	80.0%	3.1	0.17	4	6.3%	6.8%	11.7
2018	4	33.3%	81.0%	1.3	0.05	4	4.8%	8.8%	11.4
	14	38.1%	81.6%	6.8	0.11	9	4.4%	7.2%	10.9

Deep Dive

	Total Snaps		Lined Up		Man Coverage			Blitz		
Year	Pass	Run	Slot%	Box%	Trgt	Yds/Trgt	Pos%	Blitz%	Pressure%	Sack%
2018	368	438	19.4%	16.7%	12	4.3	50.0%	2.8%	45.5%	4.5%

Glossary

Avg Depth of Tackle
Average number of yards away from the line of scrimmage that the defender made his tackles

Box%
Percentage of plays the defender lined up at or near the line of scrimmage

Broken Tackles
Tackle attempts where the defender failed to bring down the ballcarrier. Counts both broken tackles (physical) and missed tackles (elusive)

BT%
Percentage of tackle attempts where the defender failed to bring down the ballcarrier. Counts both broken tackles (physical) and missed tackles (elusive)

Deserved Catch%
The percentage of targets as the primary defender that the receiver either caught or dropped the ball when the pass was catchable

Pass Breakups
The number of times the defender batted, deflected or defensed a pass

Pos% (Coverage split)
The percentage of plays where the defender was targeted that resulted in a positive EPA (a successful play for the offense)

Pressure%
Percentage of pass rushes that resulted in a quarterback hurry, hit, knockdown, or sack

Rush%
Percentage of quarterback dropbacks where the defender rushed the quarterback

Sack%
Percentage of pass rushes that resulted in a sack

Slot%
Percentage of plays the defender lined up across from a slot receiver

Tackle Share
Percentage of a team's tackles made by the defender

Safety Leaderboards

Deserved Catch Rate Allowed Leaders

Rank	Player	Team	Deserved Catch%
1	McKinley Whitfield	Tulsa	56.0%
2	Taylor Rapp	Washington	58.3%
3	Juan Thornhill	Virginia	60.0%
4	Jalen Young	Florida Atlantic	60.0%
5	Andrew Wingard	Wyoming	64.3%
6	Demetrius Flannigan-Fowles	Arizona	68.2%
7	Amani Hooker	Iowa	69.7%
8	Chauncey Gardner-Johnson	Florida	71.0%
9	Deionte Thompson	Alabama	71.4%
10	Marvell Tell III	USC	77.8%

Broken Tackle Rate Leaders

Rank	Player	Team	Broken Tackle %
1	Jaquan Johnson	Miami FL	3.3%
2	Taylor Rapp	Washington	3.6%
3	Zedrick Woods	Ole Miss	4.8%
4	Amani Hooker	Iowa	6.1%
5	Juan Thornhill	Virginia	10.0%
6	Jalen Young	Florida Atlantic	10.3%
7	Mark McLaurin	Mississippi State	10.7%
8	Mike Edwards	Kentucky	11.3%
9	Khari Willis	Michigan State	11.7%
10	Andrew Wingard	Wyoming	12.0%

Positive Play Percentage Leaders

Rank	Player	Team	Pos%
1	Taylor Rapp	Washington	16.7%
2	Chauncey Gardner-Johnson	Florida	23.5%
3	Juan Thornhill	Virginia	25.6%
4	McKinley Whitfield	Tulsa	28.6%
5	Deionte Thompson	Alabama	29.6%
6	Johnathan Abram	Mississippi State	31.6%
7	Marvell Tell III	USC	32.4%
8	Zedrick Woods	Ole Miss	33.3%
9	Andrew Wingard	Wyoming	35.3%
10	Amani Hooker	Iowa	37.2%

Average Tackle Depth Leaders

Rank	Player	Team	Avg Tackle Depth
1	Amani Hooker	Iowa	6.1
2	Andrew Wingard	Wyoming	6.3
3	Jalen Young	Florida Atlantic	7.1
4	Chauncey Gardner-Johnson	Florida	7.2
5	Marvell Tell III	USC	7.2
6	Darnell Savage Jr.	Maryland	7.5
7	Jaquan Johnson	Miami FL	8.2
8	Demetrius Flannigan-Fowles	Arizona	8.3
9	McKinley Whitfield	Tulsa	8.3
10	Juan Thornhill	Virginia	8.4

Tackle Leaders

Rank	Player	Team	Tackles
1	Juan Thornhill	Virginia	101
2	Johnathan Abram	Mississippi State	95
3	Jaquan Johnson	Miami FL	91
4	Andrew Wingard	Wyoming	88
5	Mike Edwards	Kentucky	86
6	Khari Willis	Michigan State	83
7	Deionte Thompson	Alabama	80
8	Zedrick Woods	Ole Miss	79
9	Mark McLaurin	Mississippi State	77
10	McKinley Whitfield	Tulsa	72

Pressure Rate Leaders

Rank	Player	Team	Pressure%
1	Zedrick Woods	Ole Miss	45.5%
2	Andrew Wingard	Wyoming	39.4%
3	Chauncey Gardner-Johnson	Florida	37.5%
4	Jonathan Abram	Mississippi State	37.3%
5	Juan Thornhill	Virginia	33.3%
6	Marvell Tell III	USC	33.3%
7	Mark McLaurin	Mississippi State	30.0%
8	Taylor Rapp	Washington	29.3%
9	Mike Edwards	Kentucky	27.3%
10	Sheldrick Redwine	Miami FL	23.8%

Football Terminology

Ankle Flexion
The characteristic of being able to bend one's ankles, often from an awkward position, in order to redirect one's body or change angles of pursuit.

COD
Change of Direction

COP
Change of Pace Back

Defensive Line Moves

- Bull - run straight through the lineman with power
- Speed - beats him around the edge with speed
- Push-pull - pushes lineman and grabs, pulls and sheds him away
- Rip - rips up and through the lineman with one arm
- Speed to power - speed off the edge to set up the lineman and then convert to power straight through him
- Spin - spins at the point of attack
- Swim - brings his arm over the blocker's shoulder to leverage himself past him

Defensive Line Techniques

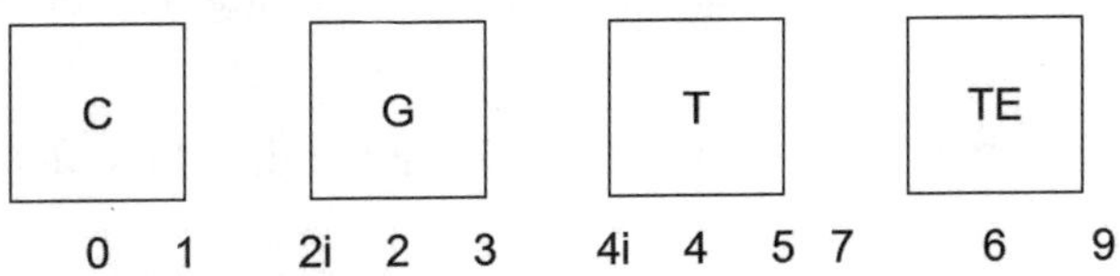

EPA
Expected Points Added, the change in Expected Points for the offense on a play

FBI
Football Intelligence

Force Defender
The player who is responsible for meeting a run in its initial stage to make the tackle, force a cutback, or otherwise alter the running track in such a way that the ball carrier is vulnerable to pursuit.

Injury Designations

Currently injured players have an injury which has affected their ability to participate in draft preparation, and may affect their ability to participate in the combine, pro days, and/or OTAs.

Long-term injury risk players have had extensive injury histories, severe injuries, and/or injuries which historically have a high rate of aggravation or recurrence.

LOS
Line of Scrimmage

Man/Gap Blocking
A run scheme which is designed to attack a specific gap, with each blocker being assigned to block a certain defensive player.

Mesh Point
The point where the QB and RB come together during a handoff, play-action fake, or read-option.

Personnel Packages (11, 12, 21, etc.)
This numbers represents the number of RBs and TEs, respectively, the offense has on the field. For example, 21 personnel means there are 2 RBs and 1 TE on the field.

POA
Point of Attack

Reduce Down
(of a defensive end) Aligning on the interior of the defensive line, usually on third downs and in other passing scenarios.

Sam, Mike, and Will Linebackers
Strongside, Middle, and Weakside Linebackers

Set the Edge
(of a force or contain player) to prevent a ball carrier from running outside of the offensive tackle.

Single High Coverage
Any coverage in which a safety is playing zone in the deep middle of the field (e.g. Cover 1, Cover 3).

Trash Navigation
(of a linebacker) The practice of scraping gaps and engaging blockers as necessary while visioning the ball carrier in order to provide run support.

Two High Coverage
Any coverage in which two safeties are in deep zone coverage (e.g. Cover 2, Cover 4).

Y-TE vs H-TE
The Y-TE is the more traditional in-line TE and is usually bigger and used as a blocker. The H-TE is more athletic and is often moved around depending on formation.

Zone Blocking
A run scheme in which each blocker is assigned to block whatever defender enters their area of assignment, with the runner ultimately attacking a gap based on how the blocking influences the leverage of a keyed defender.

4-digit height code
Player heights are expressed in a 4-digit code, with the first digit representing their height in feet, the second and third digits combining to represent inches, and the fourth digit representing eighths of an inch (e.g. 6043 is 6-foot-4-and 3/8 inches).

This book is all about finding the next big thing in the NFL. At SIS, we've created what we believe is the next big thing in football analytics, a system called Total Points. It takes granular charting data on every offensive and defensive player and divides up credit for what happens on each play using Expected Points Added. While it only exists at the NFL level for now, it represents a level of analysis that we strive to improve upon and extend to college players, revolutionizing the way we talk about prospects statistically. As you come to the end of this inaugural edition of the Handbook, enjoy this look into what will be coming in future years.

Introducing Total Points

Alex Vigderman and John Shirley

Matt Ryan won the 2016 NFL MVP award with an incredible campaign. He set career bests in completion percentage, yards, touchdowns, and interceptions, and led the league in touchdown rate and whichever raw or adjusted yards-per-attempt metric you prefer. In 2017, his numbers fell off substantially across the board, including a near-halving of his touchdown total. This year he is off to a torrid start, on pace to at least match the numbers he put up two years ago. So what gives? What happened last year?

It turns out that 2016 wasn't much of a down year at all, at least not one that was reflective of Ryan declining. In 2017, Falcons would-be pass-catchers dropped more than 60 percent more passes than they did the year before (and 35 percent more than they did in 2018) while Ryan's catchable pass rate was about the same. Add in that his receivers averaged just under a yard less per reception after the catch, cutting his totals quite a bit.

There were some serious red zone troubles, though, and that ineptitude crept into 2018 as well. Ryan's catchable pass rate in the red zone dropped off by nearly 10 percentage points from 2016 to 2017, and his receivers' catch rate on catchable passes dropped by more than 12 percentage points. These numbers have an outsized impact perceptually because of where they came on the field, but in such a small sample they're hardly predictive. What we'd like to be able to do is determine what a player is really responsible for and make sure he gets credit for it, no more and no less.

Sports Info Solutions has developed a system called Total Points that seeks to do just that using our wealth of charting data and the Expected Points framework. Using that system, Ryan was the best passer in the NFL in both 2016 and 2017, which makes his statistical rebound in 2018 more of a continuation of a trend than anything. In the space below, we'll introduce the system and how it's used to evaluate every player on the field.

Expected Points to Total Points

Before we get to the more complex Total Points system, let's make sure that we're set on the concept of Expected Points.

Football is a very tough sport to evaluate statistically. To resolve the issue of the overall complexity of the game, many analysts have settled on a common language when talking about the impact of different events during the game. That language is Expected Points (EP). At any point in time in a game, the Expected Points is the average value of the next score of the game, regardless of when it occurs or who scores. This allows us to understand how valuable just a change in field position is, regardless of whether there was a score on that drive or not.

The value of any individual play can be calculated as Expected Points Added (EPA), the difference in EP before and after a given play. Having EPA as a currency allows all sorts of different play results and events to be compared apples-to-apples, taking into account the fluctuating value of yards and downs as the other changes. And this allows for really interesting analysis when applied on a holistic level. For example, EPA shows that a "staying-ahead-of-the chains" run of 4 yards on first down is most often a negative play. The rare exceptions include plays at the outer end of field goal range.

Where the typical EPA model struggles, though, is player analysis. "Traditional" EPA-based analysis of players might read like, "Player X was worth 27 EPA catching passes in 2017," but that really means "Player X's team gained 27 EPA on plays in which Player X caught a pass in 2017." There isn't any real attribution of who is responsible for that added value. Which is why SIS sought to develop a more useful and robust model that really takes advantage of the wealth of data available, a model called Total Points.

Total Points takes the common currency of EPA and distributes the value gained or lost on a play to the different players involved based on their impact on the play. Using the wealth of SIS charting data available, this affords an unprecedented assessment of the value provided individually by each player on the field.

Take these two incomplete passes as an example:

1. The quarterback misses on a quick slant, throwing it way behind the receiver.

2. The quarterback is forced to escape the pocket after the left guard blows a block. Despite that, he delivers a strike to a receiver streaking down the sidelines who drops it.

Most traditional evaluation systems would consider these plays basically the same. The pass was incomplete in each case. But so much more happened to inform the evaluation of the players involved.

For Play 1, the quarterback was offered a clean pocket and still threw off-target, so Total Points absolves the receiver of blame and punishes the quarterback. For Play 2, the situation is the opposite. The pass was on-target and the receiver dropped it, so he gets blamed while the quarterback receives credit as if the receiver had caught it. On top of that, the offensive line's failure will make the quarterback look even better in that scenario.

These are two plays with the same in-game outcome but very different player performances, and Total Points helps distinguish that. As an example, assume the EPA on both plays above was -0.5. Using basic EPA, the quarterback and receiver would both be assigned -0.5 EPA, the full value of the play. With respect to Total Points, they might be respectively assigned -0.5 and 0 Total Points for Play 1 but 0.2 and -0.7 Total Points for Play 2, which takes into account their individual contributions to the outcome.

A Tour Around Total Points

Without digging too far into the details, here is an overview of the different considerations entering into Total Points. While Total Points is the name for the overarching system, offensive Total Points are called Points Earned and defensive Total Points are called Points Saved. This distinction helps clarify between totals of players on different sides of the ball that would otherwise be on the same scale.

When looking at these positional leaders, it's important to remember what Total Points is best suited for when it comes to player analysis. Total Points is useful to differentiate between players at the same or similar positions, especially within similar aspects of the game -- for example, comparing the performance against the run of a linebacker and a defensive tackle. This isn't as true when crossing between these aspects. For example, because of the added value of passing from an Expected Points perspective, players involved in the passing game will have more extreme Total Points (good or bad) than players involved more in the running game.

Passing

As was touched on in the pass examples above, the relationship between the quarterback and the receiver can get fairly involved. The core assumption of passing Points Earned is that each throw has a certain expected outcome based on information like the route, the depth, and the coverage. From that point, the passer and receiver split responsibility for how well they perform above that expectation. Throwing off-target passes and deserved interceptions (caught or not) will bury a signal-caller, while he will be rewarded for leading receivers to more yards after catch and making something out of a broken pocket. The receiver is then evaluated in the context of his route, so 5 yards after the catch on a screen nets less credit than the same amount on a curl.

QB Total Points Earned, 2018			Pass Catcher Total Points Earned, 2018			
Player	**Team**	**Points Earned**	**Player**	**Pos**	**Team**	**Points Earned**
Drew Brees	NO	78	Julio Jones	WR	ATL	45
Patrick Mahomes	KC	75	Travis Kelce	TE	KC	43
Philip Rivers	LAC	55	Geore Kittle	TE	SF	41
Matt Ryan	ATL	44	Odell Beckham	WR	NYG	40
Tom Brady	NE	42	T.Y. Hilton	WR	IND	39

Drew Brees of the Saints edged out Patrick Mahomes of the Chiefs by a slim margin that essentially renders the two as having had equally valuable seasons. Brees excelled at throwing the ball downfield, completing an NFL-best 58 percent of his throws that went at least 15 yards beyond the line of scrimmage, and at avoiding the sack. He took 17 in 15 games.

Mahomes racked up yardage and touchdowns in bulk, throwing for 5,097 yards and 50 scores. He had more Points Earned on third and fourth down than anyone else in the league, thanks to 14 touchdowns and an average of 9 air yards per completion (third-most among quarterbacks).

Since we're looking at accumulated value, playing an entire season has value. That's what vaults Julio Jones of the Falcons into the No. 1 spot, though on a per-play basis, he's a smidge behind

Odell Beckham Jr. of the Giants. Jones bounced back from an off-year to lead the NFL in receiving yards (1,677). In addition to his standout receiving numbers, Beckham got a spike from two long touchdown passes.

Among tight ends, Travis Kelce emerges a hair ahead of George Kittle. Kelce caught 69 percent of targets, three percentage points better than Kittle, though both had an 88 percent on-target catch percentage. The Chiefs' success on third down was partly due to Kelce's success. Kelce caught 25-of-33 third-down targets, leading to 22 first downs. Kelce had one fewer third down reception than tight end leader Zach Ertz, but had 10 fewer targets.

Offensive and Defensive Front

Line play remains one of the more elusive facets of the game from an analytical perspective. Total Points seeks to evaluate the offensive line by starting from a baseline of a clean play and punishing blockers for indicators of poor play, like blown blocks, running back bounces, and other point-of-attack events (e.g., QB hits, run stuffs, and batted passes). Pass-rushers and in-box defenders are correspondingly credited for being involved in those disruptive events and docked for allowing too many cleanly-blocked plays. Each team's performance in the trenches then informs how the players behind them are evaluated; poor run blocking makes a good run look better, and an excellent pass rush makes good coverage look less impressive.

One thing to keep in mind is that while SIS collects a good amount of data on these otherwise under-represented position groups (especially on run plays), there is still a fair amount of uncertainty about how responsible any given player is for some events on the field. Total Points reflects this by producing a lower Points Saved or Points Earned on those plays, so that there isn't too much credit being given one way or another. As a result, performance by the offensive line and defenders on run plays will have a much tighter range of Total Points than others. As SIS expands its data collection even further this will become less and less of a factor.

Offensive Line Points Earned

Player	Pos	Team	Pass Blocking	Run Blocking	Total Blocking Points Earned
Joe Thuney	G	NE	6	3	9
Trent Brown	T	NE	6	3	8
Ronnie Stanley	T	BAL	6	2	8
Jake Matthews	T	ATL	7	1	8
Andrew Whitworth	T	LA	2	5	7

The Patriots offensive line had a phenomenal year, as they allowed the third-lowest pressure rate and created the seventh-most rushing yards before contact in 2018. This success is reflected by two Patriots, Joe Thuney and Trent Brown, at the top of the Total Points leaderboard. Joe Thuney was credited with only four blown blocks in 1,051 snaps during the regular season.

Defensive Line Points Saved					
Player	Pos	Team	Pass Def Points Saved	Run Def Points Saved	Total Points Saved
Frank Clark	DE	SEA	30	-5	26
Aaron Donald	DT	LA	25	-6	19
J.J. Watt	DE	HOU	23	-4	19
DeMarcus Lawrence	DE	DAL	23	-4	19
Jerry Hughes	DE	BUF	19	-4	15

It should be unsurprising that this defensive line leaderboard is filled with some of the league's best pass rushers. By creating pressure on the QB and getting sacks, these players are incredibly valuable to their teams. Aaron Donald had an amazing season considering that he is the only defensive tackle in the top ten of Total Points Saved and eleven Total Points higher than the next highest DT (Chris Jones).

Rushing

Rushers are so clearly impacted by the play of the offensive line that much of the time analyzing running backs is spent trying to separate their performance from that of their linemen. Evaluating the offensive line's Points Earned separately allows the evaluation of the back to start with this already taken care of. Total Points acknowledges the role that the back has in his yards before contact and bounce/cutback rate, two metrics that have tended to be attributed more to the line in the past. Analysts using other Expected Points models have contended that running backs are largely irrelevant from a value perspective in the modern NFL. Total Points, for the most part, agrees, although those who are able to consistently break through tacklers and catch the ball out of the backfield will still be valued by Total Points.

Running Back Points Earned					
Player	Pos	Team	Rushing Points Earned	Receiving Points Earned	Total Scrimmage Points Earned
Christian McCaffrey	RB	CAR	10	24	34
Saquon Barkley	RB	NYG	20	12	32
Derrick Henry	RB	TEN	29	-2	26
Melvin Gordon	RB	LAC	19	4	23
Alvin Kamara	RB	NO	4	18	23

It's not enough to run the ball. Someone who hopes to lead in this stat needs to catch it too. Christian McCaffrey of the Panthers does both well and ranks No. 1 in Total Points, ahead of Giants rookie Saquon Barkley. He ranked 14th in Points Earned on rushes and 20th in Points Earned on receptions (first among running backs). McCaffrey had 107 catches on 124 targets in 2018 (86 percent catch rate) compared to 80 catches on 113 targets last season (71 percent), thus allowing him to do what was needed more often. He finished the season as the only player with at least 75 targets and no drops.

Pass Coverage

Unsurprisingly, Total Points rewards ball-hawking defensive backs for defending passes and forcing interceptions. Beyond that, though, the sure tacklers and shutdown defenders finally get their due statistically. Like with receivers, defensive backs are evaluated compared to the expected yardage on the route, so making a quick tackle on a slant or shallow cross does not go unnoticed. Along with that, each receiver and defender in coverage is evaluated for how likely he is to be targeted given elements like where he lines up, how deep he is, and the type of coverage on the play. Defensive backs who consistently deter throws are credited for doing so, and are correspondingly dinged for being peppered with targets.

Secondary Total Points Saved					
Player	Pos	Team	Pass Def Points Saved	Run Def Points Saved	Total Points Saved
Damontae Kazee	S	ATL	32	5	37
Adrian Amos	S	CHI	27	2	28
Anthony Harris	S	MIN	23	2	25
Kevin Byard	S	TEN	23	1	24
Harrison Smith	S	MIN	21	3	23

Damontae Kazee had an outstanding sophomore season in 2018, tying for the league lead in interceptions while also deterring targets in his direction. A good portion of his Points Saved are a result of intercepting seven passes despite being targeted only 21 times. He was also targeted on only 3.8 percent of his coverage snaps, which ranked 8th among safeties with at least 200 coverage snaps. Run Defense Points Saved also favors Kazee, as he is the top-ranked secondary player with five Points Saved.

Conclusion

The Total Points system is a critical step forward in evaluating individual player contributions. It allows for the division of credit that simple EPA isn't able to produce. The system has already gone through some updates since it was originally introduced in September 2018, all of which are accounted for in the analysis above. The biggest of those was a play-calling adjustment that tweaks a player's Total Points to account for contextual factors he has no control over but still affect his performance (the most obvious of those being the decision to run or pass). Future updates are on the horizon to continue to improve SIS's premier football statistic, including an eventual NCAA model of the Total Points system.

Sports Info Solutions

Sports Info Solutions, originally founded as Baseball Info Solutions, has been delivering baseball data and analysis with the highest level of accuracy, detail, and timeliness for nearly two decades. We added football tracking in 2015, empowering us to dissect the many intricacies presented each week across the NFL and NCAA FBS.

The company provides the most accurate data in a timely manner using state-of-the-art technology. The commitment to service, customization, and customer support has allowed SIS to remain at the forefront of the sports data industry. We service teams, agents, companies, and fans.

SIS captures statistical snapshots of every on-field event. This produces an exhaustive database that includes traditional statistics and advanced analysis. SIS has leveraged this database to assemble extensive pitch-charting and defensive data, as well as producing ground-breaking metrics such as Defensive Runs Saved (DRS) and Independent Quarterback Rating (IQR).

John Dewan, the principal owner of SIS, has been a leader in sports analysis for more than 30 years. His experience dates to his time as Executive Director of Project Scoresheet, the Bill James-led effort that pioneered the new wave of baseball statistics that have become common in today's vernacular. This led to the incorporation and development of STATS Inc. from a bedroom office to its sale to News Corp in 2000. Without those efforts, many of the statistics and analytics that we all take for granted may not even be available at all.

The remainder of the Sports Info Solutions team includes former professional & collegiate players, coaches, and scouts, as well as research, programming, and database management experts.

If you would like to contact Sports Info Solutions for data inquiries, potential job openings, or additional information, you can reach us at:

Sports Info Solutions
41 S. 2nd Street
Coplay, PA 18037
610-261-2370
www.sportsinfosolutions.com

Acknowledgments

Hello!

This is the first edition of *The SIS Football Rookie Handbook*, our biggest foray into football writing to date. We have been fortunate enough to grow our football business over the last few years, allowing us to produce a work this comprehensive. Many people put in long hours, nights, and weekends to be able to get this book to you before the 2019 draft. This is our attempt to thank all of them for their efforts.

John and Sue Dewan are the principal owners of Sports Info Solutions. They founded the company in 2002 with Steve Moyer as Baseball Info Solutions, then changing the company's name to Sports Info Solutions when we began covering football in 2015. John brings a wealth of knowledge and experience to overseeing the *Handbook* process both for this book and *The Bill James Baseball Handbook*, providing final editorial approval on everything that makes it into the book. Sue is the logistical mastermind that ensures the company is able to continue operating while we undertake this enormous effort.

Rob Dougherty is the President of Sports Info Solutions, leading our ever-expanding endeavors in both baseball and football. Rob brings many years of experience working in the sports data and media industries to the table and has seamlessly stepped in to coordinate our efforts with the publisher and other fiduciary duties that often go unappreciated.

Our growing presence in football continues to flourish under the leadership of Director of Football, Matt Manocherian and the guidance of Football Operations Coordinator, Dan Foehrenbach. Matt and Dan have kept our football operation running smoothly, moving things forward and adding clients, widening our reach in the industry. Nathan Cooper and John Todd have been Matt's right-hand lieutenants throughout the production of this book, ensuring both its completion and its high quality. Brian Reiff in the R&D Department and Tricia Wilson in IT Department also both deserve special acknowledgment, Brian for his incredible work formatting and compiling the book, and Tricia for managing the key technical aspects of the football operation.

Tim Kwilos is the Vice President of Operations and Administration at SIS, and in many ways, he is the glue that holds the company together. Besides making sure that the trains run on time, he oversees the operations of both sports, leads the admin team, and plays an integral role in all business decisions.

This book wouldn't be possible without the data and reports in it, and we have the Football Operations Department to thank for all that they do to collect it and make sure it is the most accurate source available. The work of operations associates Justin Stine, Mike Churchward, Josh Hofer, Cole Ratliff, and John Verros has been invaluable and is greatly appreciated, along with Senior Video Scouts Segev Goldberg, John Shirley, and Evan Butler.

Matt Manocherian is also the Director of our R&D department, which takes our collected data and analyzes it from a broad range of statistical perspectives. Joe Rosales leads our research efforts in both sports, helped by Lindsay Zeck, Brian Reiff, Alex Vigderman, Mark Simon, Andrew Kyne, Nate Weller, John Shirley, and Bryce Rossler.

Providing the technical expertise that powers the company's engine is the IT Department. Led by Director of IT, Craig Saboe, the rest of the department features Patrick Coyle, Tricia Wilson, Ben Stanczak, Will Creager, Brandyn Bechtel, Joe Gownley, and Tim Paul.

In Business Development, Corey March and Patrick Rowley are responsible for coordinating the communication of our data, research, and analysis to the public and fostering our relationships with clients.

Our baseball operations department keeps our business in that area running smoothly, with a staff that includes James Mehall, Ted Baarda, Jon Vrecsics, Dan Casey, Todd Radcliffe, Nathan Phares, and Jason Paff.

Human resources and office management is spearheaded by Carol Olsen, who works with Melanie Milbauer to make sure that our work environment is always pleasant and running smoothly.

Jason Trifilo, our Accountant/Bookkeeper, plays an instrumental role in keeping the business running, the lights on, and the finances in order, with resolute determination.

We are especially grateful for all of our outstanding Video Scouts. Their dedication and attention to detail provide the foundation of our business. Our full-time Senior Video Scouts include Noah Gatsik, Nick Rabasco, Derek Tarconish, Dan Wallie, Kyle Price, and Ken Gaffney. The rest of our Video Scouts include Nick Aiello, Chris Battinieri, Ian Berg, Kerby Callison, Austin Cochran, Elijah Cornejo, Daniel Davis, Jeff Dean, Conor Dickinson, Patrick Dougherty, Justin Drybala, Jordan Edwards, Cam Farnham, Zachary Fernandez, Ken Garron, Nick Giella, Aaron Gray, Jonny Guerra, Gennady Gusak, Dallas Hagenbuch, Brian Hammond, Ben Hrkach, Mark Johnson, Wyatt Jones, Dillon Josephsen, Kenny Kirkpatrick, Nick Martino, Jermel McElveen, Kyle Milton, Walter Moore, Alex O'Brien, Jeremy Percy, Ronan Potts, Ian Riley, Marc Roche, Brian Rogers, Bryce Rossler, David Salway, Jake Schwanitz, Drew Schweitzer, Tony Shields, Alexander Snorton, Adam Villio, Sammy Visconti, Stephen Williams, and Rocky Wilson.

Our partners at ACTA Publications, President Greg Pierce, Tom Wright, Mary Eggert, Mary Rickey, Abby Pierce, Brian Tobin, Ian Courter, Mary Doyle, Hugh Spector, and Isz.

Thank you to all of our friends in the football industry who have embraced us over the last few years and helped to make this book possible.

And finally, thank you for reading!

Index